D1524803

STUDIES IN MEDIEVAL AND RENAISSANCE MUSIC 17

A Critical Companion to Medieval Motets

Studies in Medieval and Renaissance Music

ISSN 1479-9294

General Editors
Tess Knighton
Helen Deeming

This series aims to provide a forum for the best scholarship in early music; deliberately broad in scope, it welcomes proposals on any aspect of music, musical life, and composers during the period up to 1600, and particularly encourages work that places music in an historical and social context. Both new research and major re-assessments of central topics are encouraged.

Proposals or enquiries may be sent directly to either of the editors or to the publisher at the addresses given below; all submissions will receive careful, informed consideration.

Professor Tess Knighton, Institucio Mila i Fontanals/CSIC,
c/Egipciaques 15, Barcelona 08001, Spain

Dr Helen Deeming, Department of Music, Royal Holloway College,
University of London, Egham, Surrey TW20 0EX

Boydell & Brewer, PO Box 9, Woodbridge, Suffolk IP12 3DF

A Critical Companion
to Medieval Motets

edited by

Jared C. Hartt

THE BOYDELL PRESS

First published 2018
The Boydell Press, Woodbridge

ISBN 978-1-78327-307-2

The Boydell Press is an imprint of Boydell & Brewer Ltd
PO Box 9, Woodbridge, Suffolk IP12 3DF, UK
and of Boydell & Brewer Inc.
668 Mt Hope Avenue, Rochester, NY 14620, USA
website: www.boydellandbrewer.com

A CIP catalogue record for this title is available
from the British Library

The publisher has no responsibility for the continued existence or accuracy
of URLs for external or third-party internet websites referred to in this book,
and does not guarantee that any content on such websites is,
or will remain, accurate or appropriate

Typeset in Adobe Arno Pro by
Word and Page, Chester

For the 5 J's

CONTENTS

FIGURES

The editor, contributors, and publishers are grateful to all the institutions and persons listed for permission to reproduce the materials in which they hold copyright. Every effort has been made to trace the copyright holders; apologies are offered for any omission, and the publishers will be pleased to add any necessary acknowledgement in subsequent editions.

MUSIC EXAMPLES

TABLES

CONTRIBUTORS

Margaret Bent	Emeritus Fellow, All Souls College, University of Oxford
Jacques Boogaart	Associate Professor (retired), University of Amsterdam
Catherine A. Bradley	Associate Professor, University of Oslo
Alice V. Clark	Professor, Loyola University New Orleans
Suzannah Clark	Professor, Harvard University
Karen Desmond	Assistant Professor, Brandeis University
Lawrence Earp	Professor Emeritus, University of Wisconsin-Madison
Sarah Fuller	Professor Emeritus, Stony Brook University
John Haines	Professor, University of Toronto
Jared C. Hartt	Associate Professor, Oberlin College Conservatory
Elizabeth Eva Leach	Professor, University of Oxford
Dolores Pesce	Avis Blewett Professor of Music, Washington University in St. Louis
Gaël Saint-Cricq	Maître de conférences, Université de Rouen
Jennifer Saltzstein	Associate Professor, University of Oklahoma
Matthew P. Thomson	Fitzjames Research Fellow, Merton College, University of Oxford
Stefan Udell	Ph.D. candidate, University of Toronto
Anna Zayaruznaya	Associate Professor, Yale University
Emily Zazulia	Shirley Shenker Assistant Professor, University of California, Berkeley

PREFACE

Music, like many art forms, underwent numerous changes and developments in the medieval period. In the thirteenth and fourteenth centuries in particular, a genre of music – *motets* – emerged as a dominant vehicle for composers. In fact, many scholars would consider motets to constitute the most important genre of *polyphony*: that is, instead of penning a stand-alone melody (monophony), composers would write and/or arrange two or more melodies to be performed simultaneously (polyphony). Moreover, medieval motets are intrinsically involved in the early development of polyphonic music, especially in regards to the development of rhythm and its notation; the study of motets throughout the two centuries in question reveals a fascinating evolution of polyphonic experimentation and mastery.

Yet, it is nearly impossible to come up with a precise definition for the genre of medieval motets. Briefly put, beginning in the early 1200s, motets provided an outlet for composers to set poetry to music, but, intriguingly, composers often set two or more different poems to be sung *at the same time*. Frequently, these simultaneous poems would be sung against yet another melody, the tenor, which was almost always textless and in a lower register than the texted voices, and which was usually borrowed, sometimes from a chant source, sometimes from a vernacular popular tune. This description does not account for all medieval motets – for instance, there is a significant body of surviving monophonic motets – but it does sum up a good deal of the extant repertory.

The subject matter of motets varies widely. Some motets feature vernacular French poems that employ the conventional tropes of 'courtly love'. These texts might be sung against a tenor of liturgical origin, thus inviting the listener and/or reader to draw connections between the meanings of the tenor source and the poetry. Other motets serve an admonitory function, perhaps warning or counselling a king about inappropriate behaviours, or perhaps lamenting the current political climate. Still others celebrate a particular feast day or a specific person or place. Latin texts were likewise common, and sometimes composers would even set concurrent French and Latin poems.

But why would a composer set two or even three different poems to be sung at the same time? How is the listener supposed to understand the text? Gleaning meaning from motets has resulted in abundant scholarship and differing viewpoints. Some argue that the motet poems might be read aloud or even sung individually before a performance of the complete texture so that the listener could more readily comprehend its subject matter. Others regard motet composition as a quasi-intellectual exercise for the composer and contend that the listener ought to simply enjoy the polyphonic, polytextual sound.

Unfortunately, the majority of medieval composers remain anonymous to us today. Not until Guillaume de Machaut (*c.* 1300–77) can a substantial body of motets be firmly attributed to a single composer. Due in part to this uncertainty, relatively little is known about motet patronage in the thirteenth and fourteenth centuries. Thankfully, however, hundreds of motets survive in dozens of manuscripts, many of which are beautifully illuminated (and many of which are available online), and it is through these manuscripts that we are able to see and hear these gems today.

The Introduction first illustrates the breadth of the genre by briefly considering ten examples, then provides chapter summaries that highlight many of the (often thorny) topics approached by the

Companion's authors. The first eight chapters address issues of genre, relationships between the motet and other musico-poetic forms, tenor organization, isorhythm, notational development, social functions, and manuscript layout. The last nine chapters consist of case studies that address a variety of specific pieces, compositional techniques, collections, and subgenres. The volume as a whole explores the rich interplay of musical, poetic, and intertextual modes of meaning specific to the genre, and the changing social and historical circumstances surrounding motets in medieval France, England, and Italy.

The chapters below often employ specialized terminology. Curious readers can refer to the glossary that appears near the end of this *Companion*, as well as to the index, which points to the use of various terms in the context of specific pieces.

ACKNOWLEDGMENTS

I am grateful to Caroline Palmer, who approached me with the idea for this *Companion* some years ago at the International Congress on Medieval Studies in Kalamazoo, Michigan. I thank her for her guidance and tremendous enthusiasm throughout the entire process of bringing this book to fruition. I thank Jennifer Bain for her advice in the earliest stages of planning the volume, and Elizabeth Eva Leach for her support and wise words throughout all stages of the project.

I am also grateful to Oberlin College for financial support for the setting of the volume's music examples – executed beautifully by Timothy Symons (www.cantusfirmusmusic.co.uk) – and for funding a student assistant, Gregory Manuel, who helped in numerous ways during the last few months of getting the volume ready for publication.

Finally, I thank all seventeen contributors, without whom, of course, the *Companion* would not be possible. I greatly appreciate their responsiveness to my countless emails and queries, and thank them all for their unwavering commitment to the project.

ABBREVIATIONS

CITED MANUSCRIPTS CONTAINING MOTETS

ArsB	Paris, Bibliothèque de l'Arsenal, 3517
Ba	Bamberg, Staatsbibliothek, Lit. 115
BarcA	Barcelona, Biblioteca Nacional de Catalunya/Biblioteca Central, BM 853
Bes	Besançon, Bibliothèque Municipale, I, 716 (lost; only index survives)
Boul	Boulogne-sur-mer, Bibliothèque municipale, 119
Br	Brussels, Bibliothèque royale de Belgique, 19606
C	Bern, Burgerbibliothek, 389
Ca	Cambrai, Mediathèque municipale, A 410 (olim 386)
CaB	Cambrai, Mediathèque municipale, B 1328
CaB 165	Cambrai, Mediathèque municipale, Inc. B 165
Cgc 512	Cambridge, Gonville and Cauis College 512/543
Ch	Chantilly, Bibliothèque du Château de Chantilly, 564
Châl	Châlons-en-Champagne, Archives départementales de la Marne, 3.J.250
Cl	Paris, Bibliothèque nationale de France, nouv. acq. fr. 13521
Cpc 228	Cambridge, Pembroke College, 228
D308	Oxford, Bodleian Library, Douce 308
DRc 20	Durham, Cathedral Library, C.I. 20
F	Florence, Biblioteca Medicea Laurenziana, Plut. 29.1
Fauv	Paris, Bibliothèque nationale de France, f. fr. 146
Ferrell 1	Kansas City, private library of James E. and Elizabeth J. Ferrell
fr.845	Paris, Bibliothèque nationale de France, f. fr. 845
fr.1589	Paris, Bibliothèque nationale de France, f. fr. 1589
GB-OH	London, British Library, Add. 57950
GB-Ir 30	Ipswich, Suffolk Record Office, HA 30: 50/22/13.15
Graz	Graz, Universitätsbibliothek 409
H	Modena, Biblioteca estense universitaria, α.R.4.4
Ha	Paris, Bibliothèque nationale de France, f. fr. 25566
Her	Leuven, Universiteitsbibliotheek, two parchment flyleaves
Hu	Burgos, Monasterio de las Huelgas, 9
I-Gr 224	Grottaferrata, Biblioteca del Monumento Nazionale, Kript. Lat. 224
I-MFA	Montefiore dell'Aso, Biblioteca-Archivio di Francesco Egidi, s.s. Egidi
Iv	Ivrea, Biblioteca Capitolare, 115
K	Paris, Bibliothèque de l'Arsenal, 5198
k	Paris, Bibliothèque nationale de France, f. fr. 12786
Lbl 1210	London, British Library, Sloane 1210
Lbl 24198	London, British Library, Add. 24198
LoA	London, British Library, Egerton 2615

LoB	London, British Library, Egerton 274
LoC	London, British Library, Add. 30091
LoHa	London, British Library, Harl. 978
Ma	Madrid, Biblioteca nacional, 20486
Mach A	Paris, Bibliothèque nationale de France, f. fr. 1584
Mach B	Paris, Bibliothèque nationale de France, f. fr. 1585
Mach C	Paris, Bibliothèque nationale de France, f. fr. 1586
Mach E	Paris, Bibliothèque nationale de France, f. fr. 9221
Mach F-G	Paris, Bibliothèque nationale de France, f. fr. 22545 and 22546
McVeagh	London, British Library, Add. 41667
Mesmes	Chansonnier de Mesmes (lost)
Mo	Montpellier, Bibliothèque interuniversitaire, Section de médecine, H.196
Mod	Modena, Biblioteca Estense, α.M.5.24
MüA	Munich, Bayerische Staatsbibliothek, gallo-rom.42
MüB	Munich, Bayerische Staatsbibliothek, lat. 16444
NL-Lu 342a	Leiden, Bibliotheek der Rijksuniversiteit, Fragment L.T.K. 342a
Noailles	Paris, Bibliothèque nationale de France, f. fr. 12615
NYpm 978	New York, Pierpont Morgan Library, 978
O	Paris, Bibliothèque nationale de France, f. fr. 846
Ob 7	Oxford, Bodleian Library, E Mus 7
Ob 20	Oxford, Bodleian Library, Latin liturgical d. 20 (includes fragments formerly catalogued as Ob Auct F. inf. 1.3, Ob Bodl. 862, Ob Hatton 31, and photographs of non-Bodleian fragments)
Ob 213	Oxford, Bodleian Library, Canon. Misc. 213
Ob 271*	Oxford, Bodleian Library, Bodley 271*
Ob 594	Oxford, Bodleian Library, Laud Misc. 594
Onc 362	Oxford, New College, 362
Oxf Add.	Oxford Bodleian Library, Add. A. 44
P	Paris, Bibliothèque nationale de France, f. fr. 847
Pic	Paris, Bibliothèque nationale de France, Collection de Picardie 67
Pn 571	Paris, Bibliothèque nationale de France, f. fr. 571
Pru	Princeton, University Library, Garrett 119
Ps	Paris, Bibliothèque nationale de France, lat. 11266
Q15	Bologna, Museo Internazionale e Biblioteca della Musica di Bologna, Q15
R	Paris, Bibliothèque nationale de France, f. fr. 1591
Reg1490	Vatican, Biblioteca Apostolica Vaticana, Reg. lat. 1490
Robertsbridge	London, British Library, Add. 28550
Roi	Paris, Bibliothèque nationale de France, f. fr. 844
S	Paris, Bibliothèque nationale de France, f. fr. 12581
Sab	Rome, Convento di Santa Sabina, Biblioteca della Curia generalizia dei Domenicani, XIV L 3
Str	Strasbourg, Bibliothèque municipale, 222 C. 22 (lost)
StV	Paris, Bibliothèque nationale de France, lat. 15139
To	Toledo, Biblioteca Capitular, BCT 98.281
Tort	Tortosa, Biblioteca de la Catedral, C 97

Trém	Paris, Bibliothèque nationale de France, nouv. acq. fr. 23190
Troyes 1949	Troyes, Bibliothèque municipale, 1949
Tu	Turin, Biblioteca Reale, vari 42
TuB	Turin, Biblioteca Nazionale Universitaria, J.II.9
U	Paris, Bibliothèque nationale de France, f. fr. 20050
V	Paris, Bibliothèque nationale de France, f. fr. 24406
W1	Wolfenbüttel, Herzog August Bibliothek, Cod. Guelf. 628 Helmst.
W2	Wolfenbüttel, Herzog August Bibliothek, Cod. Guelf. 1099 Helmst.
WoC	Worcester, Dean and Chapter library, Add. 68.
X	Paris, Bibliothèque nationale de France, nouv. acq. fr. 1050

OTHER CITED MANUSCRIPTS

F-Arras 444	Arras, Médiathèque municipale, 444
F-Dm 526	Dijon, Bibliothèque municipale, 526
F-LA 263	Laon, Bibliothèque municipale, 263
F-Pn f. fr. 372	Paris, Bibliothèque nationale de France, f. fr. 372
F-Pn f. fr. 837	Paris, Bibliothèque nationale de France, f. fr. 837
F-Pn f. fr. 1593	Paris, Bibliothèque nationale de France, f. fr. 1593
F-Pn f. fr. 2186	Paris, Bibliothèque nationale de France, f. fr. 2186
F-Pn f. fr. 23111	Paris, Bibliothèque nationale de France, f. fr. 23111
F-Pn f. fr. 24729	Paris, Bibliothèque nationale de France, f. fr. 24729
F-Pn lat. 1112	Paris, Bibliothèque nationale de France, lat. 1112
F-Pn lat. 7378A	Paris, Bibliothèque nationale de France, lat. 7378A
F-Pn lat. 10482	Paris, Bibliothèque nationale de France, lat. 10482
F-Pn lat. 13091	Paris, Bibliothèque nationale de France, lat. 13091
F-Pn lat. 14452	Paris, Bibliothèque nationale de France, lat. 14452
F-Pn lat. 14741	Paris, Bibliothèque nationale de France, lat. 14741
F-Pn lat. 15181	Paris, Bibliothèque nationale de France, lat. 15181
GB-Cu 710	Cambridge, University Library, Add. 710
GB-Mr [96] 66	Manchester, John Rylands University Library, [96] 66
GB-Ob 264	Oxford, Bodleian Library, Bodley 264
I-Rvat 307	Vatican, Biblioteca Apostolica Vaticana, Barb. lat. 307

OTHER ABBREVIATIONS

B	breve
C	color
DIAMM	Refers to *Digital Image Archive of Medieval Music* at http://www. diamm.ac.uk. Login required.
Grove	Refers to *Grove Music Online* at http://www.oxfordmusiconline.com. Author and entry information is provided in the text itself or a footnote. When a print edition is referred to specifically, a complete citation appears in the bibliography.
L	long
M	minim
mo	motetus

S	semibreve
T	talea
tr	triplum

It has become standard in scholarship of the thirteenth-century motet to refer to tenors, texts, trouvère songs, and refrains not only by name but also by number. Accordingly, upon first mention in each chapter, motet tenors and texts are identified by the numbers assigned to them in Ludwig 1910–78 and Gennrich 1957. For tenor voices, if identifiable, an M indicates a chant segment used for the Mass while an O indicates a chant used for the Office. Songs are identified with RS numbers provided in Spanke 1955. Refrains are identified with vdB numbers provided in van den Boogaard 1969.

It has also become customary to identify the motets of the fourteenth-century composer Guillaume de Machaut by number. M1, for instance, refers to his Motet 1, *Quant en moy vint premierement Amours/Amour et biauté/Amara Valde*. These M-numbers are distinct from those that identify tenors of thirteenth-century motets; throughout the volume, the intended meaning of each M-number is clarified by its surrounding context.

Authors refer to specific pitches by using the following in italics: *A B C D E F G a b c d e f g a′ b′ c′ d′ e′*, in which *c* corresponds to C4 (middle c). Non-italicized, upper-case letters are used to refer to a pitch in general, without specific reference to octave.

INTRODUCTION

Approaching Medieval Motets*

Jared C. Hartt

T HE TITLE OF THIS VOLUME may seem rather straightforward, but it has been deliberately
chosen to reflect one of the book's main points. *A Critical Companion to Medieval Motets*
– rather than *A Critical Companion to the Medieval Motet* – signals that the motet, essentially, cannot be regarded as a single thing: not only do motets change drastically throughout the
thirteenth and fourteenth centuries (and beyond), but even motets that are contemporaneous
with one another often exhibit such wildly different characteristics that one would be hard-pressed
to come up with a suitable definition for the genre.

What then are medieval motets? Combing through various musical dictionaries and textbooks,
one will typically find the motet defined as a polyphonic composition with two differently texted
upper voices operating over a pre-existing tenor line drawn from chant.[1] To be sure, there exist
hundreds of medieval motets that fit this description. But there also exist hundreds of motets
that do not. Perhaps the most effective way to convey a sense of the sheer breadth of the genre
is through a glance at a handful of contrasting examples discussed throughout the volume; these
motets range from the first decades of the thirteenth century to the onset of the fifteenth century,
the scope of the *Companion*.

Take for instance the subgenre of two-voice motets. *Salve salus, hominum/Et gaudebit* is a short
work that appears in **F**, one of the earliest motet sources. As shown in Example 4.3 (p. 81 below),
the melody of its tenor, *Et gaudebit*, is drawn from the Alleluia for the feast of the Ascension and
proceeds in a pattern that alternates long and short notes. The motet's texted Latin upper voice
(the motetus or duplum, interchangeably) is declaimed in the same basic rhythms with poetic lines
that are almost all of the same length. Like the majority of medieval motets, its composer remains
unknown to us today. We can compare this with another two-voice motet, *Fines amouretes/Fiat*,
that appears in the slightly later **W2** manuscript. As is illustrated in Example 9.1 (p. 195), its upper
voice is in French and contains a refrain in lines 9, 10, and 11 (enclosed in quotation marks) that

* I extend my sincere thanks to Gregory Manuel, a student from my undergraduate Medieval
Motets course in 2016, who very enthusiastically read all of the volume's chapters in May and
June 2017 and provided written responses to each. Since this *Companion* is aimed not only at
specialists in the field, but also at upper-level undergraduate students interested in medieval
motets, as well as graduate students of all levels, Greg's summaries, reactions, and questions
were immensely helpful in formulating this introduction; indeed, many of Greg's insightful
observations appear throughout.

[1] See, for instance, the 'Motet' entry in the *Harvard Dictionary of Music*: 'The term motet denoted
a particular structure: a tenor derived from chant that serves as the foundation for newly
composed upper voices; the resulting composition is heterogeneous both in the musical style
of the individual voices and in their texts'. Randel 2003, 589.

also appears within the allegorical verse narrative *Roman de la poire*; this motet exhibits the close relationship between the genres of motet and secular song. Just a few pages earlier in **W2** appears another two-voice motet, *Onques n'amai tant/Sancte Germane*, provided in its entirety in Example 12.1 (pp. 246–7). Again, its motetus is in French, but this entire voice is borrowed, having already existed as the first strophe of a monophonic song. Although its tenor incipit may suggest the tenor melody was drawn from a liturgical source as in the other two motets just discussed, it was almost certainly composed afresh to provide appropriate counterpoint with the secular upper voice.

A large number of motets, however, possess more than two voices: one such motet is *Celui en qui je me fi/La bele estoile de mer/La bele, en qui je me fi/[Jo]han[ne]*, which appears in the second fascicle of the so-called Montpellier codex (**Mo**), the most extensive source of thirteenth-century motets. A look at Example 10.2 (pp. 215–17) reveals that three different French poems are sung simultaneously above the tenor, thereby exhibiting a decidedly polytextual texture.[2] The last fascicle of **Mo** contains the motet *Par une matinee/O clemencie fons/D'un joli dart* (Example 12.3, (pp. 256–60)). Its tenor is not liturgical, but rather a borrowed secular song, and the refrain-ABABX-refrain structure inherited from this song serves to organize the entire motet. Moreover, its two upper voices proceed in different languages: French in the triplum, Latin in the motetus. The upper-voice rhythms of both of these motets are much freer in nature than the predominantly modal rhythms of the earlier examples.

In stark contrast to all the aforementioned works stands *Tres haute amor jolie*, shown below in Example 11.2a (p. 234), an instance of a *mono*phonic motet. This brief piece appears alongside fourteen others in its source – the chansonnier **fr.845** of non-Parisian origins, from either Picardy or Artois – preceded by a rubric naming the pieces as 'motets'. And sixty-three motets of this hitherto largely ignored subgenre appear in another chansonnier, **D308**, from Metz. Continuing to move even further from Paris and returning to polyphonic textures, *Jesu fili Dei/Jhesu fili virginis/Jesu lumen veritatis* is a motet of English origins from the early fourteenth century whose beginning appears in Example 13.1 (p. 264). Its tenor occupies instead the middle register, while the two outer voices are declaimed homorhythmically.

On the continent in the fourteenth century, three further examples will suffice to continue illustrating the broad scope of the genre. Guillaume de Machaut's *Hareu! hareu! le feu/Helas! ou sera pris confors/Obediens usque ad mortem* (M10) is provided in its entirety in Example 15.1 (pp. 303–5), as well as in Figure 8.5 (p. 188), a reproduction of the folios that contain the motet in Machaut's earliest complete works manuscript, **Mach C**. Significantly, Machaut was one of the first motet composers to ensure his name would be remain firmly associated with his compositions. The lengthy tenor melody, stated twice but with shorter note values the second time, is divided and organized into regularly repeating rhythmic patterns, as indicated by the annotations in the example. The upper-voice poems, written by Machaut, are sung in much faster rhythms than the tenor, and express the courtly love rhetoric typical for motets of the period. This motet stands in contrast to his later *Tu qui gregem/Plange regni respublica/Apprehende arma et scutum/Contratenor* (M22), in which the upper voices are both Latin and address current political events of the late 1350s. As shown in Example 16.1 (pp. 324–5), M22 begins with an extended introitus, sung first by the motetus voice only, then joined by the triplum. Only later does the entire four-voice texture begin; the fourth voice here is not a texted quadruplum, but is instead an untexted contratenor that shares its range and much slower note values with the tenor. Finally, *O felix templum/O felix templum* is an Italian motet from *c.* 1402 whose two upper voices share a single text honoring a

[2] Bars 1–4 of the example provide the Latin duplum as it appears in a two-voice version of the motet.

bishop of Padua; the freely composed tenor, which is not organized into repeating rhythmic units, serves more as an accompaniment to the dueting upper voices. Excerpts from the uppermost voice are illustrated in both original and modern notation in Example 5.8 (p. 126).

With just a quick glance at these ten specimens, the extensive variety that exists within the genre is thus evident. Medieval motets are not necessarily polytextual. Nor are they necessarily polyphonic. Nor do they necessarily feature a pre-composed tenor. As such, plausibly the most accurate – albeit unsatisfyingly general – definition appears in the *Encyclopedia Britannica*: 'a style of vocal composition that has undergone numerous transformations through many centuries'.[3] Although this definition also accounts for motets beyond the thirteenth and fourteenth centuries, and while it could actually describe musical genres beyond the motet as well, it captures the broad scope of the motet genre that is made abundantly clear in the chapters and myriad music examples comprising this *Companion*.

The 'motet' entry in *Grove* seems to accommodate the majority of the motets from our group of ten; however, it still excludes the monophonic, English, and Italian examples. The entry also offers a summary of the genre's origins:

> It originated as a liturgical trope but soon developed into the pre-eminent form of secular art music during the late Middle Ages. The medieval motet was a polyphonic composition in which the fundamental voice (tenor) was usually arranged in a pattern of reiterated rhythmic configurations, while the upper voice or voices (up to three), nearly always with different Latin or French texts, generally moved at a faster rate.[4]

Thus, we are told about the motet's liturgical origins and its polyphonic texture, as well as the 'fundamental' role of the tenor, which also implies the tenor's chronological priority within the motet composition process.

The *Companion*'s seventeen chapters make clear, however, that we have moved from this once fairly well-agreed-upon history of thirteenth- and fourteenth-century motets to a much more plural understanding that is contested in certain key areas. We now have varying viewpoints on the origins of the genre that resist, challenge, and sometimes even invert the standard teleological narratives of the genre's history. The previously assumed trajectories from clausula to motet, sacred to secular, and Latin to French, are all questioned, often through engagement with a substantial body of songbook motets frequently overlooked in scholarship. The bias toward not just French, but more specifically Parisian, sources and their repertories is both highlighted and corrected in many chapters. Motets of English provenance are brought back into play in current scholarship through discussions of their unique generic and notational characteristics.

The determinacy and foundational role of the tenor is also contested in several instances. The fraught terms 'isorhythm' and 'isorhythmic motets' are reconsidered. The development of notation – intrinsically linked to the development of the motet – is presented in a new light. The overriding general fixation with polytextuality in scholarship is addressed and rectified.

Dividing into two broad sections, the *Companion*'s first eight chapters address several of the aforementioned fundamental topics individually, delving into questions of genre, the motet's origins, the role of the tenor, isorhythm, motet notations, the various functions of motets spanning both centuries in question, and aspects of manuscript layout and culture. The second section consists of nine chapters we might consider case studies; these chapters exhibit a variety of

---

[3] See https://www.britannica.com/art/motet.
[4] See 'Motet, §I: Middle Ages' by Ernest H. Sanders and Peter M. Lefferts in *Grove*.

musical, textual, and musico-textual approaches to a broad range of the repertoire spanning the thirteenth and fourteenth centuries in both France and England.

In Chapter 1, Elizabeth Eva Leach considers issues of genre and origins through the lens of the substantial motet collection in **D308**, a chansonnier copied in Metz. As Leach points out, that the sixty-three motets in this manuscript have been largely ignored to this point is significant, yet perhaps unsurprising since they are recorded only as texts without musical notation. Reflecting on the fact that **D308** is the sole extant source to contain motetus texts with concordances in both polyphonic motet sources as well as in sources of notated monophonic motets *entés*, Leach ponders several questions: what can the collection in **D308** tell us about the genre of motets? How might these motets have been performed? What would the scribe or readers of **D308** have called these pieces? And perhaps most tantalizingly, through a detailed look at two **D308** motets specifically, does this large group of pieces indicate that there were actually a greater number of monophonic motets than previously thought – in short, did some motetus voices known to us today only in their polyphonic contexts first exist in monophonic forms?

In considering the origins of 'motet', both as a genre and as a term, Leach argues that the word came to encompass polyphonic liturgical works only later through analogy, and suggests that the pieces typically referred to as 'motets' today are best regarded as a hybridization of pieces arising through the retrofitting of monophonic French pieces with a tenor and (often) upper voices, and those arising from the addition of words to melismatic liturgical polyphonic discant (clausulae). Her chapter thus pushes back against some of the most common narratives surrounding motet origins discussed above – in particular, the notion of the motet's genesis as a polyphonic elaboration on liturgical chant segments, and the notion of its historical progression from sacred Latin texts to eventually including secular French texts – and at the same time, through her discussion of how a monophonic motet might be adapted into a polyphonic work, Leach challenges the presumption of the tenor as necessarily being the foundation of a motet.

With a similar penchant for disrupting tidy origin stories, Catherine A. Bradley demonstrates in Chapter 2 that the traditional view of motets as derived from clausulae is too simplistic. Disputing any totalizing chronological approach, she does not argue conversely that clausulae necessarily tend to come from motets, but rather that the written transmissions of motets and clausulae fail to fully capture the complex ecology of their performances, and that we should therefore approach genre distinctions with greater flexibility.

Working with the motet *Homo quam sit pura/Latus* and its corresponding clausula *Latus 4*, Bradley compares various existing versions of the clausula (in **F** and **W1**) to suggest that *Latus 4*'s own circulation must have been influenced by the motet's circulation. In surveying other clausulae in these manuscripts, she concludes that most clausulae in fact serve as rather poor rhythmic indicators for their motets, therefore discouraging the conclusion that these clausulae were designed for the purpose of serving as rhythmic guides. Moreover, she argues that clausulae are often not as necessary as one might think for the accurate rhythmicization of a motet; rather, concrete tenor rhythms, vertical harmonies, syllable stress, and familiarity with performance practice might have made it fairly easy for experienced singers to work out the rhythms despite notational ambiguity.

Bradley also demonstrates the slippage between conductus, conductus motets, motets, and clausulae in order to show the various modes of transforming one genre into another. Instead of reading the particular ordering of the early motet manuscripts by genre as a sign of generic fixity, she instead suggests that this ordering represents a kind of struggle against generic flexibility, and that scholars have taken these distinctions too literally. Through her consideration of issues of performance, ephemerality, and the problems with the written archive, Bradley, in essence, reads the motet manuscripts as much for what they hide as for what they show.

Alice V. Clark, in the third chapter, considers varieties and functions of the tenor in medieval motets, foregrounding the tenor's development and varying roles in the compositional process. Clark focuses on the tenor in France, but also usefully considers the frequently differing tenor functions in motets of English and Italian provenances. While many of the *Companion*'s chapters aim to show different ways in which the tenor and upper voices are mutually implicated and intertwined, Clark instead steps back and highlights the ways in which the tenor differs sonically and organizationally from the other motet voices, regardless of whether or not the tenor comes first in a given compositional process.

To begin her tracing of the tenor in the thirteenth century, Clark considers motets derived from clausulae, which already contain a rhythmicized and organized tenor and upper voice. She explains that the departure of motets from clausulae allowed for motets to expand further beyond the meaning of their chants, and allowed for the selection of tenors from sources beyond solo portions of responsorial chants, even including, at times, secular sources. She argues that there is an important distinction between a thirteenth-century framework in which upper-voice material tropes the tenor in order to expand on its local meaning and its liturgical context, and a fourteenth-century framework in which the tenor itself is selected to expand, often via a shared word, on the material of the upper voices. Clark shows that a tenor might be selected by a motet composer not only to accord with the upper-voice poetry (as outlined somewhat ambiguously in Egidius de Murino's oft-cited treatise), but also that tenors are sometimes carefully selected to afford opportunities for composing cadences. Clark highlights the difficulty modern listeners face in hearing the lengthy repeating tenor structures as the fundamental organizational principle of motets, yet argues that one can learn to hear these structural, repeating patterns with practice.

In Chapter 4, Lawrence Earp provides a thorough historical contextualization of 'isorhythm', addresses the term's shortcomings, and offers instead a new framework through which four-teenth-century motets ought to be considered and analyzed. He suggests that usage of both 'isorhythm' and 'isorhythmic motet' precipitates a tendency to read fourteenth-century motets that do not happen to employ precise rhythmic repetition as somehow less developed, and furthermore, that the term makes it difficult to account for the kinds of repetition present in thirteenth-century motets. Earp demonstrates how poetic declamation served as an instigator for rhythmic content in much of the earlier motet repertory, and that isoperiodicity in English motets – some of which date well into the fourteenth century – has its origins in such declamation patterns. This sets the English concept of isoperiodicity apart from French isoperiodicity, which instead emerged through a deprioritization of poetic declamation.

In outlining Friedrich Ludwig and Heinrich Besseler's use of the term within their narra-tive of motet development, Earp intervenes by arguing that the fourteenth-century motet is more appropriately characterized by the aesthetic impulse to saturate all levels of a work with meaning; this semiotic operation has been obscured by the overuse of the term 'isorhythm', which prioritizes exclusively precise rhythmic repetition and reifies such repetition as a narrative endpoint. Accordingly, through analysis of a number of specific motets, Earp demonstrates the variety of methods through which composers might embed a certain meaning within all levels of a motet's organization. Prioritizing this kind of semiotic saturation as a core principle of the fourteenth-century motet, he argues that literal isorhythm is but one of many ways through which meanings might be embedded. Earp proposes that the general task of analysis, from this point, is to survey both the range of motet subject matter and the range of techniques through which this subject matter is rendered musically.

Karen Desmond, in the next chapter, traces the development of rhythmic notation in medieval motets. She shows how the evolution of the motet placed various demands on notational systems, precipitating a cycle in which notational ambiguities continually arose and attempts to address them engendered new kinds of ambiguities – eventually resulting in the direct correspondences between specific visual signs and specific rhythmic durations that characterize modern notation. Desmond argues that this clarity, however, comes at the cost of the flexibility and nuance of the earlier, more ambiguous notation. Consequently, she suggests that we should not be too eager to accept later scribes' versions of earlier motets as definitive; their more precise notations might obfuscate some of the rhythmic play afforded by the ambiguity of the earlier versions.

Desmond selects several motets for examination, each of which is present in at least two different sources corresponding to different stages of the development of notation. In so doing, she demonstrates some of the methods through which motet scholars can reconstruct rhythms from ambiguous notation – harmonic considerations, for instance, might resolve some of these ambiguities – all the while invoking contemporaneous theoretical writings. Desmond also considers the rhythmic notations in fourteenth-century English motets, noting in particular the variety of notational practices often found within a single source. She likewise describes Italian notation, highly influenced by the French *ars nova* style, and compares two versions of a specific motet extant in both an Italian notation style and in *ars nova* style. Her discussion of mensuration indications rounds off her contribution; she considers motets that play with differences in mensuration, either between voices or as a structural marker. Her myriad examples (in both 'original' and 'modern' notation), tables, and figures are particularly instructive as her argument unfolds.

To address the various functions of motets in the thirteenth century, in Chapter 6 Dolores Pesce inspects several works in a family of motets based on the *portare* tenor. In the process, Pesce introduces ways in which diverse musical, sonic, literary, and textual concerns are synthesized in motet composition in order to form a cohesive whole. She demonstrates the means through which the Marian and Christological associations of the *portare* tenor have been elaborated and allegorized by upper-voice material. She also shows how the tenor can likewise serve as a source for sonic content, outlining how upper-voice syllables often mirror the vowel sounds of the tenor and coincide assonantly at important points, thereby unifying a motet. Moreover, she illustrates how vernacular refrains may have been chosen for their assonant sounds matching those in the motet voice(s), and furthermore, that a motet itself could be the source of refrain material for a vernacular devotional work. In contemplating that many motet refrains were not in fact quotations, she argues that motet composers rather aimed to make such 'pseudo-refrains' appear as if they were quoting another work in order to perform a certain learnedness, often through citing a general literary tradition of drawing connections between divine love and courtly love.

Pesce also addresses issues of textual audibility, demonstrating methods through which composers might ensure textual clarity at key moments – an important issue considering the performativity of learnedness that she elucidates from the citational tendencies of motet texts. Turning to how the motet can function as a site of musical exploration for a composer, Pesce considers tonal aspects of motet composition; in particular, she demonstrates how cadential strength and weakness might be employed in order to shape a motet into a cohesive whole.

Pesce thus offers a firm foundation for the kinds of devotional and courtly love themes that Jacques Boogaart takes as a starting point in Chapter 7, in which he highlights political commentary as a new function for fourteenth-century motets. To explore this thematic possibility, Boogaart begins with a discussion of the motet *Scariotis falsitas / Jure quod in opera* from the manuscript of the interpolated *Roman de Fauvel* (**Fauv**). Like Pesce, he argues that the audience of such motets would likely have needed to be well learned in order to understand the allegories and quotations obfuscated by the polytextual context; moreover, he draws on existing writings by theorists that support the notion that fourteenth-century motets were appropriate for erudite audiences and that singers of motets were revered for their high degree of musicianship. He suggests that motets may have been performed and critiqued as part of a society of learned musicians, and outlines the function of the motet as a means to praise or admonish certain nobles within ceremonies, mentioning only a limited number of functions of motets within the liturgy.

Boogaart discusses how the admonitory function of many fourteenth-century motets was gradually replaced by a more celebratory one, a trend that continued into the fifteenth century. The fact that more composer attributions have been made in the fourteenth century – either directly as in Machaut's case, or less directly as in many motets composed by his slightly older contemporary Phillipe de Vitry – allows Boogaart to consider another function of four-teenth-century motets: as personal, intellectual endeavors by their composers. He addresses this function by discussing a few motets by Machaut that engage with earlier motets attrib-uted to Vitry and shows that the two composers often come to different personal conclusions about topics such as love. In particular, Boogaart discusses Machaut's M10 and its engagement with Vitry's motet *Douce playsence/Garison selon nature/Neuma quinti toni*, and entertains the intriguing possibility that such a dialogue between the two motets may have come about from in-person discussions.

In Chapter 8, John Haines and Stefan Udell introduce many of the most important manuscript sources for motets, and consider the shifting cultural contexts in which they were produced as well as the specifics of their organization and layout (mise-en-page). Through discussion of several sources – accompanied by numerous full-page reproductions of select folios containing complete motets often also discussed in other chapters in the volume – they demonstrate that, in contrast to the 'sameness' typical of printed works, variations in presentation of the same material in different manuscripts can be especially informative. They likewise show how layout in a single source can lend a further layer of meaning to a motet.

After outlining the process of manuscript production, Haines and Udell argue that medieval motet sources were created at a midway point in the history of the manuscript in general, which, they state, was transitioning from a 'sacred object' to a commodity circulating among a growing urban bourgeois class. In particular, they point to Arras, the home of the **Roi** and **Noailles** chan-sonniers – two sources of great import that are focused upon and viewed in a different light later in the volume by Gaël Saint-Cricq – as exemplifying the trend of book manufacturers catering to growing numbers of bourgeoisie and university students. The authors also argue that manu-scripts such as **Fauv** were partly intended as tools of edification, with various linkages of meaning unfolding across the manuscript. Their discussion of a specific motet in **Fauv**, *La mesnie/J'ai fait*, demonstrates how layout itself can be a meaningful compositional parameter. Haines and Udell additionally describe the kinds of information imparted by erasures – they show that errors are often of a sort suggesting that scribes were copying visually from an example rather than notating from musical memory – and also consider questions of patronage.

In Chapter 9, Jennifer Saltzstein provides the volume's first exemplum chapter with a multi-faceted study of a thirteenth-century two-voice motet, *Fines amouretes/Fiat*. Two-voice motets have received much less scholarly attention than their multi-voiced counterparts, largely due to their lack of contrasting upper-voice texts which often provide ample opportunity for intertex-tual play. Saltzstein, however, shows that, far from presenting an escape from intertextual play, this motet presents an opportunity to focus on another kind of intertextuality – that unfolding between a motet and its borrowed refrain.

Noting that *Fines amouretes/Fiat* features a refrain introduced in the motet text as a song performed by the speaker, Saltzstein turns to Thibaut's *Roman de la poire*, a romance that fea-tures this same refrain among many other lyrical insertions. While Saltzstein does not aim to fully resolve the chronological questions of which came first – the motet or the romance – she is interested in the heretofore under-considered possibility that Thibaut may have quoted these refrains from the motet repertoire. In particular, she enables this possibility through drawing on Bradley's argument that some of earliest Latin motets were most likely contrafacta of French originals, with which Thibaut may have been familiar. Thibaut's possible familiarity with the motet repertory is further reinforced by verses that conjoin multiple borrowings from different motet texts. She explores the notion that this compositional process might recall the genre of the motet *enté*, thereby indicating another possible point of connection between Thibaut's romance and the motet repertory. Saltzstein likewise uses the two-voice motet to unsettle the presumption of an exclusively educated audience. She demonstrates that vernacular culture saturated the lives of motet composers in important ways, and speculates as to the musical value of these works even for listeners not learned in their intricacies.

Suzannah Clark, in Chapter 10, considers two motets, *Quant define/Quant repaire/Flos filius eius* (**Mo** 127) and *Celui en qui/La bele estoile de mer/La bele, en/[Jo]han[ne]* (**Mo** 20), for three and four voices, respectively. Despite the decidedly polytextual aspects of these motets, Clark illustrates how *mono*textual interplay between the upper voices features prominently. Intriguingly, she argues that these monotextual moments are not about sameness but rather emphasize difference, and thus resonate with the polytextual aesthetic underpinnings of the genre.

Clark suggests that **Mo** 127 requires an 'ecological listener': the motet conjures two diametrically opposed landscapes at once, and asks listeners to hold this tension in their head as these landscapes pivot on shared words. She thus argues that textual listening here is not simply about picking up on a few key words that stick out of the texture, as is the case in many other polytextual motets. Turning to **Mo** 20, she outlines the vast network of motets to which it belongs, a network that also includes two- and three-voice versions in both Latin and French. Contrary to prior scholarship, she demonstrates that the French texts preceded the Latin iterations, and that the two-voice version in fact constitutes a nucleus that was in turn expanded, rather than the four-voice version having been stripped of its voices. Clark shows that the quadruplum (the last added voice) and motetus, both poems in which the protagonist professes his love for his lady, are unified through several monotextual moments, but the quadruplum is likewise unified with the triplum, a Marian address, through the sharing of musical material and parallel voice leading. Thus, while the quadruplum's text on its own addresses the earthly lady, by being joined musically with the triplum, it likewise addresses the Blessed Virgin.

In Chapter 11, Gaël Saint-Cricq turns to thirteenth-century motets found in trouvère chansonniers as a way of providing insight into the genre's circulation outside of Paris. These songbooks of borderland provenance offer a substantial repertory of over 200 different motets. Noting the high degree of motets that circulate only in chansonniers and do not correspond to motets in the major Parisian polyphonic repertory, Saint-Cricq demonstrates that these motets come from a culture of their own, separate from the clerics in Paris, and instead part of the world of the provincial trouvères. Thus, the more typical narratives of a liturgical-to-secular trajectory and the determinacy of the tenor are insufficient to account for the non-Parisian repertory found in trouvère chansonniers.

Beginning with **Noailles**, the thirteenth-century chansonnier of Artesian origins containing the greatest number of motets, Saint-Cricq shows that the motets in this manuscript are well integrated with the other genres in terms of visual presentation and shared scribal hands, and thus were not simply additions to the manuscript, but instead were explicitly intended for inclusion. He argues that rondeau-motets combine the polyphonic structure of the motet with the repetition schemes of the chanson; as such, rondeau-motets undermine the presumption that the tenor is necessarily the determining voice. Turning to the fifteen monophonic motets in **fr.845**, Saint-Cricq raises the possibility that musical repetition might underpin the meaning of the term motet *enté* (in which case different words would be 'grafted' onto the same music), but suggests that both quotation and musical repetition are important to the subgenre. Like Leach, he notes how these pieces have received very little prior attention, and in turn advocates for the position that these monophonic pieces in fact constitute a significant part of the motet genre in general. Saint-Cricq also offers a typology of borrowings between motets and chansons, and concludes by arguing that the mutual imbrication of motet and chanson material allows us to reconsider the motet as a firm part of local trouvère practices, and that questions of trouvère authorship thus become relevant to motet scholarship.

Matthew P. Thomson, in Chapter 12, focuses on one specific type of motet-song interaction outlined by Saint-Cricq – when a stanza of a monophonic song is used to create a motet – and provides three case studies with three different emphases. Moreover, Thomson uses 'otherness' as an analytic optic through which to view the finished motet and the ways in which it integrates, or decidedly does not integrate, its quoted material.

In *Onques n'amai tant/Sancte Germane*, chosen to illustrate how musical elements of a quoted upper voice shape the motet's texture, Thomson shows that the tenor, unusually, is freely composed, which allows it to accommodate the borrowed motetus. Demonstrating that the level of detail of correspondence between the tenor and the borrowed song goes further than the general structure of the song form in question, he argues that the quoted nature of the motetus is readily perceptible because it is so determinate of the tenor content; its compositional centrality makes its status as a borrowing or insertion audible. Thomson then discusses *Bien me doi/Je n'ai que que/Kyrie fons* to illustrate various means through which the text of a pre-composed monophonic song (the motetus) can influence the structure and content of the motet's other voices. He argues that unlike *Onques/Sancte*, the quoted material in this motet is integrated in a way that is harder to detect; instead, it is intertwined imperceptibly with the triplum text. *Par une matinee/O clemencie fons/D'un joli dart* is then examined to demonstrate ways that a motet can expand both musically and textually on its quoted song, which here constitutes the tenor. Thomson details the various kinds of alterations necessary to accommodate the presence of a voice that is structured as a song and argues that the three voices are all differentiated, and thus that the quotationality or 'otherness' of the tenor is foregrounded through its structural compositional centrality.

In Chapter 13, I consider motets in England, which have been much less studied than their French counterparts. Focusing on a representative subgenre, the duet motet with medius cantus – that is, unusually, the tenor lies in the middle rather than lowest voice position – I discuss and analyze three such motets and propose a reconstruction of the missing tenor for the third. Although duet motets with medius cantus constitute just one of several kinds of the motet in England, and although this subgenre is not paradigmatic of the entire English motet practice, these motets do illustrate many of the genre's most salient characteristics. Further, this specific type of motet is generally not found on the continent, and thus constitutes an interesting subgenre ripe for examination.

Jesu fili Dei/Jhesu fili virginis/Jesu lumen veritatis and *Rosa delectabilis/[Regali ex progenie]/Regalis exoritur* share many features, including isoperiodicity, assonance, and sacred Latin texts. Both motets are also tonally coherent, often centering on F, but both also feature different intermediary competing tonal centers. After having detailed the common characteristics of these two motets, and in response to the fact that the tenor of the recently discovered motet *Majori vi leticie/Tenor/Majorem intelligere* is missing, I draw upon the pervasive features of the genre in order to offer a reconstruction of this tenor and in turn suggest a potential match. Noting how the outer voices of duet motets with medius cantus often unfold in consistent ways (in terms of rhythm, phrase lengths, and counterpoint) I consider whether such motets might have been improvised around their middle-voice tenors. I interrogate the propensity to read these works only in comparison to continental motets and suggest that we instead view English motets as a functionally distinct repertory.

Returning to the continent in Chapter 14, Anna Zayaruznaya reconsiders the role of the tenor and the process of tenor construction in *Colla iugo subdere/Bona condit cetera/Libera me*, composed by Philippe de Vitry. Like A. Clark, Zayaruznaya draws on Egidius de Murino's theoretical writings that suggest that composers had some sort of *materia* in mind before selecting their tenors; however, Zayaruznaya emphasizes that we cannot be sure whether the word *materia* refers to a general topic or theme, musical elements, already-composed upper-voice texts, or perhaps a combination of these things. In addressing this uncertainty, Zayaruznaya takes interest in *Colla/Bona* because the repetition structure of its tenor differs from that of the upper voices. She then details an instructive hypothetical reverse-engineering of *Colla/Bona*.

In imagining how one might work with the *Libera me* tenor were it to have preceded the composition of the upper voices, Zayaruznaya argues that the tenor would be most suitable for a penitential motet or a lament, of which *Colla/Bona* is neither. The alternative compositional narrative she offers is that Vitry began with the topic of condemning courtiers in favor of a simpler life (a topic that also features in some of his other works) and then proceeded to write the upper-voice texts. Thus, Zayaruznaya proposes that the motet's structural concerns were largely worked out before the selection of the tenor; in other words, significant upper-voice *materia* had already been developed before the tenor was selected. As such, Zayaruznaya makes an important intervention into the presumption that tenor material comes before upper-voice poetry and structuring. But at the same time, her piece also makes evident the complexity of synthesizing – rhythmically and structurally – multiple poems and pre-existing musical material into a fourteenth-century motet.

In Chapter 15, Margaret Bent performs an in-depth analysis of *Hareu! hareu! le feu/Helas! ou sera pris confors/Obediens usque ad mortem* (M10), a motet composed by Vitry's slightly younger contemporary, Guillaume de Machaut. Although Bent mostly focuses on this single motet (M10), her chapter offers – through demonstration – various analytical frameworks with which one might approach any of Machaut's twenty-three motets, and by extension, *ars nova* motets in general.

Bent begins with the same issue of *materia* explored by A. Clark and Zayaruznaya but here demonstrates that the mutual interdependence of the tenor material and the upper-voice material complicates simplistic understandings of the tenor as merely preceding the upper voices. In particular, Bent points out that Machaut's tenors were often not taken from the beginning of their sources, but rather borrow specific words that resonate with upper-voice texts. At the same time, she complicates the issue by showing ways in which upper-voice material is dependent on tenor material in M10. In other words, Bent's and Zayaruznaya's chapters complement each other because – while both argue for a complex understanding of the interface between tenor and upper-voice material – Zayaruznaya demonstrates how the tenor is dependent on the upper voices, and Bent demonstrates how the upper voices are dependent on the tenor (which is not to say that the tenor necessarily came first). Neither author presumes that one aspect of a motet wholly or completely precedes the other; they are more interested in the complexities and intricacies of compositional processes. Bent makes this mutual complexity clear in her discussion of the difficulty of placing monosyllabic lines of poetry in the upper voices in order to have hockets coincide with talea division points in the tenor.

Bent does not subscribe to a methodological divide between analyzing text and music and turns instead to the interplay between musical motives and words as a subtle kind of 'word painting'. Further, recalling her article that has since influenced several scholars in their use of the term 'isorhythm' (an influence that is evident throughout this *Companion*), Bent again intervenes in the overuse of the term in favor of a more discerning analysis of repetition, difference, play, and meaning.

In the next chapter, Sarah Fuller turns to a four-voice Machaut motet, *Tu qui gregem/Plange regni respublica/Apprehende arma et scutum/Contratenor* (M22). Both upper-voice poems take the form of political exhortations; this motet thus provides an example of the new political function of fourteenth-century motets discussed in Chapter 7 by Boogaart. After outlining the historical context surrounding the motet – a time characterized by war with the English, siege, nearby peasant revolts, and weak leadership – Fuller takes a specific analytical approach, one that explores how various musical aspects reinforce textual meaning and mirror this time of crisis.

Fuller outlines some unusual aspects of the tenor and suggests that the rupture of its expected pattern reinforces the upper-voice texts through mirroring the political crises of the time. Also, eschewing the term 'isorhythm', Fuller instead argues that periodicity is a useful concept for articulating the design of a motet. Her in-depth consideration of instability/stability as not only a structural parameter of the motet but also a textually/politically meaningful one is likewise significant; in her mapping of the motet's tonal structure, she shows how musical instability and stability follow the text in hinting at an interplay between anxiety and hope. She likewise maps the upper-voice poetry, which is itself fairly regular; however, its structure is obscured by differing musical periodicities. Fuller also highlights audible, meaningful moments in the triplum text, as well as Machaut's manipulation of the motetus range, which, at one significant moment, occupies the highest register in a passage expressing hope. She discusses the relationship between modern analytical visual presentations of motets (she calls this the 'score illusion'), the part-by-part presentation of motets in the original manuscripts, and the real-time experience of listening to or performing this music. Even though Fuller engages with structural details, she cautions against seeing motets as 'frozen architecture' – her focus on stability and instability serves as one way of understanding how some of these structural details might translate into affective experience.

While Machaut's M22 may be securely dated to 1358–60 due to its internal political references, the motet *Portio nature/Ida capillorum* – the subject of Chapter 17 by Emily Zazulia – cannot be dated with any type of certainty: as Zazulia elucidates, the motet, which lauds St Ida who lived some 200 years before the motet's conception, may have been composed as early as 1342 but as late as 1376. Compounding the issue is that the motet contains stylistic features that seem to contradict external evidence as to its date of origin. As such, Zazulia confronts the difficulty of weighing stylistic evidence against the kinds of evidence provided by the motet's sources, attributions, and texts.

Zazulia demonstrates a range of methods that have been used by scholars for dating a motet, and considers the potential shortcomings of each of those approaches. She also elucidates how the motet makes use of a homographic tenor: drawing on Bent's critique of the overapplication of the term 'isorhythm', Zazulia argues that the tenor here is not isorhythmic and its unfolding instead comprises two distinct processes not reducible to isorhythm: mensural reinterpretation and diminution. In the end, she does not arrive at an answer as to the date of *Portio/Ida* – but this is not her point. Instead, this uncertainty serves as a useful way of troubling an overreliance on any single form of evidence, whether stylistic or external. In particular, Zazulia shows that what seems like 'hard' evidence – the ascription of the motet to a named composer, for instance – may in fact be much more ambiguous than it appears upon a closer look, and that the details of both the music and other historical sources may complicate the picture.

As the chapter summaries above illustrate, several broad themes recur throughout the volume in addition to the major contested areas mentioned toward the beginning of this introduction. For instance, many chapters engage with the various tools through which a motet composer might craft a cohesive or unified work from such seemingly disparate parts. Earp proposes that, for the *ars nova* motet, cohesion might come about through the use of a single governing concept that permeates every layer of the work. He also invokes the potential for periodic structures to function as a unifying device, pointing out that overlapping periods prevent simultaneous phrase endings and therefore delay cadences in order to sustain momentum. In my chapter, I highlight composers' use of isoperiodicity in the motet in England as a similar means of achieving compositional cohesion. The issue of tonal coherence is discussed in Pesce's chapter with regard to thirteenth-century motets, in my chapter with regard to the motet in England, and in Fuller's chapter with regard to a fourteenth-century *ars nova* motet. Sonic convergences, yet another means of achieving compositional unity, are discussed in Pesce's and S. Clark's chapters. Leach and Thomson consider the intricacies involved in aligning various kinds of borrowed or quoted material within a cohesive whole.

Another recurring theme involves the ways in which motet composers might represent textual meaning musically. Bent invokes the concept of 'word painting' in her analysis of a Machaut motet and demonstrates how a recurring melodic motive comes to represent 'amours'. More generally, upper voices often expand upon the meaning and context of the tenor, as is evident in several of the motets in the chapters below. As Zayaruznaya shows, though, this does not necessarily mean that the tenor is compositionally foundational or originary; rather, the tenor might be selected later in the composition process in order to mirror existing upper-voice words or phrases. And yet another way in which textual meaning might be imparted is discussed by Haines and Udell: in looking at **Fauv** in particular, they show how meaning might be represented visually, through mise-en-page.

While a great deal can be learned through looking at manuscripts, several scholars also discuss the problems associated with the written archive. Bradley demonstrates that layout tends to blur the generic fluidity exhibited between motets, clausulae and conductus. Desmond argues that the updated notation of subsequent motet versions should not necessarily be taken at face value, as the original rhythmic flexibility may be obscured. Fuller discusses the differences between a motet as found on the page as compared with a motet in performance. And while Zazulia cautions against an overreliance on composer ascription in the case of one particular motet, Boogaart, on the other hand, precisely because of composer attributions, is able to speculate on the possibility that Machaut and Vitry may have shared ideas with one another.

The concept of borrowing likewise arises throughout much of the volume, an unsurprising fact given the common practice of using pre-composed tenor melodies. But it is not just the tenor that is frequently borrowed; as many chapters attest, the refrain plays a crucial role not only in the geneses of particular motets, but also in the development of the genre as a whole. Leach, for instance, prioritizes the use of refrains in her genealogy of the genre. Saltzstein, Pesce, S. Clark, and Saint-Cricq all illustrate the importance and prevalence of refrains in motets. And as Thomson has shown, an entire song strophe may be borrowed and serve as the 'foundation' to which a tenor is added, similar in some ways to one of the *portare* motets discussed by Pesce, whose motetus voice is structured as rondeau, which in turn led the motet creator to structure the tenor along similar lines.

These instances of borrowing – or when works simply share material – often necessarily bring up questions of chronology. For example, in Leach's chapter, chronological questions arise concerning the relationships between trouvère refrains and motets in **D308**, as well as between **D308** motets and their concordances in **Mo**. Bradley shows the fluidity present in the relationships exhibited between motets and clausulae. Saltzstein entertains the possibility that secular romances might have quoted from a motet repertoire that would have been familiar to the trouvères. And issues of chronology likewise arise when motets do not necessarily share material; for instance, when comparing works with one another in attempt to date a motet, Zazulia demonstrates the thorny issue of using style for the purposes of dating, and elucidates the potential dangers in doing so.

Another prominent topic concerns textual audibility and inaudibility. Although the purported inaudibility of words within polytextual motets has received a lot of scholarly attention, Saltzstein in particular corrects the general lack of attention to the two-voice motet, the text of which necessarily does not need to compete with others in order to be heard. Pesce demonstrates procedures employed by thirteenth-century composers for ensuring that key words are audible in a three-voice setting. S. Clark challenges an interpretation of monotextual convergences as being simple moments of heightened audibility and demonstrates that the meanings of shared words can in fact be diametrically opposed. Such concerns regarding audibility and inaudibility are pertinent not only to textual aspects of motets but also to structural aspects: A. Clark points to the difficulty modern listeners have in hearing talea structures as the fundamental organizational principle of motets, yet she argues that one can learn to hear these patterns. Bent states that tenor talea organization can be made audible through hockets in upper voices, which often mark talea junctures. Yet Earp argues that rhythmic repetition is but one technique among many that elaborate on the core theme of a motet, and that we should not presume rigid 'isorhythm' to be necessarily foundational to the motet or the endpoint of the genre's development. It therefore remains contested whether 'isorhythm' is a foundational compositional principle that we should learn to listen 'for', or whether the concept tends to function as a kind of scholarly red herring, leading us to overlook more sensuous or specific local features of a given motet.

In sum, this book is partly a debate genre, and partly a polyphonic motet of its own making. The *Companion* is multi-voiced – with seventeen different voices, in fact – and can be synthesized using allegory and analogy, but this can be difficult. Much like a section of hocket, its voices pop up and say their own thing, but still remain part of a larger overall texture.

1

The Genre(s) of Medieval Motets

Elizabeth Eva Leach

MARK EVERIST began the final chapter of his 1994 monograph with the statement that 'The motet is a genre'.[1] Certainly, musicologists broadly seem able to agree that certain musical pieces are medieval motets when they encounter them. Nonetheless, the questions of whether *the* medieval motet is a genre, and if so, how this genre arose and what characteristics define it, have become more difficult to answer in recent years, not least on account of the ongoing work of Everist and those who have studied with him. As many of the contributions to this volume attest, there is significant flexibility and generic porousness between clausulae and motets, conductus and motets, and songs and motets.[2] This chapter suggests that this might be because those things termed motets today are themselves a hybridization of other genres whose transmission history – comprising items largely collected retrospectively after significant use, adaptation, and further hybridization – makes it difficult, perhaps impossible, to uncover the multiple pathways through which this universe of medieval motets came about. Observing the shapes of galaxies in still images allowed astronomers to develop a taxonomy[3] and then to model galaxy formation using physical laws, deriving a dynamic history for each object based on present observations.[4] The frozen snapshot offered by surviving manuscripts might seem analogous to these telescope images, but musicologists have no such firm laws from which to track back, so are forced to make more speculative arguments from close readings, musical and notational analysis, and assumptions about chronology. This chapter will look again at issues of genre, origins, and evolution using the evidence of the large motet collection in **D308**. Lacking notation, this collection has been generally disregarded, yet it provides the sole meeting point for two kinds of motets that never otherwise appear together: examples of the so-called motet *enté*, a monophonic subgenre only otherwise found in **fr.845**, and the motetus texts of a number of widely transmitted 'mainstream' polyphonic motets.

To read most textbooks or dictionaries of music is to be told that the motet as a genre arose through the trope-like and mainly syllabic Latin texting of the upper voice(s) of a discant clausula, a polyphonic and rhythmically patterned elaboration of a melismatic section of liturgical chant. As such a genre, the motet's defining features might be polyphony, polytextuality, and rhythmic patterning. This narrative implies, too, that the earliest motets were Latin, with parental clausulae; later developments encompass a *vernacularizing* move (as French texts were combined with or

---

[1] Everist 1994, 148.
[2] See the chapters by Catherine A. Bradley, Gaël Saint-Cricq, and Matthew P. Thomson below.
[3] Hubble 1936.
[4] Lintott *et al.* 2008.

replaced Latin ones), and a related *secularizing* move from the ecclesiastical to the courtly orbit, eventually visible in a *compositional* move to use some other tune as a tenor, either appropriated from secular repertoires or newly composed.

This neat teleological story has looked suspect and ragged, especially around its edges, for almost as long as it has been told. Various figures, starting with Yvonne Rokseth in the late 1930s and including scholars such as William Waite, Wolf Frobenius, Fred Büttner, Franz Körndle, Wulf Arlt, and most recently Catherine A. Bradley, have questioned both the universal trajectory from clausula to motet and the idea that Latin texts necessarily preceded French ones.[5] Nearly all more recent discussions by specialists hedge their retelling of the classic version of events with manifold caveats and exceptions.[6] In addition, the generic subdivisions within the motet as a historical genre have been questioned, refined, and even dismissed, while modern emphasis on the alluring polytextual play in three- and four-voice motets has arguably skewed our interpretative view of motets, of which a large number survive in only two parts.[7]

While the standard narrative doubtless correctly describes the generation of many thirteenth-century polyphonic pieces that we today call motets, this chapter will problematize it further by focusing on the significant collection of motets copied in **D308**. With no indication of any tenors, these motets are copied purely as poetic texts; each consists of a single voice part, all motetus parts where this can be ascertained through concordances. They are short texts with refrains, often split between opening and closing lines, sometimes additionally internally, and sometimes only at the end; some texts have more than one refrain. In asking what kind of a collection the unnotated motetus texts in **D308** present, this chapter will raise the prospect that a greater witness to the monophonic motet genre than has hitherto been suspected may lie hidden within the mainstream polyphonic transmission.

THE MEANING(S) OF 'MOTET'

It is now widely accepted that the term 'motet' is a diminutive of the French 'mot' ('word'). Michael Beiche, in his entry on the term in the *Handwörterbuch der musikalischen Terminologie* (Dictionary of Musical Terminology), notes that the earliest Latin witnesses do not provide reliable evidence as to the origins of the musical use of the term.[8] In an article first published in German in 1970, Klaus Hofmann reflects on then-recent studies of the etymology of the term 'motet(us)'. He argues that far from originating as a Latin polyphonic genre, the genre called 'motet' was, at its outset, a short, vernacular, monophonic genre – basically a song snippet, or what we would today call a refrain.[9] This is not a refrain in the sense of a repeating refrain found

---

[5] For a useful summary, see Catherine A. Bradley's chapter in the present volume.

[6] See, for example, Peraino 2011, 195.

[7] Everist (1994, 149) dismisses the 'straightforwardly taxonomic' subgenres of rondeau-motets and motets *entés* as either 'so general, or identify[ing] so small a portion of the repertory, that they leave a large part of the repertory undifferentiated' and goes on to propose a theory of modes, drawing on Alistair Fowler and Iurii Tynianov as a way of talking about musical features. Roesner (2007) analyses a single two-part motet that he places at the boundary of motet and accompanied song, while noting its typicality. See Jennifer Saltzstein's chapter below where she stresses the importance of the two-voice motet repertory.

[8] Beiche 2004, 2.

[9] Hofmann 1970. The prominence of this article in scholarship has been increased by the availabilty of an English translation by Rob C. Wegman; see https://www.academia.edu/3335701/Hofmann_ Klaus_On_the_Origins_and_Early_History_of_the_Term_Motet. See also Beiche 2004, 6–7.

identically at the end (and/or beginning) of each stanza in a refrain-form song. Instead it is a refrain in the sense of those bits of quotable text to a catchy tune that circulated in and out of narratives, motet voices, and songs in the long thirteenth century.[10] This earliest use of the term would thus explain the sense of 'motet' in the designation 'motets *entés*' ('grafted motets') as rubricated in **fr.845**. While admitting the motet *enté* as a genuine subgenre of the motet, Everist does not find the classification particularly meaningful since it pertains to only fifteen pieces, mostly *unica*, and with no concordances in the mainstream motet repertoire.[11] Even by extending the subgenre to include motets transmitted monophonically in other sources (but not labeled 'motets *entés*' or necessarily defined by refrain usage), Judith Peraino comments that the number in the group are 'too large to be simply aberrations and too small to suggest a coherent "genre"'.[12]

Hofmann argues that the term became extended to refer to the motet-carrying melody in its entirety (the 'motetus' voice), and at the same time – *totum pro parte* – to any whole polyphonic piece of which that melody was part.[13] While this trajectory is supported and elaborated by Beiche, he notes in addition the astonishingly small number of witnesses to the terminological usage in Latin music treatises given the large number of surviving musical pieces.[14] Hofmann explains this paucity by positing that the term did not originally apply to the Latin-texted pieces of which the music treatises mainly speak and which dominate the earliest notated musical transmission. Instead, he argues that Latin-texted pieces that operated musically (and musico-poetically) in a similar way to the vernacular motet eventually came to be called motets by analogy in later thirteenth-century music theory, with this terminological change being completed by the time Johannes de Grocheio was writing.[15] Thus, although a central reference source like *Grove* might give the motet a simple origin in a liturgical trope that 'soon developed into the preeminent form of secular art music during the late Middle Ages' it seems instead that its origins are much more complex:[16] two separate genres developing jointly in the early thirteenth century – a Francophone musical genre setting a single-stanza poetic expansion of a short poetic refrain text (the 'motet') and an entirely different genre that saw the textual troping of the upper voices of Latin clausulae – were retrospectively yoked together under the term 'motet' in second half of the same century, perhaps because they both used some form of textual expansion/troping, and also because they had already interacted and hybridized musically with each other on account of already being themselves hybrid forms.

Before the application of the term 'motet' was universalized, the earliest examples of what we would now consider Latin motets are labelled as tropes or prosulae in the sources, if they have any designation at all; early theorists who discussed their compositional and notational aspects considered them a variety of discantus and thus not in need of any further label, and referred to the voice part as a duplum.[17] So, while by labelling these earliest Latin polyphonic and polytextual

---

[10] See the extensive treatment of the refrain in Butterfield 2002 and Butterfield 2003.

[11] Everist 1994, 75–89: ch. 4, 'The *motet enté*'.

[12] Peraino 2011, 192.

[13] Hofmann (1970, 144) mentions that by the time of Jean de Meun's continuation of the *Roman de la Rose* (*c.* 1270) the term was used for both the duplum part and the whole polyphonic complex. See also Beiche 2004, sections III–IV.

[14] See Beiche 2004, 8. Beiche does not cite or discuss Hofmann 1970 in this regard but only in passing on p. 3 in connection with a translation of Odington's phrase 'motus brevis cantilenae' as the strophe of a short song (rather than relating to the idea of movement).

[15] Hofmann 1970, 148–9; 148 cites *Discantus positio vulgaris* applying 'mothetus' to both the duplum and the motet setting as a whole, and giving examples of both with Latin texts.

[16] For the *Grove* quotation, see the entry 'Motet, §I: Middle Ages' by Sanders and Lefferts.

[17] See Hofmann 1970, 149.

compositions 'motets' we may be replicating a terminological usage that is medieval, the label is probably not as early as the 'motets' in question themselves. Hofmann's arguments imply that refrains, not Latin motets, are really 'the earliest motets' in the term's contemporaneous sense, and those polyphonic pieces that came to form one early subset of the genre were originally an unrelated form of discantus, included only later, by casual or analogical back-application of what had become a rather general term, under the generic label of 'motet'.

In literary sources, the word 'motet' was often employed within a narrative to introduce the performance of a borrowed refrain. The need to denominate a piece would not have applied, however, to notated sources of those musical pieces we now designate Latin motets, which therefore would have had less of a need to provide generic labels. Is it possible, then, that these pragmatic concerns account for the chronological lag between the usage of 'motet' in early literary sources and its later usage with regard to sacred polyphonic musical sources? That is to say, might the traditional caveat that absence of evidence is not necessarily evidence of absence be pertinent here? Perhaps this is the case, although I am not necessarily convinced by a rigid distinction between literary and musical sources. A literary work that describes the singing of musical interpolations whose texts it also provides in full is arguably also a musical source, especially when musical notation of that refrain was planned, as evidenced by features of layout (whether or not it was executed). One might go further and suggest, as I have done elsewhere for the whole of **D308**, that verbal notation alone is sufficient to prompt singing when one knows the song, which seems especially plausible in the case of a short, interpolated vernacular 'motet' (that is, a refrain).[18] Thus, any assumption that manuscripts of *Méliacin*, *Renart*, and *L'Art d'amours* are not musical motet sources relies on an already accepted definition for the motet as necessarily polyphonic.

Ardis Butterfield has closely linked the refrain and the motet and pointed out the preponderance of motet-based refrains among refrain-interpolated narratives.[19] Jennifer Saltzstein has shown that the refrain did not originate, as once thought, in *rondets de carole*, and that there is a whole host of refrains that only ever circulate in different motet voices.[20] Peraino has studied monophonic motets that she notes 'represent a sustained collective interest in creating songs that cross-pollinate monophonic and polyphonic repertories'.[21] Nonetheless, the persistent standard narrative has been difficult to shake off. Peraino, observing that 'for a medieval audience of vernacular song, the word "motet", perhaps more often than not, signaled the quotation of a refrain rather than polyphony', does not go on to argue that therefore the monophonic motet is rather closer to the original sense of the term than any of the musical complexes that musicologists now term motets.[22] In her essay in the present volume, Saltzstein uses Thibaut's quoting of refrains from French motets as evidence that vernacular motets came 'closely on the heels' of the Latin origins and argues that **D308**'s 'reuse of motet lyrics in other song genres suggests enthusiasm for motet texts among late thirteenth-century courtiers at considerable remove from the scholastic circles that apparently created the motet genre in early thirteenth-century Paris'.[23] Her 'apparently' would be overcautious if those scholastic circles did not create the motet genre as such, but merely created some musical pieces that could later be readily subsumed under that label. That what we think of as the earliest motets might only

---

[18] See Leach 2015.

[19] Specifically in *Chauvency*; see Butterfield 2012. See also Butterfield 2002 and Butterfield 2003.

[20] See Saltzstein 2013b.

[21] Peraino 2011, 192.

[22] Peraino 2011, 195, 197.

[23] Salzstein in the present volume, pp. 199 and 202.

have become termed motets by analogy with a parallel genre, whose origins were vernacular and monophonic, could be a reality obscured by this retrospective application of 'motet'.[24]

Both Gaël Saint-Cricq and Peraino have stressed that the existence of the monophonic motets in a number of songbooks, and the devotion of entire gatherings to them in three of these sources, should in itself not merely lead us to note the broad remit of the word 'motet', but also dissuade us from treating the motet genre as being by definition a polyphonic one.[25] The idea that pieces with distinct and separate origins might lurk below the smooth surface of the single genre of 'the medieval motet' is already hinted at by the notated musical sources, which show a bifurcation between motet books and songbooks. Saint-Cricq points out that when songbooks transmit a corpus of motets they are not 'exogenous additions oddly tacked onto songbooks: they were intended for the original program of the trouvère anthologies'.[26] And yet over half of the motets that are copied in songbooks are never copied as part of what Saint-Cricq terms 'the central tradition', that is, the motets in motet books from a principally Parisian orbit; and the collections in songbooks show a far greater proportion of *unica*. These observations hold true for **D308**, where the motets are copied by the same scribes as the six genres of the trouvère song collection that precede them (making the motets part of the manuscript's original contents), yet forty-four of sixty-three texts are *unica*.[27] As shown in Table 1.1, nineteen motets in **D308** have concordances, but I will be forced to ignore Mot24 since its other copying context is unclear, as is the relation of the notation to the text, which is fragmentarily transmitted.[28] Among the remaining eighteen concordant motets, five occur both in songbooks and in motet sources (shaded dark grey in the table), while four occur elsewhere only in the motets *entés* of **fr.845** (shaded light grey) and nine occur elsewhere only in polyphonic motet books.[29] The comparative statistics adduced in Saint-Cricq's chapter in the present volume show that **D308** is relatively large for any motet source, and that it is typical of the songbook sources for motets in its inclusion of motets within its planned contents and its high degree of *unica*.[30] Atypical, however, is that **D308** has concordances not only with texts in the polyphonic motet repertoire of the non-chansonnier sources, but also with the monophonic motets of **fr.845** that are labeled motets *entés*. This fact is significant because it

[24] The early vernacular meaning of 'motet' did not immediately disappear when the term began to be applied to a broader selection of musical pieces. Vernacular literary sources that cite refrains continue to refer to them as motets, whether in a narrative or lyric context. Nor did the extended usage of 'motet' as referring to the entire monophonic piece in which a short refrain text featured disappear either, although, as mentioned above, the number of monophonic motets that are copied as such is relatively small.

[25] See Peraino 2011, 194–5 and Saint-Cricq's chapter (p. 231) below.

[26] See Saint-Cricq in the present volume, p. 228.

[27] See the statistics giving proportions of *unica* in both motet and songbook sources in n. 13 of Saint-Cricq's chapter below.

[28] *C'est la jus condist au lai praielle* (Mot24) is on the back guard leaf of Ca, which has two identical lines of musical notation, one each above the first and second quatrains of text. These are non-mensural, each containing 5+9 pitches, separated by a stroke as if they each set a short and then a long poetic line. It is unclear, however, how they might relate to the text, which has lines of 9, 7, and 6 syllables (9´a 7b 6b 6´a 9´a 7c 6c 6´a), although it tantalizingly implies that this is a copy of this work as a monophonic motet. I thank Gaël Saint-Cricq for helping me with queries about this source.

[29] Typically for D308 the pieces with concordances in the given genre subsection cluster around a particular part of the subsection, usually the beginning, while the later parts of the subsection tend to be more densely populated with *unica*.

[30] See Table 11.1 in Saint-Cricq's chapter below.

Elizabeth Eva Leach

Table 1.1. Concordant motets in D308

No.	Incipit	Motet voice	Tenor	fr.845	Roi	Noailles	Reg1490	Mo	W2	Other polyphonic motet sources	Max no. of voices	Refrain (vdB)	Melody also preserved with Latin texts?	Clausula in F?
1	Trop suix joliette	722	Aptatur (O46)	–	–	–	–	X	–	Ba; Ps	4	[1126] (absent from D308)	–	–
2	Trop longement m'ait faillit	397	Pro patribus (M30)	–	X	X	–	X	X	Ba; Cl; [Her]; Ps	3	411	X	X
4	L'autrier juer m'an alai	651	Eius (O16)	–	X	X	–	X	X	Ca; Cl	4	338	X	X
6	Bone compaignie	91	Manere (M5)	–	–	–	–	X	–	[Bes no.53]	4	370	–	–
9	Biaus Deus revairai je jai	1091	–	no. 15	–	–	–	–	–	–	1	538	–	–
14	Dex, je ne puix la nuit dormir	480	Et vide et inclina aurem tuam (M37)	–	–	–	–	X	X	Ba; StV (marginal incipit only)	4	535	–	–
15	Sor tous les malz est li malz d'amors	579	Alleluya (M78a)	–	–	–	–	–	X	–	2	(1747)	X	–
18	É Amors! Morai je por celi	10	Omnes (M1)	–	–	–	X	X	–	Ba	3	504; 796	–	–

19	Amors qui tant m'ait grevei	544	Alleluya: Domine (M66)	–	–	–	X	–	3	(not in vdB)	X	–
20	Mercit de cui j'atandoie	792	Fiat (O54)	–	X	X	X	StV (marginal incipit only)	2	1308	X	–
21	Biaus cuers desireis et dous	477	Audi filia (M37)	–	–	–	X	–	2	216	–	–
22	Quant li noviaus tans replaire	100	Surge et illumina\<re\> (M9)	–	–	X	–	–	2	210	–	X
23	Ne puet faillir a honor	570	Descendentibus (M74)	–	–	–	X	Ba	3	158; (457); 785; (1364); 755	–	–
24	C'est la jus condist au lai praielle	1102	–	–	–	–	–	[Ca back guard leaf]	1?	(1837)	–	–
28	Mesdixans creveront	1082	–	no. 6	–	–	–	–	1	1322	–	–
30	E[n] non Dieus, c'est la raige	271 = RS 33	Ferens Pondera (M22)	–	X	X	X	–	2	665; 1447	–	–
44	Hé Diex! je n'i puis durer	1089	–	no. 13	–	–	–	–	1	(818)	–	–
50	Douce dame debonaire	1077	–	no. 1	–	–	–	–	1	604	–	–
52	J'ai trovei	167	Seculum (M13)	–	–	–	X	–	2	(984)	–	–

seems to provide an otherwise entirely missing link between the motets *entés* and the 'mainstream' motets transmitted in large thirteenth-century polyphonic, polytextual collections like **Mo**.

THE MOTET SUBSECTION OF **D308**

Overall, **D308** is a large complex book copied in early fourteenth-century Metz, containing French narrative poetry, prose, and an extensive chansonnier divided into eight genre subsections.[31] The first six of these genre subsections have similarities in their copying. All six are subject to an internal table of contents at the head of the chansonnier section of the manuscript, which lists incipits and gives each item a number. After the table of contents, each of the first six genre subsections begins at the top of a recto, the previous subsection ending with blank lines and even blank pages as necessary in order to achieve this layout. Except the first subsection (the *grans chans*), each has an initial illumination. The last two genre subsections, however, are not introduced in these ways. The motet section starts on fol. 243v with no rubric or illumination, after only three blank lines following the final *sotte chanson*; the first rondeau follows without any break on fol. 247v. The motet and rondeau subsections do not feature in the internal table of contents for the chansonnier section and are not numbered by the rubricator. Otherwise, however, the section looks similar to the others, with the texts copied as prose with large red or blue initials for each new piece, and by the same scribes as the rest of the chansonnier.[32]

Mary Atchison argues that, because the layout of **D308** provides 'no indication of the shift from the motets to the rondeaux, except through the poetic forms of the texts', the manuscript therefore presents the two genres as a unified group.[33] However, the exception Atchison notes seems rather salient, since the formal distinctiveness of the rondeau texts, with their heavily repetitious structures, would make the shift clear to any reader. Moreover, the rondeau repetitions are generally written out in full, making them easily visible. No other genre subsection could have been so readily signalled by its form alone, since all of the other sections show a wider variety of formal types. Therefore, the motets and rondeaux actually continue the arrangement by genre, setting aside the minor issue of there being one motet text in the rondeau subsection. And far from these two subsections being somehow separate from the rest of the chansonnier, there is textual as well as scribal evidence that they are well embedded within the book as a whole.

Questions remain, though. Why is there no rubricated label for the motet and rondeau sections? And what, if they had labeled the motet section, would they have called it? This omission is frustrating given that **D308** alone contains a mixture of things labeled 'motet *enté*' transmitted monophonically and only in **fr.845** and the motetus texts of more regular polyphonic, polytextual motets in the 'mainstream' tradition. The generic organization of **D308** implies that all of these items fall within the same genre. This might help situate the seemingly isolated motets *entés* of **fr.845** more squarely within the overall motet tradition of which they have been considered barely a part. In a more radical interpretation, pursued here as a thought experiment building on some suggestive – but far from conclusive – hints in the textual variants between **D308**'s Mot4 and Mot6 and their concordances, we might also consider the possibility that some (perhaps even many?) of the motetus parts known to us today only in their polyphonic settings could have begun their lives as monophonic motets *entés*.

---

[31] See Leach 2015.

[32] Complete images are available online at http://digital.bodleian.ox.ac.uk/inquire/p/ dd9d1160-196b-48a3-9427-78c209689c1f.

[33] Atchison 2005, 80.

MONOPHONIC CONCORDANCES

D308's four motet texts with purely monophonic concordances have a transmission pattern that is isolated from the other concordances in the source; see Mot9, Mot28, Mot44 and Mot50 (lightly shaded) in Table 1.1. They exist with notation solely in **fr.845**'s collection of motets *entés* where they are copied without any indication of a tenor part. In addition to being motet *enté* no. 15 in **fr.845**, *Biaus Deus revairai je jai* (Mot9) is also copied within the poem *Méliacin*, where the motet is laid out in a similarly monophonic presentation, although only the initial spatial layout survives since notation and staves were never entered.[34] Of the four concordances between **fr.845** and **D308** only refrain vdB 818 in *Hé Diex! je n'i puis durer* (Mot44) is not transmitted elsewhere.[35] (Refrains without other attestations are enclosed in parentheses in the table.) The other three concordances have refrains well attested elsewhere, all occurring in motets,[36] and those in Mot9 and Mot28 also occur in *chansons avec des refrains*.[37] The refrain vdB 1322 of *Mesdixans creveront* (Mot28) is particularly widely copied, occurring additionally in the four sources for *L'Art d'amours*, a *Salut d'amour* and the continuation of *Le Court d'amours*.[38] Mot28 possesses an unusual three-line refrain, being disposed in its grafted version at the beginning, middle, and end of the poem.

The types of refrain citation in the four concordances with **fr.845**'s motets *entés* seem congruent with the general pattern of refrain citation in the rest of the motet section in **D308**. Overall only the first and last in the contiguous section of the first sixty-three texts, of which one is duplicated, lack a refrain entirely (Mot1 and Mot63).[39] Among the sixty-three, forty-four motets have a refrain that is split between first and last lines of the text.[40] A further eight texts have final refrains; all but one are attested elsewhere. This leaves nine motet texts that have a combination of at least two refrains, of which six motets have at least one of those attested elsewhere; four of these nine include a split refrain as at least one of their multiple refrains.[41] The presence of split refrains in 76% of the texts of **D308**, therefore, lends some credibility to Ludwig's assessment that the motet

---

34 See, for example, the layout visible in the online images of **fr.1589**: http://gallica.bnf.fr/ark:/12148/btv1b8447872k/f112.item.

35 Although the refrain vdB 818 is similar to vdB 1094 in Mot41 and to vdB 846 in *Pour noient me reprent* (384) in **Reg1490** fol. 17v; **StV** fol. 290r (incipit only); **W2** fol. 239v, where the text is 'Hé, je n'i puis durer, non, sans la bele Marion'; it is not the same melody.

36 See the entries for refrains at http://medmus.soton.ac.uk/view/abstract_item/.

37 This genre strikes me as exceptionally ripe for reexamination to test the idea of 'motet' meaning 'refrain' in the early period, since the *chanson avec des refrains* is a stanzaic song interpolating various things contemporaries might have termed 'motets'.

38 Three of the four sources for *L'Art d'amours* even have it twice, once in a section glossing how it is necessary to be defiant against gossips and later illustrating the parties counter to love. The *Salut d'amour* that contains it starts 'Amors qui m'a en sa justise' and is uniquely in **F-Pn f. fr.** 837, fol. 271v. For a full listing, see http://medmus.soton.ac.uk/view/abstract_item/1322.html.

39 Mot1 omits the terminal refrain that is part of this text in concordant versions, but had those versions not existed, it is likely that scholars would have viewed the first and last lines of Mot1's text as a split refrain, although it is not attested elsewhere.

40 I do not entirely share the perturbation detectable in some scholarship about the potential for an unattested refrain to be a fiction, since I think the defining feature of a refrain is not that it is quoted but rather that it is potentially quotable, glossable, expandable, flexible; we are clearly missing texts and it may be that where we do have other attested uses, chronology is difficult to establish and/or points to the motet as the origin in any case.

41 This brings the total of split refrains up to the forty-eight mentioned by Saint-Cricq in his chapter; see p. 232 below.

texts in **D308** are 'almost exclusively' ('fast ausschließlich') motets *entés*.[42]

If the users of **D308** knew the melodies for these songs, the texts of the manuscript could easily be sung. And if the four **D308** motets with monophonic motet *enté* concordances were sung, it seems possible that the other motets in the collection would also have been sung to known melodies. It is worth testing this hypothesis with those other fourteen motets for which concordances in polyphonic sources exist. Could the users of **D308** simply have sung the motetus parts of these pieces,[43] perhaps with a vielle providing the tenor known from those concordant sources?[44] In many cases this seems entirely possible, but there are some cases where significant differences between the poetic structure of the text in **D308** and the text of the motetus in the polyphonic sources would not only make the provision of the tenor problematic, but would actually render it impossible to sing the **D308** text to the melody known from elsewhere without making some adjustments. In what follows, I will propose some adjustments in specific cases and then reflect on what those adjustments might reveal (or at least suggest) about the music for the motets in **D308**.

POLYPHONIC CONCORDANCES

Peraino's table 4.1 of 'Monophonic motets in major sources' reveals that the other sources with monophonic motets, excepting **Reg1490**, have a lower percentage of concordances with the polyphonic repertory than **D308**: only one of the eleven in **Roi** and none of those in **fr.845**, **Noailles**, or **X** have a concordance, although the sample sizes in these cases are quite small.[45] It would be easy to assume that the late copying of **D308** makes it a late source for these texts, so that if the poems differ so as to make them unsingable to the motet melodies we know from earlier sources it may be concluded that **D308** is in error and/or that its users were no longer singing these motets. But late sources do not always carry late copies; ample concordances between the **D308** and the chansonnier **U**, the earliest copied trouvère source, suggest that (at least in these cases) **D308** provides a copy of some of the *earliest* renderings of many texts. While it cannot be proven that this is the case with all the texts in **D308**, as a starting point I will avoid making any easy assumptions about chronology; instead, where the text of a motet makes it difficult to sing to the notated version known from other sources, I shall attempt to reconstruct a version that will work, and only then ask what this hypothetical version might tell us about whether it is later or whether it might antedate the known version. Ultimately the radical hypothesis that will be tested here is whether **D308**'s motetus parts, as known musically by the book's users, were earlier monophonic versions of melodies we now only know in polyphonic motet contexts. Investigation

---

[42] Ludwig 1910–78, 1/1: 307. On the dispute over the term *enté* see Everist 1994, Butterfield 2003, and Saint-Cricq's chapter, pp. 231–2 below.

[43] Despite the frequent rejection of the possibility of performing music from unnotated sources from anonymous readers of journal articles and in questions at conferences, everything about the contents of this source points to it inhabiting a court with a thriving musical culture of which this book is one of the prime documents. See Leach 2015.

[44] Accompaniment is described for two of the set-piece evening entertainments indoors at *Chauvency*, the robardel and the *jeu du chapelet*; see Regalado 2006. This description might even point to a forum in which an improvised accompaniment could have provided a testing ground for the polyphonization of monophonic motets.

[45] Peraino 2011, 190–1: eight of the nine listed for **Reg1490** have polyphonic concordances. I have omitted her inclusion of **Mo**, since this is itself a source of polyphonic repertory, and the single examples adduced in **Mesmes**, **Fauv**, and **O**, all of which are also in polyphonic sources, definitely represent too small a sample size.

of differences in the readings of the poetry between **D308** and the polyphonic sources preserve some hints that this might indeed be the case.

All but two of **D308**'s polyphonic concordances can be found in the most comprehensive collection of polyphonic motets, **Mo**, where they are copied in fascicles 2, 5, and 6, and thus belong to the 'old corpus'. The other two, *Sor tous les malz est li malz d'amors* (Mot15) and *Quant li noviaus tans replaire* (Mot22), are found otherwise only in **W2**. The pattern of these concordances aligns **D308** in this respect with any 'mainstream' thirteenth-century motet collection.[46]

D308 has copied its motet texts as a section of sixty-three one-voice motets, by implication monophonic motets, so why would it include a high proportion of texts from polyphonic motet voices? As noted above, other monophonic motet collections have virtually no such concordances, and certainly not a high proportion. Looking at the complete set of fourteen polyphonic concordances, six motets are found only in two-part settings; the rest can be found in various voice combinations up to four-voice textures. Striking, however, is that in all cases, even where the **D308** text is found elsewhere in three or four-part contexts, the **D308** text is that of the motetus voice, the voice which, if there is any source that carries a merely two-part version of the motet, will be the voice preserved there with the tenor.[47] This fact can be read in two ways, depending on whether or not the compilers knew the polyphonic, polytextual versions of these melodies. If, on one hand, the scribe has consciously chosen to copy only the motetus text when those of other voice part(s) were known, it would associate these texts with a sung performing tradition; otherwise there would be no reason to exclude the triplum or quadruplum texts, which present similar kinds of poetry but would not make clear musical sense sung on their own with the tenor. If, on the other hand, the scribe had no knowledge of the text's circulation within polyphonic motets, it would suggest the existence of a substantial repertoire of monophonic or two-part motets available to the compilers, hinting that all these motets originated either as something resembling the motets *entés* of **fr.845** or as something closer to the 'accompanied songs' of **Mo** fascicle 6.[48]

Thereafter, the kinds of performance these motetus texts point to might also be understood in different ways. The copies in **D308** might signal opportunities for polyphonic performance, since it would only require one singer to know the melody of the copied text and the other to know the chant melisma and its disposition into repeating rhythmic and pitch units in order to produce a performance of a musically coherent two-part motet. Conversely, it might signal that

---

[46] Again, it should be noted that the sample size is relatively low, but the tenors with which these motetus texts are associated elsewhere nonetheless offer additional information about the nature of D308. Three have Office-chant tenors (Mot1, Mot4, and Mot20); the other eleven have Mass-chant tenors, reflecting a fairly normal bias towards the use of Mass chants in thirteenth-century motet collections. Of the Office chants, O16 is a standard chant in the collection of the *Magnus Liber*, but O46 and O54 do not have any organum or *Magnus Liber* connections. Of the Mass chants, the use of M1, M13, and M37 (which is used in two motets, Mot14 and Mot21) is fairly widespread, and M5, M9, M22, and M30 are also standard and in the *Magnus Liber*. That leaves just M74 and the unidentified chant M78a as being unique to the D308 motets. In summary, apart from four chants – O46 and O54, M74 and M78a – D308 looks much like a list from a thirteenth-century motet collection in a motet book, according with the presence of these motets in the old corpus of Mo. I thank Catherine A. Bradley for a discussion of the points in this note.

[47] I use this as the designation of a voice with motetus function, since the order of the voices in layout is often indicative, but not always so. Several later thirteenth-century motets, notably those by Adam de la Halle, have the voice that is laid out as if it is the motetus finishing on a higher pitch than that of the triplum. Contrapuntal function, layout, and labelling are sometimes at odds in this repertoire, but not in these cases.

[48] The term is Roesner's; see Roesner 2007.

these pieces are motets in the sense of the first extension of the term posited by Hofmann, that is, that they are monophonic motets *entés* not yet (at the chronological point from which **D308**'s sources date) ensconced within a polyphonic context. If indeed all motets in **D308** were performed monophonically, the manuscript's unique mixture of motets *entés* and 'mainstream' polyphonic motets might no longer seem so odd. In other words, *despite* their polyphonic concordances, we could infer that these fourteen motets were originally monophonic motets that were adapted for polyphonic performance before being copied into other sources, and that although **D308** is a source later in date than the manuscripts transmitting those polyphonic concordances, it preserves in these instances an earlier state of the repertory.

This is a radical proposal that can be neither proved nor disproved; however, as a thought experiment, it serves to problematize some traditional chronological presumptions. As noted above, of the fourteen concordant motets, five are also copied in songbooks, which might reinforce the proposal. Perhaps working against the proposal is the fact that five can be found with alternative devotional texts in Latin, which could suggest that they belong to the more liturgical, discantus tradition, and represent musical structures that were never monophonic. However, three motets (nos. 2, 4, and 20) are in both groups, that is, they have Latin texts in other sources but are also copied in songbooks. This might suggest, on the contrary, that in these cases, the Latin texts postdate the French ones. Luckily for my present purposes, the details of Mot4's text in **D308** are rather suggestive in this regard, and a closer look at this piece will complicate the picture even further.

L'AUTRIER JUER M'AN ALAI (651; **D308** MOT4; **MO** 21)

Mot4 is a version of the widely copied motetus part in **Mo** 21, *L'autrier jouer m'en alai par un destor* (651). The motets in which this melody appears represent one of the most studied and discussed complexes in the repertoire.[49] In terms of its origin story, the melody of motet voice 651 has two seemingly contradictory features: it is both the upper voice of a textless clausula in **F** (the earliest surviving source of the music), and also possesses a trouvère refrain (vdB 338) found in Guillaume d'Amiens's dance song *C'est la fins*.[50] In addition, there are multiple texts in Latin for the motetus and triplum voices, glossing to various degrees the Christological and Marian resonances of the liturgical tenor, *Flos filius eius*. Prior to Bradley's 2013 article on this motet, scholars had tended to accept that it had progressed from clausula, through Latin textings, to French textings presenting an allegorical form of the original Marianism, and therefore tended to conclude that the untexted clausula borrowed from the melody of the trouvère song.[51] Bradley, however, argued that the 'music of the motetus in particular ... suggests that it was conceived in conjunction with its accompanying French text' and thus that the motetus melody with the French text represents the earliest version, a claim that 'is further confirmed by the song-like construction of the motetus melody, comprised of pairs of repeated melodic figures'.[52] Her argument concentrates on rejecting, for this specific case, the normative idea that the clausula predates the corresponding motet, and thus does not explicitly address the question of whether or not the

---

[49]   For a full listing of its members, see Bradley 2013, 40.

[50]   Found in **Reg1490**, fol. 119v; see Everist 1994, 66–8.

[51]   Bradley 2013, 41, ns. 117–19; see also Everist 1994, 43–50, 66–8; Huot 1997, 95–6; Planchart 2003; S. Clark 2007, 46–7 n. 32. Bradley (2013, 41 n. 116) notes earlier hints at French-motet priority in Rokseth 1935–9 and Frobenius 1987.

[52]   Bradley 2013, 53.

earliest French motet version was monophonic. The rather different textual presentation of the motetus in **D308** has not to date figured in any of the manifold discussions about this motet, but its differences with the version on which all other sources substantially agree are suggestive. If **D308** is read as presenting a monophonic version of the motet, it is interesting to imagine what relationship – both musical and chronological – this monophonic motet might have had to the melody of the motetus voice of the polyphonic motet.

First I would again like to question what might seem a reasonable assumption, that **D308** is a late source and therefore might well transmit a corrupt and incomplete version of the motetus text. In fact, the various sections and subsections of **D308** generally transmit very good texts. While the current contents of **D308** result from a fifteenth-century binding, it is likely that the original context for the chansonnier section included the preceding item, Jacques Bretel's *Tournoiement de Chauvency*, which is part of the same physical structure and shares scribes and illuminator with the song section.[53] And while it is physically separate, the first item, Jacques de Longuyon's *Voeux du Paon* also has the same illuminator and scribes.[54] **D308**'s version of the opening item, Jacques de Longuyon's *Voeux du Paon*, is in the same family as, and transmits remarkably close readings to the base text chosen by its modern editor for this source, and has more illuminations than any other manuscript of this very widely transmitted work, although that may be explained by it being copied close to its time and place of composition.[55] Jacques Bretel's *Tournoiement de Chauvency*, too, appears in its most highly illuminated version and while the text is abbreviated at the beginning (omitting seven of the seventeen jousts from the first two days and the evening's entertainments on the feast's first night), its readings are often preferable.[56] The chansonnier's frequent concordances with **U** link its readings to the earliest textual tradition for many of the songs. Moreover, looking specifically at the motets, **D308**'s concordances with the monophonic motets in **fr.845** show few textual variants, none of which are significant or obviously negligent. I therefore suggest that – at least as an opening strategy – we take the shorter text in **Mot4** as legitimate in its own right rather than a result of scribal carelessness or epigonal tradition.

I begin by asking the question of whether and how it might be possible to sing the shorter text presented in **D308** to the music that survives in the notated tradition for the motetus, taking the version of **Mo** as a convenient 'standard' version. The fact that the **D308** text is shorter than that in the other sources of this poem and that the melody will therefore need to be similarly abbreviated (exactly *how* is discussed below) strongly suggests that this text could not have been sung with the tenor of the motet version, since the tenor pitch sequence, a double cursus of twenty-five pitches (from the word 'eius'), preceded by the seven pitches belonging to 'flos filius', would need to be abbreviated in such a specific manner that it would be difficult to produce a workable performance. This suggests that unless we are looking at poetic rendering *not* designed for singing, the version in **D308** is a monophonic motet.

Table 1.2 compares the versions of the text in **Mo** and **D308**, which I have laid out first so as to align similar lexical content, which I have also given in bold face. Lines 1–2 are virtually identical

53   See catalogue item IV-10 in Stones 2013, 1/2: 41.

54   See Atchison 2005.

55   Casey 1956 edits from **GB-Ob 264** (fol. 209), dated 1338, because it is the only one of what Casey terms the 'P group' – his central and most reliable tradition for the text – to contain both the prequel and sequel of the *Voeux* and 'because of its regularity in part I and because of its great beauty' (xxxvii). Nonetheless he notes D308, which he gives the siglum P1, 'is written in the dialect of Lorraine and may be an earlier text than P. It has many independent lines in both parts of the text' (xxxvii) and 'cannot be classed with any group or subgroup' (xxiv).

56   See the notes in Delbouille 1932; see also Regalado 2006 and Atchison 2012.

Table 1.2. Textual comparison of D308 Mot4 and Mo 21

a. Aligned by sense units

D308 Mot4				Mo 21	
1	L'autrier juer m'en alai	7a	7a	L'autrier jouer m'en alai	1
2	Par .i. destor.	4b	4b	Par .i. destour	2
			7a	En .i. jardin[a] m'en entrai	3
			4b	Pour coillir flour	4
3	**Genti pucelle trovai,**	7a	7a	**Dame plaisant i trovai**	5
4	**Cointe d'ator;**	4b	4b	**Cointe d'atour**	6
5	Eus ot vairs et **lou cuer gai,**	7a	3a	**Cuer ot gai**	7
6	Plain de dousor;	4b			
7	Et **chantoit:** 'Dex,	7a	7a	Si **cantoit** en grant esmai:	8
			3a	'Amour ai.	9
	ke ferai?		3a	*Ke ferai?*	10
8	*C'est la fins, la fins*	5x	5x	*C'est la fins, la fins,*[b]	11
9	*C'ai ke nuns die, j'amerai!'*	8a	8a	*Quoi ke nus die, j'amerai!'*	12

b. Aligned by versification

D308 Mot4				Mo 21	
1	L'autrier juer m'en alai	7a	7a	L'autrier jouer m'en alai	1
2	Par .i. destor.	4b	4b	Par .i. destour	2
3	**Genti pucelle trovai,**	7a	7a	En .i. jardin[c] m'en entrai	3
4	**Cointe d'ator;**	4b	4b	Pour coillir flour	4
5	Eus ot vairs et **lou cuer gai,**	7a	7a	**Dame plaisant i trovai**	5
6	Plain de dousor;	4b	4b	**Cointe d'atour**	6
			3a	**Cuer ot gai**	7
7	Et **chantoit:** 'Dex, **ke ferai?**	7a	7a	Si **cantoit** en grant esmai:	8
			3a	'Amour ai.	9
			3a	*Ke ferai?*	10
8	*C'est la fins, la fins*	5x	5x	*C'est la fins, la fins,*[d]	11
9	*C'ai ke nuns die, j'amerai!'*	8a	8a	*Quoi ke nus die, j'amerai!'*	12

[a] vergier: **Mo, Cl, W2**
[b] C'est la fins: **Roi** and **Noailles**
[c] vergier: **Mo, Cl, W2**
[d] C'est la fins: **Roi** and **Noailles**

in both sources. Looking at the lexical content and rhyme words, it appears at first that **D308** lacks lines 3–4 of **Mo**'s version, since lines 3–4 of **D308** resemble the content of lines 5–6 in **Mo** 21. If one tries to skip lines 3–4 of the **Mo** version and sing straight from line 2 to line 5, however, problems arise at **D308** line 5, which is too long. There seems no obvious way to work around a structure that both omits and adds lines compared to the notated version, regardless of the order in which one imagines them to have been composed. I therefore decided as an experiment to try singing the text of **D308** to the music of **Mo**, regardless of the lexical content; this works because the first six lines of both texts actually have entirely the same poetic versification: three couplets, 7a 4b. This comparison is shown in the layout of part b of Table 1.2. After the first six lines, omission of melodic material will become necessary in order to sing the **D308** text; however, the difference between the texts becomes purely one-directional, with **Mo**'s version having three three-syllable lines (lines 7, 9, and 10) that are not present in **D308**. If the music for these short lines is simply omitted, the resulting monophonic version is not only poetically more regular but also contains parallel phrases that make this version even more song-like than the **Mo** 21 version. Example 1.1 shows the hypothetical monophonic version of this melody that would fit the text of **D308** and makes clear the musical parallels between lines 5 and 7.[57]

Example 1.1. Hypothetical monophonic motet melody for D308 Mot4

This is a hypothetical reconstruction of a melody for this motet, but on that heuristic basis, we can ask which of these two versions might have come first. On one hand, we might imagine that the **D308** version – in a late manuscript and the sole witness to this textual tradition – represents a later abbreviation, perhaps omitting the musical elements that only really make sense with the accompanying tenor (if we imagine they wanted to sing a well-known polyphonic motet's motetus monophonically), or perhaps simply adapting the poetic structure to present something more

---

[57] In case the leap of a seventh between the end of line 6 and the start of line 7 is thought unconvincing it should be noted that a similar leap is to be found between lines 4 and 5 in *Biaus Deus revairai* (Mot9 in **D308**) using the melody from its concordance in fr.845, as well as between lines in trouvère songs. In the putative version of Mot4, the leap serves to mark out the transition line, introducing the impassioned song of the lady in a way different from, but equally as striking as, that in the **Mo** version.

regular (if we imagine it is simply a poem, not designed for singing). On the other hand, one could take a bolder position and imagine that the **D308** version is a precious glimpse of an earlier history of this piece as a monophonic motet, and that the version in **Mo** represents an expansion, perhaps necessitated by considerations pertaining to polyphonization.

The latter view gains, I think, some traction from the poetic differences between the texts. The version in **D308** has an opening six lines in which the 'je' goes out along a byway (lines 1–2), finds a lovely 'pucelle' ('young girl'; lines 3–4) and describes her eyes and heart (lines 5–6), before saying that she is singing (line 7) and then quoting her song directly (lines 7–9). The **Mo** version starts with the same two lines, going out on the byway (lines 1–2), but then he enters a garden or orchard to pick flowers (lines 3–4). It is in that specific more confined space that he finds a pleasing 'dame' ('lady'; lines 5–6) with a merry heart who is singing in great dismay that she has love (lines 8–9) before the refrain follows as in the **D308** version. The **Mo** version has a more elevated status for the woman the narrator encounters, and situates her specifically in a garden or orchard, where the narrator is picking flowers. The woman's status and her position in a garden where there are flowers ready to be cut have been taken as Marian signals.[58] These Marian signals are absent from the **D308** version, which is nevertheless coherent on its own terms, despite its comparative brevity: it is, instead, a fairly standard pastourelle poem in lexis and narrative sequence. If the **Mo** text is an expansion of a monophonic original which was more like **D308**'s text, it would be easy to posit that the added lines were suggested at the point of polyphonization because of the Marian liturgical source of the tenor melisma.[59]

The differences between the two texts might be used to investigate the implications for the musical aspect of the two versions. What follows attempts an entirely hypothetical imagining of how the composer of the first polyphonic version might have developed it from the mono-phonic motet version. On this analysis, positing for the sake of argument a monophonic motet with **D308**'s text and music resembling that in Example 1.1, the use of a refrain from a well-liked refrain song provides a D-final and an authentic range for the tune within which it is used. The composer of the first polyphonic version then chose a very well-known tenor melisma that had a final on D but a plagal range (see Example 1.2, which shows an edition of just the motetus and tenor parts of the four-part version in **Mo**, with the text of **D308** underlaid beneath that of **Mo** for easy comparison, and not to imply that the **D308** text could be sung to the two-part version). The 'eius' melisma has twenty-five pitches; the song has fifty-three syllables, so the tenor, moving at the same basic pace as the upper part, would have needed to be a double cursus plus a few notes. In addition, however, the rhythmically prominent C at pitch 10 of the 'eius' melisma in the particular tenor rhythmicization of the chant chosen here would have required trying to find a prominent melodic G or c to sound with that tenor pitch, whereas the tonal terminations of the lines in the monophonic motet before the refrain are D, a, F, and E. Looking for internal uses of G or c in the melody thus became the chief constraint on the alignment with the tenor. The two

---

[58]   See Huot 1997, 95–6.

[59]   Moreover, lines 3 and 5 are identical with lines 2 and 3 of another motetus text in **Mo**, **Mo** 112. The motetus in **Mo** 112 begins with the same line as Mot4 and shares its line 2 with a line in its associated triplum text (line 3). The shepherdess in the triplum text opens her direct speech with 'amors ai', which corresponds to line 9 of **Mo** 21. If the text of **Mo** 21 represents an expansion on the **D308** text Mot4 through the insertion of lines 3–5, one might posit that these lines could have been readily suggested by the sharing of the highly conventional opening first line with that of another motetus part, whose continuation lines thereby became the source for lines 3 and 5, while the 'amors ai' in its triplum text formed a useful short line later. See the discussion of this piece in Butterfield 1993.

G pitches in lines 1 and 2 come too early for the tenth note of the cursus, and using the G in line 3 would lead to a dissonance of a seventh (D/c) in line 4. Thus, especially given that the double tenor cursus would not have been long enough if used alone, it made sense for the composer to begin with the seven pitches preceding the 'eius' melisma (those setting the words 'flos filius' at the opening), which are not part of the repeating pitch structure of the tenor.[60] The use of these seven pitches ('Flos filius') had the additional merit of ensuring overlapping phrase structures in the first six lines of the piece, while also opening up a compositional 'buffer' of six perfections, which could be used to insert short 'fillers' as required, mainly for contrapuntal reasons. In this case, three inserts, each of two perfections, were added to evade problems with vertical sonorities. The first insert introduces the first coordinated rest between the tenor and motetus parts (end of **Mo** 21's line 7) and allows the start of the second cursus to occur with the start of a melodic/ poetic line. Bradley cites the music-textual rhyme between this first short line, 'Cuer ot gai', and the second 'Amors ai', which has the same contour a third higher, as one of the features that makes it more convincing that this melody was specifically composed for this French text.[61] I am merely arguing that the point at which that particular musico-poetic parallel was inserted was not in my hypothetical monophonic version, but at the point of polyphonization; further, it might be that the reason for making these two lines not only parallel with each other but also with the very opening motif was precisely to introduce compelling new parallels given that they introduce temporal distance between the two phrases setting lines 5 and 7 of the **D308** version, making *their* melodic and rhythmic parallelism less overt.

Importantly, the second of the three-syllable insertions (**Mo** 21 line 9, 'Amors ai') takes care of the tricky tenor C at pitch 10 of the color in the second cursus. The compositional solution is to replicate exactly the pitches that were above tenor pitches 8–10 of the first cursus in the second, despite the rather different poetic position (occupying the last note of line 3 and first two of line 4; both boxed in Example 1.2). The immediate further insertion of 'Qu'en ferai' avoids what would otherwise have been parallel unisons between tenor and motetus for pitches 11–12 and also serves to set apart the refrain more obviously.[62]

So, *if* the **D308** text gives us a glimpse of an earlier version and *if* the music of that text is plausibly reconstructed in Example 1.1, my argument shows how a poetic structure might be adapted at the point that a monophonic motet is polyphonized in order to produce a workable contrapuntal structure. My analysis is highly speculative, however, and will not convince everyone, not least because we are so familiar with how perfectly the melody seems to exist in its **Mo** 21 version that it is difficult not to imagine it as having always existed in that form. But if the **D308** version *were* the original, and if the users of **D308** did not know the polyphonic version, there would be no reason for them to find the monophonic version deficient.

It is a further question whether modal rhythm or something like it was already a feature of the monophonic motet or whether it was introduced at the point of the addition of the tenor. Several features make a rhythmically patterned performance plausible: the monophonic motet is a single stanza so does not have to negotiate the competing rhythmic demands of different stanzas sung to the same melody, it is largely syllabic, and, in cases where the refrains of monophonic motets are

---

[60] This is a procedure used in several other motets on the 'eius' melisma.

[61] See Bradley 2013, 50. Note that the version in the songbooks **Roi** and **Noailles** ornaments the word 'cuer' with three pitches *F-E-F*, but does not do this for 'Amors', making the parallel less clear.

[62] In addition, it was necessary to adjust the chant, removing the pitch *E* from metrically prominent positions in this mode and replacing it with *D*; instances are marked in Example 1.2.

Example 1.2. Tenor and Duplum from Mo 21 with D308 Mot4 text underlaid

concordant with, for example, those in *Renart*, they are often found with mensural notation suggesting fixed ternary rhythm. The performance of refrains described in both *Renart* and *Chauvency* (with which **D308**'s motets have many refrain concordances, although not in the **D308** copy of *Chauvency*),[63] is also bound up with dancing and instrumental accompaniment, strongly implicating some kind of patterned rhythmic delivery. Perhaps this was even something that, together with not having later strophes, differentiated monophonic motets from monophonic songs.

BONE CONPAIGNIE (91; **D308** MOT6; **MO** 33)

Bone conpaignie is another motet that appears both within **Mo**'s fascicle 2 (as a motetus voice in **Mo** 33) and, in an abbreviated form, in **D308** (Mot6), although the abbreviation occurs at a different place than that seen above in *L'autrier juer* (Mot4).[64] Unlike Mot4, this motet is not copied in any songbooks. The texts of the versions in **Mo** and **D308** are given in Table 1.3 and the music in Example 1.3, with the **D308** text provided beneath the **Mo** text purely for purposes of easy comparison. The first three quatrains, occupying the first tenor cursus, are relatively similar between the two sources and set up a balanced, song-like structure in which the music of each quatrain divides into two equal-length phrases, each ending with the b-rhyme (-ée) being sung to a perfect long and then a long imperfected by a rest. The first phrase seems answered by the pitches of second: *g-g* (perfections 7–8) answered by *c-c* (15–16); then *f-e* (23–4) answered by *c-b* (31–2). The second quatrain (perfection 17) starts identically to the first. The a-rhyme changes (from -ie to -eis/-és) in the third quatrain, but otherwise the third quatrain is set similarly, starting from the upper *g* with *g-g* (39–40) answered by *a'-g* (47–8). Line 11 here, in the same position in the tenor's first cursus as the refrain citation will be in the second, anticipates the first line of the refrain music (compare perfections 41–44 and 89–92); it also introduces the topic of the refrain 'bons vins . . . assés' ('enough good wine'), for which the speaker in the refrain will cry out when it is lacking.

The differences between **Mo** and **D308** appear in the second cursus. I am assuming that **D308** first has an error in lines 13–14, misplacing the rhyme word by reverting to a more natural word order. This quatrain proceeds as if it is going to be a cbcb rhyming quatrain with line 15 using the c-rhyme; however, this line is followed by three lines that all have the c-rhyme (lines 16–18) and then a single line refrain (line 19), with the unique rhyme '-in'. The text in **Mo** has a short, five-syllable line for line 15, which uses the b-rhyme rather than the c-rhyme suggested by the rhyme scheme established to that point. Then a quatrain follows that is entirely absent from **D308** (lines 16–19); this quatrain has two lines ending in unique sounds (-é and -oit) that are not part of the rhyme scheme (the versification is fairly free with its mixture of five-, six-, and seven-syllable lines but has a tight use of only three rhymes until the refrain's final and unique terminal '-in' sound), so this quatrain sticks out as being irregular. In addition, this quatrain has a first-person speaker, whereas the preceding text consists entirely of third-person description. The content of the quatrain presents a scene concerning clerics disputing logic, entirely unprepared in the previous description of feasting in good company; therefore, this quatrain seems to belong to a more monastic, cathedral, city, or university context, rather than to the entirely courtly context of the **D308** version. Following this quatrain, line 20 in **Mo** is the same as line 16 in **D308**, but there are two further divergences in the text. The version in **D308** repeats the imperative 'buveis'

---

[63] See Butterfield 2012 and Atchison 2012.

[64] There is another motet from Mo's fascicle 2 that appears in abbreviated form in D308, *Trop suix joliette* (722; D308 Mot1; Mo 34), but it will not be discussed here for reasons of space.

Table 1.3. Textual comparison of D308 Mot6 and Mo 33

	D308 Mot6			**Mo** 33	
1	Bone conpaignie,	5'a	5'a	Bone conpaignie,	1
2	cant elle est bien privée,	6'b	6'b	quant ele est bien privée,	2
3	maint jeu, mainte druerie	7'a	7'a	maint jeu, mainte druerie	3
4	fait faire es sellée.	5'b	5'b	fait fere a celée.	4
5	Mais cant chascuns tient s'amie	7'a	7'a	Mes quant chascun tient s'amie	5
6	cointe et bien parée,	5'b	5'b	cointe et bien parée,	6
7	lors est par droit bone vie	7'a	7'a	lors a par droit bone vie	7
8	chascuns d'aus **menée**.	5'b	5'b	chascun d'aus **trovée**.	8
9	Li maingiers est atorneis,	7c	7c	Li mengieres est atornés	9
10	et la tauble aprestée,	6'b	6'b	et la table aprestée,	10
11	de boins vins i ot asseis,	7c	7c	de bons vins y a assés	11
12	par cui joie est menée.	6'b	6'b	par qui joie est menée.	12
13	Apres maingier font les deis [a]	7c	7c	Apres mengier font les dés	13
14	venir [b] a l'asamblée	6'b	6'b	venir en l'asamblée	14
15	sor la tauble **sant poseis**	7c	5'b	sour la table **lée**,	15
			7x	**Et si ai sovent trové**	16
			6'b	**maint clerc, la chape ostée,**	17
			7y	**qui n'ont cure, que le soit**	18
			6'b	**logique desputée.**	19
16	Li ostes siet par deleis,	7c	7c	Li hostes est par delés,	20
17	ke dit: 'buveis, **buveis**',	6c	4c	qui dit: 'bevés',	21
18	et cant vins faut, si crieis:	7c	7c	et quant vins faut, si criés:	22
19	'ci not faut .i. tot de vin!'	7d	7d	'ci nous faut un tour de vin,	23
			6c	*et* [c] *diex, car le nos donez!'*	24

[a] MS: venir

[b] MS: les deis

[c] The two dots under 'et' and the lack of a note above it in the manuscript show 'et' to be an error; it has therefore not been counted as a syllable for the sake of the meter.

('drink!'), giving a smooth and more regular closing section in contrast to the odd short line 21 in **Mo**'s rendering. And **Mo** then has a second line in its refrain, entirely lacking **D308**.

The lines that are in **Mo** but not in **D308** look poetically ill-fitting, which suggests that they may be a later addition. These lines insert clerics (where they were previously absent) and a first-person speaker into what appears otherwise to be an objective report of a courtly festivity; moreover, these lines break with the tightly organized rhyme scheme of the surrounding text. In terms of purely poetic form and content, therefore, it looks like **D308** is the original version and the notated motet version is an expansion. Musically, however, the extra lines of **Mo** make perfect sense: they ensure that the melody is the right length for an entire second cursus of the tenor. If we take the musical regularity to suggest that the **Mo** version is the original, and we imagine the scribes of **D308** removed the lines in question in order to make the text more suitable in a courtly environment, this would render polyphonic performance of the motet in **D308** very unlikely, since the tenor singer would need to omit pitches 10–21 of the second cursus of a 36-note color, an alteration arguably difficult to arrive at without a notated tenor. Similar to the case of Mot4, the alternative hypothesis is that **D308** presents a monophonic motet, which, at the point of its expansion into a polyphonic version, required textual adaptation, mainly through the addition of lines, in order to fill the entire double cursus of a tenor that otherwise fits quite neatly with the existing melody.[65] Example 1.3 makes the comparison with **Mo** 33 clear, displaying that its additional quatrain occupies precisely four iterations of the tenor's rhythmic pattern, a unit that coincides with the poetic quatrains in the first cursus, while Example 1.4 shows a hypothetical monophonic version for Mot6. The adaptation in the melody of Example 1.3 required in Example 1.4 to accommodate the different text is not difficult, but it does not make as much musical sense as that shown for Mot4. There is the addition of a breve imperfecting a long to accommodate the three syllables of **D308**'s 'sant poseis' where **Mo** has only the two of 'lée' (boxed X) and I have simply directly repeated the first 'buveis' figure for the second (boxed Y).

As well as adding notes in those two places, two melodic omissions have to be made. The first omission (perfections 61–76) seems neat enough, although the resulting leap of a sixth is unique in this melody. While this example may be less conclusive musically than Mot4 (since musical motivations for either expansion or abbreviation of the melody are difficult to adduce), it renders a *poetically* more regular motetus text (which is also more topically fitting, with no references to the logical disputations of clerics). The final four perfections and their breve upbeat also have to be omitted, since **D308** does not give the second line of the refrain, whereas **Mo** 33 does.[66] The anticipation of the refrain melody at the end of the first cursus (boxed X in Example 1.3) differs in its continuation from the refrain proper (boxed Y in Example 1.3), since the refrain proper has to terminate with a somewhat surprising fa-mi ending (*f-e*) to fit the ending of the chant on *a*. This ending draws the motet away from the otherwise pervasive *c*-based and melodic *c-g* axis, which makes some sense given the final pitch of the tenor and the provision of a polyphonic cadence, but might have seemed tonally odd when rendered monophonically. **D308** avoids such a strange *e* ending: instead, if one just stops singing where the text runs out, the ending on *g* replicates the

---

[65] That the text chosen is a clericalization of the repertoire might suggest that the people responsible for the addition of a liturgical tenor to a pre-existing courtly monophonic motet were clerics (although this does not rule out this happening in a courtly context, since clerics were to be found there too).

[66] The refrain's other attestation, in **Fauv**, accords with **Mo** 33, which **Fauv** certainly postdates and thus may cite. The dates of **D308** and **Fauv** are very close but Yolanda Plumley argues that **Fauv** postdates and was familiar with at least some of the repertoire of **D308**. See Plumley 2013, 33–42, esp. table 1.1.

Example 1.3. Tenor and Duplum from Mo 33 with D308 Mot6 text underlaid

Example 1.4. Hypothetical monophonic motet version of D308 Mot6

ending of the first half of the motet (corresponding to the end of the first tenor cursus). Poetically, the second line of the refrain as given in **Mo** 33 is unnecessary; the **D308** version simply ends with the host crying out that 'we are out of wine here!', with the conclusion of the second line of the refrain ('for God's sake give us some more!') being implicit. On its own terms, therefore, the Mot6 version makes perfect sense, particularly poetically and, more arguably, also musically.

CONCLUSION

D308's extensive motet collection adds complexity to the picture of the generic aspects of thirteenth century motets, although it is frustratingly difficult to draw firm conclusions because of the lack of notation. Three performance possibilities seem to present themselves: 1. they are merely poems, not to be performed with a melody; 2. they are monophonic motets; 3. they are polyphonic motets, whose tenors, while not mentioned, might have been supplied by users of the book suitably equipped with supplementary materials in their memory or written in ephemeral forms. The first possibility I tend to reject. When in romances like *Méliacin*, beast allegories like *Renart*, and versified histories like *Chauvency*, things called motets are performed, *sung* by courtiers, by minstrels or heralds, they are either refrains or single-stanza songs with refrains in them somewhere, often split between opening and closing lines, and appear to be short songs that are well known.[67] And 'mainstream' motets, whether in motet manuscripts or chansonniers, always have at least provision for music. My assumption, therefore, is that the short motets in **D308**, too, would have been sung by the commissioners and early users of this manuscript, even if the manuscript itself was not needed in the performance context.

It is very difficult to determine whether these motets were known as monophonic or polyphonic pieces given how many lack full concordances, even if among these *unica* the refrain melodies at least are frequently known. As a collection, **D308**'s motets seamlessly combine two known but seemingly distinct repertories – the motets *entés* of **fr.845** and motetus-voice texts from widely copied 'mainstream' polyphonic motets – with a third group of unique motets that might thus be assumed to reflect motet production that remained local to Metz. No other source combines any two of these three repertories. Although collected in a chansonnier section arranged explicitly by genre, no title for these pieces is given, raising the tantalizing question of what kind of generic type the compilers of the manuscript would have considered these pieces.

While the number of polyphonic concordances far outweighs the number of monophonic concordances in **D308**, this is hardly surprising given how many examples of the former and how few of the latter have otherwise come down to us. If all the motets in **D308** are designed for a polyphonic performance with tenor, this would provide unique evidence of the later polyphonization of the repertoire known only monophonically in **fr.845**. If, on the other hand, they are all designed for monophonic performance, **D308** would then provide monophonic versions of fourteen motets only otherwise known in polyphonic versions. What almost all the motets of **D308** share is refrain usage, predominantly, but not exclusively, with the presence of a split refrain. This aligns them more closely with the motets *entés* of **fr.845** than with the 'mainstream' motet tradition. This might lend support to the idea that, like the motets *entés* of **fr.845**, the motets of **D308** could have been

---

[67] For example, Haines (2010, 186–91) notes that two of Renart's songs (no. 4 and no. 71a in Haines's edition) and one each by Harouge the leopardess (no. 33), Wuace the marmot (no. 35), and Symon the monkey (no. 41), are introduced as motets. As well, one of the refrains that **D308** presents for the purpose of the Tuesday night entertainments at Chauvency-le-Chateau in *Le Tournoiement de Chauvency* presents its three lines at the beginning, middle, and end of a stanza-long song that is introduced as a 'motet' in *Méliacin*.

performed monophonically. If that is indeed the case, the question arises of whether a hypothetical monophonic motet reconstructed from a motet within the 'mainstream' polyphonic tradition is a later reduction of an earlier polyphonic motet, or whether it might represent a 'lost' earlier version, which is here in D308 preserved ossified in a late source on account of geographical (or sociological) isolation from subsequent developments. The hypothetical monophonic versions of the motets presented here certainly show different states of well-known pieces, states I think we should take seriously as representing versions that were known to different constituencies, audiences and (in D308's case) courts, from the better known versions, but their relative chronologies remain uncertain. Having floated the possibility in this chapter that the motets in D308 might represent earlier states of motets not otherwise known to have been monophonic, the strongest evidence remains that from Mot4, but even that remains inconclusive.[68]

The necessity of making interpretive assumptions means that musical analysis of this repertoire will remain controversial but also indispensable, a requisite complement to understanding textual and poetic structure. Worth noting in this regard is the citation in a unique Latin-texted motet in the fourth fascicle of Mo, Mo 66, of the melody of a widely used refrain, vdB 1424: 'N'onques nul ne les senti/Les maus d'amors/si com je sent' ('No one ever felt the pains of love like I feel them').[69] The melody occurs at the end of the motetus where it bears the words 'videat in gloria/fidelium ecclesia!' ('he may be seen in glory by the church of the faithful'). Only the shared melody links this line to the refrain, but it raises the possibility that the music of Mo 66 originally existed with a French text for this voice part that ended with the refrain (see Figure 1.1), and perhaps even that the voice part was originally a monophonic motet; further, the decision to use the 'eius' tenor at the point of polyphonization was possibly linked to this refrain's similar terminal use in a voice that is part of another motet on that same tenor, Mo 22: Hé sire que vous vantés (659). Given the prevalence of contrafaction in motet voices, those French motets that received later Latin contrafact texts, perhaps as a convenient use of ready-made examples from a flourishing parallel genre, perhaps as a deliberate attempt to render sacred a secular genre running out of control, might offer one point of terminological connection allowing 'mainstream' motets to come under the generic umbrella of the motet.[70] The term motet, applying to the refrain ('motet') and by extension to the whole duplum voice in which it appears ('motetus') and thus the polyphonic complex of which

---

[68] Paying careful attention to the errors in the copying of tenors for motets in Roi and Noailles, Wolinski (1996) suggests that their scribes copied from a shared exemplar, which had in turn been copied from sources that transmitted the motets in monophonic form, but the exemplar's scribes knew that motets are polyphonic pieces and thus attempted to supply a known and/or half-remembered version of the tenor of a polyphonic version by various workarounds, including importing missing bits of the tenor from other sources of the same tenor, or writing out repeats. But perhaps the reason the motet exemplar lacked tenors was not because they had been lost or not written down, but because these motets were originally monophonic. It is slightly dizzying and disorientating to think that large numbers of motets we know only as polyphonic might originally have been monophonic, but that should not deter us from considering this possibility seriously.

[69] The last line is 'or je les sent' ('[but] I feel them now') in most other sources; the reading here is from Mo. This refrain is also found in two different chansons avec des refrains in later, unnotated stanzas, as well as in a dit with refrains. The motet copies are the only ones with musical notation for the refrain; see http://medmus.soton.ac.uk/view/abstract_item/1424.html.

[70] See the discussion of the interplay between sacred and secular elements in Huot 1997. The standard view that secular and vernacular texts followed sacred Latin ones seems to me to be based on assumptions of increased secularization as a teleological measure of modernization in the Middle Ages. Clear indications of contrary projects can be seen, for example, in the work of Gautier de Coinci, who specifically re-purposes secular trouvère song as Marian. See the essays in Krause and Stones 2006, as well as Quinlan 2017 and Büttner 1999.

that duplum was part (the motet as a polyphonic genre), might well have continued to be used for that same sounding polyphonic object, even when, as in **Mo** 66, a Latin text now obscures all but the melodic identity of the original refrain. Retrospective application of the term 'motet' to Latin-texted pieces that were *originally* Latin textings of liturgical clausulae might then have seemed unexceptional, especially when pieces with all these varied histories might end up side-by-side in large, retrospective notated collections.

Figure 1.1. Shared refrain melody in Mo 66 and Mo 22 (BIU Montpellier/IRHT [CNRS])
Above. Mo 66, fol. 105r (fascicle 4), end of motet voice *Mater virgo pia* (691)
Below. Mo 22, fol. 29v (fascicle 2), end of motet voice *Hé sire que vous vantés* (659)

To conclude, one might invoke Anna Zayaruznaya's idea of the 'creature concept', which she developed to discuss fourteenth-century motets that explicitly thematize monstrosity. The 'creature concept' provides a non-regulative alternative to later music's 'work concept', an alternative that allows for growth, change, and hybridization in a given musical object without a complete loss of identity.[71] If linked by anything, motets are fundamentally linked through their propensity to hybridize disparate materials in the medieval sense explained by Caroline Walker Bynum as that which 'forces contradictory or incompatible categories to coexist and serve as commentary each on the other'.[72] For Bynum, such hybridity is inherently visual, but for these musical pieces it is both visual (the hybrid on the notated page, whether with musical notation or without, hybridizing the refrain at head and tail with the new body of the motet *enté*), and aural, thus capturing and fascinating both 'teachable senses' of vision and hearing. Welcome to the motet creature zoo.

---

[71] See Zayaruznaya 2015a, 67–9.
[72] Bynum 2001, 31.

2

Origins and Interactions:
Clausula, Motet, Conductus

Catherine A. Bradley

F
OR OVER A CENTURY, scholars have debated the origins of the motet and especially the motet's relationship to another genre, the clausula. A high proportion of motets recorded in the earliest manuscript witnesses dating from around the 1240s exist also in the alternative form of clausulae, which lack any upper-voice text. This presents a chronological conundrum: do motets represent clausulae with added texts, or are clausulae instead motets stripped of their words? The accepted hypothesis remains that advanced in 1898 by Wilhelm Meyer, that motets derived from clausulae. For Meyer, the clausula's liturgical heritage in the established genre of organum lent weight to its precedence, while the process of motet creation – the addition of syllabic text to pre-existing melismas – mimicked the earlier plainchant practice of prosula.[1] Friedrich Ludwig immortalized Meyer's hypothesis in his monumental and still indispensable catalogue of the entire thirteenth-century repertoire by referring to clausulae with related motets as 'sources' ('Quellen').[2] Nonetheless, several scholars hesitated to accept the invariable priority of clausulae in all cases, and although such expressions of doubt initially met with dispute and resistance, they have had a more favourable reception in recent scholarship.[3]

In 2011, Fred Büttner confirmed Yvonne Rokseth's 1939 suggestion that the unusual collection of forty clausulae with accompanying vernacular motet incipits in the Saint Victor manuscript (StV) in fact represented motet transcriptions.[4] Büttner had previously argued in favour of a motet origin for a clausula controversially identified by William Waite in 1954 as one of twenty-one irregularly notated clausulae that seemed to represent motet transcriptions in the more 'central' 'Notre Dame' manuscript F.[5] The same clausula-motet family featured also as part of Wolf Frobenius's more wholesale reversal of the conventional 'clausula-first' chronology in 1987, motivated by Frobenius's conviction that French motets containing melodic snippets associated with secular vernacular refrains could not derive from liturgical clausulae.[6] Frobenius's provocative

---

[1]   See W. Meyer 1898.

[2]   Ludwig 1910–78.

[3]   Smith (1989, 141–6) offers a useful historiographical overview of debates concerning the clausula-motet relationship.

[4]   See Rokseth 1935–9, 4: 70–1. Rokseth's hypothesis was refuted by Stenzl (1970) and the priority of StV clausulae over related motets was assumed until the publication of Büttner's 2011 monograph.

[5]   See Büttner 2002 and Waite 1954, 101.

[6]   Frobenius 1987.

article was disregarded in subsequent scholarship, but Franz Körndle has recently offered a more favourable re-evaluation, while acknowledging that Frobenius's grander proposition – extending claims about vernacular motets and refrains to encompass Latin motets with related clausulae – was on the whole too radical.[7] Building on the work of Frobenius, Büttner, Körndle, and Wulf Arlt, I have previously argued that several clausulae in **F** stemmed from vernacular motets, advocating the possibility of local reversals of the general clausula-to-motet chronology.[8]

The transcription of vernacular motets as clausulae seems to have been an exceptional practice. Nevertheless, the presence of textless French motets in **F**, appearing alongside other genuine clausulae presumably intended for liturgical use, belies the outward impression that this manu-script – the earliest extant motet collection – records only Latin-texted pieces. This undermines the conventional scholarly tendency to assume that Latin motets, particularly those with sacred texts that trope their tenor plainchants, must pre-date those in the vernacular. And since **F** attests that the composition of motets in French evidently occurred from an early date, this could account for the vernacular etymology ('little words') of the generic designation 'motet'.[9]

A fluidity in clausula-motet relationships – that motets may be made by texting clausulae, just as clausulae are occasionally motets stripped of their texts – is often obscured by general linear chronological narratives, which straightforwardly trace the origins of motets to Latin, liturgical clausulae. Yet even for motets that do seem to embody the normal 'textbook' progression of adding sacred Latin texts to clausulae, close analytical engagement with different instantiations of the same basic musical material can reveal complex and multidirectional generic interrela-tionships. Precisely such a case is the chief concern of this chapter. I seek to demonstrate that a fundamental flexibility pertains, not only to the chronological relationship between clausulae and motets and to generic identity as a Latin motet or a conductus, but also to the existence of clausulae and motets within an interactive realm of practice and performance, rather than as fixed written objects.[10]

The nature of clausula-motet relationships, even those which enact the same basic chronology, may be strikingly different in particular cases. On the one hand, a Latin motet created through the addition of new text (and perhaps also an additional musical voice) to an older clausula might then sever any connections to its original clausula, perhaps also shedding its plainchant tenor voice to become a conductus. On the other hand, a new motet (or conductus) version of an earlier clausula could retain close connections with this parent material, and subsequently influence the way in which the clausula was sung and transmitted. Ernest H. Sanders and Peter M. Lefferts acknowledge this possibility in their entry for the medieval motet (Motet, §I: Middle Ages) in *Grove*:

> Given the processes of writing and rewriting that are the hallmark of the early motet, many clausulas in the vast Florence collection (*I-Fl* Plut.29.1) may stand there already as modified on account of their careers as pre-existent sources for motets.

---

[7] Körndle 2010, 117–19.

[8] See Bradley 2013.

[9] On the vernacular etymology of 'motet', see Page 1993a, 59–60. Hofmann 1970 also underlined the connection between the term 'motet' and the vernacular refrain or 'motto'. See also Elizabeth Eva Leach's discussion in her chapter in the present volume.

[10] This chapter builds on Rankin 2008, which also underlines the relationship between musical reworkings and performative cultures. While Rankin sets aside questions of chronology, I engage directly with local chronological questions as a means of demonstrating and investigating flexible chronological and generic interrelationships.

Yet Sanders and Lefferts's admission of exchange between clausula and motet was paradoxically motivated by an essentially static conceptualization of clausulae as vital notational models for the 'composition or rehearsal' of early motets.[11] David Rothenberg's 2016 observation succinctly reiterates this position:

> Since the modal notation in use throughout the mid-thirteenth century relied on ligature patterns to indicate rhythm, it could not notate syllabically texted musical genres like motet and conductus, which demanded individual notes, not ligatures, for individual syllables. Motets, therefore, were notated without rhythm, and one needed to refer to an untexted, rhythmicized version of the clausula on which a motet was based to discern its rhythm. The discant clausula – and by extension the tenor – was the compositional starting point because there could not be a motet without a clausula.[12]

This chapter develops and substantiates the proposition that traces of a multidirectional and interactive relationship between clausulae and motets reside in surviving notated sources, demonstrating the form that such traces could take and ways in which they might be uncovered. To this end, I examine an interrelated network of clausulae and motets – *Latus 4* and *Homo quam sit pura* (231)/*Latus* (M14) – whose shared musical material is recorded in the earliest principal manuscript sources of thirteenth-century polyphony, **W1** (dated to the 1230s) and **F** (1240s).[13] I propose that a motet, created through the addition of text to a pre-existing clausula, subsequently influenced the transmission of this clausula in **F**, motivating the introduction of pitches that are notably absent from the version of the same clausula in **W1**.[14] Yet significantly, the relationship between this clausula and motet in **F** is such that it simultaneously undermines the likelihood that the clausula was modified to serve as the motet's notational guide. This offers a basis to challenge the presumption that early motets really required rhythmic props in the form of clausulae. Emphasizing the complexity of chronological and generic interactions in the compositional milieu from which motets emerged, this chapter seeks also to unsettle still pervasive conceptualizations of clausulae and motets as principally written and notationally dependent entities.

---

[11] Sanders and Lefferts, 'Motet, §I: Middle Ages' in *Grove*. Sanders had earlier remarked at greater length (1973, 508–9): 'while in a culture whose continuity largely depends on memory and oral tradition, habits of writing and reading differ from ours, to identify the rhythm of an upper voice of a motet from its notation in one of the Notre-Dame manuscripts is a task that could hardly have been less perplexing to a musician of the early 13th century than it is to us. Under these circumstances it seems difficult to imagine the composition or the rehearsing of a motet without the aid of a melismatic model'.

[12] Rothenberg 2016, 231.

[13] Clausula designations follow those in Smith 1980. Smith's numbering system reproduces Ludwig's (see Ludwig 1910–78), intended to reflect both the relative chronology of individual clausulae as well as the sequence in which they appear in manuscript sources.

[14] Smith (1992, 31) is the only scholar to have identified a specific instance in which a motet (*Hodie Marie concurrant* (441) / *Regnat* (M34)) derived from a clausula (the version of *Regnat 7* in **W1**) seems subsequently to have influenced that clausula's transmission (the version of *Regnat 7* in **F**). In this case, Smith's argument depends not on the straightforward relationship between the number of notes in a phrase and the number of syllables, but on the particular rhythmic arrangement of a phrase which affects text stress. While Smith's case is convincing, it nevertheless depends on the strictly by-the-book interpretation of ligature patterns and of Latin word stress, two aspects that can be handled with some latitude in clausulae and motets respectively. Smith himself has shown that motets also made rhythmic alterations of a similar magnitude to clausulae for reasons that seemed 'elusive' (1989, 163). Susan Allison Kidwell (1993, 181–5) has documented the fairly frequent mis-accentuation of Latin texts in early motets.

The melisma *Latus* from the Alleluia verse for Easter Day, *Pascha nostrum immolatus est Christus,* was one of the most popular clausula and motet tenors of the early thirteenth century. F alone records eleven different clausulae on the *Latus* tenor, many of which seem to have been conceived in the climate of motivic play that is the hallmark of the clausula genre.[15] The musical design of the two-voice clausula *Latus 4* is typical in this regard (see Example 2.1, which presents the version of this clausula recorded in **W1**).[16] Melodic figures in the upper voice or duplum are frequently repeated and reworked against changes in the underlying tenor chant quotation. The clausula's opening melodic gesture (labelled A) is immediately repeated up a fourth (A′). Then follows a second melodic idea (B), which recurs frequently in different contexts: repeated literally, down a step (B′), and down a third (B″). In perfections 33–4 the pitches of the B″ motive are rearranged, introducing a falling third shape that leads to a cadence on *G* at perfection 35, a pattern echoed at perfections 49 and 53 (marked by dashed boxes in Example 2.1).[17] And perfections 41–4 extend the B′ motive, with internal repetition of pitches. A final melodic idea, C, introduced in perfections 57–9 and initiating all subsequent phrases, combines features of the A and B motives. Motive C resembles the B motive in its initial three pitches and is simultaneously a literal inversion of the opening A motive. The closing phrase of the clausula (perfections 69–71) presents an altered version, C′, of the C motive: c-$b^\flat$-$b^\flat$-a-c rather than c-$b^\flat$-a-$b^\flat$-c. The use of the established C motive at perfections 69–71 would have produced a stronger consonance with the tenor in perfection 70 (a fifth rather than a sixth), moving in contrary motion towards the final cadence. Yet the internal pitch repetition in the altered C′ version echoes that found in perfections 41–4, the comparable culmination of repetitions of the B motive. Consequently, melodic intensification through internal repetition prepares the clausula's two most decisive cadences, on the lower final pitch, C, in the tenor at perfections 47 and 71.

This intricate musical aesthetic of intense motivic repetition and reworking seems more characteristic of clausulae than of newly composed motets.[18] Significantly, the *Latus 5* clausula (see Example 2.2), which directly follows *Latus 4* in **W1**, represents a continuation of the compositional game of *Latus 4*.[19] *Latus 5* begins with the same opening A motive. It repeats this motive at perfection 9, and also transposes the A material up a step (labelled A″) at perfections 13, 17, 21, and 53. The B′ motive occurs at perfections 5 and 57, while B″ and C motives feature especially prominently. In perfections 25–48, the B″ and C motives are in turn sounded three times in literal succession above changes in the underlying tenor melisma. These two clausulae on the

---

[15]   On motivic play in clausulae see, for example, Arlt 1995.

[16]   Folio numbers for clausulae follow the conventions established in Smith 1980, where fol. 57r-3 refers to the third complete clausula on fol. 57r.

[17]   The $b^\flat$ in perfection 53 of the duplum produces a tritone above the tenor *E*. As discussed in n. 28 below, the F clausula and motet have an upper-voice *a* at perfection 53, which avoids this dissonance. Significantly, the F clausula (but not the F motet) also offers a variant reading of the tenor, with *F* (not *E*) in perfection 53. Could the clausula $b^\flat$ in W1 have been intended to sound a consonant fourth against a tenor *F*, rather than the copied tenor *E*? By contrast, the tenor *E* must be intentional in the F motet, where it sounds an octave with the triplum *e*. In terms of the quoted plainchant melody a 'correct' version is impossible to establish: Rankin (2008, 127) notes that precisely this part of the *Latus* plainchant is unstable across its various extant clausulae settings.

[18]   In Bradley 2014a, 281, I contrast the reworking and transposition of small motivic cells in a clausula-derived Latin motet, with the more obviously song-like, typically un-transposed, and larger-scale melodic repetitions of a newly composed vernacular motet.

[19]   These two clausulae do not appear side-by-side in F, where *Latus 4* is on fol. 158v-1 and *Latus 5* appears on the preceding recto (fol. 158r-2).

Example 2.1. *Latus 4* clausula, **W1**, fol. 57r–3

Latus tenor, therefore, are preoccupied with the same circumscribed stock of duplum motives, showing off various combinations and manipulations of their shared musical material in both duplum and tenor voices.

Example 2.2. *Latus 5* clausula, W1, fol. 57r–4

The *Latus 4* clausula has a strikingly regular phrase structure, as comparison with its *Latus 5* counterpart reveals. In *Latus 4*, tenor and duplum voices consistently phrase together in units of four perfections. The single exception occurs at perfections 41–8, where an extended eight-perfection phrase with internal pitch repetitions leads towards a cadence on the lower tenor C final in perfection 47. Despite this consistency of phrase length, the type of cadence at phrase endings is subject to variation. Most commonly each duplum phrase closes with a two-note paroxytonic cadence followed by a breve rest (for example, perfections 7–8 in Example 2.1), but oxytonic cadences – single ternary longs followed by a rest of the same duration – are interspersed on five occasions (marked by boxes in Example 2.1). Interestingly, these more emphatic oxytonic cadences are exclusively associated with duplum cadences on *c*, arguably characterizing and reinforcing the significance of this, the final, pitch.[20]

The musical material of this two-voice *Latus 4* clausula is found also as the basis of the motet *Homo quam sit pura/Latus* (see Example 2.3).[21] *Homo quam sit pura* appears in the earliest extant collection of motets in F in a three-voice version: this monotextual or conductus motet – so called because the two upper voices present the same text in rhythmic unison (as in a polyphonic conductus) – has an additional triplum above the clausula tenor and duplum. Unusually for a motet text, *Homo quam sit pura* also carries a poetic attribution, to Philip the Chancellor (the text and translation are given as Table 2.1).[22] Philip's text is a trope on the Easter theme of the *Latus* tenor, in which Christ, speaking in the first person, tells of the sacrifices he made for mankind in his crucifixion.

Table 2.1. Text and translation of *Homo quam sit pura*

1	Homo quam sit pura	6a	-ura	p	Man, how pure is
2	michi de te cura	6a	-ura	p	my love for you
3	prout probat plura:	6a	-ura	p	just as it suffers many things:
4	dolor et pressura,	6a	-ura	p	grief and oppression,
5	verberum tritura,	6a	-ura	p	the thrashing of whips,
6	lancee fixura,	6a	-ura	p	the piercing of the lance,
7	vinctus in cathena	6b	-ena	p	having been bound in chains
8	nulla victus pena,	6b	-ena	p	overcome by no punishment,
9	potus in lagena	6b	-ena	p	the drink from the flask
10	mirra felle plena.	6b	-ena	p	a vessel filled with gall.
11	Cesa gena, omnis vena	4b+4b	-ena	p	Struck on the cheek, every vein
12	sanguine cruenta.	6c	-enta	p	spewing blood.
13	Stupens hec tormenta,	6c	-enta	p	Aghast at these torments,
14	condolet natura:	6a	-ura	p	nature feels my pain:
15	veli fit scissura,	6a	-ura	p	there is the tearing of the veil,
16	solis lux obscura,	6a	-ura	p	the obscured light of the sun,
17	patent monumenta	6c	-enta	p	the tombs open forth
18	dum sum immolatus.	6x	-atus	p	while I am sacrificed.

[20] The final pitch receives the same emphasis in the duplum of *Latus 5*, where oxytonic cadences are also consistently on *c*. Unlike *Latus 4*, however, not all *c* cadences in *Latus 5* are oxytonic (see for instance, Example 2.2, perfections 43–4).

[21] Frobenius (1987, 23) is the only scholar to have challenged the priority of *Latus 4* over *Homo quam sit pura*, on the questionable grounds that the very 'uniform' ('eintönig') style of the clausula must have been the result of its conception for a motet text. Since *Homo quam sit pura* is exceptional in its regularity, and motet texts (including those which Frobenius considers to be conceived *ab initio*, and not modelled on any pre-existing clausulae) are generally much more varied, this argument is problematic. And although Baltzer singles out *Latus 4* as 'an excellent example of neat and regular phrasing' (1974, 1: 248), she by no means implies that it is strikingly unusual for this reason or anomalous in its clausula context.

[22] This translation is adapted and modified from that in Payne 2011, 62.

Example 2.3. *Homo quam sit pura/Latus*, F, fols. 385v–386r
(*continues on next page*)

Musically, *Homo quam sit pura* differs in two significant respects from its related clausula in **W1**. Not only does the **F** motet feature an additional triplum voice, but it consistently employs paroxytonic cadences throughout, adding 'extra notes' at the end of phrases on five occasions (marked by boxes in Example 2.3). Thus, every box indicating a perfection rest in Example 2.1 now contains a duplex long pitch and a breve rest. Both of these differences seem to confirm the chronological priority of the two-voice clausula in **W1**. The motet triplum is integrated within the musical idiom of *Homo quam sit pura*: it complements several of the melodic repetitions of the motetus (for example, in perfections 21–2, the triplum matches the motetus by repeating perfections 17–18 down a step).[23] In addition, the triplum borrows some motetus motives (compare perfections 41–2 of the triplum with perfections 5–6 of the motetus, for instance). However, the triplum does not exhibit the same exhaustive working-out of material as the motetus. Furthermore, it occasionally obscures certain motivic features in the motetus: in perfections 1–8, for example, the triplum does not serve to highlight the immediate (transposed) repetition of the A motive. It is probable, therefore, that the triplum was a later addition, sensitively accommodated to an existing two-voice composition.

The 'extra notes' at the end of five phrases in *Homo quam sit pura* seem similarly to represent later additions, in this case textually motivated. The actual number of notes in a phrase is undeniably of greater importance in a motet, where there is a direct correlation between syllables of text and individual pitches, than in a melismatic clausula. Moreover, the standardization of cadence types in *Homo quam sit pura* has a significant impact on the motet text, permitting an almost isosyllabic poetic structure of six syllables per line (see Table 2.1).[24] The syllable count

---

23 I reserve the term 'duplum' for the melismatic upper-voice of a two-voice clausulae, and label this texted upper voice 'motetus' in the context of a motet.

24 In Table 2.1 'p' indicates a paroxytonic text stress, on the penultimate syllable of the line.

suggested by the *Latus 4* clausula in **W1**, by contrast, would involve an irregular alternation between five- and six-syllable lines.

The poetic regularity of *Homo quam sit pura* is disturbed only once, by an eight-syllable line (line 11) in perfections 41–4. This single irregularity seems further to confirm that text was accommodated to the music of a pre-existing clausula here. Had the music and text of this motet been conceived together, it is arguably less likely that a lone octosyllabic line should have been introduced into an otherwise exclusively six-syllable poem. Working with a pre-existing clausula, on the other hand, it is difficult to see how the creator of the motet could have maintained an isosyllabic structure in perfections 41–4 without spoiling the climatic effect of these four perfections in preparing the structurally important cadence at perfection 47. Instead, the added motet text incorporates a single anomalous eight-syllable line, and enhances the repetitive and climactic musical effect of perfections 41–4 through the use of internal rhyme (‘*Cesa* **gena**, *omnis* **vena**’).

The proposition that a motet text, specifically created for the *Latus 4* clausula, should treat its musical model with such sensitivity is all the more convincing if the poet in question was indeed Philip the Chancellor. Although Philip himself is not credited with any musical compositions,[25] he is known to be the author of prosula texts crafted for organa attributed to Pérotin, and was skilled in the art of fitting words to pre-existing music.[26] It is therefore realistic to imagine that, in fashioning *Homo quam sit pura*, Philip saw the potential to add ‘extra’ notes at the end of five phrases in *Latus 4*, a change that had significant consequences for his poetic text, with only negligible impact on the musical character of the clausula. On the other hand, however, Philip evidently recognized that insisting on a six-syllable line text throughout would require a more substantial musical reworking of perfections 41–8, representing a greater compromise to the musical and tonal design of the clausula model.

In terms of a chronology, it is, on the whole, much more convincing to imagine that notes were added to an irregular clausula than that they were taken away from a regular motet. Given the strong and memorable connection between the number of syllables in a text and the number of notes in a phrase, it is hard to see why a flexible interchange between oxytonic and paroxytonic endings in the **W1** clausula would ever have arisen were the motet *Homo quam sit pura* already in existence. The cadential variety of the **W1** clausula and the resulting emphasis on the final pitch *c* is lost in the motet through the consistent use of paroxytonic cadences. Yet, the added text and triplum in the motet version compensate for this, in at least some respects. On two occasions, at perfections 27–8 and 47–8, the cadence on the final pitch *c* is marked in *Homo quam sit pura* by the introduction of a new poetic rhyme: ‘*-ena*’ in line 7 and ‘*-enta*’ in line 12 (see Example 2.3 and Table 2.1). Similarly, the triplum reinforces these *c* cadences harmonically, either sounding *c* in unison with the motetus (perfections 48, 60, and 72) or continuing the sonority of the tenor (in perfection 28 the triplum sounds *f* above the motetus *c*, matching the underlying tenor *F* in perfection 27).

The standardization of cadence types in *Homo quam sit pura* has a convincing textual, rather than musical, explanation. In view of this, the version of the melismatic *Latus 4* clausula recorded in **F** (see Example 2.4) is all the more remarkable. The cadences of the *Latus 4* clausula in **F** match,

---

[25] See Payne 2011, xxii. Philip is credited with the creation of the text *Homo quam sit pura*, but not with the composition of the triplum voice in **F**. This triplum, which is unique to **F**, could represent a later addition to the two-voice *Latus 4* material, whose earliest motet instantiation was also in two voices.

[26] On Philip as a creator of prosulae and his ‘deep assimilation of the music he glosses’, see Payne 2011, xvi.

not those of the clausula in **W1**, but rather the consistent paroxytonic cadences of the motet (marked by boxes in Example 2.4). This strongly suggests an interactive relationship between clausula and motet versions of the *Latus 4* material that is borne out by extant written sources. Although *Homo quam sit pura* was derived from a pre-existing clausula, as preserved in **W1**, the associated motet text influenced the subsequent transmission of its related clausula, as evident from the form in which *Latus 4* is found in **F**.

Of course, it could be argued that the creator of the motet *Homo quam sit pura* simply had no knowledge of the **W1** version of *Latus 4*, and was acquainted with the clausula only in the very regular form preserved in **F**, simply adding a text to this version. I do not deny that *Latus 4* could have existed in several versions before any association with a motet text. Rebecca A. Baltzer noted that clausulae of precisely this type 'sometimes vary between their different transmissions, for what is a masculine [oxytonic] phrase ending in one copy may be made feminine [paroxytonic] in another by the repetition of the final note'.[27] Yet given the very strong correlation between the number of notes in a cadence and the syllables of an associated text, it seems more convincing to imagine that the existence of an associated motet text might serve to fix cadence types in a related clausula, than to imagine that a motet was created with reference to one particular version of a clausula, which had an otherwise fairly flexible existence.

Despite the kinship between the *Latus 4* clausula in **F** and its related motet in the same source, closer scrutiny belies the conclusion either that *Latus 4* and *Homo quam sit pura* stemmed from the same exemplar, or that the clausula was adjusted to better serve as a notational model for the motet. Certain melodic variants between the motetus and clausula duplum in F represent different approaches to motivic patterning, and this suggests that these two pieces were independent or alternative versions of the same basic material. In perfection 4 of Example 2.3, for instance, the 'extra note' in the F motetus is $b^\flat$, with the result that perfections 5–8 (motive A′) are a literal transposition of the preceding A phrase. In the F clausula, however (Example 2.4), the 'extra' duplum pitch (absent from the version of *Latus 4* in **W1**) reiterates the *c* in perfection 3, emphasizing this, the final, pitch and producing the repeated-note cadence that is more characteristic of the material in general.

The closing phrase of the F clausula and motet also differs. In the clausula, the motet's final 'extra' note is absent, and *Latus 4* continues instead with a short concluding melisma over a held tenor note, a conventional and formulaic closing gesture employed in a majority of the *Latus* clausulae in **F**. The F versions of *Latus 4* and *Homo quam sit pura* additionally approach this cadence in different ways. While perfections 69–70 of *Latus 4* have the same altered, repeated-note C′ motive (c-$b^\flat$-$b^\flat$-a) found also in the **W1** clausula, *Homo quam sit pura* presents the C motive in its unaltered form (c-$b^\flat$-a-$b^\flat$).[28] These distinct clausula and motet versions in F have different

---

[27] Baltzer 1974, 1: 248.

[28] On an earlier occasion, however, both F clausula and motet share a duplum reading that differs from the W1 clausula: both have *a* in perfection 53, rather than $b^\flat$ in the W1 clausula. At the same time, as discussed in n. 17 above , the W1 clausula and F motet share a tenor *E* in perfection 53 (despite the resulting $E/b^\flat$ tritone in the W1 clausula), while the F clausula has a tenor *F*. Aspects of the W1 clausula and *Homo quam sit pura* in F are also mixed in the F clausula in perfections 61–2. In the W1 clausula, perfections 61–2 simply repeat the C motive (c-$b^\flat$-a-$b^\flat$) of the preceding phrase. By contrast, the F motet transposes the C motive up a step in perfections 61–2 (d-c-$b^\flat$-c). The F clausula has d-c-a-$b^\flat$: this matches the related motet in the same source in perfection 61, but follows the W1 clausula in perfection 62. These small differences between the three versions – the F clausula variously independent, or aligning with the W1 clausula, the F motet, and a combination of the two – indicate a highly complicated textual transmission.

Catherine A. Bradley

Example 2.4. *Latus 4* Clausula, **F**, fol. 158v–1

motivic rationales and harmonic or climactic effects, as discussed above. Such variant readings of this phrase presented in **F**, therefore, reflect alternative tastes or approaches, rather than mere scribal corruptions.

If the **F** clausula was intended as a notational model – perhaps rhythmically adjusted through the addition of extra pitches in order to better function as such – why was its correspondence with *Homo quam sit pura* not more exact? It is difficult to account for the clausula's small motivic differences, its lack of the final 'extra' pitch, and its additional closing melisma. These features confirm that *Latus 4* and *Homo quam sit pura* were not 'cross-referenced' and standardized by the scribe of **F**, a circumstance typical, more generally, of pieces recorded in both clausula and motet forms in this manuscript.[29] In my 2011 Ph.D. dissertation I undertook a comprehensive examination of the relationship between motets in **F** and their related clausulae and passages of discant recorded within organa in **F**, considering also clausula and discant concordances in **W1** and **W2** where extant.[30] This study focused principally on rhythmic variants in clausulae that would impede the presentation of an associated motet text. It found that, of the fifty-six motets in **F** with related clausulae or discant extant in the same source, exactly half (twenty-eight) of these motets had related *sine littera* materials that would be demonstrably poor notational props.[31] That is, the extant clausulae or discant passages in **F** offered rhythmic information that actively conflicted with rhythms implied in their related motets. Since thirteen motets in **F** lack any extant *sine littera* materials altogether, no fully accurate rhythmic models are in existence for nearly sixty percent (forty-one out of sixty-nine) of the motets in this source.

This raises the larger question: do we – and did readers, singers, or composers in the thirteenth century – really need *sine littera* clausula models to work out the rhythm of motets? Hans Tischler has offered compelling rhythmic realizations for the four motets in **F** that are unique to this source and lack any extant clausulae concordances.[32] Tischler's transcriptions seem as near to incontrovertible 'solutions' as can be achieved for motets with surviving clausulae and/or concordances in later more rhythmically prescriptive mensural notations. Since motet tenors are melismatic, ligated *sine littera* as in clausulae, the rhythmic foundation of motets can be securely established. Although the syllabic upper-voices of a motet are presented in unligated *cum littera* notation, their harmonic relationship to the tenor is a useful rhythmic guide, as are the stresses and rate of declamation implied by their accompanying texts. Such rhythmic clues in texted upper-voices, in combination with the concrete rhythmic information provided by the melismatic tenor, have proved to be sufficient for modern-day editors. An oral or aural familiarity with these motets for

---

29   I have proposed that clausulae which represent motet transcriptions in **F** and related Latin motets in the same source may have derived from the same exemplar, see Bradley 2013, 37, 45, and 53. However, since this shared exemplar was a copy of a vernacular motet, which required adaptation to be rendered both as a clausula and to fit a Latin contrafactum text, the clausula and motet versions of this musical material in **F** do not match one another closely as a result.

30   See Bradley 2011, 257–74.

31   To be deemed a poor notational prop in my 2011 study, a clausula must differ rhythmically in several significant respects from its related motet. For example, the lack of 'extra notes' in the version of *Latus 4* in **W1** qualified this clausula as a poor motet model – since there are not enough pitches available for the associated text – but the small rhythmic and melodic variants between the version of *Latus 4* in **F** and *Homo quam sit pura*, were not considered significant. Rhythmic variants of the kind identified in Smith 1989 were also of insufficient magnitude to disqualify a clausula as a notational model.

32   See Tischler 1982 nos. 62, 63, 73, and 76. Tischler's mode-one rhythmicization of no. 76 is musically and textually convincing, achieved even though the copy of this two-voice motet is incomplete and lacking its accompanying modally notated tenor.

a thirteenth-century singer or reader would have made their rhythmic interpretation even more straightforward.

In the case of the motet *Homo quam sit pura*, any pre-existing sense of 'how the music goes' would seem to obviate the need for rhythmically prescriptive notation. The same basic modal pattern repeats itself, interrupted only by the anomalous eight-perfection phrase at perfections 41–8, where internal poetic rhymes, as well as repeated pitches, hint that the extra notes and syllables in this longer phrase require a presentation that is speeded up, rather than slowed down. As is the case for a majority of three-voice monotextual or conductus motets in F, there exists no *sine littera* rendering of the triplum voice. Though in textual unison with the motetus, the tripla in these three-voice motets often have additional melismas (or sustained notes in the place of motetus melismas) that are not expressly prescribed in any extant rhythmic notation, but can nonetheless be easily fitted around the motetus. See, for instance, perfections 11–12 in Example 2.3.

The necessity of a clausula model to determine the rhythm of *Homo quam sit pura* is therefore questionable. Indeed, it could even be argued that the *Latus 4* clausula might obfuscate rather than illuminate in this regard. The clausula's very short phrase lengths do not permit an extended presentation of the first-mode rhythmic pattern. No sooner has a ligated group of three notes been followed by a group of two than the phrase is practically over. Modal ligatures in the single more substantial eight-perfection phrase (perfections 41–8) are disrupted by a preponderance of repeated pitches. And although the phrases of this clausula are rhythmically simple and regular, the continual use of ternary long notes at cadences is technically a moment of *extensio modi*, that is, these notes exceed the duplex long and breve values of mode one as strictly defined. The extended single notes at the end of phrases – which stand apart from the three-note and two-note ligatures of the modal pattern – could disorient a reader.[33]

Questioning the necessity of clausulae as notational models unsettles scholarly perceptions of this more established and untexted genre as indispensable in the creation of motets. The case of *Homo quam sit pura* is particularly useful in challenging another respect in which the influence of parent clausulae on their motet offspring is considered decisive. This is the idea that perhaps the most characteristic textual feature of the earliest motets – their lack of regular line lengths and conventional poetic forms – resulted from their creation as prosulae, syllabic texts added to pre-existent melismatic clausulae and therefore determined by purely musical structures.[34] It must be acknowledged that *Homo quam sit pura* is an exceptionally regular text, and by no means characteristic of early Latin motets – which frequently mix poetic lines of varying syllables – or of vernacular ones, in which syllable counts are, if anything, even more inconsistent. Yet though exceptional, the motet *Homo quam sit pura* demonstrates that motet texts created as prosulae need not necessarily be irregular. Motet creators had only to select source clausulae, like *Latus 4*, that had regular phrase structures in the first place. By dint of a few small alterations – standardizing cadence types, for instance – they could make these clausulae more regular still. Both Baltzer and Susan Kidwell have observed that the clausulae that were texted as motets tended, on the whole, to be the more irregular ones, while strictly patterned clausulae like *Latus 4* proved generally less

---

[33] I have elsewhere refuted the idea of clausulae as notational props to explain the transcription of motets as clausulae (Bradley 2013, 57–61). I argue that *sine littera* motet transcriptions in F are in fact poor notational models, since their ligature patterns are often irregular, a consequence of the transcription process and attempts to express *sine littera* the short-note melismas characteristic of motet voices that are actually easier to show in *cum littera* notation.

[34] See, for instance, Holford-Strevens 2011, 234.

popular as motet sources.[35] There were surely instances in which the process of adding a text to a given clausula made poetic irregularity a practical necessity, but it seems that motet creators also relished such irregularity for its own sake, just as they occasionally took advantage of the possibility to fashion regular motets from pre-existing music.[36]

The clausula-motet relationship can be flexible chronologically, therefore, and poetic responses engendered by the creation of motets from clausulae can also take multiple forms. It is problematic to presume that motets were necessarily dependent on clausulae for their rhythmic information – and hence their conception and/or realization – and equally that the poetic irregularity which characterizes the motet as a genre was a purely prosaic consequence of the process of texting clausulae. Extant instantiations of the *Latus 4* and *Homo quam sit pura* material illustrate the potential for multidirectionality in clausula-motet relationships, and the possibility for musical exchange between motets and clausulae without any practical notational purpose. Yet the case of *Homo quam sit pura* also encapsulates another important flexibility in generic interactions in the early thirteenth century, in this instance between Latin motets and conducti.

In terms of its component parts and compositional process, *Homo quam sit pura* seems to be a conventional early Latin motet: it derives from a two-voice clausula, on a plainchant tenor. These origins and its categorization in **F** notwithstanding, the motetus voice *Homo quam sit pura* was recorded without its accompanying tenor as if it were a monophonic conductus in the fragmentary Châlons-en-Champagne manuscript (**Châl**, fol. 5v), whose scribe intermingled motets and conducti, with monophonic sequences and lone motetus voices.[37] Although the motetus of *Homo quam sit pura* appears in conjunction with its *Latus* tenor in the Dominican manuscript at Santa Sabina in Rome (**Sab**, fol. 135v), it marks the end of a group of monophonic conducti here. Moreover, the two-voice motet is a strophic piece in **Sab**, presented with two additional stanzas of text, a characteristic very typical of conducti but highly unusual in motets.[38]

The music of *Latus 4* is also associated with an alternative, or contrafactum, motet text. The practice of contrafaction was very common in the early motet repertoire, where new texts – in Latin or in the vernacular – were created as substitutes for existing ones, often reproducing and/or reworking the poetic structure of earlier motet texts, and engaging with their semantic content. In this case, the text *Homo quam sit pura* was replaced by *Stupeat natura*, a contrafactum tentatively attributed also to Philip the Chancellor, and which displays similar mutability in its identity as a motet or a conductus.[39] *Stupeat natura* appears as a two-voice motet in **W2** (fols. 177v–178r) and also in **MüB** (no. 15, fol. 2av).[40] In the Tortosa manuscript (**Tort**, fol. 140r), however, the motetus of *Stupeat natura* is presented without its associated tenor, and this conductus-like status is confirmed by the presence of the motet text, copied without any accompanying musical notation,

---

[35] See Baltzer 1974, 1: 256–7 and Kidwell 1998.

[36] I question in greater detail the idea that irregularity in motet texts is a necessary consequence of the prosula process in my forthcoming monograph; see Bradley forthcoming 2018.

[37] See Everist 1994, 40. Given the fragmentary nature of **Châl** it is difficult to be certain that the motet tenor was never copied here, however, Tischler (1982, 3: 62, no. 21) considers it most likely that the tenor was absent in this source from the outset.

[38] Only six Latin motets are known to set strophic texts, see Payne 2011, xxi.

[39] On the tentative attribution of *Stupeat natura* to Philip, see Payne 2011, xiv. For a transcription and translation of the text, see Payne 2011, 158–9.

[40] Although the end of *Stupeat natura* is missing in the **MüB** fragments, it is safe to assume that the *Latus* tenor would have appeared in this collection of motets, for which the tenors of other pieces are generally extant.

in two further sources.[41] *Stupeat natura* is found under the rubric 'conductus' within a group of conductus texts in **Graz** (fol. 2r), and with an additional strophe of text.[42] These two strophes are accompanied by a further three strophes in the copy of *Stupeat natura* in **Oxf Add.** (fol. 129r–v), another collection of conductus texts.

Homo quam sit pura and *Stupeat natura*, with their highly regular texts and multi-strophic versions, are particularly well qualified to appear as or alongside conducti. As texts, they are also noticeably lofty in their poetic tone and accomplished in the use of subtle word play, poetic characteristics more typically associated with the conductus tradition than with motets.[43] Yet this kind of flexibility in the presentation of early Latin motets without their tenors, as conducti, applies also to pieces with more irregular and characteristically motet-like Latin texts.[44] Similarly, the vast majority of three-voice conductus motets – in which the motetus and triplum share the same Latin text, like a polyphonic conductus, but still above a plainchant tenor – are disseminated also as straightforward two-voice motets (a plainchant tenor and a motetus). A particular piece, then, may appear both as a motet and as a conductus,[45] just as it may combine certain features associated with both genres, a plainchant tenor or a shared upper-voice text, respectively. These generic transformations are easily achieved: take a motet tenor away and you have a conductus; add a motet triplum which shares the text of the motetus and you have a conductus motet.

Such slippage between conductus motets and conducti was exploited for practical purposes by thirteenth-century scribes. **W1**, for instance, presents in the two-voice conductus fascicle the motetus and triplum voices of four pieces typically recorded in other sources as conductus motets with plainchant tenors, and apparently created by adding texts to clausulae.[46] Similarly, the quadruplum, triplum, and motetus of two pieces transmitted elsewhere as four-voice conductus motets – *Latex silice* and *Serena virginum* – appear in **W1** as three-voice conducti.[47] Although both motets have related clausulae and seem to be prosulae, they betray conductus-like features: a multi-strophic text and a melismatic cauda in *Latex silice*, and the use of the conventional closing exhortation 'Benedicamus Domino' ('Let us bless the Lord') in *Serena virginum*. It seems likely that there was not enough material for a separate motet section in **W1**, but that the hybrid character of these conductus motets nonetheless encouraged and facilitated their inclusion among conducti.

Practical necessity appears also to have influenced generic classification in **F**, when the scribe presented *Latex silice* and *Serena virginum* alongside three-voice conducti, as in **W1**, but nevertheless

---

[41] The motetus voice of *Gaudeat devotio* is also presented as a single melody on the reverse of this flyleaf in **Tort** (fol. 140v), but it is telling that this motet carries the rubric 'super N[ostrum]', acknowledging the existence of a tenor, while *Stupeat natura* has no such corresponding indication.

[42] A few other of the conductus texts in **Graz** have what appear to be later neumes added above them.

[43] *Homo quam sit pura* employs the technique of *annominatio*, a play on the range of meanings produced by slight phonetic alterations. See in Table 2.1, for example, the use of 'pena' ('punishment') in line 8, contrasted with 'plena' ('filled') in line 10.

[44] For example, *Deo confitemini* (131) /*Domino* (M13) and *Laudes referat* (140) /*Quoni[am]* (M13) are typical motets, without any hybrid conductus-like characteristics, and apparently derived from clausulae, yet they are presented as two-voice conducti without their tenors in W1 and Ma.

[45] In the vernacular realm, a comparable generic flexibility exists between French motets and monophonic songs. See the chapter in this volume by Matthew P. Thomson.

[46] *Deo confitemini* (fol. 107r); *Laudes referat* (fol. 107r–v); *Gaudeat devotio* (fols. 107v–108r); and *Qui servare puberem* (fol. 115r–v).

[47] These pieces are found in separate fascicles. *Serena virginum* (fols. 13r–15r) follows three-voice organa and precedes three three-voice conducti in fascicle 2. *Latex silice* (fol. 81r–v) appears alongside three-voice conducti in fascicle 8.

made space to copy separately the accompanying *Latus* and *Manere* tenors at the end of each piece.[48] Although **F** has collections of three-voice conductus motets (presented in two-part score with tenors appended) and two-voice motets (with motetus and tenor copied successively), *Latex silice* and *Serena virginum* are the only four-part motets in this source. It was therefore most efficient to separate these two conductus motets from their generic counterparts and to include them instead in the section ruled for three-voice conducti, where they were not out of place. In contrast to **W1**, however, the scribe of **F** retained the pieces' defining motet characteristic, their plainchant tenors, in this conductus context.

The hybrid nature and notational layout of conductus motets facilitated their location within either generic context, conductus or motet. Nonetheless, the copying of these pieces in manuscripts like **W1** and **F**, which were painstakingly ordered and which grouped pieces according to number of voices as well as genre, necessarily imposed a generic fixity.[49] It is clear that the scribe of **F** struggled to deal with the kinds of generic mixing and cross-fertilization characteristic of early motets. A three-voice piece in the conductus motet fascicle, *Veni doctor previe* (fols. 390v–392v), is effectively an organum with duplum and triplum voices that share a syllabic text. The unusual presence of this troping text (perhaps a prosula, though no untexted version of the organum survives) must have prompted the piece's inclusion in the motet fascicle.[50] Since the tenor of *Veni doctor previe* had many held notes in the organum style, however, the composition had to be copied in three-part score. This conflicted with the mise-en-page of a fascicle ruled for the presentation in two-part score of the upper-voices of surrounding conductus motets, whose modally notated tenors were copied separately at the end of each piece.[51] Here the scribe's dilemma about how best to classify and accommodate this unusual piece upset the otherwise very tidy appearance of **F** and is thus plain to see. But there are other occasions on which **F**'s tidy appearance surely conceals comparable generic conflicts. In the liturgically ordered clausula fascicle, for instance, genuine passages of discant derived from or for use within liturgical organa are interspersed with textless transcriptions of vernacular motets. A concern for order and taxonomy here gives the misleading appearance of uniformity to clausulae that seem to have functioned and been conceived in markedly different ways.

Surviving manuscript sources may conceal generic confusion and multiplicity under a neat and beautiful exterior, necessarily 'fixing' the genre of a piece that circulated in various forms. Nonetheless, comparisons across and within thirteenth-century records offer ample proof that the same music could exist as a clausula, a motet, or a conductus, and that even just within the

---

48 *Latex silice* (228)/*Latus* (fols. 230v–231v) and *Serena virginum* (69)/*Manere* (M5) (fols. 235r–237v), do not appear side-by-side in fascicle 6 of **F**, but are separated by five three-voice conducti.

49 I have suggested (Bradley 2015, 194–6) that **F** might also give an artificial impression of the extent of conductus motets as a generic phenomenon. The collection of twenty-six conductus motets in **F** represents almost the complete extant repertory of this type, and eight of these twenty-six pieces survive in conductus motet versions only in **F**. It is possible that the scribe and compilers of **F** wished to create a tranche of material substantial enough to fill and be worthy of a dedicated fascicle and that they therefore expanded existing two-voice motets into conductus motets through the addition of new tripla.

50 On the conception of *Veni doctor previe* and the relationship of the version of this piece in **F** to its two concordances in **LoA**, see Zimmermann 2008, 304–5.

51 Interestingly, the only other similar piece in **F** – the three-voice troped organum *Beatis nos adhibe* – was copied at the end of fascicle 6 (fols. 250r–252r), following three-voice conducti. Here the layout in three-voice score was more successful, and the status of the piece as a *Benedicamus Domino* trope made its presence among conducti appropriate, despite the presence of a plainchant tenor.

category of the motet there was enormous potential for variety concerning the number of voices and the addition or combination of new contrafactum texts and new strophes of text. This substantial written testimony to diverse instantiations of the same basic compositional material is surely just a partial reflection of oral and performative practices in which voices could easily have been added and taken away, texted, re-texted, and de-texted, without any recourse to notation.[52] Of course, the study of medieval motets necessarily depends entirely on written evidence. Yet even though performative and chronological flexibilities can never fully be recaptured, this does not simply render redundant or impossible the question of linear chronologies at a local level. Close analysis of extant written versions of the same musical material offers a productive basis on which to ask whether it seems most likely that music and/or text has been added or taken away and how this addition or removal has been effected, and to consider the impact of these processes. Engagement with such chronological and compositional questions on a small scale promotes a more nuanced understanding of the elusive reworkings, generic transformations, and flexibilities that characterized the wider musical climate of the early thirteenth century.

---

[52] This emphasis on reworking in the oral domain does not undermine the importance of writing and copying in creating new versions of pieces. I have demonstrated elsewhere that the scribe of F may have worked with exemplars in different forms from the version that appears in this source, proposing that the scribe, as he copied, undertook the fitting of text to clausulae (Bradley 2015, 168–84) and the substitution of contrafactum motet texts (Bradley 2013, 20–2).

~ 3 ~

Tracing the Tenor in Medieval Motets

Alice V. Clark

I N THE LATE FOURTEENTH CENTURY, Egidius de Murino wrote an elementary treatise on
how to compose a motet. The first step, he told his readers, was to select a tenor appropriate
for the theme of the motet:

*Primo accipe tenorem alicuius antiphone vel responsorii vel alterius cantus de antiphonario et
debent verba concordare cum materia de qua vis facere motetum.*[1]

First take the tenor from some antiphon or responsory or another chant from the antiph-
onal, and the words should concord with the matter of which you wish to make the motet.

After that, Egidius says, the tenor is arranged into phrases and given rhythm (a process he calls
'ordering and coloring'), and the other parts are added – contratenor first, if there is one, then
triplum and motetus. The upper-voice texts, according to this account, are added only at the end,
by dividing the music and the words and combining them 'as well as you can'.[2]

It is important to remember that Egidius is writing for beginners, so he takes each stage in
turn, while the experienced poet-composer would surely work on several levels simultaneously.
The choice of a specific tenor may reflect not only a general sense of subject matter, but also the
knowledge of certain key words, if not entire lines, of the upper-voice texts, or specific melodic
features that the composer intends to work out in the polyphonic framework. In perhaps an
extreme (but not unique) case, Anna Zayaruznaya makes a convincing argument that the composer of *Colla/Bona* had already written the texts and worked out the periodic structure of the
motet before choosing the tenor and giving it a repetition pattern that is at odds with its upper
voices.[3] Moreover, a motet that borrows a tenor used in another motet creates a further dialogue
that goes beyond general subject matter to include various aspects of structure, text, and music.
The ways in which a composer might work out tenor choice and other aspects mentally resist the

---

[1] Edited and translated by Daniel Leech-Wilkinson in Leech-Wilkinson 1989, 1: 18 (Latin) and
21 (English). Anna Zayaruznaya, in Chapter 14 of the current volume, translates '*materia*' as
'stuff', and I agree with her that her word has the flexibility that Leech-Wilkinson's 'matter' loses
when he glosses it as 'the message of the upper-voice texts'. Egidius acknowledges that his work
is intended for '*parvuli*' (line 88, Leech-Wilkinson 1989, 1: 19, translated on p. 22 as 'children').

[2] '*sicut melius potes*', line 52, Leech-Wilkinson 1989, 1: 19.

[3] See her contribution to this volume. Margaret Bent also argues that the quote from Ovid that
concludes the triplum text of *Tribum que non abhorruit/Quoniam secta latronum/Merito hec
patimur* 'was primary to those texts, and must have been chosen at least as early as, or before, the
Genesis source of the motet tenor'; Bent 1997, 89. Lawrence Earp also discusses *Tribum/Quoniam*
in his contribution to this volume.

kind of clear linearity Egidius's description gives us. For analytical purposes, however, there is value in separating these stages, considering first the reasons for selecting a tenor, then how it is arranged in a way that provides a suitable foundation for the text and music of the upper voices. We will focus mostly on chant-based motets in France, the largest surviving corpus of medieval motets, then consider more briefly French motets based on secular songs, as well as the distinctive motet traditions of England and Italy, in which the treatment and functions of tenors often differ significantly from French practices. Through all of this regional and historical variation, however, we might trace a fundamental stratification between the tenor and other motet voices – whether structural, thematic or rhythmic – as something special to medieval motets, distinguishing them among contemporaneous and subsequent musical styles alike.

THE MOTET TENOR IN FRANCE

Many of the earliest motets are thought to be based on clausulae; in such cases, the tenor has already been set out in a mensural pattern, and an upper voice (or more than one) is already written. Susan Kidwell has considered some practical reasons an early motet composer might select a specific clausula as the foundation for a two-voice Latin motet.[4] In terms of tenor organization, Kidwell finds that 'motet composers had a strong preference for clausulae with patterned, fifth-mode tenors'.[5] The difference comes in aspects of upper-voice rhythm and phrase structure, where she finds that clausulae are favored that use a variety of rhythms rather than keeping to the regular patterns of the rhythmic modes (a feature she calls 'modal purity') or that use irregular phrase lengths that break the regular patterns of poetic declamation Lawrence Earp describes elsewhere in this volume.[6] The result is a combination of a regularly patterned tenor and overlapping, often irregularly patterned, upper voices, which distinguishes the motet from the conductus and becomes a hallmark of the motet in France.

Many early motets serve in a sense to trope their chant source.[7] This is not exactly the process Egidius outlines, where the tenor is chosen on the basis of the 'matter' of the motet to come. Rather, upper voices that trope their tenor add to the meaning of the chant or its liturgical source, while in later motets the tenor serves to add value to the discourse of its upper-voice texts. As an illustration of the earlier procedure, Gerald Hoekstra discusses a two-voice Latin motet on the tenor

---

[4] Kidwell 1998. She specifically excludes French-texted motets for the purposes of her study, because, as she notes, 'they seem to reflect different practical and aesthetic concerns' (74). Toward the end of the article she briefly examines ways that conductus motets, two-voice French motets, and three-voice motets differ slightly from the basic features of the early two-voice Latin motets she studies there.

[5] Kidwell 1998, 77. Her Table 2 categorizes tenors in her control group and motet group by rhythmic mode, showing that there are no items in the motet group that mix modal patterns, and only eight (out of fifty-five total) that are unpatterned, far fewer than in her control group. On the turn from the largely unpatterned tenors in the earliest clausulae toward the more patterned tenors in the later clausulae in Kidwell's control and motet groups, she cites Baltzer 1995, xlii–xliv.

[6] As Earp notes, early motets often create upper-voice phrases of four beats, but 'disruptive phrases' are often added to this regularity; see p. 78 in Earp's chapter below.

[7] On early motets as tropes of their tenors see Kidwell 1996. Kidwell notes that troping is usually seen as commentary 'on the feast of their parent chant' (153), though she argues for an extension of the process to include not only commentary but also exhortation, in the manner of medieval preaching. The focus is still on the parent chant and its liturgical source, and Kidwell and others would argue that the resulting motet at least could be performed within the liturgy itself. See also the contributions by Catherine A. Bradley and especially Dolores Pesce in this volume.

Et gaudebit that not only ends with the word *gaudebit* but also uses other words of the Ascension chant from which the tenor is taken, expanding on them in the manner of a classic trope:[8]

Alleluia. Non vos relinquam orphanos: vado, et venio ad vos, et gaudebit cor vestrum.	*Non orphanum* te deseram ... Cum iero, *veniam* ... *Cor* penitus *gaudebit.*
Alleluia. I will not leave you as orphans: I am going, and I will come to you, and your heart will rejoice.	I shall not abandon you like an orphan ... When I go, I shall come again ... Your heart will rejoice from its very depths.

Hoekstra goes further to argue that the French triplum added to this motet in **Mo** and elsewhere becomes a kind of gloss by extension, and that even the three-voice French motet created by replacing this Latin motetus with a French one maintains a troping relationship with the tenor. The French triplum echoes the Latin motetus, he argues, by declaring:[9]

> Mes je la truis tant docete
> et loial vers moi
> et de vilenie nete,
> que ja ne m'en partirai ...

I find her so sweet and true to me, and free of guile, that I shall never leave her ...

> Or je la trouvai,
> tant par est bien faite,
> touz le cuer m'en rehaite ...

She is so wondrously fashioned that the moment I found her all my heart rejoiced in her ...

According to Hoekstra, this narrator merges with the one of the Latin text that tropes the chant, so that 'the [French] poem is heard allegorically as a love song of Christ for his Church'.[10] It appears more likely, however, that this is a case where the Ascension chant adds value to the love song, not the other way around. This motet, therefore, comes closer to Egidius's later dictum that the tenor should serve the 'matter' of the motet.

The process of reworking motets through adding or subtracting voices and texts extends beyond those motets that appear to be based on pre-existing clausulae. Creators of such motets

---

[8] The chant text appears in Hoekstra 1998, 37; the motetus text and a translation appear on pp. 44–5. The motet is based on a two-part clausula in F (no. 246, fol. 174v). See also Pesce's discussion of *Ecclesie vox hodie/Et florebit* in this volume.

[9] The text and its translation appear in Hoekstra 1998, 36–7.

[10] Hoekstra 1998, 46. When the Latin motetus is replaced by a French one, Hoekstra argues the allegorical interpretation continues and is indeed expanded by the new text, where the knight who attempts to get a young woman to abandon her shepherd becomes 'the allurement of wealth and power that seduced some clergy' (47). This may well be – as the author puts it shortly thereafter – 'fanciful', or at least start to move beyond the level of trope toward other forms of symbolic play. Not all allegorized readings, or forms of play between sacred and secular, are tropes.

may not do the actual musical arrangement of the tenor or even the upper voices, but by adding, changing, or subtracting upper-voice words and melodies, they rearrange what the motet means, and what the tenor brings to that meaning.

The waning of the reliance on clausulae during the thirteenth century opened up more possibilities for tenors drawn from diverse parts of the liturgy. Tenors continued to be taken from the solo portions of responsorial chants (great responsories, graduals, alleluias) appropriate for clausulae and other forms of Notre-Dame polyphony, but other options began to proliferate. Gordon Anderson summarizes the gradual shift: for the earliest layer (represented by the motets in F and W2) only two chant sources that are not responsorial chants appear (both Benedicamus Dominos), while the next layer (to c. 1260) includes tenors drawn from an offertory, a communion, three sequences, two Kyries, one Benedicamus Domino, one antiphon, and four *neumas*. In the later thirteenth century,[11] the process is taken further, with tenors taken from one introit, four sequences, seven Kyries, one Ite missa est, two Benedicamus Dominos, three antiphons, and four *neumas*, in addition to twenty-nine motets based on secular songs. Even where responsorial chants continue to be used as tenor sources after the earliest layer of motets, composers are less bound to draw from the solo portions of those chants. As Anderson notes, all the early motets based on responsories use the solo portions of their chant source, but in his second group choral sections begin to be used; this practice continues to some degree into the fourteenth century, in which both responsorial and non-responsorial chants appear.[12]

In other words, while the earliest motets use tenor sections that are appropriate for liturgical polyphony (i.e., the solo portions of responsorial chants), by the mid-thirteenth century such liturgical propriety is no longer needed. At this point, the rationale for selection can change toward the thematic concerns (the 'matter' of the motet) that Egidius mentions. These have been studied more fully in the fourteenth-century repertory, but an interest in exploiting the potential for a carefully selected tenor to elaborate a pre-formulated theme through its text or its context can be traced in the thirteenth century as well. This approach is illustrated in the proliferation of motets with French texts, which opens the door to intertextual connections that go beyond issues of liturgical propriety. For instance, Sylvia Huot has discussed the use of a Pentecost chant to underpin a motet whose three upper voices give the different perspectives of three sisters singing about love. Their divergent songs on the same theme, which all begin with the same words (*Trois serors sor rive mer/chantent cler*), are linked with the experience of Pentecost, where the disciples spread one message through divergent languages.[13]

This thematic rationale for choosing a tenor, in order to exploit in some way its words and/or their biblical or liturgical context, becomes particularly valuable in the fourteenth-century motet.

---

[11] G. Anderson (1976) defines this group as including the motets of fascicles 7 and 8 of Mo, Tu, and Ba. Karen Desmond discusses the current dating of these Mo fascicles in her contribution to this volume.

[12] G. Anderson 1976, 124–7. He does not discuss the sections of chant used for graduals or alleluias, but the implication of a shift from solo to choral moments in the borrowed chant is clear. In Machaut's motets, for instance, six tenors come from antiphons (two from Marian antiphons), seven from the middle or end of the respond of a responsory, and one from the respond of a gradual, all moments associated not with soloists but with the choir. Only one uses the beginning of a responsory, and two a responsory verse.

[13] Huot 1997, 53–5. The motet is *Trois serors ... La jonete* (343a)/*Trois serors ... La moiene* (343b)/*Trois serors ... L'aisnee* (343c)/*Perlustravit* (M25). See also S. Clark's discussion of this motet in her chapter.

For example, *Apollinis eclipsatur/Zodiacum signis lustrantibus/In omnem terram* has a tenor taken from an offertory used for the Common of Apostles; here not only does the motet composer seem to refer to the biblical source of the tenor (Psalm 18:5, 'Their sound hath gone forth *into all the earth …*'), but it also sets up a parallel between the twelve Apostles evoked in the tenor, the twelve signs of the zodiac discussed in the upper-voice texts, and the twelve living musicians named in its top voice.[14]

Sarah Fuller has examined melodic features that appear to have influenced the selection of tenor fragments in the fourteenth century,[15] but surely at least some of these features shaped the selection of tenors in the second half of the thirteenth century as well. The most important of these is the concern for a descending step as the final interval, allowing for the strongest type of cadence available. As she notes, all but two of the twenty motets by Guillaume de Machaut based on chant or chant-like melodies end in this way;[16] tenors that do not descend to the final at the end are similarly rare in the wider fourteenth-century repertory.

It is also remarkable that a substantial majority of fourteenth-century chant-based tenors end on *F* and *G*, with a smaller group ending on *c* (or in one case *C*) or (more rarely) *D*. This suggests a strong preference for major-third tonalities: though a *G* final can have minor thirds above it through the use of *b*♭, it is generally only the tenor that has a signature, if any.

The finals of chant-based tenors do not, however, completely line up with the modal finals of the chants from which they come. Among Machaut's twenty chant-based motets, for instance, two of the F-final tenors come from chants in mode 7, with a G final, while one of the G-final tenors is taken from a chant in mode 6, with an F final. In other words, a chant-based tenor often does share a final with the mode of its chant source, but it does not always. This reinforces the notion that the harmonic processes used in motets, while not tonal in the functional sense of the common practice period, are also not usefully described in terms of modality.[17]

Many of these features can be seen in the tenor of Guillaume de Machaut's motet 4, *De Bon Espoir, de Tres Doulz Souvenir/Puis que la douce rousee/Speravi* (M4). The tenor is taken from an introit for the first week after Pentecost;[18] this shows how the choice of a tenor has moved

---

14   The biblical translation used here is the Douay-Rheims 1899 American Edition, accessed through the Bible Gateway app; the verse appears as Psalm 19:4 in the King James Version and elsewhere. The motet is edited in Harrison 1968. Bent and David Howlett have explored these and other aspects of the group of fourteenth-century musician motets, but their work remains largely unpublished, save for the brief discussion in Howlett 2005.

15   The classic statement here is Fuller 1990.

16   The two exceptions are Machaut's M22 and M23. The three motets built on secular songs do not follow this standard pattern; each ends with an ascending step to the final.

17   As Fuller (1990, 201) notes, 'The modal system, invented to classify melodies, could not be extended routinely to polyphony, to complexes of lines and successions of two- and three-note sonorities'. She further argues that 'Tonal structures in Machaut's motets seems guided more by individual characteristics of a plainsong tenor and the possibilities it offers than by *a priori* conventions of pitch relationships' (213). She observes that most of the fragments Machaut selects 'conform to their [modal] finals', but that the composing-out of these tenors can lead to reinterpretation of characteristic features.

18   The complete text of the chant is: 'Domine, in tuo misericordia speravi: exultavit cor meum in salutari tuo: cantabo Domino, qui bona tribuit mihi. [Ps.] Usquequo Domine oblivisceris me in finem? usquequo avertis faciem tuam a me?' The introit is most often assigned to Pentecost 1, but occasionally to the Sunday after the Octave of Pentecost, or the Sunday after Trinity; clearly the variation is due at least in part to the inconsistent celebration of Trinity Sunday in the later Middle Ages.

away from the responsorial chants of the Notre-Dame school, and the use of a chant that is *not* assigned to a major feast similarly shows that factors other than liturgical propriety are at play. The introit comes from Psalm 13(12), with the antiphon (from which the tenor is taken) drawn from verse 6; the only significant variant is that, where the psalm uses the future tense *exultabit* (will rejoice), the chant uses the past *exultavit* (has rejoiced), creating a parallel with the previous verb *speravi* (I have hoped).

Given the relatively unmarked status of the Sundays after Pentecost, it is likely that liturgical context was not a major factor in the selection of this tenor, though it was in some other motets by Machaut and his contemporaries. Perhaps particularly interesting is a group of tenors taken from Lent or especially Holy Week, with which Machaut or another motet creator seems to be making an explicit comparison between the narrator, who often speaks of his suffering for love, and the Passion of Christ.

In M4, Machaut may have been responding not to the liturgical or biblical context of the tenor but rather simply to the word *speravi* – I have hoped. Elizabeth Eva Leach has noted the extent to which hope is a central theme in Machaut's works, most notably providing a key figure in his *Remede de Fortune*, where Esperance (Hope) teaches the inept narrator how to love properly – and in the process to create poetry and music in the new style of the fixed forms.[19]

The chant melody is remarkably consistent among a variety of northern French sources, including two manuscripts from Châlons-en-Champagne (a town near Reims formerly called Châlons-sur-Marne), which for Office-based chants often provide the closest reading to Machaut's melodies.[20] There are, however, several Mass books from Reims itself, and three of them (including a fourteenth-century manuscript from the cathedral) provide a slightly more distant reading. These sources share a third leap that is filled in by stepwise motion in Machaut's tenor; the Reims manuscripts include a second such leap. These variants may be compositional alterations, designed to make the tenor melody completely stepwise (with one repeated pitch at the penultimate position), a feature found in several of Machaut's tenors,[21] or to make what is in the northern French sources a seventeen-pitch melody into one that can be evenly divided into smaller units.

Once the tenor is selected, Egidius tells us to 'order and color' it. This is usually taken to refer to the process of dividing the melody into segments and giving each a repeated rhythmic pattern, generally referred to today as a 'talea'. (The term 'color' usually refers to the tenor pitches; the two terms seem to have been used rather interchangeably in the Middle Ages, but the separation here is useful.)

It has been a central tenet of the traditional definition of the medieval motet that its structure comes from a repeated rhythmic pattern in the tenor. The sway of this compositional feature, and the modern term 'isorhythm' often used to describe it, has been questioned, most notably by Margaret Bent, in part because it tends to limit attention given to examples that do not fit the paradigm.[22] It is also true that there are important subgenres of the motet that do not use such patterns. Nevertheless, regularly repeating tenor patterns *are* a major feature of the chant-based

[19] Leach 2011b, ch. 4.

[20] A. Clark 1996, 27–34; the comparison of the M4 tenor to chant readings appears on p. 189.

[21] The other fully stepwise tenors are M3 (with several repetitions of pitch) and M9, whose tenor consists entirely of alternations between *a/F* and *g/b♭*, as discussed in Fuller 1990, 204. If Machaut's source was one of the Reims manuscripts, he could have used the sixteen-pitch melody with its two leaps of a third and divided it into four taleae, but if the seventeen-pitch version was the one he knew, he would have to do something to make it fit into equal taleae.

[22] Bent 2008b. See also the chapters by Bent and Lawrence Earp in this volume.

motets of the later thirteenth and fourteenth centuries as practiced in France, the group of works currently under consideration, and the process of creating such a structure seems to be what Egidius describes in his treatise.

For modern listeners, this notion of creating musical structure through a repeating rhythmic pattern in the lowest voice, rather than through melodic repetition especially but not only in the top voice, is one of the ways in which the medieval motet as practiced in France seems most strange, second only to its use of multiple simultaneous texts in a resolutely non-imitative polyphonic texture. The difficulty of hearing this talea structure increases in fourteenth-century motets, in which the rhythmic patterns become much longer, and use much longer note values, so that they become foundational in an architectural sense (as at least one medieval theorist has noted) as their audibility decreases.[23] But even as scholarly focus has shifted to a reading of repeated tenor structures as less audible than organizational, some scholars (including myself) have learned to hear these structures reasonably well.[24] Moreover, composers came to use upper-voice features, especially rests and hocket passages, to call attention to the tenor's talea repetitions.[25]

The repetition of small rhythmic units was a feature common to the tenor organization of many clausulae; in the clausulae on *Latus* discussed by Catherine A. Bradley in the previous chapter in this volume, for instance, the tenor consistently moves in a pattern of three longs followed by a long rest. Such patterning, often limited to a couple of measures in transcription, was part of many motets from an early stage. We have already seen that Susan Kidwell identified tenor patterning as a common feature in the clausulae most favored by early motet composers.[26] Even as newly composed motets came to use patterns that gradually became longer and more complicated, such tenor patterns remained a fundamental structural principle for the French motet. This can be seen, for instance, in the first-mode pattern of three-long units that under-pins **Mo** 81, *Ja pour mal/Hé, desloiaus mesdisant/Portare*, discussed in Dolores Pesce's chapter. The staggering of phrase lengths between the three voices seen in this motet, so that all three voices never rest together – and even two voices only rarely rest at the same time – creates the characteristically continuous texture of the genre. These features will continue to be important in fourteenth-century France.

A few thirteenth-century chant-based motets use other procedures. For instance, Pesce shows that the creator of *Mout me fu grief/Robin m'aime/Portare* organizes the motet, including its chant-based tenor, according to the form of the borrowed rondeau that appears in the motetus. This rondeau, she argues, shifts the tonal emphasis of the tenor, concluding that 'motet composers considered the chant as raw material that could be manipulated to different tonal ends, even to the point of altering some notes and adding others'.[27]

---

[23] Johannes de Grocheio calls the tenor 'that part on which the others are founded, as a foundation is for the parts of a house or building. The tenor rules them and gives them their quantities, as the bones do to the other parts of the body'. Translated in Busse Berger 2005, 221.

[24] See, for example, A. Clark 2004.

[25] Earp articulates this feature in terms of periodicity in his contribution to this volume. Hocket is a technique that alternates short notes in two (or more) voices, creating a kind of broken or hiccupping effect. In the thirteenth century entire pieces were created using this technique, but by the fourteenth century it was mostly used in motets, as a rhythmic effect that often marked the final cadence of a talea. For more on the development of the hocket, and especially questions about how composers, scribes, and performers handled text given to hocket sections in motets, see Schmidt-Beste 2013.

[26] Kidwell 1998, 77, discussed above.

[27] See Pesce 1997, 37, as well as her contribution to the present volume.

The expansion of rhythmic options created by the *ars nova* notational systems espoused by Philippe de Vitry and others allowed the faster note values of the upper voice to be paired with longer note values in the tenor (and contratenor, where present). This leads to a basic stratification between texted upper voices that move in semibreves, minims, and occasionally breves, and untexted lower voices that move in breves, longs, and occasionally maximas.

In M4, Machaut's eighteen-pitch melody is repeated (for a total of thirty-six pitches), then divided into three taleae (see Example 3.1); after these are stated, the melody is repeated in what is usually called diminution, with each note reinterpreted as the next smaller note value.[28] This is the most common form of diminution, often leading to a 2:1 reduction as occurs here. It is worth emphasizing, however, that diminution and other forms of mensural manipulation do not always lead to such tidy formulas, since mensural notation allows for longs, breves, and semibreves to be subdivided variously into two or three components, and moving to a different note value may require interpreting the notation in a different way.[29]

The disposition of a tenor into taleae is about more than numbers: the composer has the ability to shape this melody in a way that allows or discourages cadences. This shaping is especially important at the ends of taleae and before rests; descending steps at these moments can enable a strong cadence, especially if the second pitch of the descending step occurs at a strong mensural position. Whether or not these descending steps become cadences, however, depends on the upper-voice pitches, rhythms, and text setting presented over them. The strongest cadential scheme possible combines a descending step in the tenor with ascending half steps in motetus (to the fifth above the tenor) and triplum (to the octave above the tenor), sustained for at least a breve.[30] Other forms of upper-voice motion can weaken a cadence, or turn what could have been a cadential moment into a non-cadential phrase end, or even negate any sense of closure. So while the tenor talea on its own can suggest potential cadence points, the three-part texture (or four-part texture with contratenor) reinforces or undercuts that potential.

In this motet, each talea has a total of twelve pitches, spread over seventeen longs; see again Example 3.1. The first begins on *F*, the final, then rises a fourth before reaching a long rest; the talea subsequently alternates pairs of notes and rests, with a result that the last tenor note of the talea (*G*) is approached by a rising step, on the second breve of the long unit – slightly weak harmonic motion (relative to the stronger descending step), in a weak mensural position. As illustrated in Example 3.2 (the complete first talea), the upper voices do not treat this phrase end as a cadence: the triplum stops on the fifth above the tenor in long 16 (L16), but lacks strong cadential motion; the motetus continues to a phrase end a breve later.

Far stronger in their cadential force are two earlier moments, both ending on a G sonority. The beginning of L9 meets all the musical criteria for a strong cadence: as shown in the example, the tenor descends by step, the motetus and triplum rise by half step, and the G sonority they reach is held for at least a full breve in all parts. The cadence falls at the end of the third line of the triplum text but in the middle of the motetus's second line, the only factor that might weaken

---

[28] This can be written out, as it is in the version of M4 given in **Ferrell 1** and **Mach A**. See also Figure 8.5 in this volume, which shows M10 as it appears in **Mach C**, where the diminution section is likewise fully notated – the first diminished talea begins toward the end of the second tenor system on fol. 215r. On the distinction between 'true' diminution and other temporal relationships, as interpreted by various theorists and embodied in the motets and songs in Ch, see Bent 2009.

[29] This is explained, for instance, in Bent's 'Isorhythm' entry in *Grove*, as well as in her chapter in this volume. See also Emily Zazulia's contribution for a good example of the complexity possible in these techniques.

[30] Fuller 1986.

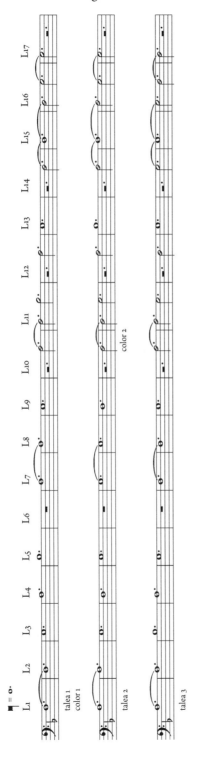

Example 3.1. M4 tenor, divided into taleae.

This example is similar to Example 14 of Hartt 2010a but is newly edited from Ferrell 1 as presented in Earp 2014. Ligatures are not indicated. The example here includes only the undiminished taleae, but the diminished talea are written out in the manuscript itself.

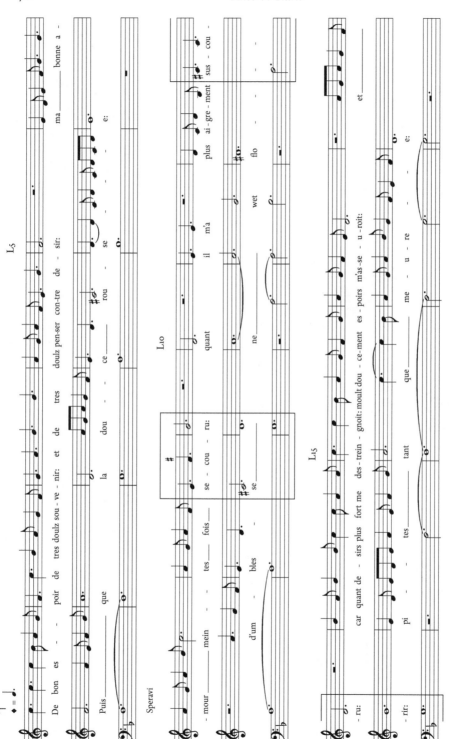

Example 3.2. M4, talea 1.

This is newly edited from Ferrell 1 as presented in Earp 2014, except that two errors are corrected. (These are both in the motetus: in L9 and L12 a B appears in the source where an L is needed.) Ligatures are not indicated, nor is the plica on the motetus's opening breve. Text abbreviations are silently expanded, and *u* and *v* are used in modern senses; apostrophes are added where sense requires them, but punctuation remains as in the manuscript.

it. Another cadence comes shortly after, at L13; here, it is the motetus, temporarily higher than the triplum, that moves to the octave. Both upper voices conclude their lines of poetry together (the triplum's fourth line and the motetus's second), thereby creating an even stronger cadence.

This talea pattern – two internal cadences (at L9 and L13), plus a talea end that is not really cadential – continues in taleae 2 and 3, but the internal cadences are weakened, often by the addition of thirds to what might otherwise be a perfect consonance of fifth plus octave. Because motetus motion continues through what might have been a cadence on *F* at the end of talea 3, our ears are led to the diminution section. Here, breve 9 (B9), which corresponds to L9 in the undiminished taleae, continues to be a transitory cadence point, while the more continuous melodic motion carries the listener to the final cadence on *F*.

What Machaut does in M4, in other words, is first divide his tenor melody in a way that gradually allows for stronger cadences at the end of the talea (ascending step to *G*, descending step to *G*, descending step to the final, *F*); however, he then gives the tenor a rhythm and the upper voices melodies that tend to undercut the cadential force of those moments. He sets up two possible alternative cadence points within the first talea, at L9 and L13, but goes on to weaken the force of these two points in subsequent taleae.

Many motets include some form of upper-voice reflection of the tenor's talea structure. This can range from a simple use of breves and breve rests at the same points in each talea (fairly common) to a wholescale repetition of all or nearly all rhythms (a technique some scholars have called 'pan-isorhythm').[31] Many motets have some form of repeated rhythmic activity (often including hocket) leading to the final sonority of the tenor at the end of each talea, sometimes transitioning into the next talea. In M4, there is no hocket, but the upper-voice rhythms repeat almost exactly from one talea to the next.[32]

Moreover, this is one of a group of Machaut's motets that uses exact melodic repetition to underline the talea structure.[33] In each undiminished talea, the motetus melody decorates its motion from *d* (at the beginning of L5) to *e* (at the beginning of L6) with a pattern that is repeated (see Example 3.2); moreover, in taleae 2 and 3 this pattern is given to the word 'desir', which appears in the triplum at the same point in the first talea. Sarah Fuller notes that the first statement of this melody is part of an avoided potential cadence at the end of the first phrase of the motet that sets up 'a problematic relationship between F and G', the final and the step above it.[34] The decorated *d* of the motetus melody, appearing at first to be a harmonic goal (approached in taleae 1 and 3 by a *c♯*), turns out to lead to a phrase end on *e* at L6, an audible sign of a desire that leads away from stability toward further motion. Moreover, the focus of this melody on *d* and *e* does not reinforce F, the final of the tenor (and of the chant from which it is taken). This further makes the pattern a destabilizing feature in harmonic terms, even while it underlines the motet's structure through its regularly placed instances within taleae.

What is most important here is that the 'ordering and coloring' of the tenor melody into taleae already sets up potential repercussions for the upper voices in terms of harmony, rhythm, phrase structure, and even melody, and that in motets of this type the tenor was clearly organized with these upper-voice implications at least somewhat in mind. The fourteenth-century motet in France, unlike its earlier relatives, represents a single creative act; a mature composer such as

---

[31] See Bent's 'Isorhythm' entry in *Grove* and Earp's contribution to this volume.

[32] Ursula Günther notes the 'deviations' in Günther 1958, 31 n. 17. The complete rhythmic structure of M4 appears as Example A1 in Hartt 2010a, 230–1.

[33] I discuss these in A. Clark 2004.

[34] Fuller 1992b, esp. 234–41.

Machaut would have worked out the later stages mentally even while working on what Egidius calls the first and second steps.

While chant (on its own or as part of a clausula) is the seed from which many motets grow, in the thirteenth century songs and refrains also appear as generating material.[35] These vernacular melodies are often used in the upper voices, as in the first example discussed by Matthew P. Thomson in this volume, in which a newly created tenor bases aspects of its form and motivic structure on the borrowed song above it. In other cases, the borrowed songs appear as tenors, as in Thomson's third example, in which the song form is reflected through melodic repetition in the upper voices. And in other cases, there is a more complicated relationship between the rhythm and structure of the borrowed song and the upper voices of the motet. Mark Everist has argued that these pieces, while limited in their influence on later motets (even the song-based motets of Guillaume de Machaut), had a critical role in the creation of the polyphonic secular song of the fourteenth century.[36]

This subgenre of motets with song-based tenors effectively ends with the three examples by Machaut.[37] These represent a kind of song-motet hybrid that seemed to suit Machaut the experimenter, who used motet-like repeated rhythmic structures and bitextuality in certain songs as well. The tenors of Machaut's song-based motets move at a rhythmic level closer to that of the upper voices than we have seen in his chant-based motets, so they are experienced more as true melodies, in counterpoint with the upper-voice melodies; they use the same rhythms and forms of their sources (as far as we can tell), and sometimes are transmitted with their texts as well. There is, in other words, no analogy to the 'ordering and coloring' stage Egidius outlines: Machaut's secular-song tenors are quoted outright, with their rhythm and their form intact.

The process of tenor selection in these motets is less clear. Scholars tend to believe that all three songs existed before Machaut used them, but there is little evidence. *Je ne sui mie certeins*, the tenor of M20, does not appear elsewhere. The text of *Pour quoy me bat mes maris* (used in M16) is found in **D308** in a slightly different form, and the words *Fins cuers doulz* (attached to the tenor of M11) appear in an anonymous *Salut d'amour*, each of whose stanzas ends with a refrain (vdB 754).[38] It would seem that these texts did at one time circulate with melodies, which have been lost, but it was likely their words that first attracted Machaut's attention. Still, he combined the forms of these tenors with the basic principles of talea-based motet construction in ways that make these three pieces unique, and in the case of M11, he further exploits the musical symbolism of the hard and soft hexachords (*dur* and *doulz* here) to expressive ends.

THE MOTET TENOR IN ENGLAND

The type of motet discussed so far – built on a pre-existing tenor often taken from chant – exists in medieval England, although it is relatively rare.[39] The English motet is marked by much greater

[35] Pesce and Jennifer Saltzstein discuss the use of refrains in upper-voice texts in Chapters 6 and 9, respectively, of this *Companion*; see also Saltzstein 2013b.

[36] Everist 2007.

[37] The most recent study of these motets is Hartt 2009.

[38] The *Salut d'amour*, found in F-Pn f. fr. 837, is edited in Schultz-Gora 1900; stanza 27, lines 196–202, is found on p. 364.

[39] Jared Hartt covers the motet in England more thoroughly in his contribution to this volume; here I will simply summarize some basic features, focusing on ways in which the English motet

stylistic diversity, including examples without any pre-existing material.[40] For example, *Virgo regalis* is built on a *pes*, a short newly composed melodic pattern stated nine times. Over the *pes*, the two upper parts engage in voice exchange, swapping texted and untexted phrases. The upper-voice text begins by quoting an antiphon for St Catherine of Alexandria, then goes on to trope it, but in a manner general enough to allow the motet to be adapted to honor other female saints, as suggested by a note in its source manuscript.[41]

Virgo regalis exemplifies many of the basic features of the motet in England, insofar as generalizations can be made given the variety of compositional approaches present. Nearly all English motets have Latin sacred texts, avoiding the fourteenth-century French propensity for Latin-texted occasional and French-texted amatory works. English motets with multiple texts exist, but many have a single text used in both upper voices. Melodic repetition often appears, in the form of the rondellus technique in which melodic phrases are exchanged among upper voices, and/or in the use of a *pes* tenor in the lowest voice. In motets based on chant or song, the borrowed material can appear in the bottom voice. However, it can also appear in the middle voice, as in the motets discussed in Jared Hartt's contribution to this volume. Chant may even appear in an upper part, with its text, so it becomes 'foundational' in a melodic rather than harmonic or architectural sense. In all cases, the tenor moves at a rhythmic level closer to that of the other voices, without the extreme rhythmic stratification of the French motets of the fourteenth century, in which tenor lines move at a pace much slower than that of the upper voices.

Example 3.3. *Ballaam* tenor organization

This is newly edited from color images of Mo, fols. 393r–394v. Ligatures are not indicated. The threefold repetition of the first double stanza (making four statements of the first tenor unit) is indicated by *t[res]* and *iii* added in very light ink at the bottom of fol. 393r. The first tenor unit is written again on fol. 393v without these instructions. The second tenor unit has the words *istud t[res]* and *t[res] iii* written below it in the same light ink, indicating a similar fourfold statement.

does and does not follow the bottom-up compositional strategies we have seen operating in France.

[40] The essential starting point here is Lefferts 1986, on which much of this section is based.

[41] The motet is edited in Sanders 1979, 98–9; the manuscript (**WOc**, xxviii fol. 1v) includes a heading that names Eadburga. Peter M. Lefferts notes that the motet is 'essentially suited for any Virgin-Martyr with a four-syllable name'; see Lefferts 1992, 176. Lisa Colton observes that the motet text tropes the antiphon for St Catherine of Alexandria; see Colton 2017a, 74–5.

Balaam de quo vaticinans/Ballaam is an example of an English motet built on chant in its lowest voice, but it operates differently from most French motets.[42] Rather than using a short fragment of chant in its tenor, it uses the pitches from two double stanzas of its sequence source in an interesting way; see Example 3.3. Because the first stanza has melodic repetition within it, the motet creator divides it so that two statements of a five-long phrase are followed by a coda of four single longs; this pattern is stated four times. The second stanza, which begins similarly to the first, then appears, giving phrases of 4+4+5 longs; this again is stated four times. The extensive use of melodic repetition sounds rather more like a *pes* than the rhythmic patterns found in French motets.

Above the tenor, the upper voices paraphrase the chant text and engage in modified voice exchange. The result is a motet that is thoroughly English but that apparently came close enough to French tastes to allow it to be copied in the eighth fascicle of **Mo** (early fourteenth century), as well as in a fragment now held in Oxford, **Onc 362** (*c.* 1320), in which only the duplum survives.

The greater emphasis in English motets on text declamation (as discussed by Earp in this volume) and on melody-based structural principles such as *pes* and rondellus, combined with the generally decreased use of techniques such as polytextuality and highly stratified textures mixing very long and very short notes, appear to be signs of a stronger concern for music as pure sound, rather than music as embodiment in sound of inaudible harmonies – a concept critical to the motet as practiced in late-medieval France. The greater concern for pleasing sound as a value may also underpin the use of 'isoperiodic' structures discussed by Earp and the tonal coherence in motets discussed by Hartt elsewhere in this volume. This is not to say, of course, that French motets are not designed to be pleasing as sound, or that English motets cannot make use of symbolic or intertextual devices; it is only to say that certain geographic differences in musical priorities are, in general, evident between English and French motets. An English interest in pleasing sound would further seem to align with the preference for imperfect consonances apparent in many of these pieces, a feature that would strike fifteenth-century French composers and inspire the creation of a new style.

THE MOTET TENOR IN ITALY

Another motet type can be seen in what is now Italy, especially from the Veneto. Here as in England, manuscript sources are fragmentary, and so too are many pieces. Nevertheless, Bent has traced in the surviving material a set of unique features.[43] Many Italian motets are written in honor of doges, bishops, and cities; even motets in honor of saints seem often to have more of a civic than a devotional purpose.[44]

Like the tenors of most French motets, those of most Italian motets have a foundational or harmonic rather than melodic function, and they move more slowly than the upper voices. However, they are not generally based on chant or other pre-existing melodic material, nor are they organized according to a repeated rhythmic pattern like the French talea. Some motets do use large-scale rhythmic repetition that involves all voices, dividing the piece into two halves with identical rhythmic profiles, an approach rarely found outside Italy. The upper voices generally share range and rhythmic activity, and sometimes text as well. This accompanied-duet texture,

---

[42] This motet is edited in Harrison 1980, 8–12.

[43] The basic introduction to the genre is Bent 1992a.

[44] Benjamin Brand has shown the intersections of political and spiritual interests in an Italian motet in Brand 2003.

especially when combined with canonic imitation in the upper voices at the beginning of the motet, can be compared to that of the *caccia*.[45] Like the *caccia* – but unlike motets composed in France – Bent sees these motets as 'conceived from the top parts down'.[46]

Marce, Marcum imitaris demonstrates many of the features of this genre, as well as issues relating to transmission. It appears in two fragmentary Italian sources, but even combining the two is not sufficient to make the piece completely performable.[47] The tenor is freely written without substantial repetition of melody or rhythm, and the two voices above it share a single text in honor of Marco Cornaro, Doge of Venice between 1365 and 1368. Following a long imitative passage reminiscent of the *caccia*, the upper voices move largely together, without the overlapping phrases or distinctions of range and rhythmic motion frequently present in the upper voices of French motets.

EPILOGUE: INTO THE FIFTEENTH CENTURY

By the early fifteenth century, diplomatic contacts surrounding the Hundred Years' War and Papal Schism allowed increased influences among the musics of France, England, and Italy. In the world of the motet these international influences can be seen most clearly in the works of Guillaume Du Fay.[48]

Vasilissa ergo gaude, dated by Heinrich Besseler to 1420, is an early work of Du Fay.[49] It is based on a tenor drawn from chant, but this tenor is treated in a manner more similar to that of Italian motet than the French. Aside from the opening long, the tenor and contratenor move mostly in breves and semibreves – at a rhythmic level close to that of the upper voices – and therefore avoid the extreme stratification of fourteenth-century French motets. Rather than putting the tenor and contratenor through a series of taleae, Du Fay uses the Italian technique of bipartite rhythmic repetition in all voices following the canonic opening in the upper voices. The borrowed tenor and addition of a contratenor are the only truly French features here.

In other ceremonial motets Du Fay freely uses polytextuality, chant tenors, and talea structures, as well as the Italian techniques he employs in *Vasilissa ergo gaude*. But at the same time he created a new style of motet, with a single Latin sacred text and an emphasis on the rhetorical presentation of that text in music. This new motet did not immediately replace the synthesis of medieval procedures represented in pieces such as *Vasilissa ergo gaude*, but it did signal the gradual decline in influence of the medieval motet.

Focusing mostly on the basic features of motet materials and construction, this chapter shows that the tenor serves a variety of roles, making it difficult to describe a singular process through which medieval motets are made. Many of these differences are regional, and the French type

---

[45] Bent 1992a, 104.

[46] Bent 1992a, 98. A couple of paragraphs later, she states, 'We can at least say that from the start the Italian motet was less bound to tenor priority than was the French, and that any such dependency receded further during the century' (99).

[47] This motet is edited in Fischer and Gallo 1987, 197–201. The fragmentary sources are **I-GR 224** and **I-MFA**.

[48] The combination of French and Italian motet styles has sometimes been attributed to Johannes Ciconia, but Bent has argued that most of the features in his motets that appear to show French influence come from the scribe of **Q15**; see Bent 1987 and Bent 1992a. She also argues that the motets in the Cyprus manuscript **TuB** are fundamentally Italianate; see Bent 1995.

[49] Edited in Besseler 1966, no. 7. The tenor comes from the gradual *Concupivit rex decorem tuum*.

has traditionally been taken as the norm, due to historiographical biases and patterns of source survival that have tended to shape scholarly narratives and marginalize divergent practices. In France, the tenor often serves as the foundation in more ways than one: it frequently uses pre-existing material, usually sounds as the lowest voice (alone or in combination with a contratenor written against it), and interacts in interesting ways with the texts and melodies written above it, often generating and/or supporting them in terms of both theme and structure. Here we can see something of the typical medieval reliance on authority, as musicians base their own work on that of others. In Italy the tenor is a new creation that sounds foundational but is more likely written after the upper voices, which it accompanies. English motets possess a great unity of subject matter, but tremendous diversity of structural processes; the repertoire includes motets that foreground chant sources audibly, motets in which chant serves a more structural role, and motets that are not based on chant at all. As in Italian motets, however, even where the tenor is not the conceptual foundation, it often sounds as such due to a textural separation from the upper voices, as Peter Lefferts has remarked:

> What is essential to the character of these motets – what seems to have made them motets in English eyes – is the stratification of function, range, melodic material, and to a lesser degree, rhythmic activity, between those voices that are texted, hence in the foreground of the composition, and that voice (or those voices) never texted and serving as a structural skeleton or foundation.[50]

This idea of stratification of voices may in the end serve to bring together the different styles of motets we have seen here, and indeed to separate them from the new style of motet that became more prominent in the fifteenth century, where techniques such as pervasive imitation make all voices fundamentally equal.[51] Whether the subject of a motet is love, politics, or faith; whether the goal seems to be pleasing sound or the play of audible and inaudible harmonies; whether the tenor drives the meaning of the motet or is added and reshaped later in the compositional process, the stratification between tenor and texted voices lies at the heart of the medieval motet.

---

[50] Lefferts 1986, 4.

[51] It could also account for the inclusion of *chaces* and even Mass movements along with motets in the index of the Trémoïlle fragment (Trém). See Bent 1990.

— 4 —

Isorhythm

Lawrence Earp

Son plaisir consiste à inventorier les manières possibles de traiter une matière donnée.[1]

S CHOLARS TODAY generally agree that 'isorhythm' ought to mean what it says, a term describing segments of music literally exhibiting the 'same rhythm', duration for duration.[2] This is the lesson of Margaret Bent's influential 2008 article 'What is Isorhythm?' By then, the literal sense of the term had already been normal usage in the work of many scholars, including, besides Bent herself, Ernest Sanders and Daniel Leech-Wilkinson.[3] As a designation of genre, however, 'the isorhythmic motet', a looser and vastly more inclusive usage was still generally accepted, and Bent's call for strict consistency between the nominal and adjectival forms of the term effectively limits its application as a generic designation to a small and incohesive assemblage of works, leaving the category without historical relevance. As compensation for a focused reinterpretation of this and many other terms, Bent offers a new terminological precision capable of distinguishing procedures that had been wrongly grouped together in earlier analyses (an example is the sphere of possibilities that had been subsumed under the term 'diminution'), thereby celebrating a newly revealed diversity of compositional procedures that had not been sufficiently appreciated previously.

Friedrich Ludwig, who coined the term in the early twentieth century, pursued a more general goal: to write a synthetic account of a period of music history. The discovery of the Ivrea codex (**Iv**) in 1921, which added a number of new motets to the repertory, allowed Ludwig's student Heinrich Besseler to flesh out a detailed narrative. For Besseler, the style of motet pioneered by Philippe de Vitry was an innovation that not only swept away the enormous diversity of late thirteenth-century motet types in France, but also, in its essentials, remained dominant for well over one hundred years, from *c.*1316 up to the late motets of Guillaume Du Fay in the 1440s.[4] This broader narrative recedes in Bent's sharpened critical perspective, despite the probability that Philippe de Vitry would have recognized Du Fay's *Nuper rosarum flores* as a motet. In my revised account, Vitry still figures as the key player, though the point of departure for this episode

---

[1] Cerquiglini 1985, 51. ('[The fourteenth-century's] delight lay in taking stock of all possible manners of treating a given subject'.)

[2] Some recent definitions are: 'the application of the same rhythm to different melody' (Bent 2008b, 128); or, 'the repetition of rhythms independently of pitch' (Zayaruznaya 2015a, 3).

[3] Sanders 1973, 561 n. 268, quoted in Bent 2008b, n. 17; Bent 2001; Leech-Wilkinson 1989. Current to this writing, see the segment 'Upper-voice rhythm' in Margaret Bent's chapter below.

[4] Besseler 1927; cf. also Sanders 1973, 556 and Leech-Wilkinson 1989, 1: 28.

in music history depends more on literary factors than musical ones. It should be possible to maintain a coherent historical narrative even as we embrace the diversity that Bent has described.

Considering the repertory to which it is usually applied, advanced **Fauv** motets through Du Fay, the term 'isorhythm' has long caused confusion. In the first place, it seems most relevant only to later stages of the development, when 'isorhythmic motets' incorporate large-scale rhythmic correspondences ('pan-isorhythm'), prejudicing early works, which exhibit much less literal rhythmic recurrence, as not quite worthy of the name.[5] In the second place, now thinking back to earlier developments, there is the nagging misgiving that even the earliest motets exhibit repeating rhythmic patterns, at least in the tenor: why do we not apply the term 'isorhythmic' to them? It will be necessary to piece together exactly what Ludwig and Besseler were trying to capture with the term.

Besseler's history of the medieval motet in France distinguishes three stages: 1. the early motet up to *c.* 1250; 2. a variety of new motet styles from *c.* 1250 to **Fauv** (*c.* 1316), spanning the activity of Franco of Cologne and Petrus de Cruce; and 3. a new consolidation of stylistic possibilities in the 'isorhythmic motet' invented by Philippe de Vitry *c.* 1316. Early thirteenth-century motets pit a tenor delivered in short ostinato patterns of four or eight beats against an upper part whose rhythmic profile is determined by poetic declamation. The vast majority of the diverse declamation patterns of poetry in the early motet define phrases of four beats, or, when concatenated, eight or even twelve beats. An early motet absolutely regular in this regard is *O Maria, maris stella* (448)/*Veritatem* (M37).[6] Here lines of eight syllables with accent on the penultimate syllable (paroxytonic stress) alternate with lines of five syllables with accent on the antepenultimate syllable (proparoxytonic stress), in short, 8p 5pp. The rhythm generated by the couplets remains consistent through seven phrases, broadening only in the eighth and final phrase, a 5p line (Example 4.1a presents the first phrase, 4.1b the last).[7]

More commonly, composers of early motets liked to play off the fixed phrase lengths articulated by an ostinato tenor pattern by introducing disruptive phrases of one, two, three, or six beats in upper voices. In the best works, varied phrase lengths can lend shape to an entire motet. For example, *Agmina milicie celestis* (532)/*Agmina* (M65), on a text by Philip the Chancellor and music likely by Pérotin, establishes a certain narrative continuity, again in phrases of eight beats, by concatenating 7pp lines with ˘6pp lines (I indicate musical enjambment with the shorthand

---

[5] I speak here of the normal usage of the term 'isorhythmic motet' before Bent 2008b, which, as stated earlier, effectively eliminates use of the term to define a genre. For the term 'pan-isorhythm', see Apel 1959, 139.

[6] Ed. Tischler 1982, vol. 1, no. 35; overview of sources and scorings in van der Werf 1989, motet 448. The transmission picture for this motet is complex. To simplify the discussion, I consider the work only in its form as a two-voice motet and as a three-voice conductus motet, not in its later revision as a double motet, *O Maria, virgo Davitica* (449)/*O Maria, maris stella/Veritatem*.

[7] I have freshly edited all musical examples in this chapter from the source given in the example's caption. In Example 4.1a, the last pitch of the tenor and the word 'gracie' in the motetus are lost in **Châl** due to a diagonal rip in the lower-right corner of fol. 14r; they are supplied from the redaction in W2, fols. 125r–126r. Sources transmit several slightly different endings of the tenor and motetus. The version given in Example 4.1b after **Châl** can be compared to the editions of Tischler 1978, vol. 2, no. 52 (**Mo**) and G. Anderson 1977, no. 75 (**Ba**) as well as Tischler's comparative edition, given in the previous note. The long mark near the end in all three voices of Example 4.1b indicates an elongated notehead in **Châl**, signaling the lengthening of a standard declamation pattern in *cum littera* notation. In this and subsequent musical examples, notes with small noteheads indicate plicas.

notation ˘6pp). The tenor ostinato serves these lines faithfully (Example 4.2a).[8] Later in the motet, the confusion of reason in the face of articles of faith is expressed in a passage in which line after line of text breathlessly stumbles over the next, concatenated to form an unbroken sixteen-beat phrase (7pp ˘4pp ˘4pp ˘4pp ˘4pp ˘6pp), finally falling silent (Example 4.2b);[9] the pattern established at the beginning then resumes to round off the work, celebrating Mary's victory over the sophists.

In lesser hands, phrase overlap in the early motet – now an accepted convention – can become an almost mindless pursuit. Four-beat phrases in the motetus set the popular and easily composed 7pp patterns of poetry in *Salve, salus hominum* (221)/*Et gaudebit* (M24) (Example 4.3).[10] The insertion of a single syllable 'dum' ('while') in line 7 willfully offsets the motetus by one beat, which then for the most part resumes regular 7pp lines. Heedless, the tenor runs throughout in three-beat bars, with a couple of two-beat bars thrown in now and again. The perplexing irregularity of phrasing indeed causes all reason to stand agape ('stupet omnis ratio', line 3). At the end, both parts relent just in time to achieve a simultaneous cadence.

Each of these examples relies on regular declamation patterns that we might just as well label 'isorhythm'. But for Ludwig and Besseler, such regularity was part and parcel of a natural, healthy state of Latin and French declamation.[11] All this changes with the Franconian and Petronian motet, Besseler's middle stage of the development, *c*. 1250 to *c*. 1316. It is in this context that Ludwig and Besseler begin to use the term 'isorhythm'.

In Besseler's view, the slowing of tempo occasioned by the fracturing of modal rhythms and the advent of mensural notation brought three results.[12] First, important cadences – a long followed by a breve rest – take on a wholly different meaning, now demarcating a period (what I have been calling a 'phrase' up to this point), in which a passage of rapid declamation terminates with a long held note. Second, text declamation, and accordingly the nature of melody itself, changes. Occurring first in the triplum and later spreading to the motetus, a freely varied prosody replaces the regular alternation of verse accent. The third result of the slowing of tempo in the Franconian/Petronian motet is a revolution in hearing and experiencing music. All this will have important consequences:

> With the destruction of the equality of voices, the fracturing of the overall modal impetus and the disintegration of the original unity of music and word, the foundations of motet

[8] Ed. Tischler 1982, vol. 1, no. 34 and Payne 2011, no. 10; overview of sources and scorings in van der Werf 1989, motet 532. In StV, *ultra mensuram* durations are normally indicated with two unison figures, indicated in the example with a long mark over the affected note (Tischler transcribes these as a dotted quarter tied to a quarter followed by an eighth rest).

[9] 'The eloquence of/the wise men of Greece,/the shrewdness of their/sophistries and teachings,/and their learning/all fall silent./After these contests/she rejoices in rest...' (trans. Payne 2011, 58).

[10] Ed. Tischer 1982, vol. 1, no. 63; overview of sources and scorings in van der Werf 1989, motet 325. In the example, the asterisks below the tenor mark repetition of the cantus firmus; the long mark above the penultimate note in the motetus indicates an elongated notehead in F. The pitch at the beginning of text line 9 in the motetus is a *c* in the source; in addition, two emendations in the tenor follow Tischler.

[11] On the 'healthy' aspect of declamation in the early motet, see for example Ludwig 1904, 206, one of many similar characterizations in his writings.

[12] Whereas formerly the duration of a long might accommodate the quick declamation of two or three syllables, now a long will accommodate four to seven syllables: paradoxically, an increase in fast values in the new mensural notation meant that the tempo of the basic values of long and breve had to broaden. See Besseler 1927, 150–1.

Example 4.1. *O Maria/Veritatem* (first and last phrases). Châl, fols. 14r and 15r–v

Example 4.2. *Agmina milicie/Agmina* (opening and excerpt). StV, fols. 258r and 258v

Example 4.3. *Salve, salus/Et gaudebit*. F, fol. 409r

composition as practiced up to then were shaken. Now it is a matter of harnessing the forces that had been released from their former coherent unity, to generate by dint of artistic labor that which is no longer a given: the *problem of form* arises.[13]

Such 'artistic labor' manifests itself in two areas according to Besseler: in ad hoc rhythmic structuring of the tenor, and in strategies of articulating periods in the now prominent triplum. As an example, consider a Franconian motet in the seventh fascicle of **Mo**, *Plus joliement* (292)/*Quant li douz* (293)/*Portare* (M22) (Example 4.4).[14]

The syllable count of each line given above the staves of the triplum and motetus provides an index of the fractured prosody.[15] In the motetus, only the first line is declaimed in the standard alternating pattern; the other three text lines in the example are concatenated with the first line to form an overarching period of 12L (in the remainder of the work, not illustrated, motetus periods are variously 3, 4, 7, or 10L). Meanwhile, the triplum has three periods of 4L each, the text declaimed in a brittle and unpredictable manner. The 4L periods defined by the triplum cadence with the motetus and tenor on *c* (L4), *F* (L8), and again on the *c* at the beginning of the tenor repeat (L12). Exactly the same cadence points are supported in the continuation of the motet, though upper-voice period lengths may vary. The tenor, here the venerable *portare* stated four times, is subject to a particular rhythmicization that requires mensural notation.[16] Besseler labels all such tenors 'isorhythmic' (of course not necessarily producing an 'isorhythmic motet') to distinguish them both from the old modal tenor patterns and from the many late thirteenth-century motets that are built on pre-existing secular songs.

Overall, the tenor period of 11L, with harmonic pillars on *c*, *c*, and *F* (at the first, fourth and eighth longs of each statement), yields an impressive fourfold strophic structure, repeated each time with very little adjustment except at the end to allow the final cadence to fall on the G in L11 of the tenor. On some iterations, voice exchange between triplum and motetus lends some variety for a few perfections, but the sonorities are essentially identical each time through. In short, a purely musical conception lies behind this work, repeating blocks of music that in a sense are analogous to the rhythmic periods in fourteenth-century motets. Here, corresponding bars in each tenor statement call forth not only rhythmic repetition, but nearly strophic melodic and harmonic repetition. The text is adapted willy-nilly to the musical layout, except that in both voices the *-er* rhyme always falls on the long note at the end of a period. Thus the image of the lover singing joyously at the opening of the triplum (chant*er*) rings throughout the work: 'I want to sing more joyfully than ever: I mustn't ever refrain from it' ('Plus joliement c'onques mais voel chant*er*. Je ne m'en doi nulement deport*er*').

The irregular period lengths typical of late thirteenth-century French-sphere motets, coordinated only by a common rhyme syllable, are well represented in *Plus joliement/Quant li douz*,

---

[13]   'Mit der Zerstörung des Stimmengleichgewichts, dem Bruch der modalen Gesamtbewegung und dem Zerfall der ursprünglichen Verbindung von Musik und Wort sind die Grundlagen der bisherigen Motettenkomposition erschüttert. Es handelt sich jetzt darum, die verschiedenen aus der unmittelbaren Einheit entbundenen Kräfte zusammenzubringen, in künstlerischer Arbeit zu erzeugen, was nicht mehr ursprünglich gegeben ist: das *Formproblem* tritt auf' (Besseler 1927, 152). All translations are mine unless otherwise noted.

[14]   Ed. Tischler 1978, vol. 3, no. 257; overview of sources and scorings in van der Werf 1989, motet 292/293.

[15]   The 'mute e' of paroxytonic lines, not counted in French versification, is indicated with a '+'; thus, '7+' actually indicates eight syllables.

[16]   On the *portare* motets, see Dolores Pesce's chapter below.

II

Example 4.4. *Plus joliement/Quant li douz* (L1–L12). **Mo**, fol. 279r–v

but the work also shows that strophic repetition of a larger harmonic framework is found among the experiments of that rich era of motet production.[17] Full coordination of period structure, true isoperiodicity, is also found among late thirteenth-century experiments, most strikingly in a motet from the eighth fascicle of **Mo**, *Se je chante* (514)/*Bien doi amer* (515)/*Et sperabit* (M49)

[17]   See Everist 2007. The sorts of melodic correspondences ('isomelism') that Everist highlights in motets on secular tenors can appear in other types as well, as the example of *Plus joliement/Quant li douz* amply demonstrates. William Dalglish (1972, 38) dubs it a 'variation motet'. Cf. also Lefferts 1986, 54–6; Lavacek 2015, 132–3.

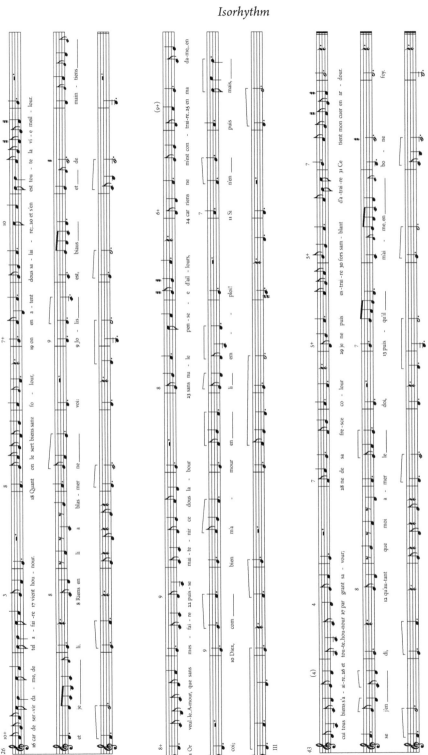

Example 4.5. *Se je chante/Bien.* **Mo,** fols. 357v–359v

(Example 4.5).[18] Here there are three statements of an old *et sperabit* tenor, a full thirty-six notes laid out in 17L. Each statement divides into three segments, 6+5+6L, the first terminating in a striking altered *c♯* in the tenor harmonized identically in each statement, the second featuring a brief hocket segment that involves the motetus at each iteration, and the third ending with a well-directed cadence on the final, *G*.[19] A generalized strophic harmonic framework is less evident than in *Plus joliement/Quant li douz*, though *Se je chante/Bien* could well be a later effort by the same composer. All of the 7- and 9-syllable lines in the motetus are declaimed in the old manner according to standard patterns, though of course the slower tempo and fractured note values mask this. There is some coordination of text structure to periodic structure, a quality systematically carried out in many fourteenth-century motets.[20] On the other hand, there are four instances in the triplum in which the rhyming syllable of one line elides with the first syllable of the next line, further confusing the verse structure. What is most striking in the work is the aspect of isoperiodicity, the consistent location of rests (not just in the tenor but also in both upper voices) quite apart from issues of declamation. Besseler considered *Se je chante/Bien* as just one more experiment among the many motet types found in the late thirteenth century. However, one cannot rule out the thought that even if it did not initiate a 'school', it may by chance have been known to Philippe de Vitry, or, owing to the uncertainty of the date of the eighth fascicle of **Mo**, was perhaps a late and peripheral reaction to Philippe de Vitry.[21] In either case, it will soon become clear later why I would rather regard this work as the end point of the compositional plan seen in *Plus joliement/Quant li douz* – a heightening of strophic tendencies – than as the beginning of the history of the fourteenth-century 'isorhythmic' motet.

Ludwig's first detailed discussion of isorhythm occurs in his 1904 article analyzing the collection of fifty motets that Coussemaker had published from **Mo**, in connection with two works, *Amor vincens* (732)/*Marie preconio* (733)/*Aptatur* (O45) and *On parole* (904)/*A Paris* (905)/*Frese nouvele*.[22] Several scholars have cited his commentary on the second of these, where the term 'isorhythmic' first appears,[23] but Ludwig laid the groundwork in his discussion of the earlier motet. What is unusual about *Amor vincens/Marie preconio* is the predictable mapping of the upper-voice period structure – the location of phrases as defined simply by rests and not by syllable count of the poetry – against the 16L tenor melody, which is stated in three iterations plus the beginning of a fourth (6L).[24] After an initial 6L period, the motetus voice articulates 4L periods throughout, except at the very end. As a consequence of this structure, the motetus consistently bridges across the cadence at the end of the three 16L tenor statements. For its part, the triplum maintains a pattern of 6+4+6L in each iteration, thus exactly coinciding with the 16L tenor. Ludwig remarked that these characteristics are 'strongly evocative of a stylistic principle that completely dominates

[18] Ed. Tischler 1978, vol. 3, no. 311; discussed and partially edited in Sanders 1980a, 352–3.

[19] The hocket passage appears to be purely formal, without any discernable rationale stemming from the text, unlike the amusing hocket passage in *Entre Copin* (866)/*Je me cuidoie* (867)/*Bele Ysabelot* (ed. Tischler 1978, vol. 3, no. 256).

[20] See motetus L7–L13 of each iteration and triplum L5–L6 of each iteration. For the fourteenth century, the classic study of this aspect of text setting is Reichert 1956.

[21] On the date of **Mo**'s eighth fascicle, see Bradley and Desmond 2018.

[22] Coussemaker 1865. *Amor vincens/Marie preconio* ed. Tischler 1978, vol. 3, no. 283 after **Mo**; the clearer version of **Ba** is ed. G. Anderson 1977, no. 59; overview of sources and scorings in van der Werf 1989, motet 732/733. *On parole/A Paris*, ed. Tischler 1978, vol. 3, no. 319, is an *unicum*.

[23] Sanders 1980a, 351; Kügle 1996, 1219; Bent 2008b, 123.

[24] Each ⁶⁄₈ bar of the editions cited in n. 22 above spans 2L.

in the fourteenth-century motet'.[25]

In the discussion that immediately follows, Ludwig noted that this regular periodicity goes against the usual practice of the early motet, in which the period structure of the upper voices is independent of the fixed tenor ostinato (recall Examples 4.2b and 4.3). He repeated the point when he returned to a consideration of *Amor vincens/Marie preconio* in the *Repertorium*. Now employing the term 'isorhythm', he again emphasizes the rhythmic recurrence (to be understood in the broad sense of 'regular recurrence', and not in the sense of literal rhythmic repetition) of periods over a repeating tenor pattern, the 'isorhythm of the upper-voice periods in the individual tenor statements'.[26]

Ludwig's discussion of *On parole/A Paris*, quoted in Bent's article, may give the impression that he reserved the term 'isorhythm' for exact rhythmic correspondence: the motetus 'realizes a structure rhythmically exactly identical (isorhythmic)'.[27] Yet the focus here on the object *Bau* (structure), and the reference immediately following to 'the isorhythmic treatment of the individual periods', makes it likely that he had always considered isoperiodicity the essential element of the new style.[28]

The 'isorhythmic motet' as Ludwig and Besseler understood it thus embraces all works that exhibit a rational and predictable period structure, works that exhibit 'periodicity'; or, as Ludwig expressed it, 'isorhythm of the upper-voice periods in the individual tenor statements'. While Besseler never questioned the overall outline of the development, his discomfort with Ludwig's term is palpable at one point:

> The designation 'isorhythm' was established by Friedrich Ludwig at a time when the development and significance of Vitry could not yet be surveyed owing to the lack of the manuscript *Iv*.[29] For the upper voices of the earliest works (not the tenors), strictly speaking only the designation 'isoperiodic' ought to have been applied, but it seems more appropriate [*doch scheint es zweckmäßiger*] to maintain uniform nomenclature.[30]

One would like to know what lies behind the qualification *zweckmäßiger* in the last sentence: does Besseler mean 'more practical', or 'more expedient', or even 'more politic'? Twenty-five years old when he wrote his Habilitationsschrift, perhaps Besseler felt obligated to retain the term invented

---

[25] 'erinnern stark an ein Stilprinzip, das in der Motette des 14. Jahrhunderts absolut herrscht' (Ludwig 1904, 218). Besides *On parole/A Paris*, which Ludwig discusses near the end of the 1904 article, two more works are isorhythmic in Ludwig's sense. *Se je chante/Bien*, discussed above, is so described in Ludwig 1910–78, 1/2: 551. In addition, an incomplete motet in the seventh fascicle of **Mo**, *Nus ne se doit* (601a)/*Je sui en melencolie* (601b)/*Ave verum corpus* (M84) (ed. Tischler 1978, vol. 3, no. 276), served as Besseler's first example of the new style (Besseler 1927, 167).

[26] 'Isorhythmie der Oberstimmenperioden in den einzelnen T.-Durchführungen' (Ludwig 1910–78, 1/2: 444), trans. Bent 2008b, 125.

[27] 'der Motetus [führt] … einen rhythmisch exakt gleichen (isorhythmischen) Bau durch' (Ludwig 1904, 223), trans. Bent 2008b, 123.

[28] 'der isorhythmischen Behandlung der einzelnen Perioden' (Ludwig 1904, 223), trans. Bent 2008b, 123.

[29] Here Besseler references Ludwig 1902, 41; Ludwig 1904, 224; Ludwig 1905, 622 *et passim*; and Ludwig 1906, 411.

[30] 'Die Bezeichnung "Isorhythmie" wurde von Fr. Ludwig zu einer Zeit aufgestellt, als die Entwicklung und Bedeutung Vitrys infolge Fehlens der Handschrift *Iv* noch nicht zu übersehen war [there follow the references given in n. 29 above]. Für die Oberstimmen der frühesten Werke (nicht die Tenores) wäre, streng genommen, nur die Bezeichnung "Isoperiodik" angebracht, doch scheint es zweckmäßiger, an der einheitlichen Benennung festzuhalten' (Besseler 1927, 201 n. 1). The note is cited in Sanders 1980a, 351; Kügle 1996, 1220; and Bent 2008b, 125.

by his teacher. In any case, Besseler's preferred term, the 'isoperiodic motet', would have avoided a lot of misunderstanding in the long run. 'Isoperiodicity' can encompass a variety of musical techniques and procedures brought to bear on the construction of form. It is not easy to construe its exact meaning without digging deeper, and this is an advantage: the problem with 'isorhythm' has been that the term is too easily interpreted in the wrong sense.

As early as 1963, Ernest Sanders repurposed the term 'isoperiodic' to apply to a large group of early fourteenth-century English motets in which equal-length periods are staggered between upper voices.[31] *Solaris ardor Romuli/Gregorius sol seculi/Petre tua navicula/Mariounette douche* provides an example.[32] The tenor, a French song 'Mariounette douche', is formally independent of the upper voices, both as regards melody (ABBAA) and period structure (see Example 4.6 and Table 4.1). All three texted voices set completely regular poetry, each voice declaiming twelve isometric 8pp lines, which are ingeniously articulated in overlapping periods that are independent of the tenor periods. The quadruplum has the simplest solution, concatenating two text lines to form mostly 8L periods (the first pair of lines is stretched to 9L), followed by a rest before the next pair begins (upper-voice rhythms in Example 4.6 omit occasional short melismas in order to show declamation patterns in their basic form). The triplum is complementary, overlapping at a point halfway through the quadruplum periods (for example, bars 13–14). The motetus rushes a bit at the outset to establish an earlier point of overlap (bars 7–8), and indeed the first two lines of the motetus are the only lines in the entire work that exhibit exceptional declamation patterns: the two other patterns for 8pp lines – one utilized at the opening of the triplum and quadruplum, the other, with an anacrusis, utilized everywhere else except the first two lines of the motetus – would not have been out of place in the earliest motets. Table 4.1 shows the distribution of texts lines and periods that fill out 54L in each voice.

The use of a single basic unit of 8(+1)L is what makes the motet isoperiodic, an appropriate term for such motets, as long as we understand that the English phenomenon is totally unrelated to French isoperiodicity.[33] English isoperiodic motets mark the culmination of a line of development extending back to the earliest motets, in which declamation patterns of rhythmic Latin poetry formed upper-voice periods (Examples 4.1–4.3 above). In contrast, France broke the link to its first stage of motet composition, cultivating motets in the vernacular that by the late thirteenth century brought on an unprecedented freedom of declamation. Thus this branch of the English development, rooted in text declamation, marks the culmination of a fundamentally different aesthetic point of departure from that of Vitry's early experiments associated with the *Roman de Fauvel* project, in which text declamation plays a decidedly secondary role.[34]

---

[31] Sanders 1963, 215–51; 1973, 543–6; Sanders 1980b, 625. Peter Lefferts builds on Sanders to distinguish a variety of types; see Lefferts 1986, 27–92 (esp. 59–75) as well as his discussion of individual motets, 223–310.

[32] Ed. Harrison 1980, 22–4 (music); 177–8 (text and trans. ed. Peter Lefferts). Example 4.6 omits ligature brackets in the tenor. Further examples of this type are discussed in Hartt's chapter below.

[33] Sanders (1973, 543 n. 196) inadvertently implies that Besseler and Handschin used the term for English works. Besseler's discussion of one example of a similar procedure found in a continental motet, *De facili contempnit* (843)/*Propositum quidem negocii* (844)/*Egregie* (ed. G. Anderson 1977, no. 79), makes it clear that he did not regard this sort of structure as isoperiodic in his sense (Besseler 1927, 180). For both Ludwig and Besseler, the fact that periods in the new 'isorhythmic' motets were unconnected to prosody was essential.

[34] For this reason, speculation regarding the influence of one geographical repertory on the other is premature and potentially off base. Arguments are reviewed in Lefferts 1986, 74.

Example 4.6. *Solaris/Gregorius sol/Petre* (tenor and upper-voice periodicity). **Onc 362, fol. 89r**

Table 4.1. Phrase structure of *Solaris/Gregorius/Petre*. **Onc 362, fol. 89r**

L(+rest)	8pp lines
	Quadruplum (54L)
9(+1)	Solaris ardor Romuli/ˇsolvit gelu Britannie
8(+1)	mundana corda populi/ˇa scoria resanie
8(+1)	cometa cum signifera/ˇdum lucem moderancie
8(+1)	dedere dena sidera/ˇquater in ortu Cancie;
8(+1)	que tenebras perfidie/ˇdemere flamme fidei
8	quocumque fluctus hodie/ˇclaudent Anglos equorei.
	Triplum (54L)
13(+1)	Gregorius sol seculi/ˇIovem de cancro Romuli/ˇmisit in libram Anglie
8(+1)	de medio qui populi/ˇtulit lunam perfidie
8(+1)	Zodiaci per singula/ˇtransit signa tripharie
8(+1)	lucescens sine macula/ˇdecursoque summarie
8(+1)	cursu se finxit firmiter/ˇmansurum eternaliter
4	in gradu Cantuarie.
	Motetus (54L)
7(+1)	Petre, tua navicula/ˇvacillat aliquociens,
8(+1)	resultat set pericula/ˇpost plurima multociens.
8(+1)	In insula Britannie/ˇfides olim convaluit,
8(+1)	timore sed vesanie/ˇgentilis diu latuit.
4(+1)	Sequacem per Gregorium
4(+1)	tuum pati consulitur
9	per Augustinum monachum/ˇet fidei reducitur.
	Tenor (54L)
11(+1)	*Mariounette douche*
8(+1)	
8(+1)	
11(+1)	
11(+1)	

Anna Zayaruznaya has recently singled out a motet transmitted in the *Roman de Fauvel*, *Je voi douleur/Fauvel nous a fait/Autant m'est* (**Fauv**, fol. 9v), as 'the earliest clear superimposition of a body onto a specific piece of music'.[35] She thereby draws attention to a work that, on further reflection, is even more epoch-making as an early attempt to express a poetic topos in musical form, in other words, to create 'program music'. Odd as it may seem, I maintain that more than anything else this is the basic attribute of the tradition that has been dubbed the 'isorhythmic motet'. In *Je voi/Fauvel*, a French tenor resembling a thirteenth-century dance song, but carry-

---

[35] Zayaruznaya 2015a, 46 (discussed 46–52, with edition); also ed. Schrade 1956b, 25. See also the analysis in Everist 2007, 398–400.

ing a text appropriate only for the *Roman de Fauvel*, is stated four times, articulating 6L periods. Fauvel, explicitly named in the manuscript, sings it: 'Autant m'est si poise arriere comme avant' ('I don't really care as long as the back weighs the same as the front'). The text evokes the 'mestier de la civiere', which Nancy Freeman Regalado has described as 'the stretcher or dung-barrow game where what goes forward also goes back', an image that epitomizes the *Fauvel* project.[36] By moving backwards and forwards in the book – engaging in 'reciprocal reading' – moral lessons are stated and restated through allusions, parallels, echoes, and new contexts. 'As we play with the patterns the compilers inscribed so abundantly in this manuscript, we discover with delight how evident meanings are repeated at every level, how signifying relations emerge out of the way each piece is placed into the whole'.[37]

Thus the triplum and motetus texts of *Je voi/Fauvel* have their part in reinforcing and augmenting the lesson of the tenor, but do so by means of circular rondeau-like text forms in isometric seven syllable lines, ABaabAB:

Triplum

Je voi douleur avenir	*I see misery coming*
car tout ce fait par contraire.	*since everything is done by its opposite.*
Chemin ne voie tenir	No one wants to keep to the road or path
Ne veut nul par quoi venir	by which one can come
puist a bien n'a raison faire.	to act in accordance with good or reason.
Je voi douleur avenir	*I see misery coming*
car tout ce fait par contraire.	*since everything is done by its opposite.*

Motetus

Fauvel nous a fait present	Fauvel has given us the present
du mestier de la civiere.	of the handbarrow game.
N'est pas homs qui ce ne sent.	There's not anyone that does not recognize this.
Je voi tout quant a present	At present, I see everything
aler ce devant derriere.	going backwards.
Fauvel nous a fait present	Fauvel has given us the present
du mestier de la civiere.	*of the handbarrow game.*

Tenor *Fauvel*

Autant m'est si poise arriere	*I don't really care as long as the back weighs*
comme avant.	*the same as the front.*

Initially the motet appears to follow the rondeau-like schema suggested above, for line 3 of the triplum and motetus are set to the same music as line 1, accompanied by the first four longs of the tenor. We imagine that the tenor will somehow yield, adhering to the upper voices as the rondeau unfolds, resembling one of the many late thirteenth-century motets structured on a rondeau refrain.[38] This gambit turns out to be deceptive, however. Fauvel barges ahead with his full six longs in four iterations, for it is his nature not 'to act in accordance with good or reason'.

---

[36] Regalado 1998, 470.

[37] Regalado 1998, 470.

[38] For motets on rondeau tenors, see Everist 2007. The most familiar example, *Mout me fu grief* (297)/*Robin m'aime* (298)/*Portare* (M22), has an overall form determined by a full rondeau in the motetus, the plainsong tenor strategically rhythmized and chromatically altered to fit; see Pesce 1997 and her contribution to this volume.

The upper voices go on to declaim their three lines in three 4L phrases, now draped over the two 6L iterations in the tenor. The result for the overall form is a palindrome, which of course 'weighs' the same at the beginning as at the end, and which is an important symbol of reversal in the *Roman de Fauvel*.[39] In addition, the equivalency of 3×4L (triplum and motetus) and 2×6L (tenor) in this middle section of the motet recalls the sort of play between perfection and imperfection that was a primary concern for partisans of the *ars nova*.

The overall structure of the musical work ratifies its poetic content, and this is what I mean when I describe *Je voi/Fauvel* as an early example of a sort of program music. Although the strategies it employs in order to express a particular poetic image are not broadly adaptable to new works, it marks the moment of a transformation of the motet as a genre, a development that will continue with slightly different compositional procedures. Compositionally *Je voi/Fauvel* is a one-off experiment, but a prominent composer involved in the *Fauvel* project, where 'evident meanings are repeated at every level',[40] soon achieved a breakthrough, the ability to coordinate all voices of a motet in the unified expression of an idea, now infinitely adaptable to new content. This cumulation of expression is effected by periodicity, and works utilizing the new procedure are those that Ludwig and Besseler termed the 'isorhythmic motet'. By approaching this development as the product of a literary impetus, as a new aesthetic, I hope to change our perspective, to imbue the early 'isorhythmic' works with fresh value. Too often, modern analysis has privileged later developments, works that exhibit more and more isorhythm (in the literal sense), as if a motet by Dunstaple or Du Fay finally realizes a goal only dimly understood by Vitry and Machaut. Further, I hope that modern analyses can achieve a needed focus by taking a motet's subject as the point of departure.

Besseler attributed three epoch-making works in **Fauv** to Philippe de Vitry. The first, *Firmissime fidem teneamus/Adesto sancta trinitas/Alleluya*, is not much more of an 'isorhythmic motet' than *Je voi/Fauvel*, since it lacks upper-voice periodicity, but it does contribute to the emerging *ars nova* motet in other ways.[41] It is not even certain that it was integral to the *Fauvel* project; it may have existed independently, slightly prior to or alongside *Fauvel*, pulled into the project *a propos*.[42] In any case, it does share in the 'reciprocal' aesthetic of *Fauvel*. Although the subject of the work is the Trinity, scholars have noted that imperfect relationships are curiously pervasive in it. In the end, the many levels of imperfection are subsumed into the ultimate level of perfection, the maximodus level defined in the *Notitia artis musice* of Johannes de Muris. In the first section, couched in perfect maximodus, imperfect modus, imperfect tempus, and major prolation, there are eight tenor taleae, each occupying nine longs; in the accelerated section each tenor talea occupies only three longs ($8×9L:8×3L = 72:24$), thus stating the cantus firmus three times faster ($72:24 = 3:1$).[43]

In this manner, the work effectively composes out a principal argument of early *ars nova* theory.[44] Indeed, it teems with imperfect bars. It is the sort of work that Jacobus aimed at in his

---

[39] On motets 'saturated with themes and structures of reversal and inversion in music and text', see Bent 1998b, 45–6 and n. 21.

[40] Regalado 1998, 470.

[41] Ed. Schrade 1956b, 60–3. See the analysis of Robertson 1997, esp. 53–7; Zayaruznaya 2015a, 203–6.

[42] Robertson 1997, esp. 72–4; Robertson 1998, 520.

[43] I adopt Sanders's notion of 'sectional acceleration' (Sanders 1975, 28–9, esp. n. 17), rather than the more commonly used 'diminution section'.

[44] This is the subject of Vetter 1987, although he overemphasizes the extent of imperfection in the work. A more detailed discussion of this issue in the context of the anonymous motet *Beatius/Cum humanum* appears in Zayaruznaya 2015b.

indictment of partisans of the *ars nova*: 'they make excessive use of imperfection in practice. They employ more imperfect notes than perfect; more imperfect modes than perfect; and consequently more imperfect measures'.[45] This sort of objection must have been in the air for some time, since Johannes de Muris had provided an answer to the question even before Jacobus expressed his objection in writing:

> In God, who is most perfect, there is one substance, yet three persons ... Very great, there-fore, is the correspondence of unity to trinity ... the binary number, since it falls short of the ternary and is of lesser repute, remains imperfect. But any composite number formed from these may properly be considered perfect because of its similarity and correspondence to the ternary. And time, since it belongs to the class of continuous things, is divisible not only by ternary numbers, but is endlessly divisible – to infinity.[46]

Muris may well have reflected on *Firmissime/Adesto* in penning this statement, and the motet stands as a monument of practical music-making that takes a modernist stance as controversies surrounding *ars nova* rhythm unfolded around it. In this polemical sense, it belongs among the most modern works of **Fauv**, completely apart from its function as a Trinity motet.

Two other works probably also by Philippe de Vitry, *Tribum, que non abhorruit/Quoniam secta latronum/Merito hec patimur* and *Garrit Gallus flendo dolorose/In nova fert animus/N[euma]*, were composed – perhaps in this order – specifically for **Fauv**.[47] In these two works, upper-voice phrases mesh with the repeating tenor at regular durational intervals, and thus exhibit isoperiodicity. Further, the interlocking structure assures that all three voices participate in staging the poetic subject. This deep integration of a polyphonic work, whereby 'evident meanings are repeated at every level', and the totality of the musical structure involves itself with a subject, is the essence of the new motet, not our modern tabulations of greater or lesser amounts of identical surface rhythms ('isorhythm' in the strict sense), which unduly privilege only one of a host of musical devices available to the composer.

Margaret Bent has thoroughly analyzed many facets of *Tribum/Quoniam*, building on the close relationship of the texts of this and two other **Fauv** motets to political circumstances surrounding the quick fall of King Philip the Fair's minister Enguerrand de Marigny after Philip's death in 1314.[48] Both upper voices end by quoting hexameters that reflect on Marigny's situation, the triplum quoting Joseph of Exeter and the motetus quoting Ovid. Bent shows that the quotations were the point of departure for the upper voice texts, preceding even the choice of tenor, which itself relates to political circumstances.[49] Further, important word roots are disposed proportionally in the work, musical 'consonances' occur in association with certain key words, the upper voices paraphrase the tenor chant in blocks, and some textual and musical details relate *Tribum/Quoniam* and *Garrit/In nova*.[50]

My reading of this motet, and of all motets in the remainder of this chapter, focuses on directly palpable structural and musical aspects that appear to be inspired by the message of the texts.[51]

---

[45] Jacobus, *Speculum musice*, Bk. 7 §45, trans. Strunk 1998, 272.

[46] Johannes de Muris, *Notitia artis musice*, Bk. 2 §2, trans. Strunk 1998, 262–3.

[47] On attribution of *Tribum/Quoniam* to Vitry, see Bent 1997, 101 n. 9. Bent does not suggest an order of composition: see Bent 1998b, 39 *et passim*.

[48] Bent 1997 and Bent 1998b; see also Schrade 1956a.

[49] Bent 1997, 89.

[50] Bent 1997, 84, 95–9.

[51] See the oft-cited mention of Egidius de Murino concerning the *materia* of a motet, e.g.,

For the purposes of this exercise, I do not concern myself with arcane matters that might figure in a deeper analysis, though I acknowledge that such matters might well have been explicated to contemporary listeners by the composer himself. Imagining a form-generating program for a work will look mainly to surface features that seem to demand explication, features that push against norms and defaults. Two points of departure are possible: either one may begin by noting something out of the ordinary in the music that appears to demand an exterior stimulus and then seek an explanation in the text, or else one may begin with the text and imagine ideas that might elicit a musical response and then look to the music for potential answers. In either case, something exterior to the music will have prompted the composer to make fundamental decisions about the conduct of the work. In brief, I argue that the motets we are considering were not conceived primarily as 'absolute' music, despite their undeniable architectural qualities, but are more akin to 'program' music, works that respond to a poetic subject, which then determines at least some of the details of the architecture.

As we have seen, Bent's analysis highlights the importance especially of Ovid's proverb to the upper-voice texts: 'All human affairs are hanging by a slender thread,/and with a sudden fall things which were strong crash'.[52] But the image of the slender thread is equally essential to the musical structure. Against convention, the tenor of *Tribum/Quoniam* is the middle voice, and never provides the harmonic foundation; instead, the motetus, the voice that carries Ovid's admonition, serves as the foundation.[53] The unusual disposition is established by the introductory segment that confirms F as the central pitch before the tenor chimes in with the fifth, c, to initiate the unfolding of color (the melody of the tenor) and talea (see Example 4.7).[54] Thus harmonically the tenor is a 'slender thread' woven through the middle of the texture. Meanwhile, the upper voices literally repeat two segments of music, each eight breves (four bars) long, locked into corresponding positions in each of the three periods. Despite their corporeal presence, the two isomelic segments – A and B – can equally be perceived as thin threads, distant from the tonal center F: the tenor pitch e (supported by a in the motetus) launches the segments, which then land on d (supported by G in the motetus). That this sequence occurs no fewer than six times as the tenor unfolds depends on the rhythmic disposition of a particular cantus firmus with particular melodic properties, in this instance, eighteen notes – *Merito hec patimur* – split into six fragments of three notes each, in which the last pitch of fragments 1, 3, and 5 supply the e, and the first pitch of fragments 2, 4, and 6 supply the d, platforms for three statements – ABA – beginning in bars 10, 22, and 34. Now the threads twist again for an additional three statements over the second iteration of the color – BAB – beginning in bars 46, 58, and 70. Further, a striking series of parallel octaves followed by parallel fifths, evident especially in each A-segment (bars 10, 34, and

---

Leech-Wilkinson 1989, 1: 21; A. Clark 1996, 6; Hartt 2010b, 57–8; and the chapters by A. Clark, Zayaruznaya and Bent in this *Companion*.

[52] 'Omnia sunt hominum tenui pendencia filo,/Et subito casu quo valuere ruunt' (Ovid, *Epistulae ex Ponto* IV); trans. Howlett 1991.

[53] 'The duplum deceptively usurps the tenor's role as the true foundation of the piece' (Bent 1997, 95).

[54] In the example, the twelve-breve (six-bar) introductory segment is omitted; bar numbers correspond to the edition in Schrade 1956b, 54–6. The example gives the entire tenor; the beginning of the second color is marked by the asterisk at bar 43. In the triplum and motetus, I have entered all rests, as well as those segments of the upper voices that recur in predictable positions over the tenor, showing 'periodicity' (empty bars have free music). Compare the examples in Fuller 2006, 103; and Bent 1997, 90–1 (this example gives the full extent of identical recurring passages in the upper voices).

Example 4.7. Periodic structure in Vitry, *Tribum/Quoniam*

58), audibly mark the isomelic passages.[55] One wants to hear the Winter wind whistling through Marigny's bones, which twisted on the gallows at Montfaucon for over two years, until 1317; at the very least one can argue that the parallel intervals – here and elsewhere in the work – make for thin and insubstantial harmony.

The most progressive musical work in **Fauv** is Vitry's masterful motet *Garrit/In nova*.[56] Quotation of the opening of Ovid's *Metamorphoses* at the start of the motetus voice already states the work's subject – transformation – a subject that permeates *Fauvel* in the sense that political transformations threaten society: 'In nova fert animus mutatas dicere formas' ('I am moved to speak of forms changed into new bodies').[57] What Vitry succeeds in doing is to transfer the essence of this message into the very core of the musical structure of the motet, such that the totality of the work reifies the notion of transformation. Vitry accomplishes this first through the absolutely unprecedented rhythmic design of the tenor, which mutates from perfect to imperfect time and back again by means of what must be Vitry's notational innovation, the use of red ink to signify a change to imperfect notes and rests. In the original notation, the note shapes form a palindrome, the *jeu de la civiere* that had been expressed in a different way in *Je voi/Fauvel*. The difference is that in *Garrit/In nova* both upper voices dovetail with the tenor at the instant of each mensural transformation, partaking in the stage play and confirming its significance.[58]

The replication of a single concept on as many levels as possible is fundamental to the new style of motet. There is no development, no teleology in this art. Besseler commented on the curious nature of repetition in isoperiodic motets: 'Isorhythmic periods are bound together only by mechanical ordering, not by a genuine inner relationship between before and after, now and earlier. They present, so to speak, a timeless replication of a particular rhythmic course'.[59] Couched here in terms of absolute music, the point relates equally well to the aesthetic of the *Fauvel* project, for this static sort of repetition serves to confirm a basic subject in each work, repeatedly replicated.

After the completion of **Fauv**, there was no turning back: the distillation of form and content in these two works, expressions of 'reciprocal reading', turned out to be primary documents of an artistic revolution.[60] Vitry continued to compose motets for new contexts following the new compositional principle. As far as we know, these new works are individual occasional motets, not groups of works aimed at some overriding artistic project of the sort that had inspired the two highly advanced **Fauv** motets. New works on new subjects, such as *Colla iugo/Bona condit/Libera me, Cum statua/Hugo/Magister invidie, Tuba sacre/In arboris/Virgo sum, Douce playsence/Garison*

---

[55] On parallel part writing, see Bent 1997, 103 n. 31.

[56] Ed. Schrade 1956b, 68–70; Hoppin 1978, no. 59; Bent 1997, 90. On the dating and positioning of *Garrit/In nova* in Fauv, see Bent 1998b.

[57] *Garrit/In nova* 'could be said to be a motet about bestial transformation' (Bent 1997, 95). A quotation from Joseph of Exeter, discovered by David Howlett, occurs at the end of the triplum (Holford-Strevens 2005, 64).

[58] For a chart of the periodic structure of this work and further discussion, see Earp 2015a, 28–30.

[59] 'Die isorhythmischen Perioden sind nur durch eine mechanische Ordnung verbunden, nicht durch eine echte innere Beziehung zwischen Vorher und Nachher, Jetzt und Früher. Sie stellen sozusagen eine zeitlose Vervielfältigung eines bestimmten rhythmischen Ablaufs dar' (Besseler 1927, 202).

[60] Bent has noted other influences as well: 'The opportunity to exercise and develop new notational possibilities in the early fourteenth century must also have been stimulated by the *Fauvel* project, another sense in which *Fauvel* may have prompted the compositions rather than being prompted by them' (Bent 1998b, 43).

selon nature/Neuma quinti toni, culminating in *Vos quid/Gratissima/Gaude gloriosa*, *O canenda vulgo/Rex quem metrorum/Rex regum*, and *Impudenter circumivi/Virtutibus laudabilis/Alma redemptoris*, established a style rich with potential and worthy of imitation.[61] Guillaume de Machaut, around ten years younger than Vitry, immediately absorbed the lessons of these works, as did other composers, though the anonymous works do not always attain the level of integration of form and content seen in the models that Vitry provided.[62]

The next task – one that far exceeds the scope of this chapter – is to survey the repertory to discover the range of subjects treated and the range of musical techniques that were brought to bear in realizing these subjects musically.[63] Motets of Vitry and Machaut provide obvious case studies, since both men were distinguished poets strongly influenced by the *Fauvel* aesthetic of replication of meaning. Vitry confirms this by his probable active participation in the *Fauvel* project itself, Machaut by the multiple expressions of certain ideas in different forms and genres that can be traced throughout his work.[64]

In coming to terms with the range of musical techniques that express meaning in the *ars nova* motet, issues of reception and chronology, including developments in the history of notation and musical grammar, need to be considered. For example, looking at the three early Vitry motets considered above and the 'middle period' motets of Vitry just listed, various devices are found: accelerated sections (freely handled in *Firmissime/Adesto*, *Douce/Garison*, and *Vos/Gratissima*, strictly proportional in *Colla/Bona*, *Tuba/In arboris*, *O canenda/Rex*, and *Impudenter/Virtutibus*), hocket segments (*Cum statua/Hugo*, *Tuba/In arboris*, *Vos/Gratissima*, *O canenda/Rex*, and *Impudenter/Virtutibus*), introductory segments placed before the beginning of the tenor talea (texted in *Tribum/Quoniam* and *Impudenter/Virtutibus*, untexted in *Tuba/In arboris*), shifts between perfect and imperfect modus (*Garrit/In nova*, *Douce/Garison*, *Tuba/In arboris*), as well as 'super-taleae', instances in which upper-voice periodicity subsumes multiple tenor taleae into larger blocks (*Tribum/Quoniam*, *Cum statua/Hugo*, *Vos/Gratissima*).[65]

Composers' eager pursuit of such musical devices to express a subject raises an important caveat for modern analysis, for text painting can contravene what we may regard as settled facts of style development and musical grammar. We have noted that the parallel perfect intervals in

---

[61] Surely we can add *In virtute/Decens* on the earlier end of the list of Vitry works, following Leech-Wilkinson 1982–3, 5–8 and 18–19; and Zayaruznaya 2015a, 107–8 and 131–8.

[62] Owing to the apparently non-chronological order of Machaut's M1–17, the cycle proposed by Robertson (2002, 79–186) seems more likely a program imposed ex post facto, based primarily on tenor snippets, although of course some motets may have been composed to fill in gaps in the series, with repercussions for the analysis of subjects of the motets.

[63] The task has actually been underway for some time in the work of many scholars. Thus, strategies for conveying duplicity in Machaut's M15 (Bent 1991), or strategies to match isoperiodic forms with images (Zayaruznaya 2015a), or, going the other way, different subjects that all utilize internal cadences undermining the eventual final (analyses in Boogaart 2001a; Boogaart 2001b; Fuller 1990; Fuller 1992b; Hartt 2010a; Hartt 2010b; Lavacek 2015; etc.), and many others: all this needs to be coordinated into an overall theory of the 'program' motet in this period.

[64] See, for example, Cerquiglini 1985, 15–103; Huot 1987, 242–301; Plumley 2013, 279–408. Daniel Leech-Wilkinson demonstrated how the same point can be made in a purely musical sense, 'sound worlds' that appear in different musical genres in different contexts (Leech-Wilkinson 1993).

[65] Sanders describes the practice the other way around, as 'tenor taleae with internally repetitive rhythmic patterns' (Sanders 1973, 558 n. 257). The term 'super-talea' was coined by Boogaart (2001b, 1: 107), to capture Reichert's German term 'Großtalea' (Reichert 1956, 202). Zayaruznaya (2018) treats this topic in detail.

Tribum/Quoniam help to convey a message, and must not be considered as evidence of inept composition. The free accelerated section in *Vos/Gratissima* is not necessarily related to chronology (most accelerated sections reduce the tenor proportionally), but is more likely a formal musical response to a text that proclaims the need to hurry ('eya properate!'). Further, what appears to be an orthodox final cadence of this motet in Schrade's edition is incorrect, for the upper voices are in such a hurry at the end of a curtailed final period that they cadence a breve before the tenor (the penultimate long in the tenor is perfect, syncopating across the barline).[66]

On the other hand, a gradually shifting horizon of expectation does seem to operate in many instances. Once the invention of the minim stem and minim rest allowed composers to reintroduce fast hocket segments into their motets, they treated the innovation carefully at first, to assure that the text setting was appropriate.[67] Extended accelerated sections whose proportionally reduced periods are replete with isorhythmic hockets are found in many motets, but in what appear to be the earliest examples, Vitry used the device without text, as a means to convey a poetic subject. In *O canenda/Rex quem*, the untexted accelerated section responds to the paean in the motetus to Robert of Naples, 'whose virtues, mores, race, and the deeds of his son I cannot write; may they be written above the heavens'.[68] In *Impudenter/Virtutibus*, the untexted accelerated section seems to respond to the prayer that concludes the texted portion of the triplum: 'O Virgin mother Mary, *so burn my spirit*, obeying your love, that I may avoid unprofitable love'.[69] Later, such accelerated sections, now fully texted, became accepted conventions, matters of a shifting horizon (multipartite sections in proportional diminution do not contradict the static replication of meaning in the motet: they only supply new facets of a single jewel).

It cannot be denied that it is sometimes difficult to identify the subject that a motet depicts. As one example of directions that analysis can take in the pursuit of this goal, consider Machaut's *Quant en moy vint premierement Amours/Amour et biauté/Amara valde* (M1), a motet that Jacques Boogaart has already analyzed with careful attention to the relationship of the subject to its musical realization.[70] The work's many perfections make it a model motet, appropriate for the opening of Machaut's cycle of motets. On the level of mensuration, the *integer valor* section utilizes modus perfectus, tempus perfectum, and prolatio major, allowing for a rare threefold proportional reduction of values in the accelerated section. Further, the voices are ordered by gradus: the tenor proceeds exclusively in longs and breves, the motetus mostly in breves and semibreves, the triplum in semibreves and minims. Regarding the text, M1 has an extraordinarily clear poetic structure that Machaut adapted nearly perfectly to the talea structure. Conflict is found in the tonal aspect, however. Despite a tenor that has an *F* final, cadences throughout the work privilege *G* and to different degrees downplay *F*. The situation is most critical at the very end of the work, where the triplum sets a sententious phrase, 'Grant folie est de tant amer/Que de son dous face on amer' ('it is great folly to love so much that one makes a bitter thing of that which is most sweet

---

[66]   Ed. Schrade 1956b, 76–81. In this ungrammatical cadence, Vitry provided a model for Machaut's use of this sort of ending for a variety of other programmatic purposes in M4, M9, M10, M15, and M17 (Boogaart 2001b; Bent 2003 on M9; Hartt 2010b, 67–70, 86–7 on M10; Bent's chapter below on M4, M10, and M15). The danger of a non-simultaneous ending is averted in M20 by a *deus ex machina*, the final 'Amen' in the upper voices (Earp 2014, 1: 34 n. 42).

[67]   See Zayaruznaya 2013.

[68]   Trans. Howlett 1991.

[69]   Trans. Howlett 1991 (italics added).

[70]   Boogaart 2001b, 1: 211–39; 2: 562–9 (edition), 673–5 (examples); Boogaart 2001a, 14–16. For much of this paragraph, I paraphrase Boogaart. Compare also the analysis in Robertson 2002, 110–13.

to him').[71] Boogaart has noted an additional punning interpretation: 'that from a sweet sound [son dous] one makes a bitter one',[72] which perfectly describes the motet's close. Just before the final cadence, there is a directed progression to G, which then slips quickly and unsatisfactorily to the true final, F. What should be sweet, the resolution to the final, is thereby rendered bitter. But, as Boogaart points out in the course of his analysis, play between the soft (F) hexachord and the hard (G) hexachord is built into the tenor itself (the chant snippet may have been altered by Machaut to heighten the effect).[73] Some outrageously harsh sonorities depicting cruel Desire directly follow mutation to the hard hexachord – such play is part of the strategy of expressing the subject. Yet it is still possible to debate fruitfully exactly what the subject is: is it that the ideal of perfect love is prone to a bitter outcome, is it the ultimate unattainability of love, or is it the bitter frustration of a cleric's love service to the patron? Is it that Hope (F) is not sufficient in the battle with Desire (G)?[74] Even if one cannot reach ultimate satisfaction in an individual analysis, the hermeneutic goal enriches the exercise, giving focus to relevant questions that might be posed.

The question as to why the motet increasingly takes on schematic qualities as it moved into the second half of the fourteenth century – in old terminology, the tendency towards pan-iso-rhythm – now looms. Besseler considered this development a degradation and attributed it to a lack of imagination:

> Wherever the motet was no longer borne by a strong and individual personality such as Vitry's, but descended into a guild affair, its rational side as exaggerated constructivism perforce came more and more to the fore. Thus for younger generations *subtilitas* became the watchword, ingenious formal designs and a sophistication of isolated sonorous effects.[75]

The tendency towards pervasive isorhythm may have undergone the same sort of development outlined above for accelerated hocket segments, at first prepared and subject-appropriate, later becoming a convention as the horizon shifted. For example, one might argue that an apparently very early example, the musician motet *Musicalis sciencia/Sciencie laudabili/Tenor*, utilizes pervasive isorhythm in response to a subject that is overtly *musical*.[76] Thus, part of the explanation may lie in the growing separation between poets and composers after Machaut.[77] In addition, poets and composers had become more focused on lyrical song forms, easier to compose and easier to consume. Already with Machaut, who composed his last three motets (M21–3) after a hiatus of about ten years since M20, there is a more generic feel: all three works are stylistically

---

[71] Trans. Colleen Donagher in Robertson 2002, 295.

[72] Boogaart 2001a, 15; Boogaart 2001b, 1: 212 and 218.

[73] See the overview of chant sources, none of which precisely capture Machaut's tenor, in A. Clark 1996, 186, discussed 54–6; further discussion in Boogaart 2001b, 2: 220–1.

[74] Boogaart concludes that 'the essence of Love's "perfection" lies in striving after it, not in its fulfilment' (Boogaart 2001a, 16).

[75] 'Gerade dort, wo die Motette nicht mehr, wie bei Vitry, von einer starken und eigenartigen Persönlichkeit getragen wurde, sondern wieder zu einer zunftmäßigen Angelegenheit zurücksank, mußte ihre rationale Seite als überspitzte Konstruktivität immer mehr hervortreten. So wird bei den jüngeren Generationen die *subtilitas* zur Parole, die raffinierte formale Durchbildung und Verfeinerung der klanglichen Einzelwirkung' (Besseler 1927, 219).

[76] Ed. Harrison 1968, no. 33.

[77] Compare Leech-Wilkinson's comments on *Portio nature/Ida capillorum* (Leech-Wilkinson 1989, 1: 176–7). Emily Zazulia discusses the issues surrounding the dating of this work in her chapter below.

uniform.[78] Likely associated with political assemblies surrounding the English siege of Reims, as a group their grand style conveys a ceremonial function, completely apart from any poetic content addressed by an individual motet's music.[79] Philippe Royllart's state motet *Rex Karole/Leticie, pacis* of 1375 became the definitive model for the ceremonial style, with its rhythmically animated hockets echoing back and forth at the end of each talea, a texture that still admirably served nearly forty years later for Ciconia's state motets. In such works, the isoperiodic French-sphere motet took on an official function with appropriately large musical proportions and public textures that could be reproduced from work to work. Here subject was less important than function.

Which motets of the second half of the century are oriented towards a particular subject and which are generic, perhaps even epigonous? This is also a matter for further analysis. It was, however, possible even for the last composers in the style to respond creatively to a subject, to do something new, while adhering to highly conventional forms. A well-known example is the evocation of the temple in Du Fay's *Nuper rosarum flores/Terribilis est*.[80] Another example is Dunstaple's *Veni Sancte Spiritus et emitte/Veni Sancte Spiritus et infunde/Veni Creator Spiritus/Mentes tuorum*, a motet conventional for the time in its three large sections proportionally reducing 3:2:1, with two taleae in each section isorhythmic in all voices, each introduced by a duet.[81] But by having the superius paraphrase the first two phrases of the cantus firmus, the hymn *Veni creator spiritus*, in each of the six duets, Dunstaple succeeded in serving his subject by permeating the entire motet with the Holy Spirit, even segments that traditionally had been free of the cantus firmus.

For Ludwig and Besseler, the music historical narrative of the development of the motet in thirteenth- and fourteenth-century France had a clear trajectory. The domination of motet rhythm by declamation patterns in the old motet, a healthy state, was challenged in the late thirteenth century by the advent of mensural notation and the concomitant slowing of tempo, allowing for longer periods and irregular text declamation. Potentially chaotic results for overall musical form were compensated in the fourteenth century by a new synthesis, the victory of a principle that rigorously coordinated period structure with tenor talea. Thus does the dialectic operate in music history writing. In my revised narrative, I acknowledge a diversity of musical initiatives surrounding motet periodicity in the late thirteenth century, but I see the new direction in the fourteenth century as the musical realization of an inherently literary phenomenon, the *Fauvel* project and its focus on reciprocal replication of a subject in myriad forms, the *mise-en-abyme*. Let us applaud the growing tendency to analyze the *ars nova* motet in terms that go beyond those of absolute music, and welcome new insights into this important chapter of music history.

At this point, when both 'isorhythmic motet' and 'isoperiodic motet' seem compromised in one way or another, Sarah Fuller's term '*ars nova* motet', borrowed from her chapter in this collection, may provide an option for an overarching term to associate with this historical phenomenon. On the other hand, some may balk at ranging *Nuper rosarum flores* among works of the *ars nova*. Vitry's discovery that isoperiodicity can serve to cumulate the individual efforts of the voices to

---

[78] Long ago I pointed to a codicological irregularity that may explain the lack of the highly 'pan-isorhythmic' motet *De Bon Espoir/Puisque la douce rousee/Speravi* (M4) in **Mach C** (Earp 1983, 140–2), and I still favor this interpretation; the possibility, however, that M4 was indeed composed after M20, between the time **Mach C** was finally completed (early 1350s) and the main portion of **Ferrell 1** (late 1360s), cannot be excluded.

[79] For the context of these works, see Sarah Fuller's chapter below.

[80] Wright 1994; Trachtenberg 2001; Utz 2016, 201–5.

[81] Bent 1981a, 52–71.

stage a particular extra-musical subject gave composers the most powerful means of pushing the new aesthetic forward over the years, but, as we saw earlier in the cases of *Je voi/Fauvel* and *Firmissime/Adesto*, it is also possible for non-isoperiodic motets to participate in the new aesthetic: isoperiodicity is but one musical parameter among many that can single-mindedly focus a motet on a subject. Perhaps in the end, we may prefer the more neutral label 'late-medieval motet'.

— 5 —

Notations

Karen Desmond

T HE TRAJECTORY of music notation's development is inextricably linked with the genre of
the motet. The thirteenth-century motet made new demands upon the existing notation
system, specifically with respect to the notation of rhythm. The syllabic settings of texts
in the motet's upper voices required a notation that could distinguish durations between *single*
notes drawn as *individual* note shapes. In polyphony, prior to the emergence of the motet, the
grouping of notes in ligatures indicated specific rhythmic patterns, but when one pitch was associated with one syllable of text, these ligatures were broken apart. There were syllabic settings
of texts that used single note shapes prior to the motet – the conductus, for example – but the
coordination of one or more syllabically set upper voices that sang different texts accompanied
by a slower-moving tenor led notators to seek a greater specificity with respect to the relationship
between notational glyph and the duration it signified. This would eventually result in the one-
to-one correspondence between graphic appearance and duration inherent in modern notation.
The current chapter examines four specific moments along this trajectory, where notational
ambiguities were resolved with codifications that in turn fostered further ambiguities. I focus
first on a selection of motets transmitted in more than one manuscript that offer opportunities to
examine how the same musical content was represented in older and newer notations, with the
caveat that the timeline of notational developments is complex, and often cannot be represented
in tidy chronologies. I close with an example that demonstrates how fourteenth-century motet
composers experimented with the precision afforded by newly invented techniques of notation, a
precision that had a direct impact on the stylistic development of fourteenth-century polyphony.

NOTATIONS *CUM LITTERA*

The *cum littera* notation of the first motet manuscripts – literally 'with text', that is, music settings
that are syllabic rather than primarily melismatic – is often described as rhythmically ambiguous.
While the patterning of ligature groups indicated specific rhythmic patterns in Notre-Dame discant, in motets, ligatures are used infrequently, especially in the texted upper parts, since single
note shapes better accommodated motets' predominantly syllabic text settings. Subsequent to the

* Sincere thanks to Catherine A. Bradley, Jared Hartt, Mary Wolinski, and Thomas Payne for
their insights on this chapter's content. For general surveys of medieval polyphonic notation
see Wolf 1904, Apel 1953, Parrish 1959, Rastall 1983, Earp forthcoming. Also see the subsections
in the *Grove* 'Notation' article by Hiley and Payne ('Polyphony and Secular Monophony to
c. 1260') and Bent ('Polyphonic Mensural Notation, c. 1260–1500'). In *Die Musik in Geschichte
und Gegenwart* see Lütteken 1997.

earliest motet manuscripts, later notators of motets devised methods that more plainly indicated the specific rhythmic durations of single notes and single ligatures. The first motet examined here exemplifies this shift. It is found in one of the earliest motet sources (**W2**), but also in two later thirteenth-century sources (**Mo** and **Ba**).

The three-voice motet *A la cheminee* (453)/*Mout sont vallant* (454)/*Par verite* is copied across a single opening of **W2** (fols. 212v–213r); see Figure 5.1.[1] The voice beginning 'A la cheminee' occupies the lower five staves of the verso page; on the facing recto, a second voice, beginning 'Mout sont vallant', occupies the first two-and-a-half staves, and the tenor ('Par verite') follows directly from the end of the third staff and continues on the fourth and fifth staves. In the later **Ba** version (fols. 6v–7r) the 'A la cheminee' voice is in the position of the motetus, with an alternate triplum voice that begins 'Chanconete' (455). The tenor in **Ba** has a Latin incipit 'Veritatem' that corresponds to the chant source of the tenor's pitches, which is the plainchant gradual *Propter veritatem*. **Mo** (fols. 39v–40r) transmits a four-voice version, with 'Chanconete' as quadruplum, the melody of 'Mout sont vaillant' as triplum, but with a different text, 'Ainc voir' (456), and 'A la cheminee' as motetus (as in **Ba**). **Mo**'s tenor has the same French text as **W2**, which parodies the Latin text of the gradual.[2]

In the three-voice version presented in **W2**, the two upper voices have the same ambitus (*F-f*), but the 'A la cheminee' voice is more rhythmically active: it occupies twice as much manuscript space as the motetus, and its text is twice as long. Despite this, in their discussions of this motet, Hans Tischler, Edward Roesner, and Mary Wolinski call 'A la cheminee' the motetus voice, since it occupies that position in both **Ba** and **Mo**.[3] To avoid confusion in the following I refer to the voice parts by their textual incipit rather than by voice label.

The 'A la cheminee' voice in **W2** is notated mostly in *notae simplices* (single note shapes), with only three two-note ligatures. Thus, almost every text syllable is set to a single pitch. The shapes sometimes have the appearance of longs (▪), with a short downstem on the right side (see, for example, the last three notes of every phrase apart from the third, which includes a two-note ligature), and sometimes of breves (▪) (see, for example, the first few notes of the first, second, and fourth phrases). The notation is ambiguous, but the singers (we presume) would have known which mode to sing. Many motets in early sources such as **W2** and **F** have corresponding clausulae from which the mode and/or more specific rhythmic details could possibly be gleaned (though, this is not the case here, since no clausula survives for this motet).[4] But beyond the assumption

---

[1]   For a discussion of the context of this motet that praises the patricians of Ghent, and a new edition of the music, see Lievois and Wolinski 2002. Also see Wolinski 2008, 12–14, for a new edition of the poems and an English translation. A comparative edition of the motet appears in Tischler 1982, 977–9. As noted in Wolinski 2008, 13, the **W2** tenor text extols the virtue of Rhenish wines over the French, while the **Mo** version extols French wines. The **Mo** version of motet is edited in Tischler 1978, 1: 50–1, and the **Ba** version in G. Anderson 1977, 16. Roesner (1984, 370–4) discusses this motet's notation in some detail within his review of Tischler 1982.

[2]   Roesner (1984, 373–4) writes of the three versions: '**W2** undoubtedly preserves no. 145 in the notation in which it was initially conceived, with **Mo** and **Ba** being independent – equally "correct", but equally restrictive – "clarifications" of it'. Roesner (1984, 372) also notes that in the motet's original state the tenor must have carried the text 'Propter veritatem' and that the 'repetition of pitch in bar 19 to accommodate an extra syllable in the French parody confirms that the latter was a replacement for the Latin original' (the chant does not have this pitch repetition).

[3]   See Tischler 1982, Roesner 1984, and Wolinski 2008.

[4]   Bradley, in the current volume, illustrates the 'multidirectional and interactive' relationship between clausula and motet (p. 45), and, through a case study of a network of *Latus* clausulae

that the singers would have known how the piece 'goes', is it possible that the apparent palaeo-graphical differentiation of the *notae simplices* in **W2** transmits distinctions in durational value? Perhaps the notator grouped together the last three notes of all phrases (except the third) – through the addition of downstems – in order to indicate second mode. Such an observation, however, would need to be supported in a systematic study of all of the second-mode motets notated by this scribe in **W2**. The standard way to end phrases in second mode, when notated in ligatures, is with a three-note ligature; in this syllabic motet the phrases end with a grouping of three notes tagged with descending stems.[5] The rhythmic interpretation of these last three notes in second mode is either BLL or BLB, depending on whether the vertical stroke that follows this grouping is interpreted as a long rest (in all three parts), thus ♪♩ ♩.♯,[6] or as simply a divider of syllables or phrases, thus ♪♩ ♪♩: I have opted for the first option in my transcription (see Example 5.1), to allow for the long rests that seem to divide each statement of the tenor's *ordo* (a common feature of tenor patterns in *ars antiqua* motets).[7] The three two-note ligatures notated in the 'A la cheminee' voice confirm its second mode: a two-note ligature indicates BL in either mode one or mode two, but here the two-note ligatures are located in positions in phrases one and three relative to the *notae simplices* that imply a second-mode pattern persisting for the entire phrase.[8]

The notation of the 'A la cheminee' voice then is perhaps not as ambiguous as it first appears. It largely breaks down into a series of breves that can be quite nicely articulated in groups of twos (BL), with occasional two-note melismas in ligature that confirm this patterning, and each phrase concludes with a three-note grouping that completes the modal pattern, differentiated in the notation with descending stems.[9]

and motets, challenges the prevailing hypothesis that clausulae functioned as notational models for the motet. See also Bradley 2011, 257–74, which found that for half the motets of F that have related clausulae or discant passages in the same source, the related clausula or discant would have been a poor 'notational prop' for the motet.

5   If the reader/singer saw a pattern of ligatures grouped as 3+2+2+2 etc., they would recognize it as mode 1, where a longer duration begins the pattern (LBL BL BL BL rest, that is, ♩ ♪♩ ♪♩ ♪♩ ♪♩ ♮); if the pattern of ligatures was 2+2+2+3, then they would know to sing mode 2, commencing the phrase with a short duration (BL BL BL BLB rest, that is, ♪♩ ♪♩ ♪♩ ♪♩♪ ♯).

6   Where the last long is worth three breves (in the modern values used here, ♩.), called a long 'beyond measure' in contemporaneous theory sources.

7   The edition of the motetus voice at L12–L14 differs slightly from that preserved in W2. At the beginning of the second staff of the motetus voice in W2 is an *F*, which appears to be a wrong note, and is crossed out by the scribe. The pitches that follow to complete the phrase are *c* and *a*. In the Mo version of this voice the *a* followed by a second *a*, which is followed by an *E*. I follow Mo's reading here, but have written the two longs on *a* as a single duplex long to accommodate the fewer number of syllables in the W2 text (the alternate text in Mo has a 7-syllable line here, whereas the line in W2 is six syllables).

8   The first three notes of the motet have to be interpreted as BBB in order for this voice to line up properly with the tenor. Breaking up the expected modal pattern (in this case BL) into notes of shorter duration is termed 'fractio modi' (that is, the 'breaking-up' of the mode). Most often the long is broken into two breves, as is the case here.

9   The ligatures in the W2 version take on the function that Curran (2014, 142) ascribes to the *notae simplices* in the notation of Cl; in other words, the ligatures of W2's version of this motet delimit the modal context: '. . . [in Cl the notator] proceeded with a modal idea of perfection, one involving an unequal subdivision in LB or BL. The succession of ternary perfections is visually articulated by pairs of figures, each component of a pair which corresponds to one or other of the two perfections' unequal parts. One seldom has to read far before reaching an unambiguous simplex note that delimits the modal context in which remaining figures must be interpreted. The particular forms chosen for the figures may (and often do) indicate the values

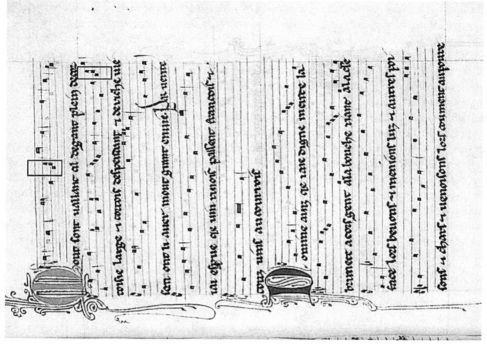

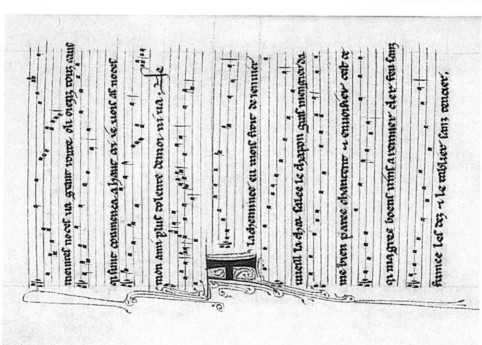

Figure 5.1. *A la cheminee/Mout sont vaillant/Par verite* in W2, fols. 212v–213r

Example 5.1. Transcription of first three phrases, L1–L24, of *A la cheminee/Mout sont vaillant/Par verite* from W2, fols. 212v–213r

108

108   Karen Desmond

The tenor voice has mostly the same note shapes as the 'A la cheminee' voice (apart from a couple of longs with elongated noteheads), yet the singer knows all the tenor notes must be sung longer than those in the upper voice since the tenor part occupies a significantly smaller share of the page (and since tenors were most often structured as a patterned series of pitches sung on notes of longer duration). The tenor's pitches divide into equal groups of four, marked by vertical strokes (with one – presumably – erroneously omitted between the third and fourth phrase), and which line up with the phrases in the upper voices indicating a pattern of three duplex longs followed by either a single long or a single long followed by a long rest (again depending on whether the vertical strokes in the tenor function as dividers of phrases or as actual distinct pauses or rests). To accord with the choice made in the 'A la cheminee' voice, the latter is rendered in Example 5.1.

The notator deployed a greater variety of notational signs in the 'Mout sont vallant' voice, including vertical strokes that represent either rests or marks of alignment, some noteheads that are horizontally elongated, a plica (toward the beginning of the third system of Figure 5.1), and more ligatures (eight in all, both two-note and three-note).[10] In this voice, the ligatures do not always mean the same thing.[11] For example, in the two instances of three-note ascending ligatures boxed in Figure 5.1, the first is best read as either as SSL (♫♩) or BBB (♫♩) since the three notes fill one perfection (see L5 of Example 5.1), but the second as BLL (♪♩ ♩.) since it occupies two perfections (ambiguity of three-note ligatures is a common feature of modal notation). However, all five of the two-note ligatures in the 'Mout sont vallant' voice can be sung as BL (♪♩), conforming to their use in the 'A la cheminee' voice. The elongated longs are also of interest. They all occur in the first phrase of the 'Mout sont vallant' voice and all denote longs that Johannes de Garlandia would term 'beyond measure' ('ultra mensuram'), that is, longs worth three breves (♩.). These extended shapes appear in other works (see the organum prosulae elsewhere in **W2**) often to suggest a relative, rather than absolute lengthening, based on the context.[12]

The motet notation of **W2**, like other of the earliest motet sources (**F**, **MüA**, and the chansonnier manuscripts, **Roi** and **Noailles**), is a flexible notation. The graphic signs do not have a single meaning, but they do nudge towards a particular interpretation. The deployment of ligatures and the inflection of certain note shapes in *A la cheminee/Mout sont* assists in the rhythmic coordination

of their constituent notes with greater mensural precision; but they need not do so for the script to be construable, and for polyphony to proceed, because it is at the level of the perfection that the discantal grammar of a motet is articulated'. Regarding the differentiation of shapes to show ligature groupings, Thomas Payne points out that in F differentiation of the *notae simplices* shapes is sometimes used to show un-ligatable groupings in ligature notation, for example, when there is a series of unison pitches (pers. comm., April 10, 2017).

[10] Plicas are found in both voices and used to effect *fractio modi*. The plica of the 'A la cheminee' voice will be discussed below.

[11] The barlines in Example 5.1 mark groupings of two modal units (aligning with the duplex longs in the tenor), and do not indicate where the vertical strokes occur, which can instead be seen in the image of W2 in Figure 5.1.

[12] A good example is the two-voice W2 prosula *Vide prophecie* (fol. 167r) (equivalent to the respond section of Pérotin's organum quadruplum *Viderunt omnes* V. *Notum fecit dominus*, and with a text attributed to Philip the Chancellor). I thank Thomas Payne for pointing me to this work. For example, the first four phrases of the upper voice begin LBLBLL, and the scribe draws the bolded L as a horizontally elongated long. It indicates a long beyond measure, worth 3B. For an edition of the prosula see Payne 2011, 3–10, which editorially marks these elongated single longs with tenuto marks. Another notational technique to indicate elongation in W2, and specifically to differentiate a duplex long of 6B, is the use of a longer-than-usual vertical descending stem; see Payne 1996, lxxxvii.

Example 5.2. The 'A la cheminee' voice in **Mo**, fol. 40r and **Ba**, fols. 6v–7r,
with the original note shapes indicated above each staff

of the three voices, even though the primary information imparted by the notation is pitch, aligned with the poems' textual declamation. This lack of durational specificity was addressed in the versions of this motet transmitted in the later thirteenth-century sources **Ba** and **Mo**, whose notations to a greater or lesser extent conform to the precepts of mensural notation codified by *ars antiqua* theorists such as Lambertus and Franco of Cologne.[13]

The 'Mout sont vallant' voice is texted in **Mo** as 'Ainc voir', but recall that this voice does not appear in **Ba**'s version of this motet. All eight ligatures in this voice in **Mo** are found in the exact same form as they were notated in **W2**. The first three-note ligature cannot be interpreted according to Franconian rules since its three notes occupy the duration of a single perfect long just as they did in **W2** (interpreted SSL in Example 5.1's transcription of **W2**), whereas according to Franco's rules such a ligature ought to occupy the duration of two longs.[14]

Turning to the 'A la cheminee' voice, Example 5.2 shows all five phrases as notated in **Ba** and **Mo** (the *notae simplices* and ligatures are indicated above each staff). Since these sources are later, the scribes now follow many of the Franconican rules of mensural notation. For example, **Ba**'s notator adheres to the following: 1. the breve imperfects the long that follows it; 2. two breves between two longs are a *brevis recta* and a *brevis altera*, rendering a 1:2 ratio where the second breve is held twice as long as the first; 3. a long followed by two breves is perfect, that is, worth three breves. The version of 'A la cheminee' in **Ba** has no ligatures, but does retain the single plica long on the *d* at L30 in the fourth phrase that is also found in **W2** (this figure is notated as a two-note ligature in **Mo**). The rhythm of 'A la cheminee' as notated in **Ba** is absolutely identical for every phrase but the last, which has a slightly different ending to close the motet. In **Mo**, some of the flexibility observed in the **W2** version remains; almost every phrase of the **Mo** version has a slightly different rhythm. Only the third phrase of **Mo** has the rhythm that **Ba** uses for every phrase.

In sum, precision and conformity are gained in the Franconian notation of **Ba**, but the flexibility and the nuances of musical expression found in the original notation of **W2**, and which were retained to some extent in the **Mo** version, are lost in **Ba**.

TOWARDS THE SPECIFICATION OF 'TEMPUS'

As mentioned above, in the last quarter of the thirteenth century theorists outlined a set of very specific rules relating to the contextual interpretation of the long and breve symbols. The notation of contemporaneous motet manuscripts (like **Mo** and **Ba**) reflects the precision afforded by these rules at the level of the long and breve, which were the predominant units of text declamation in most *ars antiqua* motets. *Ars antiqua* theorists also specified the duration of the semibreve note shape. They allowed for two durations depending on context: the minor semibreve, worth ⅓ of a breve, and the major semibreve, worth ⅔ of a breve. Ternary relationships were the rule, where a long was worth three breves, and a breve three semibreves, though a duplex long was worth twice the value of a perfect long (see Table 5.1).

---

[13] Franco's treatise is edited in Reaney and Gilles 1974 and Lambertus's in C. Meyer and Desmond 2015.

[14] Franco outlined rules for interpreting ligatures; a three-note ligature always represented BBL, where the two breves take up the value of one long.

Table 5.1. Species, names, shapes, and durations of notes in the Franconian system

Species	Subspecies	Note shapes	Duration (relative to the proper breve)
long	duplex long	◤	6
	perfect long	◦	3
	imperfect long	■	2
breve	'altera' breve	■	2
	proper breve	■	1
semibreve	major semibreve	◆	2/3
	minor semibreve	◆	1/3

In early motets, semibreves featured as melismatic decorations to melodic lines, where the primary units of text declamation were the long and the breve. Thus *notae simplices* specified the pitches for each syllable of text, or a two- or three-note ligature could substitute for one of the *notae simplices*. If this ligature replaced the breve, either in the form of a three-note conjunctura (◆◆◆) or a two-note c.o.p. ligature (◢ ◣), the text syllable received a melisma of three or two semibreves.[15] But, just as when the ligatures of modal polyphony were broken up into the long and breve *notae simplices* in order to accommodate the text syllables of the motet, once semibreves were given individual text syllables in motets, further theoretical codification was again necessary, since there was only one note shape for the semibreve (◆). The use of semibreves as individually drawn notes within a syllabic context was thus most likely the impetus for the codification of their two possible durations in Lambertus and Franco. Only a handful of motets in **Mo**'s old corpus – fascicles 2–6, thought to date from the late 1270s or 1280s – have semibreves as *notae simplices*. They occur in pairs and almost exclusively as opening gestures of phrases, in the pattern of SSBB.[16] This pattern – SSBB – was codified by Lambertus as his sixth rhythmic mode.[17]

Franco also gives examples of strings of semibreves notated as *notae simplices* separated into groupings of two and three by using a short stroke or dot that he calls a *divisio modi* ('division of the mode'). But motets with strings of semibreves separated by dots of division are not found in **Mo**'s old corpus.[18] They are a characteristic feature of several motets copied in the later fascicles of **Mo**, both in fascicle 7 (copied in the 1290s) and in fascicle 8 (which was completed possibly as late as the 1310s).[19] Thus, this style of textual declamation using strings of semibreves appears

[15] The abbreviation c.o.p. is for 'cum opposita proprietate' ('with an opposite property'), which is the term used by theorists to designate ligatures that have an ascending stem attached to the first note of the ligature in contrast to the standard form of the ligature. C.o.p. ligatures could have several pitches, but the first two notes are always two semibreves.

[16] In fascicle 2, **Mo** 20 and 23 have SSBB syllabic patterns in the quadruplum. Those with SSBB patterns in the triplum in fascicle 3 are nos. 36, 37, 38, 39, 40, 44; fascicle 4 are nos. 52, 53; fascicle 5 nos. 76, 77, 84, 102, 103, 119, 123, 124, 143, 144, 164.

[17] Lambertus exemplified it in his treatise by citing a phrase from the otherwise unknown motet *O virgo virginum celi domina*. C. Meyer and Desmond 2015, 108–9.

[18] **Mo** 40 is an exception in that it contains contains two separate instances of a group of four semibreves (but without a dot of division), where each four-semibreve group occupies the time of one breve. For an analysis of the significance of the groups of four semibreves in this motet see Curran 2013b, 168–84, esp. 181–2.

[19] On the dating of **Mo** fascicle 8 see the 'Introduction' to Bradley and Desmond 2018 and the essays by Stones, Baltzer, and Curran in the same volume.

to be a newer stylistic idiom since it is found only in these later fascicles of **Mo** and in other later manuscripts, including **Tu**, **Fauv**, and a number of English sources (to be discussed below). The question is whether in *all* of these sources groups of two or three semibreves notated as *notae simplices* ought to be interpreted following the rules outlined in Franco (that is *minor-major*, or *minor-minor-minor*), especially since some of these sources contain even larger groupings of semibreves (from four up to seven in the time of a single breve), the interpretation of which was not specified in Franco's *Ars cantus mensurabilis*.

Leaving aside the fraught question of how groups of four or more semibreves might have been sung, even attempting to determine how groups of two and three were sung is problematic.[20] Theory treatises are of some help, but exactly how these semibreves were interpreted in the transition between *ars antiqua* and *ars nova* is unclear. In the French *ars nova*, as outlined by the various witnesses to the Vitriacan tradition, the duration occupied by the breve – the *tempus* – is conceptualized in the same way as the duration of the long.[21] That is to say, the breve, just like the long, can be perfect and divisible into three equal parts, *or* imperfect and divisible into two equal parts. *Ars nova* composers wrote motets where the long consistently divides into two equal breves, which are considered to be 'in' imperfect *modus*; they also wrote motets where the breve divides into two equal parts and are 'in' imperfect *tempus*. In the Italian *ars nova* a similar dichotomous distinction was made between the perfect *divisiones* of the breve, which are based on a ternary breve, and the imperfect *divisiones*, which are based on a binary breve.[22] In the *ars antiqua*, however, as described in the theory treatises, the breve is only ever equally divisible into three, and if two semibreves occupy the duration of one breve, those semibreves are *unequal*.

To further explore this ambiguity, the next example presents *Super Cathedram Moysi/Presidentes in thronis/Ruina*, a three-voice motet that survives in the interpolated *Roman de Fauvel* manuscript (**Fauv**, copied *c.* 1317–22) as well as in a later source, **Br** (possibly copied in the 1330s), in a newer notation. *Super/Presidentes* is considered to be one of the more old-fashioned motets in **Fauv**. Semibreves notated as *notae simplices* are found only in the triplum, where there are no more than three semibreves per breve.[23] Unfortunately two of the motet's other sources are fragmentary and do not transmit the triplum; another source (**CaB 165**) transmits the motet in full in a notation similar to **Fauv** (see Table 5.2).

---

[20] For an analysis of the patterns of semibreve groups in the Petronian repertory of Mo see Maw 2018.

[21] Most *ars antiqua* compositions have ternary longs as described in Franco. The seminal study on the binary long in the thirteenth century is Sanders 1962, which found only six thirteenth-century compositions unquestionably measured by binary longs. One of these is a motet in Mo's eighth fascicle – *Amor potest conqueri* (933)/*Ad amorem sequitur* (934)/*Tenor* – though this may be a fourteenth-century composition, given the most recent hypothesis regarding the production of this fascicle (see n. 19 above). Several compositions in **Fauv** have binary longs. Subsequently, *ars nova* theorists described the measure of the long as 'modus'; thus, a motet measured with ternary longs is in perfect *modus* and one measured with binary longs is in imperfect *modus*.

[22] For charts of the Italian *divisiones* and the French *ars nova* mensurations, see Tables 5.5 and 5.6 below.

[23] *Super/Presidentes* is cited in two *ars nova* treatises as an example of a motet in perfect *modus*.

Table 5.2 Manuscript sources of *Super/Presidentes*

Manuscript	Complete or Fragmentary	Comments
Fauv, fol. iv	Complete	Undifferentiated semibreves with dots of division, no descending stems
Br, recto	Complete	*Ars nova* notation with minims, no dots of division
CaB 165, fol. i_v[a]	Complete	Undifferentiated semibreves with dots of division, no descending stems
Troyes 1949	Fragmentary (tenor only, and last line of triplum text)	
Ob 271*, fol. Bv	Fragmentary (motetus fragment only)	No stems on the semibreves of the motetus fragment

[a] This follows the foliation on DIAMM. Fragments now bound in **CaB 165** used to be part of **CaB**. Lerch 1987, which reconstructs the order of these fragments, lists this page as fol. 8v.

A passage from *Super/Presidentes* that compares the triplum of **Fauv** and **Br** is given as Figure 5.2. Examples 5.3a and 5.3b offer two interpretations of this passage in modern notation, the first with a ternary breve, the second with a binary breve (arrows in Figure 5.2 mark the beginning of the transcribed passages). Example 5.3a follows Franconian rules for the interpretation of the semibreves, so groups of three semibreves are equal (three minor semibreves, see the groupings at L33 on 'in-**de-bi-te**' and '**re-ga-li**-bus'), and groups of two are iambic patterns with a minor followed by a major semibreve (for example, see the SSBB pattern of L34 – which, incidentally, is the same pattern as Lambertus's sixth rhythmic mode mentioned above). In Example 5.3b a group of three semibreves is transcribed as ♪♪ ♪, where the longer duration is at the end of the grouping, a practice described by some theorists (again see 'in-**de-bi-te**' and '**re-ga-li**-bus' in Example 5.3b). The last note of the three is equivalent to Franco's minor semibreve, and the first two together occupy the duration of a minor semibreve: these shortest notes were called 'semibreves minimae' by some theorists (the 'least' or 'smallest' semibreves).[24]

A third interpretation, following the more specific notation of **Br**, is given as Example 5.3c. The **Br** scribe copied *Super/Presidentes* in *ars nova* notation that indicated imperfect *tempus* (see Figure

[24] This term – *semibrevis minima* – is not found in the group of treatises that disseminate Vitry's *ars nova* theories. However, in his fourteenth-century treatise *Speculum musicae* within a discussion of the *ars nova* theories of Vitry, Jacobus quotes from an unidentified author who appears to favour the style of notation used in **Fauv**, and who listed the varieties of semibreves as 'semibreves maiores, minores et minimas', that is, *semibrevis major*, *semibrevis minor*, and *semibrevis minima*; see Bragard 1955–73, Bk. 7 §34: 66. The first two are found in Franco; the *semibrevis minima* is apparently a catch-all term for all notes shorter than a *semibrevis minor*. On Jacobus as a witness to Vitry's *ars nova* theory see Desmond 2015. One of the earliest witnesses to Vitriacan theory, sometimes referred to in the literature as Wolf Anon. 4 (edited in Wolf 1908), did not differentiate the durations of two shorter notes that subdivide the *semibrevis minor*, and did not use *ars nova* terminology for these two shorter notes. Wolf's Anon. 4 did not use the term *semibrevis minima* either, but merely stated that the two notes combined were worth one *semibrevis*.

5.2). There are no dots separating the semibreve groups, and minim stems indicate the pitches to be held for the shortest duration. That is to say, in the **Br** version, every pair of semibreves is understood as equal (♪♪) and every group of three shorter notes that takes the place of a breve is notated as SSM (♪♪♪), confirming the binary division of the breve into two semibreves. Table 5.3 outlines these three different interpretations.

Table 5.3 Choices of transcription for breves subdivided into two or three

Original notation	Modern transcription	Note names	Comments
♦♦♦	♩♩♩	minor semibreve–minor semibreve– minor semibreve	Franconian (see Example 5.3a)
♦♦	♪♩	minor semibreve–major semibreve	
♦♦♦	♪♪♪	*semibrevis minima–semibrevis minima–* minor semibreve	binary breve, *semibreves minimae* not differentiated (see Example 5.3b)
♦♦	♪♪	minor semibreve–minor semibreve	
♦♦↓	♪♪♪	perfect semibreve–imperfect semibreve–minim	*ars nova*, imperfect tempus (see Example 5.3c)
♦♦	♪♪	perfect semibreve–perfect semibreve	

Leo Schrade followed the **Br** interpretation when he edited this motet – indeed he transcribed all the newer **Fauv** motets as if they were in imperfect *tempus*.[25] It is far from clear, however, whether this was the intent of the original notation in **Fauv**, since, unlike **Br**, **Fauv** does not have these groupings with minims that unambiguously denote imperfect *tempus*. The version of *Super/Presidentes* in **CaB 165** has the same *ars antiqua* notation of **Fauv** with undifferentiated semibreves separated by dots of division, even though elsewhere in the Cambrai fragments minim stems are consistently used.[26]

Other late *ars antiqua* sources have these same ambiguities with respect to the differentiation of groups of two and three semibreves. Example 5.4 is a passage excerpted from a motet unique to **Mo**'s eighth fascicle, *Je cuidoie bien metre jus* (703)/*Se j'ai folement* (704)/*Solem* (**Mo** 332), transcribed here with the original note shapes and dots of division, but arranged in score. Examples 5.5a and 5.5b provide alternate modern transcriptions first with a ternary breve and then with a binary breve. While a full analysis of the linguistic and versification patterns in the

---

25 See Schrade 1956b. Only nos. 17, 20, 31, and 32 have a group of three semibreves transcribed as three equal notes (♩♩♩).

26 Discussed by Lerch 1987, 1: 63–6. This motet is notable for its older-style notation in the Cambrai fragments: Lerch (1987, 1: 63) remarks that almost all the other motets in this source are notated in a 'voll ausgebildeter Ars-Nova-Notation'.

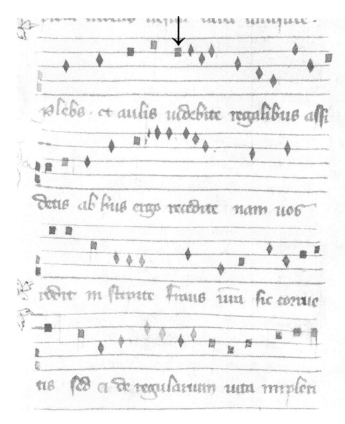

Figure 5.2. Excerpt of *Super/Presidentes* triplum in **Fauv**, fol. 1v (BnF) and **Br**, recto

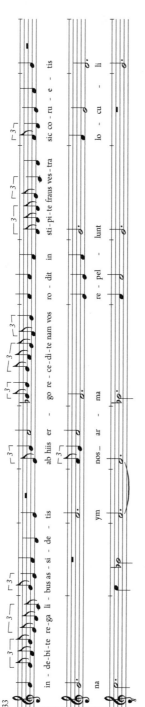

Example 5.3a. *Super/Presidentes*, triplum, L33–L41, transcribed from **Fauv** with ternary breves

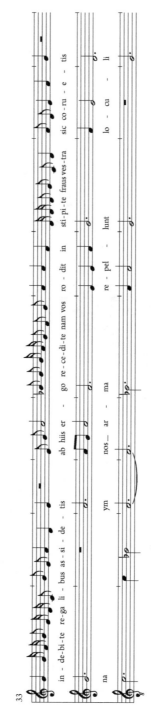

Example 5.3b. *Super/Presidentes*, triplum, L33–L41, transcribed from **Fauv** with binary breves

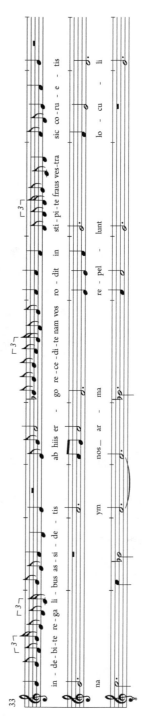

Example 5.3c. *Super/Presidentes*, triplum, L33–L41, transcribed from **Br** in imperfect *tempus*

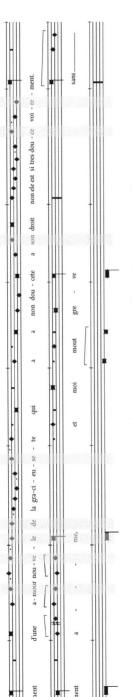

Example 5.4. *Je cuidoie/Se j'ai folement*, L5–L10, transcribed with original note shapes

Example 5.5a. *Je cuidoie/Se j'ai folement*, L5–L10, transcribed with ternary breves

Example 5.5b. *Je cuidoie/Se j'ai folement*, L5–L10, transcribed with binary breves

texts of these motets might be of some help in deciding whether the breve is ternary or binary, in many cases the evidence of the texts is equivocal. Another aspect of the musical setting that could potentially add support for one interpretation over another is patterns of consonance and dissonance. Looking specifically at semibreves pairs in *Je cuidoie/Se j'ai folement*, the tendency is for perfect consonances (here, octaves, unisons, or fifths) to be placed on the second semibreve of the pair: over the course of the motet's entire triplum more than three times as many of the second semibreves make fifths or octaves with the tenor as compared to the first semibreves. (In Example 5.4, all the perfect consonances within semibreve pairs that occur between the triplum and the tenor are highlighted by grey boxes.) And, unless the semibreve pair occurs at the beginning of a perfection (in which case it is most often a repeated-note figure where both the first and second note make a perfect consonance with the tenor, see for instance L7 in Example 5.4), the second semibreve of the pair *always* receives the perfect consonance, with only one exception in the entire motet. The internal evidence of this motet might point then to a ternary evaluation of the breve, with an iambic patterning to the semibreve pair, where the second semibreve receives a longer duration, following the rules set forth in Franco, *if* one believes that it is more likely for a consonant interval to be sustained for a longer duration than an imperfect or dissonant one.[27] Also, with this iambic patterning, the dissonances in this motet are held for the shorter duration: in Example 5.5a, at the triplum and tenor on 'non dou-', the (mildly) dissonant fourth *D/G* would be shortened and the third *D/F* would get ⅔ of the value. One anonymous commentary on Franco's treatise links exactly these criteria to the major semibreve: 'the first or second semibreve ought to be sung as the major ('greater') semibreve according to [whichever has] the greater concord' ('secundum maiorem concordantiam debet prima vel secunda semibrevis maior pronuntiari').[28]

The consonance-dissonance patterns differ in *Super/Presidentes*. In *Super/Presidentes* a significantly higher percentage of perfect consonances between the triplum and tenor occur on the first semibreve of a semibreve pair, with only a handful of instances where it occurs on the second semibreve. Does this evidence point towards an equal interpretation of the semibreve pairs in *Super/Presidentes*, or even as unequal but in a trochaic pattern (♩♪)? It is difficult to say with certainty, but it seems likely that the semibreve pairs ought to be interpreted in a different manner than the pairs of *Je cuidoie/Se j'ai folement*, with less emphasis in *Super/Presidentes* on the second semibreve of the pair.

Composers and scribes of motets soon exerted more control over the rhythmic duration of notes shorter than the breve, and codified the semibreve and minim in *ars nova* theory. Like modern editors of medieval motets, medieval scribes offered their interpretations of the older motets in what was their own 'modern' notation (that is, the new *ars nova* notation), making the rhythms of notes shorter than the breve clear and straightforward where there was previously ambiguity and flexibility. We should be wary of uncritically applying all of their interpretations to this transitional notation. A number of **Fauv** motets, for example, are extant in later manuscripts in *ars nova* notation, as just observed with **Br**'s version of *Super/Presidentes*. Invariably, the scribes of these later manuscripts notated the **Fauv** motets in imperfect *tempus*.[29] The evidence

---

[27] Roesner 1990 outlines a hypothesis for 'the emergence of *musica mensurabilis*' where perfect consonances receive a longer duration than imperfect or dissonant intervals.

[28] Gallo *et al.* 1971, 69.

[29] Several **Fauv** motets have concordances in other manuscripts and those concordances have ascending stems on some semibreves indicating groupings: *Super/Presidentes* (see above for the concordant sources), *Detractor/Qui secuntur* (**Pn** 571), *Trahunt/Ve qui gregi* (**Br**), *Se cuers/Rex* (**McVeagh**), *Servant/O Philippe* (**Pn** 571), *Tribum/Quoniam* and *Firmissime/Adesto* (which both have several later concordant sources including **Br** and **Robertsbridge**), and *Garrit/In*

of the medieval updaters must be taken into account, of course, since these scribes were closer to this repertory than we are today. But ought all the **Fauv** motets be interpreted in the same way? During the time of **Fauv**'s compilation, composers appear to have been actively engaging with the ambiguity of the lengthened breve, text declamation on the semibreve, and the possibility of the binary or ternary subdivisions of the breve. Perhaps the best solution for a modern transcription is the under-prescriptive sort given in Example 5.4, with the options for the interpretation of the semibreves laid out for the performer in a preface or critical commentary.

SEMIBREVES IN FOURTEENTH-CENTURY ENGLISH AND ITALIAN NOTATIONS

Compared to the both the French and Italian traditions, English motets demonstrate both heterogeneity and idiosyncrasy in notational practice. Peter Lefferts has observed: 'The English go their own way in matters of notation'.[30] Many of the *ars antiqua* French motet sources mentioned thus far were notated by a single scribe and present a single 'house style' of notational practice notable for its internal consistency, even while it may deviate in some details from the codifications found in contemporaneous theory.[31] By contrast, the best-known collection of medieval English polyphony, the Worcester fragments, includes motets in pre-mensural, insular English, Franconian, and post-Franconian (so-called 'Petronian') notations side-by-side.[32] This variety of notational practices deployed within a single source is true of several other of the more substantial English fragmentary sources, including, for example, **DRc 20**, **Lbl 1210**, **Onc 362**, and **Ob 7**.

The three diverging traditions of fourteenth-century notation – French, Italian, English – responded in different ways to the ambiguity presented by the subdivision of the breve discussed in the previous section.[33] Similar motet notations to those found in **Mo**'s later fascicles and **Fauv**, with strings of semibreves separated by dots of division, are found in several English manuscripts. These notations are often referred to in the scholarly literature as 'Petronian'. Given that this complex of notational practices is broader in scope than the practices associated by theorists with Petrus de Cruce, Margaret Bent has made recently made a compelling case for abandoning the 'Petronian' descriptor and adopting a more neutral one such as 'post-Franconian', which I follow

---

nova (**Pic**). On the updating of these and other transitional motets into *ars nova* notation see Desmond 2018b.

[30] Lefferts 1986, 104. The comprehensive survey of English fourteenth-century motet notations is Lefferts 1986 in ch. 4 'Motet Notations' (93–154) that also offers a good summary of thirteenth-century practice (104). On English notation see also the contributions of Handschin 1949, Handschin 1951, Dittmer 1953, Dittmer 1954, Dittmer 1957, Sanders 1962, Wibberley 1975, Bent 1978, and Lefferts 2001.

[31] Each of the three motet fascicles in **W2** was notated by a dedicated music scribe (fascicles 8–10), and while several music scribes worked on **Mo**, it is the case that a single scribe notated the music of fascicle 8, as is also the case with **Cl**, **Ba**, and **Fauv**. For a discussion of house style as it pertains to the identifying scribal preference for particular figures and their interpretation, see Curran 2014, 139.

[32] For a catalogue of English thirteenth-century sources see Lefferts 2012, including detailed descriptions of the three reconstructions that have been made of the Worcester fragments. Lefferts's catalogue is unpaginated. For studies of Italian notation see in particular Gallo 1966 and Gallo 1984, esp. 304–33.

[33] For the French response to the ambiguity of the semibreve, see ch. 4 ('Arts Old and New') of Desmond 2018a.

here.[34] The post-Franconian notations may comprise groups of undifferentiated semibreves as described in the previous section, or descending stems may be added. In eleven of **Fauv**'s motets, for example, some semibreves have descending stems (usually the first semibreve of a group of two or three).[35] Various theory treatises state that these descending stems indicate a longer duration for the semibreve so tagged, and that they were used to alter the standard durational patterning of the semibreve groups (although in some instances they are used for clarification and not to substitute an alternate pattern for the one expected).[36] These descending stems are also found in English and Italian theory and practice, and had a similar function.

Medieval English polyphony, in general, demonstrates a preference for trochaic (long-short) rather than iambic (short-long) rhythmic patterns.[37] This is true of the older insular long-breve notation (which utilized the distinctively English lozenge-shaped breve), where, of the relatively large repertory extant in this notation, only three mode-two compositions are known.[38] In support of a similarly trochaic interpretation for the semibreve pairs notated as *notae simplices* in English sources, scholars have pointed to the evidence of alternately notated versions of some compositions. For example, the motet *Thomas gemma Cantuarie/Thomas cesus/P*[rimus tenor]*/Secundus tenor* is notated in stemless paired-semibreve notation in the volume of the Worcester fragments known as 'Reconstruction II' (**Ob 20** [formerly **Ob 862**, fols. 12v–13r], fols. 34r, 35r), but it is notated in Franconian long-breve notation that clearly indicates the first mode in its two other sources (**Pru**, fol. A2 and **Cgc 512** fols. 254v–255r).[39] And several theorists, both English and continental, do allow for the possibility of the trochaic interpretation of semibreve pairs.[40]

Lefferts, in his study of fourteenth-century English motet notations, distinguishes two varieties of post-Franconian insular notations: the first, which he describes as the 'circle-stem notational complex', consists of patterns of breve subdivision within a long-breve context, the use of dots to mark the breve groupings and descending stems to mark the major semibreve, and the occasional use of either a small circle (*signum rotundum*) or upward stems to indicate smaller values. The second, which he terms 'breve-semibreve notation', is similar but tends to have a more limited range of note values primarily moving in breves and major and minor semibreves (with no longs and very few minims). This notation is used primarily in the English cantilena repertory but also in some motets. Lefferts allows that some ambiguities in interpreting English motet notations remain, as for example, when an English ternary breve-semibreve composition 'has accumulated enough minims . . . to look Continental'.[41]

---

[34] Bent 2015, 42–3. For a discussion of the theoretical references to Petrus de Cruce, and the citations of motets with more than three semibreves per breve, see Bent 2015, 26–43.

[35] For a listing and discussion of the eleven Fauv motets with descending stems see Table 2 of Desmond 2018b. For a comprehensive discussion of the tagged semibreves (*semibreves caudatae*) of **Fauv** and the interpretation of semibreve pairs in general, see Roesner *et al.* 1990, 32–8.

[36] For a discussion of these passages in the context of the Vitriacan theoretical tradition see Desmond 2018a and Roesner *et al.* 1990, 32–8.

[37] Sanders 1963, 275–6; Bent 1978, 66–9; Lefferts 1986, 117–24.

[38] Lefferts 1986, 107.

[39] Reconstruction II of the Worcester fragments comprises a fragment once with the call number Ob 862 and now catalogued as Ob. lat. liturg. d.20, fols. 23r–35v, as well as fragments ix and xxxv from WoC. Bent 1978, 67, discusses the notational updating of *Thomas gemma/Thomas cesus*. See also Levy 1951, 229.

[40] The statements from the theorists are listed in Lefferts 1986, 118–19, and discussed in Bent 1978, 66–9, and Roesner *et al.* 1990, 35–6.

[41] Lefferts 1986, 142.

The first example (from Lefferts's list of 'circle-stem' motets) demonstrates how English notations, though not yet conferring a single durational value on the semibreve with descending stem, did deploy it within contexts that clarified how the semibreve groupings ought to be interpreted. The three-voice motet *Rosa delectabilis/Regalis exoritur mater decoris* is preserved uniquely in **Onc 362** (fols. 90v–91r).[42] Groups of two to four semibreves, often syllabically set, proliferate across the two texted voices, which are equally active, and dots of division separate the semibreve groups. The semibreve groups deployed in this motet are listed in Table 5.4. This particular combination of patterns allows for only one interpretation of the breve. That is, it must be ternary, and the majority of the semibreve pairs are sung trochaically. Example 5.6 provides the opening of this motet with the forms of the original notation placed above the staves.[43] As the modern transcription of the semibreve patterns in Table 5.4 demonstrates, semibreves with a descending stem could have two different durations, either ♩ or ♪ (that is, either a *major* or *minor* semibreve) depending on context; compare in Example 5.6 the syllables (bolded here) of '**Re**-gi-na' and 'pre-**no**-bi-lis' with '**Ro**-sa' and 'de-le-**cta**-bi-lis' in the triplum, for instance.

Table 5.4. Semibreve patterns in *Rosa delectabilis/Regalis*

Original notation	Modern transcription
◆ ◆	♪ ♩ or ♩ ♪
↑◆ ◆	♩ ♪
◆ ◆ ◆	♪ ♪ ♪
↑◆ ◆◆ ◆↑	♪ ♫ ♪
↑◆ ↑◆ ◆ ◆	♪ ♪ ♫
◆ ◆ ↑◆ ↑◆	♫ ♪ ♪

Most of the semibreve pairs in this piece are tagged with a descending stem on the first semibreve explicitly indicating a trochaic interpretation of the pair (as in the just mentioned '**Re**-gi-na' and 'pre-**no**-bi-lis' at the beginning of L6 and L7 in the triplum, as well as ex-**o**-ri-tur and **tol**-li-tur at L3 and L7 in the motetus). The opening pair of semibreves in the triplum (and similarly at the beginning of L3, shortly thereafter), however, are melismatic. The first pair are drawn in ligature (and thus cannot be differentiated by the addition of a descending stem), but the second pair are drawn as separate semibreves without stems. Ought both of these gestures at L1 and L3 be edited and performed as iambs, as Frank Harrison chose to do in his edition of this piece?[44] In my transcription in Example 5.6, I opted for a trochaic interpretation of both of these pairs, given the consonances at these moments (particularly the octave at the motet's opening between the triplum and motetus), the overarching dominance of trochaic patterns in this motet, and at L3, the trochaic rhythm in parallel with the motetus.[45]

[42] For an analysis of this motet see the chapter by Hartt in this volume. See also Lefferts 1986, 69–71.
[43] In this motet the descending stems confirm without a shadow of doubt the ternary breve, whereas in **Fauv**, since there are only two patterns with the descending stems, arguments can be made for either a ternary or binary breve depending on context. See Desmond 2018b.
[44] Harrison 1980, 36–9.
[45] Caldwell (1981, 467), on the other hand, argues in support of an iambic interpretation of any unmarked semibreves.

Example 5.6. *Rosa delectabilis/Regalis exoritur mater decoris/Regali ex progenie*, L1–L7, transcribed from **Onc 362**, fols. 90v–91r

A second example is taken from the motet [Triplum]/*Frondentibus florentibus silvis/Floret*. It is extant in two fragmentary sources, one of which has had its notation updated by a later hand. The motetus and tenor are extant in **Ob 7** (p. ix), and the motetus on staves 8–11 of **Ob 594** (reverse image of flyleaf on rear board).[46] The **Ob 594** motetus is notated in a post-Franconian notation, with groups of two, three, and four semibreves separated by dots of division, and the occasional descending stem. The **Ob 7** version of the motetus originally had stemless semibreves, but as can be seen in Figure 5.3, a later hand updated it systematically, erasing and altering ligatures and

[46]   See Bent's report on **Ob 594** in Lefferts *et al.*, 1982, 342–7. Bent reconstructed the triplum of the motet on the 'strong' possibility that it is found on the first seven staves of **Ob 594**, where the visible notes fit well with the motetus voice.

adding ascending stems to the lozenge shapes in order to unequivocally indicate *ars nova* rhythmic patterns, such as SMSM and SSM (the same hand also made alterations to the tenor, but not shown in this figure). The upper staff of Example 5.7 has a reconstruction of the original notation of the motetus and an interpretation in modern notation, with the later updated version presented in the lower staff. The original notation had groups of two to four undifferentiated semibreves, which may have been interpreted according to either a binary or ternary breve: I have opted for a ternary breve in this transcription of the original version. The differences in the interpretation of the two- to four-note groupings can be seen in longs 5, 9, 11, and 14–17. With the addition of the minim stems, the later hand forced the motetus voice into a binary breve mensuration, not unlike the way in which the **Fauv** motets were updated in their later concordant sources on the continent, all of which were rendered in an unambiguous imperfect *tempus* mensuration.

The sort of updating observed in **Ob 7** prefigures a trend in English sources that by the last third of the fourteenth century sees most motets notated in the French *ars nova* notation formulated on the continent around a few decades earlier. For example, the only motet notated in **NYpm 978**, *Candens crescit lilium/Candens lilium columbina/[Quartus cantus]/[Tenor primus]* (fols. 7v–8r), within a source that otherwise transmits cantilenas and settings of the Mass Ordinary, was originally notated in Franconian notation with undifferentiated semibreves in both of its earlier sources: the Reconstruction II volume of the Worcester fragments (**Ob 20** [formerly **Ob 862**, fol. 6v], fol. 28v) and **Cpc 228** (fol. 2v). In **NYpm 978** the melismatic semibreve groups have been updated with the addition of ascending minim stems to conform with the standard Vitriacan imperfect *tempus* patterns.[47]

Table 5.5. Italian *divisiones*, with the divisio names and common meter signatures indicated

	Imperfect	Perfect
	■	■
1st div.	◆ ◆ *binaria (.b.)*	◆ ◆ ◆ *ternaria (.t.)*
2nd div.	◆◆ ◆◆ *quaternaria (.q.)*	◆◆ ◆◆ ◆◆ *senaria perfecta/ytalica (.p.)*
	◆◆◆ ◆◆◆ *senaria imperfecta/gallica (.i.)*	◆◆◆ ◆◆◆ ◆◆◆ *novenaria (.n.)*
3rd div.	◆◆ ◆◆ ◆◆ ◆◆ *octonaria (.o.)*	◆◆ ◆◆ ◆◆ ◆◆ ◆◆ ◆◆ *duodenaria (.d.)*
	◆◆◆ ◆◆◆ ◆◆◆ ◆◆◆ *duodenaria (.d.)*	

By the end of the fourteenth century in Italy too, the notation of Italian motets betrays the influence of French *ars nova* notational practices.[48] In the early decades of the fourteenth century, Italian theorists codified the patterns of durations shorter than the breve into a system of

---

[47] The scribe similarly updated the cantilena *Salamonis inclita mater.*

[48] See Table 1 of Bent 1992a, 122–5, that lists the Italian motet repertory *c.* 1300–1410.

Figure 5.3. Excerpt of [Triplum] / *Frondentibus florentibus silvis / Floret* motetus in Ob 7, p. ix

Example 5.7. Beginning of motetus *Frondentibus*, B1–B18,
with a reconstruction of the original notation in the upper staff, and the updated notation in the lower staff

divisiones, that is, subdivisions of the breve, which could be either imperfect or perfect (see Table 5.5, which outlines the divisions according to Marchetto da Padova's *Pomerium*).[49] Similar to other post-Franconian notation systems, dots mark the groups of semibreves that constitute a breve grouping, though many of the extant Italian sources also signal the higher levels of *divisiones* through the use of ascending stems. Descending stems could also be deployed – the so-called 'via artis' – that indicated a pattern different from the one expected (the 'via naturae', where the descending stem indicated a lengthening).

The repertory of Italian motets written before the last quarter of the fourteenth century is relatively small, and while notated in Italian 'trecento' notation, they frequently do not display the full range of breve subdivisions the Italian *divisiones* enabled. By the end of the fourteenth century, most copyists begin to notate Italian motets in either French *ars nova* notation or a 'mixed' notation heavily influenced by French *ars nova* practices. The motet *O felix templum/O felix templum* by Johannes Ciconia (composed *c.* 1402–5), as an example, is extant in two early fifteenth-century Italian manuscripts: **Q15** and **Ob 213**.[50] In **Ob 213**, even though most of the manuscript is copied in white mensural notation, *O felix templum* is one of a small handful of compositions copied in Italian black notation.[51] By contrast, the scribe of **Q15** notated this Italian motet in (black) French *ars nova* notation. Bent and Hallmark, in their commentary to their edition of this motet, note that *O felix templum* was originally conceived in Italian notation, a conclusion supported by the motet's rhythmic style, and 'several notational anomalies'.[52]

Though **Ob 213**'s *O felix templum* does not display some of the overt features of Italian notation – such as the *pontelli* that separate breve groupings, or letters that signify the overarching breve *divisio* (provided in Table 5.5) – nonetheless there are significant differences in the two versions. For example, minim triplets in *senaria perfecta* in **Ob 213** are notated as void noteheads in **Q15** (♩). Both techniques indicate three minims in the time of two, rendered as triplets in the transcription given as Example 5.8. Additionally, Italian theorists document various forms of alteration of the standard note shapes to indicate alterations in the expected pattern of the breve division; for example, the semibreve form with an oblique stem in **Ob 213** (◆) is notated as a semibreve with a dot of addition in **Q15** (◆ ·).[53] Both forms indicate a semibreve 1½ times its usual duration.

MENSURAL COMBINATIONS IN *DOUCE / GARISON*

Around the time that the ambiguity between the binary and ternary breve had been resolved in the French *ars nova*, and four possible combinations of mensuration had become codified (see Table 5.6), a series of motets were composed that, by means of specific notational techniques,

---

[49] Vecchi 1961.

[50] Color images (**Q15** fols. 252v–253r and **Ob 213** fols. 22v–23r) are available on the DIAMM website.

[51] Before the fifteenth century, music sources were copied in what is termed black notation where the noteheads were filled in with ink; **Ob 213** is one of the first sources to be copied in void notation, also termed white notation, where the noteheads are not filled in. Fallows (1995, 6) writes that the scribe of **Ob 213** was presumably transcribing most of the music of this source from full-black to void notation as he worked. Five pieces were notated in full-black notation, and three of these, including *O felix templum*, were apparently the first pieces copied.

[52] Bent and Hallmark 1985, 205. Minim triplets in Italian notation are more usually flagged to the left, though here in **Ob 213** are flagged to the right.

[53] Dots of addition were explicitly defined in French *ars nova* music treatises from around the middle of the fourteenth century. They were used in imperfect mensurations to designate notes as perfect, thus worth 1½ times their usual duration.

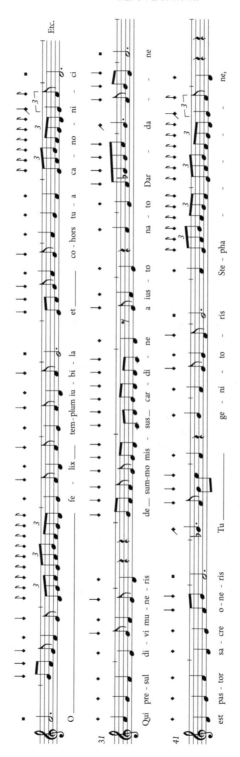

Example 5.8. B1–B10 and B31–B50 of the cantus I voice of Johannes Ciconia, *O felix templum*, transcribed from Ob 213, with original notation indicated above staff

play with the superimposition of different mensurations between the individual voice parts of a motet or the juxtaposition of different mensurations to articulate formal divisions. The division at the level of the long (into breves) was termed *modus*, and was either perfect (ternary) or imperfect (binary); the division at the level of the breve (into semibreves) was also either perfect or imperfect (*tempus*). Thus a mensuration of imperfect *modus* and imperfect *tempus*, was based on a binary long and a binary breve (in a modern notation, such a piece might be transcribed in $\frac{2}{4}$).[54] In the course of a motet, the mensuration could change. One of the techniques devised to explicitly indicate mensural change was coloration – a technique where passages of one voice, in the earlier *ars nova* usually confined to the tenor, are notated with red ink to indicate a change of *modus* or *tempus*. Only a handful of French *ars nova* motets use coloration: among these are *Garrit gallus/In nova fert/N[euma]*, *Tuba sacre fidei/In arboris empiro/Virgo sum*, *Douce playsence/Garison selon nature/Neuma*, *Almifonis melos/Rosa sine culpe/Tenor*, and two of Machaut's motets, *Aucune gent/Qui plus aimme/Fiat voluntas tua/Contratenor* (M5) and *Felix virgo mater/Inviolata genitrix/Ad te suspiramus/Contratenor* (M23). Mensuration signs are found infrequently in the earliest *ars nova* motets: two examples are *Douce/Garison* and *Zolomina zelus/Nazarea que decora/Ave Maria*. *Douce/Garison* will be considered in more detail here since it deploys both these techniques.

Table 5.6. The four mensuration combinations outlined in the Vitriacan *ars nova* treatises

	Perfect *tempus*	Imperfect *tempus*
Perfect *modus*		
Imperfect *modus*		

Douce/Garison is noteworthy in **Iv** – a manuscript that probably dates from the 1380s – for the scribe's use of mensuration signs.[55] The central witnesses to the theoretical tradition that transmitted Vitriacan *ars nova* theory all single out *Douce/Garison* for its mensuration changes, citing the motet as an example of 'partly perfect, partly imperfect' *tempus* and 'mode also' ('Tempus partim perfectum et partim inperfectum et modus etiam continetur in Garison').[56] The mensuration

---

[54] The prolation level – the subdivision of the semibreve into minims – was only ever ternary and trochaic in the earliest *ars nova* motets, for example, a typical pattern in an imperfect *tempus* voice was ♦♦♦♦ (transcribed in modern notation as ♩♪♩♪). For more on the absence of a discussion of prolation in the earliest *ars nova* treatises see Desmond 2015, 476–7, and for the predominance of the ternary trochaic patterns of semibreves and minims in the early *ars nova* music repertory see Earp 2015b.

[55] For the dating of Iv see Kügle 1997, 75.

[56] This statement is found in three of the *ars nova* witnesses that cite *Douce/Garison*: the F-Pn lat. 7378A witness, edited in Reaney et al., 1964, 69, and the I-Rvat 307 and F-Pn lat. 14741 witnesses presented in the same volume, 26–7. The later Vitriacan witness, known today as Ps. Theodonus, specifically mentions the mensuration signs of this motet (Sweeney and Gilles 1971, 43).

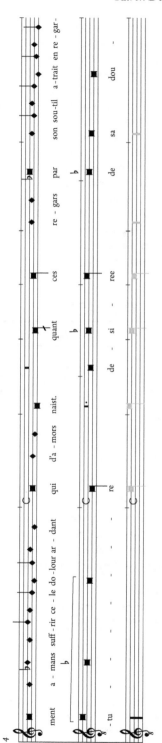

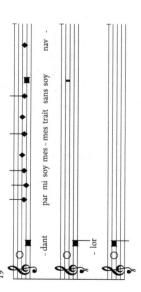

Example 5.9. Excerpt from *Douce/Garison*, L4–L11, showing mensuration changes and coloration

changes in *Douce/Garison* are noted in all three voices by **Iv**'s scribe with either a small circle (O indicating perfect *tempus*) or a small semicircle (C indicating imperfect *tempus*). The changes in *modus* are indicated by the use of red notation in the tenor, rendered in grey in Example 5.9. This red notation of *Douce/Garison* was also singled out by the central Vitriacan theoretical witnesses.

More significant than the tenor's use of coloration to signify *modus* changes, however, are the changes in *tempus* in *Douce/Garison*. The **Fauv** motet *Garrit/In nova* does have oscillations between perfect and imperfect *modus*, and these are clearly indicated to the tenor singer by the change in ink color in this part.[57] But *Garrit/In nova*'s triplum and motetus mostly move in breves and semibreves, so the singers of these parts would not really have needed to know the prevailing *modus*. The upper-voice singers of *Douce/Garison*, on the other hand, and particularly the singer of the triplum, would have to know the prevailing *tempus* division in order to know whether to interpret their paired semibreves as equal or unequal semibreves. It would have been quite difficult for singers to articulate and catch each of these rapid changes in mensuration without the circle and semicircle mensuration changes specifically indicated in the notation. For example, if the singer of the triplum part was not aware of the mensuration change at L5 in Example 5.9, the singer could easily have sung the paired semibreves of 'd'amors' at L5 as *semibrevis-semibrevis altera*.

The changes in mensuration are regularly placed in this motet, and once the singers had sung through the piece a couple of times, they would have become accustomed to where the changes in *modus* and *tempus* fell, and would have absorbed the various cues within the music itself that accompanied these changes. But, for at least a singer's first or second read-through, the mensuration signs were a crucial part of this motet's notation. Similar oscillations between perfect and imperfect *tempus* are found in the motet *Zolomina/Nazarea*, and are specifically signaled with mensuration signs in **Iv** and in the concordant source **BarcA**.

Unlike the examples explored in the first three sections of this chapter, such experiments with notation are no longer directly related to issues of text declamation or to ensuring co-ordination between the voices, but instead play with the precision and metrical possibilities afforded by the developments in motet notation, and create, I would argue, a new aesthetic for motet style in the middle of the fourteenth century.[58] Mensuration and proportion signs, in particular, grew in number and diversified by the early fifteenth century, culminating in their innovative deployment in several fifteenth-century motets, as demonstrated, for example, in Guillaume Du Fay's *Nuper rosarum flores* and Antoine Busnoys's *In hydraulis*.[59] And so, again it is a proliferation of new signs (this time mensuration and proportion signs), and their sometimes inconsistent use, that highlights music notation's potential for ambiguity and misunderstanding, as present-day scholars continue their attempts at deciphering the contextual relationships between the passages of music that scribes marked up with these signs, but which these scribes no doubt deployed for the purposes of their readers' clarification.

---

[57] The upper voices of *Garrit/In nova* declaim mostly in breves in semibreves, and have no ambiguities with respect to altering breves or imperfecting longs. All their longs are imperfect, apart from one very clearly indicated perfect long by means of the addition of a dot of perfection at L55 in the triplum.

[58] See ch. 6 of Desmond 2018a. In this *Companion*, see the chapter by Zazulia on the mensural manipulations of later motets including *Portia/Ida* and *Sub Arturo/Fons*.

[59] On mensuration and proportion signs and their treatment in fifteenth-century music theory see Busse Berger 1993, and more recently DeFord 2005 and DeFord 2015.

6

Thirteenth-Century Motet Functions:
Views through the Lens of the *Portare* Motet Family

Dolores Pesce

T HIS CHAPTER, devoted to how the motet functions in the thirteenth century, draws its examples largely from a motet family based on the chant fragment *portare*; this melodic segment appears in the *Alleluia: Dulce lignum* (M22) for the celebrations of the Cross: its Invention on 3 May and its Exaltation on 14 September. A number of Parisian chant sources, including **F-Pn lat. 1112**, fol. 169v, shown in Example 6.1, use the word *sustinere* instead of *portare*, a fact that is not necessarily significant because the words are employed interchangeability in the Office liturgy for the feasts of the Cross.[1] As indicated below the example, the text and melody also appear in a Marian version, *Alleluia: Dulcis virgo*, for the Octave of the Assumption, with the word *portare*. In this contrafactum, the image of the Cross bearing the weight of Christ changes to one of Mary carrying him, presumably both before birth and later as the infant Jesus.[2] Thus, the chant segment possesses both Marian and Christological connotations, an essential fact as we turn to the exegetical function of motets.

As discussed in Catherine A. Bradley's chapter, many of the earliest thirteenth-century Latin motets result from the addition of a syllabic text to the upper voice of discant clausulae of the *Magnus liber organi* or its supplements. These new Latin texts allude to the plainsong from which the tenor chant melisma is taken or even to other liturgical items for the same feast. These motets thus function as exegetical vehicles in which the hermeneutic modes are applied to the Scriptural passages associated with the feast. Of the four hermeneutic modes – *historia, allegoria, tropologia*, and *anagoge* – the tropological figures strongly in the early Latin motet repertory. A new Latin upper-voice text often tropes the tenor chant, giving it a moral interpretation or significance apart from its direct meaning.

---

[1] See Figure 8.3 in the chapter by John Haines and Stefan Udell for a facsimile reproduction of a motet where the tenor is presented with the word *portare*.

[2] See Pesce 1997, 38–40, for a discussion of the manuscript evidence related to the two textual versions of this particular chant melody.

Example 6.1. Melody and texts for the *portare/sustinere* chant segment

Alleluia: *Dulce lignum, dulces claves,* dulcia ferens pondera, que sola fuisti digna *sustinere* regem celorum et Dominum.

Alleluia: Sweet wood, sweet nails, bearing the sweet weight, you alone were worthy of bearing the Lord, king of heaven.

Alleluia: *Dulcis virgo, dulcis mater,* dulcia ferens pondera, que sola fuisti digna *portare* regem celorum et Dominum.

Alleluia: Sweet virgin, sweet mother, bearing the sweet weight, you alone were worthy of carrying the Lord, king of heaven.

The *portare* motet family contains only one motet related to a clausula; in this case, the motet carries a French rather than Latin text, and scholars believe that the motet version preceded its corresponding clausula.[3] Therefore, we must turn outside the *portare* family for an example of an early clausula-based Latin motet that likely functioned in a liturgical context: just as the clausula had a place in the liturgy, so too might this next creative layer, the early Latin troping motet.

The motet *Ecclesie vox hodie* (524)/*Et florebit* (M53) from **W2**, fol. 160r–v, is based on clausula no. 102 from **W1** (= **F**, no. 141). Its tenor is taken from the *Alleluia: Justus germinabit sicut lilium: et florebit in aeternum ante Dominum* (The **just** shall **spring** as the **lily**: and shall **flourish forever** before the **Lord**), which is based on Hosea 14, a passage in which the Prophet urges Israel to repent of its sinful ways because in doing so it will deserve God's forgiveness and blessings. The new motet text utters the highlighted words of the chant in its unfolding:

> Let the voice of the Church today review the solemn feast days of the **just**; and let it gain aid by virtue and praise. Let the devotion of the faithful **spring** as the **lily** and let [the Church] examine itself in its own careful scrutiny: Love feeds Hope, which steadfastness of Faith fortifies; thus let this festival be pleasing to the **Lord**, and may it **flourish forever**.

Whereas some troping motets frame the motetus text with words from the tenor chant, this example interweaves words from the Alleluia verse into a moralizing message urging the Church to scrutinize its behavior carefully, to exemplify Faith, Hope, and Love, and thereby flourish under God's protection. This exegesis of the Alleluia verse reveals a knowledge of the book of Hosea beyond chapter 14, now applied to a Christian setting. The prophet Hosea challenged and condemned first the priests of Israel as responsible for their society's immoral behavior and self-centeredness, next its upper class, then all people. The motet text creator appropriates that message, directed here to the Christian Church, though it is unclear whether the message is aimed at the Church hierarchy or all Church members. The mention of Faith, Hope, and Love (Corinthians 14:14) gives a New Testament spin to Hosea's urging to address others' needs through just practices and social concerns. Not incidentally, the moralizing function of motets could prevail over the exegetical, in that a motetus text could provide a moral sermon on any feast day, regardless of the tenor incipit.

---

³ This motet, Mo 188, and its clausula relationship will be discussed further below.

This particular motet does not partake of another aspect of early motet composition, whereby the new Latin text bases its end rhymes on the final sound of the tenor incipit; in such cases, the tenor is the source not only of upper-voice semantic content, but also of its sonic content. As will become apparent, exploration of textual–sonic interplay was an important function of the motet throughout the thirteenth century.

The earliest layer of motets also reveals two-part French examples based on clausulae or on pre-existent Latin motets, that is, as French contrafacta. These French-texted motets are initially fewer in number than the Latin. Their vernacular texts point to a performance setting other than within the liturgy, a context about which Christopher Page offers plausible speculation. Referring to two-part French motets such as those in fascicle 10 of **W2**, Page suggests an attribution to the singers within the Notre Dame Cathedral chapter who did not have secure positions and sought additional work. These singers may have created the motets for the *caroles*, the 'public dances that were a conspicuous feature of festive life in northern France during the thirteenth century and which may have mediated between the market-place realities of festivity and the more sheltered milieu of the motet'.[4] Page's evidence is both internal and external. He notes that the texts of the two-part French motets stand apart from typical trouvère texts in their shorter length, light rhythmic character similar to popular dance songs or *caroles* (a term also used for the dances performed at the *caroles*), and their emphasis on the rhetoric of the pastourelle, which tells of a knight attempting to seduce a shepherdess, who outwits him. According to Page, whereas courtly love was the mainstay topic of the trouvères, hardly any named trouvères of substance wrote pastourelles before 1240–50. Thus he considers it unlikely that trouvères were responsible for the early two-part French motets. Notre Dame Cathedral chapter singers, who fell under the broader rubric of clerics, would be more likely candidates.[5]

To support his conjecture, Page cites contemporary documents. Some moralizing motet texts themselves comment on inappropriate behavior of clerics, including their fondness for *caroles*. Robert of Courson, who taught in Paris, compiled a *Summa* between 1208–12/13 in which he refers to masters of organum as performers of vocal polyphony. As clerics of lowly status, the singers could be hired by members of the senior clergy who wished to incorporate more elaborate music into the liturgies of their churches, but Courson also mentions that they sang for an audience of 'young and ignorant persons'; this phrase in particular suggests the attendees at the Parisian *caroles* of St. Germain-des-Prés.[6]

Turning to the mid-century, surviving evidence indicates that by 1230 a vogue for French motets was in full swing. Their rhetoric drew largely from the courtly love tradition (*fin'amor*) of the trouvères:[7] a man loves an unattainable lady of high status, which brings him pain, but also ennobles him. Significantly, this courtly rhetoric infiltrates devotional literature, such as *chansons pieuses* addressed to the Virgin Mary and devotional French motets.[8] This appropriation of courtly

---

[4] Page 1993a, 52 and throughout ch. 2. See also Page 1989, ch. 5, esp. 118–23.

[5] Page 1989, ch. 6, esp. 148–9.

[6] Page 1989, 145–7. Page also discusses Courson's commentary in 1993a, 57–64.

[7] Gaston Paris first employed 'courtly love' (*amour courtois*) in 1883 in the journal *Romania* (Paris 1883). The term is controversial today because Paris defined it in relation to Victorian mores and because it does not capture the entire range of attitudes toward love voiced in this repertory. Nonetheless, it remains a useful shorthand expression to refer to the conventional tropes of courtly love often featured so prominently in these motets.

[8] *Chansons pieuses* are collected in Järnström and Långfors 1910–27. Mark Everist has found some eighteen examples of devotional motets scattered among the major sources for the vernacular motet as well as in smaller sources. See Everist 1994, ch. 7, esp. 126–39.

love language outside the courtly sphere signals the lack of a clear line between sacred and secular realms of thought. A confluence of factors accounts for such melding.

Most importantly, the thirteenth century witnessed the rise of a vernacular literary tradition that began to rival Latin for the first time. To legitimize itself, this vernacular tradition imitated Latinate writing practices, in particular the hermeneutical modes of exegesis and the notion of *auctoritas*, the latter achieved by quotation and citation of established authors and their texts. An illustrative example, the *Roman de la Rose*, states its intention to both entertain and teach others about the Art of Love. Composed *c.* 1230 by Guillaume de Lorris, it was augmented *c.* 1275 by Jean de Meun, who appropriated the discourse of the academic prologue or *accessus ad auctores* to situate Ovid, one of the three canonical writers of Latin literature, as an *auctor* of Love. De Meun thus legitimized his own poetry at the same time that he created a tradition of vernacular commentary focused on Ovid's work.[9]

Leaving aside the *Roman de la Rose*, much vernacular literature of the thirteenth century is anonymous, attributed by scholars today to the clerical class, which included priests and members of the church hierarchy, secular clergy, as well as scholars connected to the academic professions, from university masters to students of local cathedral schools. As Jennifer Saltzstein states, 'It will be productive to envision these anonymous authors as part of a *writing* community united by common ways of learning, common skills, and a common body of knowledge'.[10] Stephen Jaeger goes a step further in his reference to the 'vast subterranean influence of worldly clerical culture' in vernacular works written by clerics who divided their lives between cathedral communities and secular courts.[11] Alastair Minnis likewise writes of a clerical culture working in the service of the secular elite.[12] The very existence of monumental motet collections such as the Montpellier (**Mo**) and Bamberg (**Ba**) Codices attests to a powerful secular elite. By commissioning these collections, the owners enhanced their own prestige while they simultaneously fostered a thriving genre.

Thus we can place the thirteenth-century French motet into a picture of authors grappling with the relationship between Latinate writing practices and a contemporary vernacular culture whose members were seeking affirmation of their own learnedness. French motets quote well-known refrains and proverbs as vernacular *auctoritates* on the subject of *fin'amor*. Likewise, they partake of the allegorical mode, particularly in cases where a text seemingly about courtly love invites an interpretation related to the Virgin Mary; that is, the text lays itself open to an imagined spiritual meaning.[13]

TEXTUAL MEANING

The *portare* family of motets offers a wide range of examples illustrating how motet creators engaged in the learned play of troping, citing authority, and inviting allegorical interpretation. In doing so, they take advantage of the inherent dual semantic resonances of the chant itself – Christological and Marian.

As mentioned above, the *Alleluia: Dulce lignum* is associated with two feasts of the Cross, its Invention and Exaltation. A contrafact chant version, *Alleluia: Dulcis virgo*, survives in two thirteenth-century northern French chant sources, in one case connected with the Octave of the

---

[9] Saltzstein, 2013b, 31. For a full discussion of academic prologues to Ovid, see Minnis 2001, ch. 1.

[10] Saltzstein 2013b, 38. Emphasis added.

[11] Jaeger 2001, vii.

[12] Minnis 2009, 12.

[13] Huot 1997 is a seminal study on the role of allegory in the thirteenth-century motet.

Table 6.1. Thirteenth-century motets based on the chant segment *portare* or *sustinere*

Mo		Ba	Cl	Other sources	
5, 81	*portare*	68 *portare*	53 *portare*		
5, 91	*portare*	51 *portare*	16 *sustinere*	**Bes**	text incipit
5, 96	*portare*				
5, 142	*portare*				
5, 148	*portare*			**Bes**	text incipit
5, 159	*portare*				
6, 233	*portare*			**Noailles** 77	*portare*
7, 257	*portare*			**Tu** 16	*portare*
7, 259	*portare*	56 *portare*		**Bes**	text incipit
7, 265	*portare*	81 *portare*		**Bes**	text incipit
7, 296	*portare*				
8, 305	*portare*				
8, 335	*portare*				
3, 41	*sustinere*	19 *portare*	18 *sustinere*	**MüB** 15	no tenor
				LoC 13	*sustinere*
				Bes	text incipit
6, 188	*sustine*			**W2** 257	*sustinere*
				Noailles 37	*portare*
				Roi 20	*portare*
			41 *portare*		
8, 322	[tenor]				

The first number in the left column refers to the fascicle number in Mo, while the second number follows the motet numbering in Tischler 1978. Numbers for other manuscripts refer to item numbers within the manuscript according to Reaney 1966.

Assumption of the Virgin Mary, in the other within a list of nine Marian Alleluias, but without feast association.[14] This Marian association of the *portare* chant segment is congruent with the extraordinary growth of the cult of the Virgin in Western Europe in the twelfth and thirteenth centuries, in part inspired by the writings of theologians such as St Bernard of Clairvaux (1090–1153), who identified her as the bride of the Song of Songs in the Old Testament. The Virgin was worshipped as the Bride of Christ, Personification of the Church, Queen of Heaven, and Intercessor for the salvation of humankind.[15] This increased devotion to the Virgin Mary is evident in the Latin texts of the thirteenth-century motet corpus. Furthermore, as mentioned earlier, Mary is the addressee of devotional French works such as *chansons pieuses*, which appropriate courtly love language.[16]

[14] Pesce 1997, 39.
[15] French cathedrals were often dedicated to 'Our Lady', and many cities placed themselves under her protection.
[16] Everist (1994, 131) states: 'A strikingly large proportion of *chansons pieuses* are paraphrases of *chansons courtois*, *chansons de femme* and *chansons d'ami*'.

These combined factors open the possibility of reading French motet texts, nominally about a courtly lady, as allegories of the Virgin Mary, particularly in motets based on *portare*, with its Christological and Marian associations.

The motet family based on *portare* or *sustinere* consists almost exclusively of newly composed motets, with only one, **Mo** 188, related to a clausula. Table 6.1 lays out the total picture of surviving *portare/sustinere* motets, with **Mo** containing the largest number, followed by **Ba** and **Cl**.[17] The following discussion offers an interpretation of the textual meaning in six of the motets.

Mo 41, *Au doz mois de mai* (275)/*Crux, forma penitentie* (274)/*Sustinere*, and related versions represent the only *portare* motet that explicitly includes at least one Latin-texted voice treating the subject of Christ's crucifixion. For all versions of this motet, the motetus text, a string of appellations to the Cross, tropes the Latin chant text by incorporating the highlighted words:[18]

> Crux, forma penitentie,
> gratie
> **clavis, clava** peccati, venie
> vena, radix **ligni** iusticie,
> via vite, vexillum glorie,
> sponsi lectus in meridie,
> lux plenarie
> nubem luens tristicie,
> serenum conscientie:
> Hanc homo portet,
> ha[n]c se confortet,
> crucem oportet,
> si vis [lucis] vere
> gaudia **sustinere**.

The Cross, shape of penance, key of grace, staff of sin, vein of pardon, root of the tree of justice, path of life, banner of glory, the Bridegroom's bed at mid-day, light that totally dispels the cloud of sadness, the bright sky of conscience – let mankind carry it, comfort itself with it. You must bear the Cross, if you desire the joys of the true light.[19]

In terms of surviving triplum texts, **Ba** 19 and **MüB** 15 each present a different Latin text – respectively *Cruci Domini sit cuntis horis laus parata* (277) and *Arbor nobilis super alias venerabilis* (276) – both of which join the motetus in addressing the Cross. In **Ba** 19 the two upper voices utter the syllable 'Cru-' together at the outset and 'sustinere' at the close to create a rhetorical frame that highlights the motet's troping function. **MüB** 15's triplum text also ends with 'sustinere', though its utterance does not coincide exactly with the motetus's. Though both Latin triplum texts elaborate the chant's message, neither plays upon its exact words to the degree evident in the motetus.

17 Mo contains a total of sixteen *portare/sustinere* motets, distributed among its fascicles as follows: fasc. 3, one; fasc. 5, six; fasc. 6, two; fasc. 7, four; fasc. 8, three. Ba features five and Cl four examples, with at most one or two appearances in other sources, not including the no longer surviving Bes, which contained the text incipit of five *portare* motets. Cl 41 has no concordance, therefore bringing the total of *portare/sustinere* motets to seventeen.

18 The line 'Hanc homo portet' also is possibly a reference to *portare*, because of the fact that chant sources fluidly associate this chant segment with *portare* and *sustinere*.

19 English translations of Mo motets here and throughout are adapted from the fourth volume of Tischler 1978.

Mo 41's triplum, by contrast, offers a French pastourelle in which the author has happened upon a shepherdess who laments the loss of her lover Robin. The author overhears the shepherdess uttering these words: 'Robin, doz amis, perdu voz ai; a grant dolor de vos me departirai' ('Robin, my sweet beloved, I lost you; in great grief will I take leave of you'). In the context of the chant incipit, motetus text, and the fact that these cited words about losing a loved one are musically highlighted (to be discussed below), the triplum may be interpreted allegorically as referring to the sorrow of loss experienced by Mary and others who witnessed Christ's crucifixion on the Cross. Thus, all three surviving triplum texts in some way engage with the Christological resonance of the tenor chant.

Mo 81, *Ja pour mal, que puisse avoir* (278)/*Hé, desloiaus mesdisant* (279)/*Portare*, a three-voice French motet, also deals with suffering and is laden with multivalent meanings. In the triplum, a male expresses the pain of love, then assures the lady that he will willingly suffer for her; in the motetus, he addresses first his slanderers, then informs the lady directly that he will not abandon her because of the pain he experiences at the hands of the slanderers. A different version of this motet appears in **Ba** 68: the motetus carries a Latin text about St. Nicholas fasting, *Nicholaus igitur plenus gracia* (280),[20] while the triplum offers a different French text (and music) in which the male speaks of the pain caused by the slanderers who have hemmed him in so that he cannot go to his lady, *Pour celi que j'aim et pris* (281). While framed within typical courtly love rhetoric, the sorrowing male lover of these texts also invites an allegorical interpretation as a spiritual lover in the tradition of the Song of Songs, in which the bridegroom who longs for his bride is like the soul longing for union with God. More specific to the Cross associations of the tenor, the suffering lover could also, in the manner of parody, evoke the Christological Man of Sorrows, who loved then suffered when he was rejected by his people, as prophesized in Isaiah 53.[21] From the thirteenth century on, the Man of Sorrows developed as a devotional image of contemplation: it depicted Christ, usually naked above the waist, with the wounds of his Passion prominently displayed on his hands and side, often crowned with the Crown of Thorns. In light of this representational development, the suffering lover of the motet could have been understood by its listeners on at least three levels: as a man reacting to unrequited love by an earthly woman, as a spiritual lover in the tradition of the Song of Songs, and as the Christological Man of Sorrows.

Of the *portare* motets that invite Marian interpretations, only one, **Mo** 322, *Marie assumptio* (931)/*Huius chori suscipe cantica* (932)/*Tenor*, alludes directly to Mary's Assumption, the feast associated with the chant.[22] Yet motet creators may have intended French texts nominally about the courtly lady as allegories of Marian worship. Among the possibilities, a simple allegorical reading allows thoughts of Mary when the poet praises the beauty of an earthly woman using attributes usually applied to Mary. Such descriptions can, in the case of *portare* motets, also play into the tenor association with the Assumption, whose liturgy draws heavily on the Song of Songs with its praises of the beloved's beauty.

In Mo 322, both upper voices directly relate to Mary's Assumption. The triplum opens with these lines extolling her new position in heaven:

[20] This text deserves further attention for possible sexual connotations.

[21] The expression 'Man of Sorrows' is taken from Isaiah 53:3: 'He is despised and rejected of men, a man of sorrows and acquainted with grief; and like one from whom men hide their face He was despised, and we did not esteem Him'. Mark, Luke, and John reflected back on Isaiah's prophecy of the Messiah in their descriptions of Christ's arrest, suffering and death: 'everything the prophets have written about the Son of Man will be fulfilled'.

[22] The sole manuscript source, **Mo**, does not identify the tenor chant by name, and only the first twelve of its twenty-one pitches match the *portare* melody.

Marie assumptio afficiat gaudio filios ecclesie
que honore regio ac mundi dominio decorator hodie
ac glorie pari gradu filio consortio celestis milicie

May the assumption of Mary put joy in the hearts of the children of the Church;
she is adorned today with royal honor and worldly dominion
and with a level of glory equal to the Son's in the fellowship of the heavenly hosts.

These lines trope Christian beliefs grounded in Scripture. Line 1 acknowledges that Christians experienced joy and hope by reflecting on Mary's Assumption: she symbolized their trust in being lifted up and united with Christ, summed up in 1 Thess. 4:17: 'Then we which are alive and remain shall be caught up together with them (those dead in Christ) in the clouds, to meet the Lord in the air: and so shall we ever be with the Lord'. Line 3's explicit reference to Mary sharing in her Son's glory in heaven relates to the Scriptural promise that those who share in the sufferings of Christ will share in his glory, captured in Romans 8: 16–17: 'The Spirit itself beareth witness with our spirit, that we are the children of God: And if children, then heirs; heirs of God, and joint-heirs with Christ; if so be that we suffer with him, that we may be also glorified together'. Christ's suffering, even if not mentioned explicitly, is a subtext within the motet because the tenor *portare* also relates to the Cross. Mary was a central figure at the Crucifixion: she stood at the foot of the Cross, experiencing her Son's suffering vicariously. If a listener made this connection, they could have found hope in the thought that their own suffering could bring them into the heavenly union symbolized by Mary's Assumption.

In the motetus text, on the other hand, a chorus of voices addresses Mary in the familiar topos of man's intercessor, empowered through her Assumption into heaven: 'Tu, medica suavis peccatori atque fori celestis sindica' ('You, sweet physician of the sinner and his advocate in the heavenly court'). The chorus of voices requests that she:

nos amori regnantis applica
et abdica de inferiori,
ut requie fruamur celica.

recommend us to the Ruler's love
and disown us from the devil,
that we may enjoy heavenly peace.

The speakers acknowledge Mary's intermediary role in helping sinners resist the power of the devil and in bringing God's love upon them. They focus on what Mary can do for humankind, rather than on what human beings can do for themselves. Whereas the triplum text leaves unexpressed a hope for man attaining what Mary achieved through her Assumption, the motetus text ends with that wish: 'that we may enjoy heavenly peace'. Both texts are ultimately about hope epitomized through the figure of Mary.

Mo 265, *Mout me fu grief li departir* (297)/*Robin m'aime, Robin m'a* (298)/*Portare*, invites three possible interpretations, one Christological, one related solely to Mary, and one to the Cross and Mary.[23] The motetus text and music are taken from Adam de la Halle's *Le Jeu de Robin et de Marion*, a pastourelle expressing the simple love of the shepherdess Marion for the shepherd Robin. The triplum text offers the rhetoric of the courtly lover who grieves for his departed lady, a distressed man in contrast to the happy woman of the motetus text. Taken alone, the triplum's

---

[23] The following interpretation of this work is based on my 1997 article, 42–4.

expression of 'pained love' and 'languishing for love' could, as was true for **Mo** 81, lead to reflections on spiritual love in the tradition of the Song of Songs, or the suffering lover could evoke in the manner of parody the Christological Man of Sorrows. But in view of the joyful motetus text, one also has to consider a tradition that viewed the Cross itself as paradoxically the site of suffering *and* joy – through Christ's mortification, man's spiritual redemption was made possible. The motet's projection of both suffering and joy may relate to this tradition.

A Marian interpretation of the motet might be triggered in several ways, most directly through the triplum's list of attributes for the coveted woman: 'blanche et vermellete comme rose par desus lis' ('white and vermillion as rose set against lily'), 'blanchete comme flour de lis' ('white as a lily'). Because the lily and rose are traditional symbols of Mary, a circle of associations occurs: a woman's earthly appearance leads to thoughts of Mary, which in turn dignifies the woman. Likewise, mention of the woman's worthiness and goodness, in language reminiscent of the Virgin, 'Dame de valour', invites an allegorical interpretation of the earthly woman as Mary, further dignifying the woman as an object of worship. Another allegorical Marian reading arises when the male lover of the triplum mentions the departure of his sweetheart, which grieved him deeply. If we consider the possible liturgical connection with the Assumption, the departure could be interpreted as signifying Mary's assumption into heaven. On the other hand, the appearance of 'Marion' in the motetus text may be a playful allusion to Mary, who figured prominently in the French imagination throughout the twelfth and thirteenth centuries.[24]

Finally, if the chant summoned dual images, of Mary bearing Christ in the womb and as an infant, and of Christ's crucifixion, the composer may have intended to bring into focus two emotions experienced by Mary, one joyful and life-giving, the other sorrowing. As mentioned above, Mary was, after all, a central figure at the Crucifixion. Similarly, if the composer had in mind the feasts of the Cross and the Assumption, two opposing emotions of Mary would again come into play, her sorrowing posture at Christ's crucifixion and her rejoicing reunion with the King of Heaven. These paired emotions of Mary seem significant in view of the upper-voice texts which contrast joy and pain, fulfillment and loss, in both cases with the woman in a central role.

Our next examples focus on the rhetorical role of refrains within thirteenth-century motets. The origins of refrains have engendered much discussion, with some scholars arguing for their connection to a lost, oral song tradition, the *rondet de carole*, which accompanied round dances at the festive *caroles* mentioned earlier in this chapter. This view holds that the refrains, as a vestige of that tradition, passed orally into the written contexts where they now survive. Among the scholars who have problematized this view, Jennifer Saltzstein has examined the entire intertextual refrain corpus in relationship to identified markers of oral transmission in comparable repertories. She concludes that their distribution patterns do not indicate a strong connection between the intertextual refrain and the *rondet*. Furthermore, that the refrain melodies' identities are remarkably precise across their sources suggests they may have circulated as written artifacts.[25] Saltzstein's study lends weight to other scholars' conjecture that some refrains were newly composed 'to look and function like quotations but may not actually have been drawn from a prior source'.[26] Despite the inconclusive origins of many textual fragments that are labe-

---

[24] See Warner 1976, particularly 'Part Five Intercessor', 273–331, which includes discussion of folktales and miracle stories in which the interceding Virgin plays an active, even physical, role in solving the immediate problems of her devotees.

[25] Saltzstein 2013b, ch. 1.

[26] Saltzstein 2013b, 12. Saltzstein refers to work by Paul Zumthor, Eglal Doss-Quinby, Maureen Boulton, and Ardis Butterfield.

led 'refrains' in the scholarly literature, we can reasonably conclude that they were meant to give the impression of quoted materials. Thus, refrains relate to the Latin learned tradition of citing *auctoritas* and, as such, function as a rhetorical device for proving one's learnedness on a subject, including the Art of Love.

Mo 91, *Ne sai tant Amors server* (283)/*Ja de boine amor* (282)/*Portare*, presents two final refrains simultaneously. One relates to a vernacular translation of Ovid's *Ars amatoria*, *L'Art d'amours*, a translation supplemented with lengthy interpretive glosses that include many refrains. The refrain that concludes **Mo** 91's triplum (vdB 639) appears in Book 1 of *L'Art d'amours*, whose composition likely dates to the first third of the thirteenth century.[27] The translation itself is a testament to the vernacular impetus to build upon the *auctoritas* of the ancients, though some scholars have argued that the translation and glosses even compete with the source text for the reader's attention.[28]

The triplum's refrain occurs at the end of a male's complaint about his difficulties sleeping at night, caused by the scorn of a lady.[29] The words that precede the refrain carry clear sexual undertones: 'quant je m'i doi reposer, ne me sai de cele part torner, que penser ne m'i face fremir' ('when I need to rest, I don't know on which side to turn so that my thoughts don't make me tremble'). The male then utters refrain vdB 639: '*qu'eles me tienent en mon lit, amors, quant je me doi dormir*' ('*This is how Love treats me at night, when I should be sleeping*'). (Here and for the remainder of the chapter, quoted italicized text indicates a refrain or a portion thereof.)

Within *L'Art d'amours*, this refrain concludes a gloss of a passage that advises a man how to court a woman and get her to respond to his advances, with particular focus on his appearance. Ovid states that a male lover should be 'pale' or 'white' because the woman will believe his discoloration results from his pining away for her (*Ars amatoria*, 1: 715–30). The following excerpt is taken from the *L'Art d'amours* gloss of this passage, which begins with another sleep-related refrain, vdB 535 (lines 2056–66):

> Et de ce chantent li jouvencel:
> *Dieux! Je ne puis la nuit dormir,*
> *Li maulx d'amer m'esveille!*
> Pour ce moult vault a estre pales et descoulourés, car il semble que
> ce soit des maux d'amours, et lors en ont elles pitié, et lors y mettent
> elles leur entente et y pensent et de nuit et de jours, et puis qu'elles
> y commencent a penser, li plus fort en est fait, car quant plus pense
> on a amours, et plus fait amours grief assaulx. Et de ce chantent elles
> en leur vois:
> *Elles m'y tiennent en mon lit,*
> *Amours, quant je me doy dormir.*

The youth sing of this:
God! I cannot sleep at night, the pangs of love wake me up!

---

[27] Roy (1974, 56–7) states that the first two books were written after 1214–15, but within the first third of the thirteenth century, while the third book was written after 1268, but before the thirteenth century ended.

[28] Saltzstein (2013b, 44–5) summarizes these viewpoints.

[29] Saltzstein (2013a, 353) discusses four intertextual refrains shared between *L'Art d'amours* and the motet repertory, all of which deal 'either literally or as a euphemism, with the concept of sleep'. Her discussion includes those in **Mo** 91. Prof. Salztstein and I reached our conclusions about **Mo** 91 independently. I am grateful for her sharing her work prior to its publication in the *Musica Disciplina* 2013 issue that appeared in early 2017.

Because of this it is worth much to be pale and discolored, for it seems that it is from the pangs of love, and then the women feel pity because of it. Then the women meditate upon it, and they think about it night and day. When they begin to think about it, the most can be made of it. For the more one thinks of love, the more love makes a serious assault. The women sing of this in their way:

This is how Love treats me at night, when I should be sleeping.[30]

This gloss of Ovid's *Ars amatoria* emphasizes that a woman wants to be desired, and can be convinced of a male's heartfelt love for her if she sees signs of his distress, specifically his 'pale and discolored' countenance, which the glosser attributes to lack of sleep over her. In response, the woman is, in turn, 'assaulted' by love, which keeps her up when she should be sleeping. We hear two statements of love's sleep-depriving effect, the second assuredly in a female voice, balancing the male voice that opens the passage. In short, the translator/glosser conveyed a message that men and women can be similarly affected by love.[31]

Can one plausibly conjecture that the motet creator knew the refrain through familiarity with *L'Art d'amours*? Manuscript evidence is insufficient to make this determination, given that the motet is transmitted in multiple sources believed to have been copied after 1260, while *L'Art d'amours* survives only in fifteenth-century manuscripts. Bruno Roy has dated Book 1 of *L'Art d'amours* to the first third of the thirteenth century based on his study of its contents, including the texts it incorporated and those it apparently influenced.[32] Relying on Roy's dating, it seems reasonable to assume that the motet creator could have accessed the refrain through *L'Art d'amours*. If that was the case, the motet creator transferred the refrain from a female to male speaker; rather than adopt *L'Art d'amours*'s equal attention to men and women's experience of love, the motet creator instead projects the more typical courtly love rhetoric of the man who suffers the pains of love.

A second refrain (vdB 538) concludes the motetus, following a male speaker's assertion that his heart will never abandon his loved one, though she gives him no joy: '*Hé Dieus, la verrai je ja, la bele qui mon cuer a?*' ('*O God, will I ever see her, the fair one who possesses my heart?*') This widely circulated refrain presents a more typical *fin'amor* sentiment of willing suffering in the name of Love,[33] versus the more physically explicit complaint of the triplum refrain. Thus, within this one

---

[30] The French text is taken from Roy 1974, 152–3; the English translation is adapted from Blonquist 1987, 67.

[31] In reference to the audience of *L'Art d'amours*, Baldwin (1994, 23) suggests that the clerical translator of *L'Art d'amours* was attempting to reach an audience at the border of the clerical and aristocratic worlds. Though he makes no explicit mention of women being present, one can entertain that possibility by following his other claims: First, the audiences for romances would have included knights and their ladies (35). Second, the commentary at times approaches the diction of the fabliaux, which themselves were transmitted in late thirteenth-century manuscripts alongside romances and thus could have reached the same audiences (42). Third, by extension, one might argue that the commentary, partaking of fabliaux-like diction, was also presented to the audiences of romances – knights and their ladies. Saltzstein (2013b, 44–5) summarizes scholars' views that *L'Art d'amours* softened much of Ovid's misogyny, lessening the condemnation of women, in order to reach a broader audience in which women would be present.

[32] Roy 1974, 54–9.

[33] This refrain text is circulated in thirteen extant sources: aside from its usage in the motet under consideration, which is transmitted in four sources (of which **Bes** contains only a text incipit), it also appears in five sources of the narrative *Méliacin ou le Cheval de fust* written by Girart d'Amiens in 1285, as well as in songs and motets within chansonniers. The refrain melody that appears in this motet (**Mo** 91) is also found on fol. 189v in the chansonnier fr.845, dated to 1270–80.

motet, a listener would hear two aspects of the unrequited love topos. In the case of the triplum refrain, the motet creator may have been tapping into the specific authority of the *Ars amatoria*, while the motetus refrain seems to arise from a broader vernacular literary culture.[34]

Mo 188, *Douce dame sans pitié*, a two-voice French motet, is the sole *portare* motet that possesses a clausula version, found only in **StV** (dating from the second half of the thirteenth century or possibly around 1300).[35] Since 2011, the scholarly consensus holds that the clausulae in **StV** with accompanying vernacular motet incipits in fact represented motet transcriptions.[36] The motet's courtly love rhetoric is typical, ending with the refrain (vdB 623): '*Douz cuers, alegiés mes maus, qu'il ne m'ocient!*' ('*Tender heart, relieve my suffering, so that it may not kill me*'). This refrain, without music, also appears in a spiritual treatise, the vernacular *Le livre amoretes*, which speaks of one's hope in Christ. Anne Ibos-Augé identifies this work as 'a short XIIIth century anonymous devotional treatise'.[37] The treatise survives in two copies: **F-Pn f. fr. 23111**, which dates from the end of the thirteenth century, and **F-Pn lat. 13091**, which was assembled in the fourteenth-century in the Benedictine Abbey of Saint-Thierry. Refrain vdB 623 appears only in the second source. Based on her initial study of this devotional treatise, Ibos-Augé argues that its author drew upon numerous lyric fragments, most belonging to the corpus of French refrains, as part of his didactic intention of revealing to his reader parallels between courtly and divine love. Significantly, the author may have taken some of the refrains from motets, as in the present instance, where, aside from the vdB 623's occurrence in the second *Livre* source, it appears only in the motets *Douce dame sans pitié* (**Mo** 188) and *Un chant renvoisié et bel* (926)/*Decantatur*.[38] Given the refrain's lack of concordances outside the motet repertory, the creator of **Mo** 188 may have included this instance of direct discourse to give the impression of quoted materials, that is, a pseudo-refrain: because it sounds like a refrain, it was capable of suggesting his learnedness. In any case, if the *Livre* author took vdB 623 from the motet *Douce dame sans pitié*, we gain an expanded view of how motets functioned within the learned culture of the thirteenth century: the motet genre could itself be the source of refrain material for a vernacular devotional work.

TEXTUAL PROJECTION

Given that the thirteenth-century motet displayed its creators' command of exegesis and appreciation for *auctoritas*, one would expect that words and phrases related to the tenor and/or upper-

---

[34] Salzstein (2013a, 364–5) notes that melody of the second line of the triplum refrain 639 largely doubles the tenor or motetus melody notes. Because the triplum refrain 639 is coincident with motetus refrain 538, Salzstein concludes that the motet's creator decided to set up a two-part scaffolding between tenor and motetus, thereby 'limiting the options available for a more independent triplum melody in the final phrase' (365). Although a plausible explanation, it does not support Saltzstein's two-part conclusion: 'the triplum refrain was a textual, not a musical, quotation, another factor that suggests that *L'Art d'amours* was the motet maker's source' (366). The melody of the first line of refrain 639 unfolds largely independent of the motetus and tenor melodies, and therefore could have been quoted from another source.

[35] Dating is according to Büttner 2011, 41. Fred Büttner discusses the relationship between the StV clausula and the motet version; see Büttner 1999, 255–61 and 323, and Büttner 2011, 366–70.

[36] Büttner confirmed Yvonne Rokseth's suggestion that the StV clausulae were motet transcriptions; see Büttner 2011 and Rokseth 1935–9, 4: 70–1.

[37] Ibos-Augé forthcoming.

[38] Three other manuscript sources for *Douce dame sans pitié* are considered early witnesses to the motet: W2, Noailles, and Roi (see Table 6.1). *Un chant renvoisié et bel/Decantatur* is found in ArsB, fol. 14r–v.

voice text rhetoric would project clearly. Achieving clear projection presents a challenge within the three-voice motet, where two texts occur simultaneously. Some performers today employ layered performance as one way to ensure that the textual message is heard: motetus with tenor, triplum with tenor, then all together. But a survey of the *portare* motets reveals that some motet creators carefully positioned important words and phrases to be heard clearly even in the three-voice texture. A listener familiar with the tenor chant and courtly love rhetoric could thus easily tune in to the highlighted upper-voice language snippets.

Ba 19, with its two Latin texts on the subject of the Cross, illustrates such careful textual positioning.[39] The motetus incorporates words found in the tenor chant: an ascending melodic gesture projects 'clavis' ('key'), 'clava' ('staff') in a register above the triplum; 'ligni' ('of the tree') begins to sound during a rest in the triplum. As discussed above, simultaneous utterances frame the motet: at the outset, both voices address the Cross on the syllable 'Cru-', and at the end, both sing 'sustinere'. Other key troping words not found in the tenor chant text are exposed via a rest in the other upper voice or via high registeral placement: e.g. 'penitentie' ('of penance'), 'peccati' ('of sin'), 'peccata' ('sins'), 'ac laudandum hoc lignum' ('praiseworthy is this tree').

Example 6.2. Text Setting in Ba 19, perfections 34–45

The most striking musical setting of rhetorically important words occurs in the triplum at perfections 38–45 (see Example 6.2): 'carne sua mortificata' ('by his body given over to death') ascends well above the motetus by step; the line then leaps in four of its next five intervals, an atypical melodic unfolding in this genre. The long durations given to the five successive syllables of 'mortificata' also draw attention to this key word.[40] Significantly, the creators of the other two versions of this triplum likewise set this musical phrase with text possessing strong rhetorical impact: in MüB 15, the text reads, 'Pie relevavit sanguine' ('Piously he raised [them] up by his blood'); and in Mo 41, 'Robin, doz amis, perdu voz ai' ('Robin, my sweet beloved, I lost you'). The French text, labeled a refrain by van den Boogaard (vdB 1628), appears only in this motet complex, suggesting another possible instance of a motet creator writing direct discourse in the manner of a refrain to display his learnedness. Whether a true refrain or pseudo-refrain, this address to Robin highlights a sense of loss that is compatible with the tenor association of the Cross. Regardless of which version came first, the texting of this phrase reveals thoughtful creative responses to a distinctive musical phrase.

---

[39] See Pesce 1986, 96–7, 100–1, and 105, which treats the text setting in Ba 19 and other versions of this motet.

[40] The following phrase 'que in cruce fuit sacrificata' likewise stays in a high register, and, like 'mortificata', 'sacrificata' unfolds its five syllables as long notes (rendered as dotted quarter notes in Tischler's edition).

TEXTUAL SOUND EXPLORATION

In her case studies of some early clausula-based Latin motets, Catherine A. Bradley has revealed upper-voice texts which emphasize the sonic content of the tenor chant fragment. For instance, in *Alpha, bovi, et leoni* (762)/*Domino* (**F**, fol. 407r–v), lines 1–8 of the motetus end with the '-i' rhyme, and lines 9–15 with the '-o' rhyme, thus 'mimicking the succession of vowels at the end of the tenor word *Domino*'.[41] In another motet, *Christe via veritas* (516)/*[Adiu]tori[um]* (**F**, fol. 404r–v), the predominance of '-uto' and '-ium' rhymes 'echoes the complete word of the tenor chant on which the motet is based: **Adiutorium**'. Moreover, the motet maintains a correspondence between its music and the sonic features of its text: recurring musical shapes are invariably matched by recurring phonetic sounds, both at phrase endings and in cases of internal rhymes. In Bradley's words, 'this motet also exploits the ability of a text to reinforce and enrich aspects of the inherited musical material with another layer of sound patterns'.[42]

The interest in sonic exploration exemplified in the early clausula-based motets continues throughout the thirteenth-century. A *portare* three-voice motet from the end of the century, **Mo** 305, *Mout ai longuement Amour* (301)/*Li dous maus d'amer* (302)/*Portare*, reveals a French equivalent to the Latin tradition of having upper-voice texts incorporate sounds from a Latin text incipit. Van den Boogaard identifies a motetus refrain, vdB 626, '*Douce est li maus d'amer*' ('Sweet is the pain of love'). This phrase does not survive outside the motet, which itself has no concordance, so its status as an inherited refrain is open to question. The so-called refrain captures a common sentiment of courtly love lyrics, which the creator also articulates at the motetus beginning but with a different word order, 'Li dous maus d'amer'. Pertinent to sonic exploration, the refrain rhyme '-er' emerges as the predominant end rhyme of the motet as a whole: of 31 total lines, '-er' appears eight times, while the next most prominent rhyme, '-our', sounds five times. 'Amour' occurs in the opening lines of the triplum, 'Mout ai longuement Amour de fin cuer loiaument servi' ('I have long and loyally served Love with a true heart'), and as the final word of the motetus, 'quant a li requis s'amour' ('when I asked her for her love'). Thus, in this late thirteenth-century motet, two key words of the textual rhetoric, 'amer' and 'amour', generate a predominant sound scheme for the motet, with the two rhymes appearing simultaneously in the final sonority, 'remu**er**' against 's'**amour**'.

Another *portare* three-voice French motet, **Mo** 148, *Si com[e] aloie jouer* (288)/*Deduisant com fins amourous* (289)/*Portare* attracts attention to its sonic interplay (see Table 6.2). Its triplum incorporates three instances of direct speech; the first two present a single refrain, and the third instance presents two refrains (see the italicized text). All but vdB 1489 appear elsewhere and therefore are proper refrains. vdB 1489 occurs three-quarters of the way through the triplum, but also at the end of the motetus, and thus unifies the upper voices. The line endings of the three proper refrains unfold as follows: 1. vdB 532, *aler, ami, merci*; 2. vdB 750, *trovees*; 4. vdB 1781, *le voi*. These three refrains share an end rhyme '-er' (rhyme a) or its pronounced assonant equivalent, '-ees' or '-oi', the only exception being the first refrain's '-i' ending for its second and third lines (rhyme b). The sonic connection of the three proper refrains suggests that the creator of **Mo** 148 may have adopted them not only for their expressed sentiment, but also because of their unifying rhyme sound.[43] In turn, that sound dominates the triplum rhyme scheme as a whole.

---

[41] Bradley 2012, 151–7.

[42] Bradley 2012, 162 (full discussion 157–62).

[43] For a discussion of the refrains and their transmission history, see Pesce 2013.

Table 6.2. Poetic form in **Mo 148**

triplum line		vdB refrain	rhyme	syllable count	number of perfections
1	Si com[e] aloie jouer		a	7	4
2	l'autrier, trois dames trovai.		*a*	7	4
3	L'une s'esmut de cuer gai		*a*	7	4
4	a chanter:		a	3	2
5	'Dieus, je n'i os aler	532	a	6	4
6	a mon ami!	532	b	4	2
7	Coment avrai merci?'	532	b	6	3
8	Puis a dit tout sanz delai:		a	7	4
9	'Fines amouretes ai trovees,	750	a'	9	6
10	bien seront gaitees'.		a'	5	4
11	Puis a dit de cuer joious:		c	7	4
12	'Pleüst a Dieu, que chascune de nous	1489	c	10	4
13	tenist la pieau de son mari jalous	1489	c	10	4
14	et mes doz [amis] fust avec moi!		a	9	5
15	Touz li cuers me rit de joie, quant le voi;	1781	a	11	6
16	du tout a lui m'otroi'.		a	6	3

motetus line					
1	Deduisant		d	3	2
2	com fins amourous,		c	5	3
3	m'en aloie tout pensant;		d	7	4
4	trois dames trovai parlant		d	7	4
5	et disant,		d	3	2
6	que trop sunt envieus		c	6	3
7	lor mari et trop gaitant.		d	7	4
8	L'u[n]ne dit en sospirant:		d	7	4
9	'Duel ai trop grant,		d	4	2
10	quant si au desoz		c	5	3
11	nos vont nos maris menant;		d	7	4
12	or voisent bien espiant,		d	7	4
13	nos les ferons cous;		c	5	3
14	a leur couz		c	3	2
15	nos irons jouant.		d	5	3
16	Dieus les face mourir toz		c	7	4
17	a no vivant!		d	4	2
18	S'em proi a genouz:		c	5	2
19	Pleüst a Diu, que chascune de nous	1489	c	10	4
20	tenist la piau de son mari jalouz!'	1489	c	10	4

An italicized rhyme is an assonant equivalent to, or a variant spelling of, the rhyme with the same letter. A rhyme accompanied by a prime indicates a feminine ending.

The refrain-like utterance (vdB 1489) found only in this motet, '*Pleüst a Dieu, que chascune de nous, tenist la piau de son mari jalous!*' ('*May it please God that each of us have the skin of her jealous husband*'), presents the rhyme '-ous' (rhyme c).[44] As Table 6.2 indicates, while rhyme c occurs in the triplum only in lines 11–13, it sounds in nine of the twenty lines of the motetus (a tally that includes all assonant equivalents and variant spellings: '-eus', '-ouz', and '-oz'), while the other eleven lines use '-ant' (rhyme d). Rhymes d and c figure in the opening two lines: 'Deduis**ant** com fins amour**ous**' ('Amusing myself like a true lover'). Regardless of whether the motet creator first penned the opening lines or the pseudo-refrain, the '-ous' sound is a unifying feature of the motetus text, and a linking feature between the two upper-voice texts.

Aside from the refrain-derived rhymes that dominate this motet, it reveals another aspect of sonic play whereby the two upper voices pronounce certain sounds either simultaneously or in quick succession.[45] Among the many instances are these three: in perfections 19–20, one hears '*ami*' against '*mari*'; in perfections 21–2, '*gai-*' on the pitches *c-b* is followed immediately by '*-vrai*' on the higher pitches *d-c*; in perfection 42, the end rhyme '*cous*' sounds against the phrase opening word '*Pleüst*'.[46]

MUSICAL EXPLORATION

Newly composed thirteenth-century motets often explore two musical aspects: 1. the tonal possibilities of the foundational tenor chant segments, whereby a given tone within the chant is enhanced by sonority choice, intervallic progressions, and other devices; 2. large-scale structure, including imposing a secular form on the motet as a whole, or determining a motet's structure through the rhythmic organization of the tenor chant fragment and its repetitions. Through these explorations, motets function as musical, as well as textual, proving grounds for their creators.

The *portare* chant segment has two tonal emphases (see Example 6.1): *c* opens the segment, *G* ends it; *c* appears a total of five times, *G* a total of four. My recent study of three *portare* motets in the last two fascicles of Montpellier, **Mo** 296, 305, and 335, concluded the following: 'Despite the limited harmonic vocabulary and registral span of this repertory, a composer could and did mold a motet in subtle ways to enhance *portare*'s C and G foci, treating them relatively equally or sublimating one to the other'.[47] This study also shows how the creator of **Mo** 296 went so far as to truncate the chant segment, producing an *F* ending that is cleverly prepared in the course of the motet. In other words, the creator carefully diverted the listener from an expected *G* ending. To what degree is tonal exploration evident in earlier motets based on *portare*?

For the three late *portare* motets (**Mo** 296, 305, and 335), directed progressions contribute strongly to a sense of tonal emphasis. 'Directed progression' refers to an interval succession that can be perceived as moving towards a goal, as having a tendency to resolution: it involves stepwise contrary motion from an imperfect consonance (third or sixth) to a perfect consonance (unison, fifth, or octave). Based on her observations of fourteenth-century repertory, Sarah Fuller devised this terminology,[48] which I in turn adopted in my studies of thirteenth-century motets, where the

[44] Table 6.2 reproduces the text as it appears in **Mo** 148, where the triplum and motetus offer variant spellings of vdB 1489.
[45] See Suzannah Clark's chapter in the present volume for a discussion of instances of shared words, and even entire lines of poetry, in the upper voices of two **Mo** motets.
[46] An edition of **Mo** 148 appears in Tischler 1978, 2: 168–70.
[47] Pesce 2018, 253.
[48] Fuller 1986 and Fuller 1992b.

same tendency progressions are essential to the tonal design of each work.[49]

More detailed observations on interval succession are germane to the present discussion of tonal organization in earlier *portare* motets:

1. 6→8 and 3→5 progressions, by contrary stepwise motion outward, present the strongest syntax of tendency followed by resolution, though other compositional factors such as rhythm and motivic usage can affect the degree of closure. 3→1 progressions reveal contrary motion inward, and project a lesser degree of closure than 6→8 and 3→5.

2. Directed progressions can be further distinguished according to whether the stepwise motion is by whole or half step. Half-step motion creates a stronger tendency to resolution than does a whole step.

3. The music also reveals interval successions in which one voice moves by step, the other by leap, such as 6→5 and 3→8; depending on context, some instances of 6→5 and 3→8 may be perceived as having some degree of tendency, but with an attenuated effect in comparison to 6→8 and 3→5.

4. Perfect to perfect intervals, which have no tendency and are thus neutral, also occur in this repertory.

Finally, directed progressions can vary in their impact according to how many voices articulate the progression, the duration of the phrase ending or following rest, voice-leading and registral considerations (including voicing of sonorities), as well as linear motion in one voice which overlaps a phrase ending in another, which can weaken a sense of tonal stability. Sonorities that appear other than at phrase endings, particularly at phrase beginnings, may also play a major role in tonal shaping, assisted by register and voice leading. Significantly, calculated voice leading can at times emphasize a tone, even if not a sonority *per se*.

With this background in mind, we turn to **Mo** 81, whose tenor presents the *portare* chant segment four times, with the same first-mode rhythmic pattern superimposed throughout. Because the two upper voices duplicate one another fairly often, a two-voice rather than a three-voice musical texture occasionally emerges. The tenor and upper voice(s) frequently move in parallel fourths or fifths, and in octaves on occasion. These features identify this motet as fitting into an early layer of motet composition.

The reduction (see Example 6.3) marks all phrase endings in one or both upper voices by a vertical line drawn between the staves. All upper-voice phrase endings, articulated by rhyme and usually by a hold and/or rest, call some attention to themselves; we experience them as a sort of breathing indicator, whether regular or irregular. In the following discussion, I consider tenor phrasing only when that voice forms a phrase ending with one of the upper voices. Numbers below the staff identify all directed progressions, with those at a phrase ending enclosed within a box. Parentheses indicate an interval succession that is interrupted by a tenor rest, yet is heard as a completed progression. Each of the four tenor statements is subdivided into four units of equal length, with each unit consisting of three perfections. As will become apparent, the upper voices are laid out similarly over the four statements, though with subtle distinctions that affect the tonal emphases. Despite the limited triplum range, *c–a´*, overlapping with motetus *a–g*, sonority voicing works hand in hand with directed progressions to suggest a deliberate tonal shaping by the motet creator. Statement 3 plays a lesser role in this shaping, because it contains the highest degree of parallel voice leading and therefore a reduced number of directed progressions.

[49] Pesce 1990 and Pesce 2018.

Example 6.3. Reduction of Mo 81

Mo 81 reveals some emphasis on C in the first two tenor statements, but less so in the latter two. Leaving aside the opening tenor *c* momentarily, the first tenor *c* in the second unit of statements 1, 2, and 4 is prepared by a 3→1 directed progression at a phrase ending;[50] in all four statements the unison is harmonized with an *f*, that is, an unstable fourth that weakens a sense of arrival on *c*. But C emerges nonetheless as tonal focus because of what occurs immediately after: in statements 1, 2 and 4, the second tenor *c* of unit 2 (marked with vertical arrows) sounds a unison *c* with a motetus phrase beginning, a tone further emphasized by the triplum's descending stepwise motion *f e (d) c*, though there is no accompanying directed progression. The third statement offers the same melodic gesture, but not in connection with a phrase beginning. These *c* unisons call attention to themselves as the only examples of unisons other than the two to be discussed

---

[50] In statement 3, the *c* does not technically coincide with the triplum phrase ending, but the fact that the accompanying internal rhyme '(va-)lour' picks up on the rhyme '(do-)çour' at the end of the preceding phrase lends credibility to hearing this position as a phrase ending.

below (also marked with vertical arrows). The unisons on the second tenor *c* of unit 2 might even be heard as the delayed emphasis on *c*, which had been deflected through the *c/f* voicing at the beginning of the unit.

The other occurrences of *c* in **Mo** 81 receive varying degrees of emphasis. The tenor *c* that opens each unit 4 is approached by a leap in that voice from G to *c*. Statement 1 accompanies the tenor leap with a tendency progression (3→1), with all three voices sounding the unison *c* as a momentary point of arrival. On the other hand, in statements 2 through 4, the tenor *c* is not preceded by a directed progression, and is accompanied with a top note of, respectively, *e*, *f*, and *g*; *c/e* and *c/g* lend some emphasis to C, though less than would be the case if the top note were *c*. Like the *c* that opens unit 4, the first *c* of unit 1 in statements 2, 3, and 4 is also approached by a tenor leap from G to *c*, but in none of these instances is it accompanied by a directed progression. Its top notes also change over the four statements: *g*, *c*, *g*, and *f*, thus again drawing attention to C in varying degrees (the *f* instance will be discussed below). The unison *c* that begins the second statement recalls the unison *c* just heard at the beginning of unit 4 of statement 1 (both marked by vertical arrows), and, by association, assumes more aural importance because of its voicing. Thus, a tonal emphasis on C is most acute at the end of statement 1 and through the first half of statement 2.

How does the motet creator treat G? The tenor G at the end of each unit 2 always falls at a phrase ending, though it is never preceded by a directed progression. Nonetheless, this G always carries its octave *g* as the topmost sounding pitch, and we hear a G sonority in its most stable configuration, *G/d/g*. The same stable sonority resounds on the second tenor G in unit 3 in statements 1, 2, and 4;[51] contrary to what happened in unit 2, the sonority does not occur at a phrase ending, but *is* preceded by a directed progression. In each unit 4, we hear two directed progressions in succession: 3→5 to *a*, followed immediately by 3→5, 6→8, or $_{3}^{6} \overset{\rightarrow}{\rightarrow} _{5}^{8}$ to G. Whereas the *a* carries its fifth, *e*, above, the G consistently sounds its more stable octave, *g*, thus solidifying the impact of the *G/d/g* sonority already heard in units 2 and 3.

In addition to the recurrent G sonorities, the treatment of C in statement 4 contributes to a sense of G as a satisfying final sonority. The statement opens on the same *c/f* interval that next sounds at the beginning of unit 2, thus weakening C's presence until the unison *c* occurs in unit 2. Furthermore, because the tenor *c* at the beginning of unit 4 is harmonized with *g* in the top voice, *g*'s importance is reinforced during the final approach to the *G/d/g* sonority. Thus, despite the presence of a fair number of parallel interval progressions, **Mo** 81 strategically uses directed progressions and sonority voicing to create a subtly changing tonal palette.

An additional fascicle 5 motet, **Mo** 142, provides another view of tonal treatment. It is one of three *portare* motets that truncates the chant melody but still ends on the expected tone G of the inherited chant segment (**Mo** 91, 142, and 148).[52] Large-scale rhythmic organization of the tenor chant fragment and its repetition factors into this discussion.

Sixteen of the seventeen *portare* motets reveal a rhythmic treatment of the tenor in which a repeating rhythmic pattern (talea) is applied to a repeating melodic segment (color).[53] Fifteen of the sixteen motets always make the color repetitions coincident with the beginning of taleae,

---

[51] Statement 3 places *d* in the uppermost voice.

[52] Mo 148 actually ends on *c* because the entire chant is transposed a fifth below its usual pitch level. Two motets truncate the chant to end on different tones: Mo 296 on *F* and Mo 96 on *a*.

[53] The exception, **Mo** 265, is discussed in the text below.
     Talea and color are terms associated with the concept of isorhythm that is attributed to fourteenth-century repertory, with incipient manifestations in thirteenth-century motets. Many scholars now eschew the expression isorhythm, but continue to find talea and color useful terms, a position adopted in this discussion.

Example 6.4. Reduction of Mo 142

Mo 335 being the exception.[54] Of the fifteen, the talea remains the same throughout the motet in nine cases: **Mo** 81, 91, 96, 148, 159, 233, 257, 259, **Cl** 41; in six cases, the talea is not the same for all color repetitions: **Mo** 41, 142, 188, 296, 305, 322.

Mo 142 falls into the latter group: as shown in Example 6.4, in the course of its four statements of the color, the talea remains the same for two, then changes on the third, and yet again on the fourth. Truncation of the tenor color begins in statement 3, where twenty notes are reduced to fifteen, then to twelve in statement 4. All color segments still end on *G*, but the incidence of *G* decreases by one in statement 3 and by two in statement 4. The truncation of statement 3 is paired with a more compressed talea rhythm: it contains only three rests versus the seven of statements 1 and 2.[55] The talea of statement 4 returns to the rhythmic components of the opening talea, though they are rearranged.

Because of the tenor truncation, which gradually diminishes the chant presence of *G*, the motet creator faced the challenge of making the final *G* a convincing point of arrival. As this analysis reveals, a deliberate approach to positioning directed progressions, sonority voicing, and voice leading contribute to the motet's cohesive unfolding. Given the fairly constant phrase overlap between triplum and motetus, this motet does not draw as much attention to its phrase endings as do many other motets. Nonetheless, directed progressions still play a role in the tonal unfolding. Example 6.4 indicates all directed progressions involving *c* and *G*, with those at a phrase ending enclosed in a box.

Significantly, the motet creator never emphasizes C through a 6→8, 3→5 or 3→1 progression. Instead he foregrounds C sonorities through consistent voicing, *c/g*: C is in essence 'asserted' rather than established by tendency motion. Yet its stability is challenged at the outset by the fact that its highest sounding tone is a *g*, rather than its octave *c* (see, for instance, perfections 1, 2, 5 and 7). On the other hand, from perfection 8 onwards, each G sonority typically carries its octave *g* in the highest voice, thereby sounding its most stable configuration. Furthermore, it is fairly consistently accompanied by a tendency progression of 6→8, 3→5 or $\frac{6}{3} \to \frac{8}{5}$.[56]

Yet the motet creator complicates this G emphasis through voice leading and sonority voicing. In perfections 11–12, a 3→5 progression in the motetus and tenor leads from *a/c* to *G/d*, with an octave *g* added above when the triplum simultaneously begins a new phrase. Because the triplum and motetus continue their linear motion over the next several perfections, a sense of coming to rest on G is delayed until perfection 16, when a $\frac{6}{3} \to \frac{8}{5}$ progression from *a/c/f* to *G/d/g* occurs. But even there, the motetus continues its linear motion *d-e-f*, reaching *g* at the beginning of statement 2 over tenor *c* at the same moment that the triplum begins a phrase and draws attention to itself by its pitch *c′*, the highest of the motet. The resulting *c/g/c′* sonority is thus emphasized, as calculated voice leading and sonority voicing return the focus to *c* at the beginning of statement 2.

The next two tenor statements offer subtle changes from the tonal plan of statement 1. Statement 2 essentially unfolds like statement 1, first asserting a C sonority, then emphasizing G through directed progressions at perfections 24–5, 26–7 and 30–1. But then the final *G/d/g* sonority moves

---

[54] Mo 335 contains three 20-note tenor statements (colores). Because each brief talea contains only three pitches (each talea can be notated as three dotted half notes and one dotted half rest), the start of each color necessarily falls at a different point in the talea: the first color begins on the first note of the talea, the second color on the third note, the third color on the second note.

[55] This calculation does not include the 'introductory' *c* followed by a breve rest that occurs before the color 'proper' begins.

[56] The exceptions occur when the tenor motion is *b-G* (see perfections 7–8, 22–3, 36–7, and 46–7). The instance at perfections 22–3 is further complicated by the tenor G carrying a dissonant sonority rather than *G/d/g*.

smoothly to a simple *c/g* sonority at the start of statement 3; statement 2 eschews the registral change that had occurred at the juncture of statements 1 and 2, when, over the tenor *c*, the triplum entered on the highest pitch of the motet, creating a striking *c/g/c′* sonority. Statement 3 has roughly the same distribution of *c/g* and *G/d/g* sonorities as its equivalent spots in statements 1 and 2, but is nearly devoid of directed progressions. Our ears focus on a somewhat static sound palette bordered by *g* on the upper end. But statement 3's final *G/d/b′* sonority suddenly pulls the ear towards the C sonority that begins statement 4: the G sonority's triplum moves downward through *b′-a′-g-f*, while the motetus moves upward through *d-e-f*, creating a dissonant tension when the two *f*'s form a seventh with the tenor G. Both *f*'s find resolution in the $\frac{5}{3}$ sonority on C that begins statement 4, the triplum *f* moving to *g* and the motetus *f* to *e*. Thus, dissonance transforms the *G/d/b′* sonority into a preparation for the *c/e/g* sonority that follows.

Statement 4, whose tenor is now truncated to include the tone G only twice, inherently emphasizes *c*, but with a nuanced treatment that prepares the final directed progression to a *G/d/g* sonority. As Example 6.4 shows, a *c/g* sonority sounds at two phrase endings (perfections 42–3 and 45–6), both prepared by the lesser tendency progression 6→5: *a/f* moves to *c/g*.[57] The ear expects the sixth *a/f* to move outward to the octave *G/g*, more generally because of the voice-leading conventions of this repertory, but more particularly because the listener has heard multiple 6→8 progressions to G throughout the first half of the motet. Therefore, when the 6→8 progression to G eventually occurs in the last two perfections (48–9), the ear is primed to hear the final *G/d/g* sonority as a satisfying arrival point. Furthermore, the 6→8 directed progression is embellished by successive dissonances over the tenor *a*, creating additional tension to enhance the strength of this tendency progression and firmly establish G as the final tonal focus. Thus, this motet with a uniquely constructed tenor reveals a calculated approach to sonority voicing and voice leading, in tandem with a judicious use of directed progressions, resulting in a cohesive tonal unfolding.

The *portare* motet family also reveals some distinct exploratory structural procedures. **Mo** 322 stands apart for a number of reasons; see Example 6.5. Carrying an incipit of 'tenor' rather than *portare* or *sustinere*, the motet's tenor consists of three colores, only the first of which relates to *portare*, and then only through the first twelve of its twenty-one pitches. Color 1 appears twice, with the same superimposed talea of eighteen perfections. The second color also sounds twice, accompanied by a new, color-specific talea of twenty-four perfections. A third color, with its own rhythmic profile, sounds once to end the piece.[58] Unlike in other *portare* motets, a sense of sectional individuality results from the use of multiple colores/taleae, coupled with two other features. First, the third talea no longer contains the perfect long (dotted-quarter-note) rests found in taleae one and two and becomes instead a string of perfect long notes. The compression of the third talea versus the openness of the second talea with its evenly spaced rests creates the sense of a relatively more active final section, despite the fact that this section also contains twenty-four perfections and that the upper voices engage in consistent motion throughout the motet. And second, **Mo** 322 also reveals a frame-like effect in that colores one and three are apparently intended to be textless, perhaps sung as melismas.[59]

Another example of individualized structure occurs in **Mo** 265, discussed above for its many possible textual interpretations. Its creator not only adopted the *portare* chant segment in the

[57] A 6→5 progression to *c* also occurs in statements 1 and 2, perfections 6–7 and 21–2.

[58] As Example 6.5 shows, color 3 consists of four 3-note units, each of which repeats itself before moving on to the next 3-note unit.

[59] **Mo** 322 has no concordances, so this textless presentation of colores 1 and 3 in Mo cannot be compared to other transmitted versions.

Example 6.5. Rhythmic organization of **Mo** 322 tenor

tenor, but also inserted into the motetus the rondeau *Robin m'aime, Robin m'a* from Adam de la Halle's *Le Jeu de Robin et de Marion*.[60] The rondeau unfolds *A B a a b A B*, where capital letters refer to refrain text, lower-case to new text, with all letters consistently linked to the two musical segments *a* and *b*. Responding to this rondeau structure, the motet composer does not present the chant segment straightforwardly, but instead breaks it into two sub-segments *a* and *b*, which are then presented in tandem with the motetus's unfolding of the rondeau *a* and *b* musical segments.[61] Significantly, the secular pre-existing element, rather than the chant fragment, directs this motet's unfolding.

CONCLUSION

Thirteenth-century motets reveal their creators' learnedness and ingenuity in melding newly composed music and text with pre-existing materials: chant from the singing tradition of the Church, and vernacular refrains derived from the courtly love tradition. Within this synthesizing framework, the creator's arsenal of approaches included exegesis and allegory, textual sound exploration, subtle working out of a tonal plan, and structural experiments linked to tenor rhythmic organization and secular *formes fixes*. Likely created by clerics for their own communities as well as for a growing literate lay audience, these motets were intellectual and sonic gems designed to tantalize the minds and ears of their listeners.

---

[60] The motet is provided as Figure 8.3 in this volume, but as it appears in the concordant Ba 81.

[61] Pesce (1997, 28–37) discusses the tonal design of this motet in full.

7

A Prism of its Time: Social Functions of the Motet
in Fourteenth-Century France

Jacques Boogaart

I N AN OFFICIAL LETTER in 1346, King John of Bohemia, Count of Luxembourg, absolved the
Dominican order of an old allegation that they had murdered his father, Henry VII, Emperor
of the Holy Roman Empire, by poisoning the Mass wine during communion. The crime would
have taken place at Buonconvento near Siena in 1313, in the midst of a campaign during which
the emperor intended to unite the warring city-states of northern Italy under the imperial crown.
John's letter, written in the year of his own death in the battle of Crécy, mentions the *romancij,
chronicae & moteti* (romances, chronicles and motets) that had been composed in response to
his father's alleged murder.[1] One such motet, *Scariotis falsitas/Jure quod in opere/Superne matris
gaudia*, survives as the fifth musical piece in the *Roman de Fauvel* (**Fauv**).[2] Its texts proclaim the
wickedness of the Dominicans and the horror of their crime. Many of the motets in **Fauv** criticize
the clergy and the mendicant orders; even the pope himself (at that time Clement V, the first
of the Avignon popes) is accused of currying favor with the monstrous Fauvel who aspires to
dominate the world. Pope Clement had initially supported Henry's enterprise in Italy but, at the
instigation of King Philip the Fair of France, had abandoned his cause. Philip's past reign and
his evil counselors are likewise heavily criticized in **Fauv**. Thus, the motet places us in the midst
of the political turmoil in France and Italy at the beginning of the fourteenth century. Since the
manuscript probably originated in circles of French court officials,[3] and since John of Bohemia, who
was a long-standing friend of the French royal house (and, incidentally, Guillaume de Machaut's
first patron), often sojourned in Paris, he may have known or heard the motet about his father's
death. John's rejection of the accusation came no less than thirty years after the alleged murder,
so he too may have initially given credence to the allegation uttered in the motet.

Scariotis falsitas/Jure quod in opere reveals one of the newer functions of the motet during the
fourteenth century, beyond the traditional concerns with amorous and devotional subjects. In
the previous century, political topics were more proper to the conductus, although there are some
thirteenth-century motets criticizing the hypocrisy of the clergy.[4] With the gradual abandonment
of the monotextual conductus genre, the subject of politics shifted to the polytextual motet, which

---

[1] Baluze 1761, 326. Interestingly, this is a rare occurrence of the Latin word *romancius* in the sense
    of the French *roman*.
[2] Text and translation in Strubel 2012, 140–3; music edition in Schrade 1956b.
[3] See especially Wathey 1998.
[4] About the transformation of two old conductus into motets, see Welker 1998.

enabled more possibilities for dialogue and textual contrasts. This shift also implies an important change in the intended public: a conductus was far easier to understand and more rhetorically straightforward, therefore appealing to a large audience; a motet required of its audience more experience and discernment. To what kind of listeners, then, was the message of this motet addressed? Likely it was intended for persons with knowledge of classical Latin literature, able to recognize the quotation from Lucan's *Bellum civile* with which the triplum of the motet ends, 'servat multos Fortuna nocentes' ('Fortune preserves many wicked men'), or at least familiar with collections of stock quotations from the Latin classics, such as the *Florilegium Gallicum*, in which this phrase featured.[5] Many Latin motets, not always political, end with such sentential expressions.[6] In a similar vein, motets in French, usually dealing with courtly love but sometimes also with devotional subjects, featured quotations from vernacular poems, which may often have been the springboard for the new text. It was already a long tradition in the thirteenth-century motet to cite refrains from songs such as the pastourelle, as Dolores Pesce has elucidated in the previous chapter. In the fourteenth century, however, the loftier *grand chant* of the trouvères also came to be seen as a rich source of quotable material.[7] This implies that listeners and singers in both centuries would have possessed the necessary erudition to recognize these borrowings and understand their meaning within their new context. In what follows, I pursue many threads introduced by Pesce in her discussion of musical and poetic functions of the thirteenth-century motet, but focus primarily on the changing social functions of the motet in the fourteenth century.

TESTIMONIES OF THEORISTS

Testimonies as to how, for whom, and in what kind of surroundings motets were performed during the fourteenth century are few and far between. The late-thirteenth-century theorist Johannes de Grocheio (his *Ars musice* has traditionally been dated *c.* 1300 but may well be from earlier, around 1275) gave one of the very few, and therefore often cited, descriptions of the various musical genres and their social functions in the Paris of his day. According to him, motets were sung 'in the presence of the educated (*litterati*) and of those who are seeking out the subtleties of the arts'. The motet should 'not be celebrated in the presence of common people because they do not notice its subtlety nor are they delighted in hearing it'; for them, simple songs were better suited. Grocheio does not detail what benefit motets brought to singers like he did for the monophonic genres: *chansons de geste*, for instance, were appropriate for the aged to help them through their suffering, and cantilenas for young people in order to keep their minds far from depraved thought. His only comment about the motet is that 'it is customarily sung at their (the *litterati*'s) feasts for their enhancement, just as the *cantilena* that is called a *rotundellus* at feasts of the common laity'.[8]

Although Grocheio's testimony is probably too early to account for the reception of the motet in the fourteenth century, his description closely matches that of the theorist Jacobus de Ispania/Jacques de Liège (late 1320s).[9] In the seventh book of his enormous *Speculum musice*,

---

[5] See Holford-Strevens 2005, 60.

[6] See Bent 1997 and Wathey 2005.

[7] Boogaart 2001a, 64.

[8] Edited in Mews *et al.* 2011, 84–5.

[9] Margaret Bent has recently proposed a new identification of this theorist (Bent 2015); this has, however, been refuted in Wegman 2016. On Jacobus and the date of his *Speculum*, see Desmond 2000.

dealing with polyphony, Jacobus recalls 'a certain company of some able singers and judicious laymen'[10] who sang and listened to new- and old-style motets and compared them, preferring the old ones; Jacobus exalts the old practice and deplores modern developments and speculations in mensuration. Thus, it appears that *ars antiqua* motets were still sung at this time, as is confirmed by a few extant collections like **Fauv** or **Iv** that contain motets in both the old and new styles. Jacobus also mournfully remarks that although the moderns sometimes do make beautiful motets, 'their manner of singing, in which the words are lost' renders the texts unintelligible, as was observed in 'a great company of judicious men'. They almost exclusively compose motets and songs, and no longer appreciate the beautiful organa, conductus and hoqueti of the past.[11]

The last bit of testimony comes towards the end of the fourteenth century: Arnulf de St Ghislain (*c.*1400), in his treatise *Tractatulus de differentiis et gradibus cantorum*, divides musicians into four classes, the lowest being the ignorant whose singing is like the howling of the beasts and whom he harshly bans from the realm of music. He admits to his second class those who do not possess sufficient knowledge but who listen avidly to better musicians; moreover, some members of this class are skilled instrumentalists. Third are the professionals in theoretical matters who may give advice to performers but who do not practice music. His great admiration, however, goes out to the expert singers, whom he considers the highest class: these able musicians sing according to 'modus, measure, number and color' ('modus, mensura, numerus et color'). He does not use the term motet, but his choice of words strongly suggests that he is referring to motets or complex polyphonic compositions at the least. Among the expert singers number women as well, whom Arnulf, in an intriguing remark, compares to Sirens, able to 'divide tones in semitones and semitones into indivisible microtones'.[12]

OCCASIONS AND SUBJECTS

Both Jacobus and Arnulf speak about a great society (*magna societate*) or a throng (*turba*) of able and learned musicians who listen to each other or sing themselves. From their reports we gather that composers and connoisseurs of motets assembled at festive occasions, which were very possibly comparable with the traditional poetical *puys* in the cities of northern France where trouvères contested in showing their skills. A few motets criticize certain practices like incorrect word splitting in hockets (for example, *Musicalis sciencia/Sciencie laudabili/Tenor*) or incoherence of text (*In virtute/Decens carmen/Clamor meus/Contratenor*),[13] and could have been presented at such occasions as model pieces of correct writing or as a mode of criticism. Thus, a context in which makers of motets discussed, praised, and criticized each other's work is easily imagined. Daniel Leech-Wilkinson and Karl Kügle have shown many connections between individual *ars nova* motets, both in musical structure and in the structure of the texts.[14] Apparently, a restricted number of motets were avidly studied and analyzed as springboards for new compositions. In a comparable way it is also worthwhile to investigate the motet repertory for relationships in subject matter, accomplished, for instance, through a common tenor or a

---

[10] Strunk 1998, 277–8; Latin text in Bragard 1955–73, 7: 46–8.

[11] Strunk 1998, 273.

[12] Edition, translation, and commentary in Page 1992.

[13] Both works have been edited in Harrison 1968; *Musicalis sciencia/Sciencie* has most recently been discussed in Zayaruznaya 2013 and Zayaruznaya 2015a, 74–81; *In virtute/Decens carmen* in Zayaruznaya 2015a, 70–105 and 235–6.

[14] See Leech-Wilkinson 1982–3 and Kügle 1997, 89–147, esp. 139 ff.

related theme.[15] The works of Vitry and Machaut offer some examples that will be discussed in the last section of this chapter.

The theorists confirm that the motet was primarily the domain of an intellectual caste, as an elitist genre that demanded literateness, musical expertise and careful reflection.[16] Through its intellectual prestige, the motet became a fitting adornment for ceremonial occasions like coronations and at other times an instrument to admonish or praise kings and nobles; further below I will go a little deeper into this latter aspect. Yet the thirteenth and fourteenth centuries also saw the rise of the bourgeoisie and the cities; what of them? Was their repertory indeed confined to monophonic songs as Grocheio reported (and as seems evidenced still in the early fifteenth-century Bruges song collection, the *Gruuthuse* manuscript, which preserves much earlier repertoire)[17] or could they also have practiced polyphony? There are very few references to performances of motets in cities during the fourteenth century. One exception is the yearly miracle plays by the guild of the Parisian goldsmiths; there, reportedly, sacred motets were sung at the end of each play.[18] Regrettably no such work has been preserved, but the mention suggests that motets may have been performed at similar public occasions. A more tenuous testimony appears in Froissart's *Joli buisson de Jonece*, an allegorical dream vision in which, near the end of his story, the author evokes the singing of 'a motet newly sent to him from Reims' during a feastly journey to the god of Love.[19] Whether this might record a poetic reflection of real events, such as the singing of motets during processions or parades, is doubtful; monophonic song seems more likely for such occasions.

Within the liturgy motets had little place; they were permitted during Mass only after the Sanctus and at the end, at the Ite missa est (one such motet is *Se grasse n'est/Cum venerint/Ite missa est*, which concludes the Tournai Mass). In the Office, a motet could occur at the end after the Benedicamus Domino. In a saint's Office, a motet may have been sung in his or her honor, such as Machaut's M19, *Martyrum/Diligenter/A Christo honoratus* for St Quentin, which could have found a yearly performance in the collegiate church of Saint-Quentin; its triplum describes the saint's vita and miraculous deeds while the motetus spurs those present on to honor him in song.[20] Some lesser-known saints, forebears of noble or royal families, who are revered in motets and whose motets might have been sung at their name days are St Louis of Toulouse and St Ida of Boulogne (*Flos ortus/Celsa cedrus/Quam magnus pontifex* and *Portio nature/Ida capillorum/Contratenor/Ante thronum trinitatis*).[21] And, of course, continuing a long tradition from the early thirteenth century onward, many motets were still being written in honor of the Blessed Virgin Mary.

---

[15]   In the thirteenth century a small number of melismas were used over and over again by anonymous composers; see the chapters by Alice V. Clark and Dolores Pesce in this volume. During the fourteenth, shared tenors are the exception rather than the rule; where they occur, they invite further investigation of the connections between motets.

[16]   See Bent 1992b.

[17]   Edited in Brinkman and de Loos 2015.

[18]   See Plumley 2013, 176–9.

[19]   It is discussed in Huot 2003. A motet from Reims would almost certainly be a work by Machaut; Huot gives some suggestions.

[20]   Robertson (2002, 69–75) discusses several occasions where this motet may have functioned; for example, the completion of the choir stalls with scenes from St Quentin's life.

[21]   Both are edited in Harrison 1968. See Emily Zazulia's chapter in this volume for a detailed analysis of *Portio nature/Ida capillorum*.

Subjects of motets thus ranged from political and criticizing, admonishing and polemical, celebratory and laudatory to amorous, devotional or both at once; more than in any other genre, all aspects of fourteenth-century culture found a place in the motet, which can truly be called a prism of its time.

COMPOSERS

While hardly any thirteenth-century motets can be connected to a composer's name (with the exceptions of Adam de la Halle and Petrus de Cruce), individual compositional personalities begin to take shape in the fourteenth century. Philippe de Vitry (1291–1361) was universally lauded as the most famous fourteenth-century composer, specifically with regard to motets. Although he 'signed' a few of his motets by including his name in the text, it has been notoriously difficult to securely fix his surviving oeuvre.[22] A number of attributed motets are polemical, for instance the three political motets in **Fauv** that mock the downfall of Enguerrand de Marigny.[23] Another motet attacks one (unidentified) Hugo whom Vitry accuses of being a hypocrite (*Cum statua/Hugo, Hugo/Magister invidie*). In a later motet he compares the poet Jean de Le Mote (first half of the fourteenth century) to this despicable Hugo (in *Phi millies/O creator/Jacet granum/Quam suf-flabit*).[24] His victims must have been quite erudite to understand Vitry's complex wordings and mythological allusions. Vitry and Le Mote, together with Guillaume de Machaut (*c.*1300–77) and the otherwise unknown Collart Haubiert, are the names that Gilles li Muisis (a chronicler and poet from Hainaut) hails as the best of France's poet-composers in his *Méditations*.[25] An intriguing reference to this Jean de Le Mote is found in an unattributed motet, *Mon chant/Qui dolereus/Tristis est anima mea*, probably written in remembrance of William, Count of Holland, Zeeland, and Hainaut, who died in 1337; it quotes lines from Le Mote's *Li regret Guillaume*, which was written in William's memory.[26] The most complete composer 'portrait' we have, however, is the one that Guillaume de Machaut drew of himself in various works, most notably in his late *Livre dou Voir Dit*.[27]

Apart from Vitry and Machaut, we have only a few ascribed single pieces and a number of composer names without connection to any known motets. A few so-called musicians' motets (the aforementioned *Musicalis sciencia/Sciencie* as well as *Apollinis eclipsatur/Zodiacum/In omnem terram*) together transmit some forty different composer names including those of Johannes de Muris, Vitry and Machaut. The named composers are presented as a circle of friends or colleagues; they are abundantly praised in *Apollinis/Zodiacum*, but are advised to respect the rules of rhetoric in *Musicalis sciencia/Sciencie*. One work has been ascribed to Denis le Grant (d. 1352), the chace *Se je chant mains que ne suelh*,[28] quoted in a ballade by Machaut. Egidius de Pusiex is purported to have composed the motet *Portio nature/Ida capillorum* and Bernard de Cluny *Apollinis/Zodiacum*, one of the most well-known motets of the century and a dazzlingly

---

[22] For all supposed ascriptions to Philippe de Vitry, see the lemma 'Vitry, Phillipe de' in *Grove*.

[23] Discussed in Bent 1997 and Bent 1998b.

[24] See Zayaruznaya 2015a, 106–41 and 250–5.

[25] Lettenhove 1882, 1: 88–9; Plumley 2013, 197–8.

[26] Plumley 2013, 231–7; edition in Harrison 1968 and Plumley 2013, 240–6.

[27] For a survey of the documentation on Machaut's life, see Earp 1995, 3–51. The most complete and detailed recreation of Machaut's life and ideas is Leach 2011b.

[28] Kügle argues that the chace may have been regarded as a subgenre of the motet; he is supported by the index of **Trém**, in which this chace is listed among the motets (Kügle 1997, 151–3).

complex piece according to David Howlett's analysis of its texts.[29] The Chantilly codex (**Ch**) provides further names: Philippe Royllart wrote a motet for King Charles V, *Rex Karole/Leticie, pacis/[Virgo prius ac posterius]/Contratenor*; Egidius de Aurolia and J. de Porta wrote *Alma polis/Axe poli cum/Contratenor/Tenor*; Johannes Alanus wrote *Sub Arturo/Fons citharizan- tium/In omnem terram*, which honors a circle of English musicians and was probably inspired by the earlier piece *Apollinis/Zodiacum*.[30] It is not clear whether all of the named composers in these works wrote motets. These musicians would have belonged to the social circles of court officials or were members of the lower or higher clergy. Some of them are associated with both circles, such as Vitry and Denis le Grant, who became bishops of Meaux and Senlis, respectively.

SOURCES

Sources that could tell us something about the purpose or dissemination of motets are few and rather diverse in nature; many sources were probably lost in the wake of the nearly constant warfare during this 'calamitous' century.[31] The first important source, **Fauv**, is an exceptional document. The genesis of this marvelously illuminated manuscript is generally placed in the circles of the French court administration at the occasion of the royal successions following the death of Philip the Fair in 1314; its completion is dated 1316/17 or slightly later. Ostensibly, the romance was initially meant as an admonition for the new king, Louis X, then, after his sudden death two years later, for Philip V, 'qui regne ores' ('who reigns now', as the manuscript notes); the warning, however, may have addressed a wider target audience.[32] This satirical story was originally written by a court official, Gervès du Bus, and several versions are extant. In **Fauv**, the story was expanded with illuminations and musical insertions, allegedly thanks to a Breton clerk, Chaillou de Pesstain; it comprises no less than 167 musical pieces, monophonic and polyphonic, among which feature thirty-four motets. The motets are unevenly dispersed throughout the story, with a greater density at the beginning and at the end. They are both old and new in style, and certainly were made by a variety of composers, among whom at least two distinct personalities have been recognized, a not-yet-identified 'Master of the royal motets' who practiced a somewhat more conservative way of composing, and, according to most scholars, Philippe de Vitry, who then must have been in his twenties and who was responsible for the modern works in the *ars nova* style.[33] The motets mostly form part of the storyline; in several cases the texts of older pieces were adapted to fit the new context. To find such coherence between motets that are otherwise of very divergent natures and structures is indeed exceptional.[34]

The half-horse, half-human protagonist Fauvel is the embodiment of evil; his name is an acrostic of six vices: Flaterie, Avarice, Vilanie, Variété (fickleness), Envie, Lascheté (cowardice). Fauvel has his throne in a princely hall whose walls are decorated with portraits of deceivers from all social classes and with 'songs, lais and many ballades, hockets, motets and little songs that did not deal with love stories but with tried-and-tested frauds that Master Swindler had dictated ...

---

[29] Howlett 2005. On Egidius de Pusiex as the composer of *Portio nature/Ida capillorum*, see Emily Zazulia's contribution below.

[30] All these works have been edited in Harrison 1968.

[31] Tuchman 1978.

[32] See especially Wathey 1998.

[33] See Leech-Wilkinson 1995.

[34] See Dillon 2002, ch. 6, for a general discussion of the musical insertions in **Fauv**.

They were well written and notated in music, with flats and false melodies'.[35]

However, the motets in **Fauv** for the most part indict these evils and vices; many criticize social, political, and ecclesiastical abuse with fiery language, as general complaints or attacks directed at specific persons. Towards the end of its second part, three motets attributed to Vitry mock the downfall of Enguerrand de Marigny, the corrupt adviser to the Philip the Fair who was tried and hanged by Philip's successor in 1315.[36] His fate serves in a more general way as an *exemplum* for future counselors. One other motet attributed to Vitry, the Trinity motet *Firmissime/Adesto Sancta Trinitas/Alleluya benedictus*, may be briefly singled out for its provocative message, in this case not by its words but by its music. The work is remarkable for several reasons, but foremost for its bold choice of mensuration in imperfect (duple) note values.[37] The *ars antiqua* maxim that mensural perfection is superior to imperfection was formulated by Franco of Cologne (*c.* 1260–80) with an appeal to the Trinity:

> The perfect long is said to be the first and principal, for in it all the others are included and all the others are reducible to it. It is called perfect because it is measured by three tempora, the ternary number being the most perfect number because it takes its name from the Holy Trinity, which is true and pure perfection.[38]

This fundamental tenet was still upheld as late as 1321 by a modern theorist, Johannes de Muris, in his *Notitia artis musice*.[39] In various versions of the treatise *Ars nova* (assumed to reflect teachings by Vitry) the Trinity motet is cited as an example of a motet with *im*perfect longs and breves. Other structural numbers in the motet feature duple proportions as well.[40] Thus, a motet in honor of the Trinity undermines the very trinitarian basis of *ars antiqua* theory; it has rightly been called an 'early manifesto of the *ars nova*'.[41]

An interesting concordance to the motet corpus in **Fauv** is the Brussels rotulus **Br**, which transmits five of the Fauvel motets (including the Trinity motet) but in slightly modernized notation, as well as a small number of other works. The rotulus clarifies by the addition of flags how the semibreves minimae, ambiguous in **Fauv**, are to be read;[42] moreover, it is a precious witness to how motets could travel and be transmitted in a handy format.

The chronologically next important source, Machaut's motet corpus, presents an entirely different case. It is exceptionally well preserved in no less than five beautifully written and decorated

---

[35]   Edited in Strubel 2012, 276–9; commentary in Dillon 2002, 117–20.

[36]   The Marigny motets are discussed in Bent 1997, Bent 1998b, and Wathey 1998.

[37]   For more on this aspect of the motet, see Lawrence Earp's discussion in Chapter 4 of this *Companion*.

[38]   Strunk 1998, 229. Before Franco, Magister Lambertus had already expressed this same basic tenet; see Rebecca A. Baltzer's entry 'Lambertus, Magister' in *Grove*.

[39]   'That all perfection lies in the ternary number follows from many likely reflections. In God, who is most perfect, there is one substance, yet three persons; he is threefold yet one, and one yet threefold. Very great, therefore, is the correspondence of unity to trinity'. Strunk 1998, 262–3.

[40]   For example, the hymn text in the motetus is doubled by interpolated verses. See the arguments in Vetter 1987, counterarguments in Robertson 1997, and further discussion in Zayaruznaya 2015a, 203–16. The maxima is a duplex longa and only the semibreve probably has a ternary subdivision, as in **Br**; however, in **Fauv** the semibreves are unspecified and could thus be both perfect or imperfect. Edition of the motet in Schrade 1956b and in Vetter 1987.

[41]   Vetter 1987. Another later motet praising the Trinity, also ascribed to Vitry (*Tuba/In arboris/Virgo sum*), uses both binary and ternary mensurations (on the modus level; the tempus is imperfect).

[42]   See Karen Desmond's chapter in the present volume for a discussion of this notation specifically.

codices and one paper copy dating from the 1340s, 1360s, 1370s and 1390s; they contain Machaut's complete works in various stages of growth.[43] These books were clearly intended to be part of a noble or even royal library.[44] It is the largest collection of motets (twenty-three) we have by a single author comprising almost a quarter of the surviving *ars nova* repertoire. Even within his musical oeuvre these motets have a somewhat special status: in contrast to most of his other lyrical works, the motets are transmitted nowhere else as texts only (with just one exception in a peripheral manuscript).[45] Machaut indeed includes the motet in his late Prologue to his works within the list of forms he had practiced, but otherwise the composer is completely silent about his works in this genre. Among Machaut's motets, it is most easy to determine the social function of the six Latin works; these are related to ceremonies and furthermore provide an overview of the various solemnities during which a motet could be sung. M18, *Bone pastor/Bone pastor/Bone pastor* and M19, *Martyrum/Diligenter/A Christo honoratus* are celebratory pieces for the churches of Reims and Saint-Quentin where Machaut held prebends. M9, *Fons/O livoris/Fera pessima*, is an allegorical political diatribe, probably meant as an attack on Edward III of England although it is not entirely clear for which occasion it was intended; it might refer to the initial homage of Edward to Philip VI in 1329 and his later claim to the French throne which started the Hundred Years' War in 1337.[46] The last three motets of his corpus, M21, M22 and M23, are grand four-voice works, written at the time of the English devastation of France and the siege of Reims, during which Machaut served as a watchman.[47] Machaut's seventeen French or French-Latin motets are devoted to the art of courtly love and ponder the various difficulties an aspiring lover encounters in his quest for perfect love. It is not clear what their social function may have been; since Machaut served for many years as John of Bohemia's secretary, is it possible that they were performed at John's court? The motets seem too learned a kind of music for courtly entertainment. That they would be veiled allegories hiding a Christian message as Anne Walters Robertson has hypothesized seems, to the present writer at least, not very likely either: why would Machaut, canon at Reims Cathedral, have needed to hide a spiritual message under a courtly clothing, and for whom would that message have been intended?[48] Given the motet's status as a learned genre, we may perhaps assume that in his motets Machaut set out his contemplations on courtly love and its problematics, which were deepened by the spiritual dimension of the tenors.

The Ivrea manuscript (**Iv**) was apparently made for a small community in the Piedmontese town of Ivrea but contains music originating from courtly circles centered around Orléans and thus actually belongs to the northern French cultural sphere.[49] In contrast to the codices described above, it is not a preciously decorated manuscript. Still, it features the largest collection of motets

---

[43] Chronologically ordered their sigla are **Mach C, Ferrell 1, Mach B, Mach A, Mach F-G** and **Mach E**. For all information about these and other manuscripts containing works by Machaut, see Earp 1995, 77–128; further discussion in Earp 1989 and Earp 2014. **Ferrell 1** has been edited in facsimile, see Earp 2014; the other manuscripts can be consulted at http://gallica.bnf.fr.

[44] See Earp 2011 and Earp 2014.

[45] The texts of his most famous motet, M8, a diatribe against Fortune, appear in only one such source. See Earp 1995, 114 [item 46].

[46] The suggestion that King Edward III was the target of the motet was Kurt Markstrom's (1989); however, he unconvincingly endeavors to explain *all* the images in the texts as allegorical clothings of real events and persons. See Boogaart 2001a, 5–11. A detailed analysis is given in Bent 2003.

[47] Earp 1995, 38–40. The most extensive discussion of the possible functions of these motets is in Robertson 2002, 119–223.

[48] Robertson 2002, 79–188; critical arguments in Boogaart 2004b.

[49] See the conclusions from the codicological and scribal evidence in Kügle 1997, 75–9.

in any surviving fourteenth-century book, thirty-seven in total. In **Iv**, all the various types of motets are found: laudatory for kings and nobles, celebratory for saints, polemical and amorous; in this regard, it is probably the most representative collection of motets. Despite its having been copied around 1380, a few motets date back to the thirteenth century, others are quite modern, but none of its repertoire extends beyond *c.* 1359. The book also contains several *unica*. **Iv** is the richest source for the works of Vitry, to whom perhaps as many as eleven or twelve motets can be ascribed. Nevertheless, as Kügle concludes on grounds of his physical research of the manuscript, the motets of **Iv** may seldom have been heard in Ivrea itself.[50]

Apart from these codices, little else remains from the northern regions where the motet flourished most. The Cambrai fragments (**CaB**) contain motet materials in both *ars antiqua* and *ars nova* styles.[51] The fragment Trémoïlle (**Trém**) is the remnant of a once very large codex that had belonged to Philip the Bold, Duke of Burgundy. It must have been one of the vastest collections in France; more than seventy motets as well as a number of songs are listed in its tantalizing index. Its oldest part was copied no later than 1376 but apparently new pieces were added later.[52] Its scribes probably had access to many important sources, including the works of Machaut, who normally guarded his works, restricting them to books he controlled himself. The appearance of Machaut's works in this index could be explained by his close contacts with members of the royal family. **Trém** itself must have contained nine motets by Machaut and possibly eleven by Vitry; besides the index, only a few fragments of these works survive.

A few sources stem from southern France and northern Italy. The beautiful manuscript **Ch**, one of the main repositories of the *ars subtilior* chanson, ends with thirteen fairly complex motets from the later fourteenth century. It is an early fifteenth-century manuscript from Italy, perhaps made for a Florentine purchaser, but its repertoire is French, and again seemed destined for noble circles, as indicated by the dedicatees of the songs, who include Count Gaston de Foix-Béarn and Jean, Duke of Berry.[53] A manuscript in Modena, **Mod**, contains three more late motets. These codices, along with a number of small fragments, testify to the propagation and dissemination of the *ars nova* motet in southern Europe.

Most of these musical sources show hardly any signs of intensive use. Thus, little can be gleaned from them in terms of their practical function for music making. Rather, the purpose of these books was, it seems, to conserve (and for their owners, to possess) impressive works of music and poetry on parchment, as mementos of living performances.

Lastly, a special and interesting type of dissemination is the transmission of motets as literature without music.[54] A number of German manuscripts from humanist circles assembled texts with related subject matter from twelfth- and thirteenth-century writers such as Philip the Chancellor or Walther of Châtillon, as well as fourteenth-century writers such as Philippe de Vitry. Seven motet texts (perhaps even nine, depending on their attribution) by Vitry have thus been preserved, sometimes even with text readings superior to their musical sources.

---

[50] Kügle 1997, 205.

[51] See Lerch 1987.

[52] See Bent 1990.

[53] A facsimile edition appears in Plumley and Stone 2008; see also their 'Introduction'. The motets of **Ch** and **Mod** have been edited in Günther 1965 and/or Harrison 1968.

[54] Wathey 1993 and Zayaruznaya 2010, 55–63.

THE PUBLIC SPHERE: MOTETS FOR KINGS AND NOBLES

A great number of motets were written for public occasions, both political and ecclesiastical. The first part of the Fauvel story ends with two so-called royal motets, celebrating King Louis X and his successor Philip V. The first, *Se cuers joians/Rex beatus/Ave*, was written for Louis's coronation in 1315 and has the interesting characteristic of being bilingual with each language representing a different domain: the French triplum text evokes the world of courtly love, while the Latin motetus counsels the young king. Elizabeth Brown has argued that the triplum text, 'written in French, the language of the beast Fauvel', is critical of its dedicatee and 'anticipates the bestial desire that Fauvel feels for Dame Fortune', whereas, contrastingly, the Latin text sets the example of a just prince.[55] However, in the French text itself nothing seems to warrant this interpretation; it evokes an ideal lover, completely in the style of the *Roman de la Rose*, as young, full of joy, cheerful and noble. These four characteristics make him exactly the lover ladies should be looking for.[56]

Se cuers joians, jonnes, jolis	If a heart that is joyful, young, cheerful
Et gentis aimme, c'est raisons;	and noble, is in love, that is reasonable and right;
Car au joians est ses deliz	because for the joyful [heart] it's his pleasure,
Et au jonnes sa nourreçon	and for the young his apprenticeship,
Et au joli est sa droicture	and for the cheerful it's his right condition,
Et au gentil est sa nature.	and for the noble [heart] it's his nature.
[...	...]
Dames, pensez d'itieus choisir!	Ladies, take care to choose such [lovers]!
Car bien puet et doit avenir	For surely can and must
Gentilz, jolis, jennes, joians	a noble, joyful, young and cheerful [heart]
Au bien dont il est desirans;	arrive at the wellbeing for which he is desiring;
N'autres ne doit d'amours joïr!	no one else should find joy in love!

(triplum, lines 1–6, 19–23)

The motetus text advises the new king to follow the example of his famous forebear St Louis (King Louis IX). Thus, *both* texts evoke the image of an ideal prince, behaving courtly and reigning wisely.[57] The work is followed by the motet *Servant regem/O Philippe/Rex regum et dominus dominancium*, written for Louis's successor and brother Philip V, who was crowned in 1316.[58] Its texts counsel the young Philip to behave as a good king, to listen to the advice of honest men, and, like in the preceding motet, to follow in the example of his great-grandfather.

Another royal motet with an interesting combination of texts is *O Philippe franci qui generis/O bone dux indolis optime/Solus tenor*, appearing in **Iv**. Its triplum text addresses King Philip VI; the motetus addresses his son, Duke John of Normandy (who would later become King John II the Good). The recommendation to Philip is to reign by virtue and prudence; he is, somewhat surprisingly, warned about the vices of several of his subjects: the peoples of Reims, Sens, Lyon,

---

[55] E. Brown 1998, 62, 64.

[56] Translations, unless otherwise indicated, are mine.

[57] Louis did indeed not live up to the ideals evoked in the motet. Had it been written after his death and especially for **Fauv**, it could indeed have been meant as a critical work. However, the lines introducing the motet recall the memory and the valiant deeds of St Louis, with a warning: if his successors Philip III and IV had followed his example, they would not have taken to love Fauvel. The author announces that he will recite a motet about St Louis. It seems therefore that the work is a remembrance of Louis's coronation.

[58] Discussed in Dillon 1998.

Bourges and other cities. The motetus admonishes Duke John to repress his first impulses, to fight for the church, to be just and to love his country. In Machaut's M22, *Tu qui gregem/Plange regni respublica/Apprehende arma/Contratenor*, an unnamed duke (but in all probability John the Good's son Charles, Duke of Normandy and later King Charles V) is spurred on to take action and to lead his people wisely. In the motetus, the poet laments the bad government of France and hopes that from now on its state of affairs will improve.[59] When he became king in 1364, Charles was honored in Philippe Royllart's motet *Rex Karole, Johannis genite/Leticie, pacis, concordie/[Virgo prius ac posterius]/Contratenor*. The triplum reminds Charles of the good deeds of his father (John II) and prays that he may bring peace; the motetus, a prayer to Mary for peace, evokes the biblical story of Esther, Haman and Mardocheus; the oppression and liberation of the Jewish people here parallels the oppression of France by the English.

Gradually, such celebratory texts lost their admonitory character and developed into flattering lauds, set in impressive musical constructs and sometimes obscure language. Vitry wrote a few celebratory motets; one such example, *O canenda/Rex quem metrorum/Rex regum/Contratenor*, praises Robert d'Anjou, King of Naples. Vitry's late motet *Petre clemens/Lugentium/Non est inventus similis illi* (1342) glorifies Pope Clement VI, a personal friend of the composer. This grand work served, as Andrew Wathey has demonstrated, as propaganda for Clement's continued stay in Avignon despite urgent pleas to let the Papal See return to Rome.[60] Three motets by unknown composers exalt Count Gaston de Foix-Béarn, who bore the epithet Fébus, likening him to the sun-god Phoebus Apollo. Gaston held an important strategic position, as his lands bordered the English territories in southern France. In *Altissonis aptatis/Hin principes/Tonans*, the triplum compares him to mythological heroes while the motetus names the many enemies that Fébus will conquer. *Febus mundo/Lanista vipereus/Cornibus equivocis* defends his loyalty to France against suspicions of his siding with the English, but does so in cryptic wordings (such language became typical in late fourteenth-century motets). The musically complex motet *Inter densas/Imbribus/Admirabilem est nomen tuum/Contratenor* is again a praise of Gaston, who is described in the texts as a magnificent prince, surrounded by knights and poets. The imagery of lush gardens and woods refers to Gaston's love of hunting.[61] This celebratory function of motets is the one that remained longest, continuing well into the fifteenth century. Guillaume Du Fay's grand motets, which combine the traditions of the French and the Italian ceremonial motet, thus stand in a long tradition.[62]

THE PRIVATE SPHERE: MOTETS FOR REFLECTION

Perhaps the most interesting motets – because they can tell us something about the conceptual worlds and the imaginations of their composers – are those that we can suppose were written to proclaim personal convictions or reflections. Such motets hold even more intrigue in instances in which we can suppose that various makers exchanged thoughts or reacted to each other's work.

---

[59] Such a complaint was also uttered in the **Fauv** motet *Nulla pestis est gravior/Plange, nostra regio/Vergente*. Its motetus text may have inspired the motetus of M22. See Sarah Fuller's chapter in this volume for a detailed analysis of M22.

[60] Discussed in Wathey 1993, 133–40; Bent 1998a, 15–19.

[61] All of these motets are edited in Günther 1965 and/or Harrison 1968.

[62] The fourteenth-century Italian motet is almost exclusively celebratory and written in Latin. See the chapters by Alice Clark and Karen Desmond in the present volume for further discussion of the motet in Italy.

An example is Machaut's use of Vitry's motet *Douce playsence/Garison/Neuma quinti toni*. The work is well known to have been the musical model for Machaut's earliest four-voice motet, M5, *Aucune gent/Qui plus aimme/Fiat voluntas tua/Contratenor*, in which Machaut took Vitry's talea and added a contratenor with the talea in retrograde.[63] Elsewhere I have argued that Vitry's texts formed the inspiration for another motet, M10, *Hareu/Helas/Obediens*, and moreover that M5 and M10 have a close structural connection.[64] Their tenors even express the same idea in different wordings; that is, subjection and obedience to the will of the lady and love: *Fiat voluntas tua* ('Thy will be done') in M5 and *Obediens usque ad mortem* ('Obedient unto death') in M10 (Vitry's tenor, the Neuma chant, has no special connotation). Vitry's triplum text describes in the voice of an outside observer, almost as that of a physician, how love's fire is ignited and is fanned through the lover's windpipes by his sighing, and how love's pain can be accepted because of the pleasure given as a final reward; in the motetus the speaking voice is the lyric I, who does not wish to be healed from love's pain because of the pleasure love brings in the end. (The complete poems and translations appear in the Appendix to this chapter.) It is my impression that this work has a slightly amused tone whereas Machaut's texts in M10 are far more committed and melancholic.[65] Machaut observed a chiastic reasoning in Vitry's texts and imitated this construction while reversing the ideas. Briefly: Vitry's triplum begins with 'Douce playsence' ('Sweet pleasure'), with which his motetus ends, 'playsence pure' ('pure pleasure'); the triplum ends with the idea of fulfilment, 'la planté' ('fullness', 'abundance'), with which the motetus began, 'Garison' ('Healing'). In a similar construction, Machaut's triplum starts with the outcry 'Hareu, hareu, le feu, le feu' ('Help, help, the fire, the fire') and ends on 'morir malgré Nature' ('to die in spite of Nature'), whereas the motetus begins with dying, 'moy qui ne vail nès que mors' ('me, fit for nothing but death') and ends with fire, 'N'en feu cuers humeins ne puet longue duree avoir' ('Nor can a human heart survive for very long in fire'). Additionally, Machaut's opening 'Hareu, hareu' quotes the midpoint of Vitry's triplum text. The kinship and opposition between both motets is clearest in the contrast of Vitry's opening line of the motetus, 'Garison selon Nature' ('Healing according to Nature'), and Machaut's closing line of the triplum, 'morir malgré Nature' ('to die in spite of Nature').

Shared tenor melodies or tenor words suggest other exchanges of ideas between Vitry and Machaut. Two of Vitry's motets show a relationship with two of Machaut's possibly earliest motets (M12 and M17); in Machaut's corpus the two are exceptional for their bilingual texts, with a French triplum and Latin motetus and tenor, and for their experimental structural features.[66]

In the motet *Vos, quid admiramini/Gratissima/Gaude gloriosa/Contratenor* Vitry expresses his rejection of earthly love and women, and his worship of the Blessed Virgin as an almost mystical marriage. In both upper-voice texts the speaking voice is a lyric I.

| Vos, quid admiramini, | You virgins, why are you amazed |
| Virgines, si virgini | if we have deigned to wed |

---

[63] For an extensive analysis, see Leech-Wilkinson 1989, 1: 88–104.

[64] Boogaart 2001a, 51–72.

[65] For the texts and translation of M10, see the analysis by Margaret Bent in the present volume; they are discussed in Brownlee 2005.

[66] M17 experiments with long-term syncopation in the tenor, similar to the examples in the well-known treatise of Egidius de Murino; see Boogaart 2001a, 47–50. M12 is an experiment with upper-voice isorhythm; during each of the nine tenor taleae some repeating rhythms are heard in the upper voices, but when three taleae are combined into one overarching 'super-talea', a much clearer isorhythmic pattern appears in the triplum and motetus; see Boogaart 2001b, 102–10 and Zayaruznaya 2010, 119–20.

Pre ceteris eligende	the Virgin who is to be forechosen
Dignati fuerimus	above the others,
Nubere, dum nupsimus	so we wed the one
Tamquam valde diligende.	who is so much to be loved.

(triplum, lines 1–6)

Earthly ladies are very unfavorably compared with the Virgin:

Ista lux, vos nubila,	She is light, you are wrapped in clouds,
Ista velox aquila,	she is a swift eagle,
Vos colubres gradientes	you creeping snakes,
Ista super ethera	she reigns beyond the heavens,
Regnat; vos in misera	you languish, in deprivation,
Valle languetis egentes;	in the vale of misery.

(triplum, lines 13–18)

Peter Dronke has suggested that the motet has a rather lighthearted, 'flippant', tone,[67] but one may also infer a more earnest intention. In an earlier motet attributed to Vitry and clearly related in theme and tone, *Impudenter/Virtutibus/[Alma redemptoris]/Contratenor*, the motetus text abundantly praises Mary, while in the triplum the poet describes the conversion of his earthly and physical love into a spiritual love for the Virgin:

Impudenter circumivi	Shamelessly I wandered around
Solum quod mare terminat;	the earth that is bound by the sea;
Indiscrete concupivi	indiscriminately I desired
Quodquod amor coinquinat.	whatever love defiles.
Hic amo forsan nec amor,	Now I love, perhaps am not loved,
Tunc pro mercede crucior,	then for reward I am tortured;
Aut amor nec in me amor,	or I am loved and there is no love in me,
Tunc ingratus efficior.	then I have become ungrateful.
Porro, cum amor et amo,	Furthermore, when I am loved and do love,
Mater Eva est media	mother Eve is in between,
In momentaneo spasmo	in a momentary spasm
Certaminis materia,	of struggle with matter,
Ex quo caro longe fetet	after which the flesh longtime stinks
Ad amoris aculeos.	of the stings of love.
Quis igitur ultra petet	Who therefore strives any further
Uri amore hereos?	to be burnt by love-sickness?[68]
Fas est vel non est amare?	Is it right to love or is it not?
Fas est quam ergo Virginem	Right it is therefore [to love]
Que meruit baiulare	the Virgin, who deserved to bear
Verum Deum et hominem.	the true God and Man.

(triplum, lines 1–20)

---

[67] Dronke 1968, 2: 406–10.
[68] For the meaning of 'amore hereos', see Lowes 1914. I am grateful to Dr Eddie Vetter for his suggestions for the translation.

'Mater Eva' probably refers to the original sin, of which the poet wishes to be cleansed. Returning to *Vos quid/Gratissima*, in the motetus the poet declares his love for the Virgin; the text ends with an amorous dialogue between a king and a queen, which seems borrowed from the *Song of Songs*.

O regina, tuum amplectere	O queen, embrace your [lover],
Astringendo pectus cum ubere!	clasping [my] breast tightly to [your] bosom!
O rex regum, oculum oculo	O king of kings, join eye to eye
Et os ori junge pro osculo,	and mouth to mouth for a kiss,
Ac inspira verbum in labia	and inspire the word on [my] lips,
Quo recepto fiat caro dia.	which, once received, may make the flesh divine.

(motetus, lines 9–14)

The choice of this imagery can be explained by the complete tenor words *Gaude virgo gloriosa, super omnes speciosa*, from the Marian antiphon *Ave regina coelorum*. The direct source for the words *super omnes speciosa* is Sapientia 7:29, a praise of Wisdom: 'Est enim haec *speciosior* sole et *super omnem* stellarum dispositio' ('For she is more beautiful than the sun, and above all the order of the stars').[69] This apocryphal bible book was traditionally ascribed to Solomon, as was the Song of Songs. In the poetic tradition Dronke characterizes as 'sapiential', the Virgin Mary is seen as a personification of Wisdom.[70] The one who is 'beautiful above all', then, is Sapientia, whom Solomon longs for as his bride. 'She reacheth therefore from end to end mightily and ordereth all things sweetly. Her have I loved and have sought her out from my youth, and have desired to take her for my spouse, and I became a lover of her beauty' (Sapientia 8: 1–2). Vitry probably elaborated his text in this sense, 'courting' Wisdom as personified by the Virgin Mary. A few lines in the triplum suggest this interpretation:

Ista virgo regia	She, the royal virgin,
Dulcis est amasia	is a sweet mistress,
Mea sponsaque pia.	and my devout bride.
Rex ego sum, hec regina.	I am king, she queen.
Quid tanta referimus?	Why do we tell all this?
Nos qui cuncta novimus,	We, who know all,
Dignam preelegimus	have preferred to choose her as worthy
Et ut rosa hanc pre spina	and as this rose above the thorn.

(triplum, lines 19–27)

Machaut wrote his M17 on the same tenor but selected a shorter fragment restricted to the words *Super omnes speciosa*.[71] In this motet, *Quant vraie Amour/O series summe rata/Super omnes speciosa*, he elaborates a very different viewpoint about love from Vitry's: the idea of a bond that may never be broken. The motetus text consists of a rather complex chain of reasoning leading to a lover's complaint:[72]

---

[69] Translations from biblical texts are from the Douay-Rheims-Challoner version.

[70] Dronke 1968, 1: 87–97.

[71] Machaut transposed the melody up a fifth, resulting in a very high tenor.

[72] The translation owes much to the advice of Dr Holford-Strevens, to whom I express my thanks. Barton Palmer refashioned my translations of Machaut's texts; they are taken from our edition of the motets; see Boogaart *et al.* 2018.

O Series summe rata,	O, Order perfectly proportioned,
Regendo naturam,	who by governing Nature
Uniformam per causata	maintains a uniform bond
Tenens ligaturam,	through all that is generated,
Argumentis demonstrata	demonstrated by proofs
Non pati fracturam,	not to suffer breakage;
Cum sit Amor tui nata	since Love is Thy daughter,
Spernatque mensuram,	and [yet] scorns measure,
Melle parens irrorata,	appearing [at first] sprinkled with honey,
Post agens usturam,	[but] afterward scorching,
Dans quibus non est optata	giving to those who do not desire it
Mitem creaturam,	a gentle creature
Que sola sit michi grata	who, alone, should be pleasing to me
Michique tam duram,	and [yet] is so hard on me,
Mirans queror mente strata	I complain, my mind confused,
Talem genituram.	wondering at such a begetting.

(motetus, complete)

In contrast to the perfect Universal Order who reigns over all generated things by an unbreakable bond, Love, who is his 'daughter', behaves irrationally and capriciously. The I complains about a 'creature' Love has given him that is at the same time pleasing and unyielding (clearly the courtly lady) and does not understand the chain of events that has led to this result.[73] In the triplum text, *Quant Vraie Amour*, a bond between a girl and a lover is forged. When a second lover tries to woo her, he does not stand a chance, even if he has suffered all the pains of a lover; Love was ordained by Nature not to be broken. The text concludes:

S'il par sa druerie	if he in his lovesickness
Maintient qu'Amours soit faussee,	maintains that Love has played him false,
Quant il n'i trueve mie	because he finds in her nothing
Merci d'amant desiree,	of the lover's reward he desires,
Combien qu'il l'ait comparee	though he has dearly paid for it
Par moult dure hachie,	with misery quite hard to bear,
N'en doit estre Amour blasmee,	then Love should not be blamed for all this,
Mais de tant plus prisie	but all the more esteemed
Qu'elle ensieut, comme ordenee,	for following, as was ordained,
Nature, qui l'a formee	Nature, who formed Her
Sans estre en riens brisie;	without showing any break;
Car qui .ij. fois vuet denree,	for he who wants to have the same goods a second time,
Le marcheant conchie.	fouls the merchant.

(triplum, lines 18–30)

[73] The motetus text probably refers to Alain de Lille's *De Planctu Naturae*, specifically its most famous poem 'O Dei proles genitrixque rerum', in which Love's perverted behavior is the subject of Nature's complaint. The triplum text was inspired by Boethius's praise of Love's power to maintain the world's order, in *De consolatione philosophiae*, II, m. 8, 'Quod mundus stabili fide'; see Boogaart 2001a, 41–7. As is well known, Boethius was an important source for Machaut's poetry; *Remede de Fortune* was modeled on the *Consolation*, transposed to the world of courtly love.

In both the motetus and triplum the lover fails to understand Love and complains. The tenor words can be interpreted as the wisdom he longs for in order to comprehend the disturbing role of Love in the ordered cosmos. Thus, Machaut elaborates a similar association with the book of Wisdom, but in a manner more proper to his conception of courtly love, in which faith is never to be broken. The shared idea between the two motets appears to be the association of the tenor words with the books of Solomon.

Another two motets by both composers relate in subject, elaborated differently in each. Both works share the same tenor words, although in this case the words stem from different chants. Freeing oneself from court service is the subject of both Vitry's *Colla iugo/Bona condit/Libera me* and Machaut's *Helas! Pour quoy/Corde mesto/Libera me* (M12).

Colla/Bona is one of the most widely disseminated motets by Vitry.[74] The tenor was taken from an antiphon for Holy Wednesday, 'Libera me de sanguinibus' (text from Ps 50:16): 'Deliver me from blood[-guiltiness], O God, thou God of my salvation: and my tongue shall extol thy justice'. In the motetus, freedom is lauded; better to be your own master than a slave:

Vincit auri pondera sue potestatis	To be one's own master is better than masses of gold.
esse. Vobis funera, servi, propinatis	You slaves, you administer death to yourselves
mala per innumera dum magis optatis.	when, among countless evils, you desire [even] more.

(motetus, lines 7–9)

The triplum is a plea to free oneself from service at court:

Colla iugo subdere curias sectari,	One puts one's neck under a yoke by attending at courts,
quarum sunt innumere clades, mores rari.	at which disasters are innumerable, good habits few.

(triplum, lines 1–2)

Soon after, it is expressed that it is better to be poor and free:

Malo fabam rodere liber et letari	I prefer to nibble a bean and rejoice as a free man
quam cibis affluere servus et tristari.	than to abound with provisions and be sad as a slave.

(triplum, lines 7–8)

And, courtiers must flatter and betray others to get rich:

Aulici sunt opere semper adulari,	The duties of a courtier are always to flatter,
fictas laudes promere lucraque venari	to utter feigned praises, and to hunt for profits,
ab implumis tollere plumas et conari	and to try to take feathers away from the unfeathered,
dominis alludere, falsa commentari.	to play up to lords, to compose false things.

(triplum, lines 9–12)

---

[74] It is discussed in Wathey 1993, 140–4, and in the present volume by Anna Zayaruznaya. The translation is David Howlett's, printed in Wathey's article and Zayaruznaya's chapter.

In this context the tenor words are meant as a prayer to be freed from the guilt that attending at courts inevitably brings. The triplum text contains several Latin quotations and ends with a line from Lucan's *Pharsalia* that was already used in a Fauvel motet: 'Nulla fides pietasque viris qui castra secuntur' ('there is no faith or piety in men who follow camps').[75] The first words of the triplum, *Colla iugo*, have been presumed to be a quotation from Ovid's *Remedia amoris* (line 90). Perhaps, though, since the context in Ovid is rather about throwing off the yoke of love, it is also possible that a Boethian poem was the source, the context of which seems more fitting. In *De consolatione* III, m. 1 ('Qui serere ingenuum volet agrum'), Philosophia teaches her pupil, who is seeking true happiness, that he must first learn not to strive after earthly riches,[76] precisely the purport of Vitry's motet.

Tu quoque falsa tuens bona prius	So must you too, who now have eyes only for false goods,
Incipe colla iugo retrahere	first begin to draw your neck from the yoke,
Vera dehinc animum subierint.	that then the true may slip into your mind.

(lines 11–13)

Machaut's motet, *Helas!/Corde mesto*, elaborates the theme of freedom from court service in his preferred domain, courtly love. The tenor was taken from a responsory from Lent II (text from Gen. 32: 9–11): 'Deliver me from the hand of my brother Esau, for I am greatly afraid of him'. The story of Jacob and Esau, from which this text stems, is full of duplicity and reversal of position. Both upper-voice texts have an essential reversal at their midpoint, which is made audible in the music.[77] The motetus text begins as a lover's complaint about unrewarded service. He bemoans the caprices of blind Fortune who smiles to the wicked but lets down the good. Following Boethius's lessons, the poet decides to ignore her tedious behavior, taking to prayer instead.[78]

Corde mesto Cantando conqueror,	With sad heart singing I complain,
Semper presto Serviens maceror,	a servant always ready, I weaken,
Sub honesto Gestu totus teror,	by honest deeds I waste away to nothing,
Et infesto Casu remuneror.	and a hostile fate is my reward.
In derisum, Fortuna, te ponis;	Into a laughing stock, Fortune, you make yourself;
Das arrisum Expars rationis	you giggle, devoid of reason,
Et obrisum Malis; sed a bonis	and you smile at the wicked; but the virtuous

---

[75] Lucan, *Pharsalia* X, line 407; quoted in the motet *Detractor est/Qui secuntur castra/Verbum iniquum et dolosum* (trans. in Strubel 2012, 168–71).

[76] Edited in Stewart *et al.* 1978, 230–1.

[77] The reversal is made audible by the register: until the midpoint the motetus is generally the higher voice; after it, the triplum takes its normal position. The register change is marked by brief melodic imitation. Boogaart 2001b, 102–9 and Zayaruznaya 2009, 204–9.

[78] Zayaruznaya rightly distinguishes three different 'realms' in the three stanzas of the text: courtly, philosophical, and religious, while also recognizing the division into two; see Zayaruznaya 2009, 192–4, 200, and 204–9. See also Huot 1994, 233–5; she interprets the motetus text as a 'complete rewriting of the French triplum: a transformation of courtly sentiment into spiritual conversion'. This is of course a plausible interpretation, though I prefer to read the texts as parallels. Parallelism of courtly love and Christian faith is also found in the conclusion of M20, *Trop plus/Biauté paree/Je ne sui mie*, where the lover prays to both God and Amours to help him serve his lady, so that she may consider him as her friend.

Tollis risum Et abis cum donis.   you deny your laugh, stealing away with your
                                                        gifts.

Spernens cece Fortune tedia   Spurning the irksomeness of blind Fortune,
Utor prece Cum penitencia,   I take to prayer with penitence,
Culpe fece Ut lauto venia,   so that, scrubbed clean of guilt's filth by
                                                        forgiveness,
Michi nece Promatur gloria.   in death glory will be mine.

(motetus, complete)

In the triplum text, which is filled with paradoxical sentences and possibly quotes from several trouvère chansons,[79] the lover first complains bitterly about his unattainable lady and wishes he had never seen her, but after the midpoint he accepts his lot and even wishes nothing else than to suffer. He concludes that, notwithstanding his pain, he will continue to serve his lady:

Par tel raison suis povres assasez,   By such logic, I am both deprived and satisfied,
Quant je plus vueil ce dont sui   Since I desire most what grieves me the worst:
    plus grevez:
Dont ne doit nuls pleindre   So no one should be upset about what I endure
    ce que j'endure
Quant j'aim seur tout ce qui n'a   In that I love above all the one who
    de moy cure   cares nothing for me.

(triplum, lines 31–4)

In Machaut's motet, then, the wished-for freedom consists in a stoic virtue, combining insight, resignation, and perseverance in the struggle with the paradoxes of Love and Fortune. In this case the connection between Vitry's and Machaut's motets might be sought in the Boethian associations.

These few examples show how motets could be composed as an exchange of ideas between the two best poet-composers of the fourteenth century, who pondered, each in his own preferred sphere, on subjects of mixed secular and spiritual character, away from the cruel reality of their time. Their ideas about love appear to be very different. Whether the connections are the result of a personal encounter and discussion, or of emulation of Vitry by Machaut, the younger artist, remains unknown; since M5, M12 and M17 seem to belong to Machaut's earliest productions, it is possible that they are the fruit of a meeting between the older and the younger composer. Admittedly, these motets demonstrate but one aspect of the manifold functions motets could assume in the fourteenth century, but an aspect that may bring us a little closer to the conceptual universe of these 'philosophers' in words and music.

[79] I have traced one poem by Gace Brulé from which several lines are quoted; see Boogaart 2001a, 31–2.

APPENDIX

PHILIPPE DE VITRY,
DOUCE PLAYSENCE / GARISON / NEUMA QUINTI TONI,
TEXTS AND TRANSLATIONS

Triplum

Douce playsence est d'amer loyalment,
Quar autrement ne porroit bonement
Amans suffrir cele dolour ardant,
Qui d'amors naist.

Quant ces [ses] regars par son soutil attrait
En regardant parmi soy mesmes trait,
Sans soy navrer,

L'impression de ce qu'il veut amer,
Jusqu'a son cuer, lors estuet remembrer
Et souvenir

Du gentil corps qu'il vit au departir.
Puis le convient trembler, muer, fremir
En tresailant

Et soupirer, cent fois en un tenant,
Le[s] dous soupirs qui livrent au cuer vent
Par les conduis,

Por quoy Desirs, qui est a celle duis,
Esprent et art et croist en ardant, puis
Fayre le doit.

Areu, hareu! cuers humains ne porroit
Cel mal soufrir, se playsence n'estoit
Qui souvent l'oint.

Mays on porroit demander bian apoint
Comment lo mal puet plaire qui si point,
et je respons:

En esperant d'avoir bon gueredon.
Por en saisir quant il leur sera bon
Enviet pluseurs

En traveyllant, sans cesser, nuit et jour.
Donques doit bien l'amoreuse dolour
Venir a gré,

En attendant la tres aute planté
Dont bonament a pluseurs saoulé.

It's a sweet pleasure to love loyally,
for in no other way a lover truly could bear
that burning pain
which is born from love.

When his look, by its subtle attraction,
draws into itself through looking
– without wounding itself –

the impression of the one he wants to love,
right to his heart, then he must remember
and imagine

the noble figure he saw at parting.
Next, he must tremble, change color,
shiver and shudder,

and sigh, a hundred times at once,
the sweet sighs that bring air to the heart
through the windpipes,

by which Desire, who is the channel to her,
kindles and burns and grows in burning,
since it must do that.

Help, help! A human heart could not
suffer that pain, if there were not pleasure
that often soothes it with balm.

But one might most rightly ask
how such a pain can please which stings so much,
and I answer:

in the hope to have a good reward.
To obtain that, when it will be for their good,
  spurs many on

to labor for it, unceasingly, day and night.
So Love's pain should indeed be
very welcome,

as one awaits the very great abundance
with which she has truly inebriated many [lovers].

Motetus

Garison selon Nature	Healing, in line with Nature,
Desiree [desire] de sa dolour	from its grief is desired by
Toute humaine creature,	every human being,
Mais je qui ai d'un ardour,	but I who have been enflamed by fire,
Naisant de loyal amour,	engendered by loyal love,
Espris de garir n'ay cure.	do not care to be healed;
Ains me plaist de jour en jour	rather, such burning pleases me
Adés plus telle ardeure,	better from day to day,
Nepourquant elle est si dure	although it is so harsh
Que nuls hons n'auroyt vigour	that no man would have the strength
Du soffrir, sans la douchour	to suffer it, if there were not the sweetness
Qui vient de playsance pure.	that springs from pure pleasure.

NEUMA QUINTI TONI   **NEUMA OF THE FIFTH TONE**

— 8 —

Motets, Manuscript Culture, Mise-en-page

John Haines and Stefan Udell

W HEN, TWO CENTURIES AGO, the royal courtier turned music archivist Jean-Benjamin de Laborde stumbled upon some thirteenth-century motets, he mistook them for monophonic songs – songs, he claimed, that had short hymn melodies tagged on at their end. The reason for the hymn, Laborde surmised, was to show the original Latin melody from which the Old French song before it was derived.[1] If he had actually compared the melodies, Laborde would have realized how different the Latin chants were from the Old French songs that preceded them. In fact, the French antiquarian had no idea that he was looking not at two separate melodies, but at two voices meant to sound together: the one an Old French melody or motetus, and the other a Latin chant fragment or tenor. Then again, Laborde's easy dismissal of the bilingual motet reflected the general attitude of his day towards counterpoint of the Middle Ages. As his contemporary Charles Burney wrote concerning organum of Gothic Antiquity (as he called the Middle Ages), such music would 'neither please nor instruct the modern contrapuntist'.[2] No wonder musical antiquarians of the eighteenth century had little interest in the medieval motet.

What had confused Laborde about the motets he had unwittingly uncovered was their mise-en-page, their layout on the page. These polyphonic pieces are laid out in part format where one voice follows the other, rather than score format which presents simultaneously sung voices one on top of the other, a clearer visual representation of their mode of performance. The early motet's layout would continue to confound scholars until just over a century ago, when a professor of Latin philology by the name of Wilhelm Meyer finally linked the earlier Latin organum to its bilingual descendant the motet, thereby correctly identifying Laborde's 'hymn incipits' as tenors, the lower voice of a polyphonic motet. To be fair, the polyphonies of Adam de la Halle had been known for decades before Meyer's discovery, but this was because the rondeaux of Adam were laid out in the more transparent score format.[3]

A few years after Meyer's serendipitous discovery, the first real scholar of the motet, a newly graduated doctor of history in his mid-twenties by the name of Friedrich Ludwig, set out to catalogue all extant sources containing medieval motets. Between 1897 and 1902, during what he called 'meine Studienreisen', Ludwig transcribed every bit of early medieval polyphony he could find in libraries all across Europe, filling up over thirty thick books with his transcriptions.[4] The task Ludwig had set before him of unravelling the motet was ambitious and, frankly, monumental. To

---

[1] Laborde cited in Haines 2004a, 198 n. 53.

[2] Burney cited in Haines 2004a, 169.

[3] Haines 2004a, 165–78.

[4] Ludwig in Haines 2003, 141. Some of Ludwig's notebooks do contain monophony as well.

175

make matters worse, Ludwig was a stickler for detail, and so he only published during his lifetime the initial volume of his motet catalogue, a work he titled *Repertorium organorum recentioris et motetorum vetustissimi stili* ('Catalogue of Very Late Organa and of Motets in the Earliest Style'). By the time the final section of this work appeared forty years after his death, thanks to Ludwig's students the entire *Repertorium* spanned three thick volumes, a still incomplete version of the master's total work.[5] Still today, researchers on the medieval motet owe their greatest debt to Ludwig's seminal spade work for having launched the study of the motet as a scientific enterprise within the booming industrial university of High Capitalism.[6] For the foreseeable future, at least, Ludwig's *Repertorium* will remain an indispensable guide to the study of the motet, provided medieval studies can keep pace with the humanities' seemingly inexhaustible potential for academic commodification.

To anyone discovering the medieval motet for the first time, like the young Ludwig it is easy to become overwhelmed by the genre's web of manuscript sources as well as these pieces' sometimes disconcerting layouts. The present chapter will provide a general survey of the manuscripts from the thirteenth and fourteenth centuries containing motets, with attention to the cultural context of these books on the one hand, and on the other to the main types of layout found in them.

MANUSCRIPT PRODUCTION AND LAYOUT IN THE MIDDLE AGES

For the most part, the medieval sources that survive with notated motets are collections, and usually medieval books of the highest quality (labelled 'high-grade' in this chapter) that contain more than just motets. It is possible to divide these books into two different types: sources with musical contents and sources that contain both literary works and musical ones.

Of the first type, sources that contain only musical pieces, we can distinguish three different kinds. Firstly are thirteenth-century collections of polyphony, the most famous of these for the motet being the manuscripts known as **Mo** and **Ba**, both produced sometime in the last few decades of the century. Some polyphonic collections also include some monophonic works, such as the monophonic conductus section found on fols. 415r–462v of the Notre Dame manuscript **F**. Secondly are anthologies of mostly monophonic songs, the so-called chansonniers – the focus of Gaël Saint-Cricq's chapter in this *Companion*. These sources include motets interspersed among songs, while some also feature brief sections devoted entirely to motets, like the motet gathering found in **Roi** (with motets on fols. 205r–210v). Thirdly are fourteenth-century collections of polyphony, such as **Iv** (with motets throughout), and **Ch** (with motets on fols. 60v–72v). It is worthwhile noting that the medieval books mentioned in this paragraph are not devoted to a single composer. Rather, they feature multiple composers, many of whom are anonymous.

The second type of extant motet source is a collection that combines literary (i.e., textual) and musical works. We begin with manuscripts containing the works of Adam de la Halle, most notably the book that comes closest to Adam's own edition of his works, **Ha**, where the famous Artesian's motets are found on fols. 34v–37r. Secondly are miscellanea, heterogeneous sources

5   Ludwig 1910–78. Subsequent reprints of vol. 2 and of both parts of vol. 1 were variously edited by Friedrich Gennrich and Luther Dittmer. Dittmer shared with me (John Haines) in a letter dated 15 February 2016 that 'in 1964 Heinrich Besseler, suffering the effects of a stroke, entrusted to me Ludwig's manuscript of vols. II and I,2 of the *Repertorium* ... We still must learn from the master Ludwig'.

6   On Werner Sombart's historical divisions of capitalism and specifically 'Hochkapitalismus' (as distinct from the medieval 'Frühkapitalismus'), see Sombart 1919, 2: 12, and more recently Arrighi 2010, 28–86; on Ludwig's cultural context, see Haines 2003.

that happen to include motets. Such is **Cl**, a mainly literary tome that features a small section of motets (fols. 370r–390v). Thirdly is the romance of Fauvel in the edition (**Fauv**) made by Chaillou de Pesstain, a literary animal story interspersed with musical pieces, some of which are motets. Finally, there are the complete-works manuscripts of Guillaume de Machaut. At least one of these, the book known as **Mach A**, was created under the supervision of the French composer himself.

From the perspective of our print-biased predilection for sameness, the sources just listed present a disconcerting, not to say sloppy, diversity. The reason for this is simple: to state an obvious but important point when it comes to the Middle Ages, no two books are the same. A deluxe manuscript, for example, can present the same contents as a more modest one but reorganize and augment the contents following a sophisticated structure, as argued below for **Fauv**.

All of the books under consideration in this chapter were handmade; the word 'manuscript' comes from the Latin expression *manu scripto*, meaning 'written by hand'. The handwritten books that have come down to us are the end products of an extensive copying process going back to earlier sources and drafts that unfortunately no longer survive. It is important to stress that only a minority of artifacts have come down to us from the total writing activity in the Middle Ages. Not surprisingly perhaps, it is the most expensive books that have been preserved. These books can tell us something about the majority of lost sources, for they were composed using a variety of exemplars that circulated among scribes and bookmakers at the time. Nevertheless, our view of medieval music writing in general and of the medieval motet in particular is stilted, much like the archaeologist holding the single surviving brick from an ancient palace that has long vanished from view.

One of the main interests of the surviving anthologies and collections, therefore, is what they can tell us about the various lost exemplars that preceded them – what they can tell us, in short, about medieval manuscript 'culture', to use a still fashionable academic term. In the Middle Ages as in Antiquity, the writing up of high-grade books involved a hierarchy of activities that all started with some kind of note-taking. This was nearly always done on a humbler writing surface than the high-grade parchment of surviving sources, media such as the ubiquitous wax tablet or parchment roll. The famous image of Machaut writing on a parchment roll attests to this preliminary activity.[7] Because they were generally more modest looking than the extant parchment codices, these low-grade media have not survived.

In the Middle Ages, as in Antiquity, the writing out of any text – including musical ones such as the surviving sources of the motet – followed three main stages.[8] First came the initial noting down, often in shorthand on a temporary surface such as wax (*notare*, following Roman nomenclature). Second, an outline and draft of the layout (*formare*), especially in the case of the most expensive books with an often intricate mise-en-page. Finally, this draft was revised and corrected to produce the final version (*emendare*). To repeat, little to nothing of this evidence survives for music. Yet we know from literary reports on the medieval writing process as well as the sources themselves (their paleography and codicology) that such a process was both inevitable and necessary in the making of a beautiful book like **Ch** or even **Roi**, for example. Thus the extant sources represent the endpoint of a complex writing process, from our point of view an 'invisible' transmission that we will never fully know.

As for the final *emendare* phase of the extant collections or anthologies, as we might call them, we can ascertain how these were produced with a greater amount of certainty. The typical process involved a series of tasks, the first of which was to prepare and cut the parchment. A typical parchment book took up the hides of several animals and cost a great deal more than today's books – at least several months' salary of a trade medieval worker.[9] Then the contents for the future codex had to be determined based on available exemplars. It is clear from some sources that not all exemplars were available at the time of compilation. One third of the Latin tenor voices in **Roi**, for example, were not copied down probably for this reason, as discussed below. Then began the preparation of the writing surface by pricking the edges of gatherings and tracing the ruling across folios, that is, across two pages.[10] Once this grid was established on the page, the actual writing could begin. (Throughout this chapter, the word 'page' will be used to refer to a single side, recto or verso, of a parchment folio, a nod to common practice even though 'page' usually refers to the numbered paper of printed books.) As a rule, the texts for musical pieces were inscribed first, which would enable the scribe to skip two or three ruling units, depending on how space was needed for the musical staff.

Either around this time or shortly after it, a scribe would trace in red ink each individual staff line, often hundreds of them at a time – without a doubt the most tedious task of all. For nearly the entire Middle Ages, the tracing of each red staff line in music books was done freehand. Gradually, in the early 1300s, a multi-nib fork instrument came to be used to trace staff lines. Unfortunately, we will never know exactly how this transition took place, since the earliest surviving music 'rake' ('rastrum'), as it has sometimes been called, dates from the eighteenth century.[11] Finally, the musical notes could be written down, along with other finishing touches ranging from rubrication to painting and illumination.

Out of what kind of milieu did these extant sources of the motet – sources that had been carefully laid out and planned, written up, notated, rubricated and illuminated – arise? In the broader history of the book, the surviving motet sources stand at a midway point between the time-honored handcrafted codex as a sacred object for most of the Middle Ages and the book as a commodity in the early mercantile days of capitalism.[12] The thirteenth century marks a major step in this transformation, a significant change in how human beings view the handmade artifact that is the book. Gianfranco Folena has identified the 1230s as the songbook's decade of transition from castle to city, from the noble patron owner to the new urban merchant.[13] And indeed, it is during this time that emerges a new urban bourgeois buyer who ultimately heralds the global book-buying customer of the modern era (from the 1500s onwards).

For most of the Middle Ages, books containing music were written up in scriptoria or writing workshops, most of which were in some way connected with the Church. Books with music were produced by monks or clerics working either in monasteries or churches, trained in the Latin liturgy. Most book production in Western Europe was linked to church-related activities and was almost exclusively in Latin, the language of learning. It was not until the last few centuries of the medieval millennium that new centers of book-making activity emerged in urban centers that were growing at an unprecedented rate. These new bookmaking ateliers catered on the one hand to a growing number of university students and on the other to an emerging bourgeoisie that, in the case of the motet, is epitomized in the city of Arras. Two of the motet's earlier sources, **Roi** and **Noailles**, were chansonniers either produced in Arras or by an Artesian scribe working elsewhere. For, in the wake of the Fourth Crusade, the production and consumption of Old French books

[9]   De Hamel 1992; Schramm 1933, 141.
[10] The pricking and ruling process is described and illustrated in Haines 2008, 333–6.
[11] Haines 2008, 363–7.
[12] Jardine 1996, ch. 6.
[13] Folena 1990, 135.

had become a cosmopolitan activity: French literature was well on its way to assuming cultural dominance. From around 1200 onwards, international demand grew significantly for books in Old French ranging from chronicles to songbooks, both across Europe and in French colonies in Greece and the Levant.[14]

In hindsight, we can see that this development around 1200 would lead only a few centuries later to the early modern commodification of the book. This is not surprising, for the Crusades, funded by a new international monetary system, were the warm-up act for Europe's bigger gambit in the late 1400s, the invasion of the Americas and the official birth of capitalism. Or, to paraphrase Giovanni Arrighi, it was during the Crusades that the late-medieval first systemic cycle of accumulation gave way to the modern interstate economic system.[15] With respect to the manuscript culture of the motet, then, the thirteenth and fourteenth centuries constitute a fascinating and crucial period. This period presents us with an ever-widening gap between the old book and the new: between a parochial auteur like Gautier de Coinci and an international composer like Pérotin whose Parisian works were disseminated as far as Scotland,[16] between an old-fashioned sentimentalist like Eudes of Nevers who took a French songbook with him to Acre as a reminder of his beloved Burgundy, and a new global mercenary like William of Villehardouin, whose eclectic anthology of songs and motets showed off his cosmopolitan status as the wealthy son of French emigrants and the Prince of Frankish Greece.[17]

This is the manuscript culture out of which arose the earliest motets, those musical pieces combining Latin chants and new Old French melodies. What is surprising is how little we know of the patrons and provenance of many of these books, especially those from the motet's first phase in the thirteenth century. For example, where, exactly when, and for whom was produced the thirteenth century's most ample and luxurious book of motets, **Mo**, are not known. Compiled sometime at the end of the thirteenth century, with over three hundred pieces representing nearly a hundred years' worth of motet composition, **Mo** first emerges out of historical obscurity two centuries after its initial production with its first known owner, Estienne Tabourot of Dijon.[18] Generally speaking, more is known about fourteenth-century sources, a high point being the books compiled by Machaut. Fairly accurate dates can be surmised by identifying illuminators of the manuscripts and when they worked, through mention of events and people in his poetical works, and through a handful of historical documents which place Machaut in the service of certain nobility. Nevertheless, the patronage and original use of these manuscripts remain conjectural.

Taking what little we do know about the original commission of thirteenth- and fourteenth-century books as a whole, it is nevertheless possible to distinguish two types of contexts and users. On the one hand, we have people moving in the traditional ecclesiastical environment, either churches, most famously the Cathedral of Notre Dame for manuscripts like the aforementioned made-in-Paris **F**, or monastic houses such as the Abbey of St Jacques in Liège for **Tu**. On the other hand, are wealthy secular patrons of the book such as the Prince of Frankish Greece mentioned earlier, whose songbook **Roi** was likely commissioned by an anonymous French nobleman, possibly Charles of Anjou.[19] Given the expensive quality of these books as well as the high social

---

[14] On this development, see Haines 2013, esp. 68 n. 54, and Haines forthcoming.

[15] Arrighi 2010, 37–48 and 111–29. See also Wallerstein 2011, 38.

[16] Everist 1990.

[17] Having arrived in Acre in 1265 with several Old French books in hand, including a songbook, Eudes died within a year; Haines 2013, 70.

[18] Wolinski 1992.

[19] Haines 2013, 58.

status of their destined users, they were generally carefully planned and sketched out. In fact, some cases present us with an astoundingly intricate structure. This can be seen best in **Fauv** discussed below and in Machaut's collected-works manuscripts, where music is used within and in relation to textual works in complex ways. Such intricately organized manuscripts were likely devised for the edification of patrons, for them to discover and follow the meaningful linkages set by the compilers of related content on the same page or across the manuscript.

MOTET LAYOUTS OF THE THIRTEENTH CENTURY

In a few of the earliest sources of the motet, such as **LoA**, motets are presented in a score format, with the motetus and tenor moving on the page one on top of the other in parallel fashion. This score format was the same one used for the motet's immediate polyphonic predecessor, organa. But in short order the score layout for motets would be abandoned in favor of part format, with the voices given one after the other. The exact reason for this switch from score to part layout is unclear, but likely has to do with the fact that the tenor voice takes up much less space than the upper voice or voices: as detailed in Chapter 3 of this volume, most tenors in early two-voice motets are short excerpts of a larger Latin chant, given in long notes with a text that is often restricted to a single word. From a purely monetary point of view, part layout makes sense: less precious parchment space is used up if the tenor's long-held notes are given in condensed form following the syllabic motetus, rather than taking up an entire staff below the motetus following the layout of most organa.

One of the intriguing questions regarding the copying out of early motets is whether the immediate exemplars that were used by the scribes for collections like **Roi** and **Noailles** had both motetus and tenor, or whether these scribes or their editors needed to locate two different exemplars at different times, one with the newly invented Old French tunes needed for the upper voices and the other with the existing Mass and Office chants to be used as tenors. We consider the latter possibility in the following comparison of layouts in manuscripts **Roi** and **Noailles**.

An important factor influencing the layout of a given motet was whether its book's individual pages had been initially split into two columns or not. Taking the opening page of motets in **Roi** (fol. 205r shown in Figure 8.1), we can see that it is divided into two main columns.[20] Like most music books, this double-column layout is the same throughout the entire book; in this case the two columns each measure 75mm x 215mm. Here again, the modern reader is struck by the handmade nature of the medieval book, as column dimensions vary from one codex to the other; at least for the books under consideration here, there was no one universal column measurement. This mapping out of pages into columns was done at the earliest stage of compilation, right after the ruling process described earlier in this chapter. After the horizontal ruling lines were traced across a folded parchment folio or binion, a second grid was established on each individual page. This grid defined both the writing block and the page margin areas. Following carefully made prick marks, a series of vertical lines were drawn for left and right margins and two columns, if needed. Only then could writing begin. Looking at the page shown in Figure 8.1, we see that it contains three full motetus voices with their tenors. In fact, the latter have blank staves; only the motetus staves have music notation.[21] At the bottom of the page begins a fourth motetus, pointing to a layout problem that would worsen later in the thirteenth century as more upper

---

[20] The style of the diagrams in this chapter builds on the diagrams given in Apel 1953 and Switten 1995, 8.

[21] The motets in Roi are listed in J. Beck and L. Beck 1938, 1: xxiv–xxv.

voices were added to motets, the problem of motets starting and finishing on different pages. We will address this shortly.

The contents of the motet section in **Roi**, compiled in the 1250s, are strikingly similar to those of manuscript **Noailles** compiled a few decades or so later. A comparison of **Roi**'s opening motet page (Figure 8.1) and that of **Noailles** (Figure 8.2, fol. 179r) is instructive, for they both open with the exact same motets but in different layouts. In Figure 8.2, we can see that **Noailles**'s page, unlike **Roi**'s, has a single-column layout; its writing block measures 145mm x 205mm, slightly less than **Roi**'s (162mm x 215mm). The crucial difference between the two lies in **Roi**'s two columns as opposed to **Noailles**'s one. A glance at both pages makes clear that while **Roi**'s double-column layout allows for more to fit on its page, the result is a crowded, less elegant look. While **Noailles**'s single-column layout 'breathes' more, it can only fit two and a half motets compared to **Roi**'s three and a half.[22] We also notice that **Noailles**, unlike **Roi**, has musical notes in both the tenor and motetus voices. Ludwig once suggested that the greater number of missing tenors in **Roi**'s motet section – fourteen of its thirty-six motets lack music notation for their tenors – implied that **Roi**'s scribe was more familiar with copying Old French songs than Latin chant melodies.[23] A simpler explanation for this lacuna, however, could be that those who ruled **Roi**'s pages and drew its staves failed to allot enough space for some tenors because these did not yet have the exemplars available for the tenor voices. As seen in Figure 8.2, tenor 1 in **Noailles** takes up three or four times the space that is allotted for it in **Roi** (Figure 8.1).[24]

Like **Noailles**, two other early important sources of the motet, **F** and **W2**, employ a single-column layout. In **F** we find 26 conductus motets followed by a section containing 40 two-voice motets and 3 three-voice motets; all are in Latin. Since the upper voices of the conductus motets share one Latin text, they are written in score format, but to save space, the tenor is notated on its own immediately after the upper voices conclude. Interestingly, these motets are ordered according to the tenor chant's placement in the liturgical calendar. For the rest of the motets in **F**, the voices are always written successively, one after the other, but the liturgical ordering no longer consistently holds.[25] Of **W2**'s over 200 motets, not only are there far more three-voice polytextual motets than in **F**, but there are also dozens that employ French poetry in the upper voice or voices. All of the motets in **W2** are laid out on the page following the same principles as in **F**. The predominant ordering principle, however, differs: for instance, at fol. 145r begins a series of 19 two-voice Latin motets, arranged not according to the tenor incipit but instead alphabetically by the first letter of the motetus text. Several additional alphabetical series of motets ensue.

As to the process of copying tenor and motetus voices from exemplar to final copy, we can learn more from patterns of erasures that are found in certain manuscripts. In these cases, the notes that scribes have erased by scratching out with a penknife are still visible on the parchment. Thus we see both the original melodic error and its correction or alteration. The types of error found for music – transposing a melody up or down a second or a third, for example – confirms that scribes were copying from written exemplars and not making up the music as they went.[26] In most cases, scribes seem to have looked at the exemplar, taken in a half dozen notes, looked down to write these out, and returned to the exemplar again.[27] One notable source of musical

---

[22] A list of motets in **Noailles** (as well as those in **Roi**) appears in Everist 1989, 357–63.

[23] Ludwig 1910–78, 1/1: 299–305.

[24] Wolinski 1996 likewise offers suggestions for copying rationale.

[25] See Catherine A. Bradley's chapter for further discussion of the organization and layout of F.

[26] Haines 2004b.

[27] Haines 2004b, 74.

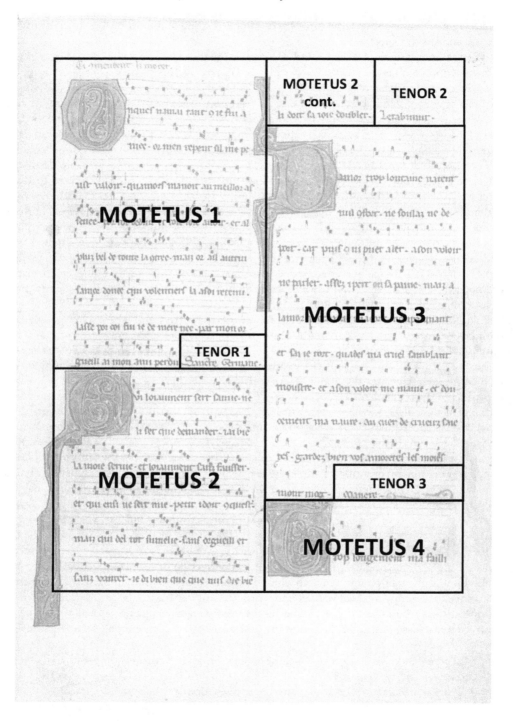

Figure 8.1. Layout of the opening page of motets in **Roi**, fol. 205r (BnF)

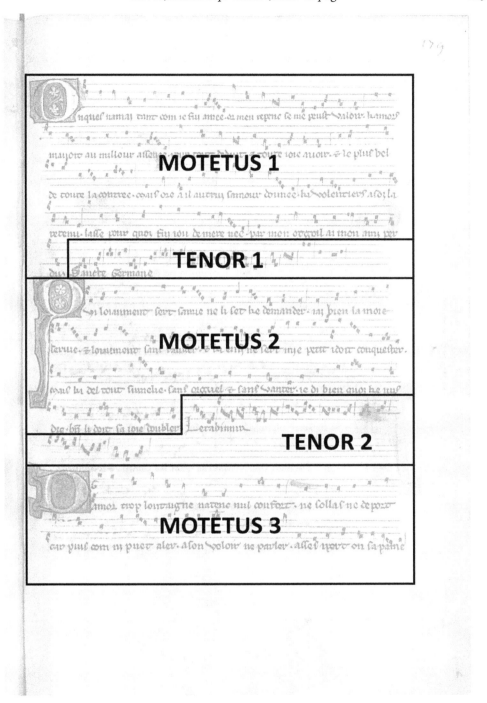

Figure 8.2. Layout of the opening page of motets in **Noailles**, fol. 179r (BnF)

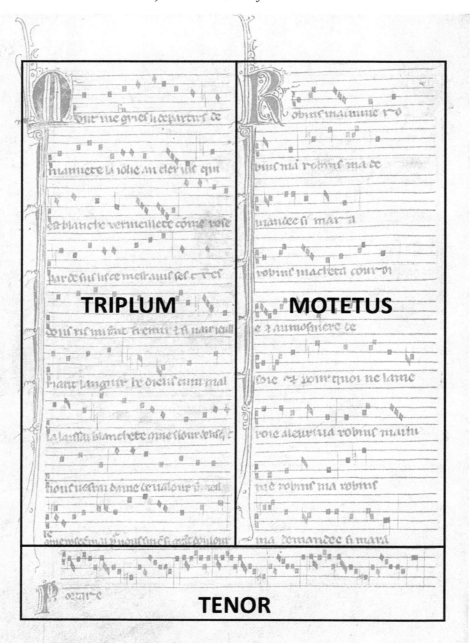

Figure 8.3. Layout of *Mout me fu/Robin m'aime/Portare* in Ba, fol. 52v

erasures for motets is manuscript **Cl**, whose motet collection was probably copied sometime in the 1260s. The patterns of erasures in this book is interesting in that it suggests scribal fatigue. In the first half of the motet libellus, few errors occur. But, beginning at the halfway mark, errors increase until a concluding 'burst of accuracy culminating at the final folio which is entirely free of erasures'.[28] Which is to say, medieval scribes were human beings like the rest of us.

The thirteenth century culminates in two of the most lavish collections of motets from the Middle Ages, manuscripts **Mo** and **Ba** mentioned earlier.[29] The main challenge for the editors of each book was a motet corpus that most often featured more than one upper voice, so predominantly three- and four-voice motets rather than the two-voice type (motetus and tenor). **Mo** uses several different layouts for its more than 300 motets.[30] For instance, the 17 four-voice motets that begin at fol. 23v present the quadruplum and triplum each in their own column on a verso, and the triplum and tenor each in their own column on a recto. The three-voice motets in the next several sections of **Mo** employ a single column format: the triplum appears on the verso, the motetus on the recto, and the tenor runs across the bottom of the entire opening. In the later sections of **Mo**, however, three-voice motets are typically presented with two columns per page: the triplum occupies the left column, the motetus the right column, and the tenor spans the bottom of the page. This last type of layout was also used for the 100 motets in **Ba.** One of the more straightforward cases is shown in Figure 8.3, **Ba**'s fol. 52v. Triplum and motetus run in two columns side by side for most of the page; the lowest staff with the tenor runs across the whole writing block. Thus this three-voice motet is made to fit neatly on a single page. With **Ba** and the last sections of **Mo** we have left the simpler part layout of the motet for something more complex, pointing the way to the fourteenth century. While there is no discernable ordering principle within each section of **Mo**, **Ba** arranges its 100 motets alphabetically based on the first letter of the motetus (not triplum) voice.

MOTET LAYOUTS IN THE FOURTEENTH CENTURY

A new layout practice was established in the first source of motets in the fourteenth century, the so-called Fauvel manuscript, **Fauv**, written up around 1316. Aside from the *Roman de Fauvel*, the manuscript also contains a section of dits, chansons, and a historical chronicle in verse. The *Roman de Fauvel*, which heads the manuscript, is a *roman à chansons*, or a romance with interpolated music, and is the most sophisticated of its kind.[31] This copy of the Fauvel romance incorporates 169 pieces in its poetical structure, 34 of these being motets. The location of a motet is determined by its relation to the text, images, and other musical pieces to produce meaning within the larger narrative of the story; consequently, the layout of the motets in **Fauv** differs from the criteria in the other manuscripts we have seen so far. Far from haphazard musical supplements, not only are the Fauvel motets placed at pivotal points in the story, but they also serve to delineate the structural layout of the romance. Most of the motets are concentrated at either ends of the romance as the

---

[28] Haines 2004b, 67.

[29] Although these manuscripts can be dated at roughly the end of the century, it is important to note that the motets in Mo especially provide examples of the genre that span a period of at least fifty to sixty years.

[30] Tischler (1978, xxix–xxxi) provides useful diagrams and a discussion of the types of page layouts present in **Mo**.

[31] The medieval expression *roman* or 'romance' simply means a story that is not in Latin but in a Romance vernacular, in this case Old French.

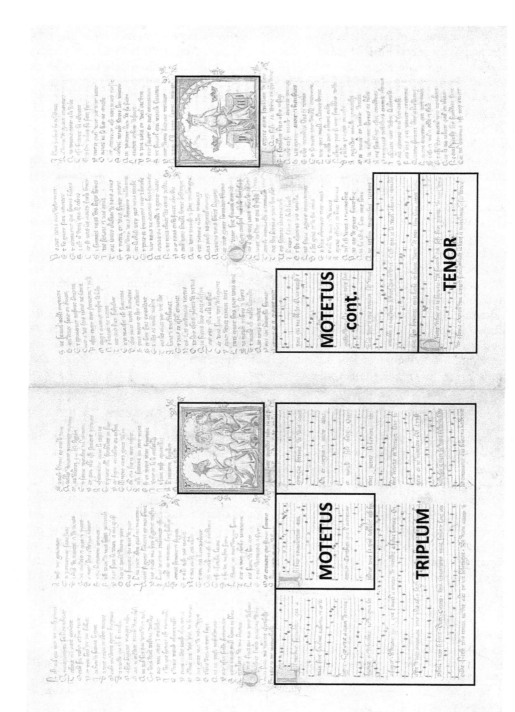

Figure 8.4. Layout of *La mesnie fauveline/J'ai fait nouveletement/Grant despit* in Fauv, fols. 15v–16r (BnF)

first and last items, thus highlighting their importance as structural markers. The majority are Latin texted and many are previous works that were adapted or simply inserted into the romance. Of the rest, four are bilingual motets (Latin and Old French) and four have the vernacular in all three voices. Some of these are likely unique to the manuscript. It is obvious from their content that several were specifically composed for the romance.[32]

As the largest manuscript examined in this chapter (462mm x 330mm), **Fauv** easily accommodates several full pieces on a single page, yet there are four motets copied across openings (from verso to recto) and one across a page turn (from recto to verso). These appear to have been placed this way intentionally. Of these motets, possibly the most interesting in terms of layout is the motet on the opening of fols. 15v–16r, *La mesnie fauveline/J'ai fait nouveletement/Grant despit* (Figure 8.4). It has one of the most involved layouts of all the motets, fully integrated as it is in the larger structure of the romance, surrounded by its relevant text and images. The motet coincides with Fauvel's arrival at Fortune's home (called *macrocosm*) and it marks the end of the romance's first third; here begins a dialogue between Fauvel and Fortune. Likewise, at the two-thirds point of the romance, where Fortune takes her leave of Fauvel, ending the dialogue between the two, there is a motet on fol. 30r: *Aman novi probatur exitu/Heu! Fortuna subdola/Heu me! Tristis est anima mea*.[33] Thus *La mesnie/J'ai fait* on fol. 15v–16r corresponds both structurally and narratively to *Aman novi/Heu! Fortuna* fifteen folios later. The broader architectural planning of *La mesnie/J'ai fait* is matched by the specifics of its text, clearly composed for this location of the romance: it summarizes the verses that immediately precede it, where Fauvel gives a speech to his courtiers and prepares to approach Fortune to ask her hand in marriage.[34]

A closer look at *La mesnie/J'ai fait* makes clear just how intricately the motet is interwoven into the romance. As can be seen in Figure 8.4, *La mesnie/J'ai fait* is surrounded by text and images. The image on fol. 15v (left side) shows Fauvel at left edge of the frame facing to the right and towards his courtiers, the Vices, to whom he is talking. On the facing folio is Fortune, sitting and holding out two crowns and looking across the opening to Fauvel with displeasure. This cross-folio interaction is mirrored in the motet layout. The tenor, in Fortune's voice, is copied on the folio with the image of Fortune. The triplum, the voice of the courtiers, is on the folio that they occupy. The motetus, in Fauvel's voice, is copied across the folio, representing his transition from the courtiers to his meeting with Fortune. The page break of the motetus voice splits Fortune's name (*for | tune*), highlighting the purpose in the layout. The voices are also placed in a manner that is unique to this motet. The triplum voice is written in full on fol. 15v, across the three columns. It surrounds on all sides the first part of the motetus voice in the top of the middle column's music layout – to the left, bottom, and right of it. This is likely intentional as it replicates Fauvel's courtiers surrounding him in the accompanying image.

There is also a symmetrical musical and lyrical pattern in the structure of *La mesnie/J'ai fait* designed to incorporate the motet more completely into this meaningful layout. The aforementioned page break, in the motetus voice at *fortune*, occurs at the fifteenth long plus two semibreves (or the sixteenth 'measure') of the music, reflecting the voice's page break at fol. 16. The same happens for the column break in the triplum voice, at the fifteenth long plus two semibreves (or the sixteenth 'measure') from the end of the music. In a similar symmetrical fashion, the change of column width in the motetus voice of *Aman novi/Heu! Fortuna*, the structurally corresponding

---

[32] Roesner *et al.* 1990, 16.

[33] Although the text of the triplum begins 'Quoniam novi' in the manuscript, it has been shown to be corrupt and should instead read 'Aman novi'; see Becker 1936.

[34] Roesner *et al.* 1990, 16.

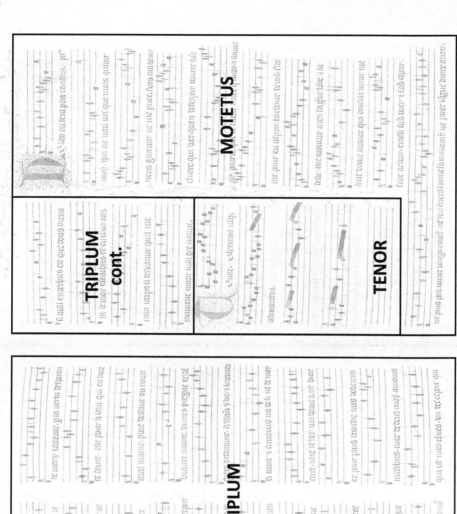

Figure 8.5. Layout of Motet 10, *Hareu! hareu! le feu / Helas! ou sera pris confors / Obediens usque ad mortem* in Mach C, fols. 214v–215r (BnF)

motet on fol. 30r, occurs at the midpoint of the voice, at the thirtieth long plus two semibreves from both the end and the beginning of the music, reflecting its location and corresponding to its local layout concerns. The symmetrical breaks in the layouts of these two motets, which would not be audible in performance but are highlighted by the layout and the specific placement of meaningful words in the lyric, reveal an approach to structure in terms of the medieval idea of *musica*, or the harmony of the spheres. The micro-structure of the motets mirror the macro-structure of the romance, as these layouts outline the equally symmetrical Fortune's dialogue previously pointed out (from fol. 16 to fol. 30).[35]

From the Fauvel romance in the early fourteenth century we move to the famed poet and composer Guillaume de Machaut later on in the 1300s. The layout schemes of the famous **Fauv** manuscript seem to have influenced Machaut. This can be seen in the precise and meaningful layouts in his poetical works and in the compilation of his large complete-works anthologies, all of which contain long-form poetical works, *romans à chansons*, a lyric poetry collection, and music sections that are ordered by genre. The ordering of the motet section has been examined in detail by Jacques Boogaart and Anne Walters Robertson; it likely mattered to the poet composer since it was retained throughout all copies of his complete-works manuscripts.[36] This is important to keep in mind when looking at the layout of individual motets in Machaut's manuscripts, since in some cases their meaningful placement within sections has an influence on their layouts.[37] Beyond their ordering, the motet sections are also highly consistent in layout and notation across manuscripts, as Lawrence Earp has noted, which is not the case for Machaut's other music sections.[38] In his first manuscript of collected works, **Mach C** (completed in the early 1350s),[39] there is a section of nineteen motets. The motet section is at the end of the manuscript and does not fit a single gathering or set of gatherings, so the section was not restricted by a set amount of space (the opposite is the case for the last example of the chapter).

The layout of Machaut's M10 (Figure 8.5) is representative of the whole motet section in **Mach C**. Mise-en-page is consistent from one motet to the next, with variations due only to the lengths of the voices. No matter the length of the motet, each one takes up two facing pages, as illustrated here. Occasionally, one finds empty staves where the scribe finished copying the notes of a voice in less than the allotted space. In general, more staff space was planned for than used; only five of Machaut's motets in **Mach C** take up all the space in the staves. As seen in Figure 8.5, there is one empty staff after the tenor part of M10's layout. The ordering of the voices here is consistent with those in the **Mo** and **Fauv** manuscripts, with the triplum first rather than the motetus. Although the order of the motets is retained in later manuscripts, the layout changes in some important respects. In **Ferrell 1**, the layout remains one motet per opening, but in a single column format and with each voice following in the order triplum-motetus-tenor. In **Mach A**,

---

[35] There are several more clues incorporated into this structural treatment, such as in the motet tenor's lyric, where Fortune predicts that she will present Vainglory to Fauvel at the end of their dialogue on fol. 30. Also, both motets play with language. Fortune sings in vernacular in *La mesnie/J'ai fait* and Fauvel sings in Latin in *Aman novi/Heu! Fortuna*, a reversal of their proper modes of speech. See Roesner *et al.* 1990, 16.

[36] Boogaart 1993 and 2001a; Robertson 2002, 79–102, 152–4. From the initial ordering in **Mach C**, there was the addition of M4 and three more at the end. **Mach E** is the only one to have a different ordering. See Earp 1989, 489–92.

[37] This idea, as relevant to **Mach A** especially, is supported by arguments in my (Stefan Udell's) forthcoming dissertation (University of Toronto).

[38] Earp 1983, 65–7.

[39] For the most recent scholarship that addresses the dating of **Mach C**, see Earp 2014, 1: 30–1.

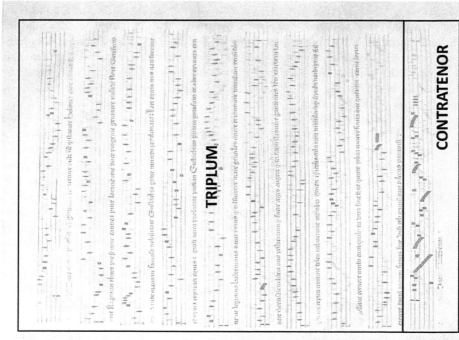

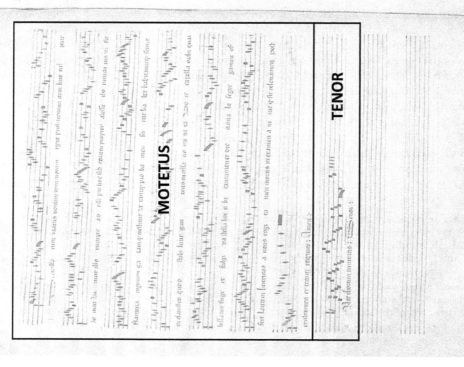

Figure 8.6. Layout of *Portio nature/Ida capillorum/Contratenor/Ante thronum trinitatis* in Ch, fols. 61v–62r (image CNRS-IRHT, © Bibliothèque et archives du château de Chantilly)

the layout is similar to **Mach C** with the main difference being that column two of the verso side contains the motetus voice, as opposed to the continuation of the triplum. The facing recto side repeats this layout with the triplum in the first column and the motetus in the second, with the tenor following the motetus voice rather than the triplum.

As mentioned earlier, there are some clues in Machaut's manuscripts that provide compelling evidence regarding their patronage. **Mach C** is a good example of this. We know from certain historical documents and from his poetry that Machaut was employed by King John of Bohemia until his employer's death in 1346.[40] Machaut likely wrote one of his most famous works, the *Remede de Fortune*, for John's daughter, Bonne of Luxembourg. Since the manuscript begins with *Jugement du roy de Behaigne*, a *dit* in honor of her father, followed by a lavish copy of the *Remede de Fortune*, illustrated by the most important of the three artists employed for the manuscript, scholars have concluded that it was likely made for her.[41] Bonne died probably from the plague in 1349 while the manuscript was still being made, but a member of the royal family, possibly her husband and the future King John II the Good, commissioned its completion as a memorial to Bonne, as is suggested by a document from the treasurer of King John II.[42] Although this is not definitive evidence, compared to previous manuscripts there is much more historical documentation with which to build such arguments for patronage.

The so-called Chantilly codex, **Ch**, likely compiled in the 1410s,[43] is a high-grade music manuscript, justly famous for its extravagant combination of music notation and artistic design. It features a motet section containing thirteen pieces. Like **Fauv**, **Ch** is a large manuscript (387mm x 286mm) and made of high quality parchment. There does not appear to be an ordering principle similar to the **Fauv** and Machaut manuscripts. Unlike the layout of **Fauv** (Figure 8.4) or that of **Mach C** (Figure 8.5), **Ch** presents its works in a single-column format (Figure 8.6); the break from the two-column format that dominated much of the previous two centuries is likely due to a wealthy patron's extravagant request. The book's writing block is an impressive 280mm x 225mm. To give an indication of size, **Mach C** has 57% of the page space of **Ch**, the whole codex being approximately the size of **Ch**'s writing block alone. Considering this, it is remarkable that each folio side of **Ch** is dedicated to only one chanson, with only a few exceptions, and each facing page opening to a single motet. In contrast to the books surveyed earlier in this chapter, including the just discussed **Mach C**, in **Ch** the book planners made no effort to put as much content as could fit on a page, in part dictated by the single column layout. As we saw above in the case of **Roi** compared with **Noailles** (Figures 8.1 and 8.2), a multiple column layout allows for a greater economy of space. Most folios in **Ch** have empty staves in their lower portions. Of all the high-grade manuscripts considered so far, **Ch** was the most lavish, and probably the most expensive if its extravagant layout is any indication.

Many medieval books, including most of those considered in this chapter, are organized in distinct gatherings that were later assembled together. For most manuscripts of this period, these gatherings or booklets were made up of four parchment sheets folded together to form eight leaves or folios, called quires or quaternions. For example, both manuscripts **Roi** and **Noailles** (Figures 8.1 and 8.2) present the majority of their songs in groups of eight-folio gatherings, with the motets placed near the end of the anthology in the form of two or more gatherings. **Ch**'s contents are similarly organized. For example, its fourth gathering contains predominantly four-voice chansons.

---

[40] Earp 1995, 8–28.

[41] For a summary of the arguments on this subject, see Earp 1989, 467–8.

[42] Earp 1995, 26–7 and Earp 2014, 1: 31.

[43] See Bent 2017, 21 and *passim* for the most recent discussion of the dating of Ch.

The motets that immediately follow are contained within a single gathering, the last one in the book. Rather than four folded sheets of parchment, however, **Ch**'s gatherings are a little larger; each is made up of six sheets (called a sexternion) yielding twelve folios. The scribes of **Ch** had to carefully mete out the total number of pieces in this allotted space: since there were thirteen motets to fit on twelve folios, the scribes began the first motet at the end of the fourth gathering of four-voice chansons and placed the last, short motet onto the gathering's very last page.

The ordering of the voices in **Ch**'s motet section forms a general yet inconsistent pattern. As seen in Figure 8.6, the voices that take up more space, the motetus and triplum, are copied at the top of each page, with the tenor and contratenor voices placed under these. Except for the **Ch**'s first motet, the motetus voice always appears on the verso side of a folio, an ordering that is contrary to the other manuscripts examined here. In some ways, **Ch**'s layout is old-fashioned. In *Portio/Ida* shown in Figure 8.6, the tenor voice follows the motetus, like the earliest examples of this chapter (Figures 8.1 and 8.2), but this order holds for only five of the motet layouts. Sometimes, the contratenor follows the motetus, and in a couple of instances, both tenor and contratenor are found below the triplum on the recto folio. There does not appear to be any reason for the latter layout, since in one case (fol. 67v), there is enough space for the tenor or contratenor voice.

CONCLUSION

If recent scholarship has come further than the eighteenth-century scholar Jean-Benjamin de Laborde mentioned at the beginning of this chapter who mistook medieval polyphonic pieces for monophonic songs, there still remains much to learn about the early motet as a product of the book-making cultures of the thirteenth and fourteenth centuries. As already mentioned, little is known about who exactly commissioned and created most of the books containing motets. Such vital questions of provenance are intimately linked to the origins of the motet itself. Whatever light future research can throw on the patrons and scribes of books like **Noailles** or **Ba** will likely tell us something interesting about the motet itself as a musical genre. The books of the fourteenth century in particular raise the specific question of why motets were laid out the way they were – at least in the extant manuscripts. For, more than likely, the music scribes of the extant manuscripts were copying from exemplars that are unfortunately now lost. What was the appearance of these original sources of the motet? Were individual motet voices taken from disparate sources or were they already written out together in these lost exemplars? And if so, were they in score format or part format? Finally, why were these books copied down in the first place? A great deal of medieval music, from lullabies to music for specific instruments, was never copied down. What about these pieces motivated literate musicians to set them down in parchment? Many of the answers to these questions are, to cite the medieval motet's first scientist Friedrich Ludwig speaking a century ago, 'a task of the musicology of the future'.[44]

---

[44] Haines 2003, 164.

9

Clerics, Courtiers, and the Vernacular Two-Voice Motet:
The Case of *Fines amouretes/Fiat* and the *Roman de la poire*

Jennifer Saltzstein

I N HIS 1993 BOOK, *Discarding Images*, Christopher Page offered a sustained critique of studies of intertextuality in the *ars antiqua* motet. Page argued that modern scholars who undertook nuanced interpretations of the relationships between the different voices of polytextual motets were operating from a personal bias toward bookishness.[1] Reinterpreting oft-cited passages of Johannes de Grocheio's *De musica* regarding the literate audience of the medieval motet, Page reacted against the scholarly tendency to view this audience as a cultural or intellectual élite who interpreted motets 'in a fashion that somehow approximates to what a musicologist, armed with dictionaries, concordances, the *Glossa ordinaria*, and more besides can accomplish'.[2] Scholars such as Sylvia Huot and others viewed the subtle, intertextual meanings that emerged when interpreting the motet voices against one another as evidence of the learnedness of their composers and audiences.[3] Page disagreed, arguing that these intertextual interpretations highlighted fortuitous, rather than intentional, connections, and hypothesizing that the motet composers of the thirteenth century were more interested in using musical structure to highlight the phonic qualities of their texts, such as the rhyme scheme and rhyme sounds. The reaction to Page's critique and his novel theory of motet aesthetics was swift and largely negative.[4] Moreover, in the decades that followed, intertextual analyses of motets, many directly inspired by Huot's work, proliferated, arguably forming the mainstream of current *ars antiqua* motet scholarship.[5] Although they successfully showcase the interpretive possibilities of the genre, these recent studies have perpetuated other scholarly biases that Page rightly criticized in *Discarding Images*. Page warned, for example, that intertextual motet interpretations overwhelmingly focused on just one source: the old corpus of **Mo**. He also noted that intertextual analyses privileged motets that featured contrasting upper voices over the more numerous examples in which the texts of the upper voices were poetically

---

[1] Page 1993a, ch. 3.

[2] Page 1993a, 86.

[3] Page's critique is primarily directed at a particular article: Huot 1989.

[4] His argument was roundly criticized in the reviews of *Discarding Images* and later in full-length articles supporting the value of intertextual interpretation. For article-length responses, see Weller 1997 and S. Clark 2007.

[5] See discussion in Dillon 2012, 32. Intertextual analyses of the *ars antiqua* motet include, for example, Butterfield 1993, S. Clark 2007, Colton 2008, Grau 2013, Hoekstra 1998, Huot 1997, and Rothenberg 2011.

similar in their theme, register, and genre.[6]

Page also argued that the focus on intertextuality had led scholars to all but ignore a substantial portion of the motet repertoire: the two-voice motet.[7] The two-voice motet repertory has arguably received less attention than it deserves, particularly from the hermeneutic perspectives that have animated so much recent research on the genre.[8] The importance of the two-voice motet in the context of the motet genre is clear: the majority of the earliest motets in Latin and French were written for two voices, two-voice motets appear in most of the major surviving motet manuscripts, and the two-voice motet was broadly cultivated, appearing in not only Parisian polyphonic sources but also chansonniers connected to Arras.[9] Indeed, the sheer number of two-voice motets should encourage us to pay them more attention. They comprise a quarter of the motets transmitted in **Mo** and a significant portion of the motet repertory as a whole.[10]

For Page, the subgenre offered an important correction to the modern critical fascination with intertextuality: 'Many of the earlier motets comprise a single, texted line over a plainchant tenor; unless there is some manner of relationship between the text and the tenor cue ... then the question of "intertextual" relations within the motet does not arise'.[11] Many of the motets in the surviving corpus thus presented the listener with a song accompanied by a tenor. These motets were untouched by the drama of upper-voice registral contrast or the mixing of poetic genres; instead, they offered accessibility and clarity of poetic and musical structure. This chapter centers on a case study: the two-voice motet, *Fines amouretes* (794)/*Fiat* (O50). This motet illustrates the accessibility and songlike nature of the two-voice motet subgenre while also attesting to the continued relevance of intertextuality. The most important intertext in *Fines amouretes/Fiat* lies not between the motet's own voices – it is accomplished through the motet composer's use of an intertextual refrain, a short phrase of text and sometimes music that circulated intertextually across thirteenth-century music and poetry.[12] Investigation of the motet's musical and poetic structure as well as its ties to the interpolated romance the *Roman de la poire* invites renewed reflection on the *ars antiqua* motet's audiences and its cultural functions.

The motet, *Fines amouretes/Fiat*, appears on fol. 238r–v of **Mo** and on fol. 230v of **W2**. A complete edition appears in Example 9.1.[13] Its tenor, *Fiat*, is drawn from the verse of an Office responsory for the feast of the Holy Trinity, 'replebitur majestate eius omnis terra; fiat, fiat' ('his great majesty shall fill all the earth. Let it be so! Let it be so!').[14] In our motet, the tenor is divided into four cursus of twenty pitches each (marked in Roman numerals in Example 9.1). The two-voice texture is divided into two distinct sections that are not governed by the tenor patterning, but rather center around the text's versification and the diegetic performance of an

---

[6] An important exception to this tendency is Grau's analysis of what she terms the 'homoglossic' motet. See discussion in Grau 2013.

[7] See Page, 1993a, 95.

[8] For studies of compositional process in the two-voice motet repertory, see Bradley 2011, Bradley 2014a, and Saint-Cricq 2013b.

[9] Two-voice motets appear in **Roi** and **Noailles**, both believed to originate in Arras, as well as in several other non-Parisian sources. See especially Saint-Cricq's chapter in the present volume.

[10] Bradley 2014b, 407.

[11] See Page 1993a, 93–5.

[12] I discuss the mechanics of thirteenth-century refrain usage in Saltzstein 2013b. On refrain usage in romance, see especially Ibos-Augé 2010. For an excellent, recent hermeneutic interpretation of a pair of two-voice motets, see Bradley 2017.

[13] The edition in Example 9.1 follows **Mo** but with *ficta* interpolated.

[14] See 'Replebitur majestate eius omnis terra; fiat, fiat' at www.cantusdatabase.org.

Example 9.1. *Fines amouretes/Fiat*

intertextual refrain.[15] The rhyme scheme is *a5′ b5 a5′ b5 a5′ b5 b4 c5 c4 d8′ c7 c4 e6 e3 e8 f6 e6*. The motetus part's first section begins with three equal phrases of six perfections each (numbered in the example); these phrases correspond with the motetus' rhyme scheme for the first six verses of the text: *a5′ b5 a5′ b5 a5′ b5*. In this opening passage, the speaker addresses a plea directly to 'True beloved', begging him to convince his lady's friend to serve as an emissary and deliver to her a song he has written (lines 1–6). In lines 7–8, the subject announces his impending performance of the song in question, which is the rather long refrain, '*A li m'envois/ne m'en tendroie mie, mie;/je l'aim trop, a li m'envois*' (vdB 101). The meaning of this refrain is ambiguous; the second verse has been translated 'I would not understand myself', following the spacing in **Mo**, which provides no space between the letters in the words 'm'entendroie'.[16] If the poet actually intended 'm'en tendroie', using the verb 'se tenir' (meaning, in this case, 'remain') rather than 'entendre', a different, perhaps more logical, translation of the full refrain emerges: 'I am going to her, I could never remain, I love her too much, I am going to her'.[17] This is the way the refrain text is segmented in its only other surviving poetic context, a concordance I will discuss further below. Neither **Mo** nor **W2** provides a space between 'm'en' and 'tendroie', which could indicate that the poet indeed intended 'm'endendroie'. However, the spacing of other words in the two manuscripts is inconsistent. The scribe of **W2** divides 'm'envois' into 'm'en vois' whereas the **Mo** scribe writes 'm'envois'; the scribes in both **W2** and **Mo** write 'enfrançois' rather than 'en François'. Thus we cannot know for certain based on the segmentation of the words what the poet intended to express in the second verse of the refrain.

The refrain is integrated into the text's rhyme scheme through a *vers de liaison* – the introduction of a 'c' rhyme ('-ois') in line 8 ('que di en françois'). This technique is often used to foster ties between a borrowed lyric and its surrounding poetic context. The motet's second section (lines 9–17, starting from the anacrusis to perfection 24) focuses on the speaker's performance of the refrain, followed by his pledge to love her loyally. The motet composer highlights the poetic structure musically in several ways. Immediately before the central passage in which the speaker performs his song (the refrain), the composer brackets the text 'ce chant ci' ('this song here' line 7, perfections 19 and 20) with rests in both voices and sets the motetus and tenor parts in the same rhythmic values; the homorhythm continues through line 8 ('que di en François'). Moreover, this is the first time in the motet that the phrase structures between the motetus and tenor align; in the opening verses, the tenor phrases overlap with the motetus structure. This sudden alignment between the two voices casts the tenor in an accompanimental role, amplifying the motetus voice and its text. This is also the only section of the motet in which the ranges of the two voices are crossed, a factor that is surprising given that the motetus voice has an unusually wide melodic range: an eleventh.[18] The voice crossing in line 7 and the homorhythmic setting and tenor alignment in lines 7–8 work together to trumpet the phrase 'this song here that I sing in French', which demarcates the intertextual refrain that follows, 'A li m'envois' (vdB 101), as the song that the speaker asks the lady's friend to deliver on his behalf. There is a realism to the way

---

[15] Saltzstein 2013b, 3–4.

[16] See Tischler 1978, 4: 68.

[17] *Analyse et traitement informatique de la langue Français: Dictionnaire du Moyen Français (1330–1500)*, 'Tenir', www.atilf.fr. I am grateful to Eliza Zingesser for her thoughts on this passage.

[18] Only six of the seventy-two fully notated two-voice motets in **Mo** use a range this wide (see nos. 192, 215, 222, 226, 242, and 246) and only one (199) encompasses a twelfth. Most use a range of an octave or a ninth. For a systematic account of the symbolic meanings of voice crossing in fourteenth-century motets, see Zayaruznaya 2009.

in which the motet composer introduces a quoted refrain into the text as a diegetic song. Further, the use of the demonstrative adjective in the phrase 'ce chant ci' objectifies the song. Emma Dillon has argued that motet lyrics that refer to their own poetry or voices through demonstrative adjectives present themselves as 'no longer products of the interior imagination, but things, now, for others to behold'.[19] At this musically heightened moment in which the motetus voice refers to the refrain he is about to sing as 'ce chant ci', we apprehend the refrain as a song within a song.[20]

The melody of the refrain also contributes to its function as a song within the narrative. The motive that opens the repeated phrase 'A li m'envois' is boxed in Example 9.1 and marked *a*. Motive *a* reappears at the repetition of 'A li m'envois' in the refrain's close, giving the refrain a rounded character that sets it apart from the rest of the motet as a diegetic song. Within the full intertextual refrain, the phrase 'A li m'envois' thus functions as an in*tra*textual refrain, repeating with the same text and melody. This repetition renders the refrain even more songlike, increasing the realism of its performance within the narrative of the motet. There is also a longer segment of music initiated by motive *a* that begins in the second half of line 11, where the refrain's opening phrase 'A li m'envois' is repeated, and that concludes at perfection 35. The longer phrase creates a kind of musical enjambment that connects the second half of line 11 with line 12, 'Si m'en revois'. The entire phrase is then repeated on the text 'Mes cuers vers li ne se desment' ('My heart will never deceive her', line 15). The melodic repetition lends further musical coherence to the motet's second section. The musical setting thus draws attention to the status of the refrain as a performed song, and uses the refrain's opening motive to structure the motet's second section.

Although it appears during its midpoint rather than at the motet's close, the refrain 'A li m'envois' also alludes, in interesting ways, to the poetic device of the *envoi*. Depending, again, on how we understand the textual segmentation ('m'envois' or 'm'en vois'?), this passage could mean either 'You send me to her' or 'I am going to her'. In either case, the phrase puns on the term *envoi*, a well-known device from troubadour and trouvère song. In the songs of the trouvères, the *envoi* appears in the final verses and its function is to designate the song's addressee, whether this is a lady, patron, or some other recipient. Often, the trouvère will open the *envoi* with a call to the song itself, asking it to go and send itself out into the world to find his beloved. The device has a curiously anthropomorphic character; the poet asks the song to come to life and traverse physical distances, then to speak for itself, conveying the poet's message.[21] The *envoi* projects the song into a world exterior to the poem;[22] this function highlights its affinity with the intertextual refrain, another musico-poetic device that suggests a relevant poetic context that is external to the musical context in which it appears. The phrase 'a li m'envois / m'en vois' evokes the device of the *envoi* by name. The motet composer could be saying that the lover himself is going to his lady, or the refrain could be written in the voice of the song as it travels to the poet's lady in the manner of an *envoi*. The tortuous way in which the *envoi* of the trouvères positions the song as the poet's emissary is also latent in the motet lyric's opening verses, where the motet composer asks 'True beloved' not to address his lady directly, but rather, to enlist one of her friends to deliver his song to her on his behalf. The motet's lyrics are permeated by notions of distance and dispatch, and its brief narrative is full of messengers and go-betweens. These themes are driven by the refrain

---

[19] Dillon 2012, 22. See a similar example in Saltzstein 2013b, 65.

[20] For other motets that use refrains internally to mimic performances of song, see S. Clark 2007, 48–54, and Saltzstein 2013b, 52.

[21] The trouvères inherited this device from the troubadours' *tornada*. See Peraino 2011, 30, and Phan 1991.

[22] Phan 1991, 57.

(where the phrase 'a li m'envois/m'en vois' appears twice in the refrain's three verses). There is a thus a clever play on genre in this motet voice, which stages a refrain as a diegetic song, then resituates that song as an *envoi*.

This refrain does indeed seem to have been sent forth; like many thirteenth-century refrains, it traveled to other texts. 'A li m'envois/m'en vois' is an intertextual refrain – in addition to our motet, it also appears in the *Roman de la poire*, an autobiographical narrative by a certain Thibaut that contains twenty lyric interpolations.[23] The *Poire* is an Old French allegorical verse narrative that combines the autobiographical perspective of the *Roman de la Rose* by Guillaume de Lorris with the technique of lyric interpolation used by Jean Renart in his *Roman de la Rose*. The narrative begins with a series of monologues that serve as exempla for the tale to follow, relaying episodes from the Classical and vernacular love stories of Cligè and Fenice, Pyramus and Thisbe, Tristan and Iseult, and Helen and Paris. After these monologues, the *Poire* commences with a tale of two lovers in which a lady picks a pear and takes a bite of it. She hands the pear to the narrator/lover/ protagonist, who takes a bite of the pear and falls deeply in love with her. The story that follows is built, fundamentally, around the lyric interpolations (or refrains) that the lovers exchange through emissaries who perform them within the narrative. The first letter of each refrain forms an acrostic that names the lady (Annes or 'Agnes'), the lover (Thibaut), and the word love ('Amors'). The two lovers communicate through these refrains and work to decode them. The narrative of the *Poire* thus resonates strongly with the themes of our motet, *Fines amouretes/Fiat*. In both contexts, a lover attempts to communicate through messages relayed to his lady in the form of refrains; emissaries deliver the messages to her by performing the refrains.

Could one of these works have quoted the refrain 'A li m'envois' from the other? If so, which work was written first, our motet or the *Poire*? In the many romances that use the technique of lyric insertion throughout the thirteenth and fourteenth centuries, it is notoriously difficult to determine whether or not the author wrote the insertions himself or quoted them from other works. In the case of the *Poire*, however, the way in which the narrative is built around the acrostic formed through the lyric insertions strongly suggests that that they were quoted from elsewhere. As Ardis Butterfield explains, 'the acrostic both generates and predetermines the whole work'.[24] In her edition of the *Poire*, Christiane Marchello-Nizia provided a detailed concordance of the insertions into the text and the other sources that survive for these refrains.[25] It is not surprising that a very high portion of the lyric insertions have concordances in works that survive. Eleven of the twenty refrains are attested in other thirteenth-century songs, romances, *saluts*, motets, and proverbs. This robust concordance base does not settle the status of Thibaut's refrains, however; the question remains whether Thibaut quoted the refrains in the *Poire* from the works that are known to us or quoted them from others that have not survived, or whether some of the authors of these other works quoted their refrains from the *Poire* itself. Answering these questions is complicated by the fact that the dating of the *Roman de la Poire* is not certain. The romance does not appear to have been widely transmitted (two complete copies and one nearly complete copy survive). It apparently postdates its two most important poetic models: the widely transmitted *Roman de la Rose* of Guillaume de Lorris (written around 1225) and the widely influential *Roman*

[23] The final, twentieth lyric insertion, the proverbial and widely transmitted refrain 'Qui bien aime a tart oblie' (vdB 1585), may be a later scribal addition unique to **F-Pn f. fr. 2186**. See Marchello-Nizia 1984, xlvii, Butterfield 2002, 248, and Ibos-Augé 2010, 308.

[24] See discussion in Butterfield 2002, 246–52, at 246.

[25] Marchello-Nizia 1984.

de la Rose of Jean Renart, which was likely completed between 1202 and 1218.[26] Marchello-Nizia noted that Thibaut drew the first lyric interpolation, 'Unques n'amai tant com ge fui amee, / Cuer desleaus, a tart vos ai veincu', from the song '*Onques n'amai*' (RS 498) by Richard of Fournival.[27] The two verses Thibaut quotes in the *Poire* do not appear consecutively in Richard's song – they are derived from the song's first verse and a modification of its last.[28] Marchello-Nizia concludes that Richard's song must have been Thibaut's source and reasons that the *Poire* would therefore have been written no earlier than the middle third of the thirteenth century, during Richard's period of compositional activity, which ended with his death in 1259 or 1260.[29] The copying of the earliest manuscript of the *Poire* around 1275 provides a *terminus ad quem*.[30]

Examining the concordances for the *Poire*'s refrains and their dating, moreover, strongly suggests that Thibaut either quoted refrains that were very old and well known to his audience, or that he may have quoted his refrains directly from some of the other surviving sources in the *Poire*'s refrain concordance base. Many of the refrains are transmitted in manuscripts that date from the first half of the thirteenth century. The *Poire*'s sixteenth refrain, 'J'ai amors a ma volenté / teles com ge voel' (vdB 912) also appears in a rondeau featured in Renart's *Rose*. The *Poire*'s eighth refrain, 'Mes cuers a bone amor quise / tant c'or l'a a sa devise', appears in the song 'Quant li dous tens s'assouage', which is found in the oldest portion of the chansonnier **U**, known to have been copied in 1231 or 1232.[31] Most interesting, for our purposes, is the dominance of the motet repertoire in the concordance base for the *Poire*'s refrains – eight of the eleven refrains in the *Poire* that have surviving concordances are connected with at least one motet.[32] Moreover, five of these refrains are transmitted in two of the vernacular motet repertoire's oldest sources: **W₂**, which dates to the middle of the thirteenth century, and **MüA**, which most scholars believe was copied in the mid century but some have argued was copied as early as the second quarter of the thirteenth century.[33] Table 9.1 provides these refrains and their concordances. Although the copying of **W₂** and **MüA** coincides with the earlier decades of the period during which the *Poire* was likely composed, the repertoire these motet manuscripts transmit may have been written long before their copying. The Latin motets in the manuscript **F**, which was copied in the 1240s, are believed to be the oldest in the motet repertoire. Whereas it was once thought that these Latin motets preceded the composition of the first vernacular motets by several decades, Catherine A. Bradley has posed convincing arguments indicating that some of the earliest motets may, in fact, be Latin contrafacta of Old French originals that are preserved in manuscripts not copied until the third quarter of the thirteenth century. It is thus possible that vernacular motet composition followed closely on the heels of the earliest Latin motets, and that French motets were composed alongside Latin ones quite early in the thirteenth century, at the genre's first stages, and copied

---

[26] On the date of Guillaume de Lorris's *Roman de la Rose*, see Brownlee and Huot 1992, 1. On the dating of Jean Renart's *Rose* see Terry and Vine Durling 1993, 1, and especially Baldwin 1997, 48–51.

[27] For an extended analysis of the motet *Onques n'amai / Sancte Germane*, which was built on the first verse of Richard's song, see Matthew P. Thomson's chapter in this book.

[28] The final verse of Richard's song is 'Car trop ai tart mon felon cuer vaincu' ('For I have vanquished my treacherous heart too late'). Doss-Quinby *et al.* 2001, 120–1.

[29] See Marchello-Nizia 1984, xlvii–xlviii.

[30] Huot 1987, 174.

[31] On the dating of U, see Lug 2012.

[32] These are insertions 1, 2, 4, 7, 11, 15, 19, and 20. On the melodic concordances of the refrains in the *Poire*, see Ibos-Augé 2010, 92–3, 197–8.

[33] See the detailed discussion in Bradley 2011, 40–3.

later in the century.[34] The motets in Table 9.1 could, therefore, have been composed decades before Thibaut wrote the *Poire*.

Table 9.1. Refrains shared between the *Roman de la poire* and the motet repertoire

Refrain	Position in *Roman de la poire*	Motet Concordances	Other sources	Motet manuscripts
'Onkes n'amai tant com je fui amée' (vdB 1427)	Insertion 1 (line 250)	*Onques n'amai* (820) / *Sancte Germane*	*Salut II, Le Court d'amours*, 'Onques n'amai' by Richard de Fournival	W2, Roi, Noailles, Her
'N'est il bien reason, or i pensez, *que cil qui mielz aime, soit li mielz amez?*' (vdB 364)	Insertion 4 (lines 890–1)	*En mon chant deslou* (8) / *Omnes*	none	MüA
'Se je n'ai s'amor, la mort m'est dounée, je n'i puis fallir' (vdB 1685)	Insertion 7 (line 1424)	*Tout leis* (46) / *Do[minus]*	*Prison d'amours, Salut II*, Hereford Proverbs	W2, MüA
'A li m'envois, / ne m'en tendroie mie, mie / je l'aim trop / a li m'en-vois' (vdB 101)	Insertion 11 (lines 2504–5)	*Fines amouretes* (794) / *Fiat*	none	W2, Mo
'J'ai amors a ma volenté / teles com ge voel' (vdB 912)	Insertion 15 (line 2793)	*Tout leis* (46) / *Do[minus]*; *Tout adés* (153) / *In seculum*	*Roman de la Rose* by Jean Renart	W2, MüA; W2, Mo, Reg1490 (no tenor)

None of this demonstrates that the motets in Table 9.1 were Thibaut's sources for the refrains they share with the *Poire*. It is always possible that Thibaut knew these refrains from other musical or poetic works that did not survive. As we saw earlier, however, it is extremely likely that Thibaut drew his first insertion from Richard de Fournival's song '*Onques n'amai*'. Moreover, Thibaut's fifteenth insertion is also the refrain of a rondeau in Renart's *Rose*; since Renart's *Rose* was one of Thibaut's literary models, it stands to reason that he may have known the refrain from this text and quoted it. Table 9.1 also highlights the presence of a long noticed network of refrains shared between the *Poire, Le Court d'amours* and a *Salut d'amour*, among others.[35] Thibaut may have been familiar with some of these works.

[34] Bradley 2013, 4–8 and Bradley 2012.
[35] Buffum 1912, 5–11; Butterfield 2002, 250; Butterfield 1997, 86; and Doudet *et al.* 2016, 50–2.

It is, however, suggestive that Thibaut's fourth and eleventh insertions survive exclusively in the *Poire* and in the motet repertoire. Further, although Renart's *Rose* was a possible source of Thibaut's fifteenth insertion, this refrain is additionally found in the motet *Tout leis/Do[minus]*, which also shares a different refrain with Thibaut's insertion 7. Although scholars once believed that *Tout leis/Do[minus]* was a so-called 'refrain-cento motet', which would contain a voice made entirely of quoted refrains, Christopher Page and Mark Everist demonstrated that introductory phrases of *Tout leis/Do[minus]* either quote from or imitate a monophonic *rondet de carole*.[36] The fact that this one motet shares two different refrains also found together in the *Poire* suggests either that these refrains were extremely widely known in other works that did not survive, or, perhaps, that one author quoted them directly from the other. The literature on interpolated romances rarely grapples with the sourcing or compositional chronology of the inserted lyrics found within thirteenth-century narratives, and as such, literary scholars have not considered motets as potential sources of refrain material found in romances.[37] Could Thibaut have quoted refrains from the vernacular motet repertory?

The early dating of the motets in question and the dominance of motets in the *Poire*'s refrain concordance base allow us to at least entertain this possibility. Indeed, the eleventh lyric insertion in the *Poire* seems to have been constructed by combining two refrains from different motet voices: *Fines amouretes* and *Quant froidure trait a fin* (535). The insertion in the *Poire* reads 'A lui m'en vois, ne m'en tendroie mie, Diex, ge l'aim tant'. This shares the first two verses from the refrain discussed earlier in the context of *Fines amouretes*: 'A li m'en vois, / ne m'en tendroie mie, mie, / je l'aim trop, a li m'en vois'. At the third verse, however, the *Poire* version uses the end of a different refrain, 'He, Diex, je l'aim tant' (vdB 819), which is found in the motet voice *Quant froidure trait a fin*. Just as Thibaut's use of non-consecutive verses from Richard de Fournival's song 'Onques n'amai' caused Marchello-Nizia to surmise that he drew his verses directly from that song, the conjoined refrain verses that comprise Thibaut's eleventh insertion suggest the possibility that Thibaut might have known these verses from the two motets. In her interpretation of the refrains that form Thibaut's acrostic in the *Poire*, Butterfield argued that textual echoes between several pairs of refrains created internal *enté* structures such that the *dit* was often framed by refrains that featured slightly varied repetitions of the same lyrics.[38] Whereas she does not address whether or not Thibaut intended to evoke the form of a motet *enté*, if Thibaut had intentionally conjured up a poetic grafting technique with strong ties to the motet repertory, this could indicate his familiarity with the motet genre.

This might all seem unlikely. The notion that the aristocratic poet who wrote the courtly romance narrative of the *Roman de la poire* was familiar with and perhaps even quoted refrains from the motet repertoire is contrary to the common image of the motet repertoire as bookish and clerical.[39] Yet the contradiction only arises when our notion of *clergie* is focused on ordained clerics charged with sermon composition or university masters and students engaged in the higher-level study of theology. In fact, the term cleric did not necessarily designate the intellectual elite

---

[36] See Page 1993a, 52 and Everist 1994, 116.

[37] Although Butterfield often notices suggestive concordances between romances and motets, she resists describing 'schemes of influence' between them. See, for example, Butterfield 2002, 98–9. See similar treatment in Huot 1997, 77–84.

[38] The motet *enté* has attracted a great deal of attention. For a comprehensive survey of literature see Peraino 2011, ch. 4.

[39] Although we know nothing about the biographies of Thibaut or Annes, they are depicted wearing the fleur-de-lis, suggesting they were members of the aristocracy. See Huot 1987, 185.

who were in command of Latin – it simply referred to all those who fell under the jurisdiction of canon law. Although he continued to argue that the *ars antiqua* motet's composers and principal audiences were clerics, Page reminded us of the broad array of people who were classified as clerics in the Middle Ages: university masters, students, parish priests, secular canons, boys learning plainchant and studying grammar, and others.[40] In a performance of *Fines amouretes/Fiat*, highly educated listeners may have attempted to interpret the relationship between the motetus lyrics and the chant tenor, delighting, perhaps, in the amusingly profane ways in which celebratory tenor incipit 'let it be so' implies a successful outcome for the lover's missive. However, clerics with less advanced educations and, potentially, lay audiences may have found a vernacular two-voice motet like this one as accessible as a trouvère song, enjoying the harmonic accompaniment of the tenor voice while following along with the Old French lyrics in the motetus part.

Even if we assume that the motet originated and circulated within a clerical milieu, this would not have precluded the genre from being enjoyed by other audiences. And indeed, scholars have found clues that some motets may have been appreciated by the laity and in certain courtly circles. Studies of **Mo** and **Cl** by Dillon and Curran have revealed an alignment between the motet and Marian devotional practices that were flourishing in the thirteenth century. These accounts point to motet texts that repurpose or refashion Marian prayers widely used not only in the divine Office, but also in prayer books used by the laity. The ordering and the program of illuminations in **Mo** may even have been designed to prompt a prayerful engagement with the motets it contains; this diminutive manuscript may have functioned like a book of hours, a medieval devotional book geared specifically toward lay women.[41] The motet collection **Cl**, which is replete with motets foregrounding Marian devotion, is preserved within a much larger codex in which the motets coexist with vernacular devotional works such as the *Conception de Nostre Dame* of Wace and stories from the *Miracles de Nostre Dame* by Gautier de Coinci. This manuscript aligns motets with vernacular translations of Latin materials strongly associated with the rise in lay literacy and effective piety that followed the fourth Lateran Council of 1215.[42] It is not difficult to imagine that a non-clerical reader could have enjoyed reading, singing, or listening to performances of the vernacular lyrics of many of the motets in **Mo** and **Cl** without attempting to perform their musical settings polyphonically. A manuscript copied at the turn of the fourteenth century, the so-called *Douce Chansonnier* (**D308**), transmits a corpus of sixty-three motet lyrics without their musical notation.[43] Interestingly, some of the other song lyrics in this chansonnier seem to have been created by repurposing and transforming the lyrics of motet voices.[44] D308 was compiled specifically for a courtly audience in Lorraine; the presence of motet lyrics in the manuscript and the reuse of motet lyrics in other song genres suggests enthusiasm for motet texts among late thirteenth-century courtiers at considerable remove from the scholastic circles that apparently created the motet genre in early thirteenth-century Paris.

The case of *Fines amouretes/Fiat* encourages us to keep a broad perspective on vernacular polyphony in the thirteenth century. It suggests the possibility that some two-voice Old French motets may have been known to a range of thirteenth-century vernacular authors, including authors of courtly romance. It also sheds light on a corner of the motet repertoire that is less allegorical, less exegetical, and perhaps less intellectual than many of the examples illuminated

---

[40] See discussion in Page 1993a, 68–84.

[41] See Dillon 2012, 285–94.

[42] Curran 2013a, 219–54.

[43] For a detailed discussion, see Elizabeth Eva Leach's contribution to this volume.

[44] See discussion in Leach 2015, 424–43.

in the existing secondary literature. This accessibility affirms elements of Page's critiques in *Discarding Images* and suggests some of the many ways that increased attention to the two-voice motet repertoire could modify our images of the motet repertoire as a whole. Yet our motet also engaged in clever play with the vernacular poetic devices of intertextual refrain quotation and the *envoi*, evidence of the composer's mastery of trouvère song and his exploration of its themes within the genre of the motet. This deep engagement with vernacular song places our motet in the company of the small corpus of motets that have a voice transmitted elsewhere as a monophonic trouvère song,[45] those motets whose upper voices are structured in *pedes cum cauda* form,[46] and many others that situate the vernacular song corpus as the motet's central interpretive subject matter. In addition to serving as a corrective against our tendency to view the motet as overly bookish and learned, *Fines amouretes/Fiat* is also an important reminder that the medieval clerics who composed motets were clearly steeped in vernacular culture – their mastery of the songs of the troubadours and trouvères is evident in many examples across the motet corpus. Whether they were singers performing polyphony in Old French for hire before lay audiences or scribes painstakingly copying vernacular manuscripts in scriptoria, medieval clerics continually brought learning and vernacular expression into new and interesting dialogues.[47]

---

[45] Friedrich Gennrich first drew attention to this phenomenon in Gennrich 1926. For a complete list of these motets, see Haines 2004a, 31–2. See also the discussion in Everist 2016, 143–4.

[46] Saint-Cricq 2013b.

[47] Robert of Courson inveighs against clerics who sell their services illicitly by performing polyphony for lay audiences, suggesting that this was a common practice among those clerics who were trained to sing polyphony. See the discussion in Page 1989, 145–7.

10

When Words Converge and Meanings Diverge:
Counterexamples to Polytextuality
in the Thirteenth-Century Motet

Suzannah Clark

A VITAL CHARACTERISTIC of the polyphonic thirteenth-century motet is polytextuality. Even two-voice motets are polytextual insofar as the tenor typically contains a melisma based on a word or two or a fragment of a word from a chant, while the upper voice contains a fully fledged text. In the case of three- and four-voice motets, the more explicit polytextual nature of the genre comes to the fore, as the upper voices each contain different texts, sometimes even in different languages. Within this verbal texture, Christopher Page has argued that an important part of the genre's aesthetic is the design of brief moments of convergence of a vowel sound, rhyme, syllable, or even a word amongst the upper voices. Page suggested that such exceptions to the heterogeneous verbal texture may have been what Johannes de Grocheio had in mind when he remarked on the artistic 'refinement' of motets. Using the motet *Par un matinet* (658)/*Hé, sire* (659)/*Hé, bergier* (657)/*Eius* (O16) as his model, Page observed that such confluence is both fleeting and rare.[1] Hence its refined status. Although perhaps not quite as rare as Page suggested, it is nonetheless the case that in a genre where the emphasis is on the differences amongst the texts, convergences seem privileged and special.

There are, however, some motets where long stretches of monotextuality seem to be the point. Striking because they are exceptions to the general rule, the most celebrated of these are even preserved in succession in the Montpellier codex as **Mo** 26 and **Mo** 27: *Viderunt. Por peu ne sui departis* (7)/*Viderunt. Por peu li cuers ne me parti* (6)/*Viderunt. Par pou le cuer ne me parti* (5)/*Viderunt om[nes]* (M1) and *Trois serors sor rive mer … La jonete* (343a)/*Trois serors sor rive mer … La moiene* (343b)/*Trois serors sor rive mer … L'aisnee* (343c)/*Perlustravit* (M25).[2] **Mo** 27 is the clearest example because all three upper voices begin with an identical text sustained for an

---

[1] Page 2000, 354 and 355. The example he uses involves the confluence of the vowel 'u' in the words 'nus' and 'nunques', which Page points out is nonetheless a carefully crafted 'dissonance of vowels' because the former is a pure vowel sound and the latter nasalized (354).

[2] Mo 26 is found on fols. 40v–41r and appears as a two-voice motet (with the quadruplum [5] from Mo and tenor but without the initial 'Viderunt' in either the upper voice or tenor) in **W2** fol. 252r and MüA fol. 2r. Mo 27 appears on fols. 40v–42r (with 343a notated as the motetus and 343c as quadruplum) and in Cl fol. 381v (with the voices as shown above). These motets contain attributes of the conductus motet. As explained in Everist 1994, 29–35, genuine examples of the subgenre contain identical texts in the upper voices throughout a piece.

entire sentence spanning two musical phrases, 'Trois serors sor rive mer/chantent cler' ('Three sisters at the seashore are singing brightly'). The textual unity of the conductus style conveys the idea of a single narrator's voice.[3] Once the narrator begins to distinguish each sister, each of whom then sings a song about her ideal lover, the motet aptly bursts into polytextuality. As a motet about the three women imagining their ideal bridegrooms, Sylvia Huot interprets it as a humorous allegory of the disciples awaiting the Holy Spirit, a meaning signaled by the use of a portion of chant from the first Alleluia of the Mass for Pentecost in the tenor. According to her, the shift from mono- to polytextuality is symbolic: it captures the effect of the 'linguistic diversity of Pentecost, where the disciples' single language gave way to a mixture of languages'.[4]

Huot identified a similar symbolism in the use of the technique in **Mo 26**.[5] The opening word 'Viderunt' in all three upper voices sets a striking tone of textual unity, not least because it is a unique example of a Latin start to an otherwise vernacular motet. Monotextuality continues into the vernacular portions of the motet, although with less crystal clarity than experienced in **Mo 27**. That is, the second lines of the motetus and triplum are identical, while the quadruplum begins with the same two words and ends with the same two syllables. The third and final line of this short motet is then polytextual until the last word once again converges on 'congié' ('leave') in all three upper voices. As Huot explains, the motet plays on the meaning of the Christmas gradual where the birth of Christ is witnessed by all: 'they all saw' ('viderunt omnes'). She argues that what all can see in this motet is 'secularized and trivialized' as three typical scenarios within the courtly love tradition play out. In the quadrulum, the hero claims he nearly left his lady but actually never will; in the triplum, he confesses his heart nearly left him when she told him to leave; and in the motetus, he says his heart nearly left him when he left her. As Huot puts it, 'The moments of unison, contrasting with those of divergence, help to stress its thematics of amorous leave-taking and of the indiscretion that allowed all to see the lovers' farewell'.[6]

In a different section of her book, Huot also discusses another motet, **Mo 127**, noted by many scholars for its pervasive textual overlap: *Quant define la verdour* (661)/*Quant repaire la dolçor* (662)/*Flos filius eius [et super hunc flo(rem)]* (O16). She highlights the strategic placement of 'amour' ('love') appearing in both voices just beyond the middle of the motet, in a rhyme position with a rest after, and of the words 'amer' appearing simultaneously as the last word of the motet – but with the divergent meanings of 'bitter' and 'love'. These coincidences sum up the 'sense of futility and despair in love' as the cornerstone of the motet.[7] However, the overlapping of text is far more extensive than these few keywords. This motet therefore deserves further scrutiny not only for the striking pervasiveness of its monotextuality but also because, as I shall argue, it demands a different kind of listening and interpretation from the symbolic unity to the 'profusion of voices' that Huot discerned in the shifts from mono- to polytextuality in **Mo 26** and **Mo 27**.[8]

In the second section of this chapter, I will examine another case of textual overlap between the motetus and quadruplum. This time, the monotextuality is aurally obscured by the contrasting text of the triplum. The four-voice incarnation of *Celui en qui je me fi* (390)/*La bele estoile de mer* (389)/*La bele, en qui je me fi* (388)/*[Jo]han[ne]* (M29) survives only in the Montpellier codex

---

[3] The edited texts and translations in this chapter are from Tischler 1978, with occasional adaptations.

[4] Huot 1997, 53–5.

[5] Huot 1997, 52–3.

[6] Huot 1997, 53.

[7] Huot 1997, 97.

[8] Huot 1997, 52.

(**Mo** 20). It belongs to a rich network of two- and three-voice vernacular versions, with two- and three-voice Latin concordances, as well as a related clausula and refrain citation. The strategy of the poet-composer of the quadruplum offers a unique critical commentary on the typical lyrical and musical construction of the motet as a genre. Taken together, my two case studies provide important insights into the medieval aesthetics of playful juxtaposition of lyric themes and contrariness for which the polytextual motet is celebrated.[9]

Quant define la verdour/Quant repaire la dolçor/Flos filius eius [et super hunc flo(rem)] survives in three sources, **W2** (fol. 214v), **Cl** (fol. 371r–v), and **Mo** (fols. 173v–175r). (For ease of reference, I shall refer to it as **Mo** 127.) Its refrain (vdB 489), which appears simultaneously in both the motetus and triplum, has no other known sources. The opening scene of **Mo** 127 is occupied by a description of flowers, birds, and a meadow, and it is not until the mention of 'fine amour' ('true love') in the motetus about two-thirds of the way through the motet that it is clear that the motet falls within the scope of courtly love and not the pastourelle. However, rather than articulating the usual combination of optimism amidst the anxiety of unrequited love, both voices complain about the pitfalls of *fin'amor*.

Expressions of love were generally tied to the beginning of the spring season, when, as the motetus reports, greenery awakens and birds return from migration and are heard to sing again. This is the time of year when protagonists are inspired to sing of the object of their affection, according to the long vernacular lyric tradition of the troubadours and trouvères – the tradition from which the love poetry of the motet emanated. In this motetus, a male protagonist observes how the arrival of spring ushers in budding leaves and flowers and the sound of joyous, singing birds. He even confesses to being filled with sadness and pain, which is the inevitable affliction of devoted men experiencing the pangs of unrequited love.

In a departure from the usual depiction of a single episode of courtly love, this protagonist divulges a disastrous personal history. In this case, his sadness and pain stem not from being in a current state of unrequited love but from a fear of repetition – the fear that he is embarking on yet another season where he will devote himself unconditionally to 'true love' (*fin'amor*) only to receive no mercy in response. Indeed, he goes so far as to reveal that this has been going on for years: he states that he has 'given all my years to true love without any return' ('j'ai mis tout mon aage en fine amor sanz nul retor'). Alas, not only have the years gone by, but on a quotidian level he is forced to think day and night about his misfortune: 'And night and day I have to think … *how I have given my heart and soul to loving well*' ('et nuit et jor m'estuet penser … *quar j'ai douné cuer et cors pour bien amer*'). In this motet, then, we hear not of an eager anticipation for the future of the season but of the painful memories of chagrins of the past:

> **Motetus**
> Quant repaire la dolçor
> que nest/pert la foille et la flour
> et par pré et par boscage

---

[9]   The idea of 'contraries' in the middle ages often centers around the interplay of the sacred and the profane or the divine and the carnal in vernacular literature; see Bolduc 2006. More broadly, contraries can involve any opposites, which as C. Brown (1998, 2) points out is summed up by the narrator towards the end of the *Roman de la Rose*: 'contrary things … are glosses of one another, and the person who wants to define one of them must keep the other in mind'. See also Regalado 1981. The elucidation of such juxtapositions is at the heart of Huot 1997, a book that revolutionized the understanding of the thirteenth-century motet.

font li oiseil grant baudor,
mon cuer est en grant tristor
et me met en mon corage;
car j'ai mis tout mon aage
en fine amor
sanz nul retor.
Et nuit et jor
m'estuet penser,
car j'ai doné,
Dieus, quar j'ai douné
cuer et cors pour bien amer.

When the sweetness returns and leaves and flowers bud/appear and birds sing ever so happily in the meadows and thickets, my heart is full of sadness and makes me pensive, for I have given all my years to true love without any return. And night and day I have to think, how, *my God, I have given, how I have given my heart and soul to loving well!*

Our hapless protagonist experiences just as painful an off-season. The fall and winter are conventionally a time when troubadours and trouvères withdraw from their relentless attempts at seduction in the spring and summer. Here, the triplum relates how, as the fall begins with its dying leaves and migrating birds, his days and nights are devoid of thinking of love's happiness. Obsessed by defeat from the spring season – or seasons, as we learn in the motetus – his heart is bitter:

Triplum
Quant define la verdour,
que muert la fuelle et la flour
et par pré et par boscage
font cil oisiel grant tristour,
qui n'i font point de sejour,
lors ne me vient en courage
de servir en nul aage
bone amour.
Pour sa baudour
ne nuit et jour
ne puis penser,
[*qui m'a doné,*]
Dieus, qui m'a doné
cors pensant et cuer amer.

When the verdure comes to an end, when leaves and flowers die and birds sing sadly in the meadows and thickets and stay not long, then have I no heart for ever serving good love again. Neither night nor day can I think of love's happiness. *Who gave me, God, who gave me a pensive body and bitter heart?*

As shown in Example 10.1 and as has been pointed out by numerous scholars, there is a striking overlap of words between the two upper-voice texts in this motet.[10] With the exception of

---

[10]   See especially Gallo 1985, 24 and Huot 1997, 96–8. See also Pesce 1986, 93–5, for the argument that skilled duplication or repetition of text aids comprehension.

the slight misalignment of 'aage' in the rhyme position of line 7 in both poems, identical text is synchronized musically throughout. As has also been observed, antonyms that provide polytextuality – particularly at the outset of the motet – are also carefully aligned: in bar 3 'muert' appears against 'nest' ('death' versus 'birth') and in bar 8 'tristour' appears against 'baudor' ('sadness' versus 'happiness').[11] Alberto Gallo concluded the following: 'Where there are parallel situations, the texts unite; where they differ, contrasts arise in the two voices, almost like verbal polyphony'.[12]

However, it is an oversimplification to say that monotextuality expresses parallelisms and polytextuality expresses difference, for, as we have already seen, Sylvia Huot has noted how both upper voices end with the word 'amer', which is only an apparent textual unity. The word is used as a homograph; in the motetus it means 'love' and in the triplum it means 'bitterness'.[13] In many ways, this homograph marks the culmination of a rich diversity of meanings that the monotextual utterances convey throughout this motet, even though there are no other instances of homography. Further scrutiny of the text and music of this motet reveals how its poet-composer generated a remarkable texture of converging words with diverging meanings. As such, its monoverbal texture exemplifies both a different sonic world and a different manifestation of the poetics of contrast that might normally be associated with the generic norms of the thirteenth-century polytextual motet.

Take for instance the phrases 'la fuelle et la flour' and 'la foille et la flour' at the end of the second line of the triplum and motetus respectively. Despite the similar words, the image in the mind's eye of the leaves and flowers in the two voices is utterly contrasting. In one voice, they are all dead ('muert'); in the other, they are coming to life ('nest'). While there is even a nice touch of using the alternative forms for the word 'leaf' – 'fuelle' against 'foille' – as if to distinguish their spring versus fall condition,[14] the real contrast is set up by the words that come before them: the antonyms 'define' ('to end') and 'repaire' ('to return') sound together and delineate the fall versus spring seasons, and the leaves and flowers are described by the simultaneous singing of 'muert' and 'nest', as noted earlier.

Significantly, **Mo** and **Cl** contain a variant at this point. Instead of 'nest', which is the reading in **W2**, it reads 'pert', which perhaps comes from 'apert', 'to open'. While the word no doubt refers to the budding leaves, it is a significant (scribal?) intervention – significant, that is, for its sonic quality and for its telltale signs of an aesthetic preference for like-sounding words.[15] It rhymes with 'muert', thus reinforcing the ubiquitous assonance throughout this motet. But in keeping with similar words signifying natural objects in different states, it is an assonance of words that have opposite meanings.

Lines 3 and 4 contain an even more pervasive overlap of words. Here, instead of polytextuality dissolving into monotextuality, the sentences are virtually identical until they reach their rhyming words, 'tristour' versus 'baudor'.[16] Unlike the typical polytextual motet, where the (third party) listener strains to hear the words and probably at most follows key words, this passage seemingly

[11] Huot 1997, 98. Observe that Tischler's edition of this motet has 'naist', a spelling which is not in any source but is a more conventional spelling of the word in Old French. The 'pert' variant will be discussed below.

[12] Gallo 1985, 24.

[13] Huot 1997, 98.

[14] Only **Mo** distinguishes between 'fuelle' from 'foille', which are alternatives for 'leaf'. There seems to be no botanical significance between these two spellings. W2 and Cl have 'fuelle' in both voices.

[15] See n. 1.

[16] I say 'virtually' identical because the article 'cil' sounds against 'li' in bar 7.

Suzannah Clark

Example 10.1. Mo 127: *Quant define la verdour/Quant repaire la dolçor/Flos filius eius [et super hunc flo(rem)]*
Edition based on Tischler 1978.

offers relief through the crystal clarity of monotextuality.[17] Yet once again, despite the identical texts about the 'pré' ('meadow'), 'boscage' ('thickets'), and 'oiseil' ('birds'), the listener must conjure up in his or her mind's eye and inner ear different land- and soundscapes. In the motetus, the meadow is filled with birds, who chirp happily. In the triplum, they sing with sadness and eventually fly away, leaving a silence. If the words are easy to hear, the demands on the listener are to imagine opposites in each voice part. This is an ecological listener, one attuned to the seasons, one who hears the opposition and sees counterimages in the sameness of the texts.

Just as the first iteration of the tenor draws to a close in bar 10, the upper voices finally express the generic norm. They launch into the typical verbal texture of a motet: polytextuality. Yet, the cacophony of language is ignited just as the triplum reports that the birds have left the scene. Their migration means there is silence in the air. Of course, there is always a certain paradox involved in speaking or singing of silence, but here it arises at the very point that this motet begins to display its generic hallmark. So, when **Mo** 127 is most generically itself, the topic in one voice is about silence, symbolized by a texture in which the words are harder to discern.

As is a feature of many motets based on the *Flos filius* chant, the repetition of the tenor is not exact, either in pitch or rhythm.[18] However, all voices set out in bar 11 by repeating the melodic gestures of the opening, as if momentarily to suggest the repeat will be exact. While they also begin polytextually, as if the motet will behave generically on the repetition, the words soon begin to converge once again. The most striking confluence in this second part of **Mo** 127 is when the words 'nuit' ('night') and 'jor' ('day') each appear simultaneously in both voices (see bars 15–17 in Example 10.1); they are emphasized by being the middle of three short phrases that are all surrounded by rests and all articulate the same rhythm and almost the same motif. These musical techniques have been repeatedly shown to be used to highlight key passages in this repertoire.[19] Here again, although the singers sing the same words 'nuit' and 'jor' simultaneously, the nature of the nights and days that our (ecological) listener needs to imagine are different, for they belong to different seasons. During the spring (the motetus), the days become longer and the nights shorter; while during the fall (the triplum), it is the opposite.

These measures are also brimming with a repeating motif. As Mark Everist has observed, the motetus moves by descending sequence in bars 15–17, a sequence in which the triplum participates for the last two iterations in bars 16–17.[20] Although certainly these repetitions serve a technical

[17] While I posit here a third-party listener taking in a performance, the consumption of motet texts involves readers and performers, who themselves are 'listeners' in the most multifaceted sense of the word.

[18] For example, **Mo** contains seven motets based on the *Flos filius* segment of the 'Flos filius eius' chant, of which two others, **Mo** 72 and **Mo** 94, have significant variations in the repetition. Conversely, see the tenor of **Mo** 21 in Example 1.2 in Elizabeth Eva Leach's chapter in the present volume, in which she delineates the repetition of 'eius' from 'flos filius'. This points to interesting ways in which composers of motets sought to select precise portions of chant melismas – sometimes even favoring certain syllables, as is the case of my second case study, **Mo** 127, which is based on 'han' of 'Johanne' – to support the upper voice(s) of their motet.

[19] For a variety of musical techniques used by poet-composers to highlight poetic meaning, see Nathan 1942, Pesce 1986, Smith 1989, Butterfield 1993, S. Clark 2007, Colton 2008, Dillon 2012, and Saltzstein 2013b.

[20] Everist 1994, 170–1. The edition in Everist shows the reading of Mo, which does not have a plica in the motetus of bar 15. Tischler's edition (from which Example 10.1 is taken) adds the plica in the motetus of bar 15, which is present in both W2 and Cl. Only W2, however, contains the plicas and ligatures at the beginning of each phrase, transcribed as sixteenth notes in Example 10.1; Cl has them in the triplum but only in bar 15 in the motetus. In all versions, the short clip

purpose, they may also be said to depict an irritating earworm experienced by the protagonist. He has been trapped – for years – in the web of *fin'amor*. The rhythmic motif that dominates bars 14–17 and resurfaces in the refrain in bar 19 is first heard to accompany the words 'en fine amor' in bar 14. As shown in Example 10.1, both voices repeat it while the protagonist claims that in the fall (triplum), he cannot think of love's happiness either night or day ('ne nuit et jour/ne puis penser') and that in the spring (motetus), he must think obsessively both night and day about how he has devoted himself to true love. Again a paradox is played out musically: whether he wants to or not, he ends up thinking of *fin'amor* and singing its motif. It is the classic case of, as George Lakoff put it, saying to someone 'don't think of an elephant'. It cannot be done: an elephant is then all one can think of.[21]

Fin'amor is an offshoot of Cupid's arrow, and the afflicted have little choice but to do its beckoning. Motif *x* is like the arrow that strikes: sung first to 'en fine amor', the protagonist is now compelled to sing motif *x*, which he does to the words 'pour sa baudour'/'sanz nul retor', and 'ne nuit et jour'/'et nuit et jour', and 'ne puis penser'/'m'estuet penser'.

For a troubadour or trouvère, being struck by love is the legendary prerequisite to composing a new song, which also plays on the fiction that the lyric 'je' is a conflation of the poet-composer and performer-protagonist. In the troubadour and trouvère repertory, the make-believe is easy to go along with since only one person – the professed 'je' – is singing. By contrast, the fact that, in a three-voice motet such as this one, there are two voices singing from the mouth of ostensibly the same protagonist situated simultaneously at opposing times of the year punctures the fiction of the performer-protagonist lyric 'I'. Or, it is perhaps the conceit of the motet that many simultaneous voices may emanate from one protagonist. Nonetheless, this moment in **Mo** 127, where *fin'amor* is explicitly named to a motif that then takes on a life of its own and consumes the protagonist's thoughts, is a moment of realism: the sounds and polyphony of motif *x* become the soundtrack of both his thoughts at night and, like the elephant, his attempts not to have those thoughts.[22] As such, it is a quintessential instantiation of Lakoff's cognitive framing 'don't think of *x*'. Motif *x* is both 'thinking of *x*' and 'not thinking of *x*'. Moreover, in the refrain, when the protagonist wonders – at least according to Tischler's proposed underlay – 'who gave me' ('qui m'a doné') a pensive mind and bitter heart, motif *x* is the giveaway: *fin'amor* did it.

For a motet that contains so much textual overlap, it seems fitting that it ends with the same refrain in both voices, a technique that is relatively rare, although we will encounter it again in my other case study.[23] This refrain is unique to this motet. After the refrain's midpoint, which is

of each phrase stands out, but the version in W2 is certainly the catchiest.

[21] Lakoff 2004 outlines the cognitive principles in framing debates in a political context. His argument is based on the psychological process whereby attempts to suppress certain thoughts instead tend to bring them to mind.

[22] Dillon 2012 draws attention to the notion of the sonic quality of the words serving as a soundtrack to the textual meaning, rather than specifically the music itself furnishing the meaning, as I argue here. For another example of a musical soundtrack, see Colton 2008, 175–9, for her analysis of *Nus ne mi pourroit conforter* (736)/*Nonne sui, nonne* (737)/*Aptatur* (O45), in which a nun complains that she is awoken by the bells for Matins as soon as she tries to sleep. The music mimics the sound of bells ringing, so she can hardly escape their sound.

[23] Saltzstein (2013b, 15) identifies the special quality of refrains that circulate exclusively amongst motets. They 'exhibit a high degree melodic stability and visual resemblance'. By contrast, the motet also enjoyed the simultaneous appearance of refrains in more than one voice part, which necessarily involved the invention of a new melody for at least one of the renditions of the refrain in order to achieve counterpoint. Where concordances external to the motet exist, they usually show that the motetus carries the intertextual melody.

marked by a rest in bar 19, the texts briefly diverge, if only to highlight the last word, which is a homograph, as observed earlier. Where perhaps there is little to distinguish this refrain from the thousands of others in terms of its sentiments, the subtle moment of polytextuality highlights how love seems at once to emanate from the protagonist ('Dieus, quai j'ai douné'), yet be thrust upon him ('Dieus, qui m'a doné') by the whims of *fin'amor*. On closer analysis, then, even in the passages of monotextuality, **Mo** 127 preserves the 'playful juxtapositions' so characteristic of the thirteenth-century motet. It is not, therefore, the case that unity of text marks parallel situations and differing texts mark contrast, as Gallo claimed.

My next example exhibits similar techniques of converging words and diverging meanings. Only in its full splendor as a four-voice vernacular motet, uniquely surviving as **Mo** 20 (fols. 24v–27r) *Celui en qui je me fi/La bele estoile de mer/La bele, en qui je me fi/[Jo]han[ne]*, does it contain passages of overlapping texts, which occur between the quadruplum and motetus parts. Unlike **Mo** 127, where the monotextuality was an aurally striking feature of the motet, in **Mo** 20 the confluence of text between the quadruplum and motetus is counterpointed against a different text in the triplum: the prevailing verbal texture is still polytextual therefore.

According to Gordon Anderson, the four-voice French motet was the progenitor of an extensive network: there are two- and three-voice motets comprising voice parts 389 and 388 (the triplum and motetus here), which Anderson regarded as written traces of hearings of **Mo** 20 with voices stripped away.[24] There are also two- and three-voice Latin motets, which he argued are contrafacta. He made his case on the basis of the uniform style of the music of all the upper parts in **Mo** 20. As is immediately obvious in Example 10.2, all phrases begin together and, with the exception of bars 3, 6, and 14, all phrases conclude and rest together. Anderson believed that, had the parts been gradually added, they would have reflected a development of styles and the parts – especially the quadruplum – would have been more independent, as indeed are the other four-voice motets in fascicle 2 of **Mo**. Using style as a determiner of compositional history is often perilous,[25] and in this case Anderson invokes that ever elusive yet trusty lost source, which stretches the credulity of his proposed transmission history. Most scholars agree with Anderson that the Old French core of **Mo** 20 predates the Latin motet largely due to the use of mode 6, the fact that the Latin text does not trope the tenor, and some oddities in the Latin underlay.[26] Indeed, if we allow for the likely possibility that the motet grew from a two-voice nucleus to four voices, it might be fruitful to ask why a poet-composer would compose a quadruplum in a regressive style and what the hermeneutic point might be behind synchronized phrases. It is to hermeneutics that I now turn as I delve into a layered appreciation of the poetic and musical interplay of the voices in this motet – privy as I am (no matter what the actual compositional history was) to its multitude of archival traces. As such, my acquaintance of the network arises by leafing through **W2**, where *Ave, plena gracia* (391)/*Johanne* (M29) on fol. 178r may be read against its vernacular counterpart *La bele, en qui je me fi* (388)/*Johanne* on fol. 236v, and then by leafing through **Mo** and finding the four-voice

---

[24] G. Anderson 1968–76, 2: 278.

[25] For more on the thorny issues surrounding musical style and compositional history, see Emily Zazulia's chapter below.

[26] G. Anderson 1968–76, 2: 277. In the course of his extensive study of the family of motets based on *Johanne* (and *Mulierum*, a melisma from the same chant), Michael Alan Anderson only mentions in passing **Mo** 20 and its kindred Latin concordances (2011, 14 n. 32, 19 n. 47, 30); he does not address their chronology, which lay outside the scope of his study.

Example 10.2. **Mo 20**: *Celui en qui je me fi/La bele, en qui je me fi/La bele estoile de mer/La bele, en qui je me fi/[Jo]han[ne]*. Bars 1–4 of duplum from *Ave, plena gratia/Johanne*. Mo 20 edition is based on Tischler 1978. The duplum excerpt is based on G. Anderson 1968–76.

motet **Mo** 20 on fols. 24v–27r and the three-voice vernacular motet **Mo** 345 on fol. 397r–v. This three-voice vernacular motet, *La bele estoile de mer* (389)/*La bele, en qui je me fi*/*Johanne*, is also copied in **Ba** (fol. 34v), and its Latin counterpart *Psallat vox ecclesie* (392)/*Ave, plena gracia*/*Johanne* survives in fragmentary form in **MüB** (fol. VIv).[27]

Its network does not end there. Each of the three upper voices in **Mo** 20 ends with a refrain: the duplum and quadruplum end with the same words of the refrain vdB 1327 but with different melodies. Intriguingly, this motet's two-voice nucleus is concordant with a clausula in **StV** (no. 31, fol. 291v). This clausula is not, however, the origin of the refrain's music; rather, the current consensus is that **StV** clausulae postdate their motet counterparts: these clausulae are motets stripped of their texts.[28] The existence of a Latin concordance might cast doubt on the status of this refrain were it not for its citation (with identical music to the motetus 388) in another motet *En tel lieu s'est entremis* (424)/*Virgo* (M48) in **Roi** (fol. 208r–v) and **Noailles** (fol. 188r), a motet which is twice copied into **Mo** with an added triplum, *Onques ne se parti* (425): **Mo** 100 and **Mo** 126 (fols. 140v–142r and fols. 173r–174r). The refrain of the triplum (vdB 717) is unique. With this network fully in hand, I turn now to my analysis of **Mo** 20, beginning with its nucleus.

The vernacular motetus consists of the standard language and concepts for the earthly love of a lady, who is identified as 'la bele' from the outset. Such secular themes of love involve, as here, cries for mercy, the desire not to be forgotten by the lady, a willingness to suffer pain for love and to pine after her day and night, the promise to abandon yearnings for anyone else, and the belief that one's heart belongs to the lady and no longer oneself. These sentiments occupy the entire text of the motetus:

> La bele, en qui je me fi,
> merci cri,
> qu'ele son ami
> ne mete mie en oubli;
> car, voir, je l'aim si,
> que point ne m'esmai de dolor
> souffrir ne de languir nuit et jor,
> mes que ne perde l'amor
> de li, par qui tout deffi.
> Mes cuers se reclaime:
> *Mes fins cuers n'est mie a moi,*
> *ains l'a, qui bien l'aime.*

To the fair one in whom I trust, I cry for mercy so that she forget not her sweetheart, for in truth I love her so much that I in no way dread suffering pain or languishing night and day as long as I lose not the love of her on account of whom I abandon all else. My heart cries out: *My loyal heart belongs not to me but rather to the one who loves it well.*

The musical setting of the opening five poetic lines is structured in such a way as to emphasize the protagonist's plea for mercy. As shown in Example 10.2, the phrase 'merci cri' in bar 3 is surrounded by rests, a musical technique that isolates critical passages to draw attention to their meaning, as we also encountered in **Mo** 127. Bar 3 is musically staged as an interjection,

---

[27]   Folio numbering of **MüB** follows DIAMM.

[28]   The idea that clausulae are precursors to the motet was called into question long ago, although this chronology dies hard. Catherine A. Bradley has written extensively on this issue and offers further evidence for a more complex view of chronology in her chapter above.

like an unplanned cry: observe how the rhythm and the melodic contour of the surrounding phrases in bars 1–2 and bar 4 (labelled a and b respectively in Example 10.2) are repeated in bars 5–6 (labelled a´) and bar 7 (labelled b´) without the intervening material in bar 3. Additionally, the rhyme '-i' of 'merci cri' dominates the soundscape of the first five lines of the motetus up to the end of bar 7. The aurally irksome vowel sound is further intensified both by the internal words 'qui' at the highest point of the melodic contour in the first bar, as well as the 'merci' of 'merci cri'.

The rest of the motetus contains other paired phrases, which are, with one notable exception, matched by rhyme, rhythmic profile, and melodic contour. Firstly, bars 8–9 and bars 10–11 are paired by their endings: both contain distinctive downward leaps, which articulate the new '-or' rhyme of the words 'dolor' and 'jor'. Indeed, the two consecutive leaps of 'de dolor' in bar 9 descend to the lowest point heard in the motetus's melodic line thus far, only for the leaps on 'nuit et jor' in bar 11 to plunge to what will turn out to be the lowest point of the entire motetus. Bars 13–14 and 15–16 form the next clear phrase-pair. This time, they are most obviously paired by their beginnings, although they also end on the same pitch. Both begin with striking leaps, housed in the same rhythm and with complementary contours. While they both end on the same pitch, *d*, accompanied each time by *G* in the tenor, the second phrase introduces a new rhyme, '-e'. Such a break in the rhyme pattern is a common technique for preparing a refrain.

Within this context of paired phrases, the material in bar 12 strikes the ear as the odd phrase out: it has no companion phrase. Much like 'merci cri', it serves as a brief moment of anxious pitter-patter as the protagonist emits a mouthful of syllables, fearing as he does losing the love of his lady. Although an isolated phrase in terms of musical structure, it nonetheless connects to the ensuing phrase through enjambment as the full sense of the textual phrase is completed with the words 'de li' in bar 13 ('mes que ne perde l'amor / *de li*') – an emphatic continuation that accentuates that he 'does not want to lose the love *of her*'. Despite the rest between phrases, then, the enjambment is underscored musically by a retaking in bar 13 of the interval *D/a* sung by the tenor and motetus at the end of bar 12, a detail that will prove important when the motet is fleshed out in three and four voices. Additionally, the words 'de li' reignite the opening '-i' rhyme, and, coupled with their musical setting, recall the cry for mercy with the same leap from *a* to *d*, albeit to a different rhythm (compare bars 3 and 13 in Example 10.2). This connection is apt: he is desperate both for her continued love and her mercy. Indeed, just as the '-i' rhyme dominated the poetic lines of the opening, so the poetic line in bars 13–14 is similarly infused with words ending in '-i': 'de li, par qui tout deffi'. The rhythm and the melodic leaps of the musical setting of this textual phrase are again tailored to supply a kind of soundtrack or onomatopoeic rendition of the increasingly desperate cries of the protagonist.

The refrain is also devised as a final moment of undisciplined music. The text's grammatical structure suggests a shape with the caesura positioned at the midpoint, as might be expected of a normative refrain phrase structure: '*Mes fins cuers n'est mie a moi, / ains l'a, qui bien l'aime*'. Instead, the placement of the rest in bar 19 suggests that the protagonist breathes in the wrong place. It is as if, when the protagonist says 'my heart cries out', the ensuing refrain is uttered compulsively. In other words, the mismanagement of the natural breathing point of the refrain, combined with the interjection for mercy in bar 3, the striking descending leaps in bars 9 and 11, and the alliteration of '-i' word endings in bars 13–14 mean we witness a song where the protagonist loses his composure for brief moments during the otherwise refined discourse and musical utterance of *fin'amor*.

Before turning to the other upper voices, it is instructive to compare the compositional design of the vernacular duplum to the Latin duplum, which does not maintain all of the elegant phrase pairings of the French motet.

Ave, plena gratia,
Pia via per Maria,
Stella maris previa
Virgo Maria,
Duc per mundi pericula
Tu nostra regula singula
Solve reis vincula,
Quia dia regia,
Mater salvatoris,
Permanes in gloria
Tui genitoris.[29]

Notably the rhythmic repetition of bars 4 and 7 in the Old French version in Example 10.2 is lost in the Latin incarnation because the interjection of bar 3 is joined to the next phrase (see the underlay of 'Pia via per Maria' ['pointing the way, Maria']).[30] The cry for mercy that was bounded by rests in the French motet is replaced by one phrase pointing the way, as it were, to the next through the extra syllable, reflecting, it seems, the new meaning of the words. By contrast, the end of the Latin text preserves the rhetorical structure of the Old French original. In an elegant response to the original, 'de li, par qui', which was a turning point back to the initial '-i' sounds of the French motet, is rendered in the Latin version 'Quia dia' in bar 13, precipitating the return of the '-ia' rhyme. The Latin rhymes thus match the changes in the French motet: '-ia' is heard consistently until bar 9, when it changes to '-a', which in turn changes to '-is' in bar 16, the point of preparation for the refrain. The entry of '-is' seems to adhere to the typical model for announcing the presence of a refrain in the French motet, even though Latin motets do not contain refrains. The Latin motet even seems to model a refrain-like adage as its final thought: 'Permanes in gloria/Tui generis' ('thou shalt forever remain in the glory of thy son'). Again, the musical caesura is misplaced, arriving as it does after the word 'tut', which also undermines the '-ia' rhyme of 'gloria'. There is no good reason to have composed a line and melody like this in the case of the Latin motet, which strongly suggests the music was pre-existent. Unlike in the French counterpart, where the refrain is spoken from the heart ('my heart cries out') and is metaphorically in direct speech, the statement in the Latin motet comes from a presumed 'we' envoicing the motet as a whole.

The poet-composer(s) of the triplum and quadruplum of the Old French motet offer interesting commentaries on the foundational two-part motet.

Triplum
La bele estoile de mer,
qui amer
doit on sans fauser,
vueil servir et henorer,
de cuer reclamer.
Virge pucele, en qui je croi,
roïne del mont, aidiés moi!
Proiés vostre fil, le roi,
qu'il me deigne conforter

---

[29] Edition of the text is from G. Anderson 1968–76, 1: 178–9.
[30] Translation of the text from G. Anderson 1968–76, 2: 274.

et geter de paine.
Nus ne doit joie mener,
se bien ne voz aime.

The lovely star of the sea whom one should love without deception is the one whom I desire to serve and honor and entreat from the depths of my heart. Virgin maid, in whom I believe, queen of the world, help me! Beg your Son, the King, that He deign to comfort me and take away my pain. *No one should be joyful unless he loves you well.*

Quadruplum
Celui en qui je me fi,
qui de fi
sai, qu'ele est a mi,
requier de vrai cuer et pri
d'amour, car en li
cuer et cors ai mis sanz retor;
souffrir s'ele osast la dolor
et la tres loial amour,
dont mes cuers, qu'ele a seisi,
sovent se reclaime:
Mes fins cuers n'est mie a moi,
ainz l'a, qui bien l'aime.

With a true heart I beg and lovingly beseech the one in whom I trust, who I in truth know is mine, in whose care I have irrevocably placed heart and soul, that she dare to feel the pain and the most loyal love which often prompt my captured heart to cry out: *My true heart belongs not to me but rather to the one who loves it well.*

As already observed, the triplum sacralizes the addressee. This split is wonderfully captured by the only monotextual moment in the three-voice motet. Both voices begin with 'la bele'. However, the word 'bele' is a different part of speech in each voice. In the motetus, it is a noun – a nickname for the earthly lady. In the triplum, it is an adjective – a complimentary modifier for the 'star of the sea', a nickname for the Blessed Virgin Mary. The quadruplum, as we shall see, takes this kind of textual confluence with divergent meaning even further. Meanwhile, the rest of the motetus and triplum provides a typical polytextual texture for motets of this time period: they contain contrasting words, contrasting rhymes, and contrasting discourses of love (one earthly, the other Marian). However, the triplum's phrase lengths and overall rhyme structure almost entirely match the motetus, a structure that is also mirrored in the quadruplum. With the exception of the aforementioned phrase endings in bars 3, 6, and 14 (where one or more voices contain a brief melismatic flourish instead of a rest), all of the other phrases of the upper voices proceed at the same pace, with their rests appearing as they do at the end of bars 2, 4, 7, 9, 11, 12, and 16 and in the 'wrong' breath of the refrain in bar 19. The rhyme schemes are also synchronized, although the rhyme endings are not uniform. The motetus and quadruplum share the same rhymes (-i, -or, and -aime), while the triplum has its own (-er, -oi, and -aine/aime).

As mentioned earlier, the motetus and quadruplum are also paired by their monotextuality and their common lyrical thread: both feature the theme of earthly love. The textual overlap includes 'en qui je me fi' in bars 1–2, the homophone 'a mi' and 'ami' in bar 4, 'souffrir' in both voices in bar 10, 'amour' and 'l'amor' in bar 12, and, once again, a simultaneous refrain (vdB 1327) 'se reclaime: *mes fins cuers n'est mie a moi, ains l'a, qui bien l'aime*', spanning bars 15–20. Compared to our previous example, this degree of overlap might seem unremarkable. Indeed, as we shall see, even the manner in which the meanings diverge as the words converge is subtler in this case. How is this achieved?

The title by which the quadruplum is known is a textual correction. **Mo** has 'De lui de qui je me fi' ('the one in whom I trust'). One wonders if the initial D was meant to be for 'Dame', but it seems in this context right to change 'de lui de qui' to 'celui en qui'. Indeed, an apt ambiguity remains: does 'celui' refer to the lady in the motetus or the triplum? The unity of text between the quadruplum and motetus for the phrase 'je me fi' ('I trust') suggests he places his trust in the vernacular lady of the motetus; however, the octave parallelism in the music in bars 2–3 joins the quadruplum's vocal line with the triplum. Therefore, while the words suggest trust in an earthly lady, the music suggests she is the Blessed Virgin Mary. Similarly, during the cry for mercy, which is highlighted as an interjection by the phrase structure of the motetus, the protagonist of the triplum declares his love for the Virgin to the same music as the quadruplum, albeit an octave lower. Thus, while the quadruplum shares with the motetus the expression of vernacular love – sometimes even using identical words – it shares its music with the triplum's music for the Blessed Virgin Mary. Moreover, in being an octave lower it dips below the tenor, as if to assert liturgical privilege.[31] The quadruplum is therefore an amalgamation of the other two upper voices. It is as if the poet-composer of the quadruplum (who may or may not be the same as for the other voices) wanted to restore the weight of the discourse of love to its earthly incarnation, while vocalizing it through the melody associated with Marian love.[32]

The next piece of shared text takes place in bar 4, where 'a mi' and 'ami' occur together. Here, the words converge yet the meanings diverge in a rather splendid way. In the quadruplum, the protagonist declares 'qu'ele est a mi' ('she is mine'), whereas in the motetus he cries out that he hopes she will not forget her sweetheart ('ami'). Using homophones, he claims she is his and he names himself as her sweetheart at the same time. The motetus and quadruplum operate in close collaboration during other textual overlaps as well. The word 'souffrir' in bar 10 refers to his suffering in the motetus but her feelings in the quadruplum. Similarly, the coincidence in bar 12 of 'l'amor' in the motetus and 'amour' in the quadruplum refers respectively to her love, which he hopes not to lose, versus his loyal love, which he claims she has seized. In this passage, the musical duplication is again significant. His loyal love for her is set to music that loyally follows the contour of the music of the triplum. Just as the triplum expresses 'Proiés vostre fil, le roi' ('Beg your Son, the King'), the quadruplum channels a prayer of 'tres loial amor' ('most loyal love') in parallel fourths that merge into a unison, as if to break into an ancient organum texture for maximum holiness. The two texts unite once more at the end for a common refrain, 'my loyal heart belongs not to me but to the one who loves it well'. Both the announcement of the refrain (bars 15–16) as well as the rhyme word at the end of the refrain (bar 20) contain monotextuality between the duplum and quadruplum and matching melodies between the triplum and duplum. That is, in bars 15–16 the triplum and quadruplum join musical forces as he hopes his pain is taken away, while his heart often cries out.

The music of the triplum and quadruplum duplicates elsewhere in the motet in passages that have no monotextual content. Observe most significantly bars 5–6, the end of bar 8, and

---

[31] I am grateful to Jared Hartt for pointing out the unusual range of the quadruplum, which frequently plunges below the tenor – a texture that persists for much of the first part of the motet.

[32] Rokseth (1935–9, 4: 256) applauded the balance of the three-voice motet, only to judge the 'later addition' ('introduction postérieure') of the quadruplum as disrupting the equilibrium in favor of the corporeal. As I suggest, an account of the music redresses the balance.

bars 13–14. These moments are drawn together through another musical means, which seem to derive from the interesting internal structural contours of the tenor.[33] Although **Mo** 20 is written over a single iteration of the syllable 'han' from the *Johanne* tenor, its particularly long melisma contains internal repetition. As annotated in Example 10.2, this repetition occupies bars 1–8 and bars 9–16. The segment of chant supporting the refrain material is different from anything heard thus far in the tenor, which further serves to demarcate the refrains from the rest of the motet. The poet-composer of the motetus camouflages the beginning of the tenor's repetition in bar 9 by extending its phrase across the point of repetition; the other voices follow suit. While this overlap creates a sense of continuity or perhaps draws the listener's attention away from the beginning of the tenor's repetition in bar 9, the return in bars 13–14 of the triplum's two-measure melodic phrase first heard in the triplum in bars 5–6 falls in the corresponding parts of the tenor's repetition. To reinforce this melodic memory, the quadruplum sings the opening tag of this phrase in bar 8, a point at which there is a repetition-within-a-repetition in the tenor (compare bars 5–6 and bars 8–10).

The distinctive counterpoint of this motet – albeit in its two-voice format – was noted by a contemporary theorist: Franco of Cologne cited the two-voice Latin motet as an example where 'It should be known also that sometimes both the tenor and the discant, for reasons of beauty, ascend and descend together'. As such, *Ave, plena gracia/Johanne* was a counterexample to the norm, which typically proceeds 'by concords, sometimes mixing them with discords in suitable places, so that when the tenor ascends the discant descends and vice versa'.[34] In this light, it becomes noteworthy that the moments of musical duplication in the triplum and quadruplum occur when the duplum moves either in parallel or oblique motion with the tenor. The other two voices together provide the contrary motion.

As Huot memorably put it: 'The motet is particularly well suited to cultivating a playful dialectic of sacred and profane discourses'.[35] The motet is unique amongst all literary and musical genres insofar as contraries can be sung at the same time. In the case of **Mo** 20, each layer of the network plays on these juxtapositions: in its simplest form, the vernacular motetus is heard against a liturgical tenor but it is also heard against its Latin contrafactum. This is little different from other literary genres: the two two-voice motets may be placed or performed alongside one another, for contemplation of now the earthly lady, now the Virgin Mary – or now French, now Latin. As intertexts go, and true to Jean de Meun's didactic valediction in the *Roman de la Rose*, it is impossible to listen to one version without the other version in mind. However, when the contrafactum text is echoed in the vernacular triplum, it brings the medieval interest in the two 'bele' figures into a kind of simultaneity of utterance that only the motet can do. And remarkably, with the addition of the quadruplum, the contrast is taken a step further. In **Mo** 20, the text about the vernacular lady is infused with the music belonging to the voice about the sacred lady, and this triplum about the sacred lady is similarly infused with quadruplum's music belonging to a part about a vernacular lady. Only the acute listener – attentive to both text and music – will appreciate the bifocal meaning of the quadruplum. Its musical and textual correspondences do not eliminate the 'poly-' expressive routines of the motet. Similarly for **Mo** 127: its textual semblances belie its vivid polarities. To grasp this requires an ecological listener, one attuned to the seasons. The motet's familiar lexicon encapsulates the discourse of desire on the one hand and,

---

[33] A brief analysis of the repetition in this chant is provided in M. Anderson 2011, 11 and 13.

[34] Cited in G. Anderson 1968–76, 2: 277.

[35] Huot 1997, 18.

on the other hand, shines light on the empty, bleak, fallow period in an amorous trouvère's life, which is rarely recounted in this repertoire. In so doing, the examples explored in this chapter epitomize the vigorous pursuit of contrast in the Middle Ages. They exhibit but an artful semblance of monotextuality.

11

Motets in Chansonniers and the Other Culture
of the French Thirteenth-Century Motet

Gaël Saint-Cricq

I N THIRTEENTH-CENTURY MOTET SCHOLARSHIP, the question pertaining to the existence of repertories and practices both from borderland provenance and culture remains an intricate issue.[1] It has been overshadowed by the evidently dominant role of Paris in both the creation and transmission of a repertory largely preserved and told in manuscripts from the Île-de-France. It has been further obscured by the dearth of documentation on the circulation and reciprocal influences among the existing sources. Several studies have nevertheless examined sources and documentation testifying to the existence of non-Parisian motet practices or repertories, but either the sources and documentation are later than the thirteenth century, or they witness practices and works stemming from Parisian central culture, thus testifying to the influence of the latter rather than the emergence of indigenous local corpora.[2]

In this search of motet repertories possibly created and preserved outside of the Parisian bosom, an ensemble of promising sources has until recently received only little consideration: the thirteenth-century chansonniers. The songbooks preserve a significant repertory of 294 occurrences of motets disseminated in seventeen sources, offering a total of 209 different works. This ensemble divides into two categories. The first contains motets that are recorded in a separate, distinct collection, in some cases identified as such by a preliminary rubric. Six sources (listed first in Table 11.1) include such collections, accounting for 225 occurrences; some of them are among the largest repositories of thirteenth-century motets.[3] The second category includes motets

---

[1] Throughout this chapter, the 'central' repertory designates the motet repertory that proceeds from the tradition of Parisian polyphony of Notre Dame, and such as it appears essentially in the main Parisian sources of the motet (**F, W2, Mo, Ba**). On the contrary, the 'borderland' or 'local' repertory designates any repertory on the fringes of these traditions and sources, therefore revealing alternative practices of the motet.

[2] For an overview of non-Parisian polyphonic sources and practices, see Everist 1989, 171–224. Examples of thirteenth-century sources from borderland provenance but that record Parisian works are **Ma, LoB, Boul**, and, *c.* 1300, **To**. The borderland source **Hu** includes in part an alternative repertory and has been the subject of recent studies, but may be dated *c.* 1325 (Bell 2004, 36) or even as late as the 1340's (Catalunya 2016, 106–8). See also the attempts to determine a borderland provenance for a cluster of motets compiled in Parisian sources, though with limited success; a summary is provided in Saint-Cricq 2009, 241 n. 5.

[3] With 91 works, **Noailles** is the fourth-largest repository of thirteenth-century motets. **Roi** originally included 48 motets according to the index, but eight are lost. **Mesmes** is a lost chansonnier, of which remains only a description by Châtre de Cangé in F-Pn f. fr. 24729, fols. 104v–105r (see

copied within the song collections themselves, without any particular distinction regarding their genre. These 59 occurrences of motets, which 'wander' amid songs, occur in all seventeen sources listed in Table 11.1. Finally, 10 further motets constitute a special case that escapes either category. Copied as additional items in the empty staves of **Roi** at both ends of the codex, they consequently do not appear as isolated motets disseminated within a trouvère song set. Nor do they constitute a separate consistent motet collection, as they are copied by different scribal hands alongside a variety of musical works, and were entered at different stages between the end of the thirteenth and the mid fourteenth century.[4]

These chansonniers stand apart from the sources containing repertory of Parisian polyphony on geographic and cultural grounds, as well as from the point of view of their contents. Indeed, as shown in Table 11.1, with the possible exception of **k**, all are non-Parisian sources, coming from Artois, Picardy, Lorraine, Burgundy and Italy, and span the 1250s to *c.* 1310.[5] Moreover, they form a counterexample to the customary types of sources for the thirteenth-century motet, namely, service books and motet books. Fourteen of the seventeen sources contain primarily songs, not excluding, occasionally, the complementary redaction of a few non-lyric texts; the three other sources (**D308**, **k**, **S**) bring together, more or less equally, vernacular literary texts and songs. Copied within the core sources of the trouvère lyric poetry, these motets therefore step out of the liturgical and polyphonic realm of the Parisian clerks and instead fall within the culture of monophonic chanson of the provincial trouvères. Finally, the content itself of the corpus offers a clear glimpse of a rather idiosyncratic repertory, perhaps illustrative of a borderland motet culture: of the 209 different motets preserved in chansonniers, 116 (55.5%) circulate in this type of source exclusively. Thus, on the basis of the extant sources, these 116 works may be said to be purely a product of the trouvères songbooks.

Admittedly, the songbook motets do not constitute a homogenous group. However, they together do provide a variety of characteristics, individual works and even clusters of works distinct from the Parisian tradition, thereby offering an original, sometimes alternative, perspective on the genre. This chapter aims to provide an overview, through a few selected examples, of some of these idiosyncratic traits and repertories, showing that the context of their redaction, that is, the chanson culture in general and the surrounding songbook and its local culture in particular, is a key to their understanding. The first section below inspects the motet collection in **Noailles** as a representative example of separate motet collections included in chansonniers, then examines one of the few series of borderland motets included in this source. The second section investigates the monophonic motet, a category found exclusively in chansonniers and that appears as the locus of a symbiosis between the genres and forms of the motet and the chanson. Finally, the last section focuses on the shared quotations between the motets in chansonniers and the song repertory, which often reveals a play on references between motets and songs belonging to the same songbook and culture.

Karp 1962) mentioning a motet collection with only the incipit of the first work. Collections in fr.845, **Mesmes**, **Roi**, and Reg1490 are preceded by a rubric.

[4] For a survey of these additions, see Haines 1998, 162–81, and Peraino 1995, ch. 3.

[5] The sections relevant to the motets in **H** and **U** are dated in the 1250s. The latest sources of the corpus are **O**, **k**, **V**, and **D308**.

Table 11.1. Thirteenth-century chansonniers with motets

Source	Provenance	# (collection)	# (amid songs)	# (other)
Noailles	Artois	91	4	–
D308	Lorraine	63	10	–
Roi	Artois?[a]	48	4	10
fr.845	Picardy or Artois	15	5	–
Reg1490	Artois	7	10	–
Mesmes	?	1[b]	?	–
C	Lorraine	–	1	–
H	Italy	–	1	–
K	Picardy or Artois	–	3	–
k	Île-de-France or Center-west[c]	–	3	–
O	Burgundy	–	4	–
P	Picardy or Artois	–	3	–
R	Artois?	–	1	–
S	Burgundy or Champagne[d]	–	2	–
U	Lorraine	–	2	–
V	Picardy or Artois	–	1	–
X	Picardy or Artois	–	5	–

[a] The provenance of **Roi** remains undecided between Artois, Picardy, Champagne, and even Morea (see Haines 1998–2002, 18, Peraino 2011, 154–84, and Stones 2013, 1/2: 160). Nevertheless, the twinship between the motet collections in **Roi** and the Artesian **Noailles** makes it very likely that at least the bulk of **Roi** originates from Artois.

[b] The provenance and the number of motets originally included in the motet section of this lost chansonnier are unknown.

[c] See Fery-Hue 2000.

[d] See Stones 2013, 1/1: 73 and 2/2: 130.

NOAILLES AND THE BORDERLAND CULTURE OF THE MOTET
IN A SONGBOOK COLLECTION

The chansonnier de Noailles was copied between the late 1260s and the late 1270s in Artois and most probably in Arras.[6] Like three other chansonniers including separate motet collections – **Roi**, **D308** and **Reg1490** – **Noailles** is a multi-layered composite source. It contains six main collections that together constitute an anthology of lyric and non-lyric works in which central repertories share space with local ones. Collection 1 is a *libellus* of fifty-five songs by Thibaut de Champagne, and constitutes the very symbol of an 'international' collection as it circulates across manuscripts of several provenances.[7] Collection 2, the main songbook, provides large sections of non-Artesian prestigious trouvère works, but the majority of these almost four hundred songs are the work of trouvères from Artois, several of whom were members of the confraternity of Jongleurs and Bourgeois d'Arras. Collection 4, the 'chansons et dits d'Arras', is known for its references to almost two hundred names associated with Arras and the confraternity. Collection 5 features a non-lyric poem whose author, Robert le Clerc d'Arras, was also a member of the confraternity. Finally, collection 6 is a set of thirty-one songs entirely composed by the Artesian trouvère Adam de la Halle. It is in the middle of these miscellanies, within which the local corpora take the lion's share, that collection 3 of motets was copied (fols. 179r–196v).

The motets that comprise collection 3 were clearly part of the compilatory project from the beginning. Indeed, the literary hand is the same as the one in charge of the majority of collections 1 and 2, while the musical hand is identical to that responsible for collection 1. The ruling pattern, the written block, and the decoration are rigorously identical to collection 2. A few distinctive material traits suggest that collection 3 was produced separately – but it is doubtless that it was immediately added to collections 1 and 2 – and that the manuscript shortly thereafter comprised collections 1 to 5.[8] In this respect, the **Noailles** motet set is illustrative of our corpus as a whole. Barring the ten additions in **Roi**, the songbook motets are always copied in tandem with the neighboring trouvère songs. This is self-evident in the case of isolated motets appearing within the song sets. But the same holds true for the other distinct collections: like **Noailles**, the gatherings in **fr.845**, **Reg1490**, **D308**, and **Roi**, although possibly produced apart from the main song section in a first phase, are always copied by a scribe also active in the surrounding song bodies.[9] Our motets do not, therefore, constitute exogenous additions oddly tacked onto songbooks: they were intended for the original program of the trouvère anthologies.

The typology of the **Noailles** motets likewise reflects our corpus as a whole: works with more than two voices are the exception, and the collection includes exclusively French motets whose

---

[6] The dating and provenance of **Noailles** relies on the evidence of its contents, of the local references scattered in various texts, and of the Franco-Picard writing of the scribes. This information and all the findings on **Noailles** included in this section are elaborated at length in the exhaustive analysis of this manuscript and its motet collection in the 'Introduction' of Saint-Cricq 2017.

[7] Apart from **Noailles**, **Roi**, too, devotes a *libellus* to Thibaut, while almost all the other thirteenth- and fourteenth-century trouvère songbooks include very large sections devoted to his songs, often found at the beginning of the song collections and sometimes preceded by a miniature and a rubric (see especially chansonniers **Reg1490**, **R**, **K**, **fr.845**, **X**, and **O**).

[8] Only collection 6 led to a true enlargement of the codex; copied *c.* 1300, it was added sometime between then and the eighteenth century.

[9] On the contents, production and structure of **Roi**, see Haines 2013. For **D308**, see Doss-Quinby *et al.* 2006, xlv–lx, and Atchison 2005, 1–106 (esp. 57–79 on scribal hands). On **fr.845**, see Elizabeth Aubrey's entry 'Sources, MS, §III: Secular monophony, 4. French' in *Grove*. On **Reg1490**, see Tyssens 1998, 15–111.

upper voices most often carry the topoï and registers inherited from the trouvère chanson. Their notation is also symptomatic of the practices and limitations of the chansonnier culture. The upper voices were copied in an unmeasured notation comparable to that of the surrounding song gatherings, at a time when motet books were already employing their own reliable mensural notation.[10] With only four tenors notated with perfect accuracy, the redaction of tenors reveals uncountable gross errors: numerous lacunae, myriad errors in pitch, fanciful patterning of the melismas lacking any sensible modal formula, erroneous tenor words, all of which testifies to insecure knowledge of polyphony, liturgy, and even Latin. These notational traits are typical of the entire corpus of motets copied in chansonniers: of the almost three-hundred occurrences, only fifteen are notated in mensural notation, and the tenors are almost always the locus of a faulty or missing notation across the seventeen sources.[11] These problems in part reveal scribes immersed in vernacular culture, sure of themselves when copying trouvère songs but clearly in trouble when faced with a polyphonic repertory.

As a small-scale model of the whole chansonnier, the **Noailles** motet collection compiles central and local corpora side by side. As striking evidence of the manuscript's originality, forty-nine works (54%) appear nowhere as motets but in **Noailles** or in the **Noailles-Roi** tandem, these two motet collections actually constituting a single 'meta-collection'.[12] These forty-nine pieces are therefore unique within the motet repertory, a remarkable trait that exemplifies the great proportion of *unica* in songbooks compared to the central motet sources.[13] Furthermore, some of the **Noailles-Roi** *unica*, on the basis of their distribution and of their unusual compositional procedures, clearly form idiosyncratic series of motets. This is true, for example, of the eight rondeau-motets peculiar to **Noailles-Roi** (**Noailles** nos. 22 to 26, 61, 68, 82), which have several times been the subject of substantial commentary. These works share together several poetic motifs; musically and textually, the upper voices of these eight pieces are built on the formal structure of the rondeau (see, for instance, motet no. 22 in Example 11.1a).[14] Accordingly, their tenor melismas are reconstructed as rondeaux to ensure formal compatibility with their motetus voices (here, see segments y and z of the tenor).[15] Friedrich Ludwig then Mark Everist pointed out the particular cyclical nature of rondeau-motets 24, 25, and 26, with their motetus voices using identical poetic formulas and their tenors built on successive portions of the *Alleluia: Letabitur iustus in domino*. Everist in turn outlined the compositional traits that clearly distinguish the rondeau-motets in **Noailles** from those preserved in the Parisian codex **Mo** and that allow one to suggest an Artesian origin for

---

[10]   See the opening folio of the **Noailles** motet collection in Haines and Udell's chapter, Figure 8.2.

[11]   Only one tenor is accurately notated in **Roi**. Among the seven polyphonic motets in **Reg1490**, only one tenor has been copied. The collections in **fr.845** and **D308** include only monophonic motets, the latter source being unnotated. Among the 59 wandering motets in chansonniers, only one tenor is notated. See also Wolinski 1996.

[12]   These two sources have the same chronology and possibly provenance, and all the motets in **Roi** are also present in **Noailles**, in the same sequence, in the same state and notation. The only notable difference between these twin collections is their dissimilar size, for **Noailles** comprises forty-three more pieces than **Roi** (see the introduction in Saint-Cricq 2017).

[13]   **Noailles-Roi**, **D308** and **fr.845** contain 54%, 69.9%, and 73.3% of *unica*, respectively, to be compared to the 39%, 41%, 2.9%, 2.8%, and 11.2% of *unica* as motets in, respectively, **Mo V**, **Mo VI**, **Cl**, **W2 IX**, and **W2 X**. Only the seven motets in the collection of **Reg1490** stand apart, with no *unica* at all.

[14]   Text of Example 11.1a edited by Eglal Doss-Quinby and Samuel N. Rosenberg.

[15]   The only exception is no. 68, whose tenor remains uncopied.

1	*Mes cuers est emprisonés*	7A
2	*en trop crüel prison.*	6B
3	Merchi, dame ki l'avés!	7a
4	*Mes cuers est emprisonés.*	7A
5	Amors, car l'en delivrés,	7a
6	s'en prendés raençon.	6b
7	*Mes cuers est emprisonés*	7A
8	*en trop crüel prison.*	6B

Example 11.1a. *Mes cuers est emprisonés* (268a)/*Et pro* (M20a), **Noailles** no. 22, fol. 184r

[second Sunday following Easter week]

Example 11.1b. *Alleluia: Surrexit pastor bonus … ovibus*, **F-Arras 444**, fol. 147r

the cluster.[16] But the notion that these eight rondeau-motets belong to a borderland repertory is further corroborated by the tenor 'Et pro' that underlies the rondeau-motet no. 22. Unknown elsewhere in the thirteenth-century polyphonic repertory and hitherto either unidentified or misidentified, this melisma actually stems from the *Alleluia: Surrexit pastor bonus... ovibus*. What has made this melody hard to identify is its omission from thirteenth-century Parisian books of plainchant and, in general, from most of the French liturgical books of the medieval period.[17] It is present, however, in all extant thirteenth-century chant books from Arras; in the two sources that provide the music for it, the portion 'Et pro' is strictly identical to the tenor; compare Examples 11.1a and b. This identification therefore roots this work, and by extension the whole cluster of rondeau-motets, even more deeply in Artois.[18]

Noailles rondeau-motets illustrate the relationship that occurs between the songbook motets and the context of their redaction. They testify to the interpenetration between the polyphonic organism of the motet and the repetitive formal types of the chanson, as opposed to the asymmetry of phrases and versification as well as the primary and determinant role of the tenor, which are native marks of the motet as a genre.[19] In sum, these pieces highlight the rooting of our motets in the local culture of their songbook, here with recourse to a local tenor, but also to the rondeau form that will be, several years later, the structure that frames the first examples of polyphonic songs, also originating from Arras, under Adam de la Halle's pen.

THE CHANSONNIER'S SPECIALITY: THE MONOPHONIC MOTET

A notable category in the motet repertory is found exclusively in the chansonniers: the monophonic motet, which takes the form of an upper voice without a tenor in the sources. Monophonic and polyphonic occurrences are equally represented in our corpus, with 147 instances each. Three gatherings, **D308**, **Mesmes** and **fr.845**, are dedicated entirely to monophonic motets. Their concentration in the chansonniers, and conversely their exclusion from Parisian motet books, points to them as a confluent of the motet and chanson genres. Their statistical significance lends them credence as a legitimate category of the genre and at least as a potential setting of a motet, as 63 of our monophonic pieces are found elsewhere in the sources with up to four voices. The use of the term 'motet' to designate these works without tenor in the rubrics of **fr.845** and **Mesmes** does not stem only from the polysemy of the word in the Middle Ages,[20] but should also extricate our understanding of the genre from its mere polyphonic context.[21]

By announcing '*Ci commencent li motet enté*', the rubrics in **Mesmes** and **fr.845** attach the additional '*enté*' characteristic to their contents, one that recurs frequently in the corpus of

---

[16] Ludwig 1910–78, 1/1: 290, 298; Everist 1994, 90–109.

[17] Hughes (2005, 51) lists only six occurrences of this chant among the two hundred French medieval sources considered.

[18] For an analysis of other series and instances of borderland culture in **Noailles**, see the 'Introduction' of Saint-Cricq 2017.

[19] For examples, several of which are recorded in chansonniers, of rearranged or invented tenors designed to adhere to a motetus by incorporating song formal types, see Saint-Cricq 2013a. On the impact of song material on the motet polyphonic structure, see also Everist 1996 and Everist 2007.

[20] For a survey of the attestations of 'motet' in medieval sources, see Hofmann 1970. See also Elizabeth Eva Leach's discussion in Chapter 1 above.

[21] A claim also found in Peraino 2011, 194–5. Her ch. 4 is entirely devoted to the examination of the monophonic motet *enté*.

monophonic motets.[22] The only medieval description of the word '*enté*' ('grafted') in a musical context,[23] albeit abstruse and much disputed, seems to define it as the interpolation of one (or more) refrain(s) at both ends of a work, with the refrain being possibly a quotation.[24] It has been traditionally maintained that a motet *enté* is a work whose voice part is framed by the two halves of a divided refrain.[25] According to this definition, the collection in **D308** is largely devoted to the motet *enté*: forty-eight of the sixty-three pieces have initial and final lines that together create a unity of meaning with a clear refrain function, twenty-seven of which are documented quotations. Additionally, although copied by different hands at different times, all ten additions in **Roi** likewise behave like motets *entés*: among the eight non-lacunary works therein, seven feature framing lines found as refrains in another source. Although many monophonic motets can also be classified as motet *entés* – and vice versa – this is by no means always the case: among the seventy-four motets *entés* with attested quotations included in the motet repertoire, thirty-three are found exclusively in polyphonic form.

As shown in Table 11.2, the collection in **fr.845** contains fifteen monophonic motets *entés*. These works have been the subject of recent discussions on the validity of the traditional definition of the motet *enté*. Indeed, the necessity for the framing lines to be a refrain quotation has been challenged since the standard refrain bibliography identifies only seven quotations in these fifteen works. This view has paved the way for an alternative definition of the motet *enté*: musical repetition, a prominent feature in these fifteen works, would be the actual procedural referent for the term '*enté*' in the rubric, as these works hinge on the grafting of the same musical material onto the diverse lines of the texts.[26] However, an examination of the works reveals that both elements under consideration – quotation *and* musical repetition – actually appear to be consubstantial. Indeed, it is not seven motets that include a documented refrain-quotation, but rather nine (see the two quotations in bold type in Table 11.2). In the case of motet no. 12, it is evidently refrain vdB 458 that is quoted. This refrain is found elsewhere without music in the last strophe of the *chanson avec des refrains* RS 816 in **O** (fol. 85v): the first limb is strictly identical to the first line of our motet, but the scribe in **O** abbreviates the second limb with 'etc.'. However, on the evidence of the versification of the song, it is most probable that the second limb should match the last line of our motet.[27] The framing lines of motet no. 3, meanwhile, certainly match refrain vdB 1801 found in the *chanson avec des refrains* RS 1957, copied without music in **C** (fol. 40r) with two variants: 'La trés bone amor jolie/me tient coente et gai'. While the lexical variant in the motet ('bone' becoming 'haute') is insignificant, the subtraction of the initial article – the first line therefore becoming hexasyllabic – constitutes a more substantial disturbance, to which we will return.[28]

---

[22] See fr.845, fol. 184r, and n. 3 above.

[23] It appears in Johannes de Grocheio's *Ars musice*, c.1275: see Mews *et al.* 2011, 70–1.

[24] See the discussions in Page 1993b, 27; Mullally 1998, 8; Peraino 2011, 212–13; Butterfield 2003, 98–9. According to Plumley (2013, 22), quotation is what the term 'cantus insertus' also used by Grocheio might refer to.

[25] See Ludwig 1910–78, 1/1: 305 and Rokseth 1935–9, 4: 211.

[26] This reassessment was proposed by Everist (1994, 75–89) then discussed in Peraino 2001 and Butterfield 2003.

[27] Indeed, in the three strophes of the song, lines 9–10 are flexible, adapting to the versification of the refrain used in lines 11–12. In the third strophe, line 10 commands a heptasyllable and a rhyme of '-er' to match the second limb of the refrain, exactly like the final line of motet no. 12.

[28] Note that while the mute '-e' at the end of a line in Old French never counts as a syllable in the metric scheme, it is nevertheless always sounded when set to music. Thus, in this motet, this hexasyllabic first line is sung on seven notes, due to the allocation of a note to the final '-e'.

Table 11.2. The monophonic motets *entés* in **fr.845** with their refrain-quotations

Work incipit	Attested quotation	Framing lines
1. Douce dame debonaire (1077)	vdB 604	*Douce dame debonaire, fin cuer amoros, / Sans jamés mon cuer retraire, toz jorz pens a vos.*
2. Hé amors morrai je (1078)	vdB 796	*Hé, Amors! morrai je / sanz avoir merci?*
3. Tres haute amor jolie (1079)	**vdB 1204**	***Tres haute amor jolie / mi tient cointe et gai.***
4. Hé dex tant doucement (1080)	–	Hé, Deus! tant doucement / me tient li maus que j'ai.
5. D'amors vient et de ma dame (1081)	–	D'amors vient et de ma dame / ma joliveté.
6. Mesdisans creveront (1082)	vdB 1322	*Mesdisanz creveront / ja ne savront / la joie que j'ai.*
7. Or ai je trop demoré (1083)	vdB 1432	*Or ai ge trop demoré / de ma dame revoer.*
8. De vos vient li maus (1084)	vdB 487	*De vos vient li maus / que je sent.*
9. Aimi li maus que j'ai (1085)	–	Aimi! Li maus que j'ai / me tient joli.
10. Quant plus sui loing de ma dame (1086)	–	Quant plus sui loig de ma dame / et je plus i pens souvent.
11. Hé dex que ferai (1087)	–	Hé, Deus! que ferai / se je n'ai merci ?
12. D'amors vient toute ma joie (1088)	**vdB 458**	***D'amors vient toute ma joie, / si ne n'en doit nus blasmer.***
13. Hé dex je n'i puis durer (1089)	–	Hé, Deus! je n'i puis durer / sans voz, bele.
14. Amoureusement languis (1090)	vdB 144	*Amoreusement / me tient li maus que j'ai.*
15. Dex la reverre je ja (1091)	vdB 538	Deus! la reverre je ja / (…)

Motet no. 3 in **fr.845** is a work finely crafted from the point of view of the poetic-musical repetition, largely stemming from the material of the framing lines, marked *I* and *II* in Example 11.2a. Framing line *II* is musically prepared by two instances of phrase 2, each of which has identical pitches; moreover, each prepares the final pentasyllabic line and the second phrase 2 anticipates the rhyme '-ai' of this final line. Throughout, phrase 2 or framing line *II* is always preceded by materials produced by the first limb of the quotation: *I* itself before first phrase 2, then the poetic-musical endings stemming from *I* (marked *end of 1*) before the second phrase 2 and before final framing line *II*. The tension resulting from the dissociation of the two limbs of the quotation therefore largely accounts for the structure of the work: the poetic-musical repetition enables a triple hearing of the juxtaposition of the poetic-musical sonorities coming from the two quotation phrases that are separated by the *enté* technique, thus reconstructing what had been separated.

Motet no. 11 in **fr.845** heightens this remarkable type of structural plan generated by the framing lines, marked *I* and *II* in Example 11.2b. These two lines – that do not match any attested quotation in this motet – trigger a relentless play of poetic repetition with the rhyme '-*ai*' coming from *I*, and the incessant pentasyllable stemming from both framing lines. Musically, the repetitions *1* or *end of 1* prompted by framing line *I*, and the repetitions of *2* or their variants *2´* stemming from the framing line *II*, succeed one another. The poetic-musical material generated by the disjunct framing lines *I* and *II*, respectively, are therefore juxtaposed four times in the course of the work.

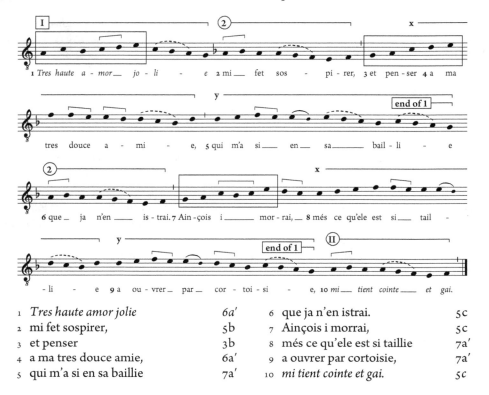

1	*Tres haute amor jolie*	6a'	6	que ja n'en istrai.	5c
2	mi fet sospirer,	5b	7	Ainçois i morrai,	5c
3	et penser	3b	8	més ce qu'ele est si taillie	7a'
4	a ma tres douce amie,	6a'	9	a ouvrer par cortoisie,	7a'
5	qui m'a si en sa baillie	7a'	10	*mi tient cointe et gai.*	5c

Example 11.2a. *Tres haute amor jolie* (1079), fr.845 no. 3, fol. 184r

Given the strategic structural crafting in works nos. 3 and 11, the incongruity of the hexasyllabic first line in motet no. 3 stands out. Indeed, the lines echoing *I* (lines 5, 8, 9 with their rhyme '-ie', and the musical ending *1* for lines 5 and 9), which alternate with lines 6 and 7 that poetically prepare the final line, are heptasyllabic rather than hexasyllabic. In this respect, the length of the first line contradicts the strategy of alternating the poetic norm of the first framing line with that of the second framing line. Moreover, an additional instance of musical repetition stemming from *I* appears in the work (see the three boxed motives in Example 11.2a), through the variation of the incipit of the first phrase; on the evidence of the two variations in the course of the work, the initial *G* of the incipit seems to be lacking. This conjunction of signals suggests that the scribes, not exactly lacking in errors elsewhere in this motet section, omitted the initial *G* and its article 'La' at the beginning of the work, and thus the two framing lines of the motet should have exactly matched the refrain vdB 1801 of the song in **C**.

The repetitive structure and the quotation process are clearly interlocked in the **fr.845** collection. With the exception of motet no. 2, all the works exhibit a repetitive framework – sometimes subtlety crafted with a play on melodic transposition (nos. 5, 6, 7, 9, 12) – aiming at filling the gap between the two limbs of the refrain. And with now nine attested quotations, the probability that the framing lines are all quotations in the collection appears strengthened. The prerequisite of quotation in the motet *enté* is shared by a number of the motets in **D308** and the additions in **Roi**, as is the procedure of grafting the poetical features of the framing lines onto the rest of the text. However, musical repetition is a feature unique to **fr.845**, and does not appear as a structural device in **Roi** and in the motets *entés* of **D308** with a musical concordance elsewhere.

1 Hé Deus! que ferai?	5a	7 car je l'aim pieça,	5c
2 se cele ne m'aime,	5b'	8 loiaument sans faindre.	5b'
3 ou mon cuer mis ai	5a	9 La mort m'est prouchaine	5b'
4 lige a son demaine.	5b'	10 se s'amor n'en ai,	5a
5 Trop sera vilaine	5b'	11 bien sai que morrai	5a
6 se pitié n'en a,	5c	12 se je n'ai merci.	5x

Example 11.2b. *Hé Deus! que ferai?* (1087), fr.845 no. 11, fol. 189r

The works in **fr.845** thus reveal the monophonic motet to be an organism in which a symbiosis takes place between the genres of the motet and the chanson, demonstrating an adaptation to one another. From the motet, it retains the monostrophic form, the tendency to use free poetic-musical structures and, on many occasions, the grafting procedure.[29] From the chanson, it adopts the sources, the monophonic setting, and on some occasions the formal types: the play on repetition in motet no. 11 produces an AAB *pedes cum cauda* form, typical of the trouvère chanson (see Example 11.2b) and occasionally used in the motet repertory.[30] This motet showcases again, like the **Noailles** rondeau-motets, the transfer of formal types from the chanson to the motet genre.

[29] We have only two examples of chansons *entées*, song RS 498 and balette RS 2065, versus seventy-four motets *entés*.

[30] On the motets using a *pedes cum cauda* form, see Saint-Cricq 2013a.

QUOTATION AND THE SELF-REFERENCE
OF THE LOCAL SONGS AND TROUVÈRES

The interpenetration between motet and chanson as witnessed by our corpus is not to be assessed only in terms of shared compositional procedures or structural features, but also in the light of shared quotations between these repertories. Quotation is a remarkable trait of the songbook motets: with 57% of the pieces including material found in another work, our 209 motets exhibit quotation more frequently than the central motet collections. Moreover, the typology of the quoted materials is also notable, as 50% of the 120 quotations included in the corpus are found in at least one chanson.[31] In our corpus, as in the motet and song repertories in general, there exists three levels of quotation between the songs and motets. First and most commonly, the motets can summon the song – and vice versa – by way of a short refrain quotation. In the second level, the shared material is not limited to a refrain, but extends to a larger scale, with the sharing of several lines and/or phrases between a motet voice and a song strophe.[32] The third degree consists of quoting an entire song strophe as a motet part[33] – or vice-versa; in this manner, 34 voices of polyphonic motets also appear as an entire strophe of a song elsewhere. In songbook motets, there exists a clear tendency for the exchange and hybridization with the trouvère chanson by way of all three levels of quotation; but more specifically, it is remarkable that this play on reference occurs more frequently with the surrounding songs of the chansonnier that contains the motets in question. Indeed, the chansons preserved in **Noailles** are the heaviest supplier of chanson quotations in **Noailles** motets, before **K**, **fr.845**, **P**, and **X**. Conversely, it is in this latter group of sources that one predominantly finds the song quotations appearing in the **fr.845** monophonic motets, none being found in **Noailles**. Likewise, the song sections in **D308** are the heaviest providers of song quotations in the **D308** motet section. By means of quotation, the songbook motets are a locus of self-reference to the surrounding chansonnier and its local culture.[34]

The **Noailles** motets are typical of the self-reference of the local song culture: of the twenty-four quotations that are shared with ascribed songs, eighteen occur in at least one song by Artesian writers, some from Arras or closely tied to the city.[35] Strong evidence is offered by the recurring presence of the trouvère Moniot d'Arras in the **Noailles** motets. Moniot was probably an Arras native, and a member of the poetic circle of the city.[36] He is particularly ingrained in the **Noailles** songbook: of the twenty songs attributed to him, fourteen are found in **Noailles**, which is the largest repository of Moniot's work. Moniot is also the most represented trouvère in the motet section, with six different quotations found in songs attributed to him. Conveniently, these six quotations display all the previously discussed degrees of quotation between a song and a motet.

---

[31] By comparison, 45.8%, 48%, 34%, and 37.4% of the upper voices in **Mo V**, **Cl** (French motets), **W₂ IX**, and **W₂ X**, respectively, include quotations. These are found in at least one song in 38.6%, 39.5%, 37.5%, and 39% of the cases. Only **Mo VI** has rates comparable to our corpus (56% and 52%).

[32] See examples in Saint-Cricq 2013b.

[33] Matthew P. Thomson's chapter in this *Companion* examines three such examples of motets that quote an entire song stanza as a motet voice.

[34] Saltzstein (2013b, 80–113) has for example surveyed an Arras corpus of refrains circulating in chansons and motets, functioning like *exempla* promoting Arras vernacular culture as a source of knowledge. Plumley (2013, 24–55) has also pointed out a cluster of quotations circulating within the different collections in **D308**.

[35] See details in Saint-Cricq 2017.

[36] See Dyggve 1938, 30–65.

Three cases (motets nos. 41, 78, 84) exemplify the short quotation of refrains. All three refrains are found only in songs by Moniot, two being exclusively preserved in **Noailles** and **Roi**. Two further motets, nos. 8 and 12, provide examples of long quotations. Each of the two again uses a quotation appearing only in songs attributed to Moniot and transmitted in various redactions, among them **Noailles**. Their way of quoting fragments of the songs is wholly original and exactly the same in both works; specifically, text and music of the song's first two poetic lines and musical phrases constitute the incipit, and the motets close with the final text and music phrase of the monophonic piece. Example 11.3a offers an edition of motet no. 8,[37] and Example 11.3b of the corresponding song as it appears in **Noailles** and **K**. The comparison between the song and the motet reveals that the quotation (italicized in the examples) involves a minimum of poetic or musical variants from one to the other. Beyond the quotation *stricto sensu*, the newly composed part of the motetus appears largely prompted by the song material: from a musical point of view, phrase *1*, corresponding to the first part of the quotation, is echoed by segments *1′* (heard twice and sampling L3–L6 from *1*) and *1″* (corresponding to L2–L6 from *1*). Similarly, segments *2* and *3*, both located in the final part of the quotation, were already heard as soon as L16 then L22 for the former, and L26 (slightly varied in *3′*) for the latter. Poetically, the two rhymes '-ee' and '-our' of the song retain their hold in the motet, and both the song and the motet resort almost exclusively to the heptasyllabic lines. A comparison of the motet to the eight notated redactions of the song is also enlightening. The song is notated a fifth lower in **K**, **fr.845**, **P**, **X**, **U**, and **V**, and only in the Artesian songbooks **Roi** and **Noailles** does it take place on the same pitches as the motet. **Noailles** alone exhibits additional significant variants, all absent from the other versions embodied by **K** in Example 11.3b. In the course of the work, the song in **Noailles** reiterates, much more than in **K**, the musical material from phrase *1* – the one quoted at the incipit of the motet. Phrase *1* is immediately repeated, just like in **K**, but the **Noailles** version then gives three segments sampled from different parts of *1*, while **K** does so only once (see *beginning*, *middle* and *end of 1* in Example 11.3b). From that point of view, the makeup of the song in **Noailles** is much closer to the motet than the song in **K**, as both the motet and the song in **Noailles** reiterate material from the first phrase. In the same way, segments *2* and *3* found in the final quotation are anticipated by *2′* and *end of 3* in the **Noailles** song just like they were in the motet, but these segments do not appear in **K** *et al.* In sum, the **Noailles** song alone is built like its corresponding motet, taking its material from both ends of the work. Motets nos. 8 and 12 are not only the products of a common compositional procedure, possibly composed by the same author in a tribute to a local trouvère, but they also specifically quote the song as transmitted in the same local version.

The last reference to Moniot d'Arras in the **Noailles** motets exemplifies another degree of quotation: the motetus of motet no. 38 is exhaustively copied, without tenor, as the last item of a collection of eight songs by Moniot in chansonnier **Reg1490**, also originating from Artois.[38] It is one of the ten cases in our corpus in which a motet is copied both in a distinct motet collection and as a wandering motetus amid surrounding songs. These occurrences bespeak a two-way hybridization between chanson and motet. First, there are works in which the transfer occurs from chanson to motet by means of an added tenor and the subtraction of the additional strophes. Such motets can often be identified through the alteration of a few pitches of the song so as to suit a pre-existing tenor or, conversely, through the arrangement of the tenor: irregular modal patterns or alteration of pitches of a pre-existent tenor, and even newly invented

---

[37]   Text edited by Eglal Doss-Quinby and Samuel N. Rosenberg.

[38]   Fol. 46v. **Reg1490** provides nine further cases. On the presence of these motetus voices at the closure of individual song collections, see Tyssens 1998, 21–2.

1	Li dous termines m'agree	
2	del mois d'avril em pascour,	
3	adont m'otroia s'amour	
4	la plus belle ki soit nee	7a'
5	et ki plus a de valour;	7b
6	s'en sui em plus grant baudour	7b,
7	k'a nul jour	7a'
		7b
		7b
		3b

8	n'en fu mais aparlee;	7a'
9	ains est loiaus et provee	7b
10	si l'emporte grant honour.	7b
11	Cuers, va i faire sejour	6a'
12	ens la tres douce contree	7a'
13	ou cele maint cui j'aour.	7b
		7b
		7a'
		7b

Example 11.3a. *Li dous termines m'agree* (593) / *Balaam* (M81), Noailles no. 8, fol. 180v

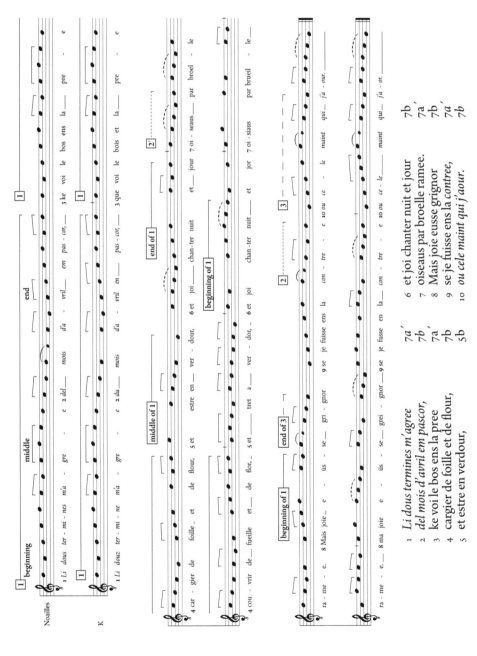

Example 11.3b. Song *Li dous termines m'agree* (RS 490), Noailles fol. 120v (above, and edition of the text), and K p. 133 (below, transposed a 5th higher)

Example 11.4. *Par main s'est levee la bele Maros* (528c) / *Florebit* (M53), Noailles no. 38, fol. 187r

1 Par main s'est levee	5a′
2 la belle Maros,	5b
3 ki sans amour n'est mie;	6c′
4 si s'en est alee	5a′
5 toute seule au bos,	5b
6 nus piés et deslaichie;	6c′
7 lors s'est escriee:	5a′
8 'Mes amis mignos,	5b
9 ki m'a en sa baillie,	6c′
10 deüst ore flors coillir	7d
11 et un chapelet bastir	7d
12 a mes beaus chaveus tenir;	7d
13 s'en fuisse plus jolie!'	6c′
14 Lors l'a coïsi, s'est saillie.	7c′
15 —'Bien viegne', fait il, 'm'amie	7c′
16 ke je tant desir a tenir	8d (5d+3d)
17 sous le raim.	3e
18 *Mignotement la voi venir,*	8d
19 *celi ke j'aim'.*	4e

melismas, are options often resorted to in order to facilitate the handling of the pre-existing song.[39] Second, the transfer may occur from motet to chanson. The most striking example in our corpus is embodied by the four motetus voices converted into songs in chansonnier **X** with added strophes, and attributed to Robert de Reims.[40] This is also the case of **Noailles** no. 38; see Example 11.4.[41] No mark of adaptation from song to motet is detectable in the motetus, and the tenor chosen as well as its pattern are absolutely conventional. Moreover, the length and versification of the text, with its nineteen lines, five different rhymes and six different lengths, are most visibly those of a motet rather than of a song, as are the heteromelism and the occasional disjointed turn of the melody. Finally, it seems clear that the repetition of segments *1* and *2* in the second half of the motetus is prompted by the reiteration of the tenor cursus from L34 onwards, and that the latter indeed determined the fabric of the upper part. This work constitutes, unlike Moniot's previous example, an instance of transfer from motet to chanson. It shows the amalgamation between these genres that is progressively made by songbook compilers; and by copying what is decidedly a genuine motet voice in order to complete a song collection devoted and ascribed to Moniot, the copyist of **Reg1490** seems to designate a trouvère as responsible for the composition of a polyphonic motet.

The motets copied in chansonniers offer an alternative perspective on the genre, which blurs the traditional history of a polyphonic genre born from Parisian liturgy, by showing it as a multifaceted genre with varied practices, provenances and influences.

From an organic point of view, a part of this corpus points to the mutual influence of chanson and motet genres, whether the compositional prerogatives and song materials intrude in the polyphonic complex, or the transfer of motets into trouvère sources is accompanied by a mutation aiming at assimilating their makeup into that of the song.[42]

From the point of view of the reception of genre, the chansonniers show the motet as progressively settling in the soundscape of the trouvère anthology. In the 1270s, **Noailles** associated the motet with the practices of the Arras 'trouvèreship' and **Roi** displayed it among the various branches of the poetic-musical secular culture alongside French and Occitan songs, lais, rondeaux, and instrumental pieces. The organizational principle in later songbooks such as **D308** or **Reg1490**, where the motet – associated with the rondeau – receives its own generic section alongside, and in the same way as, *jeu-parti*, *grand chant* or *pastourelle* among others, establishes even more firmly the genre as a must-have of the trouvère compilation.[43]

---

[39]   See among others the invented tenors of *Bien m'ont amors* (942a)/*Tenor* (**O**, fol. 21v) or *Onques n'amai tant con* (820)/*Sancte Germane* (**Noailles**, fol. 179r), recorded in songbooks and analyzed in Saint-Cricq 2013a. On the latter motet, see also Thomson's discussion and analysis in his chapter of the present volume.

[40]   It was known that Robert's songs RS 1485, RS 1852, and RS 1510 were copied as polyphonic motets in various redactions. It has hitherto escaped notice that song *L'autrier dejouste un rivage* (RS 35) corresponds to the Latin motet *Virgo gignit genitorem* (133)/*Domino quoniam* (M13) in **W2**, fol. 189v and its related clausula (**F**, fol. 156r).

[41]   Text edited by Eglal Doss-Quinby and Samuel N. Rosenberg.

[42]   Butterfield (2002, 73–121) has highlighted this blurring of generic boundaries in thirteenth-century music and literary corpora, especially through the use of contrafacta and the disruptive intermediation of refrain citations. This notion of generic hybridity between song and motet is at the core of Peraino's examination of the monophonic motet (2011, ch. 4).

[43]   See Callahan 2013 for a reflection on the evolution of the organizational principles in the chansonniers.

From the angle of the geography of the genre, the chansonniers expand the map of the motet, by spreading out its practice to diverse northern territories of the French area. It is first and foremost in Artois that songbooks outline a non-Parisian practice of the genre. From that perspective, **Noailles** is particularly enlightening. The motet section certainly constitutes a gathering of works performed and heard in Artois in the second third of the thirteenth century, joining local creations with works and stylistic traits coming from the central motet repertory.[44] The whole chansonnier appears as a compendium of the poetic-musical practice and production of the circle of trouvères and clerics orbiting around the confraternity of Jongleurs and Bourgeois d'Arras. The presence of a polyphonic collection of motets amid songs and texts typical of Arras and the confraternity therefore reveals that the performers, audiences and occasionally composers, were no doubt the same for the motets and the other collections contained in this source.

Finally, the motets in chansonniers question the role of the trouvères themselves in the history of the genre and the key people involved. Many songbook motets allow a glimpse of the presence of a number of trouvères in the repertoire. Moniot d'Arras, present in seven different motets through attribution or quoted material in the repertoire, is only one of the trouvère names. Jean Erart, Robert de Reims, Richard de Fournival and Adam de la Halle likewise recur several times, and might be associated with thirty motets among them, on the basis of the attribution in the sources, and/or of the use of a long quotation found in an ascribed song. While the link between song and motet has been discussed through the lens of modal rhythm in the chanson,[45] the question of the authorship of the trouvères in the motet repertoire has hardly been investigated since Coussemaker.[46] It might constitute, however, a key to our understanding of the confluence between chanson and motet both in the sources and in the works of the thirteenth century.

---

[44] See Saint-Cricq 2017 for further details.

[45] For a summary and an analysis of this dispute, see Haines 2001.

[46] See Coussemaker 1865, xi and ch. 6.

12

Building a Motet around Quoted Material:
Textual and Musical Structure in Motets
Based on Monophonic Songs

Matthew P. Thomson

I N THE THIRTEENTH CENTURY, polyphonic motets and monophonic songs were connected in a number of different ways, many of which are explored by Gaël Saint-Cricq in the previous chapter of this *Companion*. This chapter focuses on three concrete examples of one particular type of interaction: when a motet voice has been created by quoting the entire first stanza of a monophonic song. Each of these motets demonstrates a different manner in which a motet can fashion itself around the characteristics of a quoted song. In presenting a variety of approaches to building a motet around a song, I not only catalogue different modes of song-motet interaction, but also provide a foundation from which to consider the workings of quotation within the thirteenth-century motet.

In approaching song and motet interaction, it can often be profitable to examine the chronological relationships between motets and songs that borrow significant musical and/or textual material from each other. If, for example, a particular motet can be shown to have quoted from a song, the specifics of this intergeneric borrowing can be examined in much more detail than if that relationship remained unestablished. The three examples addressed in this chapter are part of a corpus of twenty-one motets that include an entire voice part that is also found as the first stanza of a monophonic song.[1] The networks of songs and motets in this corpus exhibit different chronologies. In all three cases examined in this chapter, it seems most likely that an earlier monophonic song was quoted in a later motet, moving it from a monophonic to a polyphonic context. In total, this seems the most probable chronology for twelve of the twenty-one cases. In five cases, the reverse seems to have happened: a motet voice was changed into a monophonic song by stripping it of its polyphonic context and adding further stanzas. In the remaining four cases, the extant evidence does not allow for a conclusion to be drawn.[2]

Looking at the interaction between song and motet from the vantage point of the chronology of specific motets and songs is complemented by the more general category of stylistic influence.

---

[1] This corpus was first addressed as such by Gennrich 1926. It was then extended and modified in Haines 2004a, 31 and Saint-Cricq 2009, 2: 143. It was further extended and considered as a full corpus in Thomson 2016. In Gaël Saint-Cricq's chapter above, he mentions a corpus of thirty-four motet voices. The difference between our numbers can be accounted for, in part, by our use of different criteria for inclusion within the corpus.

[2] For the analysis that underpins these conclusions, see Thomson 2016, chs. 1–2.

This consists not of examining the impact that particular songs have on particular motets, but of the influence that song style in general might have on motet style. Since the work of Friedrich Gennrich, scholars working on this field have often focused on motets' use of musico-textual forms that were most commonly found in monophonic songs.[3] In more recent scholarship, for example, Mark Everist has chronicled the use of rondeau form in motets, while Saint-Cricq has explored motets that use *pedes cum cauda* form.[4]

In examining its three examples, this chapter will use many of the same tools of analysis as studies that look for the general stylistic influence of songs on motets, especially concentrating on motets' use of song form. Instead of talking about motet and song style in the abstract, however, it will show how a motet could engage with the specific characteristics of a song that it quoted, demonstrating how that engagement places it in dialogue with thirteenth-century norms of quotation. In each of these three cases, the motets build themselves around a particular aspect of the song that they quote. In the first example, *Onques n'amai tant* (820)/*Sancte Germane*, the motet takes the musical motivic structure of its source song and bases the new polyphonic texture on it. The second, *Bien me doi* (611)/*Je n'ai que que* (612)/*Kyrie fons* (Nr. 3), uses the textual themes of the song as building blocks for the text of the rest of the motet. In the final example, *Par une matinee* (896)/*O clemencie fons* (897)/*D'un joli dart*, both the text and the music of the song are used as a basis on which to build a new motet.[5]

The voice part *Onques n'amai* exists as the motetus of *Onques n'amai tant*/*Sancte Germane* and as a three-stanza monophonic song.[6] As with all three of the examples, in order to show that the motet quotes the song voice in a particular way, it is first important to demonstrate that the monophonic version of this voice part pre-existed its related polyphonic motet and was subsequently turned into it. In this case, the tenor, labelled either *Sancte* or *Sancte Germane* in the extant sources, provides the necessary clues. As Saint-Cricq has shown, the *Sancte Germane* tenor shows a number of irregularities.[7] The incipit is presumably intended to refer to the chant (O27) for the feast of Saint Germane, an unusual choice for a motet tenor: while the beginning of this chant provides the basis for both two-voice and three-voice organa, it is not used as a tenor for any other extant motet.[8] More importantly, the melodic profile of the tenor provided for *Onques*/*Sancte* does not resemble that of O27, nor does it seem to correspond to any other plainchant melody.[9] The pitches of the tenor are therefore most likely to have been created for the specific purpose of turning the song *Onques n'amai* into the motet. This makes this motet-song

---

[3] Gennrich 1921 and Gennrich 1926.

[4] Everist 1988; Saint-Cricq 2013a; Saint-Cricq 2013b. *Pedes cum cauda* form describes any musico-textual form that opens with two sections that are poetically and musically the same (the *pedes*), and follows them with a different section. I use *pedes cum cauda* here, rather than AAX or ABABX which I employ later when discussing specific motets, as it has the advantage of not referring to any of these forms in particular but to the formal principle in general.

[5] The *Sancte Germane* tenor has no identifying number because it does not match any plainchant melody, as discussed shortly. In the case of *D'un joli dart*, there is no number because this tenor melody is not drawn from liturgical chant. A small number of sets of chants, such as Kyrie tropes, are given their own series of numbers (Nr.).

[6] The motet is found in W2, fols. 219av–220r, **Noailles**, fol. 179r, and **Roi**, fol. 205r. The song is found in the chansonniers **Reg1490**, fol. 68v and U, fols. 137v–138r (without notation).

[7] Saint-Cricq 2009, 1: 204.

[8] Saint-Cricq 2009, 1: 202.

[9] Saint-Cricq 2009, 1: 203.

pair a particularly interesting example of a motet adapting a song. As the tenor is not drawn from plainchant, but is new, the creator of the tenor had much more freedom than if they were trying to fit a pre-existent song and a pre-existent chant together. Although song and chant could be adapted, the basic melodic shape of both must be maintained, thereby yielding at least two sets of restrictions on how the voices can interact musically. When the tenor is newly created, one of those sets of restrictions disappears.

The motet *Onques/Sancte* places its source song at the centre of its musical conception by reflecting many of its musical characteristics in the *Sancte Germane* tenor that was newly created for it. On the most general level of form, the overall melodic and poetic ABABX structure of the song is marked in the tenor: as can be seen in Example 12.1, the tenor sings the same musical material under the first AB section (lines 1–2) as under the second (lines 3–4); the lengthy X section begins with line 5.[10] In this regard, the motet exemplifies a general stylistic influence of song on motet: a motet is adopting a musico-textual form associated with the monophonic song repertoire. It is significant, though, that this motet does more than adopt a generic song form; it also reflects the melodic detail of the particular pre-existent song voice that it quotes. The *Onques n'amai* voice has a repetitive structure that goes far beyond the repetition of the A and B sections in lines 3 and 4, and much of that repetitive structure is also reflected in the tenor. The tenor is responding not only to song in general, but to this song in particular.

The most clearly structural motive of the *Onques n'amai* voice part, both in its song and motet versions, is that which ends all but one of the poetic lines, identified on Example 12.1 as **a**. It appears in both open and closed forms, marked **a⁰** and **aᶜ**, which occur in an alternating pattern within each pair of lines: lines 1–2, 3–4, 6–7, 8–9. (Because line 5 does not end with **a**, it is not part of the open and closed structure of paired lines.) Just as **a** marks the end of a line, the motive **b** twice marks the beginning of a line, in lines 6 and 7. The repetition of this motive emphasizes that the structure of paired lines has recommenced after the break in line 5. Motive **b** – though slightly altered – also begins line 9. As well as melodic sections which mark the beginning and end of a line, the *Onques n'amai* voice part often uses the same succession of pitches to move between different sections of melody, transitional passages that are marked as motive **c**. Motives **a**, **b**, and **c** perform a specific function in the melody, always appearing in the same basic position within the line. Motive **a** always provides an ending function, **b** an opening one, and **c** enables the transition between two musical ideas.

The segments marked **d** and **e** comprise a different type of motive. They do not stay at the same point in the poetic line but move around within it, fulfilling different functions each time they appear. Motive **d** first appears as the opening of lines 2 and 4, the B sections of the opening ABAB *pedes*. When it appears again, it forms the middle section of lines 6 and 8, where it is strongly linked with the shortened version of the open line ending **a´⁰**. Motive **e** shows a similar adaptability; first heard in the middle of line 5, it appears later as the opening of line 8.

Many of these motivic relationships are reflected and reproduced in the tenor of *Onques/Sancte*. In making the tenor, the creator of the motet has almost universally matched the open-closed

---

10 In Example 12.1, *Onques/Sancte* is given in an edition prepared from W2. Although there are numerous variants between this source and both **Roi** and **Noailles** (see Figures 8.1 and 8.2 in this *Companion*), they are small-scale and mostly concern the different arrangement of the same notes within ligatures. While **Noailles** contains the same tenor as W2, **Roi** contains a tenor incipit but no notation, which is not uncommon in this source. In general, the versions of the motetus found in **Roi** and **Noailles** are slightly closer to the notated song than W2, although this is not universal. W2 was therefore chosen for this edition to demonstrate that the motivic parallels still function despite having more variants with respect to the song version.

Example 12.1. Analytical edition of *Onques n'amai tant / Sancte Germane*, based on W2 fols. 219av–220r

* Emended. Both **W2** and **Noailles** have *E*.

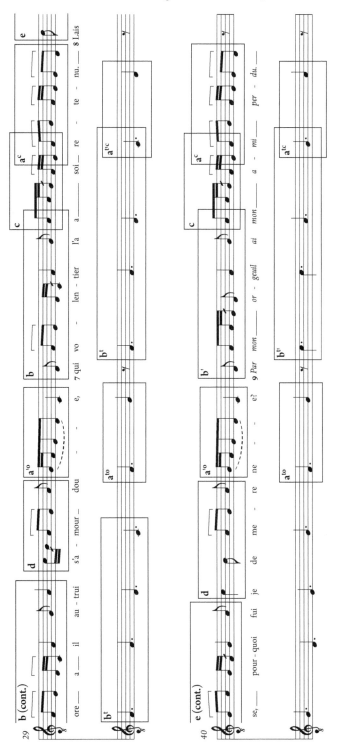

I have never loved as much as I have been loved. Now I repent, for all the good it may do me. For Love has directed me towards the best one, in order that I might have every delight and joy, even towards the most handsome man in all the land. But now he has given his love to another, who happily kept him to herself. Ah, why was I born of my mother? Because of my pride I have lost my sweetheart. (Translation mine, with thanks to Huw Grange for checking it.)

cadence structure of the motetus. As can be seen in Example 12.1, each time the motetus cadences on *C*, either by a^o or by a'^o, the tenor ends its matching phrase with the two note progression *F-G*, marked as a^{to}. A similar pattern occurs when the motetus makes a closed cadence on *D*. Each closed cadence is accompanied in the tenor by an ascending stepwise motive. With the single exception of line 7, these motives are on the pitches *G-a*, and are marked a^{tc}.

The appearances of motive **b** at the beginnings of lines 6 and 7 are accompanied in the tenor by the *F-F-D-C* figure marked b^t. This reflection is not only limited to iterations of the full **b** motive: when **b** is recalled at the beginning of line 9, the tenor sings the notes *c-c-a-G*, the same melody as b^t but a fifth higher.

It is the specificity of a reference to the motivic structure of a particular song that makes quotation a useful category of analysis here: the characteristics of the motet are built not only on a song style in general, but on this song in particular. The process of shaping a new motet around a pre-existent song is a very similar process to that of glossing: a piece of pre-existent material is extended and amplified by being placed within the context of newly created material. The song *Onques n'amai* is therefore being treated in much the same way as other quoted material in thirteenth-century lyric. Ardis Butterfield has shown similarities between glossing and the quotation of refrains, small sections of music and text which are quoted across thirteenth-century lyric genres.[11] One of the key parts of this comparison with glossing is the independence that a glossed text often retains from the gloss that surrounds it. Butterfield has argued that refrains are sometimes simultaneously within the host text but are also clearly separate from it.[12] The same is true for the motetus of *Onques/Sancte*: the fact that the tenor's structure is so thoroughly based on that of the quoted voice part means that the motetus can still be perceived quite clearly as a foreign body that has been extended and made into this new entity.[13] The *Onques n'amai* voice becomes a citation in the sense defined by Mikhail Bakhtin; it is 'the image of another's language': despite, or perhaps because of, the fact that it is at the structural heart of the motet, it retains an inherent otherness.[14]

Strategies for amplifying one voice within a motet were not only musical: in the case of *Bien me doi/Je n'ai que que/Kyrie fons*, the new motet takes on and develops the textual message already found in the pre-existent song.[15] The motetus of this motet is also found as the single-stanza monophonic song *Je n'ai que que*, inserted into a treatise on courtly love, *Li Commens d'Amours*.[16] In order to create the new motet – its opening appears in Example 12.2 – both a tenor and a triplum are added: the musical material of the tenor is taken from the chant melody *Kyrie fons bonitatis*, while the triplum has newly composed music and text. The treatise *Li Commens d'Amours*, which contains the song from which the motetus is created, recommends a particular way of gaining the affections of the woman for whom the courtly lover is constantly searching, and this method

---

[11] Butterfield 2002, ch. 15.

[12] Butterfield 2002, 255. See also Saltzstein 2010, 265.

[13] For a further exploration of this idea, see the category of 'conceptual priority' in Thomson 2016, ch. 1.

[14] Butterfield 2002, 243. For cases in which motets play with quotation and pre-existence, either by not highlighting quoted material or by basing themselves around a song voice that seems to be quoted but is not, see Thomson 2017.

[15] The motet is found in **Mo**, fols. 286r–288r, **Tu**, fol. 9v, and **Bes**, no. 24 (text incipit only).

[16] The treatise is found in **F-Dm 526**, fols. 4r–10v and **GB-Mr [96] 66**, fols. 2r–4r. It has been attributed to Richard de Fournival by Antoinette Saly. See Saly 1972.

of loving is reproduced in the song. In the motet, the new triplum text also bases itself around the treatise's recommendations, textually extending and amplifying the message of the song in a way akin to the musical glossing in *Onques/Sancte*. In the case of *Bien/Je/Kyrie*, however, the argument that the monophonic version of *Je n'ai que que* pre-existed its polyphonic relation cannot rely only on one piece of evidence, like the invented tenor in *Onques/Sancte*. Rather, it must be based on a number of small pieces of evidence, which together suggest that it is most likely that the monophonic version existed before, and was subsequently turned into, the polyphonic version.

Example 12.2. Opening of *Bien me doi/Je n'ai que que/Kyrie fons*

The first of these pieces of information is the tenor that is used for the motet. It takes its melodic material from a melody for the *Kyrie* that is most often associated with the troped text *Kyrie fons bonitatis*.[17] The melody used for the tenor in the motet differs slightly from those found in extant chant manuscripts. In two places, the note *a* in the chant manuscripts is *Fmi* in the motet tenor, while a number of times a single note in the chant sources is sung twice consecutively in the motet tenor.[18] I have suggested elsewhere that alterations to the tenor chant below a song voice

[17] In Margaretha Landwehr-Melnicki's catalogue of Kyrie melodies, this is found as number 48. See Landwehr-Melnicki 1968, 95–6. Landwehr-Melnicki's catalogue has been extended and reorganized in that of David Hiley, which enables consultation according to manuscript, as well as according to chant. Its position in Landwehr-Melnicki's catalogue means that Hiley consistently refers to this Kyrie melody as K48. See Hiley 1986.

[18] This is as compared with the most frequently occurring version of this widely transmitted chant, chiefly in F-Pn lat. 14452, fol. 134v, F-Pn lat. 1112, fol. 257v, and F-LA 263, fol. 26v. *Mi* and *Fa* are used here in their normal Guidonian sense as denoting a note that is respectively either a semitone away from the note above it or a semitone away from the note below it. *Fmi* is therefore here the equivalent of a modern F♯, whereas *Bmi* would be the equivalent of B♮. For a more detailed consideration of the musical differences between the chant sources and the tenor, see Thomson 2016, 66–7.

can sometimes form part of an argument that the song voice pre-existed the motet: indeed, there are cases in which it seems most likely that the changes to the chant have been made in order to accommodate the pre-existent pitches of the song.[19] The version of the *Kyrie fons* chant that the tenor presents certainly fits more easily with the *Je n'ai que que* voice than the versions found in the chant manuscripts, but in this case the differences between the two are not significant enough alone to demonstrate that the song existed before its related motet.

The strongest piece of evidence for a song-to-motet chronology is the textual and thematic links between the song and the treatise, and between both of them and the motet: the song is so closely linked to the themes of the treatise that it seems most likely that it was created specifically for insertion within the treatise and was therefore created before its related motet.

This connection between song, motet, and treatise does double duty within the present argument. It suggests the chronological relationship between song and motet, but it also demonstrates that the new triplum text of the motet is built around the themes drawn from both song and treatise. To consider the link between song and treatise, a short summary of the themes of both is necessary. *Li Commens d'Amours* falls into two distinct parts. The first (lines 1–88) consists of a relatively brief description of the way a lover should behave if he wishes to gain his lady.[20] The second (lines 89–594) is a series of ten *exempla*, which tell the stories of characters who exemplify the messages expounded by the author in the opening recommendations.

The song *Je n'ai que que* appears in the final *exemplum*, that of Pancharus (lines 501–71, song at lines 516–32), who is in love with the appropriately named Queen of Fémenie. Pancharus's lord, the King of Trasce, finds this love unacceptable on grounds of social class and sends Pancharus faraway 'to forget the great love and great loyalty he had for this woman' (lines 507–8).[21] Pancharus, unable to stand the pain, returns, creeps into the Queen's bedroom and, seeing two shapes in her bed, stabs the one he assumes to be another man. It transpires that the other shape in the Queen's bed was her small dog and that, in attempting to exact his jealous revenge, he has murdered his lady. Unable to bear the guilt, he kills himself with the sword with which he had stabbed the Queen (lines 537–71).

Pancharus himself sings the song *Je n'ai que que* as he is leaving the country on the instructions of his lord. This lyric interpolation is connected both textually and thematically with the treatise that surrounds it. In line 507, the narrating voice reports that the King had sent Pancharus out of the land, 'hors dou pais'. This is echoed in the song fifteen lines later when Pancharus laments that 'it is necessary for me to leave my love and go out of the land' ('laissier m'estuet m'amie / et hors del pais aler') (lines 521–2). This textual echo is matched by a thematic one: the treatise establishes a strict order for the way that lovers should proceed in winning their lady, differentiating between the roles of sight, sound, and speech. The text of the song *Je n'ai que que* is also based around this order, placing the treatise's description of the act of loving at the conceptual centre of the song. In the motet, the new triplum text is also based around this narrative, glossing the text of the song by reproducing the model of loving on which it is based.

Li Commens d'Amours begins with a recommendation to the lover that he should 'maintain his heart and body completely' (line 37) and that he should make sure that he gives no one cause to

---

[19] See, for example, the consideration of the motets *Mout me fu grief* (297)/*Robin m'aime* (298)/*Portare* and *Cil qui m'aime* (1053)/*Quant chante oisiaus* (1054)/*Portare* in Thomson 2016, 34–42, 81–9. Saltzstein (2007, 75) has also seen tenor recomposition as a signal of quotation.

[20] The line numbers refer to the edition found in Saly 1972, 41–55.

[21] 'Pour oubliier le tres grant amour et le tres grant aloiance k'il avoit a cele dame' (lines 507–8).

speak ill of him (lines 41–54).[22] After such a prelude of self-examination is complete, the lover can begin his attempt to gain his lady. The treatise stresses that all contact with the lady should begin through sight, for 'the first message of love, it is the eyes' (line 65).[23] The lover should therefore begin to woo his lady by throwing her sweet looks, which he should pair with sweet, inarticulate sighs (line 62). The combination of looking and sighing is to be for the lady alone, to gain her trust. These visual and aural cues are intended to demonstrate the loyalty that the lover would show in loving her (lines 67–8). Only once these cues have had their effect, 'when the time and place comes' (line 87), should the lover begin to speak to his lady. Articulate speech is something which should not be attempted before a connection has already been made.

The themes of sight, sound, and articulate speech are central to the song *Je n'ai que que* (and thus the motetus voice of the motet), which also stresses the order in which these senses should be used:

> Je n'ai, que que nus en die,
> nule ocoison de chanter:
> et si chant, mes che n'est mie
> de cuer pour moi deporter,
> 5 kar laissier m'estuet m'amie
> et hors du pais aler.
> Ci a dure departie;
> qui la porroit endurer?
> Or m'en convedra plourer
> 10 a tous les jors de ma vie,
> car je ne quier oublier
> son gent cors, sa segnourie,
> qui pris m'a par resgarder,
> si que ne puis autre amer.
> 15 Li douz maus d'amer m'aigrie,
> quant n'i puis parler.

In spite of what anyone may say, I have no reason to sing; and yet I sing, but it does not come from my heart, and it does not make me glad for I had to leave my sweetheart and go out of the country. This is a hard separation; who could stand it? Now I will have to weep all the days of my life, for I do not seek to forget her beauty, the nobility which captured me by sight alone so that I want to love no other. The sweet pains of love make me bitter when I cannot talk to her.[24]

When Pancharus first fell in love with his lady, it was because 'her beautiful body, her nobility / have captured me by sight' (song, lines 12–13). He made the connection with her through sight and, while the treatise never specifically states that the queen reciprocated his love, it implies that the lovers established the sight-based bond of trust that the treatise describes (treatise, lines 503–5). Once he is absent from his lady, it is the articulate speech of lovers for which Pancharus pines: love makes him bitter 'when he cannot talk to her' (song, line 16). The song therefore matches the

---

22 'De cuer et de cors netement maintenir' (line 37).

23 'Li premier message d'Amours, che sont li oeilg' (line 65). This may be a reference to lines 134–40 of *L'Art d'amours*, the widely circulated translation of Ovid's *Ars amatoria*. See Karl 1924, 66–80, 181–8.

24 Translation adapted from Tischler 1978, 4: 85.

treatise that surrounds it both textually and thematically, which suggests it was created for insertion into the treatise. Taking this evidence along with that of the variations in the tenor melody, it seems most likely that the song pre-existed and was later converted into the motet *Bien/Je/Kyrie*.

In this motet, the newly created triplum replicates the narrative found at the beginning of *Li Commens d'Amours* in a way that is more straightforward and more general than the song:

> Bien me doi sor toutes riens d'Amour loer,
> quant en si haut lieu m'a fait mon cuer douner,
> dont je le doi a tous jours mercier
> con fins amans ; car onques ne me peut grever
> 5 nus maus, ce m'est avis,
> k'Amours me feit
> sentir pour la bele au vis cler.
> Douz dieus je l'aim tant, que ne puis oublier
> sa tres grant biaute,
> 10 qui nuit et jour me fait
> a li penser et souvent souspirer,
> et sa grant valour, son sens et sa bonte,
> k'on doit bien recorder,
> k'on ne porroit mie trouver
> 15 plus vaillant de celi,
> qui si m'a saisi.
> Aymi, Dieus, aymi!
> Ne me porroie plus tenir, que je n'i
> alasse tout maintenant parler a li;
> 20 mes je la criem si,
> que mon penser ne li ose descouvrir,
> car trop m'aroit maubailli,
> [s'a] s'amour avoie falli.
> Et pour ce en chantant li pri,
> 25 k'ele me voelle retenir a ami;
> kar ausi m'en doinst dieus joir,
> comme je l'ai loiaument en boine foi servi.

I must praise Love above all else, since he has made me bestow my heart in such a high place. For this I must always thank him like a true lover; for none of the pain which love makes me feel on account of the fair one with the bright countenance will ever bother me. Sweet God, I love her so much that I cannot forget her very great beauty, which night and day makes me think about her and often sigh. Nor can I forget her great worth, the wit and the generosity which should be remembered, for one greater than she who has captured me could not be found. Alas, God, alas! I cannot hold back any longer from going now to speak to her. But I fear her so much that I do not dare reveal my thoughts to her, for I would be destroyed if I had failed to win her love. And so singing, I beg her that she consent to keep me as her lover; for thus may God give me joy from her, since I have loyally and in good faith served her.[25]

---

[25] Translation adapted from Tischler 1978, 4: 85.

The lyric persona is a lover who is only part of the way along the journey which the treatise recommends. He has fallen in love with the sight of his lady, 'the beautiful one with the bright countenance' (triplum, line 7) and cannot forget her 'great beauty' (line 9). This beauty causes him to think on her and sigh from love (line 11). He has therefore come through the first two stages of the process of loving: he has called sight and inarticulate sound to his cause. Later on in the triplum text, he resolves to progress to the next stage: his love of her means that he cannot any longer hold back from going to speak to her (lines 18–19). Despite this resolution, he fears that the first two stages of the process have not been effective. If he goes to speak to her and finds out that he has failed to gain her love (line 23), he would be destroyed (line 22). His hope rests in the fact that she will already love him by the time he asks for her love, her trust will have been won by his looks and sighs. The triplum culminates with the speaker going one step further than prescribed by the treatise: 'and so singing, I beg her / that she consent to keep me as her lover' (lines 24–5).

In *Bien/Je/Kyrie*, the creator of the motet has written a triplum text that expands on the message of the song voice found in the motetus and the treatise from which it comes: it personalizes the process of loving by speaking in the first person and provides a different perspective on how to enact the recommendations of the treatise. Just as *Onques/Sancte* glossed and amplified its source musically, *Bien/Je/Kyrie* extends the textual message of the song on which it is based.

The resulting motet also treats its song voice as a quotation by glossing it, but has a different character from that of *Onques/Sancte*. As the *Onques n'amai* voice is found in a two-voice motet, it has no other text with which to compete and feels like an independent voice part. This separation is then emphasized even further by the structuring role played by the quoted song voice. On first contact with *Bien/Je/Kyrie*, however, there is nothing that separates for the listener the *Je n'ai que que* voice from any of the others. It slips much more imperceptibly into its motet context, in which it is heard as entwined with the new triplum voice, as the texts are sung simultaneously and are similar in content and expression. Although the motet is still based around the characteristics of its quoted song voice, the homogeneity of the two upper voice texts means that the *Je n'ai que que* voice does not have the requisite otherness to be noticed as a citation of someone else's voice, and so falls beneath the surface of the new identity of the motet.

In *Onques/Sancte*, a motet glossed its source song by musical means; *Bien/Je/Kyrie* accomplished a similar task through textual means. The motet *Par une matinee/O clemencie fons/D'un joli dart* brings these two categories together, doing so in this instance by using a pre-existent song not for one of its upper voices, but instead for its tenor. The structure of this borrowed tenor voice is in turn reflected musically through the use of motives in both triplum and motetus that reoccur over the musical repeats of the tenor. Further, the tenor's structure is also reflected textually: the three stages of the triplum's pastourelle text are matched to the three sections of the tenor's musical and textual structure.[26]

The tenor of this motet, *D'un joli dart*, is found not only as a two-stanza pastourelle in **D308**, but also as the tenor to the motet *De mes Amours sui souvent repentis* (898) / *L'autrier m'estuet venue volentés* (899) / *Defors compiegne*.[27] Although the two tenors have different incipits, they are the same song: the variation results from the structural organization of the song in each tenor. The

---

[26] The motet is found uniquely at **Mo**, fols. 355v–356v.

[27] In **Mo**, the tenor is labelled as *Defors compiegne*, whereas in **D308** the pastourelle is labelled *Dehors conpignes*. The former spelling is used here for consistency. The pastourelle is found at **D308**, fol. 203v, where no notation is provided. *De mes/L'autrier/Defors* is found in **Mo**, fol. 371r–v.

refrain, 'D'un joli dart d'amours suis navrée par son regart/puis que il li plait forment m'agrée' (vdB 633), is found both at the beginning and the end of the tenor for *Par une/O clemencie/D'un joli dart*.[28] In the tenor for *De mes/L'autrier/Defors compiegne*, as well as in the monophonic pastourelle, the refrain is only at the end of the voice. Without the first refrain, the tenor and the monophonic pastourelle begin with a different incipit: *Defors compiegne*.[29]

This flexibility about refrain placement is normal for songs in the late thirteenth and early fourteenth century: the same song could be recorded in one manuscript as having a refrain at both ends of each stanza, and in another as having a refrain only at the end.[30] That the song *Defors compiegne* has been differently manipulated in two different motet tenors suggests that it pre-existed them: the motets both interpret the form of a pre-existent song. This suggestion is strengthened by the text which closes the triplum of *Par une/O clemencie/D'un joli dart*, 'Sir, your love is pleasing to me' ('Sire vostre amour forment m'agree'). This is a rather unusual ending to the triplum's pastourelle: the woman who has been approached by the knight accepts his love willingly, the opposite of her generically common rejection.[31] The woman's statement, however, chimes exactly with the final line of the *D'un joli dart* refrain, which closes both stanzas of the song: 'Because it pleases him, it gives me pleasure' ('puis qu'il li plait, forment m'agree').[32] None of the sources that contain the two motet tenors writes out the syllabic poetry underneath them, even if it could easily have been sung in performance, so the triplum interacts intertextually with text that is written out only in **D308**'s version of the song. It therefore seems most likely that the song pre-existed and was subsequently quoted in the two motets.

The upper voices of *Par une/O clemencie/D'un joli dart* use melodic repetition to reflect the structural properties of their tenor.[33] As mentioned above, the tenor of this motet has two statements of the *D'un joli dart* refrain, at the beginning and the end; see perfections 1–11 and 41–51 in Example 12.3. These refrains enclose the main body of the song, which is itself in ABABX form. Both of these structural properties are reflected in the motetus and triplum voices. The return of the refrain at the end of the tenor is marked by the upper voices singing the same musical motives in perfections 47–9 (marked **a** and **b** on Example 12.3) that they used over the analogous place in the tenor's first refrain at the beginning of the motet, perfections 7–10. The upper voices also mark the internal ABABX structure of the main body of the song. Each time that the

[28] 'I am wounded, through his gaze, by a pretty dart of love,/because it pleases him, it gives me pleasure'.

[29] Although the pastourelle does not have notation in D308, it seems likely that it employed the same melody as both the motet tenors. It is therefore referred to as 'monophonic' here due to the strong possibility that it once was found as a notated monophonic song. On the collection of monophonic motets in D308, see Elizabeth Eva Leach's chapter above. The refrain *D'un joli dart* is found notated (with some variants) in F-Pn f. fr. 372, fol. 18v, F-Pn f. fr. 1593, fol. 18r, and Ha, fol. 168r. The text of the pastourelle can quite easily to be sung to the melody found in the motet tenors (see, for example, the edition in Tischler 1978, 3: 169–70), raising the possibility that this tenor may have been texted in performance; see Saltzstein 2013b, 156 and n. 27. This possibility is given credence by the motets in the later sections of Mo with tenors that are fully texted. See, for example, *Qui amours veut maintenir/Li dous pensers/Cis a cui* (Mo, fol. 314r; Ba, fol. 32v; Tu, fol. 28r).

[30] Doss-Quinby *et al.* 2006, xxvii–xxxiv; Atchison 2005, 47–52. The structure of these songs is also discussed in Page 1998; Plumley 2013, 26–8.

[31] On the roles played by characters in the pastourelle and the extent to which those roles were determined by gender and/or class, see Dell 2008, ch. 3; Delbouille 1926; Zink 1972.

[32] This correspondence has already been noted by Walker 1982, 333.

[33] Saint-Cricq 2009, 1: 262–3 and 2: 170.

tenor moves from its A to its B section, the triplum and motetus sing the same musical motivic material, marked **c** and **d**.[34]

The musical reflection of the structure of the tenor is complemented by the text of the triplum, whose pastourelle text splits into three conventional sections. In the pastourelle's first section, a male *je* uses the tropes of a 'spring opening' to narrate his journey to an orchard, in which he finds a beautiful lady. The second section consists of the man's long address to the lady, praising her and asking her to grant him mercy. In a short closing section, the lady responds surprisingly, welcoming the man's love. Each of these sections displays a different character of voice: male narrating, male speaking, female responding. In *Par une/O clemencie/D'un joli dart*, these three sections line up with the three main units of the song tenor's refrain-song-refrain structure: the end of the first section of the triplum (male narrating, lines 1–5) coincides with the beginning of the main body of the song in the tenor in perfection 12, while the triplum's second section (male speaking, lines 6–19) concludes precisely as the tenor restarts the refrain in perfection 41, after which follows the triplum's third section (female response, lines 20–1).[35]

By basing both the musical repetitions of its motetus and triplum and the textual structures of its triplum on those of its quoted song tenor, and by creating clear intertextual reference between the triplum and the song from which the tenor is drawn, *Par une/O clemencie/D'un joli dart* accomplishes a similar task to *Onques/Sancte*: it creates a new entity in which the pre-existent material maintains its independence from the rest of the motet. In *Bien/Je/Kyrie*, the upper-voice texts were homogeneous in meaning and expression, and thus the quoted motetus lacked the otherness that would prompt its recognition as a quotation. In *Par une/O clemencie/D'un joli dart*, all three parts are quite separate. The Latin motetus, a cry to the Blessed Virgin Mary, differs in language and expression from its French triplum counterpart. This sense that the three voices have their own separate identities amplifies the importance of the tenor's influence on the musical and textual structure of the rest of the motet. There are three individual entities here, but as a whole they are ruled by the tenor: the lowest voice is therefore 'othered' and foregrounded as a quotation. Within the three voices of the motet, the quoted song tenor remains a citation of someone else's voice: its role as the structuring force of the motet affords it the otherness required to maintain its independence from the new context in which it has been placed.

The independence afforded to the tenor is even more striking when it is contrasted with other types of quotation within *Par une/O clemencie/D'un joli dart*. Anne Ibos-Augé has demonstrated that the triplum of this motet quotes both text and music from a number of other motets that are also found within **Mo**: one of these motets was *Bien/Je/Kyrie*.[36] As can be seen by comparing the opening of the triplum of *Bien/Je/Kyrie* in Example 12.2 with perfections 43–5 of the triplum of *Par une/O clemencie/D'un joli dart* in Example 12.3, the text 'Bien me doi sor toutes riens d'amour loer' ('I must praise Love above all else') is found with its accompanying music in both places. Along with a number of other quotations, this passage sinks into its context in a way that contrasts sharply with the treatment of the tenor, which is proudly foregrounded as a separate entity.

All three motets examined take on stylistic traits that have often been seen as characteristic of song, including a strict musico-poetic structure and the textual register of courtly love. The motets are

---

[34] Saint-Cricq (2009, 2: 170) provides an edition of this motet that shows these motives.

[35] Other motets also base the structure of a pastourelle text on the tenor over which it occurs. See, for instance, Evans 1983, 138–40, for an analysis of the motet *L'autre jour par un matinet* (628)/*Hier matinet* (629)/*Ite missa est*.

[36] Ibos-Augé 2014.

not only responding to song in general, however, but to songs in particular. They take the specific elements of their quoted song voices and build their new voice parts around them. In doing so, they interact with the cultural norms of quotation present across thirteenth-century lyric. They can do this through musical strategies, as in *Onques/Sancte* or *Par une/O clemencie/D'un joli dart*, or they can do it through their texts, as in *Bien/Je/Kyrie*. The new polyphonic entity can be constructed in a way that retains the otherness and independence of the quoted song voice, as in *Onques/Sancte* and *Par une/O clemencie/D'un joli dart*, or it can be constructed so that the voice part slips imperceptibly into the identity of the new motet, as in *Bien/Je/Kyrie*.

The strategy pursued in this chapter has focused on many of the issues commonly employed when addressing the general stylistic influence of song on motet, such as musico-textual form and textual register, but it has used them to talk about motets that quote specific song voices. Its combination of the general and specific allows this approach to acknowledge the importance of song form while also pinpointing the particular musico-textual strategies of song outside of general form to which creators of motets reacted. By doing so, it starts to build a picture of the way that medieval musicians viewed the interaction between these two genres.

TRANSLATION OF TEXT IN EXAMPLE 12.3

Triplum

One morning, in the joyous month of April, I went out to play; in a flowering orchard I found a pleasing lady and, singing, greeted her: 'Oh, lady of worth and beauty, full of honor and of great goodness, on your account have I been in great dismay for a long time. I know that I will die, if you do not have mercy, for the sweet thoughts which I have make me sing. I must praise above every other thing love that makes me so gay. I await mercy, and if it is pleasing to you, I will have it'. She replied like a proper lady: 'Sir, your love is very pleasing to me'.

Motetus

O font of mercy and pardon, dew from heaven, prize of life, hope of the despairing, joy of the penitent, O you who are believed to be the salvation of the peoples, be the aid of the wretched by pleading with your Son the King of All to give to us a reprieve from our sins.

(Translation adapted from Tischler 1978, 4: 105.)

Example 12.3 Analytical edition of *Par une matinee / O clemencie fons / D'un joli dart*, based on **Mo** fols. 355v–356v

13

The Duet Motet in England:
Genre, Tonal Coherence, Reconstruction*

Jared C. Hartt

E RNEST SANDERS AND PETER LEFFERTS begin their *Grove* entry, 'Sources of English Polyphony 1270–1400', with the following: 'It is an indication of the lamentable state of preservation of medieval English polyphony that, strictly speaking, a report on its MS sources has to be so negative.' The reason for this comment is that there are no surviving English sources comparable to the continental **Mo** and **Ba** codices from the thirteenth century, for instance, or to **Fauv**, **Iv**, and the Machaut manuscripts from the fourteenth, all of which contain dozens of motets. Instead, we are left mostly with a large number of thirteenth- and fourteenth-century English manuscript fragments, and within these fragments, the majority of the motets are incomplete. Significantly, though, in one source, **LoHa**, there is a list of contents of a now-lost thirteenth-century manuscript that contains 164 sacred polyphonic compositions, among them 66 motets with two upper-voice texts (*moteti cum duplici littera*) as well as 15 conductus motets (*moteti cum una littera et duplici nota*).[1] This indicates that in England, there were indeed manuscripts with extensive motet sections that simply are not extant today.[2]

Despite the lack of surviving complete sources, there remain more than enough motets from England from which to make some general observations regarding style, function, and compositional approach.[3] On the one hand, the surviving motets constitute a homogenous group in several respects. For instance, the poetry is almost exclusively Latin, the subjects are invariably sacred or devotional, and consistent declamation patterns tend to dictate the rhythm of the motet voices; this stands in stark contrast to continental motets in general, which frequently feature French

---

* I thank Margaret Bent, Karen Desmond, Lawrence Earp, Elizabeth Eva Leach, and Dolores Pesce for their comments and suggestions as this chapter developed into its current form.

1 The contents, organized by genre, appear on fols. 160v–161r of **LoHa**. Lefferts (1986, 162–5) provides the complete list. Bent (2017, 25 n. 22) entertains the possibility that it was a prescriptive table of contents of an unrealized project.

2 See also **Lbl 24198**, which Bent (1981b, 67) proposes must have been a sizeable codex due to its alphabetical arrangement and numbered headings; it contained likely more than 100 motets.

3 Lefferts lists the following numbers of motets that survive in English sources: about 60 motets from the thirteenth century, many of which are fragmentary, and approximately 130 motets from the fourteenth century, of which about 60 are completable. For comparison, about 500 survive from the continent in the thirteenth century, and more than 200 from 'the fourteenth-century French tradition'. See Lefferts 1986, 2 and 319 n. 5. See also his Appendix 3 for a list of the thirteenth-century English motet repertoire and the beginning of his Appendix 2 for the fourteenth-century English motet repertoire organized both by short title and by source.

poetry in the courtly love tradition and, beginning in the later thirteenth century, often had less and less concern with traditional, regular declamation.[4] On the other hand, the motet in England exhibits a variety of formal structures and compositional approaches. For example, about half of the English extant motets (or fragments thereof) from the thirteenth century have a tenor drawn from a liturgical source; the other half have so-called *pes* tenors, in which the foundational melody was either freely composed or converted from an already-existing popular tune. Both tenor types continued to be used in the next century, but there was an increase in the use of secular songs as tenors, though even in such cases the upper voices remained Latin and the subjects liturgical.[5] Looking through the repertoire from the beginning decades of the fourteenth century, one can find many motets featuring pervasive voice exchange; many exhibit 'isomelic' properties – that is, melodic repetition in the upper voices that corresponds to a repeating portion of a tenor melody. Furthermore, many motets are decidedly sectional while others are through-composed; many feature regularly repeating phrase periods that are staggered between the voices while others exhibit a variety of carefully calculated phrase lengths distributed among the motet texture – these can all be described as 'periodic'. And there are still other distinguishing musical, poetic, rhythmic, and formal features.[6]

One aspect of compositional approach that *does* tend to dominate the corpus of English motets as a whole, regardless of tenor origin or overall form, is the tendency for a work to be tonally unified. To be sure, not all of these motets exhibit tonal coherence, and of those that do, one motet might exhibit a greater degree of tonal unity than another. Consequently, one approach for examining a motet of English provenance is to inspect the degree to which a motet displays this quality; this will be one tack taken here.[7] It is also instructive to inspect the setting of the poetry and the various declamation patterns employed in these motets; this will likewise be a focus. Naturally, a motet's structural organization, both at the level of the tenor and as an entire texture, must also be taken into account. As such, this chapter will focus on these aspects – and how these aspects can implicate one another – in an examination of three fourteenth-century motets of English provenance: *Jesu fili Dei/Jhesu fili virginis/Jesu lumen veritatis*; *Rosa delectabilis/[Regali ex progenie]/Regalis exoritur*; and *Majori vi leticie/Tenor/Majorem intelligere*. These works are all examples of a specific subgenre, the 'duet motet with medius cantus'; that is, the tenor, which is drawn from a liturgical source, is the 'medius cantus' and occupies the middle register of the texture.[8] Strikingly, the texted outer voices feature alliterative openings, a characteristic shared by many English motets. These motets also constitute a specific subtype of periodic motets: they are isoperiodic. The third of these, *Majori/Majorem*, is particularly intriguing: it has been only recently discovered, but its tenor is missing from the source manuscript. Consequently, a reconstruction of this motet will be proposed.

---

[4] See Lawrence Earp's contribution to this volume.

[5] Margaret Bent (pers. comm.) reminds me of *Domine quis* in **Ob** 7 and *Are post libamina* in **GB-OH** that are both contrafacta, Latinized from French motets. See also Bent with Howlett 1990, 57.

[6] Lefferts (1986, 27) divides fourteenth-century English motets into two general categories, isomelic motets and periodic motets, though as he points out, these two categories are not always mutually exclusive.

[7] Although to speak of tonal coherence or tonal unity may be anachronistic, the fact that so many of these motets display such properties make these useful terms for discussion. And a motet that displays a high degree of tonal coherence is in no way a more 'successful' motet than one that is not tonally coherent; rather, assessing the degree of tonal coherence is simply one of many lenses through which to view this repertory.

[8] Duet motets with medius cantus are discussed in Lefferts 1986, 68–72.

JESU FILI DEI / JHESU FILI VIRGINIS / JESU LUMEN VERITATIS

Jesu/Jesu survives in **DRc 20**, a manuscript of otherwise non-music items that contains four fly-leaves of music inserted at each of its ends.[9] Frank Harrison indicates that the eight leaves were most likely originally part of a single manuscript and that 'there is a high probability that these leaves were in use for performance in the [Durham] Abbey community'.[10] The motet appears on fol. 2r of **DRc 20** and fills the entire page in a manner typical of several motet manuscripts: the triplum is notated first, the motetus follows, and the tenor occupies the last staff on the page.[11] Looking at the manuscript, it is not immediately evident that the tenor in fact occupies the middle-voice range of the motet, as is illustrated in Example 13.1, the motet's opening.[12]

The tenor incipit notated in the manuscript, 'Jhesu fili virginis, rex celestis agminis', matches the text of the beginning of a devotional sequence for Jesus that is found in the Dublin troper **GB-Cu 710**. There are several differences between the pitches from this source and the tenor of our motet; thus, either it is unlikely that the melody was taken from this version of the sequence in particular or, if it was, it demonstrates that composers sometimes altered their source melody when composing a motet.[13] Regardless of its specific source, the tenor melody does in all likelihood comprise an entire devotional sequence;[14] this contrasts with the typical melismatic melodies set to a word or words that are frequently used as tenors in continental motets. The tenor melody's twenty-seven pitches are neatly divided into nine equal parts and are set in a simple, regular 4L (3L+1L) rhythmic pattern; see, for instance, the first four longs in Example 13.1. Although the tenor is notated only once in the manuscript, it must be sung through twice, save the last two 4L phrases, in order to accommodate the lengths of the two texted voices.

The opening 'Jesu' in both the triplum and motetus immediately makes clear for the listener the subject of the motet: it is a prayer to Jesus. Both poems plead to Jesus, the 'most fair of judges', for guidance and to be granted peace at final judgment. The triplum especially, but also the motetus, makes frequent use of various Latin forms of 'justice' and thus exhibits a relatively high degree of assonance; see the italicized words in Table 13.1.[15]

---

[9]   Although the flyleaves contain at least a dozen motets, those contained in the last four flyleaves include several of French provenance, at least two of which have been attributed to Philippe de Vitry.

[10]   Harrison and Wibberley 1981, xi.

[11]   See Haines and Udell's chapter in this volume for specific examples from the continent.

[12]   A facsimile appears in Harrison and Wibberley 1981, 169, and color images may be found on DIAMM. The edition appears in Harrison 1980, 129–32. The lone commercial recording is Gothic Voices 1999, *Masters of the Rolls: Music by English Composers of the Fourteenth Century*. Hyperion, CDA67098.

[13]   Harrison claims in an article as well as in the critical commentary to his edition that the tenor pitches derive from this sequence, but 'not in a straightforward way' (Harrison 1967, 82, and Harrison 1980, 164). A comparison of the two melodies reveals that direct correspondence breaks down after the first three pitches. Lefferts (1990, 280), on the other hand, calls the two melodies 'musically unrelated'. See A. Clark 1996 for a discussion of chant alteration in Machaut's and Vitry's motets.

[14]   Pieragostini (2011, 350–2) has recently shown that the 'Jhesu fili' voice exists as part of yet another motet with medius cantus, but instead as the lowest voice (the motetus). The middle-voice tenor is '[I]n seculum', a popular choice in thirteenth-century motets on the continent, but the triplum voice remains missing. A facsimile of the two extant voices appears on p. 345 and a modern transcription of the two surviving voices on p. 369. The melody of the 'Jhesu fili' voice matches the sequence as found in **GB-Cu 710** much more closely than does the tenor of our motet; see Pieragostini 2011, 352.

[15]   Translations adapted from Lefferts in Harrison 1980, 199–200.

Example 13.1. *Jesu/Jhesu/Jesu*, L1–L10

Table 13.1. Poetry and translations of *Jesu/Jhesu/Jesu*

Longs	Poetry	8p and 7pp lines
Triplum (64L)		
5	[1] **Jesu** fili Dei patris,/[2] *judicum* equissime,	8+7
4	[3] nate virginis et matris,/[4] virginum mundissime,	8+7
4	[5] tu et *judex* equitatis/[6] sol atque *justicie*:	8+7
4	[7] conqueror ob feritatis/[8] vim atque malicie!	8+7
4	[9] Ensi dona mundiali/[10] *judici* non prebeo,	8+7
4	[11] aut si modo casuali/[12] quandoque non placeo,	8+7
4	[13] nichil licet ergo mali/[14] fecerim aut facio,	8+7
4	[15] tantum ipse me penali/[16] feriet *judicio*.	8+7
4	[17] Versa vice speciali/[18] munera si dedero,	8+7
4	[19] prevalebo causa tali/[20] in hoc quod desidero	8+7
4	[21] ne thesauro temporali/[22] quo cum hic caruero	8+7
4	[23] pena premat immortali/[24] quamdiu vivus ero:	8+7
4	[25] ab hac vita set letali/[26] liber abire spero.	8+7
4	[27] Conjunctor O boni mali,/[28] **da mihi quod sicio,**	8+7
7	[29] innocentique finali/[30] parces in *judicio*./[31] **Reum munda nunc vicio.**	8+7+8

O Jesus, son of God the father, most fair of judges, born of the virgin and mother, purest of virgins, and you the judge of equity and the sun of justice: I complain on account of the power of wildness and evil! I don't present offerings to the judge with a worldly sword, and if by chance in some manner at any time I don't please, even though I do and may have done nothing evil, he himself will strike me so much with penal judgement. If, after my particular vice has been turned around I shall have given gifts, I shall prevail for such reason in that which I will have desired, so that perpetual punishment not oppress [me] while I shall have lacked worldly treasure so long as I am still alive; but from this deathly life I hope to depart free. O joiner of good and evil, give me what I thirst for, and you will spare the innocent one in the final judgement. Now cleanse the culprit from sin.

Tenor (64L)

4×16

Motetus (64L)		
6	[1] **Jesu** lumen veritatis,/[2] candor eterne lucis,/[3] vitam	8+7+(2+
4	prebens sanitatis/[4] tuis virtute crucis,/[5] forma	6)+7+(2+
4	vere pietatis:/[6] conqueror ecce tibi!/[7] Tenet	6)+7+(2+
8	hic vim potestatis/[8] licitum esse sibi/[9] sicut viri probitatis, /[10] perdere quos vult eos,/[11] mundi	6)+7+8+7+(2+
4	*judex* in peccatis/[12] solver plane reso./[13] Heu! cum	6)+7+(2+
4	paxque reproborum/[14] prevalent, aspicio/[15] ad te,	6)+7+(2+

4	ubi spes *justorum*; /[16] figura quo nescio/[17] crevit,	6)+7+(2+
4	Deus, tu deorum/[18] omnium, nulla latent,/[19] te que	6)+7+(2+
4	facta perversorum/[20] lucide biti patent./[21] Tantum	6)+7+(2+
4	finis hos florere,/[22] mundi gaudere bonis,/[23] atque	6)+7+(2+
4	ceteris torquere./[24] Presidentes cum thronis; /[25] sic hoc	6)+7+(2+
4	malum vix cavere/[26] valet quis ubi donis?/[27] *Jhesu*	6)+7+(2+
4	cordium scrutator,/[28] **da mihi quod sicio,**/[29] cum sis	6)+7+(2+
6	*justus* pacis dator/[30] in tuo *judicio*./[31] **Reum munda nunc vicio.**	6)+7+8

O Jesus, light of truth, radiance of eternal light, offering a life of healing to your own by virtue of your cross, truly the emblem of piety: behold, I complain to you! This man holds that the force of power ought to be permitted to him, as to a man of probity, to destroy those who he wants to, and as a judge of the sins of the world, to absolve evildoers entirely. Alas! And while the peace of the reprobates flourishes, I look to you: where is the hope of the just? I know not how this sort of thing grew. God, from you of all gods nothing is concealed, you to whom the deeds of sinners are clearly evident. You put a stop to their flourishing, to their enjoying the goods of the world, and to their torturing of others. They preside from their seats of authority; thus who is able anywhere even barely to guard against this evil with gifts? O Jesus, examiner of the heart, give me what I thirst for, since you are the giver of just peace in your judgement. Now cleanse the culprit from sin.

The table also reveals that the poems in the triplum and motetus exhibit regular structures. Each consists entirely of alternating 8p and 7pp lines, and are in fact exactly the same length, 233 syllables each.[16] As Lawrence Earp elucidates in his chapter in the present volume, a hallmark of the motet in England is regularly declaimed Latin poetry set to periodic phrase structures. As can be seen in Example 13.1, each period in the triplum is set with a pair of 8p and 7pp lines. (A period concludes with a rest, transcribed here as ⸳ in the outer voices and ‿ in the tenor.) After the initial 5L period, there is an 8p7pp pair set to each ensuing 4L period; this occurs thirteen times until the end, at which time a trio of lines, 8p7pp8p, occupies the last 7L period.[17] In the motetus, the 8p7pp pair likewise concludes at the beginning of L5, but the first two syllables of the next 8p line are concatenated with the pair, thus extending the initial period to 6L. The ensuing 4L period thus begins on the third syllable of that 8p line, it continues through the 7pp line, and concludes on the second syllable of the next 8p line. This pattern is maintained throughout the remainder of the motet until its concluding 6L period, which begins on the third syllable of an 8p7pp8p series of lines. Thus, after the initial staggering of phrases, 4L periods ensue; these 4L periods constitute the motet's main building blocks. As such, the motet can be described as isoperiodic due to its pervasive staggered periods of equal length.[18]

Following Lefferts, English isoperiodic motets can be broken down into two categories: those that feature declamation in longs and breves, and those that also feature declamation in breves and semibreves.[19] Isoperiodic motets with B-S declamation patterns generally occur as a specific

---

[16] As explained in Earp's chapter in this volume, a 'p' (paroxytonic) line has emphasis on its penultimate syllable, and a 'pp' (proparoxytonic) line has emphasis on its antepenultimate syllable.

[17] The last period is illustrated in Example 13.3 below, to be discussed shortly.

[18] 'Isoperiodic' in the sense described by Sanders, but not by Besseler; see Earp's contribution to this *Companion*.

[19] Lefferts 1986, 59. The motet examined in Earp's chapter above features declamation predominantly at the L-B level.

subgenre: duet motets with a medius cantus, such as *Jesu/Jesu*. As shown in Example 13.1, the motet begins its first three longs as though the triplum and motetus will be declaimed in L-B patterns, but in L4 there is a sudden burst of declamation featuring syllabic semibreves. In fact, starting at L4 in *Jesu/Jesu*, and during every ensuing fourth long for the entire motet, the tenor rests and the outer voices declaim the same accelerated rhythmic pattern.

Thus, the triplum period that begins at L6 establishes that voice's declamation pattern, which repeats every 4L for the rest of the motet. The motetus's 4L declamation pattern begins at L7; it too repeats for the remainder of *Jesu/Jesu*. Taking the outer voices as a pair, syllables are always declaimed together except for the third breve of each triplum period when the motetus is at rest (e.g. L6), and at the third breve of each motetus period when the triplum is at rest and the motetus begins an 8p line (e.g. L9). The result is a nearly entirely homorhythmic texture that features frequent, regular rhythmic repetitions.

A consequence of this layout is that there are always back-to-back sustained sonorities, beginning at L5 and L6, that recur every four longs. The first sustained sonority of each pair (for example, at L5) marks an arrival, a moment of rhythmic and sonorous rest after the flurry of semibreve parallel sixths. Although the end of the motetus period does not coincide with the triplum period's conclusion at L5, but instead ends one long later, the motetus *does* sustain an imperfect long, just like the triplum, and both of these voices sound against the tenor's perfect long, thus yielding a cadential effect nonetheless. The next long of each pair (for instance, at L6) could therefore be thought of as the beginning of the next phrase. Consequently, when viewing the entire three-voice texture, it is not the tenor that dictates the motet's phrase structure, nor is it the voice that occupies the lowest register, the motetus, but it is instead the triplum.

This arrangement of the motet's rhythmic and periodic structure and the resulting sustained sonorities allow for clear moments of tonal articulation. Continuing to look at Example 13.1, the motet begins on an F_5^8 sonority; this concord stands out by virtue of being the motet's initial sound. L2 and L3 are likewise counterpointed with $_5^8$ sonorities, each time a step higher.[20] At L4, the tenor drops out, and a series of unstable parallel sixths begin. The last sixth of L4, an unstable G^{+6} dyad, resolves outward by step to an F/f octave that is joined with the c that begins the tenor's second period. This stable F_5^8 sonority at L5 is thus an aurally salient moment: it is sustained for an imperfect long, it is approached with directed voice leading, it provides rhythmic relief after the flurry of activity in L4, and it marks the moment when both triplum and motetus conclude their lines of poetry. As such, the F_5^8 sonority that began the motet continues to be given tonal emphasis.[21]

The second phrase begins on a sustained D_8^{12} sonority, providing a new momentary tonal focus. After the A_5^8 sonority in L7, a series of parallel unstable sixths again ensue, this time resulting in an $A^{+6} \rightarrow G_5^8$ progression, thus now emphasizing a G tonal center. Again, the sustained sonority, the directed progression, the rhythmic rest, as well as the conclusion of poetic lines all combine to grant tonal emphasis, but now to G instead of F.

This play between emphasizing F and G sonorities keeps up for much of the remainder of the motet. As illustrated in Table 13.2, of the sixteen phrase endings in the motet, seven feature directed

---

[20] Despite the successive $_5^8$ sonorities, the contrary motion in the outer voices precludes direct parallel octaves.

[21] Interestingly, the simple three-note ascending stepwise motive that is iterated twice in longs at the beginning of the tenor (c-d-e) is sung in breves in the triplum in L1 and in the motetus in L2 and L3 (f-g-a', G-a-b, a-b-c). As Margaret Bent emphasizes in her chapter in this *Companion*, the extent to which tenor melodic material is used in the texted voices of a motet has often been neglected in motet studies; indeed, this constitutes an avenue for further investigation in the English motet repertory.

voice leading to F_5^8 sonorities, while almost as many, six, conclude with a directed progression to a G_5^8 sonority. The three other phrases conclude on F_5^{+10}, D_8^{12}, and C_U^8 concords; each of these unique sonorities serves a specific purpose in the motet's tonal plan, and it is no accident that they occur at successive phrase endings (L29, L33, L37), culminating in the C_U^8 concord at L37, a striking aural and structural moment.

Table 13.2. Phrasing, sonorities, and cadences in *Jesu/Jhesu/Jesu*

	5L		4L		4L		4L		4L		4L	
1		*5*	*6*	*9*	*10*	*13*	*14*	*17*	*18*	*21*	*22*	*25*
F_5^8		$G^{+6}{\to}F_5^8$	D_8^{12}	$A^{+6}{\to}G_5^8$	D_8^{12}	$A^{+6}{\to}G_5^8$	C_8^{12}	$G^{+6}{\to}F_5^8$	Bb_{+3}^{+6}	$A^{+6}{\to}G_5^8$	A_5^8	$G^{+6}{\to}F_5^8$

	4L		4L		4L		4L		4L		4L	
26		*29*	*30*	*33*	*34*	*37*	*38*	*41*	*42*	*45*	*46*	*49*
G_{+3}^{+6}		$G^8\ F_5^{+10}$	D_8^{12}	$E^{+10}{\to}D_8^{12}$	Bb_{+3}^{+6}	$D^{+6}{\to}C_U^8$	G^{+10}_5	$G^{+6}{\to}F_5^8$	Bb_{+3}^{+6}	$A^{+6}{\to}G_5^8$	D_8^{12}	$A^{+6}{\to}G_5^8$

	4L		4L		7L		
50		*53*	*54*	*57*	*58*	*61*	*62* *63 – 64*
C_8^{12}		$G^{+6}{\to}F_5^8$	D_8^{12}	$A^{+6}{\to}G_5^8$	E_8^{12}	$G^{+6}{\to}F_5^8$	$G_{+3}^{+6}{\to}F_5^8$ ‖

At L29 in Table 13.2, note the conspicuous absence of the arrow that indicates directed voice leading. Instead of concluding on an unstable sixth, the semibreve patter comes to an end on a stable *G/g* octave; thus there is no directed progression to an F_5^8 sonority that we have already heard three times in the motet, including at the end of the previous phrase. Instead, an unstable F_5^{+10} concord concludes the phrase and thus F begins to be destabilized. The next phrase changes focus to D, beginning and ending on D_8^{12} sonorities, the latter sonority approached with a directed progression.[22] Previously, each phrase ending with a tenor D was counterpointed with a fifth below and a fourth above, thus yielding a G_5^8 sonority; the motet creator has therefore precluded giving G emphasis in this phrase. The next phrase begins with a very unstable Bb_{+3}^{+6} sonority at L34; Example 13.2 shows this moment in the motet. Again, instead of counterpointing the tenor's *d* at L34 with a G_5^8 sonority, the unstable Bb_{+3}^{+6} concord propels the music ahead and continues to undermine G's previous status as a tonal focus. All of these various sonorities serve a specific purpose: to undermine both previous tonal centers in order to set up the end of this phrase, and, in particular, the C_U^8 sonority at L37. As shown in the example, this moment is indeed striking for several reasons: at now our ninth phrase ending in the motet, the triplum's *c′* is the highest pitch sung at a cadence thus far; the C_U^8 sonority marks the only sustained C concord in the motet; moreover, it is the only sustained sound in the motet without *diversitas* (that is, it is the only concord that does not consist of three distinct pitches – here one hears a unison on *c*);[23] as such, it presents the only instance when the tenor sings the same pitch as the motetus and thus is the only time the tenor assumes the (shared) role of governor of sonority. Finally, and perhaps most significantly, this moment serves as an aural marker: the C_U^8 sonority coincides with the beginning of the second tenor statement and as such signals for the listener this important structural moment.

---

[22] D as pitch center is not completely new to the ear, however, as a sustained D_8^{12} sonority also began the periods at L6 and L10.

[23] See Hartt 2010a for a complete explanation of sonorities with and without *diversitas*.

Example 13.2. *Jesu/Jhesu/Jesu*, L34–L37

After this arresting moment on C_U^8, the competition between F_5^8 and G_5^8 sonorities resumes in the second (abbreviated) tenor statement. Table 13.2 reveals that, just as in the first statement, each of the next six 4L periods concludes with either a held F_5^8 or G_5^8 sonority; thus, all sustained sonorities at phrases endings are the same in the second tenor statement as they were in the first, that is, until the conclusion of the motet, which appears in Example 13.3. As is illustrated in the example, the last cadence to emphasize G occurs at L57. In the approach to this moment, however, both voices homorhythmically intone 'da mihi quod sicio' ('give me what I thirst for'), thereby rendering the words clearly audible for the listener, as was done at the motet's beginning when 'Jesu' was sung together in the outer voices. The would-be end of the next 4L period, L61, brings the focus back to F; this phrase, too, concludes with intelligible text: the important 'judicio' is declaimed in unison. Due to the regularly repeating 4L phrases, the listener has come to expect that another sustained sonority will be sung in L62. Instead, the pattern breaks with the early entrance of the semibreves, a ploy that extends the final triplum period to 7L and the motetus to 6L in order to accommodate for the offsetting at the beginning of the motet. This entire final line of poetry, 'Reum munda nunc vicio' ('Now cleanse the culprit from sin'), is likewise rendered together in the texted voices. For the first time, an unstable G_{+3}^{+6} is declaimed throughout the duration of an entire long, which therefore grants even more emphasis to the F_5^8 resolution sonority. The motet thus concludes with the same sonority with which it began. Taking all of the simultaneously intoned words from the motet, the following phrase emerges: 'Jesus […] give me what I thirst for, [… in] judgement now cleanse the culprit from sin'. The creator of the motet has ensured that its message can be clearly heard.

In sum, *Jesu/Jhesu/Jesu* is indeed a tonally unified motet: it not only begins and ends on F_5^8 sonorities, but it also has many internal phrases beginning and ending on that same concord, many of which are further emphasized through directed progressions and sonority length. But the tonal properties of this motet encompass not just unity: the composer of the motet sets up a play between F_5^8 and G_5^8 sonorities throughout the course of the motet, and towards its midpoint deliberately undermines both of these foci by employing a variety of voicings and sonority types, which ultimately also serve a specific structural function highlighted aurally by the C_U^8 concord. As we will see, competing sonorities and careful tonal planning are not unique to *Jesu/Jhesu/Jesu* in the English motet repertory.

Example 13.3. *Jesu/Jhesu/Jesu*, L54–L64

ROSA DELECTABILIS / [REGALI EX PROGENIE] / REGALIS EXORITUR

Rosa/Regalis appears in **Onc 362**, one of the richer extant sources for the motet in England;[24] it contains some eighteen motets, including one four-voice motet with three texted upper voices above a French tenor,[25] two four-voice motets with two texted upper voices and two voices of tenor function, as well as several three-voice works. *Rosa/Regalis* appears across fols. 90v–91r; the triplum occupies the verso, the motetus the recto. In contrast to *Jesu/Jesu*, the tenor immediately follows the triplum in the manuscript; this placement visually reflects the tenor's middle register position in the motet. Interestingly, this motet is a later addition to the manuscript; the music that initially appeared on these folios was erased and was in turn replaced with *Rosa/Regalis* – thus, it is a palimpsest.[26]

The tenor consists of a single statement of an entire antiphon for the Nativity of the Virgin Mary (8 September): 'Regali ex progenie Maria exorta refulget; cuius precibus nos adiuvari mente et spiritu devotissime poscimus' ('Mary, sprung from regal progeny shines brightly with mind and spirit; we most devoutly ask that we may be aided by her prayers'). Its fifty-nine notes are divided into seven groups of eight pitches with a remainder of three. As shown in Example 13.4, each group of eight pitches is divided unevenly into two 4L periods: the first contains three pitches, set as longs, the second five, set as longs and breves. This 8L rhythmic pattern occurs seven times in the motet (thus comprising fifty-six of the tenor's pitches), after which the motet concludes with a single 4L period containing the last three notes of the tenor.[27]

The 'Regali ex progenie' melody in its original form begins and ends on *F*. It has therefore been transposed up a fifth for the motet. Interestingly, the same occurs in *Jesu/Jesu*: its devotional sequence was likewise originally *F*-centered, but was transposed up a fifth. Given that these tenor melodies both occupy the middle position in their respective motets, one has to wonder if the creators of these motets wanted to maintain the pitch center of the initial tenor source in the motet as a whole; since the middle-voice tenors in such motets are most frequently counterpointed with a fifth below, the transposition allows for both motets to communicate the *F*-centering of the original melodic materials.

Additional similarities between this motet and *Jesu/Jesu* abound. For instance, the poems of the triplum and motetus of *Rosa/Regalis* are again of identical lengths (here 218 syllables); see Table 13.3.[28] The main building block of this isoperiodic motet is likewise the 4L period, as is shown in the leftmost column of the table, and the initial staggering of the periods is achieved in a similar

---

24   A facsimile of the motet is found in Harrison and Wibberley 1981, 106–7, and color images appear on DIAMM. An edition appears in Harrison 1980, 36–9; as has been noted by Lefferts (1986, 296), this edition sometimes lacks rhythmic accuracy and consistency, especially concerning the semibreve pairs which Harrison sometimes renders iambically and sometimes trochaically. I have rendered all pairs, including those in SS ligatures, trochaically. Karen Desmond discusses the notation involved in the opening of this motet in her contribution to this volume. See also Bent 1978 and Lefferts 1986. The lone recording appears on Sine Nomine 1996, *A Golden Treasury of Mediæval Music*. Amon Ra, CD-SAR 63. The motet is considered in Sanders 1963, 239–40, and in some detail in Lefferts 1986, 96–7 and 295–6.

25   This motet, *Solaris/Gregorius/Petre/Marionette douche*, is discussed in Earp's chapter above; see in particular his Example 4.6 and Table 4.1.

26   The verso and recto each also contain a work in score (as opposed to being notated in parts) on the bottom three staves, written in an entirely different hand from both *Rosa/Regalis* and the rest of the surrounding music.

27   The end of the motet appears in Example 13.5.

28   Translations from Lefferts in Harrison 1980, 180–1.

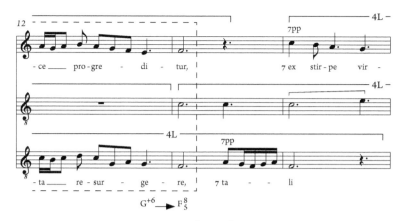

Example 13.4. *Rosa/[Regali]/Regalis*, L1–L14

Table 13.3. Poetry and translations of *Rosa/[Regali]/Regalis*

Longs	Poetry	pp lines
Triplum (60L)		
5	[1] Rosa delectabilis/[2] spina carens exoritur;	7+8
4	[3] regina prenobilis/[4] hec culpa carens nascitur.	7+8
4	[5] Hec que Jesse virgula/[6] de radice progreditur,	7+8
4	[7] ex stirpe virguncula/[8] David est que producitur.	7+8
4	[9] Hec luna formosior/[10] ut aurora progreditur;	7+8
4	[11] sole speciosior/[12] materiali cernitur.	7+8
4	[13] Eius est amabilis/[14] et graciosa facies;	7+8
4	[15] fit illa terriblis/[16] velud astrorum acies.	7+8
4	[17] Exorta conspicitur/[18] ex regali progenie	7+8
4	[19] virgo, que dinoscitur/[20] reis spes alma venie.	7+8
4	[21] Castis Dei filium/[22] hec concepit visceribus,	7+8
4	[23] quem pudoris lilium/[24] sesrvans lactat uberibus.	7+8
4	[25] Via deviantibus/[26] precor amore filii	7+8
7	[27] sis virgo peccantibus/[28] culpaque disperantibus/[29] pia mater auxilium.	7+8+8

A delectable rose arises without a thorn; this celebrated queen is born without a blemish. She who comes forth as a little twig from the root of Jesse, she is that sweet, dear virgin who is produced out of the lineage of David. She, more beautiful than the moon, comes forth like the dawn; she is perceived as more splendid that the actual sun. Here is a loving and gracious figure; she becomes worthy of awe, just as the array of stars. The virgin, arising from kingly forebears, is admired; she, who is known as the hope for wrongdoers, the soul of kindness. She conceived the son of God in her chaste womb; the lily of modesty, serving him, suckles him at her breast. I pray by the love of the son that you, virgin, blessed mother, true way to them who err, be an aid to sinners and those despairing in their guilt.

Tenor (60L)

4×15

Motetus (60L)

6	[1] Regalis exoritur/[2] mater decoris anima;/[3] naturalis	7+8+(4+
3	tollitur/[4] honoris amicicia. /	3)+8
1	[5] Nova caro	(4+
4	certinur/[6] emendata resurgere,/[7] tali	3)+8+(2+
4	et suboritur/[8] cuncta regens impendere./[9] Terre vita	5)+8+(4+
4	redditur/[10] Eve salus in gracia;/[11] nobis	3)+8+(2+
4	ac refunditur/[12] eius pax excellencia./[13] Rex turbatur	5)+8+(4+
4	emitur/[14] qui vitam orbi dederat./[15] Falso Iuda	3)+8+(4+
4	traditur,/[16] pacem reus omiserat./[17] Presta tuos	3)+8+(4+
4	excipe/[18] regina tuis emulis;/[19] conclamantes	3)+8+(4+
4	accipe/[20] nos tibi vitam servulis./[21] Des viam	3)+8+(3+
4	laudantibus,/[22] et cunctis te egregia/[23] regina	4)+8+(3+
4	orantibus/[24] bina enim remedia./[25] Tribuas	4)+8+(3+
4	egentibus/[26] peccato penitentibus,/[27] ut qui culpa	3)+8+(4+
6	miseri/[28] sunt hii pena sint liberi/[29] fineque cives celici.	3)+8+8

The royal mother arises; the soul of comeliness; she is elevated by her love of true honor. The new flesh is seen to rise again, free from sin, and to such a one is born in turn one to oversee, ruling all. Life is restored to earth, and in grace the salvation of Eve; and peace is restored to us by her excellence. The king is troubled, is bought, he who gave life to the earth; he is betrayed by deceitful Judas; sinful man gave up peace. O ready queen, rescue us from those who rival you; heed us who cry to you, and devote their life to you. May you show the proper way to those giving praise, and, O you excellent queen, give double remedy to all who pray. May you grant to the needy, and to the penitent in their sin, that those who suffer from some fault may be free from punishment, and in the end, citizens of heaven.

fashion: the first triplum period is again stretched to 5L, and the first motetus period to 6L through the addition of four syllables from the next line to the 7+8 pair. 4L periods then ensue for the remainder of the motet until 7L and 6L periods conclude the triplum and motetus, respectively.

The declamation in the motetus begins in a manner similar to *Jesu/Jesu* with a regular first-mode L-B pattern in L1 and L2; see Example 13.4. The triplum here, however, declaims syllables on each breve at its outset, albeit with occasional short melismas. In L3, declamation speeds up in both voices to the B-S level; here, though, minim pairs appear (see the beginning of L4, for instance). *Rosa/Regalis* also differs in that the parlando passages are not entirely syllabic, though they are homorhythmic – see the boxed passages in the example. Although parallel sixths feature prominently in the parlando passages, there is also a greater frequency of other intervals; for instance, there are occasional octaves (see L3, L8, L11, L12) and tenths (L8), but the last breve in each case always consists of an unstable, imperfect interval. Without exception, these boxed portions set simultaneous 8pp lines in the triplum and the motetus throughout the entire motet, and these lines always conclude on a sustained sonority that recurs every four longs. The motetus pitch of the arrival sonority is sustained either for an imperfect long (♩. in the transcription) as in L9 or as a breve ($\downarrow$.) as in L5, but even when only a breve, the pitch attacked on the next breve is always the same, as in L5, thereby continuing to render the same sonority.[29]

Like *Jesu/Jesu*, the motet begins and concludes on F_5^8 sonorities. But unlike *Jesu/Jesu*, which prominently featured dueling F_5^8 and G_5^8 sonorities, here one finds three competing sonorities: there is play between F_5^8, G_5^8, and A_5^8 throughout. As shown in Table 13.4, although each 4L phrase does not begin with a clearly delineated sustained sonority as was the case in *Jesu/Jesu*, among the fifteen concords that conclude each phrase – all of which are approached via directed voice leading – nearly half, seven, are F_5^8 sonorities, four center on G_5^8, and three on A_5^8. After alternating between F_5^8 and G_5^8 sonorities in the first three phrases, attention turns to A_5^8 for two consecutive phrases and back to F_5^8 for two phrases; then, alternation between all three centers resumes until the unexpected D_8^{12} concord at L53.

Table 13.4. Phrasing and cadences in *Rosa/[Regali]/Regalis*

	5L	4L	4L	4L	4L
1	5	9	13	17	21
F_5^8	$G^{+6}{\to}F_5^8$	$A^{+6}{\to}G_5^8$	$G^{+6}{\to}F_5^8$	$B^{+6}{\to}A_5^8$	$B^{+6}{\to}A_5^8$

4L	4L	4L	4L	4L
25	29	33	37	41
$G^{+6}{\to}F_5^8$	$G^{+6}{\to}F_5^8$	$A^{+6}{\to}G_5^8$	$B^{+6}{\to}A_5^8$	$A^{+6}{\to}G_5^8$

4L	4L	4L	7L	
45	49	53	57	58 59 – 60
$G^{+6}{\to}F_5^8$	$A^{+6}{\to}G_5^8$	$E^{+10}{\to}D_8^{12}$	$G^{+10}{\to}F_5^{12}$	$G_{+3}^{+6} \to F_5^8$

This concord at L53, along with the one at L57, stand out by virtue of their intervallic constitutions; they feature twelfths. As illustrated in Example 13.5, which shows the concluding phrases of the motet, the tenor's *D* at L53 is counterpointed not with a fifth below (and thus rendering G_5^8) as was the case in all previous instances, but instead with an octave, thereby yielding the motet's only cadential D sonority; this moment in turn serves to weaken G as tonal center in anticipation of the motet's conclusion on F. To bring the focus back to F, the next phrase concludes with a $G^{+10}{\to}F_5^{12}$ directed progression across L56–L57. Rather than simply composing a $G^{+6}{\to}F_5^8$ progression, the F_5^{12} sonority instead yields a new sound in at least two different respects: first, it is the only sonority in the motet without *diversitas*; second, the triplum's ascent to *c′* marks the motet's melodic peak.[30]

The voicing of this F_5^{12} sonority, however, is not as stable as it could be since it lacks an octave above the tenor's *F*, thereby necessitating another progression to achieve utmost finality and tonal unity. Consequently, following this climax at L57, as a sort of 'wind-down', the parlando passage

---

[29] At L9 is the only occurrence of a breve rest in the motetus following the boxed material, thus splitting the 4L period into 3L+1L. In all ensuing instances the next line of motetus poetry begins on the third breve of the long, such as in L13.

[30] The pitch *c′* occurred previously (for instance in L52 and L55 in the triplum) but this marks the first instance it is sustained at a cadence.

begins early (again, the triplum and motetus periods are extended here to make up for staggering at the beginning), and the ensuing short phrase sets the triplum's and motetus's concluding 8pp lines. The tendency sonority, G^{+6}_{+3}, is uttered for the entire antepenultimate long, again serving to grant extra emphasis to the final sustained F^8_5 sonority. Just as in *Jesu/Jesu*, the motet concludes with the same concord with which it began.

Example 13.5. *Rosa/[Regali]/Regalis*, L52–L60

MAJORI VI LETICIE / TENOR / MAJOREM INTELLIGERE

Lefferts lists four additional extant duet motets with medius cantus.[31] Like *Jesu/Jesu* and *Rosa/Regalis*, all of these works are isoperiodic, featuring either 4L or 8L period lengths, and all include declamation at the B-S level. To these six can be added two more motets of this subgenre appearing on two flyleaves in a monastery library in Bologna; these flyleaves have been recently discussed by Renata Pieragostini.[32] Neither motet is complete, however: one lacks its triplum and the other its tenor. While reconstructing a triplum may prove difficult, reconstructing a tenor in this case is arguably a less arduous task given what we know about the characteristics of the other duet motets with medius cantus. Take, for instance, *Majori vi leticie/Majorem intelligere*,

[31] Lefferts 1986, 62. Page (1997) provides a detailed discussion and new edition of one of these motets, *Zelo tui langueo/Tenor/Reor nescia*.

[32] As Pieragostini (2011, 343) explains, the manuscript, together with its flyleaves, is currently lost, as are the photos taken of it by Giuseppe Vecchi; Pieragostini worked from copies of those photos that had been made by one of Vecchi's younger colleagues.

the recently discovered motet that lacks its tenor. In her discussion of the motet, Pieragostini usefully provides a transcription of both voices with their respective poems but does not suggest a solution for the tenor;[33] the outer voices and poetry appear in Example 13.6.

Looking first at the phrase structure, a 6L period (5L+1L) begins the triplum, five 8L periods ensue, and a 10L period concludes it. The motet thus comprises 56L. The opposite occurs in the motetus: it begins with a 10L period, five 8L periods follow, and a 6L period ends it. Thus, we can surmise that the motet is isoperiodic and that the tenor might unfold as seven 8L periods.

Both voices set the poems of the triplum and motetus in a relatively straightforward fashion; the poems are nearly equal in length at 120 and 115 syllables, respectively. The triplum's first 6L period sets a single 8-syllable line of poetry, the ensuing 8L periods each set three lines of poetry mostly consisting of 7, 7, and 4 syllables,[34] while the final 10L period sets three 7-syllable lines. In the motetus, the first 10L period concatenates three lines of poetry (8, 7, and 5 syllables), the ensuing 8L periods each set three lines of poetry (7, 7, 3 or 7, 8, 3), while the last 6L period contains the final 8-syllable line.

Taking now the outer voices as a pair, notice the accelerated homorhythmic, syllabic B-S declamation at L8; similar passages recur every eight longs throughout the motet and feature primarily, but not exclusively, imperfect intervals. If the tenor indeed consists of 8L periods (7L followed by 1L of rest), then the first rest would coincide with the first parlando passage, and all subsequent rests would align with the ensuing parlando passages; this accords with the behaviors exhibited in *Jesu/Jesu* and *Rosa/Regalis*.

Other than in the parlando passages, the triplum and motetus move primarily in perfect longs, as well as in B-L, second-mode patterns. Does the tenor voice move only in perfect longs (like in *Jesu/Jesu*) or does the tenor sometimes feature more than one pitch per long (as in *Rosa/Regalis*)? If we attempt to counterpoint only one tenor pitch for each long, then the first three pitches are most likely a, a, and G: the first a yields a D_5^8 sonority to begin the motet, the next a allows for a reiteration of this concord while also being consonant with all four pitches in the outer voices, and the G allows for melodic movement by step as well as consonance with all outer-voice pitches. We run into potential trouble in the next long, however, since no single pitch is consonant with F/a and E/b (the triplum's c could be interpreted as passing in nature). Further, the space between the voices becomes very tight here, with only a third to begin the bar. Does the tenor require two pitches in this bar? Or might the tenor rest, and instead unfold in 4L (3L+1L) periods? We will return to this question shortly.

Moving ahead to L5, an a in the tenor seems plausible, and skipping to L7, c seems like the most sensible solution. These two bars could be linked with b, which, of course, is consonant with both E and D in the motetus. L8, as we have already determined, consists of a rest.

Revisiting for a moment the big picture: does the tenor consist of one statement of a lengthy melody or perhaps two or more statements of a shorter melody? There are many ways to divide 56L into equal parts, but parsing into two or perhaps three sections seems the most likely scenario given the characteristics of the other duet motets with medius cantus.[35] If the tenor statement

---

[33] Pieragostini 2011, 370–1. On p. 345, Pieragostini provides an image of the folio that contains the motet.

[34] The triplum poem's penultimate trio of lines consists of 7, 8, and 4 syllables.

[35] *Fusa/Manere/Labem* contains two complete tenor iterations plus a portion of a third statement. *Quare/Tenor/Quare* has four complete tenor statements, but the motet is much longer, consisting of 94L; interestingly, the second and fourth tenor statements are retrogrades. *Zelo/Tenor/Reor* likewise features four tenor iterations, and it, too, is a much longer motet, consisting of 130L.

Example 13.6. *Majori vi leticie/[Missing Tenor]/Majorem intelligere*

occurs three times, then *a-a-G* would need to be consonant with the outer voices in L19–L21, which it is not. But if the tenor melody occurs twice, then *a-a-G* would need to fit in L29–L31, which it does.[36] Looking ahead, our next proposed series of pitches from L5–L7, *a-b-c*, likewise fits in L33–L35. Thus far, then, it seems plausible that the motet contains two tenor statements.

Returning to L4, we hypothesized that the tenor may either consist of two pitches or be at rest. If we are correct that the tenor begins its second statement at L29, then the parlando passage at L32 answers our question: L32 should be accompanied by a rest in the tenor, and thus so should L4. In all likelihood, then, the tenor operates in 4L periods (3L+1L) and we can therefore insert a rest at an interval of every four longs within our reconstructed tenor line.

The extant outer voices of *Majori/Majorem* alone indicate that the motet exhibits careful tonal planning: the work features a clear tonal center (D) as well as other competing sonorities throughout, just like in *Jesu/Jesu* and *Rosa/Regalis*. The proposed tenor pitches thus far accord with typical sonority construction in this regard. Take, for instance, the first five phrases (one 5L phrase followed by four 4L phrases). The motet would begin with a D_5^8 sonority; this concord also concludes the phrases at L5 and L9, both of which are approached with an unstable sixth. Attention would turn to E_5^8 at L13 and L17 (thus *b* likely occupies the tenor in both instances) before returning to the original tonal center at L21. And throughout the tenor's second statement, there is again emphasis on D sonorities at L29 and L37 (but not at L33, where this time, A is instead granted emphasis), and on E sonorities at L41 and L45. The motet, of course, concludes on a D_5^8 sonority, the same concord as at the beginning.

Although the method described thus far does not provide definitive answers for every tenor pitch in the motet – for instance, is the missing pitch at L10 and at the corresponding L38 *a*, *F* or maybe even *c*? – this approach does, I propose, allow for a plausible melodic reconstruction, and the suggested pitches can in turn help to locate the source melody. Yet there is another specific feature of the extant duet motets with medius cantus that could point us in the direction of the original tenor melody: assonance. As Pieragostini reminds us: 'This predilection for homogeneity and assonance between texts is a well-known peculiarity of the English motet repertory from the late thirteenth well into the early fifteenth century'.[37] Recall the texts and tenors of our two previously examined motets: *Jesu/Jhesu/Jesu* and *Rosa/Regali/Regalis*. Might assonance play a role in determining the tenor of *Majori/[Missing tenor]/Majorem*?

Not just any source melody whose text begins with 'M', 'Ma-', or 'Majo-' will suffice. The words of the tenor source naturally should accord with the meaning imparted in the outer-voice poetry:[38]

Triplum

O Mother, you are rightly overwhelmed **today** by the power of your **joy**, which is **stronger** than **yesterday's sorrow**; because, although you saw that Jesus was silenced and killed, yet you hoped that he would be revived from death. Grief therefore did not have the power to destroy you, because hope provided for a marvelous cure for the time to come; hence the power of **joy** appears to be **stronger** than that of **sorrow**.

---

[36] The *E/a* fourth that plausibly begins L30 was evidently regarded as acceptable counterpoint: see, for instance, the series of parallel fourths in L40. Further, the fourth in L30 occupies the less lengthy first third of the bar.

[37] Pieragostini 2011, 361.

[38] Translations adapted from Pieragostini 2011, 353–4. Added emphasis is mine.

Motetus

Mankind is not able to comprehend (whether it be by way of reasoning or inspiration) which one has the more powerful nature, either **joy** or **sorrow**. **Yesterday's misery** could not be described; and **today's joy** is similar in that it cannot be described; reason has not the faculty thoroughly to understand things that are boundless. Therefore, my human judgement longs for an explanation of my fate, but is unable to investigate it.

Both poems juxtapose 'today's joy' with 'yesterday's sorrow'. Jesus's crucifixion led to 'misery' and 'sorrow', and although in the motetus it is undecided which sentiment is more powerful, the hope of his resurrection ('that he would be revived from death') leads the triplum voice to conclude that joy apparently overcomes sorrow. In our search for an M-tenor, we can also hypothesize that the original source melody may very well begin on *D* – recall that the tenors in the other two motets were transposed up a fifth – thus its first six pitches may be *D-D-C-D-E-F*.

A plausible match might be 'Majorem caritatem nemo habet ut animam suam ponat quis pro amicis suis' ('Greater love hath no man, than in that he layeth down his life for his friends'), from an antiphon from the Common of Apostles. This text, of course, refers to when Jesus told his disciples that he intended to give his life for the sake of mankind, after which he set the ultimate example of self-sacrifice by going to the Cross. The triplum and motetus poetry thus react to Jesus's crucifixion. As shown in Example 13.7, the opening pitches of our reconstructed tenor indeed match the antiphon phrase.[39] While not an exact match, the proposed source melody begins and ends on *D*, thereby exhibiting tonal unity, features the same marked leap of a fourth from *c* to *f*, and, barring repetitions and filled-in thirds, mostly agrees with the pitches set to the antiphon's first four words, 'Majorem caritatem nemo habet'. Recall that in *Jesu/Jesu* the motet tenor exhibited numerous differences from its source melody, and the tenor of *Rosa/Regalis* likewise revealed minor variants; thus is seems reasonable to suggest that here, too, an altered version of the melody may have been employed for the motet. A proposed version of the complete motet appears in Example 13.8.

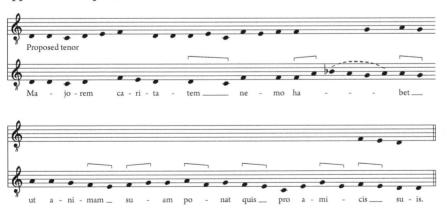

Example 13.7. Comparison of the reconstructed tenor with 'Majorem caritatem nemo habet'

[39] A search on www.cantusdatabase.org reveals that the 'Majorem caritatem' melody survives in myriad medieval sources spanning several centuries and geographic locations, the vast majority of which begin with the same ten to twelve pitches transcribed in Example 13.7. Minor variants generally ensue. The particular reading provided in the example appears on fol. 503v of **F-Pn lat. 15181**; a direct link to an image of that folio may be found on the database's website.

Example 13.8. *Majori vi leticie/[Majorem caritatem]/Majorem intelligere*

The three motets examined in this chapter provide a snapshot of one specific subgenre of the fourteenth-century motet of English provenance. Although several other motet types occur in the repertory – indeed the varieties of structures and organizational methods outnumber those of its continental counterpart – these works *do* feature a great number of the characteristics typical of the genre in general in thirteenth- and fourteenth-century England: Latin poetry, sacred subject matter, regular declamation patterns dictating the rhythm of the texted voices, periodicity (and sometimes isoperiodicity), a tendency for assonance, and tonal coherence.

One might further reflect for a moment on the tenor as middle voice and how the outer voices behave around it. Might this subgenre have been a semi-improvised practice? Was it an antecedent to faburden? It is easy to imagine moving from perfect sonority to perfect sonority in passages where the tenor sings its sustained pitches (one singer a fifth below and another a fourth above the chant pitch, while generally avoiding parallel octaves), and then, when the tenor drops out, singing the text in accelerated declamation in parallel *im*perfect intervals until the tenor joins again. With practice, astute singers could plausibly master this technique. Further study in this regard may prove fruitful.[40]

One can also further consider the unwavering use of sacred subject matter in the genre. In addition to motets that serve as a prayer to Jesus (*Jesu/Jesu*), for instance, or address the Blessed Virgin Mary (*Rosa/Regalis*), or reflect upon Jesus's crucifixion (*Majori/Majorem*), numerous extant motets are devoted to saints. Take, for example, the cult of St Catherine that proliferated throughout medieval Europe and whose legend was likewise popular among motet composers in England.[41] Lefferts lists thirteen extant St Catherine motets; this number stands second only to the quantity of motets devoted to the Virgin Mary.[42] An example of such a motet, *Mulier magni meriti/Multum viget virtus/[Tenor]*, is built on a *pes* tenor structured as two nearly identical phrases with open and clos endings, believed to have been freshly composed for the work. The motet exhibits periodic phrase structures, isomelic properties, interesting passages of accelerated declamation toward its conclusion, as well as a tenor that assumes the more conventional lowest-voice position. Despite these stylistic differences as compared with our three duet motets, this motet is still similar to the others in several respects: it features assonance, it is largely isoperiodic, it is tonally coherent (again, featuring competing sonorities ultimately giving way to its final F_5^8 concord), and its subject and function are clear: one can imagine *Mulier/Multum* being sung in St Catherine's honor on her feast day, November 25.[43]

---

[40] Niels Berentsen's recent dissertation (2016) on improvised medieval polyphony considers certain English improvisational techniques quite similar to the possibilities I am suggesting here, as well as the ways in which such improvised practices might leave discernable traces within works that are fully written out. Although Berentsen does not address the English duet motet with medius cantus in particular, he considers the instructions for polyphonic improvisation laid out in the English treatise *Quatuor principalia musicae* in conjunction with a variety of coexisting approaches through which medieval English singers could have improvised polyphonic textures.

[41] See Bent 1981b for a reconstruction of a St Catherine work, the rondellus *Rota versatilis*, as well as Gower 2016, esp. ch. 3, for a recent detailed account of St Catherine's influence.

[42] Lefferts 1986, 171.

[43] *Mulier/Multum*'s layout in its source manuscript, Cgc 512, is intriguing. If one imagines turning the page to its opening (fols. 246v–247r), it would become immediately noticeable that the motet is presented upside down. On the left (fol. 246v) appears the motetus and on the right (fol. 247r) the triplum and the tenor. If one turns the page again, the next item (the triplum of a dedicatory motet to St Peter and St Paul) begins right way up, thus the back of fol. 247r is notated in the usual orientation. One therefore has to rotate the book 180 degrees in order to make sense of the motet: the voices would then be presented in a typical layout, with the

Because the medieval motet in England generally eschewed secular topics and thus French or even vernacular texts, the repertory differs from its continental counterparts in several respects, and – perhaps consequently – has received less thorough treatment in modern scholarship. Take, for instance, the rich practice of French refrain citation seen so prominently in continental motets in both centuries in question, a practice that allows for multiple levels of meaning. Or consider the continental mix of sacred tenors with upper-voice vernacular poetry, which, again, can afford several possible readings. That these English motets do not necessarily exhibit the same *subtilitas* of textual interplay as their continental counterparts, coupled with the lack of extant complete sources mentioned at the beginning of this chapter, likely contributes to the relatively sparse attention these works have been given since becoming available in modern editions.[44] Yet the motet in England during this period simply operated within different parameters, independent of its French counterpart, and therefore embodies a different aesthetic: indeed, as Margaret Bent wrote, this repertory 'has no demonstrable continental links, and seems to have remained quite separate in style, techniques, and notation'.[45] This inclination toward sacred composition continued in the last decades of the fourteenth century, and beyond: while composers on the continent shifted their focus to the secular song but still continued to write motets primarily organized around the deliberate patterning of pitch and rhythmic elements, English composers, too, gradually shifted their focus elsewhere, in particular to settings of the Mass Ordinary, yet they continued to write motets exhibiting a rich variety of compositional approaches, including some that adopted and even expanded upon continental practices.[46]

triplum on the left and the motetus on the right. Strikingly, on the upside down fol. 246v, a large circular, spoked figure that spans nearly the entire region of the notated motetus is clearly visible as bleed-through from fol. 246r. And turning back to this folio, indeed, the only thing found on that page is the circular figure. Could it be Catherine's wheel? If so, by rotating the book – that is, by turning Catherine's wheel – the music then makes sense.

44 Significantly, Lisa Colton has very recently advocated for a reconsideration of music-text relationships in English polyphony; see Colton 2017b for an analysis of *Ave miles celestis curie*, a motet-like four-voice song dedicated to St Edmund, found in **Ob 7**.

45 Bent 1978, 65.

46 See Bent 2010, 84: 'Soon after 1400 there began a period of intense reception and absorption by English composers of French stylistic and notational influence'. For an example of such a motet, see her discussion of *Sub Arturo plebs/Fons citharizancium* on pp. 86–8 of that same article, and Bent 2017, 35 n. 37, in which she reiterates a dating of after 1400 for the motet. Emily Zazulia discusses *Sub Arturo/Fons* in Chapter 17 of the present volume.

14

Materia Matters: Reconstructing Colla/Bona

Anna Zayaruznaya

T HANKS TO THE SURVIVING TESTIMONIES of Egidius de Murino and Johannes Boen – which are backed up by cycles of rhythmic and melodic repetition so clear they can be noticed by even the novice analyst – we know quite a bit about how *ars nova* motet tenors were constructed.[1] But at what point in the process of motet composition did tenor construction take place? Did composers begin with tenors and then proceed to the upper voices, or did some aspects of upper-voice construction precede the ordering of borrowed chant notes into rhythmically patterned motet tenors? The chief theoretical witness on this point is again Murino, who indicates in a famous aside near the beginning of his treatise that chants are selected for motet tenors based on some pre-existing constraints:

> Primo accipe tenorem alicuius antiphone vel responsorii vel alterius cantus de antiphonario et debent verba concordare cum materia de qua vis facere motetum.

> First take a tenor from some antiphon or responsory or another chant from the antiphoner, and the words should be in agreement with the stuff (*materia*) out of which you wish to make the motet.[2]

While this remark patently indicates that *materia* precedes the selection of a chant for the tenor, it does not make clear what exactly 'materia' is. The word is frustratingly vague: it can mean substance, topic, subject matter, even building material; I have translated it above as 'stuff'. A range of scholarly viewpoints has been expressed on what exactly this stuff might be, and how it relates to the process of composing motets. Sometimes 'materia' has been interpreted as a broad theme, the subject-matter which a motet treats.[3] At other times it has been suggested that the upper-voice texts were fully written before the tenor was selected.[4] In most accounts this stuff is limited to the semantic realm – indeed Murino links *materia* with text specifically. When it comes to notes

---

[1] Tenor construction is discussed by Alice Clark in Chapter 3 of the present volume.

[2] Edited in Leech-Wilkinson 1989, 1: 18. Unless otherwise noted, translations are my own.

[3] Boogaart (1993, 5) interprets *materia* as a general theme, suggesting that it might have been decided on at the same time as the tenor was chosen: 'according to Egidius de Murino ... the composer must first define the *materia* with which the work deals by choosing a suitable fragment from plainchant'.

[4] Leech-Wilkinson (1989, 21) glosses 'the matter of which you wish to make the motet' thus: 'in other words, the texts'. Bent (2003, 372) provides a more agnostic assessment: 'The primary factor that led a composer to choose a tenor for a motet was to suit the symbolic, ritual or topical significance of its attached words to the subject of the texts of the upper parts (whether or not these had already been composed)'.

and pitches, the tenor is still often characterized as 'the "bones" and "foundation," defining the outlines of the whole work'.[5] In practice, this foundational metaphor implies that structures of rhythmic repetition were implemented first in the tenor, and then in the upper voices, with the latter's occasional repetition of rhythms reflecting or magnifying the tenor's form.[6]

But in a significant minority of the *ars nova* repertory – some quarter of the body of work made up by the motets in **Iv**, Machaut's oeuvre, and the newest pieces in **Fauv** – tenors and upper voices feature different structures of rhythmic repetition.[7] One of the most interesting of these is *Colla iugo subdere/Bona condit cetera/Libera me*, attributed to Philippe de Vitry.[8] In what follows I will first examine the textual and musical characteristics of the chant upon which the motet's tenor is based, seeking to extract from these a set of parameters for the kind of motet that might have been constructed upon a tenor with these characteristics, whether because the tenor was the starting point of composition, or because it was chosen to accord with some pre-determined poetic theme. I will then turn to the finished motet to compare its actual properties with the expectations derived from the tenor, ultimately seeking to describe a compositional process that might have resulted in a motet with the semantic and formal qualities of *Colla/Bona*.

The tenor pitches of *Colla/Bona* are from the Lauds antiphon for Wednesday of Holy Week, where they span the words 'Libera me de sanguinibus' ('Free me from blood'): '**Libera me de sanguinibus**, Deus Deus meus, et exaltabit lingua mea iustitiam tuam' ('**Free me from blood**, O Lord my God, and my tongue will extol thy justice'; Example 14.1).[9] The antiphon, in turn, takes its text from the *Miserere*, the important penitential Psalm 51(50), of which it closely paraphrases verse 16:

> [3]Miserere mei, Deus, secundum magnam misericordiam tuam; et secundum multitudinem miserationum tuarum, dele iniquitatem meam. [4]Amplius lava me ab iniquitate mea, et a peccato meo munda me. [5]Quoniam iniquitatem meam ego cognosco, et peccatum meum contra me est semper ... [16]**Libera me de sanguinibus, Deus, Deus salutis meae, et exsultabit lingua mea justitiam tuam.** [17]Domine, labia mea aperies, et os meum annuntiabit laudem tuam. [18]Quoniam si voluisses sacrificium, dedissem utique; holocaustis non delectaberis.

> [3]Have mercy on me, O God, according to thy great mercy. And according to the multitude of thy tender mercies blot out my iniquity. [4]Wash me yet more from my iniquity, and cleanse me from my sin. [5]For I know my iniquity, and my sin is always before me ... [16]**Deliver me from blood, O God, thou God of my salvation: and my tongue shall extol thy justice.** [17]O Lord, thou wilt open my lips: and my mouth shall declare thy praise. [18]For if thou hadst desired sacrifice, I would indeed have given it: with burnt offerings thou wilt not be delighted.

We might presume that a composer beginning with such a chant would have gone on to compose – or would select this chant if he were already planning to compose – a penitential motet, either

---

[5]   Here I quote Boogaart 2003, 14. See also the account of motet composition in Busse Berger 2005, 228–32.

[6]   'What all the procedures [along the spectrum from partial to complete upper-voice isorhythm] have in common is that they use the tenor's rhythmic structure, reflected and sometimes magnified by upper-voice rhythmic repetition, to create a more or less audible musical structure'. A. Clark 2004, 491.

[7]   For a full account of this phenomenon and the works involved, see Zayaruznaya 2018; an expanded version of this analysis of *Colla/Bona* can be found there in ch. 6.

[8]   On the attribution see Bent and Wathey 2001, 810.

[9]   For sources see A. Clark 1996, 255–6.

in the sacred register, or in the secular realm of the penitent lover who is ready to sacrifice his happiness, and his life, to the whims of his lady. A lament would also be a good match: the texts of *Garrit gallus flendo dolorose/In nova fert animus/Neuma d'Alleluia*, for example, would sit well over this kind of tenor, the pairing implying that mankind's sin has led to the fallen state of the Fauvelline world. Yet another direction for the author to pursue would have been more local to the borrowed section of the chant: he might link the blood from which the psalmist wishes to be freed with battles impending or lost, as in Vitry's *Phi millies ad te/O creator Deus pulcherrimi/Jacet granum oppressum palea/Quam sufflabit Francus ab area*, which refers grudgingly to the 1356 defeat of the French at Poitiers, or Machaut's *Christe qui lux es/Veni creator spiritus/Tribulatio proxima est/Contratenor* (M21) which reacts to the English siege of Reims in 1359–60.[10]

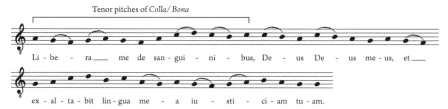

Example 14.1. *Libera me de sanguinibus,* **F-Pn lat. 10482,** fol. 163v

Beginning with – or committing early to – this particular section of *Libera me de sanguinibus* would also have formal implications for the motet being composed. The borrowed notes total 13; with so short a snippet the composer would need to state his melody multiple times – perhaps as many as four or five, or even six times, according to the testimony of motets built on similarly short segments.[11] The resulting tenor might therefore have been 52, 65, or 78 notes long. Since these multiples of a prime number do not present many options for division into sections which are not themselves 13 notes long, or which would not result in excessively long taleae (three 26-note taleae, for example), the composer might have gone on to modify his melody.[12] He might, for example, have added an extra final pitch to make 65 into 66 (which could then be arranged as six 11-note taleae); or he might have added a passing tone or tones to fill in one or both leaps in the melody, lengthening the snippet to 14 or 15 notes and thus rendering its multiples easier to divide in various ways.[13]

[10] *Phi millies/O creator* is edited in Zayaruznaya 2015a, 250–5; on its dating, see Zayaruznaya forthcoming 2018a. On the Siege of Reims and *Christe/Veni*, see Robertson 2002, 189–92.

[11] *Li enseignement de chaton/De touz les biens qu'amours ha a donner/Ecce tu pulchra et amica mea* ('M24') uses a 15-note snippet which is repeated four times; *Se pàour d'umble astinance/Diex, tan desire estre ames de m'amour/Concupisco* uses a 12-note snippet repeated four times; and *Fons tocius superbie/O livoris feritas/Fera pessima* (M9) uses a 12-note snippet repeated six times.

[12] It previously appeared that the tenor of Vitry's later *Petre/Lugentium* was built on a 33-note talea, but this voice can now be identified as a solus tenor; the original tenor consists of 15-note taleae; see Zayaruznaya forthcoming 2018a. Throughout this chapter I use the word 'talea' to mean a series of rhythms that returns periodically. In the case of tenors, which are often fully talean, talea means both the pattern being repeated and the span of music demarcated by such repetition. In the case of upper voices which are only partially taleic, I use talea to mean the rhythms repeated, and 'block' for the musical zones demarcated by rhythmic repetition. I avoid 'color' entirely because for many fourteenth-century theorists both 'color' and 'talea' meant rhythmic repetition. For more on this terminology see Zayaruznaya 2018, ch. 3.

[13] On composers altering their chant material in the course of constructing tenors, see A. Clark 1996, 66–8.

Such might be our expectations of *Colla/Bona* if its tenor chant source should have been the semantic or formal starting-point for the work's composition. But all such expectations are frustrated by the actual motet. Formally, its 13-note tenor melody is not organized into a whole number of rhythmic cycles. Rather, the borrowed notes are subject to partial repetition: in each section (the first in *integer valor*, the second in diminution) the snippet is stated two times fully and then followed by its first three notes (annotated below the staves of Example 14.2 on p. 294).[14] The obvious hypothesis that these extra notes are there to 'use up' remaining notes of a looping talea is disproven by the circumstance that the talea is also subject to both full and partial repetition: both sections feature seven loops of a simple talea followed by a remainder of one note and a rest.[15] It is hardly likely that such a haphazard scheme of rhythmic and melodic repetition would have arisen organically from the 13-note snippet 'Libera me de sanguinibus'. Rather, these 'extra bits' of chant and talea suggest that the tenor is being made to fit into something else which preceded it.

The theme treated by the texts of *Colla/Bona* is hardly less surprising from the point of view of its tenor. The poet speaks neither with the penitential voice of sinner or lover nor as a supplicant wishing to escape death or violence. Rather, the motet is an invective against greedy courtiers, comparing their rich but constrained lives with the simple but happy existence of someone who is his own master. Like the tenor's structure, this theme hardly follows from the tenor. Together these surprising formal and textual pairings put the question of *materia* into sharp relief. Just what had been decided upon about *Colla/Bona* when Vitry decided to 'take a tenor from some antiphon'?

In what follows, I offer a hypothetical narrative of composition for *Colla/Bona*. In doing so I seek to find the most probable order in which various compositional processes might have taken place to result in the motet that has come down to us. But the process of composition was certainly not as linear as my narrative suggests. At any stage the composer might have made a decision that overruled those made in previous steps. For example, even though I will posit that the triplum and motetus texts were written early on, nothing would have stopped Vitry from changing words in either voice once he perceived how the polyphonic framework aligned their poetry, provided only that the new words fit into the established meter. Such changes can hardly be gleaned in hindsight, since a retrospective reconstruction can only lead to the motet as it ultimately comes down to us, and not any of its hypothetical other versions. The finished motet hints at an order that might have made its composition manageable, and below I speculate about that order. But composition is by its nature recursive, as are many creative acts.

The thing that would eventually become *Colla/Bona* probably began as an idea to write a motet criticizing the dishonest ways of the groveling courtier. That this subject-matter was important to Vitry can be gleaned from his bucolic *Dit de franc Gontier*, whose narrator wistfully describes a meal shared in the woods by a peasant couple, Gontier and Helayne. After observing their humble but appetizing fare ('fresh cheese, milk, butter, cream and cheese, curd, apple, nuts, plums, pears, garlic and onion, chopped shallots on a brown crust, with coarse salt,') he overhears Gontier wax

---

[14] Examples 14.2, 14.3, and 14.4 follow Iv, fols. 17v–18r, and the text edition in Wathey 2005, 75. Leech-Wilkinson (1982–3, 2) incorrectly characterizes the borrowed segment of chant as 29 notes long.

[15] This is unusual but not unique: Machaut's *Tu qui gregem/Plange, regni respublica/Apprehenda arma et scutum/Contratenor* (M22), discussed in Sarah Fuller's chapter in this volume, features partial repetition of a borrowed melody in its tenor. Both *Flos ortus inter lilia/Celsa cedrus ysopus effecta/Quam magnus ponifex* and *S'il estoit nulz/S'Amours tous amans/Et gaudebit cor vestrum* (M6), analyzed in Zayaruznaya 2018, chs. 4–5, feature tenor taleae subject to partial repetition.

eloquent about his freedom from courts and tyrants:[16]

> 'Ne sçay', dit-il, 'que sont pilliers de marbre,
> Pommeaux luisans, murs vestus de paincture;
> Je n'ay paour de traïson tissue
> Soubz beau semblant, ne qu'empoisonné soye
> En vaisseau d'or. Je n'ay la teste nue
> Devant thirant, ne genoil qui s'i ploye.
>
> Verge d'uissier jamais ne me deboute,
> Car jusques la ne m'esprent convoitise,
> Ambicion, ne lescherie gloute.
> Labour me paist en joieuse franchise;
> Moult j'ame Helayne et elle moy sans faille,
> Et c'est assez. De tom bel n'avons cure'.

'I know nothing', said he, 'of marble pillars, glittering summits, walls covered with paint-ings; I do not dread a web of treachery beneath a kind countenance, nor that I will be poisoned with a golden cup. I bare my head before no tyrant, nor do I bend a knee. The doorman's rod has never pushed me back, for greed, ambition, and gluttonous lechery have not threatened to bring me within its range. My labor feeds me in my happy liberty; I dearly love Elaine, and she loves me without reservation, and that's enough. We want no splendid tomb'. (lines 19–30)

And after hearing this the narrator agrees, sighing in the final lines: 'Alas! a slave of the court is not worth a dime, but honest Gontier is worth a rare gem set in gold'.[17]

Like this *Dit* (whose chronology relative to the motet cannot be determined), *Colla/Bona* condemns courtiers as mere servants without agency while valorizing the simplicity – and even the simple diet – that comes with liberty. Unlike the *Dit*, which is strophic and not set to music, the motet needed two texts that would be compatible both semantically and structurally, and whose formal properties would in turn have implications for the musical form. Vitry chose to render both texts in tridecasyllable, with caesural rhymes splitting each line into 7+6 syllables. Both voices are monorhymed, the triplum on '-ari' (with '-ere' at the caesura); the motetus on '-atis' ('-era' at the caesura). The only departure from this scheme comes at the end of the triplum, where a 16-syllable quotation from Lucan in the final line imposes its rhyme, '-tur', on the penultimate line. A half-dozen other quotations pepper the texts (in bold in the Latin below). These borrowed snippets may have dictated the choice of the '-ere' and '-era' caesural rhymes:[18]

---

[16] 'Fromage frais, laict, burre, fromaigee/Craime, matton, pomme, nois, prune, poire,/Aulx et oignons, escaillongne froyee/Sur crouste bise, au gros sel,' lines 5–8; ed. Piaget 1897, 63–4; all further references are to this edition. The resonances between *Colla/Bona* and the *Dit de franc Gontier* are briefly noted in Besseler 1927, 204.

[17] 'Las! serf de court ne vault maille,/Mais franc Gontier vault en or jame pure,' lines 31–2.

[18] Wathey (2005, 69–71) identifies these quotations and suggests Vitry might have found them in a florilegium. On quotations as the germinating matter for motets see Bent 1997 and Zayaruznaya 2015b. Often quotations have been borrowed without their attendant meters. In *Colla/Bona*, the final couplet of the triplum jumps out of the tridecasyllabic lines, and in *Garrit/In nova*, both the famous Ovidian quotation that opens the motetus and the line from Joseph of Exeter that caps off the triplum are extrametrical. It may be that in these cases upper-voice metrical schemes were decided upon before quotations were chosen. On the quotations in *Garrit/In nova*, see Holford-Strevens 2005, 61–2.

Triplum[19]

Colla iugo subdere	curias sectari,
quarum sunt innumere	clades, mores rari.
Potens suo vivere	debet exequari.
Aliena desere,	quadra convivari
5 **pane tuo vescere,**	tibi dominari.
Si vis es, effugere	curis lacerari.
Malo fabam rodere	liber et letari
quam cibis affluere	servus et tristari.
Aulici sunt opere	semper adulari,
10 fictas laudes promere	lucraque venari,
ab implumis tollere	plumas et conari,
dominis alludere,	falsa commentari.
Ve quos habent pongere	verba que subduntur:
Nulla fides pietasque	**viris qui castra secuntur.**

One puts one's neck under a yoke by attending courts, at which disasters are innumerable, good habits few. He who can should be up to living on what is his own. Leave the property of others alone; live together in an open square; eat your own bread; be your own master. If you want money, avoid being mangled by cares. I prefer to nibble a bean and rejoice as a free man than to abound with provisions and be sad as a slave. The duties of a courtier are always to flatter, to utter feigned praises, and to hunt for profits, and to try to take feathers away from the unfeathered, to play up to lords, to compose false things. Woe to those whom the words which are placed below have to sting: there is no faith or piety in camp followers.

Motetus

Bona condit cetera	bonum libertatis.
Qui gazarum genera	tot thesaurisatis,
multiplici fallera	vos qui falleratis,
et cum libet ubera	fercula libatis,
5 si vivere libera	vita nequeatis
numquam saporifera	servi degustatis.
Vincit auri pondera	sue potestatis
esse. Vobis funera,	servi, propinatis
mala per innumera	dum magis optatis.

The good of liberty gives zest to other good things. You who lay up as treasure so many kinds of wealth, who harness yourselves with manifold ornament and at a whim sample rich dishes, if you cannot live a free life, you never taste savor-bearing things as slaves. To be one's own master is better than masses of gold. You slaves, you administer death to yourselves, when among countless evils, you desire (even) more.

The triplum is 14 lines long; the motetus, 9 – strange dimensions for two texts meant to go together, since 14 and 9 have no common factors. This mismatch has important consequences for the motet's structure. The fact that 14 is divisible by 2, and 9 by 3, may be reflected in, or precipitated by, the decision to cast the triplum in perfect modus and the motetus in imperfect – a conflict

---

[19]   Trans. David Howlett in Wathey 2005, 75–6; motetus translation modified for line 4.

Table 14.1. Duration of poetic lines in *Colla/Bona*

	Triplum line	Breves[a]	Motetus line	Breves[a]
α	1. Colla iugo subdere curias sectari	10	1. Bona condit cetera bonum libertatis. [+Untexted phrase]	15+12
	2. quarum sunt innumere clades, mores rari.	6		
	3. Potens suo vivere debet exequari.	12		
	4. Aliena desere, quadra convivari	12	2. Qui gazarum genera tot thesaurisatis, [+Untexted phrase]	12 +12
	5. pane tuo vescere, tibi dominari.	12		
β	6. Si vis es, effugere curis lacerari.	12	3. multiplici fallera vos qui falleratis,	12
	7. Malo fabam rodere liber et letari	12	4. et cum libet ubera fercula libatis,	12
	8. quam cibis affluere servus et tristari.	12	5. si vivere libera vita nequeatis	12
γ	9. Aulici sunt opere semper adulari,	6	6. numquam saporifera servi degustatis.	15
	10. fictas laudes promere lucraque venari	6		
	11. ab implumis tollere plumas et conari,	5	7. Vincit auri pondera sue potestatis	12
	12. dominis alludere, falsa commentari.	7		
δ	13. Ve quos habent pongere verba que subduntur:	12	8. esse. Vobis funera, servi, propinatis	12
	14. 'Nulla fides pietasque viris qui castra secuntur'.	8[b]	9. mala per innumera dum magis optatis.	6[b]

[a] Includes any rests following the phrase
[b] Not including a final maxima notionally lasting 4 breves

that persists throughout the finished motet. The openings of the two texts may also have played a role in this decision, matching their valence to imperfection and perfection respectively: in the worse scenario (the metrically imperfect triplum), 'one puts one's neck under a yoke by attending courts'; in the better (the perfect motetus), 'the good of liberty gives zest to other good things'.[20]

Counterpoising 3 and 2 is not a problem – Vitry did so in many of his motets, and everything fits as long as the basic building block lasts 6 breves or imperfect longs. But counterpoising 14 and 9 takes some planning, and it was to this issue that the composer presumably turned after writing his texts. To see how he faced the self-imposed challenge we must look to the finished motet. The duration of each line of the triplum and motetus in *Colla/Bona* is given in Table 14.1. It becomes apparent here that the motetus is set more regularly than the triplum, its lines generally lasting around 12 breves, with some variation in order to create staggered phrasing (that is, breves 'borrowed' for lines 1 and 6 are 'paid back' in the shortened line 9). Additionally, two

[20] On the relationship between mensural and worldly perfection in *ars nova* theory and practice, see Zayaruznaya 2015b, 140–8.

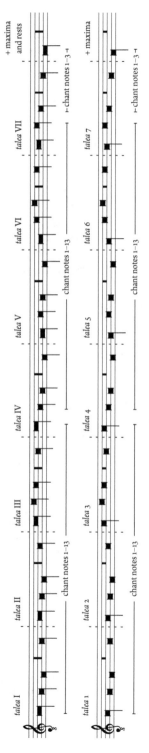

Example 14.2. *Colla/Bona*, tenor, borrowed chant notes and taleae marked (ligatures expanded)

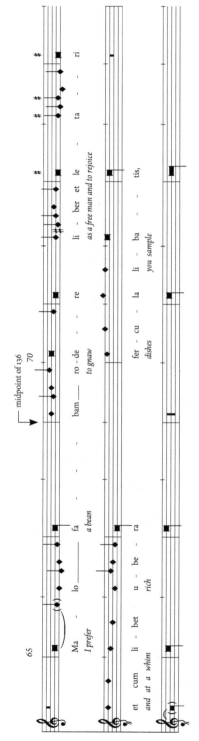

Example 14.3. *Colla/Bona*, breves 64–75

extra untexted 12-breve spans are inserted after motetus lines 1 and 2. Vitry is fond of playing with untexted singing in his motets.[21] Here the added phrases serve to decrease the difference in length between the two texts, giving the motetus two 'phantom' lines for a total of eleven twelve-breve spans. The finished length of the motet reflects this structure: it is 11×12, or 132 breves, plus a final maxima notionally lasting 4 breves.

The triplum, meanwhile, has fourteen lines, which cannot all be 12 breves in duration. To fit fourteen into eleven, Vitry groups together lines 9 and 10, and 11 and 12, setting each pair in a span of 12 breves. Additionally, the opening couplet is declaimed over 16 breves, which we might take to be twelve plus four more borrowed from line 14 for the sake of staggered phrasing. In this way, two texts of rather incompatible length are brought into alignment: the motetus has been stretched, and the triplum compressed, to eleven 12-breve units.

The different alignments between triplum and motetus summarized in Table 14.1 divide the motet into four sections. In sections α and γ, the triplum packs in more text than the motetus, whether due to the insertion of untexted lines (in section α) or the speeding-up of the triplum's declamation (in section γ). In sections β and δ, the two voices declaim at the same rate. It is much more common in the repertory of *ars nova* motets, and especially in Machaut's oeuvre, to see a motetus that consistently carries less text than the triplum. In *Colla/Bona*, the decision to have them occasionally match their rates of text-declamation seems to have stemmed from the meanings and locations of specific lines. Section δ pairs the pithy final couplets of both voices, which address the court's minions. And in section β the declamatory parity enables a superimposition of lines that are related by mentions of food (also important in the *Dit de franc Gontier*) and allusions to the differences between those who taste life as servants of the court and those who are free in their poverty. 'I prefer to nibble a bean and rejoice as a free man', the triplum declares, 'than to abound with food and be sad as a slave' (lines 7–8). And the motetus puts the same thing in a different way: 'you who ... sample rich dishes at a whim, if you cannot live a free life, never taste flavorful things as slaves' (lines 4–6). Indeed, the confrontation between beans and rich dishes staged by triplum line 7 and motetus line 4 is literally central to the motet, whose midpoint, marked by an arrow in Example 14.3, falls on the bean. Moreover, the 36-breve section β in its entirety is centrally located: the material on either side of it averages 50 breves in duration.[22] The bringing-into-alignment of these similar sentiments in the two voices likely motivated the stretching and contraction to which the texts are subject in sections α and γ.

A schematic sketch for the motet at this stage might have looked something like Figure 14.1. This figure reflects the various approaches to text coordination described above, and suggests that the triplum might declaim its extra line alone, or in a section of music that stands outside of some repetitive structure. While Figure 14.1 has no information about the specific rhythms that we might find in each section, decisions about the alignment of the two texts have implications for their periodic structures. The addition of untexted material to the motetus at two different points, for example, has potential talean implications, while the differing rates of text declamation needed to achieve different kinds of coordination between the two texts will necessarily have impact on the rhythms used to set them. Finally, the possibility of a bipartite tenor with the second part in diminution is suggested by the co-existence of blocks that are 24 breves long with those that are 12. A tenor in imperfect modus is implied by the 2:1 ratio between longer and shorter blocks, since

---

[21] On untexted passages in Vitry, see Zayaruznaya 2013, 488–93, and Zayaruznaya 2014.

[22] The lengths differ due to staggered phrasing: the triplum spends 52 breves in section α and 48 in section γ, and the motetus, 51 and 49 respectively, including the final maxima.

a tenor in perfect modus would produce a 3:1 ratio between sections.[23] The most straightforward way to make a motet with 2:1 diminution last 136 breves is to have the *integer valor* statement last 90 breves, so that the second section is 45, for a total of 135 breves – close enough.

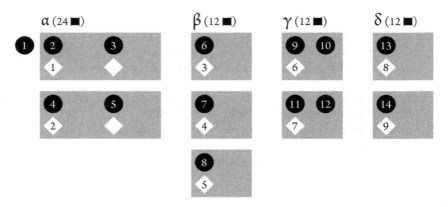

Figure 14.1. Hypothetical compositional plan for *Colla/Bona*, summarizing the co-ordination of text-lines in triplum (black circles) and motetus (white diamonds; hollow diamonds represent long untexted motetus passages)

In considering upper-voice block dimensions we move seamlessly from the upper voices to the tenor that will underlie them, and I suggest that it was at this point in the creative process that Vitry decided on a source chant to concord with this accumulated stuff (though he certainly may have had some contenders in mind already). His choice was *Libera me de sanguinibus*. The relationship between its opening words, 'Free me', and the concern with liberty, slavery, and servitude in the upper-voice texts is unambiguous. 'Libera me', however, encompasses only six notes. Adding the next syntactical unit makes it 'Libera me de sanguinibus' – 'free me *from blood*'. Blood is less relevant than freedom to the upper voices, whose texts ask to be delivered from servitude rather than death. Though bodily harm could be linked loosely with the cutthroat atmosphere at court, it is perhaps telling that only the words 'Libera me' seem to have traveled with the motet.[24] After this the antiphon turns to praise God's justice ('Free me from blood *my Lord, and my tongue shall extol thy justice*'), the invocation of which is not particularly pertinent to the motet's message. Perhaps this was a good reason to stop where he did.[25]

---

[23] For more on the relationship between tenor diminution and upper voices in which periodically recurring rhythms articulate blocks of differing sizes, see Zayaruznaya 2018, ch. 4.

[24] No surviving source for the motet includes the full tenor text; CaB fol. 5r (DIAMM foliation)/fol. 13r (foliation in Lerch 1987) gives 'Libera me' and **Trém** fol. 1v, has 'Libera me domine', which is incorrect. Other sources do not label the chant. A. Clark (1996, 107) notes that *Colla/Bona* shares its use of a tenor from Wednesday of holy week with *In virtute/Decens*, another admonitory motet, suggesting that 'both writers may have individually found a way to exploit the appropriateness of a penitential context for their criticisms'. Zayaruznaya (2015a, chs. 2–3) argues that *In virtute/Decens* is almost certainly by Vitry as well. While the coincidence may suggest that Vitry indeed found some significance in simultaneously casting aspersions and asking for forgiveness, it may instead attest to his fondness of or special familiarity with this part of the liturgy and his rather de-contextualized use of tenor labels.

[25] We can never know whether Vitry considered other chants. Machaut's *Helas/Corde mesto* (M12), which probably post-dates *Colla/Bona*, has a tenor also labeled 'Libera me', but drawn

'Libera me de sanguinibus' gave Vitry 13 notes – a nice coincidence, perhaps, with the trideca-syllabic poetry. But in other respects the snippet is less-than-ideal. Neither 13 (a prime number) nor its smaller multiples have any denominators in common with 90, which is the target length of the *integer valor* section. This means that no talea could be applied to some whole number of melodic iterations without leaving a remainder of notes unaccounted for. The ascent at the fragment's end is also problematic, since a stepwise descent in the tenor is useful for making a final cadence in a three-voice motet. Evidently realizing that neither the length of this melody nor its melodic profile were quite right for his motet's structure, Vitry used the melody and its talea as flexible building blocks that could be molded to fill out the form of the upper voices.

The tenor talea upon which he settled combines a maxima and three longs with a longa rest in the penultimate position (■ ■ ■ | ■), shrinking to a long, three breves and a breve rest in diminution (■ ■ ■ | ■). This is both a short and a nondescript pattern compared to some of Vitry's other taleae, but its avoidance of small notes and a moderate amount of rest make it versatile. In its original form it has a duration of 12 breves, and in diminution 6; it is thus compatible with the motet's 24- and 12-breve upper-voice units and superimposition of perfect and imperfect modus. As mentioned above, 90 breves of *integer valor* would be needed before diminution set in. Ninety divides by twelve to make 7.5, and 7.5 taleae would have used 30 chant notes – two cycles of 13, plus the first four notes, *a-G-F-G*. But this does not yield a descending step at the end, and thus Vitry chose to repeat only three extra chant notes, ending his first cursus with a rest instead of a *G* longa.[26] The second section features the same tenor scheme of repetition – two cycles of the chant plus three more notes stretched over seven taleae and an extra bit. The remainder here is a maxima, rather than the longa-plus-breve rest that would result from diminution, and the maxima adds the beat that makes the motet a total of 136, rather than 135 breves. With this haphazard but functional scheme of repetition settled on, the tenor's pitches were ready to dictate the motet's harmonic and melodic elements, to which the composer presumably turned at this point, working out the staggered phrasing of voices and setting the text as he went. At this stage, the motet really was composed from the bottom up as pertains to its harmonic content, in that the tenor's pitches limited the choice of pitches in the upper voices.[27] Decisions about rhythm would stem from text-setting conventions of the genre, in which each line of poetry – or a group of lines, if they are grouped – ends with a breve or a longa, usually followed by a breve rest. Thus text-setting is intimately linked with talea at line-ends, whereas the beginnings and middles of lines can have more or less individual rhythmic profiles.

As the schematic analysis of *Colla/Bona* given in Example 14.4 shows, the varying zones of triplum-motetus coordination marked in Table 14.1 have their analogues in sets of upper-voice

---

from the Lenten responsory *Minor sum*, and encompassing 21 notes. See A. Clark 1996, 195 and 245; and Zayaruznaya 2009, 205.

[26] A. Clark (1996, 46 and 166) points out that the excerpted chant melody, which ends on a *c* approached from below, would have been unsatisfactory in a final cadence, given the preference for final major-third tonalities and an 'overall favor given to F and G finals in the fourteenth century motet repertory'. This manipulation of the snippet allows the motet tenor to end on *F*. However, that does not explain the re-statement of three, rather than two, extra notes from the beginning of the chant, since ending on *G* (pitch 2) would have done just as well, and left no notes beyond the seventh talea. This 'remainder' has been described as a partial talea VIII (for example in Schrade 1956b, 85–7, and Besseler, 1927, 222), but in that case it would be a maxima followed by a longa.

[27] See, however, Lavacek 2011.

blocks with different taleae.[28] The opening four breves seem to stand on their own, giving the triplum a chance to start its extra line, and the motetus a chance to get ahead for the sake of staggered phrasing. Section α is particularly salient in the motetus, whose two long untexted spans are sung in nearly identical rhythms (see the melismas underlaid by dotted lines in Example 14.4). Section β, which houses the lines about food, consists of a shorter and almost entirely taleic 12-breve block stated thrice. Together, sections α and β make up the *integer valor* portion of the motet. In sections γ and δ the tenor speeds up, running through two of its taleae during each of the 12-breve upper-voice blocks. Section γ features a fast-talking triplum with some recurring rhythms in both voices, while both upper voices in section δ have only a sprinkling of talea.

No edition or scholarly discussion of *Colla/Bona* notes the presence of the upper-voice structures shown in Example 14.4. Instead, editors have represented the work's structure as that of its tenor – seven taleae in each of two sections, with an eighth incomplete one directly before the diminution begins.[29] But the upper-voice form of *Colla/Bona* is far more regular than the tenor's chaotic combination of whole and partial rhythmic and melodic repetitions: after a four-breve opening, the triplum and motetus are organized in blocks of two different lengths (24 breves, 12 breves) that are stated either two or three times. The total number of blocks is the same as the number of lines in the motetus: nine. This is another way of saying that the motetus's form determines the form of the whole to a large extent, though the addition of long untexted stretches in section α takes the longer triplum text into account. The tenor's combination of structured and unstructured, regular and irregular repetitions only makes sense if the upper-voice texts and their periodic structure were already in place when the composer selected his chant snippet. The alternate hypothesis – that the haphazard repetition schemes of the tenor would have been decided upon first, and would end up perfectly fitting into the more regular structures of upper voices which had not yet been written – is untenable.

There can be no doubt that a range of compositional processes was in use for the construction of fourteenth-century motets. In some cases tenors could well have been the germinating ideas behind entire compositions, the choice of their chants tantamount to a decision about what the motet would be about, and their musical and rhythmic properties acting as blueprints for the rest of the motet's voices. But *Colla/Bona* could not have begun life in this way. Here, the *materia* that preceded the choice of tenor seems to have included two completed upper-voice texts and a detailed formal plan for their coordination and declamation. Nor is *Colla/Bona* alone. Margaret Bent has shown that in *Fons tocius/O livoris* (M9) 'the triplum offers the clearest possible evidence that not only the substance of the text but the details of its word-breaks were planned together with the musical design' because of its accommodation of hocketed text without the division of words by rests.[30] It may even be that the full composition of texts preceded tenor choice and organization in the majority of cases. The theorists are mute on this point: it falls to the analyst to re-imagine the act of composition in pursuit of the stuff of motets.

---

[28] Shading in this example marks taleae in all voices, while the systems are so arranged as to vertically align like rhythms with like. In choosing what to shade I have set the bar at rhythms lasting a breve or more that repeat exactly in the majority of blocks within a given section.

[29] While Besseler (1927, 222 n. 3) notes that the upper voices group into larger blocks in the diminution section (sections γ and δ here), the larger groupings in section α are described here for the first time. Editions consulted include: Besseler 1927, 247–50; Johnson 1955, 2: 116–20; Schrade 1956b, 85–7. Gastoué 1936, 139–42, does not label taleae.

[30] Bent 2003, 380.

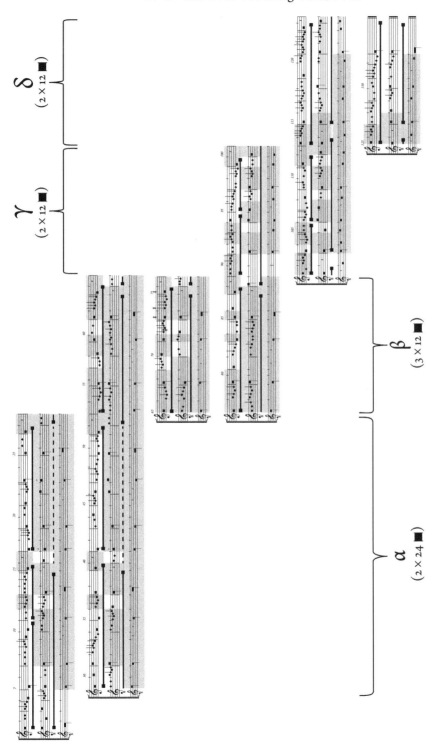

Example 14.4. *Colla/Bona,* upper-voice blocks aligned, periodically repeating rhythms (taleae) shaded, boundaries of text lines indicated with bold box-tipped lines

15

Machaut's Motet 10 and its Interconnections*

Margaret Bent

CHOICE OF TENOR

T HE MUSICAL FOUNDATION of a motet is a tenor that underpins the structure with a melody usually taken from chant. Egidius de Murino prescribes that the tenor should first be taken from an antiphon, responsory or other chant, and that the words should concord with the *materia* about which the motet is to be made. While the tenor is the musical foundation, it is not the only building block; Egidius at least implies that the verbal content of the upper parts has already been decided, whether or not the texts, or indeed any musical features, have been worked out in detail.[1] This substance (*materia*) precedes and determines the choice of tenor. In nearly all of Machaut's motets (and in many by other composers) the words and chant excerpt of the tenor are not those of the beginning of the chant, often pointing up a deliberate choice to isolate a word or phrase especially suited to the – perhaps already planned – upper-part texts.[2] This has often made it harder (and sometimes impossible) to identify the source chant, especially if it is unlabeled.

But it is not only in the disposition of the tenor as a skeleton or ground-plan for the motet that the tenor shapes its musical material. Machaut clearly also chose his chant excerpt for its musical qualities, important among them its potential to serve as the grammatical foundation for counterpoint; not only would the composer assess the number of tenor notes for its divisibility into talea units, but also its cadencing potential at tenor rests or talea divisions, especially at the end,

---

* Kevin Brownlee and I gave a joint presentation on this motet in Oxford in 1991 and again in 2001. His contribution addressed not only the verbal intertextuality within the motet texts, but also its external literary context in the *Roman de la Rose* and the *Ovide moralisé*. It was published in a *Festschrift* kindly presented to me in 2005, where he announced my contribution as forthcoming; see Brownlee 2005. Here it is, finally. Meanwhile, Jacques Boogaart has independently completed a number of highly perceptive studies of the motets. Some of the present material, drafted long ago, overlaps with his observations, which I have tried to signal where appropriate; for M10 see Boogaart 2001a, 51–5, Boogaart 1993, 24–30, and Boogaart 2001b, ch. 6. Several aspects of M10 are also discussed in Hartt 2010b. I am very grateful to Jacques Boogaart, Jared Hartt, and Sean Curran for valuable comments on an earlier draft of this paper.

[1] Leech-Wilkinson (1989, 1: 18–20) provides a revised version of Egidius's text. In Bent 1997 I have argued for *Tribum/Quoniam* that the verbal 'citations' are as much building blocks as is the tenor chosen to go with them.

[2] Especially in M1, M2, M3, M4, M5, M6, M7, M8, M9, M10, M12, M14, M17, M19, M21, M22, M23. M15 is the only one to use a chant beginning, *Vidi Dominum*. Sean Curran (pers. comm.) reminds me that tenors of early thirteenth-century motets were normally based on a single word from within a chant; the discant sections from which motets often derive are built on melismas which are usually embedded deep in a chant's structure.

at least in the three-part motets.[3] Nearly all of Machaut's three-part motets end with a stepwise descent in the tenor, which serves the final cadence. The exceptions are the three whose tenors are secular melodies (M11, M16, and M20), and whose final ascents would once have formed counterpoint against the songs' own tenors.

The four four-part motets are also exceptions to final stepwise tenor descent; they all share the tenor role with an *essential* contratenor (and would thus have been candidates for composition with the aid of a solus tenor).[4] M5 and M23 are the only motets with (interlocking) coloration in tenor and contratenor. The tenor of M21 does make a stepwise cadence, but in M22 and M23 the final stepwise descents are made not by the tenor, but by the contratenor.[5]

The extent to which tenor melodic material is integrated into the upper parts of *ars nova* motets has been under-recognized; Machaut's habitual use of that material must have influenced him in the choice of a tenor to suit the material of the texts. The dark textual content of M9, for example, is reflected in the conjunct and serpentine contour of its tenor, and by the use of motives derived from the tenor in the upper parts.[6] Conversely, for the uncertainties of Fortune in M8, Machaut chose a tenor with intervallic leaps which are echoed in the upper parts and reinforced with uncertainly swaying syncopations. Such relationships between music and text will be examined below as they apply to M10; some connections with other motets will also be noted.

If Machaut had decided in advance to include hockets, as he often does in isorhythmic passages that clearly mark talea joins (M9), or in a final diminution section (M10), and if he had further decided to adopt the discipline of not breaking words by rests (as in the hockets of M18 and M9), the texts had to be planned with monosyllables in positions which made this possible.[7] This requires a high degree of forethought and tight coordination between the disposition of the tenor, the upper voices, and the arrangement of those hockets at corresponding positions in the motet's structure, both textually and musically.[8]

---

[3] Hartt 2010b also addresses these questions.

[4] Essential, in that it underpins otherwise unsupported fourths. See Bent 1981c, update in Bent 2002, 38–46, and Bent 2008a.

[5] The lower parts of M5 are extremely problematic, with many dissonances and unsupported fourths. I would suggest emending the worst such solecism, the first colored tenor note (bar 9 and corresponding positions) from *a* to *b♭*, as it appears in **Mach C**, **Ferrell 1**, **Mach B** and **Mach E**, though in this color statement only. Although the tenor ends with a stepwise descent, it does so non-cadentially, and ahead of a final irregular cadence in the contratenor. See Boogaart 2001a, 56–72 (also 23–6), for extensive discussion of this motet, and *passim* for the extent of Machaut's quotations especially from trouvère songs. Dunstaple makes an unusual choice in his most famous motet, the four-part *Veni Sancte Spiritus/Veni Creator*, choosing a tenor excerpt that ends with a falling fifth, producing a quite exceptional cadence.

[6] See Bent 2003 and the associated music examples online. Boogaart has also pointed out the serpentine character of the tenor of M9 and the relation of the tenor to upper-part motives in M4; see Boogaart 2001a, 9–10 and 22–3.

[7] Bent 2003. See also Bent 1984, where another similarly disciplined instance is given: *Carbunculus ignitus lilie*, no. 143 in the Old Hall manuscript, **GB-OH**; reprinted in Bent 2002, 290–1.

[8] Unsignaled changes of mensuration occur in the motetus of M4, and by a different disposition within the modus in the second color of M6, whose tenor is written out only once, with repeat sign. Its concluding rest places the first breve of the second color as an 'upbeat' to the perfect modus, thus requiring different breves to be altered or not in the restatement. To a modern reader, this looks like a re-rhythmicization of the color, but it is in fact derived from homographic notation. Boogaart (2001a, 25) ingeniously construes this as overlapping telescoped taleae, removing the need to accept the fourth 'fragmentary' talea of Schrade's edition. The changes of mensuration in Rondeau 10 (*Rose lis*) are also unsignaled.

Example 15.1. *Hareu! hareu! le feu / Helas! ou sera pris confors / Obediens usque ad mortem*

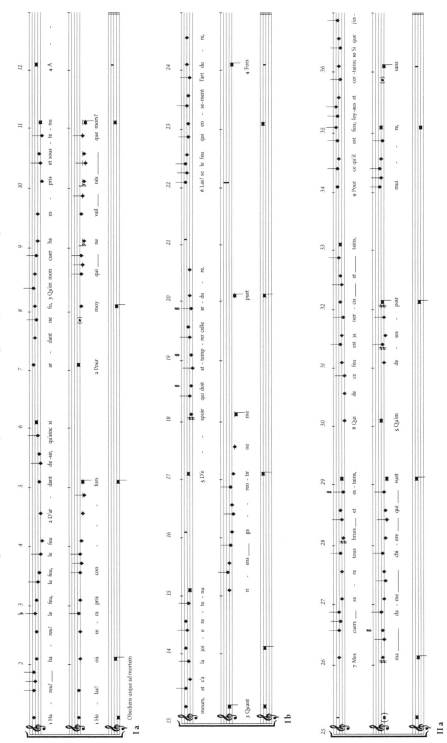

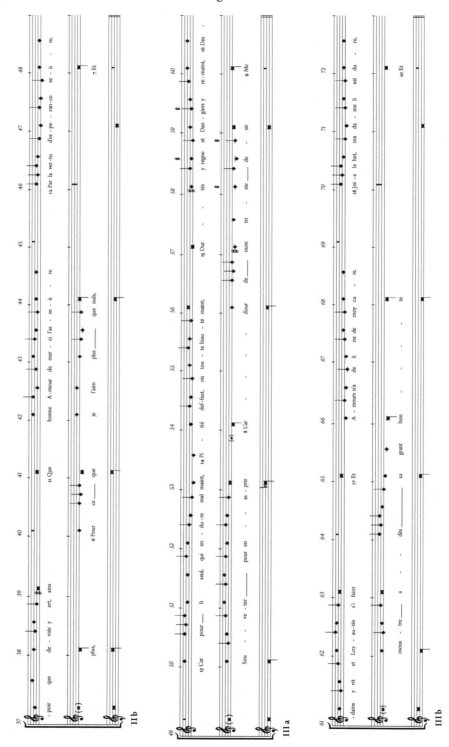

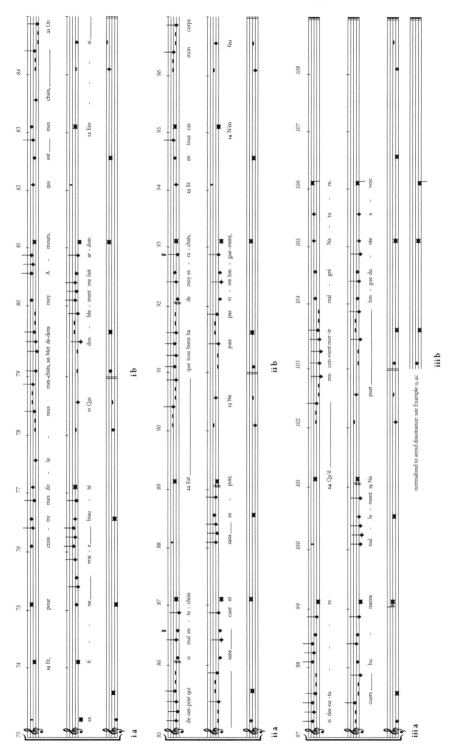

Table 15.1. M10, verses lined up with taleae

T1	1 Hareu! hareu! *le feu, le feu, le feu*	a	1 Helas! où sera pris confors	a
	2 *D'ardant desir*, qu'ainc si *ardant* ne fu,	a		
	3 Qu'en mon cuer ha espris et soustenu	a	2 Pour moy qui ne vail nès que *mors*?	a
	4 *Amours*, et s'a la joie retenu	a		
	5 *D'espoir* qui doit attemprer celle *ardure*.	b	3 Quant riens garentir ne me puet	b
	6 Las! se le *feu* qui ensement l'art dure,	b		
T2	7 Mes cuers sera tous bruis et estains,	c	4 Fors ma dame chiere qui vuet	b
	8 Qui de ce *feu* est ja nercis et tains,	c		
	9 Pour ce qu'il est fins, *loyaus* et certains;	c	5 Qu'en *desespoir muire*, sans plus,	c
	10 Si que *j'espoir* que deviés y ert, ains	c		
	11 Que bonne *Amour* de merci l'asseüre	b	6 Pour ce que je *l'aim* plus que nuls,	c
	12 Par la vertu *d'esperance* seüre.	b		
T3	13 Car pour li seul, qui endure mal maint,	d	7 Et Souvenir pour enasprir	d
	14 Pitié deffaut, où toute biauté maint;	d		
	15 Durtés y regne et Dangiers y remaint,	d	8 *L'ardour* de mon triste *desir*	d
	16 Desdains y vit et *Loyautés* s'i faint	d		
	17 Et *Amours* n'a de li ne de moy cure.	b	9 Me moustre adès sa grant bonté	e
	18 Joie le het, ma dame li est dure,	b		
t1	19 Et, pour croistre mes dolereus meschiés,	e	10 Et sa fine vraie biauté	e
	20 Met dedens moy *Amours*, qui est mes chiés,	e	11 Qui doublement me fait *ardoir*.	f
t2				
	21 Un *desespoir* qui si mal entechiés	e	12 Einsi sans cuer et *sans espoir*,	f
t3	22 Est que tous biens ha de moy esrachiés,	e	13 Ne puis pas vivre longuement,	g
	23 Et en tous cas mon corps si desnature	b	14 N'en *feu* cuers humeins nullement	g
	24 Qu'il me convient *morir* malgré Nature.	b	15 Ne puet longue durée avoir.	f

Tenor: Obediens usque ad mortem.

Italicized in the table are words associated with love, fire, burning, hope, despair, loyalty, death, desire (Amours, ardure/feu, espoir/desespoir, loyauté, mors, desir). Note how the '-oir' rhymes also highlight 'espoir' and 'desespoir' in non-rhyming positions. Brownlee (2005, 81–2) pointed out the unique triple statement of 'le feu' in tr line 1, and the emphatic repetition of 'ardant' in line 2.

Translation by Kevin Brownlee (2005, 88–9), revised incorporating suggestions from Leofranc Holford-Strevens (pers. comm., 2001) and Jacques Boogaart (pers. comm., 2016).

Triplum

Help! Help! The fire, the fire, the fire of burning desire, which has never before been so burning, which Love has in my heart ignited and maintained, and thus has taken away the joy of Hope which should temper this burning heat. Alas! if the fire which consumes it completely continues!

Then my heart will be entirely burned up and extinguished; my heart, which is already blackened and charred by this fire, because it is pure, loyal and faithful; so that I expect that it will be dead before good Love assures it of Mercy through the power of reliable Hope.

Because Pity fails only for my heart, which suffers many pains, [Pity] in whom all Beauty dwells; Harshness rules there and Refusal there remains, Disdain lives there, and Loyalty grows weak; and Love does not care for my heart or for me; Joy hates it; my Lady is harsh towards it.

And, to increase my painful sufferings, Love, who is my commander, places within me a despair which is so ill disposed that it has pillaged all my goods from me; and in every case it so de-natures my body that I must die in spite of Nature.

Motetus

Alas! where will comfort be found for me, who am worth no more than if I were dead? When nothing can protect me except my dear Lady who wants me to die in despair, nothing more, because I love her more than anyone.

And Memory – in order to stir up the burning of my sad desire – shows me continually her [=my Lady's] great goodness and her refined true beauty, which makes me burn twice as strongly.

Thus, without heart and without hope, I cannot live for long, nor can a human heart survive for long in fire.

Tenor

Obedient unto death

Machaut's chant tenors are mostly plucked from a liturgical and hence usually also a biblical context which they implicitly carry with them, all the more strongly if better known and easily identified. Ludwig identified the tenor melody of M10 as taken from the middle of the Maundy Thursday fifth-mode Gradual *Christus factus est pro nobis* **obediens usque ad mortem**, *mortem autem crucis* (Philippians 2, 8–9: 'Obedient unto death').[9] Jacques Boogaart reminds me that this chant concludes all three Tenebrae services, *mortem autem crucis* being an extension on Good Friday. He proposes, rather, an identical antiphon from the same day that is associated with the liturgical action of extinguishing the fire of the candles.[10] Death and loyalty (=obedience?) are primary ingredients of this motet, which is transcribed as Example 15.1.[11]

TENOR DISPOSITION

Machaut's tenor chant excerpts range in length from a color of ten notes (M14) to forty-eight (M23). M15 has forty notes (in a single color); M10 with thirty is close behind, but this is doubled by color repetition. Its thirty-note chant segment begins and ends on *F*, and has the rather narrow compass of a 6th up to *d*. Example 15.2 numbers the chant notes, and shows how they

---

[9] Ludwig 1926–54, 2: *60 and 3: 40 (144). Variant melodies from appropriate liturgical sources are assembled in A. Clark 1996, 194 and 244.

[10] *Christus factus est pro nobis obediens usque ad mortem*. Fer. V in Coena Domini; Fer. VI in Parasceve; Sabbato Sancto; Invent. S. Crucis; Exalt. S. Crucis. *CAO* III, nr. 1792; IV, nr. 7983, *Cantus* ID 830399. Boogaart 2001b, 242.

[11] The motet as it appears in **Mach C** is provided as Figure 8.5 in John Haines and Stefan Udell's chapter in this *Companion*. The **Ferrell 1** version is published in Earp 2014.

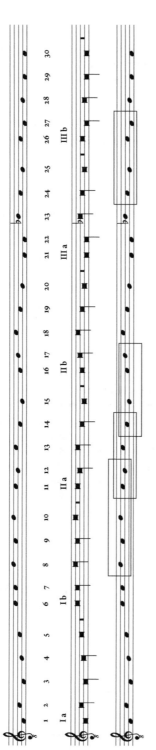

Example 15.2. The tenor of M10

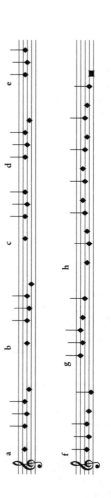

Example 15.3. Prominent motives in M10

are grouped in six rhythmically identical paired taleae or *ordines* each of five notes as Ia, Ib; IIa, IIb; IIIa, IIIb into three double (ten-note) taleae, each of which corresponds to a period of the upper parts, as laid out in Example 15.1.[12] It is surely not accidental that thirty notes from a Holy Week chant suggest the thirty pieces of silver by which Christ was betrayed 'usque ad mortem' ('even unto death').[13]

Melodically, this tenor is not as rich in symmetries as some others.[14] But segments Ia and IIIb are close to mirroring each other, and segments IIa and IIb are so nearly identical as to have caused the omission of IIb (in the first color only) by haplography in **Mach B** and **Mach E**. Each five-note talea (*ordo*) is palindromic: B L L L B, followed by a B rest. In the diminution section this becomes S B B B S. This palindromic rhythm appears with inverted values as S M M M S (Examples 15.3a and 15.3b), as a dominant rhythm in the upper parts.

In color 1, each double talea occupies 24B, in the diminution section 12B, where the same melody is written out at the next note level down. Both colores are internally isorhythmic but, because of the reduction, not with each other.[15] The second substitutes B for L, S for B, *resulting in a 2:1 reduction* ('per semi', as sometimes specified for other pieces), as counted out in the minim values of the upper parts. But although the note values often appear to be straightforwardly halved, the operation of duple and/or triple divisions at different mensural levels often makes it misleading to describe the asymmetrical *process* as a 2:1 reduction, or halving. The new values here are in fact derived by a light but unsignaled mensural transformation which changes the status of the notes. In the first color, the longs are perfect, with imperfect breves and major prolation, and they coincide with the upper-part breves. In the diminution section, the perfect longs become perfect breves, but with major semibreves (which thus do not directly mirror the corresponding imperfect breves of color 1). This also happens commonly in other fourteenth-century motets by Machaut and others, as in the diminution section of M18.[16] The now-perfect breves of the accelerated tenor undercut the clear duple tempus of the continuing imperfect breves in the upper parts, setting up an audible tension. The upper parts are in imperfect modus (i.e. with imperfect longs), while the first color of the tenor is in perfect modus, syncopated: the opening breve is not an upbeat but a 'downbeat' syncopating agent, made up to a perfection with the breve and breve rest that end each short talea.

[12] This is what Reichert (1956, 202) called a 'Großtalea'. Boogaart (2001b, 107) has referred to it as a 'super-talea', a term now adopted by Zayaruznaya (2015a, 81). I prefer either to give this the more precise designation of a double talea, or to refer to the smaller grouped taleae as *ordines*. In M10, each pair corresponds to a period of the upper parts. This also happens in M8, which has three short (4-note) *ordines* in the time of one upper-voice talea, and five of these short taleae per color.

[13] Although M10 is not about deceit it is certainly about what leads to death. M15 however is about deceit; I suggested that its 30-breve taleae might also have resonances of Judas's betrayal; see Bent 1991, 15. See also Arlt 1986.

[14] As demonstrated in Bent 2003.

[15] I advocate a more precise use of the term in Bent 2008b.

[16] Up to a point, the diminution in M10 fits the brief prescription of Muris in the *Libellus*: 'Tertio nota, quod quando tenor est de modo perfecto et tempore imperfecto, diminutio etiam fit directe per medium, sicut pro longa valente tres breves ponitur brevis valens tres semibreves'. ('Third, note that when the tenor is in perfect modus and imperfect tempus, diminution is also made by halving directly, so that for a long worth three breves is placed a breve worth three semibreves'.) Berktold 1999, 76–7. Although Muris has allowed for substitution at all levels (including minim for semibreve), he does not address the fact that in cases such as this the same relationships of twos and threes do not apply obliquely at the next level down (prolation); see Bent 2009, 207–8.

Machaut plays with the mensural status of this opening: the opening melody and rhythm of the triplum (Example 15.3a, *c′c′b′c′a′*) are echoed at the beginning of double-taleae two and three (respectively a step lower, Example 15.3b, *b′b′a′b′g* at B26 and at the opening pitch at B50), but they are delayed by a breve, emphatically recapitulating the opening motive over the first tenor long rather than the initial breve that syncopates it, creating a playful ambiguity as to where the talea starts, and whether that breve might after all be an upbeat. Thus, short passages of upper-voice isorhythm even where present are not always aligned.[17] The first full statement of the opening triplum motive is followed by the second in displaced isorhythm (B26), which in turn is in aligned identity (pitch and rhythm) with the third (B50). An expectation is set up at the beginning, and then the same rhythm, also with similar melody, signals the beginnings of the new taleae, but a breve later. As here, oblique or displaced rhythmic correspondences create subtle asymmetries; this displacement pretends to challenge the modus status of the tenor notes by making the status of the first note ambiguous (as to whether it is an upbeat to the perfect-modus tenor or a syncopating agent). Such passages are far from simplistic views of isorhythm that applaud mechanical and regular repetition as if they embodied the mature perfection of the motet.[18]

MOTIVES DERIVED FROM THE TENOR
INTEGRATED INTO UPPER VOICES

The extent to which the tenor generates the melodic material of the upper parts varies between different motets; but this little-explored use of tenor material, in addition to the tenor's well-known symbolic and structural contributions, provides a musical counterpart to the perhaps more obvious semantic textual relationship between tenor and upper parts, weaving the sacred melody into the non-liturgical musical fabric in parallel to the simultaneous presentation of related sacred and secular texts.[19]

There is a textual relationship between the 'death' and 'obedience' of the tenor ('Obediens usque ad mortem') and the upper parts (see Table 15.1), notably in 'mortem': 'mors'–'muire'–'morir', and 'obediens': 'loyaus'–'Loyautés', though such relationships are perhaps less abundant in M10 than in some other motets (for instance, M7, M9, M15). Musically, however, the chosen but pre-existent pitches of the tenor and its compositionally determined rhythms are pervasive in the upper parts of M10.

I have mentioned the derivation from the tenor of the palindromic rhythm S MMM S (Example 15.3a), the opening triplum motive. Its frequent occurrences are always prominently placed, at significant points on *c′*, nearly always with the same melodic shape, a falling third at the end. The motive is sometimes shortened to the complementary forms S MMM (Example 15.3c) or MMM S (Example 15.3d), but in all cases the three minims (which occur twenty-four times) always have the same shape (Example 15.3e).[20] These are derived (see the boxes in Example 15.2) from tenor notes 11–14 *cbca*, 24–7 *aGaF*, descending a third; tenor notes 8–11 *dcdc*, descending a step. Tenor

---

[17] A similar displacement occurs in M17, where a brief long-note isorhythmic passage in the motetus anticipates the subsequent talea joins by a breve.

[18] A similar displacement occurs in M7, where three tenor taleae are imposed on two colores both in the first and the diminution sections. The second and third taleae in the first section are isorhythmically displaced by a breve from the opening statement, as in M10.

[19] I have demonstrated instances in M9 in Bent 2003 and in the **Fauv** motets *Tribum/Quoniam* and *Aman/Heu* in Bent 1997, and Bent and Brownlee, forthcoming.

[20] These motives are also set out by Boogaart 2001b, 682.

notes 14–17, *aGab*, rising at the end, recur in tr B$_{79}$, B$_{85}$, B$_{103}$, mo B$_{88}$. The first box covers a fifth note: see Example 15.3g (and 15.3f, transposed).

The three minims of these figures mostly take a single syllable in color 1, except where they mark the double-talea joins with syllabic setting at B$_{22}$, B$_{46}$, B$_{70}$; in color 2, due to the more condensed text setting, more of these minims are syllabic. The duple-time alternations of the complementary rhythms (Examples 15.3c and 15.3d: S MMM and MMM S), subsets of the larger group, coincide with imperfect breve groups throughout. The consequences of this for the perfect breve groups of the second color were noted above.

Most of these melodic motives also occur with the rhythm S M S M. Melodic derivation from the chant is ubiquitous, though some characteristic intervals in the chant are not used, notably the rising fourth *F-b*$^\flat$ (unless one counts the rising fourth *c-f* in mo B$_5$–B$_7$).[21] However, the motetus descent to its lowest notes in B$_7$–B$_{11}$ emphasizes the progression *f b*$^\flat$ *a*, and although with a descending fifth – *F* is heard in the tenor at this point – strongly recalls the *F b*$^\flat$ *a* of the tenor notes 22–4.

The motive C DCD occurs both in the tenor (notes 7–10) and very conspicuously in the triplum at B$_{35}$ around the middle of the first section. The first imitative appearance of MMM S M appears in the motetus on *a'* and, imitating it, in the triplum on *d'*, B$_{34}$–B$_{35}$: Examples 15.3f and 15.3g. This figure is indeed a Machaut cliché, in rhythm and melodic shape, but what singles it out in this motet are its particular placements and derivation from the tenor pitches: see the first boxed group in Example 15.2. The tenor notes 8–10, *dcd*, give the same minim figure at mo B$_8$, tr B$_{35}$ (as *d'c'd'*), mo B$_{100}$, notes 11–13, *cbc* (*a*), at tr B$_1$, B$_{22}$, B$_{50}$, B$_{80}$, B$_{97}$, B$_{98}$ (each beginning on *c'*), notes 24–6, *aGa* (*F*), at mo B$_{34}$, tr B$_{46}$, mo B$_{64}$, tr B$_{70}$, mo B$_{76}$, tr B$_{91}$ (each beginning on *a'*). The figure also occurs on *ede* (mo B$_3$, B$_{40}$, tr B$_{103}$), *b'a'b'* (tr B$_{26}$), *gfg* (tr B$_{79}$, mo B$_{80}$, tr B$_{85}$, mo B$_{88}$), and in other rhythms.

The tenor-note progression *cbc* or *aGa* followed by a falling third is a frequent feature of the upper parts: see mo B$_{64}$, tr B$_{70}$, and elsewhere, transposed to *d'c'd'b'* at tr B$_{35}$. *cbca* as MMM S (Example 15.3d) appears somewhere in each talea, nearly always at the beginning:

C$_1$:   T$_1$ tr B$_1$ as *c'b'c'a'*
            T$_2$ in tenor (and transposed to *b'a'b'g* in tr B$_{26}$)
            T$_3$ tr B$_{50}$ (against 'Souvenir' in mo B$_{50}$)
C$_2$:   t$_1$ tr delayed to B$_{80}$ (density area)
            t$_2$ in tenor
            t$_3$ tr B$_{97}$–B$_{98}$ (twice with 'desnature', the first time curtailed to MMM M)

It also occurs at tr B$_{14}$ and B$_{76}$ as S M S M. Given the motet's emphasis on death, and the prominent placing of this motive, might we also hear CBCA as an allusion to the *Dies irae*?

D is the highest note of both the triplum and the tenor, at their respective octaves. B$_{35}$ is the first of only two triplum occurrences of this peak note (on 'fins, loyaus', on the minim figure *d'c'd'*, giving emphasis to loyalty = obedience?) while the motetus at the same place has 'muire', thus linking the death and loyalty of the tenor's 'Obediens usque ad mortem'.

The other appearance of the triplum's top note *d'* is at B$_{62}$, also on 'Loyautés'. These two passages are also the only occurrences in the first section of the group MMM S M (Examples 15.3f and 15.3g) outside the talea-ends, creating particular emphasis. 'Mors' coincides with the only occurrences of the lowest note of the motetus (B$_{10}$–B$_{11}$). Thus the extremes of range correspond

---

21   Boogaart (2001b, 683) sets out the derivation of triplum motives based on the outlined descending fourth of tenor notes 13–15, 18–20.

to key concepts in the tenor (loyalty is high, death is low) and are emphasized in the upper-part texts; 'Obediens usque ad mortem' literally runs the gamut.

Voice crossing is not as important a strategy here as it is in some other motets,[22] though the extremes of range are cultivated especially within the motetus, which goes below the tenor at B18 ('nothing can heal me'); it rises briefly above the triplum at B30, and more significantly at B51 for 'souvenir' ('memory'), hitting its own highest note, the triplum pitch c' which it recalls with the same motive – a souvenir.

The tenor notes 3–6 *FGac* occur up an octave in tr B5–B7 and at B79–B80, the motet's principal density point. Subsets occur as *ga'c'* in tr B13–B14, B42–B43, as the third *a'c'* in tr B33–B34 and B37, and the rising third emphatically in all three voices (*Fa, ce, a'c'*) at the start of the second color B73–B75.

What I have just called the main density point (B79–B81), three-quarters of the way through the motet, is marked by the first minim hockets (from tr B78), the coincidence of tr 'Amours' with mo 'ardoir' ('love' and 'burning'), on the highest tenor note, *d*, a direct verbal and musical cross-citation with M15 ('meschiés': see below), and mo 'doublement' ('doubly') marking the only place in the motet where the three-minim figure is heard twice in immediate succession within the same breve (B80 in mo, then tr).

The tenor also contains the sequence of notes *abcaGF* (notes 16–21 in Example 15.2), which from mo B50 is shadowed in ornamented form: *a'ga'b'* | *c'b'c'b'* | *a'b'a'g* | *f* (Example 15.3h) simultaneously with the triplum repeat of the opening (i.e. a 'souvenir'). Here at B50 the motetus rises for the only time to the high *c'* that is next-but-one the triplum's highest note. The prominent *abc* motive (tenor notes 16–18) is picked up in the tr ending *a'a'b'b'c'* (B104–B106).

The tenor chant segment ends with a repeated *F* (tenor notes 29–30, but also 21–2, and on *c* notes 6–7); this is reflected in the repeated semibreve spondees at **B1** (mo), tr B9, B20, *B24*, mo B42, tr B44, *B48*, **B68**, *B72*. There are fewer in the second color, except, conspicuously, at tr B104 and in both parts at B105 (bold = on *f*). These include the ends of each of the first three taleae (their breve numbers are italicized).

The triplum at each of the three double-talea ends in the first color contains both verbal rhyme ('-ure', twice each, lines 5–6, 11–12, 17–18; see Table 15.1) and exact and aligned musical isorhythm (B14–B24, B38–B48, B62–B72). These serve as clear markers of the talea ends. The motetus is less consistently isorhythmic here, but mo B17–B23 and B65–B71, the ends of double-taleae one and three, have the same notes and rhythms.[23] In some motets (notably M9) the talea endings are signaled by hockets: that happens here (but less insistently) in the diminution section. But in the first color's three double taleae the structure defined by the tenor is highlighted by this textual and musical rhyme in the upper parts. All six of the '-ure' feminine rhymes (the only feminine rhyme in both texts) from the first three stanzas are set to repeated-note semibreve spondees, which makes the setting of the final '-ure' couplet all the more striking: 'desnature' is broken ('dena-tured') by rests, and the final cadence on 'malgré Nature' places the feminine syllable on the final long.[24] While there is strict aligned isorhythm only in the triplum at the end of each of the first

[22] Notably Bent 2003, 382–5. Anna Zayaruznaya has developed this idea, especially in Zayaruznaya 2009.

[23] Sanders (1973) demonstrated the counting of periodicity in upper parts between rests. Such periods sometimes conform to a set of numbers different from the recurring periods themselves, but they are far from being the only criterion of tidy structure.

[24] Earp (2005, 114–15 and Example 9.11) reports the striking treatment of feminine rhymes in M10.

three double taleae, there are many shorter rhythmic correspondences, sometimes between two but not all three double taleae, or not in both parts, and there are several lateral displacements.

UPPER-VOICE RHYTHM

The twentieth-century term isorhythm has shifted application in the course of the last century and is now commonly but improperly used to cover identity in both pitch and rhythm, and diminished or mensurally transformed iterations that are therefore not 'the same', 'iso-'. We do less than justice to the music by applying 'isorhythm' as a monolithic straitjacket rather than being open to composers' inventiveness at drawing on a wide range of techniques to arouse our expectations and to satisfy or side-step them. Repetition is a fundamental, perhaps the most fundamental, musical form-building device. But fourteenth-century composers often chose to exercise subtlety and *varietas* by avoiding exact and regular repetitions. In motets, as elsewhere, it behooves us to celebrate diversity of structures and strategies – with and without isorhythm – rather than attempting to force conformity on them.

A full statement of the rhythm of the opening phrase (S MMM | S SM | SM SM) occurs at tr B_1–B_3, B_{26}–B_{28}, mo B_8–B_{10}, tr B_{50}–B_{52}; it occurs partially at mo B_3–B_4, B_{56}–B_{58}, tr B_{80}; of these, tr B_1, B_{50}, and B_{80} are at the opening pitch on c'. Smaller fragments of this imitated motive (Example 15.3c, S MMM) are at mo B_{40}, B_{56}, and in the echo of the opening at pitch at tr B_{80}. After B_{80} we no longer hear this rhythm in its full form, but its complement Example 15.3d, MMM S (already heard at B_{34}, B_{35}, B_{64}, B_{70}, B_{76}), and in tr B_{80} the last statement on c' of S MMM.

Just as the upper-part melodic material is disciplined, with significant derivations from the chant tenor, so too is the rhythmic vocabulary. Each Machaut motet sets up its own vocabulary of rhythmic norms, exercising restraint even within a palette that is already quite restricted. A motet might, for example, use trochaic rhythms almost exclusively, with one or two isolated iambs at significant points, such as the pointed iambics that anticipate the talea joins in M14 and M15, or it might make a feature of iambic rhythms so that departures from them become significant, as in Vitry's *Petre clemens*. The norms thus set up may then be observed, frustrated, or played with, reserving some rhythmic formulas for special effect or verbal or structural emphasis.[25]

ENDINGS

Only three of Machaut's motets end with $^{10}_{6} \overset{\rightarrow}{\to} {}^{12}_{8}$ cadences on F (Example 15.4a): M4, M10, and M15. There are many points of verbal and musical interrelationship between these three motets, and indeed between each of them and other motets. In this case, all three of their final cadences are anomalous. In M4 and M10, taken literally, the tenor does not arrive with the upper parts; in M15, it is the triplum that cadences later, with what we would call an appoggiatura.

The endings of M4 and M10 have been adjusted in the editions of Ludwig and Schrade so that the parts cadence together. This involves adjustment of the penultimate notated tenor value, although the diminutions are in both cases written out in the manuscripts without adjustment. M15 however is transcribed (by Ludwig, followed as usual by Schrade) with its concluding triplum appoggiatura – perhaps because a delayed upper-voice resolution sounds less offensive to our ears (more like the end of the Bach *St Matthew Passion*) than does a lower-voice dissonance (Example 15.4d). The problem of these endings remains unresolved, and has hitherto been largely swept

---

[25] This has not been much noted, but see as demonstrated in Bent 2003, 384–5 and Table 5.

Example 15.4. Final cadences of M4, M10, and M15

under the carpet. I suggested a possible emendation for the end of M15,[26] but if it is judged that its appoggiatura should stand, what is the status of others that have been regularized by both editors? Are we to take the ending of M10 literally? To allow the tenor its full notated span would require extension of the upper parts from 107 to 108 breves, making their final long perfect (possible, and yielding a nice total number), but not otherwise signaled; but more seriously, a dissonant delay in the tenor's arrival on the cadence to join the upper parts (Example 15.4c).[27] Singers, on balance, would probably have decided to arrive together, by delaying the upper parts' cadence by a semibreve, or by shortening the penultimate tenor breve, and cheating the tenor of its final semibreve and semibreve rest. It could be claimed that the diminution had simply been written out mechanically, without necessary adjustment of the ending. Ludwig simply states that the final talea should be truncated, and he may be right.[28] In favor of a dissonant ending for M10 we could invoke the textual encouragement of 'desnature' (tr B97), 'Ne puet longue durée avoir' (mo B101–B106) and 'malgré Nature' (tr B104–B106). Example 15.1 gives the dissonant version, which follows the manuscripts and the isorhythm, with the safer option of a simultaneous ending on a small stave beneath.

There is disagreement between the manuscripts at a similar crux at the end of M4 (Example 15.4b), where for the penultimate note two sources (**Ferrell 1, Mach G**) follow the diminution strictly with a long, making the tenor cadence after the upper parts, while in two others (**Mach A, Mach E**) this has been shortened to a breve, perhaps in a failed attempt to normalize the cadence, but it only succeeds in making the tenor cadence ahead of the upper parts. Neither version produces simultaneity, but a contemporary editorial attempt to do so may encourage the safer option of simultaneous arrival, both here and in M10. Taken in isolation, any of these would seem to be a self-evident case for adjustment, to avoid serious musical anomaly. But given that this problem exists in more than one motet, there is a danger of making too easy a leap to normalization.[29]

TEXT DISTRIBUTION

Machaut's motets show a full spectrum from even spacing of the text throughout the motet, or of stanza-talea correspondence (for example, the triplum of M9), to regular but spectacularly uneven spacing (as in the motetus of M9).[30] Such spacing is often purposefully contrived to bring about verbal coincidences, such as, here, tr 'Amour' with mo 'aim' in B42, tr 'Amours' and mo 'ardoir' in B80–B81, or in order to make a word like 'souvenir' in the motetus punningly coincide with a pitch repetition at triplum B50.

The 24 ten-syllable lines of the triplum fall into four six-line stanzas with rhymes aaaabb ccccbb ddddbb eeeebb (Table 15.1); the recurrent b-rhyme is '-ure', and no rhyme syllables are shared between triplum and motetus. One six-line stanza is allocated to each of the first three double taleae, the final stanza to the entire diminution section; in other words, the last three double taleae have just two lines each, an uneven distribution. The 15 eight-syllable lines of the motetus fall into

---

[26] In Bent 1991, 19.

[27] Boogaart (2001a, 54–5) and Hartt (2010b, 67–70) also address the noncoincident final cadence of M10.

[28] Ludwig 1926–54, 3: 40 (144).

[29] In M17 the tenor's L rest before the final cadential progression has to be shortened (unsignaled) to a breve rest; no other solution is possible here, so the need to adjust in that motet may encourage similar adjustments in the others.

[30] Reichert (1956) has explored this aspect in some detail for other motets.

seven rhymed couplets, plus a final line. Three lines are allocated to each of the first three double taleae, two each for the last three. This cuts across the rhyming couplets by placing three lines for each of the undiminished double taleae, in a way directly analogous to a three-on-two talea-color relationship (as in M9 and M4), or as here, the three-beat perfect breves of the diminished tenor set against the two-beat imperfect breves of the upper parts.

Thus the distribution of the text between the two color statements in the triplum is 18:6 (3:1), and in the motetus 9:6 (3:2). For each of the first three double taleae the tr-mo distribution is six lines to three, i.e. 2:1, but for the last three double taleae, two lines each, i.e. equal text distribution in both parts. The second color includes some minim hocketing, which does not exploit this equal texting between the parts; upper-part isorhythm is maintained for only a few breves including this hocket.[31] Machaut here does not embrace the discipline of syllabic hockets without breaking words. The final 'odd' line of the motetus repeats the penultimate rhyme '-oir' (of the couplet lines 11–12), integrating the last three couplets with a rhyme-scheme of their own (abbccb) which coincides with the second color. The ratio of lines between tr and mo is 24:15 = 8:5, and the ratio of syllables 240:120, 2:1 (24×10:15×8), one of few cases in Machaut of such a neat proportion.[32]

RELATION TO OTHER MOTETS

Vitry's *Douce/Garison* has a strong literary connection to M10, and indeed may have been a model for it. This was demonstrated in a detailed comparison by Boogaart.[33] But apart from a few three-minim groups, some syllabic, there is little obvious musical connection between the two motets. Boogaart also pointed out M10's strong tie with M4, 'inspired by Thibaut's *Tout autresi*', and with M1.[34] Thomas Brown remarked that the triplum text of M10 also alludes to a few verses around the midpoint of the *Roman de la Rose*, with significance for its place in the ordering of the motets.[35]

The strongest links, however, are to M15. 'Amour' is of course not an uncommon word in these motets, but the way in which it is recapitulated, with a musical allusion and a direct verbal cross-reference, suffices to establish a deliberate connection between M10 and M15. 'Amours', the first word of M15, recurs in line 24 of its triplum. It is the opening subject of M10, though the word appears there first in triplum line 4, and thereafter once in each of the four stanzas. In both motets it is placed between 'meschiés' and 'mes chiés' ('misfortunes' and 'my lord'), recapitulated at the center of a pun on 'meschiés':

---

[31] The equality of text between the upper parts is not exploited as fully for hockets here as in some other motets, such as Vitry's *Vos/Gratissima*.

[32] See the 240+120 syllables of *Apollinis*, discussed throughout Howlett 2005.

[33] Boogaart (2001a, 51–2) kindly noted that I had pointed out this connection in an earlier conference paper. Also, 'Je respons' occurs at the junction to *Douce/Garison*'s second color which, like those of Vitry's motets *Vos/Gratissima* and *Firmissime/Adesto*, is newly rhythmicized, not a diminution or homographic transformation of the first. Boogaart (2001a, 56–72) discusses the relation of Vitry's tenor to Machaut's M5.

[34] Boogaart 2001a, 52, 55, and Boogaart 1993, 28–30.

[35] T. Brown 2001. M4 also has a strong link to M9 because the shorter tenor of M9 (*Fera pessima*, an evil beast) is in fact identical with notes 3–14 of the eighteen tenor notes of M4 (*Speravi*, I hoped), although drawn from within different chants; both are serpentine and completely conjunct, with a range of only a fourth and, despite their very different textual significance, afford considerable comparative interest for Machaut's use of the same melodic material.

M15, lines 23–5:

> Mais aveuc tous ces *meschiés*
> Sueffre *Amours qui est mes chiés* |
> Que Raison, Droiture, …

But with all these misfortunes, Love who is my lord allows Reason (=ratio), Equity, Sweetness, Good Nature, Openness, Grace and Pity (a list of seven good things) to have no power against cruelty.

M10, lines 19–20:

> Et, pour croistre mes dolereus *meschiés*,
> Met dedens moy *Amours, qui est mes chiés*,
> Un *desespoir* …

And, to increase my painful sufferings, Love, who is my commander, places within me a despair …

Immediately striking is the musical setting in M10 of this 'Amours' (at B80) to the same phrase, a third higher, that 'Amours' receives at the beginning of M15 (Example 15.5). No other Machaut motet besides these two starts with this rhythm, let alone with a similar melodic shape, except M9.[36] This motive (M10, B80) refers back to its own full exposition at the beginning of M10, and to its full recapitulation at B50. As we saw above, there are several further repetitions at other pitches that are just rhythmic, or partial, but only these three (B1, B50, and B80) are on *c′*. None is on *a′*, the opening pitch of M15, though the M10 tenor contains the phrase *aGaF* at notes 24–7.[37]

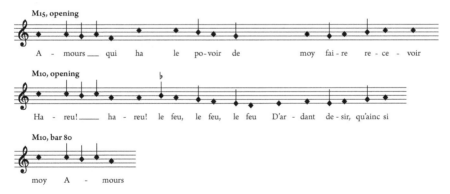

Example 15.5. Openings of M15 and M10, and the 'Amours' motive

Recall that this motive, S MMM S (Example 15.3a), is always prominently placed and usually falls a third. We might identify it as standing for 'Amours'. The other motive, complementary and of secondary prominence, places the three minims in the rhythmically inverse position, MMM S M (Examples 15.3f and 15.3g), sometimes shortened in the color-2 hockets to MMM M. Its first two occurrences are for the words 'Las' (tr B22) and 'muire' (mo B34, echoed immediately by tr B35), its last on 'me convient morir' (tr B103); it might therefore be considered to have at least

---

[36] See Bent 2003, 386, Example 11.

[37] M15's melodic material is less closely related to its tenor than some, but it does several times have the tenor's *aGa*.

some rhetorical association with trouble and death. Its first statement, in the triplum on 'Las', is at the pitch of the opening 'Amours' motive ($c'b'c'$), where it coincides in B1 with the 'las' of the motetus's opening word 'Helas'. In addition, another significantly placed word linkage between the two motets connects 'Helas', the opening word of the M10 motetus, and the middle words 'Et' and 'las' of both M15 texts: in M15 the middle words of the triplum ('Et', 84th of 168) and motetus ('Las', 31st of 62) respectively are hooked together and exposed so that one hears 'Et las' precisely straddling the midpoint of the music (the 60th breve of 120). Again, love tends to be higher in pitch than death.

The 'amour' words in the first two stanzas are linked thematically in the first two double taleae (at B13 and B42), with the phrase $c'c'g\,a'$ (over tenor c and with a unison on g). The triplum's second-stanza 'Amours' coincides with the only 'amour' word in the motetus, 'je l'aim' at B42. The third stanza's 'Amours' at B66 coincides with 'grant bonté' in the motetus, which is set in long notes to an exact repetition (pitches and rhythms) of what the motetus had at this point in talea 1. The fourth stanza's 'Amours' (B80), as we have seen, alludes to the opening, at pitch, has verbal identity with M15, and presents the 'Amours' motive that opens M15. An example of deceptive musical non-repetition in M15 occurs, appropriately, with *Faux Samblant*, the opening words of the motetus in M15, where at the final talea (B91) triplum and motetus usurpingly change places as did Jacob (the subject of the tenor), false-seemingly, with Esau.[38]

Both M15 and M10 are centrally concerned with love and death. The first triplum line of M15 tells of 'love who has the power to make me receive joy or death'. The first-person emphasis is confirmed by placing 'moi' as the middle word of its motetus. M10 laments the fiery burning, 'Ardour', of love, 'Amours' (note the assonant punning), which leads to death, 'mors'. 'Mors', as noted above, is set to a long on the only appearance of the motetus's lowest note, a, which ends its rhythmic echo of the full statement of the triplum's opening 'death' motive. To be plunged down into this death can be seen quite literally as the consequence of the 'Amours' (B12) that enters in punning juxtaposition at the octave above the sustained 'mors' (B11), whose low a is heard in unison with a tenor a – *Obediens usque ad mortem*.

A further complex of puns is exercised on 'Ardour' and 'dure', parallel to 'Amours' and 'mors'. In M15, 'Ardure' ends both the first half of the triplum text and the first half of the music. The '-ure' rhyme that, alone, runs through the whole triplum of M15's irregular scheme of 2×19 lines is also used as the closing couplet of each triplum stanza in M10. Both rhymes are extremely prominent in their tripla, and made even more so by exposed spondaic cadences in their musical settings.

These examples augment an increasing collection of punning words of division, measurement or proportion occurring at significant structural points, such as 'beyond measure', 'longue durée' etc. Such words in other motets include 'medio', 'meta', 'iterum', 'similis', 'bis', 'rursus', as well as cutting or 'hard' words (here 'dure', punning on 'talea' = 'taille'): 'bis acuto gladio', 'incidere', 'vulnere' ('twice-sharp sword', 'cut', 'wound'). Words signifying repetition such as, here, 'souvenir' and 'doublement' are also often found at talea or color repetitions (see, too, M4) as markers of actual verbal and musical recapitulations. In this case, 'doublement' also comes soon after the color's doubling of time (mo B79–B80).

I have drawn attention to 'word painting' and intertextuality of a kind little noticed in this repertory; it is often richer and subtler than the more obvious madrigalisms to which we are accustomed from later music, and at least as pervasive. Because both the music and texts of motets are self-consciously structured in counted or proportioned ways, they offer opportunities to mark

---

[38] Bent 1991, 23. See that article for further observations on symbolic and text-music relationships in M15.

structural points by making them coincide musically with appropriate words or puns that Machaut has placed with equal deliberation in the texts. We have seen how the musical material of the tenor can permeate the upper parts just as their textual material determines the choice and disposition of the tenor color, and invites an intricate web of musical and textual conjunctions. Text-music relations in fourteenth-century motets have not been favorably received, largely because of the presumed incomprehensibility of simultaneously enunciated texts, which has earned motets a bad press. But this is not the only genre which benefits from, and indeed invites, preparation and study. It is time to rethink that prejudice in the light of these connections, freed from the assumption that these pieces were designed for instant comprehension by an unprepared passive audience or, now, that motets are best heard in succession on a CD or playlist rather than being studied individually through repeated hearing or performance. Above all, these connections demonstrate (in this case as in others) that motet composition of this sophistication involves very complex planning and interaction between textual and musical components, a very different picture from the idea of a rigid isorhythmic blueprint by which the maturity of a motet is judged according to how closely it conforms. The intricacies of these compositions demand reflection and attention outside an unprepared hearing.

16

A Motet Conceived in Troubled Times:

Machaut's Motet 22

Sarah Fuller

MACHAUT'S FOUR-VOICE MOTET *Tu qui gregem/Plange regni respublica/Apprehende arma et scutum/Contratenor*, positioned twenty-second within the series of motets preserved in the late manuscript collections of his oeuvre, begins poignantly with the single word 'Plange' ('Weep') uttered at length (nine breves) by the motetus voice alone, followed by the words 'regni respublica'; see Example 16.1. It is the French kingdom's body politic (to which Machaut's original listeners belong) that is commanded to weep. On the last syllable of 'regni', the triplum enters with the pronoun 'Tu', the intimate 'you'. Only after the tenor and contratenor have entered is the referent of 'Tu' revealed – it is the person who leads the flock, that weeping body politic, the person who, as the text then reveals, has so far failed as an effective leader. The opening words of the two poems announce the complementary relationship between them, as may be seen in the texts with their translation that appear on the next page.[1] The triplum text exhorts an unnamed person in authority to step up and lead effectively, while the motetus text expresses the suffering and hope for relief of the French people who urgently need a protective, caring, and effective leader. The acute problem of leadership is hammered home rhetorically by the triplum's intensive repetition of 'dux' ('leader'), 'ducere' ('to lead') and their cognates – twenty times in as many poetic lines. The texts directly voice the concerns of those who would have heard this motet when it was first performed in Reims circa 1358–9.[2]

---

[1] Texts from Robertson 2002, 328–9. Translation adapted by S. Fuller. Italics in the Latin poems indicate recurring passages of unsettled hocket rhythms (triplum) or syncopation (motetus) in the musical setting. The tenor comes from the Responsory *Posuit coronam capiti meo* from the Common of One Martyr, whose text can be traced to Psalm 34, verse 2.

[2] For editions of M22 see Ludwig 1926–54, 3: 79–81; Schrade 1956c, 3: 22–5; Kühn 1983, 2: 11–16; Leech-Wilkinson 1989, 2: 71–3. A new edition of the Machaut motets appears in the series *Guillaume de Machaut: The Complete Poetry and Music*; see Boogaart et al. 2018. Recent recordings include Ensemble Gilles Binchois 1998, *Guillaume de Machaut Le Jugement du Roi de Navarre*, Cantus, C9626; The Clerks' Group 1999, *Guillaume de Machaut: Motets and Music from the Ivrea Codex*, Signum, SIGCD011; Ensemble Musica Nova 2002, *Machaut Les motets*, Zig-Zag Territoires, ZZT 021002.2, 2 CDs; The Hilliard Ensemble 2004, *Guillaume de Machaut Motets*, ECM New Series, ECM 1823; and Graindelavoix 2016, *Guillaume de Machaut: Messe de Nostre Dame*, Note 1 music, GCD P32110. Texts and translations are provided in the CD booklets, and may be found also in Robertson 2002, 328–9, Markstrom 1989, 38–9, and Kühn 1983, 1: 32 (German translation).

Triplum

Tu qui gregem tuum ducis,
Opera fac veri ducis,
Nam ducere *et non duci*,
Hoc competit vero *duci*.

Dux prudentium consilio
Ducat nec sit in octio
Debetque dux anteire,
Ductus autem *obedire*.

Sed si ductor *nescit iter*
Ambo pereunt leviter.
Nam ambulat absque luce
Qui ducitur ceco duce.

Sed qui habet *verum ducem*
Omni hora *habet lucem*
Et ille bene ducitur
Qui a nullo seducitur.

Unde qui ducum ductor es,
Contere nunc seductores
Et taliter nos deducas
Ut *ad pacem nos perducas*.

Motetus

Plange, regni respublica.
Tua gens ut scismatica
Desolatur
Nam *pars ejus est iniqua*
Et altera *sophistica*
Reputatur.

De te modo non curatur
Inimicis lo*cus datur*
*Fraudu*lenter,
Tu*i status deturpatur*
Sua virtus augmentatur
Nunc patenter.

Te *rexerunt imprudenter*,
Licet forte in*nocenter*
Tui cari.
Sed amodo congaudenter
Te facient et *potenter*
Deo dante dominari.

Tenor

Apprehende arma et scutum et exurge.

You who lead your flock,
do the deeds of a true leader,
for to lead and not to be led,
this constitutes a true leader.

Let the leader, counseled by judicious men,
lead, and not be passive.
For a leader should go before,
and those led should obey.

But if the leader does not know the way,
they both easily perish,
for he who is led by a blind leader
walks deprived of light.

But he who has a true leader
has light at every moment.
And he is well led
whom no one leads astray.

Wherefore, you who are leader of leaders
destroy now those who mislead,
and lead us in such a way
that you bring us peace.

Weep, body politic of the kingdom.
Your people, as though apostates,
are forsaken,
for some of them are wicked
and others are considered
duplicitous.

No one looks after you now;
positions are given to enemies
fraudulently.
Your standing is ruined;
their power now increases
openly.

They have guided you imprudently,
although perhaps innocently,
those dear to you.
But presently, they will,
God granting, make you prevail
joyfully and powerfully.

Take up arms and shield and rise up.

The lengthy motetus-triplum passage before the lower voices enter communicates the anxious tone of the Latin poems through calculated pitch and intervallic choices (Example 16.1).[3] The first phrase of the motetus starts on a strong, stable *f* but closes a half-step lower, on a protracted unstable *e*, on the last syllable of 'Plange'. The answering phrase returns to the *f*, but falls a dissonant tritone to an extended ♮ on the last syllable of 'regni'.[4] The following segment returns via *c* to *e* and reinstates the unstable ♮ before the motetus melody resolves to *c* on the last syllable of 'respublica' at the very moment the two lower voices enter, creating a stable, perfect *F-c-c-f* sonority. Not only do the outlines of the motetus phrases shift between stable and unstable pitches, but the intervals within the motetus-triplum duet also convey musical instability that chimes with the texts. The principal interval between them is a third, an imperfect interval that in the fourteenth century was heard as inherently unstable. The intervallic instability is enhanced on L7 when the triplum introduces an inflected *c♯* that audibly clashes with the preceding *c♮* in the motetus.[5] It is furthered by the perfect fourth beginning L8, an interval categorized as a dissonance, whose introduction by leap in the motetus is quite unexpected.[6] The unstable ♮-*d* third at the end of L8 finally resolves on the next long with the entry of the lower voices. The motetus moves conventionally to *c*. But the triplum, rather than meeting the motetus in a unison (the standard resolution of their minor third, according to contemporary *contrapunctus* treatises), leaps to an *f*. The contratenor entry on *c* at that moment might be understood as supplying the proper resolution of the triplum *d*. In any event, the first four-voice sonority, *F-c-c-f*, confirms the centrality of the initial motetus *f*.[7] This arresting introitus in the upper voices introduces the role that pitch emphases, intervallic qualities, and rhythmic shaping play in conveying the emotive tone of M22's texts as well as in energizing the composition.

The present study focuses on two broad areas central to understanding M22. One is the role of order and periodicity in the crafting of the work. The other is the interplay of qualities of stability and instability as the motet unfolds in performance.[8] Relations between texts and musical setting intertwine with these foci. A context for these angles of analysis is set by a brief glance at the historical circumstances within which Machaut composed this motet, the most overtly political in his musical output.[9]

---

[3] In the sources for M21 and M23, the scribes enter the word 'Introitus' below the many rests beginning the tenor and contratenor parts, thus signaling the nature of the substantial motetus-triplum openings in those motets. There is no such designation in the sources for M22. Nevertheless, given the character of M22's initial motetus-triplum passage, I will refer to it as an introitus.

[4] The square ♮, from the Guidonian gamut, signifies a whole step above *a*, or *b♮*.

[5] Similarly, the bold triplum *g♯* on L9 of T1 jars with the immediately preceding contratenor *G* and creates a linear tritone with the preceding *d*. The sharp is in **Mach A** and **Mach G**, but not in **Ferrell 1**.

[6] This fourth weakens the triplum arrival on *d*. Compare with the neighbor-tone fourth on L6 that is merely ornamental.

[7] Allsen (1992, 246–8) believes that Machaut modeled the M22 opening on that of Philippe de Vitry's three-voice motet *Tuba sacra/In arboris/Virgo sum*. There are surface similarities, but Machaut's introitus is imbued with considerably more musical tension than Vitry's.

[8] Two previous analytic studies of M22 are Kühn 1983, 1: 29–41 (a much expanded version of Kühn 1973, 138–44) and Leech-Wilkinson 1989, 1: 119–28. Neither takes the particular perspectives adopted here.

[9] Delogu (2012, 261–2) notes that in his *dits* Machaut sometimes refers explicitly to political and social concerns of his time and provides portraits of ideal rulers.

Example 16.1. M22, introitus and T1, L1–L10

HISTORICAL CONTEXT

Motet 22 is one of three late motets that Machaut created in the period 1358–60 when he had been a resident canon at Reims Cathedral for some eighteen years. The three are: *Christe qui lux es/Veni creator spiritus/Tribulatio proxima est/Contratenor* (M21), *Tu qui gregem/Plange regni respublica/Apprehende arma et scutum/Contratenor* (M22), and *Felix virgo mater Christi/Inviolata genetrix/Ad te suspiramus/Contratenor* (M23). The three differ from his twenty earlier motets (composed prior to the mid-1350s) in their extended duration, amplified four-voice texture, texts in Latin (the elevated language of the Church), and subject matter directed to serious public concerns of the time.[10] Together, the texts of these three works present a coordinated image of a society in dire straits, desperate for relief. M21 pleads to Christ and the Holy Spirit for protection against surrounding enemies (mo) and asks their help against those whose wars lacerate the community (tr). M22 takes aim at ineffectual political leaders who fail to guide the country competently (tr) and calls attention to the demoralized body politic suffering under inept rule and imminent foreign threat, looking to a true leader for deliverance (mo). M23 bewails destructive enemies, appeals for the Virgin Mary's merciful guidance to peace (tr), and requests her intervention for the physical salvation of her suffering people (mo). The tenors, melodic segments selected from liturgical chants, reinforce the messages of their respective upper voices with the weight of religious authority: M21, 'Tribulation is near and there is no one to help'; M22, 'Take up arms and shield and rise up'; M23, 'We sigh to you, lamenting and weeping'.[11]

The anxieties, appeals for divine aid, and reports of specific fears voiced in these texts are closely connected with the unsettled political and social situation in Reims (and throughout the French realm) in the period from around 1356 to 1360. The lack of leadership castigated in the triplum of M22 dates back to the Battle of Poitiers where, on September 19, 1356, the English defeated

[10] Machaut's earlier motets are for three voices (save for M5), and mainly set French texts, predominantly on courtly love subjects. Robertson 2002 provides contexts for all of Machaut's motets, and explores in depth possible religious connotations and symbolism in the first seventeen.

[11] Texts and translations of all three late motets along with tenor sources appear in Robertson 2002, 326–31. While the texts of M21 and M23 appeal for divine aid, M22 targets the human leader whose ineptness has exacerbated the current crisis and caused great suffering to the people.

the French and took captive John II, King of France, along with many other French nobles.
Under the eighteen-year-old Dauphin, who became Regent, civil order eroded. The countryside
(including that around Reims) was ravaged by militaristic companies of brigands (many of them
ex-soldiers), and in May 1358 a peasant uprising known as the Jacquerie spread pillage and killing
with assaults on castles and manors of the wealthy. In Reims itself, as early as 1356, the citizens
had risen against their Archbishop, Jean de Craon, a peer of the realm, for failing to maintain and
reinforce the city's fortifications as was his duty. Civilian authorities had to intervene to rebuild
the city walls. Those fortifications were tested when on October 28, 1359, Edward III of England
invaded France with the express aim of conquering Reims and having himself crowned King of
France in the cathedral. The English siege of Reims, which lasted from early December 1359 to
January 11, 1360, was intense but unsuccessful. It was in these perilous times with a weak Regent
and ineffective Archbishop, marauding bands of brigands and Jacquerie in the countryside, and
the serious threat of English conquest of Reims that Machaut wrote his extraordinary three late
motets whose texts express the fears of his community and their hopes for delivery.[12] The tensions
voiced in the texts of M22 are communicated not only in the introitus to M22 discussed above,
but also in compositional qualities within the body of the motet. A first step in grasping this is to
become familiar with the nature of the periodicities that shape the motet.

DESIGN AND PERIODICITIES IN M22

Composition of a French *ars nova* motet was guided by the premise of periodicity. Periodicity
was manifested poetically in the versification of the upper-voice texts and musically in recurring complex rhythmic constructs in the tenor (and contratenor, if present), and sometimes,
partially, in the upper voices as well. Before investigating core periodicities in M22, the 'score
illusion' requires comment. Modern editions permit us to see the motet as a totality with the
voices aligned synchronically and boxed in bar lines. In the original manuscripts, the voices are
inscribed independently, each in its own space field, and only each singer's ability to count longs
and breves accurately ensures precise coordination of the parts. A modern score encourages a
quasi-architectural, block-like overview of a motet's design, whereas the original performers
(and listeners) would have perceived the motet more as a series, or even cycle, of interrelated
segments and sounds unfolding over time. The composer will mentally envision the design and
sound of the whole, but realizes it as a tapestry of interweaving lines that are registered separately
in the notation.[13]

   Adhering to tradition, Machaut would have begun crafting M22 with two given elements, the
poetic texts of the upper voices (the triplum and the motetus), which he wrote himself, and a
fragment of plainsong providing pitches for the tenor voice.[14] He would impose upon the plainsong notes an individual rhythmic pattern (the talea, 'cutting') that would repeat regularly in the
tenor over the course of one or more statements of the borrowed melody (the color). Both given
elements – musical and textual – are crafted according to a periodic scheme, but their periodicities
need not coincide in the finished composition, and do not in M22.[15]

---

[12]   For more detailed information on the historical situation in France 1350–60, see Desportes 1979,
       Markstrom 1989, Robertson 2002, 189–223, and Tuchman 1978, 126–203.

[13]   On the concept of fourteenth-century polyphony as a tapestry, see Fuller 1992a, 56.

[14]   The casual suggestion in Leech-Wilkinson 1989, 1: 138, that Machaut might not have written the
       texts of M21, M22, and M23 has no basis in evidence.

[15]   Bent (2008b) has thoroughly critiqued use of the term 'isorhythm' for motets of the fourteenth

Machaut's design of the two poems is quite straightforward, as an examination of the Latin texts provided earlier reveals. The triplum poem has five stanzas of four lines each, each line a uniform eight syllables in length. The motetus poem has three stanzas of six lines each, the eight-syllable lines energetically punctuated by short four-syllable lines in the third and sixth positions of every stanza but the last.[16] Regular rhyme patterns control the line endings and define the stanzaic units of both poems. The poetic versification is, however, masked in the musical setting because the musical periodicities cut across it.[17] That is, the musical periodicities take precedence over the texts' stanzaic structures, although the latter will be evident to those singing the upper voices.

Machaut's design of the tenor foundation of M22 stands out as highly unorthodox in comparison with his usual practice. The borrowed plainsong melody, shown in Example 16.2a, consists of twenty-four notes and could easily have been arranged in regular talea segments of twelve, eight, or six notes that would coordinate exactly with the color boundaries.[18] But Machaut's talea takes in sixteen notes, so that the second talea begins two-thirds of the way through the first color and extends through the first third of the second color; see the talea markings, T, on Example 16.2a. This ensures that the pitches in the second color statement differ in rhythmic profile from those in the first. The talea's periodicity is twelve perfect longs, which are rhythmically grouped by rests, metric placement and duration as 4L+4L+4L; see Example 16.2b. What is unusual is how the expected periodicity of color and talea is disrupted toward the end of the motet. After two full statements, the color starts a third time, but breaks off midway at the eleventh note, an *F*, indicated with a dotted double bar line in Example 16.2a. All other Machaut motets have an integral number of color statements.[19] To curtail a tenor's melody partway through its course is exceptional not just for Machaut, but for his contemporaries as well.[20] The fourth talea compounds the melodic truncation by breaking off two-thirds of the way through, on its eighth long. There is a possible musical rationale behind these curtailments of the final color and talea. The borrowed melody centers on *F* over its first fifteen notes, but the last nine gravitate toward *D*. In starting a third color and cutting it short on the eleventh pitch, *F*, Machaut ensures that the motet will end in the same tonal sphere with which it began.[21] But it is not impossible that these departures from normal completions of melodic and rhythmic units also carried a symbolic message, as reflections of the troubled civic situation lamented in the texts. Unusually, the sources do not explicitly notate the partial fourth talea in the tenor and contratenor. These two voices have to supply it on the basis

---

and fifteenth centuries and suggests that 'a wider palette of descriptive terms' should be used for works musicologists have for decades labeled 'isorhythmic motets' (138). My preference is to designate fourteenth-century French motets as '*ars nova* motets' and to speak of 'periodicity' as a design principle.

[16] The final line of stanza 3 is dramatically expanded from four to eight syllables.

[17] The irregular textual positions of the periodic hocket/syncopated rhythms are indicated by italics in this edition of the Latin texts.

[18] Descriptions by fourteenth-century theorists of how to structure a motet tenor from a plainsong are summarized in Leech-Wilkinson 1989, 1: 15–24.

[19] A complete conspectus of tenor organization in Machaut motets appears in Hartt 2010b, 62–3.

[20] For another exceptional case of fourteenth-century tenor organization, see Chapter 14 by Anna Zayaruznaya in the present volume.

[21] Note that tonal closure was not a general premise in Machaut's musical oeuvre. Bain (2008, 198) observes that 64% of Machaut's polyphonic songs do not end with the same tonal focus with which they began. For his motets, only some 35% begin and end in the same tonal area (with the beginning assessed from the first full sonority). All three late motets do, however, begin and end in the same tonal sphere.

of an enigmatic verbal cue, *Apprehende arma* (the first two words of the tenor incipit), located after the full textual incipit of the notated tenor, but not aligned with the end of that voice.[22]

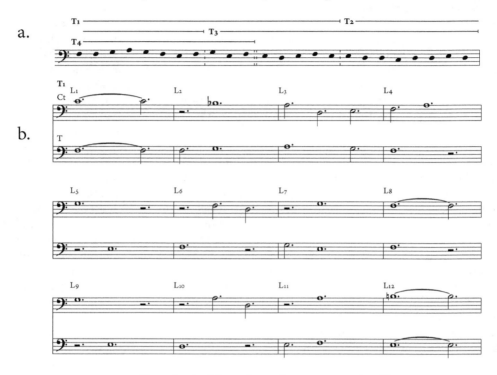

Example 16.2. M22, color and tenor-contratenor, T1

The tenor talea constitutes the foundation for periodicities in the other three voices. To the tenor in his late motets, Machaut added a companion contratenor crafted at the same slow-paced mensural level of the tenor, and with the same periodicity. It is likely that the rhythms of the tenor and contratenor voices in M22 were conceived simultaneously, because, as is apparent in Example 16.2b, they interact in slow hocket twice within the talea. L5–L7 and L9–L11 feature the same series of staggered rests and pitch attacks between the two voices that bind them inextricably in oscillation before they end their exchanges by joining together on sustained sonorities (L8 and L12). More normal continuous rhythms hold in both voices within the first four longs of each talea. The repetition of the hocket unit in the last two-thirds of each talea creates an overall rhythmic pattern of xyy within the tenor-contratenor pair, each unit four longs in duration; see the lower brackets in Figure 16.1. Hence, the combined lower-voice framework contains an internal periodicity within the twelve-long talea periodicity.

As in all three of Machaut's last motets and in several movements of his Mass, the upper voices also exhibit partial periodicities linked to those of tenor and contratenor, periodicities

---

22 The textual cue is given in **Mach A** and **Mach G**, but not in **Ferrell 1**. When present, the cue is positioned *within* the melodic line, not at its end (as a later 'Da Capo' would be). The contratenor voice has no cue. Tenor and contratenor thus have to take the initiative (as would a *dux*?) to complete the motet properly.

Example 16.3. M22, disruptive periodic rhythms, T3, L5 to T4, L1

Sarah Fuller

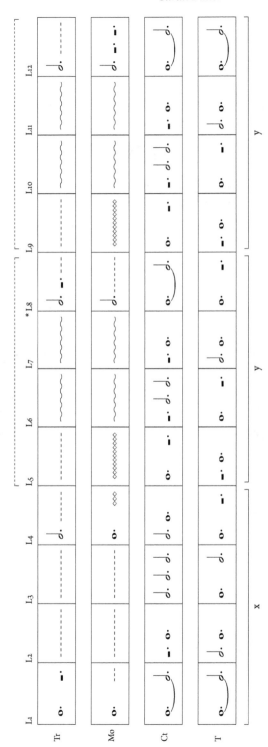

Note heads and rests indicate fixed rhythms. Dashes indicate various ordinary rhythms. The symbol ⁓ indicates fixed syncopated or hocket rhythms. The symbol ∞∞∞ indicates ordinary fixed rhythms in the motetus. The * on L8 indicates where T4 breaks off. All voices sustain a perfect long at this end point.

Figure 16.1. M22, rhythmic periodicity map

that are marked by distinctive rhythms – hocket or syncopation. In M22, the quick upper-voice syncopated/hocket passages coincide with the slow hocket passages in the two lower voices. In all four taleae, the motetus voice has a recurrent rhythmic pattern that extends from L_4 to a stable arrival on L_8. The rhythms on L_6–L_7 are syncopated; see the dotted brackets in Example 16.3. The pattern of L_5 to the initium of L_8 repeats for L_9–L_{12}. The motetus rhythmic profile thus conforms to the xyy pattern of the tenor-contratenor foundation. The triplum also joins in with a rhythmic pattern L_6–L_8, B_1 that repeats L_{10}–L_{12}. This pattern, fractured by minim rests, creates a quick hocket effect, albeit in a single voice.[23]

The rhythmic patterns and periodicities in all four voices articulate audible phrase units of four longs each within each statement of the tenor talea. The first unit begins (L_1) with a long note in every voice, and concludes (L_4) with an extended sonority in all voices, save for T_2 where the triplum carries through. The second and third units feature identical disruptive rhythms that close with secure arrivals on protracted sonorities (L_8 and L_{12}). These recurring patterns of periodicity are mapped in Figure 16.1. Note that although the regularity shown there represents one aspect of the compositional design, it is to some extent misleading, because pitches, intervals, and harmonies change with each talea iteration, as do melodic contours, text, and text declamation. The periodicity map of the talea in Figure 16.1 represents the motet as a sort of 'frozen architecture' rather than as a vibrant musical work whose multiple and varied facets are experienced during the course of a performance.[24] This discussion now turns to those varied facets that animate M22 for singers as well as listeners, in particular to the interplay between stable and unstable elements.

STABILITY AND INSTABILITY

As in Machaut's musical language generally, tensions and fluctuations between stable and unstable elements are driving forces over the course of M22. These tensions arise in the realms of rhythm, pitch, line, and sonority, which interact in intricate ways. Building upon the previous observations about periodicities, rhythmic instability in M22 commands attention. Particularly salient are the disruptive hocket rhythms in the triplum that stand out L_6–L_7 and L_{10}–L_{11} in each talea, as can be observed in Examples 16.1 and 16.3. Distinct rests at the start of semibreve units displace short minim pitches that follow, giving an effect of melodic dissolution and rhythmic and textual disruption. (In modern terms, notes are displaced off the beat.) Metric and melodic order are only reestablished when the singer lands on a stable breve L_8 and L_{12}. Simultaneously with these triplum disruptions, the motetus engages in a syncopated pattern that not only masks the start of breve units but shifts its mensural grouping from perfect (triple) to imperfect (duple) breve groupings. In effect, within L_6–L_7 and L_{10}–L_{11} of each talea, the motetus delineates imperfect rather than perfect longs (in modern terms, a hemiola effect); see the dotted brackets in Example

---

[23] This absence of a companion quick hocketing voice is rare in Machaut's oeuvre but does occur briefly in the *integer valor* talea of M21 (L_4–L_6), where, similarly, the motetus sustains syncopated notes while the triplum, fractured by rests, sings short off-beat pitches. In M22, is the lack of a true rhythmic companion to the triplum hocket rhythms possibly a symbol of an ineffective *dux*? The Anonymous of St Emmeran, in a treatise dated 1279, does mention hocketing in a single voice (Yudkin 1990, 228).

[24] Taking an 'architectural' perspective, Leech-Wilkinson (1989, 1: 122–3) and, following him, Allsen (1992, 248–50) see the introitus and curtailed fourth talea (both twenty-four breves long) in terms of an overall symmetrical form in M22. Aurally, the musical unfolding does not project such a static form, and symmetry is unlikely to have been a primary compositional premise, partly because its presumed axis is so obscured within an unsettled rhythmic passage.

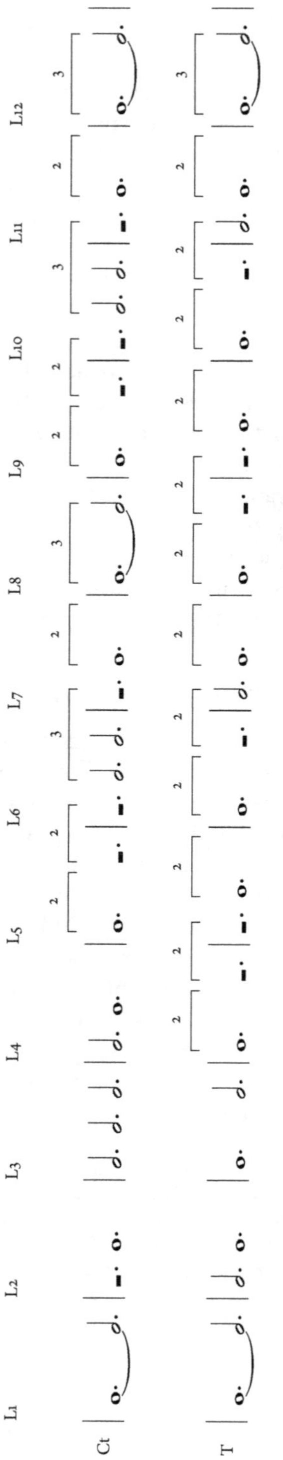

Figure 16.2. M22, metric groupings in tenor and contratenor taleae.

16.3. In doing this, the motetus supports more subtle shifts among triple and duple groupings in the lower voices, shifts that occur in both tenor and contratenor from L4 to the end of each talea. As illustrated by the markings on Figure 16.2, beginning at L4 and through L11, the tenor voice essentially produces duple breve groupings.[25] Although the written mensuration of perfect longs does not change, the actual durations of imperfect longs and dual groupings of breve rests articulate several imperfect long units.[26] Beginning on L5, one unit later than the tenor, the contratenor also shifts mensural groupings, with a mix of duple and triple units that cut across those of the tenor.[27] Because tenor and contratenor voices move slowly relative to the upper-voice activity, their departure from the official perfect modus (three-breve groupings) through actual articulation of imperfect modus groupings (two-breve groupings) may not be apparent to a listener. But it will be apparent to the singers who are producing both voices and are carefully counting durations.[28]

In the realm of pitch, qualities of stability and instability arise most audibly from the nature of primary sonorities, their duration and location within the mensural grid, the nexus of pitch relationships, and occasional half-step inflections (chromatic notes) that depart from the diatonic grid. This is to say that intervallic components, mensural position, duration, and rhythmic displacements have a material effect on perception of sonorities, their qualities of stability, of arrival, of instability, of forward inclination. The overall tonal profile of M22 is projected through sonorities of at least a breve duration in all voices that, due to the foundational rhythmic periodicities, occur regularly on L1, L4 (excepting T2), L8, and L12 of each talea. These punctuating sonorities stand out locally, but vary in stability. What is immediately clear from the conspectus of these sonorities in Example 16.4 is that F sonorities dominate at the beginning and end of M22, with T1 and T4 sounding successive F sonorities on L1, L4, and L8.[29] But the internal periodic arrivals, from T1, L12 through T3, L12, occur on E (three times), C (twice), and D (three times). This distribution is not entirely due to the pre-existent tenor, for from T2, L8 through T3, L1, it is the contratenor that anchors the C, D, and C sonorities respectively. The core tonal profile is thus one of stable beginning focus on F sonorities, a varied series of salient sonorities in the middle, with no talea ending on the same sonority with which it began, and a return to stable F focus in the shortened fourth talea. That T3 ends on a D sonority reflects the gravitation of the source plainsong from F to D centering.

Perceptions of relative harmonic stability are created not only by pitch relationships among primary sustained sonorities but also by the structure of those sonorities, their intervallic components. Scholars have extended fourteenth-century classification of individual intervals as perfect and stable or imperfect and unstable to categorize three-voice sonorities according to differing degrees of perfection and imperfection. The P (perfect) and I (imperfect) annotations below the sonorities in Example 16.4 indicate these aural differences, with modifications to accommodate

---

[25]   Tenor groupings are determined in part by groupings in other voices.

[26]   The imperfect tenor groupings align with those in the motetus voice, as can be seen in Example 16.3.

[27]   That is, the contratenor duples at L5 begin on the second breve of the tenor duples.

[28]   This is a matter of distinguishing between the formal mensuration of notation and actual temporal groupings realized in the music. See Maw 2004 on this topic. Johannes Boen, in his *Musica* of 1357, speaks of the younger generation converting perfect into imperfect; see Frobenius 1971, 77.

[29]   Square noteheads indicate tenor pitches.

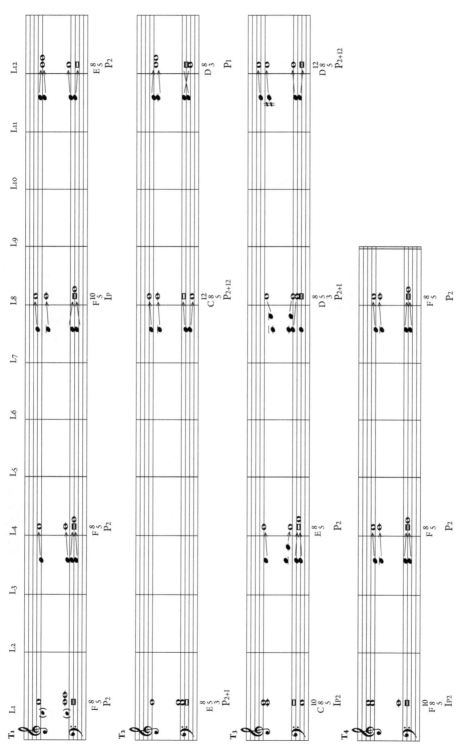

Example 16.4. M22, tonal outline.

sonorities with four distinct pitches.[30]

Space limitations preclude detailed investigation of Machaut's sonority choices here, but note that stable sonorities of just fifth and octave (with one pitch doubled) prevail in T_1 and at the end of T_4. On the instability wing, T_2, T_3, and T_4 all begin with sonorities that include imperfect consonances, and the prominent D sonorities at T_2, L_{12} and T_3, L_8 include thirds that signal continued forward motion.

Another means of creating harmonic instability is through chromatic inflections of pitches either within the context of a directed progression,[31] or individually to create an unstable interval or sonority, or to provide piquant clashes with local diatonic pitches. Chromatic inflections are relatively sparse in M22, due in part to the fact that standard voice leading for arrivals on F and E sonorities requires no adjustment of thirds or sixths. The approach to C sonorities may entail an F♯ in an inner voice, but this is not always implemented. Preparations for C sonorities on T_2, L_8 and T_3, L_1, for example, do not inflect the F because that pitch belongs to the given plainsong tenor;[32] see Examples 16.5 and 16.6. Earlier in T_2, a striking instance of F inflection occurs at L_2 where both triplum and contratenor sing extended F♯s above a tenor D; see Example 16.5. The combination of imperfect, inflected third and tenth renders the sustained D sonority highly unstable and leads to a widely spaced C sonority, $\frac{12}{8}$, on L_3. Those startling double F♯s at T_2, L_2 serve a strategy of destabilizing the D sonority and propelling it toward a C resolution.

In several instances, raised Cs clash with nearby more stable diatonic Cs. The expressive effect has already been noted at the end of the introitus, where an unexpected triplum *c*♯ enhances the following *d*, but clashes with nearby *c*♮s in the motetus voice; see Example 16.1. A similar clash occurs within the motetus line itself at T_3, L_6–L_8; see Example 16.3. Although a normal +6→8 progression with the tenor seems to motivate the motetus *c*♯ on L_7, B_1, the inflected pitch seems anomalous in context. A *c*♮ precedes it, its resolution is brief and metrically displaced, and *c*♮ is immediately reinstated in the ensuing stepwise descent of *c-♭-a*. The one moment when a motetus *c*♯ has a distinct harmonic role is at T_3, L_{11} where, with a tenor E, it provides a strong +6→8 approach to the D sonority that ends the talea. This is the only instance of an emphatic arrival on D in M22. Significantly, it occurs on the *D* that concludes the second color, just before F is reinstated and becomes the primary tonal center in the partial fourth talea.[33]

Along with inflected pitches, dissonances also contribute to the interplay of unstable and stable sonorities in M22. Although basic *contrapunctus* manuals officially excluded dissonances from a simple two-voice intervallic framework, in compositional practice they do occur. And

---

[30] On classification systems and labels for fourteenth-century three-voice sonorities see Fuller 1986 and Hartt 2010a. I have adopted Hartt's labels here, but modified them to accommodate four-voice sonorities. P2 = two perfect intervals (as $\frac{8}{5}$); P2+12 = a doubling of the fifth (as $\frac{12}{5}$); PI and P2+I = one or two perfect intervals with an internal imperfect interval (as $\frac{8}{3}$ or $\frac{8}{3}$); IP and IP2 = an imperfect interval between the outer voices, with one or two internal perfect intervals (as $\frac{10}{5}$ or $\frac{10}{8}$).

[31] On directed progressions, see Fuller 1992b. The classic three-voice formulation is $^{+6\ \to\ 8}_{+3\ \to\ 5}$.

[32] Petrus palma ociosa, in a treatise dated 1336, cautions against altering a plainsong tenor through *falsa musica*. Wolf 1913–14, 514.

[33] Note that *ficta g♯/G♯* inflections in triplum or contratenor are unlikely on T_3, L_{11} because the triplum leaps to its brief *g* from a *c*, and the contratenor G echoes the similar G at the end of T_2. Interestingly, the triplum *a*′ that heads the D sonority of T_3, L_{12} is preserved in the F $\frac{10}{8}$ sonority that begins T_4, but is taken by the motetus and transformed to imperfect intervallic status; see Example 16.3.

Example 16.5. M22, approaches to C sonorities, T2, L1–L8

some theorists actually discuss their functionality.[34] The patent dissonances in M22 occur in pre-cadential contexts, as the result of syncopated rhythms in the motetus, or from linear logic within individual voices, with pre-cadential functions being the most frequent. Typical instances may be observed in T_1, L_7; see Example 16.1. On the first breve of L_7, the syncopated motetus *a* clashes with an entering tenor *G*, but moves quickly into consonance with a ♭. The *a* reappears on B_3, this time jarring with a contratenor *G*, and again a consonant third is restored on the second semibreve. This second dissonance is pre-cadential, as all four voices then converge on an imperfect F sonority at L_8. Linear logic also obtains here, for the motetus line from L_6, B_3 to L_8, B_1 can be regarded as an overall scalar motion, *a*-♭-*c*, to a stable *c*. The dissonances work with rhythmic instability to prepare a strong cadential arrival on the breve-long F sonority. The tenor *F* of T_1, L_8 is the same point at which, in the shortened final talea, the motet will end (also with a precedential *G/a* dissonance), but the sonority a stable F_5^8 rather than an F_5^{10}.

A particularly piquant series of dissonances is heard in T_2, L_3–L_5; see Example 16.5. Parallel sevenths between triplum and contratenor occur L_3, B_3 to L_4, B_1 with triplum *a′*-*g* (the *a′* approached by leap) pitted against contratenor ♭-*a*. An even harsher clash – of triplum breve-length *d* against an entering tenor *E* – is notated in the manuscripts on the next long. Although attested in all sources, that triplum *d* on L_5, B_2 is likely a scribal error, an instance of dittography in which a scribe erroneously reiterates a previous passage or word verbatim. Beginning on L_3, B_1 of T_2, the triplum sings two linear descents from *a′*-*d*; see the dotted brackets in Example 16.5. A third descent, L_4, B_3 to L_5, B_2, is also notated as *a′*-*d*, but an endpoint on *e* (as emended in Example 16.5) fits far better harmonically with the entering tenor *E*. An octave here accords with the quality of the other breve-length (or longer) notes in the triplum, which are consistently consonant (save for the *a′* T_2, L_3, B_3). Whatever the case, line certainly plays a role in the vocal collisions from L_3 to L_5, with a series of scalar triplum descents from *a′* down a fifth or (plausibly) a fourth and a contratenor line that starts on *G*, leaps to *c* and traces a stepwise descent and encirclement (*c*-♭-*a*- *F♯*) back to *G*.[35] Tonal considerations might play a role here also. The parallel sevenths between triplum and contratenor occur above tenor *D*s that are near the end of the first color. The dissonances destabilize those D sonorities, masking the plainsong's tonal gravitation to *D*.

OTHER SALIENT FEATURES

From the periodic recurrence of upper-voice syncopations and displaced hocket rhythms followed by coordinated arrivals on sustained sonorities of breve length, both singers and listeners can gain an overall sense of coherent, cyclic design in M22. But there are other signposts that create significant relationships within the motet. One striking moment occurs at T_1, L_8 where, after a clear harmonic arrival, the start of the motetus phrase on a high *a′* is directly imitated by the triplum entrance; see the dotted brackets in Example 16.1. This imitation stands out as a rare moment of camaraderie between the two upper voices, and it recurs with the same figure, on the same pitches, at the comparable spot in T_3, L_8; see the smooth brackets in Example 16.3. The brief imitations not only launch the last phrases of both taleae, but audibly connect them, particularly since the ♫♩♪ figure occurs rarely in M22.[36] A less obvious imitation occurs mid-phrase at T_1,

---

[34] See Fuller 2013 for fourteenth-century theorists' diverse views on dissonance. Hartt (2010a, 198–203) classifies dissonant sonorities. Jackson (2003–8) reviews Machaut's dissonance practices, while Boogaart (2007) explores text-interpretative roles of dissonances in Machaut's music.

[35] The sharp on the contratenor *F*, T_2, L_2, doubtless remains in force for the subsequent *F* of L_4.

[36] The upper voices first state this figure in tandem T_1, L_3, the triplum also starting on *a′*; see

L2 where the motetus leaps up an octave to replicate the triplum's descending figure *g-f-e-*[*d*] in the same rhythm and at the same pitch (Example 16.1). Could this echoing of the triplum be a subtle musical realization of the triplum's text 'qui gregem tuum ducis' ('who lead your flock')? Since the two voices are linked in octaves during the previous two breves (T1, L2, B1–B2), this motetus leap up into the triplum registral space stands out.

Example 16.6. M22, salient triplum phrase and motive, T2, L12 to T3, L1

Although a listener's apprehension of the texts after the opening 'Plange' is veiled by simultaneous delivery and fragmentation of words in complex rhythmic passages, there are passages where significant segments of text stand out. Particularly prominent are the ends of T1, T2, and T3, where at L12 the triplum begins an animated phrase while the motetus rests and tenor and contratenor sustain perfect longs. The texts of these phrases stand forth clearly: 'Dux prudentium consilio', 'Ambo pereunt leviter' (Example 16.6), and 'Et ille bene ducitur' (Example 16.3). Each of these lines is a significant element in the triplum exhortation: the leader needing to heed prudent counsel, the danger of perishing if the leader knows not the way, the condition of being well led. The singer will realize the significance of these particular phrases, but others would need the context of the whole poem to grasp their import. Machaut further underscores the threat of 'Ambo pereunt leviter' by setting this phrase to the same familiar motive, at the same *a'* pitch level, as the imitative passages T1, L8 and T3, L8; compare Example 16.6 with the imitations in Examples 16.1 and 16.3. None of the motetus text lines in the body of the motet stands out to quite the same extent as the three triplum phrases mentioned, but the motetus voice regularly assumes prominence at the beginnings of T2, T3, and T4. Each time when it enters on L1, after the 'solo' triplum phrase, it rises above the triplum and temporarily becomes the highest voice; see Examples 16.3 and 16.5.[37] The most striking of these entrances, shown in Example 16.3, is that on T4, L1 when the motetus enters on *a'*, the apex of its range. It maintains that superior position during most of the ensuing ten-breve phrase (eight of ten breves). The text at that point looks forward to a joyful time when the kingdom will be well governed ('Sed amodo congaudenter').

the first dotted bracket in Example 16.1. At T2, L8, the two voices engage in rhythmic but not melodic imitation; see Example 16.5.

[37] These are not the only moments when the motetus rises above or, as at T1, L8 (Example 16.1) and T3, L8 (Example 16.3), equals the triplum register. The registral 'crossings' and sharings between motetus and triplum in M22 seem to have nothing to do with the symbolic turns of Fortune explored in Zayaruznaya 2009, but are more connected with imitative signposts, text emphases, and the related messages of the two upper voices.

The elevation of this text line to a high register invites the motetus singer to underscore it vocally and bring it to the attention of anyone cognizant of the written poem.

CONCLUSION

Musical understanding of M22 involves awareness on the one hand of large-scale periodicities and pitch foci, and on the other hand of details and cross-currents of mensural groupings, subtleties of harmonic formations and pitch inflections, salient interactions among the voices. Cognizance of the motet's communicative capacity entails understanding the meaning and historical contexts of its texts and being attuned to ways, both obvious and subtle, in which the musical discourse projects the spirit of the texts. The interplay of stable and unstable elements, the pointed fluctuations between metrically settled passages and arrival points and substantial passages restlessly syncopated and disturbed by hocket truncations, provide a musical portrait of the present anxieties and hopes for the future expressed in Machaut's eloquent poems.

17

A Motet Ahead of its Time?
The Curious Case of *Portio nature/Ida capillorum*

Emily Zazulia

P*ortio nature/Ida capillorum/Contratenor/Ante thronum trinitatis* presents modern scholars with a conundrum. Many aspects of the motet's advanced style and structure are at odds with the early date suggested by its text and attribution. Consequently, the work raises basic methodological questions: are we to trust extrinsic factors like source dating and compositional function even when they appear to contradict stylistic evidence? As with many fourteenth-century motets, the text of *Portio/Ida* contains an apparent clue to its origins.[1] The motet is dedicated to St Ida of Lorraine (*c.* 1040–1113), who, through her marriage to Eustace II, became Countess of Boulogne. The motetus text ends with a prayer for the soul of a certain 'Henricus', who names himself as the author of 'this song and collection of words'. While the earliest sources lack an attribution outside the motetus poetry, one late source for *Portio/Ida* names two authors: 'Magister Heinricus' and 'Egidius de Pusiex'. This has led scholars to suggest that Henricus was responsible only for the texts and Egidius for the music.[2] The sources therefore seem full of identifying clues, especially when compared with anonymous pieces or those that have generic texts.

The connection between 'Egidius de Pusiex' and *Portio/Ida* is found only in Coussemaker's 1866 transcription of a now lost source, **Str**: 'Magister Heinricus' appears in the center head of the page, in the same space Coussemaker indicated the composer of other pieces, and 'Egidius de Pusiex' is written slightly smaller and off to the right.[3] In trying to identify this Egidius, Suzanne Clercx and Richard Hoppin propose 'Egidius de Puiseus', chaplain for Hughes Roger de Beaufort, Pope Clement VI's nephew.[4] This identification would place the motet's origin at the Avignonese papal court. St Ida was never a widely venerated saint, certainly not beyond Boulogne and Calais, so

---

[1] No line-by-line translation of the motet's texts has ever been made, because, in the words of Leofranc Holford-Strevens, some late-medieval motets 'simply cannot be construed as rational human discourse'. Holford-Strevens 2011, 236. Dr Holford-Strevens assures me that a running translation is impossible but has nonetheless offered his expertise in making sense of these texts. I thank him profusely for this assistance. The edition and summary of these texts included as an appendix to this chapter are based on his work, but any errors are my own.

[2] See, for example, van den Borren 1924, 133–4, and Günther 1965, lviii. Van den Borren also raises the possibility that Egidius simply provided the contratenor, which was likely a later addition anyhow, as discussed below. This hypothesis brings to mind a suggestion later raised in Atlas 1981, which proposes that conflicting attributions in the fifteenth-century chanson repertory may indicate later stages of revision rather than misattribution.

[3] See van den Borren 1924, 133–4. Str was lost in a fire just four years later, in 1870.

[4] See Clercx and Hoppin 1959.

how did she become the subject of a motet written more than two hundred years after her death?[5] Surely she would have had special significance for the motet's commissioner. Her most prominent descendant in the Avignonese retinue was Cardinal Guy of Boulogne – Ida's great grandson seven times over.[6] Working backward from Egidius's death in 1348, Clercx and Hoppin suggest that Egidius could have written the motet in 1342 when Guy of Boulogne became a cardinal.[7]

This hypothesis about the motet's origin would appear convincing enough were it not for some stylistic considerations that seem at odds with such an early dating. These include surface-level features, such as extended chains of semibreve syncopations, as well as structural features concerning the tenor construction. Noting that these characteristics do not appear in motets from the 1340s, Ursula Günther suggested the late 1360s or early 1370s as a more probable dating.[8] Guy of Boulogne did not die until 1373, so Günther's revised dating would not invalidate him as a possible dedicatee, though it would require identifying a different Egidius. *Portio/Ida* turns up in the index of the lost **Trém** manuscript, created in 1376, forming a firm *terminus ante quem* for the motet's composition.[9] But 1376 is quite a bit later than 1342. In this chapter I consider the factors that pull *Portio/Ida* toward the 1340s on the one hand, and toward the 1360s – or even later – on the other. Confusion about the piece's dating provides a window into issues of style, source study, and narratives surrounding the development of the medieval motet. I aim to untangle these threads in order to see which contradictions can be addressed – and which cannot.

THE MOTET'S PROTAGONISTS

Who was St Ida? She was born Ida of Lorraine, daughter of Godfrey III, Duke of Lower Lorraine. She became Ida of Boulogne when she married Eustace II, Count of Boulogne in 1049. As the triplum text describes, Ida was known as the mother of crusaders and a benefactress of several religious houses. She had three sons: Eustace III, who became the next Count of Boulogne; Godfrey of Bouillon, the first Christian ruler of the Kingdom of Jerusalem; and Baldwin, the second ruler of the Kingdom of Jerusalem. The text praises them for their part in the first crusade. Godfrey and Baldwin both served as kings of liberated Jerusalem and were buried near the Holy Sepulchre.[10]

The motetus speaks of a precious relic – eleven strands of the Virgin Mary's hair – that Ida had given to the Benedictine abbey of La Capelle, one of the houses she founded. After Eustace II died

---

[5]   Ida had used her considerable means to support the crusade and later to found several abbeys in northern France. She and Eustace made gifts to a number of monastic houses and collegiate churches including the abbey of La Capelle, Les Attaques; the church of St Léger in Lens; the abbey of St Amand, east of Lens; the abbey of St Wulmer, Samer (Boulogne); Notre Dame de Boulogne; and the abbeys of Le Wast and St Bertin, east of Boulogne. See Tanner 2004.

[6]   The direct line from Ida to Guy proceeds as follows: Ida of Lorraine and Boulogne – Eustace III of Boulogne – Matilda of Boulogne – Marie of Boulogne – Mathilde of Flanders – Aleydis of Leuven – Robert V of Auvergne – Robert VI of Auvergne – Robert VII of Auvergne – Guy of Boulogne.

[7]   The ledgers of Pope Clement VI are published in Berlière 1906.

[8]   Günther 1965, lvii–lviii.

[9]   On the dating of this source, see Bent 1990.

[10] Following Godfrey's death, Baldwin accepted the title of King, which his brother had rejected, since in his view, Christ was the only true king of Jerusalem. As the first ruler of Jerusalem, Godfrey was celebrated in literature, art, and music for centuries. His acts featured in *chansons de geste*, and he became identified as the grandson of the Swan Knight. In fact, in *Le Chevalier au Cygne*, one version of the Swan Knight tale, Ida herself is said to be the daughter of the Swan Knight and Beatrix, Duchess of Bouillon. See also Gerritsen and Van Melle 2000, 260–5.

in *c.* 1087, Ida was left in charge of the family lands when her sons went off to the crusades. She was connected with powerful ecclesiastical figures including St Anselm of Bec (later Archbishop of Canterbury) and St Hugh of Cluny.[11] Herself quite powerful, Ida was able to convince St Hugh to provide monks for La Capelle and King Alphonso I of Spain to send the miraculous hairs.[12] Though it has long been recognized that the motet texts match the vita of St Ida written *c.* 1130–5 (included in the *Acta sanctorum*), they more closely follow the twelfth-century record of her miracles.[13]

What about Cardinal Guy of Boulogne, who Clercx and Hoppin name as a likely dedicatee for the motet? One of the era's most important political figures, he represented the papacy in several high-profile diplomatic missions, including between England in France in attempts to end what would come to be called the Hundred Years' War.[14] He was even considered a possible successor to Pope Innocent VI, but internal politics kept him from being elected.[15] As a descendant of St Ida (his older brother William XII was the Count of Boulogne), he seems a promising candidate to have been the motet's dedicatee. As mentioned above, Clercx and Hoppin posit that *Portio/Ida* was composed in 1342, when Pope Clement VI made Guy a cardinal, but this was only the first potential occasion in a career that would last thirty more years.

However, Guy was not Ida's only prominent descendant. His niece Joan I (1326–60), Countess of Auvergne and Boulogne, became Queen of France through her marriage to John II. Guy's own nephew, Robert of Geneva, who began his career in 1361 as Bishop of Thérouanne (the diocese containing Boulogne and Calais), went on to become Antipope Clement VII in 1378. It is not impossible that *Portio/Ida* was written instead for him,[16] but this, too, would require rethinking the identification of the Egidius named in **Str**, since the Egidius identified by Clercx and Hoppin died in 1348.

The fourteenth century saw renewed interest in launching a new crusade. Clement VI declared a crusade in 1343, but this endeavor only made it as far as Smyrna. Pope Innocent was concerned that the conflict between the English and the French would derail the possibility of uniting for a

[11] See Tanner 2004, ch. 4.

[12] There is some question about how the hairs reached La Capelle. Some sources say that the Bishop of Astorga sent them at the request of Alfonso, others imply they came from the bishop himself. See Gaiffier 1968. One other account, less well attested, suggests Ida's son Godfrey acquired the relic and tested it himself to ensure its veracity. See Pruvost 1875, 107–8.

[13] This account mentions the miracle in which the Bishop of Astorga tested the hairs in fire, but they were not harmed; this does not appear in Ida's vita. Moreover, the triplum text echoes the miracle account's laudatory prologue. Though no phrases come directly from the miracle account – presumably because they would not fit the motet texts' leonine hexameter – there is some shared vocabulary. The miracle appears in four manuscripts spanning the twelfth through fifteenth centuries. On the sources of these accounts, as well as an edition of the fifteenth-century copy, see Gaiffier 1971, ch. 2. For an edition of Ida's vita see *Vita B. Ide Vidue* in *Acta Sanctorum* (Carnandet 1866). On the dating of Ida's vita, see Gaiffier 1968, 69.

[14] See Jugie 1987.

[15] Both Guy and his nemesis Cardinal Hélie of Talleyrand-Périgord were seen as candidates, but the college was so divided that neither was able to reach the necessary voting threshold. See Johnes 1808, 97. This section is omitted from the more common Penguin edition of Froissart's *Chronicles*. See also Zacour 1960, 64–5.

[16] If this is the case, the motet would have been written at least two years before Clement's election to the papacy (due to the 1376 date of **Trém**'s index). Other possible occasions include when he became Archbishop of Cambrai in 1368 and a cardinal in 1371.

campaign east.[17] The triplum of *Portio/Ida* venerates Ida's sons as crusaders ('These sons crossed the sea, attacked the heathen...'). In this way the motet could be framed as crusading propaganda, but this notion does little to help date the piece.

It has gone unrecognized in earlier work on *Portio/Ida* that Boulogne and Calais were major sites of conflict in the 1340s during the Hundred Years' War. In fact, the abbey of La Capelle, which housed the relic in question, was destroyed during the 1346 siege of Calais.[18] It has been difficult to determine what happened to the relic during and following the siege and whether it was destroyed with the abbey.[19] The area would remain under English control into the sixteenth century. The abbot of La Capelle, Philippe de Conflans, was made Bishop of Orleans in 1349, after which point the abbey lay in ruins for seven years before Pope Innocent VI passed it into the care of a certain 'Laurent'.[20]

How these historical events relate to our motet remains unclear. It seems unlikely that the motet would not mention the loss of the relic and abbey had it been composed after its destruction. But are we to believe that this obscure relic – along with the abbey that had housed it for 250 years – was lost not five years after featuring so prominently in *Portio/Ida*? Such coincidences are not unheard of, but they do give pause. After all, the motetus text begins by emphasizing the relic's indestructibility as proof of its sacred status. If the motet were written with knowledge of the abbey's destruction, continued veneration of the relic would suggest that it was not, in fact, destroyed along with the abbey.[21] In other words, we might say that the motetus text implicitly construes the siege of the abbey as yet another test the relic faced. Perhaps *Portio/Ida* was even written in response to these events. Ultimately we are left with more questions than answers.

MIXED MESSAGES

Dating a motet based on matters of style is challenging. Few sources and even fewer pieces with secure dates make the foundation on which to build lamentably small.[22] When Clercx and Hoppin suggested Guy of Boulogne's 1342 nomination as a possible occasion for *Portio/Ida*, they remarked that 'the style of the motet *Ida capillorum/Portio nature* does not deny a date of composition

---

[17] On the role of the papacy in the fourteenth-century crusades, see Setton 1976.

[18] Desplanque 1867.

[19] Ursula Günther claims that the relic is 'still preserved and revered today in the Benedictine abbey of Notre Dame de la Capelle'; see Günther 1965, lvii. I have been unable to find any trace of the relic after 1346 except for the text of this motet. Even if the relic has survived to the present day, the abbey did not. The abbey of La Capelle should not be confused with Notre Dame of Boulogne, also rebuilt by Ida, which does survive to the present day and continues to house other relics.

[20] Despite this transaction, there is no indication that any community remained at the abbey. See Desplanque 1867, 359.

[21] It would also be ironic for the motet text to discuss seeking refuge from the wars (motetus lines 7–8) – presumably the crusades – when the relic would itself soon be lost to another war. That said, this passage is particularly difficult to parse, but has traditionally been understood as Ida spending her final years at Capella. See Günther 1965, lvii–lviii. What if we understood these 'bella' to be the fourteenth-century conflicts, rather than the crusades? In this reading, that line would celebrate the hairs having been spared by the wars at Calais.

[22] For some of the reasons dating in this period is particularly difficult, see Leach 2011a, 100–3. For earlier approaches to this issue, see Günther 1978 and Bowers 1990. On related problems in fifteenth-century music, see Milsom 2015.

around 1345' and that it 'presents no rhythmic complications despite its isorhythmic division'.[23] But our understanding of style and chronology has changed in the last sixty years. What once seemed plausible may now be difficult to reconcile.

Before diving in to specific issues of style, we should step back and look at this motet's sources, since they are complex and contain significant variants.[24] We know *Portio/Ida* appeared in at least five sources, though only two survive intact.[25] The motet appears in the main layer of **Iv**, and this copy seems to be the earliest we have, even though the manuscript itself may postdate the motet considerably.[26] The other complete concordance appears in **Ch**, from closer to 1400, or perhaps even the 1410s.[27] That *Portio/Ida* appeared in **Trém** by 1376 gives a *terminus ante quem*, but without the motet itself we cannot compare its reading against the other sources. Although we do not have access to **Str** since it was destroyed in 1870, Coussemaker made a copy of it in 1866, as mentioned above, so its reading is not completely lost. The mid-fourteenth-century Leiden fragment, **NL-Lu 342a**, which contains most of the motetus, closely matches the reading in **Str**. These two sources more often agree with **Ch** than **Iv**.[28]

Though both complete copies (**Iv** and **Ch**) transmit four voices, the motet appears to have been conceived in three parts with the contratenor added later. The contratenor is not essential to the counterpoint, which can otherwise stand on its own. Moreover, this voice often doubles one of the other voices and at times introduces significant dissonances.[29] *Portio/Ida* is hardly the only motet to be augmented with an extra voice, presumably to keep it current as four-voice textures became more favored.[30]

---

[23] 'le style du motet *Ida capillorum-Portio nature* ne dément pas une date de composition qui se siuerait vers 1345 … En effet, ce motet … ne présente aucune complication rythmique, malgré son découpage isorythmique'. Clercx and Hoppin 1959, 86–7; translation mine.

[24] Günther's edition includes a full list of variants between sources. See Günther 1965, lx–lxii (list of variants) and 57–65 (edition). The motet has also been edited in Harrison 1968, 24–9 (following **Iv**) and 30–5 (following **Ch**), though the latter edition includes a number of misreadings of the **Ch** version. A three-voice edition (omitting the contratenor) appears in O. Raitzig and A. Raitzig 2011, 47–59.

[25] These are **Iv** (fols 6v–7r), **Ch** (fols 61v–62r), **Str** (fols 74v–75r, lost), **NL-Lu 342a** (fol. 2v, fragment), and **Trém** (extant today only in the index).

[26] The dating of **Iv** remains contentious. Besseler first hypothesized that the manuscript was copied near the papal court of Avignon. This remained the accepted provenance until Günther suggested the manuscript instead came from the court of Gaston Fébus, *c.* 1365–70. Karl Kügle argues that the manuscript was copied in the 1380–90s as a retrospective collection, since its core repertory dates from before 1360, with some pieces as early as the 1310s. See Besseler 1925, 194; Günther 1978, 291–3; Kügle 1997, ch. 2.

[27] See Plumley and Stone 2008, 179–82, and Bent 2017, 21 *et passim*.

[28] These sources do not agree on voice placement: **Iv** and **Ch** both present the 'Ida capillorum' voice in the space traditionally occupied by the triplum (i.e. on the verso), whereas **Str** places the voice singing 'Portio nature' in this position. Figure 8.6 in the present volume shows the version in **Ch**. I follow Günther (and thereby **Str**) in considering 'Ida capillorum' to be the motetus, since its text is shorter and ends with authorial self-identification. See Günther 1965, lix.

[29] For example, in bar 50 an *a* in the contratenor sounds against the motetus's *g*, in bar 68 the contratenor's *b* clashes with the triplum's *a′*, each of these sounding for the length of a perfect breve. In bars 93–4 the contratenor introduces a *G* beneath a *c/g* sonority, creating an unsupported fourth at a conspicuous moment of stasis that follows one of the extended syncopated passages.

[30] In his discussion of **Ch**, Reaney (1954) suggests that *L'ardure/Tres dous/Ego rogavi* was also conceived for three voices, and that the fourth voice, a non-isorhythmic contratenor, was a later addition. Additionally, the Nuremberg copy of *Degentis vita/Cum vix/Vera Pudicicia* has an extra

Example 17.1. *Portio/Ida*, bars 1–6, readings in **Iv** and **Ch**

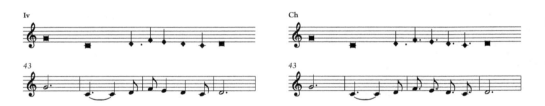

Example 17.2. *Portio/Ida*, bars 43–6, motetus, readings in **Iv** and **Ch**

The **Ch** copy of *Portio/Ida* includes a number of interesting variants. For instance, as shown in Example 17.1, in **Iv** the triplum begins on *c*, beneath the motetus's opening *f*, but in **Ch** the triplum begins an octave higher, thereby occupying the more typical highest register of the opening sonority. Note too how **Ch** transmits different text underlay in the motetus. Indeed, the motetus readings continue to differ in pitch and rhythm, sometimes to a greater degree than we might expect of more typical variants.[31] This degree of variation in the motet's concordances suggests that the motet has been updated, perhaps when it was copied into **Ch**.

The most unusual variant occurs in the motetus in bar 45, where a typical pre-cadential rhythm has been exchanged for four equal-length dotted minims that cut across the prevailing meter; see

contratenor; see Günther 1965, xxii. Other motets, including two in **Ch** and four in **Iv**, feature a solus tenor, a voice that combines the most important pitches of the tenor and contratenor to allow for three-voice performance; see Davis 1967.

[31] An example of a more typical variant occurs in bar 19 of the motetus where a pair of minims (the latter altered) on *c-e* in **Iv** is replaced by a trio of minims on *c-d-e* in **Ch**.

Example 17.2. (Note that the first dot in each example is a dot of division, which divides breve units – much like a barline – and ensures that the *d* minim imperfects the preceding *c* breve. The subsequent dotted minims in **Ch** are dots of addition, which work like modern dots, increasing each note's value by half.) Nothing like this occurs anywhere else in this motet, but **Ch** is quite clear about the reading.[32]

As Günther observes, strings of semibreve syncopations, which occur in all extant sources, also suggest a later dating for the motet. She also notes that *Portio/Ida* is the only motet in **Iv** to use semibreve syncopations in major prolation.[33] In *Portio/Ida*, this syncopation does not function like hocketing, which sometimes marks structural junctures in other fourteenth-century motets, but instead occurs at two analogous points near the end of both statements of the motetus's second talea; the first passage is shown in Example 17.3.[34] (The motet's structure will be elucidated in more detail below.) In instances where the rhythm was clearly updated, the new rhythms occur in isolated places, not in corresponding locations in the paired upper-voice taleae, suggesting that the modernization did not take the upper voices' isorhythmic structure into account. But these semibreve syncopations occur in all sources, strongly suggesting they were present from the motet's original conception.[35]

Example 17.3. *Portio/Ida*, bars 89–93, edited from **Iv**

The other precocious feature of *Portio/Ida* – the unfolding of its tenor – was undoubtedly part of the motet from its conception. The tenor must be sung four times, but rather than call for a literal repetition as do some motes from the period, *Portio/Ida* requires the singers to interpret the notated tenor line according to a different mensuration in each statement. The tenor in **Iv** is accompanied by an inscription instructing how it should be repeated: 'It is to be sung first in

32 Harrison 1968, 24–9 (**Iv**) and 30–5 (**Ch**), transcribes these bars in exactly the same way in his back-to-back editions of the two sources, thus obscuring the change in **Ch**. Günther 1965, 57–65, however, transcribes four dotted eighth notes.

33 Günther 1958, 38. Modus, tempus, and prolation refer to the relationship between larger and smaller note values at successive levels. A larger note value may contain either two or three of the next smallest value at each of these levels. Modus concerns the division of longs into breves, tempus the division of breves into semibreves, and prolation the division of semibreves into minims.

34 The corresponding instance occurs in bars 113–16.

35 The treatise *Ars cantus mensurabilis mensurata per modo iuris*, by Coussemaker's Anonymous V, cites *Portio/Ida* as an early example of syncopae: 'such syncopa I find first in the motet *Ida capillorum*' ('primo invenio in motecto Ida capillorum talem syncopa'). The musical example he gives is similar to the syncopations found in the surviving sources for *Portio/Ida*, but does not match any exactly. See Balensuela 1994, 212–13.

perfect [modus], second in imperfect [modus], third, cut in half (*per semi*) of the first, the fourth half (*per semi*) of the second'.[36] In other words, the first time through it is sung with perfect longs (each worth three breves), second with imperfect longs (worth two breves). The third and fourth statements must be sung in diminution, whereby the singer mentally replaces longs with breves and breves with semibreves; the third statement is thus sung with perfect breves (each worth three semibreves), and the fourth with imperfect breves (worth two semibreves). The final result is a four-fold tenor statement, whereby each statement is different and shorter, despite the fact that they all derive from a single notated line. (The contratenor repeats in the same fashion.) While the verbal canon might seem to indicate a single process of tenor transformation, I would argue it actually has two components: mensural reinterpretation and diminution.

The notated tenor rhythm is essentially drawn from earlier patterns in modal rhythm. The series ■■■ ■■■ | ■■ occurs four times in succession in the course of a single statement of the 32-note melodic line. We may call this the tenor's talea. For the full notated tenor, see Figure 8.6 in the chapter by Haines and Udell, which shows the tenor as it appears in **Ch**. Note the patterning: two sets of three ligated notes, a rest (vertical line spanning two staff lines), and a set of two notes; all of this then stated three more times.[37] The contratenor uses the same rhythms, but it moves the breve rest from the seventh position to the fourth position relative to the tenor's rhythm (that is, it appears directly after the first notated long). In the first tenor statement, longs are perfect, and thus the second breve of each pair of breves must be altered, doubling its duration in order to fill out the perfection. In the second statement, longs are imperfect, and breves remain unaltered. The third and fourth iterations are related in the same way, but breves replace longs and semibreves replace breves. The process by which the prevailing mensuration changes a note's perfection or causes alteration is mensural reinterpretation. Diminution is substitution – either mentally or in writing – of the initial notes with those of the next smallest value. These processes are related, but not identical.

For a long time all repeating structures in motets were grouped under the umbrella of 'isorhythm', but beginning with Margaret Bent's probe into the historiography surrounding that term, there has been a push for more nuanced readings.[38] Bent argues that 'isorhythm' should be reserved for the literal repetition of rhythmic patterns independent of melodic repetition, whereas in pieces like *Portio/Ida*, in which the tenor must be reread in different ways, the tenor should instead be considered 'homographic'. This terminological shift away from the 'rhythmic' toward the 'graphic' highlights the fact that each iteration of the tenor is identical in sight but not sound, making the term 'isorhythm' especially inapt.

Portio/Ida does feature large-scale rhythmic repetition, but it is located in the upper voices rather than the tenor. The two upper voices feature four rhythmic blocks (which we might consider taleae) that are each repeated once, forming a kind of rhyming couplet, before moving on to the next.[39] Each upper-voice talea is stated twice per full statement of the tenor. Because the

---

[36] 'Primo dicitur perfecte, secundo imperfecte, tertio sese [scisse] per semi de primo, quarto de secundo'; translation mine.

[37] Notice that there is no verbal cue provided in Ch like there is in Iv. Here the four semibreve-like figures at the end of both the tenor and contratenor tell the performers to sing their respective parts four times, but nothing in the notation indicates the changes of mensuration required to coordinate with the triplum and motetus.

[38] Bent 2008b. See also Lawrence Earp's discussion and reassessment of the topic in his chapter in this volume.

[39] On repeating structures in the upper voices of motets, see Zayaruznaya's chapter in this *Companion*, as well as her forthcoming 2018b, in which she analyzes this motet.

tenor gets shorter each time it is reinterpreted, the upper-voice blocks also get shorter (that is, shorter in total duration, but not in prevailing note values). Daniel Leech-Wilkinson suggests the motet may even have been conceived with thoroughgoing upper-voice isorhythm that has since been obscured by scribal editing.[40]

Mensural reinterpretation would become more common in the fifteenth century, but was quite rare in the fourteenth. The only other fourteenth-century motets to feature mensural reinterpretation are *Inter densas/Imbribus irriguis/Admirabilem est/Contratenor* and *Sub Arturo plebs/Fons citharizancium/In omnem terram*, both of which appear in **Ch**, as well as a motet-like Gloria in **Iv**. Diminution in the fourteenth century was much more common, though it was not signalled in the way it is in *Portio/Ida*. Instead, the diminished rhythms in the later passes were written out in breves and semibreves,[41] so the singers did not have to make the substitution mentally.[42] Twelve other pieces in **Iv** feature tenor diminution, and in every case the diminished note values are written out. Besides *Portio/Ida*, the next earliest pieces that call for diminution with verbal instructions rather than writing it out in reduced values do not appear until **Ch**.

Inter densas/Imbribus takes the mensural reinterpretation found in *Portio/Ida* to new heights. The motet's very brief tenor and its numerous repetitions highlight the process of reinterpretation: the tenor must be read eight times under eight different mensurations, as detailed in a verbal instruction. While not all possible combinations are explored, as they are in Eloy d'Amervale's *Missa Dixerunt discipuli* from the mid-fifteenth century, *Inter densas/Imbribus* features changes at the levels of major modus, minor modus, tempus, and prolation, which makes it more mensurally complex than *Portio/Ida*. *Inter densas/Imbribus*, however, does not appear in **Iv**, only in **Ch**, suggesting a later date – indeed, possibly much later: recall that **Ch** may date from as late as the 1410s.[43]

The other example of mensural reinterpretation and diminution from the earlier **Iv** is the aforementioned anonymous Gloria. This motet-style Gloria features a homographic tenor that must be interpreted in a similar manner to *Portio/Ida*, except that its upper voices change mensurations at the same time as the tenor, whereas the upper voices of *Portio/Ida* remain in imperfect tempus, major prolation throughout.[44] After beginning with perfect modus (i.e. perfect longs), the upper voices shift to imperfect modus, then to perfect tempus with minor prolation, and finally to imperfect tempus and minor prolation.[45] The tenor and contratenor change mensurations with the upper voices, reading their respective lines according to the four successive mensural situations.[46] Therefore, unlike *Portio/Ida* in **Iv** where a verbal canon cues these reinterpretations,

---

[40] Leech-Wilkinson 1989, 1: 178.

[41] See, for instance, the tenor of Guillaume de Machaut's motet *Hareu/Helas* provided in Figure 8.5 in the present volume, in which the diminished note values are clearly indicated for the singer.

[42] See Zazulia forthcoming.

[43] On *Inter densas/Imbribus*, Eloy's *Missa Dixerunt discipuli*, and mensural reinterpretation in the fifteenth century, see Wegman 1991.

[44] The Gloria is edited in Stäblein-Harder 1962, 23–5.

[45] Even in the upper voices, these changes are not directly indicated, but must be inferred from the patterns of notes. In the first section (Et in terra), breves and semibreves are both grouped into sets of three, and in the second section (Domine deus) they are grouped in twos. Longs and breves disappear from the third and fourth sections, where note values are almost entirely semibreves and minims. Again, grouping semibreves into threes (Qui sedes) and twos (Amen) convey the active mensuration.

[46] The decreasing length of each section in the upper voices combined with the indication to sing the tenor and contratenor four times gives a clue that each tenor statement must also somehow get shorter in terms of its sounding length.

here there is simply an indication – four short tic marks – to sing the line four times.

Noting that this Gloria and *Portia/Ida* have similar tenor taleae, Leech-Wilkinson has suggested that the Gloria was a precursor to our motet. The Gloria's texts feature largely homophonic text declamation in its early sections, which might point to an earlier date,[47] and its inconsistent dissonance treatment suggests it is less skillfully composed.[48] Leech-Wilkinson's hypothesis, however, may be problematic, as it seems unlikely that a development as technical as mensural reinterpretation would originate with an individual of little skill (as characterized by Leech-Wilkinson), though it is not impossible. It is also unclear which came first in the process of composing this Gloria: the decision to change mensurations at the beginning of formal sections, or the idea of mensurally reinterpreting the tenor. If the former, I could imagine the tenor reinterpretation following directly from that earlier decision, but the issue can be argued from both sides.[49] Thus, this Gloria further complicates matters surrounding our motet: although, like *Portia/Ida*, it is extant in the earlier **Iv** manuscript and features tenor transformation, it lacks the anomalous rhythmic features of *Portio/Ida* that point to a later date. At the same time, it is not clear whether or not the Gloria was a precursor to *Portio/Ida*, nor if the Gloria's tenor transformation was merely a consequence of the mensuration changes in the upper voices. Again, more questions arise.

Portio/Ida is thought to have influenced several pieces, including *Sub Arturo/Fons*, a motet of English provenance. This connection has implications for our understanding of how tenor manipulations enter the vocabulary of musical style. Like *Portio/Ida*, the dating of *Sub Arturo/Fons* suggested by external factors seems at odds with its musical structure. *Sub Arturo/Fons* is built around a homographic tenor that is read successively under three different mensurations: perfect tempus with minor prolation, imperfect tempus with major prolation, and imperfect tempus with minor prolation.[50] The motet text itself indicates that the tenor line should be read in a 3:2 proportion ('bis sub emiolia normis recitatur'), which, in the end, produces the same result as the mensural reinterpretation because the tenor contains only longs and breves. By identifying those named in the motet texts as specific English musicians, Brian Trowell has suggested that *Sub Arturo/Fons* dates from 1358 for the Windsor Garter celebration – an early date considering the motet's style.[51] Roger Bowers delayed the *terminus ante quem* to 1373, the year of the death of J. Alanus, the composer named in the motet text. But Bowers acknowledges that even c. 1370 might seem too early a date for an English motet of such complex form.[52] Moreover, the motet does not appear in any source until **Ch**, and it is copied again in the fifteenth-century sources

[47]   The homophonic text declamation breaks away in the hocketed Amen conceived in duple meter and featuring minim rests, though these characteristics do not necessarily point to a late date; these features also appear in *Post missarum/Post misse* in **Iv**.

[48]   Leech-Wilkinson 1989, 1: 170–1. Leech-Wilkinson states that the two works' taleae are the same length in breves, but this is not quite correct. Besides, counting in breves is ill-advised, since the number of breves changes depending on whether you read in perfect or imperfect modus. Counting longs instead, *Portio/Ida*'s talea is six longs in duration and is repeated four times for a total of twenty-four longs per tenor statement, whereas the Gloria's talea lasts twelve longs and is not repeated within an individual tenor statement. That said, it is not clear what effect shared length would have on determining the direction of influence.

[49]   Determining a chronology for fourteenth-century mass movements can be even more difficult than for motets, since their texts offer no insight into the circumstances of their composition.

[50]   In **Ch** a verbal canon describes this series of mensurations, while in **Q15** the tenor is headed by three stacked mensuration signs. For more on this shift from verbal canons to mensuration signs, see Zazulia forthcoming.

[51]   Trowell 1957, 74.

[52]   He justifies this in Bowers 1990, 331–5.

Q15 and a now-fragmentary bifolio from Yoxford, **GB-Ir 30**. Margaret Bent has even suggested that the J. Alanus of *Sub Arturo/Fons* is a later J. Alanus, which would move the motet's date until after 1400.[53] *Sub Arturo/Fons* is instructive because its situation resembles that of *Portio/Ida*. Both motets' proposed dates depend on somewhat speculative identifications of their named composers, but the proposed dates seem too early for the motets' styles.

I wish I were able to offer more definitive evidence regarding *Portio/Ida*'s date, since it may have important implications for our understanding of late-medieval approaches toward notation, rhythm, and the role of motet tenors. The best I can offer is a word of caution against becoming too comfortable with a given conclusion, especially when using it as the foundation for further inferences. The more times it is said that Egidius de Pusiex composed *Portio/Ida* in 1342 to cel-ebrate Guy of Boulogne becoming a cardinal, the more ingrained that hypothesis becomes. But this hypothesis depends not only on an attribution that appears in a nineteenth-century tran-scription of a now lost source, but also on identifying one specific individual to whom that name might refer. In some ways this is the best hypothesis we have, but it is not without its problems.

This ambiguity opens up two possibilities: we could conclude that we have the wrong Egidius, and the motet instead dates from the 1360s or 1370s. Or, we could conclude that the piece is, in fact, from the 1340s. In other words, to return to the original hypothesis is to interpret *Portio/Ida* as either eccentric or visionary for its time.

It is in part because of the apotheosis of tenor transformation in the fifteenth century (including, but not limited to mensural reinterpretation) that we seek its origins in the fourteenth. In this light, should the motet turn out to be from the 1340s, *Portio/Ida* appears to be an anomaly. But I cannot help but wonder: if the fifteenth-century motets with tenor transformation had never been composed, would *Portio/Ida* merely look like a strange experiment from the mid-fourteenth century? If the schematic manipulation of tenors had not become an important compositional device, it would hold less importance for our narrative about stylistic change. Almost paradoxi-cally, we might then be less concerned about a piece that features a homographic tenor because it would seem like a one-off. In other words, if this technique had not caught on, the 1342 dating might not cause such discomfort. So, perhaps we should not be so worried about sticking with the original story.

This motet might have faded from view if not for the unusual treatment of its tenor and its precocious use of syncopations. Here again questions of style rub up against questions of function. Interest in the motet appears to have continued into the fifteenth century as the copies in **Ch** and **Str** attest. Moreover, its significance was not limited to musical sources: *Portio/Ida* is cited in two surviving theoretical works demonstrating its importance for points of theory and notation.[54] *Portia/Ida* may have been recopied and updated to meet a continued interest in venerating St Ida. Or perhaps fascination with the motet's form, including its unusual tenor treatment, can explain these later copies.

The difficulties with dating this motet touch on many of the major concerns with dating pieces from this time. The surviving attributions are not straightforward, and we hold little hope of turning up an autograph copy. St Ida is an obscure enough dedicatee that the text alone might reveal the motet's intended function, but questions persist. The earliest sources are damaged

---

[53] Bent 1977, Bent 2010, 86–8, and Bent 2017, 35 n. 47.

[54] In addition to the *Ars cantus mensurabilis mensurata per modo iuris* already cited, *Portio/Ida* is mentioned in an early fifteenth-century treatise that begins, 'Differentia est inter motetos'. See Staehelin 1974.

(**NL-Lu 342a** contains only an incomplete reading of the motetus) or perhaps lost (if the motet was conceived for three voices), and evidence of later attempts to modernize it obscure aspects of style that might aid dating.[55] This case comes down to questions of whether and when to place greater stock in extramusical evidence, including attributions and text, or in our understanding of musical style. Unfortunately this conundrum can become circular: with so few datable pieces to shape our sense of stylistic development, sometimes conclusions must be built on precarious foundations.[56]

There has been a move away from a teleological view of stylistic and notational development. Instead scholars increasingly recognize that our ideas about style and chronology inform one another. Older styles – both musical and notational – often coexisted with newer ones, so determining whether a piece is old or just looks old can be a challenge.[57] But the questions are different when dealing with a piece that may be older – perhaps much older – than it looks. *Portio/Ida* therefore prompts us to rethink our narrative for how musical style changed, and how much confidence we can place in the evidence we have at our disposal. This example underscores the tenuousness of our situation as we work through the finer points of fourteenth-century musical style.

---

[55] On considering external and stylistic markers of dating early music, see Milsom 2015.

[56] Notational style also frequently serves as evidence for dating, but because different notational systems did not change uniformly, and instead existed side by side, this type of evidence is less conclusive than we might like. But so too with the extramusical evidence, which is often based on relationships that cannot be proven.

[57] For one such example, see Zayaruznaya 2015a, 139. For a similar situation in the work of Josquin, see Sherr 1988.

APPENDIX

PORTIA/IDA

Edited text and notes on its translation, based on the work of Leofranc Holford-Strevens

Triplum

> Portio nature, precellentis geniture,
> Ide recture iuste sancteque stature,
> Bolonie cure comitisse non sine iure,
> flagranti thure prefemur cantica pure;
> 5 Lotarie rore duce progenie genitore
> militie flore Godefrido cordis honore,
> inde maritate famoso nobilitate
> Eustachio grate mundi per climata late,
> e quis tres nati fuerunt et equis reparati,
> 10 equis et grati, mira probitate probati;
> Eustachius primus, Godofridus et alter opimus
> extitit, ut legimus, Baldevinus datur ymus.
> Qui transvexere mare, gentiles iniere
> et invenere tumulum Dei, cum sibi vere
> 15 Jerusalem libere duo postremique fuere
> reges, augereque Dei fidem studuere.
> Gaudentes, leti, tandem langore repleti,
> termine deleti tribuerunt membra quieti.
> Christicolis culti iuxta tumulumque sepulti,
> 20 verbigena fulti, quod possunt cernere multi,
> cum quibus in vita sine fine quiete polita
> vivere finitaque queamus carne sospita
> Carcere dimisi mundi simus fore visi
> celo gavisi cum dilectis paradisi.

1–4	Singers exhort themselves to sing, amid fragrant incense, the praises of Ida, 'of outstanding birth, just rule, saintly exaltation [*stature*]' and her rightful countess-ship of Boulogne.
1	Problematic from the start. *Portio nature* ('A portion of nature') is not connected syntactically to what follows.
2	The intended meaning of 'stature' is unclear.
5–8	The daughter of Godfrey, Duke of Lorraine and lover of chivalry, then married to Eustace, renowned for his nobility, she was beloved all over the world.
9–12	They had three sons, all knights and 'loved by the just, approved for their wondrous probity; Eustace was first [Count Eustace III of Boulogne], and second Godfrey [of Bouillon] the wealthy, as we read, and Baldwin is given them last.
13–16	These sons crossed the sea, attacked the heathen, and found God's tomb'; the last two were kings of liberated Jerusalem, and sought to expand the Christian faith;
17–20	they lived happily until their final rest in death; honoured by Christians and buried near the Sepulchre, 'maintained by the Wordbegotten [Christ], which many can see';

21–4   with them may we enjoy eternal life when our flesh is laid to rest, freed from the prison
        of the world, rejoicing with those beloved of paradise.

22   Sources have 'sopita', here emended to 'sospita'

Motetus

    Ida capillorum matris domini dominorum
    igne probatorum; cum lino nil perit horum
    vanuit illorum per adesse pir hoc, sed eorum
    propter abesse thorum cuius ussit flamma rogorum.
5 Gazam quesivit veramque probam vestivit.
    Hanc habitamque sivit in claustro quod stabilivit.
    Gaudens in cella nominata voce Capella
    orci quam bella defugere. Fulgida stella,
    hoc tibi cantamen et dictionale gregamen
10 offert laudamen Henricus avens rogitamen
    mortis in examen, anime quod sis relevamen,
    post exalamen ut tecum regnitet. Amen.

Tenor

    Ante thronum trinitatis
    Before the throne of the Trinity.

1–4   This text addresses 'Ida of the hairs of the mother of the Lord of Lords, tested in the
        fire', declaring that nothing of them perished with the cloth, through the presence of
        this fire, but through the absence of the one 'whose bed the flame of the pyres burnt'

5–8   She sought a treasure [i.e. the Virgin's hairs] and donned a true and honourable one
        and placed it in the cloister she established, rejoicing to escape wars in the cell called
        Capelle.

8–12   'Gleaming star, this song and collection of words Henricus offers in praise, desiring your
        praise on the point of death, that you may relieve his soul and, after breathing his last,
        he may reign with you. Amen'.

9   *gregamen*, **Iv**; the other two have *segregamen*, 'separated block', which makes neither
        sense nor meter.

BIBLIOGRAPHY OF WORKS CITED

Allsen, Jon Michael. 1992. 'Style and Intertextuality in the Isorhythmic Motet 1400–1440'. Ph.D. diss. University of Wisconsin-Madison.

Anderson, Gordon Athol, ed. 1968–76. *The Latin Compositions in Fascicules 7 and 8 of the Notre Dame Manuscript Wolfenbüttel Helmstadt 1099 (1206)*. 2 vols. Brooklyn.

——. 1970. 'Clausulae or Transcribed Motets in the Florence Manuscript?' *Acta musicologica* 42: 109–28.

——. 1976. 'Responsory Chants in the Tenors of Some Fourteenth-Century Continental Motets'. *Journal of the American Musicological Society* 29: 119–27.

——, ed. 1977. *Compositions of the Bamberg Manuscript. Bamberg, Staatsbibliothek, Lit. 115 (olim Ed. IV. 6)*. Vol. 75 of Corpus Mensurabilis Musicae. [Rome].

Anderson, Michael Alan. 2011. 'Fire, Foliage and Fury: Vestiges of Midsummer Ritual in Motets for John the Baptist'. *Early Music History* 30: 1–54.

Apel, Willi. 1953. *The Notation of Polyphonic Music, 900–1600*. 5th edn. Cambridge, MA.

——. 1959. 'Remarks about the Isorhythmic Motet'. In *Les colloques de Wégimont II: 1955*, 139–44. Paris.

Arlt, Wulf. 1985. 'Zur frühen Geschichte der Motette: Funktionen – historische Schichten – Musik und Text – Kriterien der Interpretation'. Unpublished paper presented at *Das Ereignis Notre-Dame*, Wolfenbüttel.

——. 1986. '"Triginta denariis": Musik und Text in einer Motette des *Roman de Fauvel* über dem Tenor *Victimae paschali laudes*'. In *Pax et sapientia: Studies in Text and Music of Liturgical Tropes and Sequences, in Memory of Gordon Anderson*, ed. Ritva Jacobsson, 97–113. Stockholm.

——. 1995. 'Warum nur Viermal? Zur historischen Stellung des Komponierens an der Pariser Notre Dame'. In *Studien zur Musikgeschichte: Eine Festschrift für Ludwig Finscher*, ed. Anegrit Laubenthal and Kara Kusan-Windweh, 44–8. Kassel.

Arrighi, Giovanni. 2010. *The Long Twentieth Century: Money, Power, and the Origins of Our Times*. London.

Atchison, Mary, ed. 2005. *The Chansonnier of Oxford Bodleian MS Douce 308: Essays and Complete Edition of Texts*. Aldershot and Burlington.

——. 2012. 'Two Versions of the *Tournoi de Chauvency* and their Connections to the Chansonnier of Oxford, Bodleian MS Douce 308'. In *Lettres, musique et société en Lorraine médiévale: Autour du Tournoi de Chauvency (Ms. Oxford Bodleian Douce 308)*, ed. Mireille Chazan and Nancy Freeman Regalado, 71–104. Geneva.

Atlas, Allan. 1981. 'Conflicting Attributions in Italian Sources of the Franco-Netherlandish Chanson, c. 1465–c. 1505: A Progress Report on a New Hypothesis'. In *Music in Medieval and Early Modern Europe: Patronage, Sources and Texts*, ed. Iain Fenlon, 249–93. Cambridge.

Bain, Jennifer. 2008. 'Messy Structure? Multiple Tonal Centers in the Music of Machaut'. *Music Theory Spectrum* 30: 195–237.

Baldwin, John W. 1994. *The Language of Sex: Five Voices from Northern France around 1200*. Chicago and London.

——. 1997. '"Once there was an emperor …": A Political Reading of the Romances of Jean Renart'. In *Jean Renart and the Art of Romance*, ed. Nancy Vine Durling, 45–82. Gainesville.

Balensuela, C. Matthew, ed. 1994. *Ars cantus mensurabilis mensurata per modo iuris*. Vol. 10 of Greek and Latin Music Theory. Lincoln, NE.

Baltzer, Rebecca A. 1974. 'Notation, Rhythm, and Style in the Two-Voice Notre Dame Clausula'. 2 vols. Ph.D. diss. Boston University.

——, ed. 1995. *Les Clausules à deux voix du manuscrit de Florence, Biblioteca Medicea-Laurenziana, Pluteus 29.I, Fascicule V*. Vol. 5 of Le Magnus Liber Organi de Notre-Dame de Paris, ed. Edward H. Roesner. Monaco.

——. 1997. 'The Polyphonic Progeny of an *Et gaudebit*: Assessing Family Relations in the Thirteenth-Century Motet'. In *Hearing the Motet*, ed. Pesce 1997, 17–27.

——. 2007. 'Why Marian Motets on Non-Marian Tenors? An Answer'. In *Music in Medieval Europe: Studies in Honour of Brian Gillingham*, ed. Terence Bailey and Alma Santosuosso, 112–28. Aldershot.

——. 2018. 'The Decoration of Montpellier Fascicle 8: Its Place in the Continuum of Parisian Manuscript Illumination'. In Bradley and Desmond 2018, 78–89.

Baluze, Étienne. 1761. *Stephani Baluzii Tutelensis Miscellanea*. Ed. Giovanni Domenico Mansi. Vol. 1. Lucca.

Beck, Jean and Louise Beck, eds. 1938. *Le Manuscrit du Roi, B. N. Fonds Français No. 844*. 2 vols. Philadelphia.

Becker, Philipp August. 1936. 'Fauvel und Fauvelliana'. *Berichte über die Verhandlungen der sächsischen Akademie der Wissenschaften zu Leipzig, Philologische-Historische Klasse* 88/2: 1–45.

Beiche, Michael. 2004. 'Motet/motetus/mottetto/Motette'. In Vol. 36 of *Handwörterbuch der musikalischen Terminologie*, ed. Hans Heinrich Eggebrecht, 1–23. Mainz.

Bell, Nicolas. 2004. *The Las Huelgas Music Codex: A Companion Study to the Facsimile*. Madrid.

Bent, Margaret, ed. 1977. *Two 14th-Century Motets in Praise of Music*. Moretonhampstead.

——. 1978. 'A Preliminary Assessment of the Independence of English Trecento Notations'. In *L'Ars Nova Italiana del Trecento* 4, ed. Agostino Ziino, 65–82. Certaldo.

——. 1981a. *Dunstaple*. Vol. 17 of Oxford Studies of Composers. London.

——. 1981b. 'Rota versatilis – Towards a Reconstruction'. In *Source Materials and the Interpretation of Music: A Memorial Volume to Thurston Dart*, ed. Ian Bent, 65–98. London.

——. 1981c. 'Some Factors in the Control of Consonance and Sonority: Successive Composition and the *Solus tenor*'. In *International Musicological Society: Report of the Twelfth Congress, Berkeley 1977*, ed. Daniel Heartz and Bonnie Wade, 625–34. Kassel.

——. 1983. 'The Machaut Manuscripts Vg, B and E'. *Musica Disciplina* 37: 83–112.

——. 1984. 'Text Setting in Sacred Music of the Early 15th Century: Evidence and Implications'. In *Musik und Text in der Mehrstimmigkeit des 14. und 15. Jahrhunderts: Vorträge des Gastsymposions in der Herzog August Bibliothek Wolfenbüttel, 8. bis 12. September 1980*, ed. Ursula Günther and Ludwig Finscher, 291–326. Vol. 10 of Göttinger musikwissenschaftliche Arbeiten. Kassel.

——. 1987. 'A Contemporary Perception of Early Fifteenth-Century Style: Bologna Q15 as a Document of Scribal Editorial Initiative'. *Musica Disciplina* 41: 183–201.

——. 1990. 'A Note on the Dating of the Trémoïlle Manuscript'. In *Beyond the Moon, Festschrift Luther Dittmer*, ed. Bryan Gillingham and Paul Merkley, 217–42. Ottawa.

——. 1991. 'Deception, Exegesis and Sounding Number in Machaut's Motet 15'. *Early Music History* 10: 15–27.

——. 1992a. 'The Fourteenth-Century Italian Motet'. In *L'Ars Nova Italiana del Trecento* 6 (1984), ed. Giulio Cattin and Patrizia Dalla Vechia, 85–125. Certaldo.

——. 1992b. 'The Late-Medieval Motet'. In *Companion to Medieval & Renaissance Music*, ed. Tess Knighton and David Fallows, 114–19. London.

——. 1995. 'Some Aspects of the Motets in the Cyprus Manuscript'. In *The Cypriot-French Repertory of the Manuscript Torino J.II.9: Report of the International Musicological Congress, Paphos 20–25 March, 1992*, ed. Ursula Günther and Ludwig Finscher, 357–75. Neuhausen-Stuttgart.

——. 1997. 'Polyphony of Texts and Music in the Fourteenth-Century Motet: *Tribum que non abhorruit/Quoniam secta latronum/Merito hec patimur* and its "Quotations"'. In *Hearing the Motet*, ed. Pesce 1997, 82–103.

——. 1998a. 'Early Papal Motets'. In *Papal Music and Musicians in Medieval and Renaissance Rome*, ed. Richard Sherr, 6–43. Oxford.

——. 1998b. 'Fauvel and Marigny: Which Came First?' In Bent and Wathey 1998, 35–52.

——. 2001. 'Isorhythm'. *The New Grove Dictionary of Music and Musicians.*, ed. Stanley Sadie, 2nd edn, 12: 618–23. London and New York.

——. 2002. *Counterpoint, Composition, and Musica Ficta*. London and New York.

——. 2003. 'Words and Music in Machaut's Motet 9'. *Early Music* 31: 363–88.

——. 2008a. 'Naming of Parts: Notes on the Contratenor, c. 1350–1450'. In *'Uno gentile et subtile ingenio': Studies in Renaissance Music in Honour of Bonnie Blackburn*, ed. Gioia Filocamo and M. Jennifer Bloxam, 1–12. Turnhout.

——. 2008b. 'What is Isorhythm?'. In *Quomodo Cantabimus Canticum? Studies in Honor of Edward H. Roesner*, ed. David Butler Cannata, with Gabriela Ilnitchi Currie, Rena Charnin Mueller, and John Louis Nádas, 121–43. Vol. 7 of Miscellanea. Middleton, WI.

——. 2009. 'The Myth of *tempus perfectum diminutum* in the Chantilly Manuscript'. In *A Late Medieval Songbook and its Context: New Perspectives on the Chantilly Codex (Bibliothèque du Château de Chantilly, 564)*, ed. Yolanda Plumley and Anne Stone, 203–27. Turnhout.

——. 2010. 'The Earliest Fifteenth-Century Transmission of English Music to the Continent'. In *Essays on the History of English Music in Honour of John Caldwell: Sources, Style, Performance, Historiography*, ed. Emma Hornby and David Maw, 83–96. Woodbridge.

——. 2015. *Magister Jacobus de Ispania, Author of the Speculum musicae*. Farnham.

——. 2017. 'The Absent First Gathering of the Chantilly Manuscript'. *Plainsong and Medieval Music* 26: 19–36.

—— and Kevin Brownlee. Forthcoming. 'Icarus, Phaeton, Haman: Did Vitry Know Dante?'.

—— and Anne Hallmark, eds. 1985. *The Works of Johannes Ciconia*. Latin texts ed. M. J. Connolly. Vol. 19 of Polyphonic Music of the Fourteenth Century. Monaco.

—— with David Howlett. 1990. '*Subtiliter alternare*: The Yoxford Motet *O amicus/Precursoris*'. *Studies in Medieval Music: Festschrift for Ernest H. Sanders*, ed. Peter M. Lefferts and Brian Seirup. *Current Musicology* 45–7: 43–84.

—— and Andrew Wathey, eds. 1998. *Fauvel Studies: Allegory, Chronicle, Music, and Images in Paris, Bibliothèque Nationale de France, MS Français 146*. Oxford.

—— and Andrew Wathey. 2001. 'Vitry, Philippe de'. *The New Grove Dictionary of Music and Musicians*, ed. Stanley Sadie, 2nd edn, 26: 803–13. London and New York.

Berentsen, Niels. 2016. '*Discantare super planum cantum*: New Approaches to Vocal Polyphonic Improvisation 1300–1470'. Ph.D. diss. Leiden University.

Berktold, Christian, ed. 1999. *Ars practica mensurabilis cantus secundum Iohannem de Muris: Die Recensio maior des sogenannten 'Libellus practice cantus mensurabilis'*. Munich.

Berlière, Ursmer. 1906. *Suppliques de Clément VI (1342–52): Textes et Analyses*. Rome.

Besseler, Heinrich. 1925. 'Studien zur Musik des Mittelalters I: Neue Quellen des 14. und beginnenden 15. Jahrhunderts'. *Archiv für Musikwissenschaft* 7: 167–252.

——. 1927. 'Studien zur Musik des Mittelalters II: Die Motette von Franko von Köln bis Philipp von Vitry'. *Archiv für Musikwissenschaft* 8: 137–258.

——, ed. 1966. *Guillelmi Dufay Opera Omnia*. Vol. 1 of Corpus Mensurabilis Musicae. Rome.

Blonquist, Lawrence B., trans. 1987. *L'Art d'Amours (The Art of Love)*. Vol. 32 of Garland Library of Medieval Literature, Series A. New York.

Bolduc, Michelle. 2006. *The Medieval Poetics of Contraries*. Gainesville.

Boogaart, Jacques. 1993. 'Love's Unstable Balance, Part I: Analogy of Ideas in Text and Music of Machaut's Motet 6, Part II: More Balance Problems and the Order of Machaut's Motets'. *Muziek & Wetenschap* 3: 3–33.

——. 2001a. 'Encompassing Past and Present: Quotations and their Function in Machaut's Motets'. *Early Music History* 20: 1–86.

——. 2001b. '"O series summe rata". De motetten van Guillaume de Machaut; De ordening van het corpus en de samenhang van tekst en muziek'. 2 vols. Ph.D. diss. University of Utrecht.

——. 2003. '*Speculum mortis*: Form and Signification in Machaut's Motet *He Mors/Fine Amour/Quare non sum mortuus*'. In *Machaut's Music: New Interpretations*, ed. Elizabeth Eva Leach, 13–30. Woodbridge.

——. 2004a. 'L'accomplissement du cercle: observations analytiques sur l'ordre des motets de Guillaume de Machaut'. *Analyse musicale* 50: 45–63.

——. 2004b. Review of Anne Walters Robertson, *Guillaume de Machaut and Reims: Context and Meaning in His Musical Works*. *Early Music* 32: 603–6.

——. 2007. 'Thought-Provoking Dissonances: Remarks about Machaut's Compositional Licences in Relation to his Texts'. *Dutch Journal of Music Theory* 12: 273–92.

——, ed. with Domenic Leo and R. Barton Palmer. 2018. *The Motets*. Vol. 9 of *Guillaume de Machaut: The Complete Poetry and Music*. General eds. R. Barton Palmer and Yolanda Plumley. Kalamazoo.

Bowers, Roger. 1990. 'Fixed Points in the Chronology of English Fourteenth-Century Polyphony'. *Music & Letters* 71: 313–35.

Bradley, Catherine A. 2011. 'The Earliest Motets: Musical Borrowing and Re-use'. Ph.D. diss. University of Cambridge.

——. 2012. 'New Texts for Old Music: Three Early Thirteenth-Century Latin Motets'. *Music & Letters* 93: 149–69.

——. 2013. 'Contrafacta and Transcribed Motets: Vernacular Influences on Latin Motets and Clausulae in the Florence Manuscript'. *Early Music History* 32: 1–70.

——. 2014a. 'Comparing Compositional Process in Two Thirteenth-Century Motets: Pre-existent Materials in *Deus omnium/REGNAT* and *Ne m'oubliez mi/DOMINO*'. *Music Analysis* 33: 263–90.

——. 2014b. 'Seeking the Sense of Sound'. *Journal of the Royal Musical Association* 139: 405–20.

——. 2015. 'Re-workings and Chronological Dynamics in a Thirteenth-Century Latin Motet Family'. *The Journal of Musicology* 32: 153–97.

——. 2017. 'Song and Quotation in Two-voice Motets for Saint Elizabeth of Hungary'. *Speculum* 92: 661–91.

——. Forthcoming 2018. *Polyphony in Medieval Paris: The Art of Composing with Plainchant*. Cambridge.

—— and Karen Desmond, eds. 2018. *The Montpellier Codex: The Final Fascicle. Contents, Contexts, Chronologies*. Woodbridge.

Bragard, Roger, ed. 1955–73. *Jacobi Leodiensis Speculum musicae Libri VII*. 7 vols. Vol. 3 of Corpus Scriptorum de Musica. Rome.

Brand, Benjamin. 2003. '*Viator ducens ad celestia*: Eucharistic Piety, Papal Politics, and an Early Fifteenth-Century Motet'. *The Journal of Musicology* 20: 250–84.

Brinkman, Herman and Ike de Loos, eds. 2015. *Het Gruuthuse-handschrift. Hs. Den Haag, Koninklijke Bibliotheek 79 K 10*. Vol. 13 of Middeleeuwse Verzamelhandschriften uit de Nederlanden. Hilversum.

Brown, Catherine. 1998. *Contrary Things: Exegesis, Dialectic, and the Poetics of Didacticism*. Stanford.

Brown, Elizabeth A.R. 1998. '*Rex ioians, ionnes, iolis*: Louis X, Philip V, and the *Livres de Fauvel*'. In Bent and Wathey 1998, 53–72.

Brown, Thomas. 2001. 'Another Mirror of Lovers? Order, Structure and Allusion in Machaut's Motets'. *Plainsong and Medieval Music* 10: 121–33.

Brownlee, Kevin. 2005. 'Fire, Desire, Duration, Death: Machaut's Motet 10'. In S. Clark and Leach 2005, 79–93. Woodbridge.

——— and Sylvia Huot. 1992. 'Introduction: Rethinking the *Rose*'. In *Rethinking the* Romance of the Rose: *Text Image, Reception*, ed. Kevin Brownlee and Sylvia Huot, 1–18. Philadelphia.

Buffum, Douglas L. 1912. 'The Refrains of the *Court de Paradis* and of a *Salut d'amour*'. *Modern Language Notes* 27: 5–11.

Busse Berger, Anna Maria. 1993. *Mensuration and Proportion Signs: Origins and Evolution*. Oxford.

———. 2005. *Medieval Music and the Art of Memory*. Berkeley.

Butterfield, Ardis. 1993. 'The Language of Medieval Music: Two Thirteenth-Century Motets'. *Plainsong and Medieval Music* 2: 1–16.

———. 1997. '*Aucassin et Nicolette* and Mixed Forms in Medieval French'. In *Prosimetrum: Crosscultural Perspectives on Narrative Prose and Verse*, ed. Joseph Harris and Karl Reichl, 67–98. Cambridge.

———. 2002. *Poetry and Music in Medieval France From Jean Renart to Guillaume de Machaut*. Cambridge.

———. 2003. '*Enté*: A Survey and Reassessment of the Term in Thirteenth- and Fourteenth-Century Music and Poetry'. *Early Music History* 22: 67–101.

———. 2012. 'The Musical Contexts of Le Tournoi de Chauvency in Oxford, Bodleian MS Douce 308'. In *Lettres, musique et société en Lorraine médiévale: Autour du Tournoi de Chauvency (Ms. Oxford Bodleian Douce 308)*, ed. Mireille Chazan and Nancy Freeman Regalado, 399–422. Geneva.

Büttner, Fred, ed. 1999. *Die Klauseln der Handschrift Saint-Victor (Paris, BN, lat. 15139)*. Tutzing.

———. 2002. 'Weltliche Einflüsse in der Notre-Dame-Musik? Überlegungen zu einer Klausel im Codex F'. *Anuario Musical* 57: 19–37.

———. 2011. *Das Klauselrepertoire der Handschrift Saint-Victor (Paris, BN, lat. 15139): Eine Studie zur mehrstimmigen Komposition im 13. Jahrhundert*. Lecce.

Bynum, Caroline Walker. 2001. *Metamorphosis and Identity*. New York.

Caldwell, John. 1981. Review of Frank Ll. Harrison, ed., *Polyphonic Music of the Fourteenth Century, xv: Motets of English Provenance*. *Music & Letters* 62: 466–70.

Callahan, Christopher. 2013. 'Collecting trouvère lyric at the peripheries: the lessons of MSS Paris, BnF fr. 20050, Paris, BnF fr. 12581, and Bern, Burgerbibliothek 389'. *Textual Cultures* 8/2: 15–30.

Carnandet, Jean Baptiste, ed. 1866. 'Vita B. Ide Vidue'. In *Acta Sanctorum* 13 April, 11: 141–6. 3rd edn. Paris and Rome.

Casey, Camillus. 1956. '*Les Voeux du Paon* by Jacques de Longuyon: An Edition of the Manuscripts of the P Redaction'. Ph.D. diss. Columbia University.

Catalunya, David. 2016. 'Music, Space and Ritual in Medieval Castile, 1221–1350'. Ph.D. diss. Julius-Maximilians-Universität Würzburg.

Cerquiglini, Jacqueline. 1985. '*Un engin si soutil*': *Guillaume de Machaut et l'écriture au XIVe siècle*. Paris.

Clark, Alice. V. 1996. '*Concordare cum Materia*: The Tenor in the Fourteenth-Century Motet'. Ph.D. diss. Princeton University.

———. 2004. 'Listening to Machaut's Motets'. *The Journal of Musicology* 21: 487–513.

———. 2011. '*Prope est ruina*: The Transformation of a Medieval Tenor'. In *Music, Dance and Society: Medieval and Renaissance Studies in Memory of Ingrid G. Brainard*, ed. Ann Buckley and Cynthia J. Cyrus, 129–42. Kalamazoo.

Clark, Suzannah. 2007. '"S'en dirai chançonete": Hearing Text and Music in a Medieval Motet'. *Plainsong and Medieval Music* 16: 31–59.

——— and Elizabeth Eva Leach, eds. 2005. *Citation and Authority in Medieval and Renaissance Musical Culture: Learning from the Learned*. Woodbridge.

Clercx, Suzanne and Richard Hoppin. 1959. 'Notes biographiques sur quelques musiciens Français du XIVe siècle'. In *Les colloques de Wégimont, II: 1955*, 63–92. Paris.

Colton, Lisa. 2008. 'The Articulation of Virginity in the Medieval Chanson de Nonne'. *Journal of the Royal Musical Association* 133: 159–88.

——. 2017a. *Angel Song: Medieval English Music in History*. Abingdon.

——. 2017b. 'Music, Text and Structure in 14th-Century English Polyphony: The Case of *Ave miles celestis curie*'. *Early Music* 45: 27–40.

Coussemaker, Charles Edmond Henri de. 1865. *L'art harmonique aux XIIe et XIIIe siècles*. Paris. Reprint. Hildesheim, 1964.

Curran, Sean. 2013a. 'Composing a Codex: The Motets in the 'La Clayette' Manuscript'. In *Medieval Music in Practice: Studies in Honor of Richard Crocker*, ed. Judith A. Peraino, 219–54. Middleton, WI.

——. 2013b. 'Vernacular Book Production, Vernacular Polyphony, and the Motets of the "La Clayette" Manuscript (Paris, Bibliothèque nationale de France, nouvelles acquisitions françaises 13521)'. Ph.D. diss. University of California, Berkeley.

——. 2014. 'Reading and Rhythm in the "La Clayette" Manuscript (Paris, Bibliothèque nationale de France, nouv. acq. fr. 13521)'. *Plainsong and Medieval Music* 23: 125–50.

——. 2018. 'A Palaeographical Analysis of the Verbal Text in Montpellier 8: Problems, Implications, Opportunities'. In Bradley and Desmond 2018, 32–65.

Dalglish, William. 1972. 'The Use of Variation in Early Polyphony'. *Musica Disciplina* 26: 37–51.

Davis, Shelley. 1967. 'The Solus Tenor in the 14th and 15th Centuries'. *Acta Musicologica* 39: 44–64.

Deford, Ruth I. 2005. 'On Diminution and Proportion in Fifteenth-Century Music Theory'. *Journal of the American Musicological Society* 58: 1–67.

——. 2015. *Tactus, Mensuration and Rhythm in Renaissance Music*. Cambridge.

De Hamel, Christopher. 1992. *Scribes and Illuminators*. Toronto.

Delbouille, Maurice. 1926. *Les origines de la pastourelle*. Bruxelles.

——, ed. 1932. *Jacques Bretel: Le Tournoi de Chauvency*. Liège.

Dell, Helen. 2008. *Desire by Gender and Genre in Trouvère Song*. Woodbridge and Rochester.

Delogu, Daisy. 2012. '"Laissier Le Mal, Le Bien Eslire": History, Allegory, and Ethical Reading in the Works of Guillaume de Machaut'. In *A Companion to Guillaume de Machaut*, ed. Deborah McGrady and Jennifer Bain, 261–75. Leiden and Boston.

Desmond, Karen. 2000. 'New Light on Jacobus, Author of Speculum musicae'. *Plainsong and Medieval Music* 9: 19–40.

——. 2015. 'Did Vitry write an *Ars vetus et nova*?'. *The Journal of Musicology* 32: 441–93.

——. 2018a. *Music and the moderni, 1300–50: The* ars nova *in Theory and Practice*. Cambridge.

——. 2018b. '"One is the loneliest number …": The Semibreve Stands Alone'. *Early Music* 46.

Desplanque, Alexander. 1867. 'Recherches sur L'abbaye de la Capelle en Calais'. *Annales du Comité Flamand de France* 9: 330–82.

Desportes, Pierre. 1979. *Reims et les Rémois aux XIIIᵉ et XIVᵉ siècles*. Paris.

Dillon, Emma. 1998. 'The Profile of Philip V in the Music of Fauvel'. In Bent and Wathey 1998, 215–32.

——. 2002. *Medieval Music-Making and the Roman de Fauvel*. Cambridge.

——. 2012. *The Sense of Sound: Musical Meaning in France, 1260–1330*. Oxford.

Dittmer, Luther. 1953. 'Binary Rhythm, Musical Theory and the Worcester Fragments'. *Musica Disciplina* 7: 39–57.

——. 1954. 'An English *Discantum Volumen*'. *Musica Disciplina* 8: 19–58.

——. 1957. 'The Dating and the Notation of the Worcester Fragments'. *Musica Disciplina* 11: 5–11.

Doss-Quinby, Eglal, Joan Tasker Grimbert, Wendy Pfeffer, and Elizabeth Aubrey, eds. 2001. *Songs of the Women Trouvères*. New Haven.

Doss-Quinby, Eglal, Samuel N. Rosenberg, and Elizabeth Aubrey, eds. 2006. *The Old French Ballette, Oxford, Bodleian Library, Ms Douce 308*. Geneva.

Doudet, Estelle, Marie-Laure Savoye, and Agathe Sultan, eds. 2016. *Lettres d'amour du moyen âge: Les saluts et complaintes*. Paris.

Dronke, Peter. 1968. *Medieval Latin and the Rise of European Love-Lyric*. 2nd edn. 2 vols. Oxford.

Dyggve, Holger Petersen. 1938. 'Moniot d'Arras et Moniot de Paris'. *Mémoires de la Société néophilologique de Helsingfors* 13: 3–252.

Earp, Lawrence. 1983. 'Scribal Practice, Manuscript Production and the Transmission of Music in Late Medieval France: The Manuscripts of Guillaume de Machaut'. Ph.D. diss. Princeton University.

——. 1989. 'Machaut's Role in the Production of Manuscripts of His Works'. *Journal of the American Musicological Society* 42: 461–503.

——. 1995. *Guillaume de Machaut: A Guide to Research*. New York and London.

——. 2005. 'Declamatory Dissonance in Machaut'. In S. Clark and Leach 2005, 102–22. Woodbridge.

——. 2011. 'Interpreting the Deluxe Manuscript: Exigencies of Scribal Practice and Manuscript Production in Machaut'. In *The Calligraphy of Medieval Music*, ed. John Haines, 223–40. Turnhout.

——. 2014. *The Ferrell-Vogüé Machaut Manuscript*, with Domenic Leo, Carla Shapreau, and Christopher de Hamel. 2 vols. Oxford.

——. 2015a. 'Cathedral and Court: Music under the Late Capetian and Valois Kings, to Louis XI'. In *The Cambridge Companion to French Music*, ed. Simon Trezise, 21–48. Cambridge.

——. 2015b. 'Tradition and Innovation in *Ars nova* Motet Notation'. Paper presented at the American Musicological Society conference, Louisville, November 14, 2015.

——. Forthcoming. 'Notations II'. In *The Cambridge History of Medieval Music*, ed. Mark Everist and Thomas Forrest Kelly. Cambridge.

Evans, Beverly Jean. 1983. 'The Unity of Text and Music in the Late Thirteenth-Century French Motet: A Study of Selected Works from the Montpellier Manuscript, Fascicle 7'. Ph.D. diss. University of Pennsylvania.

Everist, Mark. 1988. 'The Rondeau Motet: Paris and Artois in the Thirteenth Century'. *Music & Letters* 69: 1–22.

——. 1989. *Polyphonic Music in Thirteenth-Century France: Aspects of Sources and Distribution*. New York and London.

——. 1990. 'From Paris to St. Andrews: The Origins of W1'. *Journal of the American Musicological Society* 43: 1–42.

——. 1994. *French Motets in the Thirteenth Century*. Cambridge.

——. 1996. 'The Polyphonic Rondeau *c.* 1300: Repertory and Context'. *Early Music History* 15: 59–96.

——. 2007. 'Motets, French Tenors, and the Polyphonic Chanson ca. 1300'. *The Journal of Musicology* 24: 365–406.

——. 2016. 'Vernacular Contexts for the Monophonic Motet: Notes from a New Source'. In *Music and Culture in the Middle Ages and Beyond: Liturgy, Sources, Symbolism*, ed. Benjamin Brand and David J. Rothenberg, 142–57. Cambridge.

Fallows, David, ed. 1995. *Oxford, Bodleian Library Ms. Canon. Misc. 213. With an Introduction and Inventory by David Fallows*. Chicago and London.

Fery-Hue, Françoise. 2000, 'La tradition manuscrite du *Lapidaire du roi Philippe*'. *Scriptorium* 54: 91–192.

Fischer, Kurt von and F. Alberto Gallo, eds. 1987. *Italian Sacred and Ceremonial Music*. Vol. 13 of Polyphonic Music of the Fourteenth Century. Monaco.

Folena, Gianfranco. 1990. *Culture e lingue nel Veneto medieval*. Padua.

Frobenius, Wolf, ed. 1971. *Johannes Boens Musica und seine Konsonanzenlehre*. Vol. 2 of Freiburger Schriften zur Musikwissenschaft. Stuttgart.

——. 1987. 'Zum genetischen Verhältnis zwischen Notre-Dame-Klauseln und ihren Motetten'. *Archiv für Musikwissenschaft* 44: 1–39.

Fuller, Sarah. 1985–6. 'A Phantom Treatise of the Fourteenth Century? The *Ars Nova*'. *The Journal of Musicology* 4: 23–50.

——. 1986. 'On Sonority in Fourteenth-Century Polyphony'. *Journal of Music Theory* 30: 35–70.

——. 1990. 'Modal Tenors and Tonal Orientation in Motets of Guillaume de Machaut'. *Studies in Medieval Music: Festschrift for Ernest H. Sanders*, ed. Peter M. Lefferts and Brian Seirup. *Current Musicology* 45–7: 199–245.

——. 1992a. 'Guillaume de Machaut: *De toutes flours*'. In *Models of Music Analysis: Music Before 1600*, ed. Mark Everist, 41–65. Oxford.

——. 1992b. 'Tendencies and Resolutions: The Directed Progression in *Ars Nova* Music'. *Journal of Music Theory* 36: 229–258.

——. 2006. *The European Musical Heritage 800–1750*. Rev. edn. New York.

——. 2013. '*Contrapunctus*, Dissonance Regulation, and French Polyphony of the Fourteenth Century'. In *Medieval Music in Practice: Studies in Honor of Richard Crocker*, ed. Judith A. Peraino, 113–52. Middleton, WI.

Gaiffier, Baudouin de. 1968. 'Sainte Ide de Boulogne et l'Espagne. Apropos de reliques mariales'. *Analecta Bollandiana* 86: 67–81.

——. 1971. *Recherches d'Hagiographie Latine*. Brussels.

Gallo, F. Alberto. 1966. *La teoria della notazione in Italia dalla fine del XIII all'inizio del XV secolo*. Antiquae Musicae Italicae Subsidia Theoretica. Bologna.

——. 1984. 'Die Notationslehre im 14. und 15. Jahrhundert'. In *Die Mittelalterliche Lehre von der Mehrstimmigkeit*, ed. Frieder Zaminer, 257–356. Vol. 5 of Geschichte der Musiktheorie. Darmstadt.

——. 1985. *Music of the Middle Ages II*. Trans. Karen Eales. Cambridge.

——, Gilbert Reaney, and André Gilles, eds. 1971. *Petrus Picardus, Ars motettorum compilata breviter. Anonymus, Ars musicae mensurabilis secundum Franconem (Mss. Paris, Bibl. Nat., lat. 15129; Uppsala, Universiteitsbibl., C 55). Anonymus, Compendium musicae mensurabilis artis antiquae (Ms. Faenza, Biblioteca Comunale 117)*. Vol. 15 of Corpus Scriptorum de Musica. [Dallas].

Gastoué, Amédée. 1936. *Le Manuscrit de musique du trésor d'Apt*. Paris.

Gennrich, Friedrich. 1921. *Rondeaux, Virelais und Balladen aus dem Ende des xii., dem xiii, und dem ersten Drittel des xiv. Jahrhunderts mit den überlieferten Melodien*. 3 vols. Dresden.

——. 1926. 'Trouvèrelieder und Motettenrepertoire'. *Zeitschrift für Musikwissenschaft* 9: 8–39, 65–85.

——. 1957. *Bibliographie der ältesten französischen und lateinischen Motetten*. Vol. 2 of Summa Musicae Medii Aevi. Darmstadt.

Gerritsen, William Pieter and Anthony G. Van Melle, eds. 2000. *A Dictionary of Medieval Heroes: Characters in Medieval Narrative Traditions and their Afterlife in Literature, Theatre and the Visual Arts*. Woodbridge.

Gower, Gillian Lucinda. 2016. 'Iconography of Queenship: Sacred Music and Female Examplarity in Late Medieval Britain'. Ph.D. diss. University of California, Los Angeles.

Grau, Anna Kathryn. 2013. 'Hearing Voices: Heteroglossia, Homoglossia, and the Old French Motet'. *Musica Disciplina* 58: 73–100.

Günther, Ursula. 1958. 'The 14th-Century Motet and its Development'. *Musica Disciplina* 12: 27–58.

——, ed. 1965. *The Motets of the Manuscripts Chantilly, Musée Condé, MS 564 (olim 1047) and Modena, Biblioteca Estense, a.M.5.24 (olim Lat. 568)*. Rev. edn. 1998. Vol. 39 of Corpus Mensurabilis Musicae. Rome.

——. 1978. 'Problems of Dating in *Ars nova* and *Ars subtilior*'. In *L'ars Nova Italiana del Trecento 4*, ed. Agostino Ziino, 289–301. Certaldo.

Haines, John. 1998. 'The Musicography of the "Manuscrit du Roi"'. Ph.D. diss. University of Toronto.

——. 1998–2002. 'The Transformations of the *Manuscrit du Roi*'. *Musica Disciplina* 52: 5–43.

——. 2001. 'The Footnote Quarrels of the Modal Theory: A Remarkable Episode in the Reception of Medieval Music'. *Early Music History* 20: 87–120.

——. 2003. 'Friedrich Ludwig's "Medieval Musicology of the Future": A Commentary and Translation'. *Plainsong and Medieval Music* 12: 129–64.

——. 2004a. *Eight Centuries of Troubadours and Trouvères: The Changing Identity of Medieval Music*. Cambridge.

——. 2004b. 'Erasures in Thirteenth-century Music'. In *Music and Medieval Manuscripts: Paleography and Performance*, ed. John Haines and Randall Rosenfeld, 60–88. Aldershot.

——. 2008. 'The Origins of the Musical Staff'. *Musical Quarterly* 91: 327–78.

——. 2010. *Satire in the Songs of Renart le Nouvel*. Geneva.

——. 2013. 'The Songbook for William of Villehardouin, Prince of Morea (Paris, Bibliothèque nationale de France, fonds français 844): A Crucial Case in the History of Vernacular Song Collections'. In *Viewing the Morea: Land and People in the Late Medieval Peloponnese*, ed. Sharon Gerstel, 57–109. Cambridge, MA.

——. 2015. 'Manuscript Sources and Calligraphy'. In *The Cambridge Companion to French Music*, ed. Simon Trezise, 293–312. Cambridge.

——. Forthcoming. 'Aristocratic Patronage and the Cosmopolitan Vernacular Songbook: Bibliothèque nationale de France, f. fr. 844 and the French Mediterranean'. In *Musical Culture in the World of Adam de la Halle*, ed. Jennifer Saltzstein. Leiden.

Handschin, Jacques. 1949. 'The Summer Canon and its Background: I'. *Musica Disciplina* 3: 55–94.

——. 1951. 'The Summer Canon and its Background: II'. *Musica Disciplina* 5: 65–113.

Harrison, Frank Ll. 1967. 'Ars Nova in England: A New Source'. *Musica Disciplina* 21: 67–85.

——, ed. 1968. *Motets of French Provenance*. Vol. 5 of Polyphonic Music of the Fourteenth Century. Monaco.

——, ed. 1980. *Motets of English Provenance*. Texts ed. and trans. Peter Lefferts. Vol. 15 of Polyphonic Music of the Fourteenth Century. Monaco.

—— and Roger Wibberley, eds. 1981. *Manuscripts of Fourteenth Century English Polyphony*. Vol. 26 of Early English Church Music. London.

Hartt, Jared C. 2009. 'The Three Tenors: Machaut's Secular Trio'. *Studi Musicali* 38: 237–71.

——. 2010a. 'Rehearing Machaut's Motets: Taking the Next Step in Understanding Sonority'. *Journal of Music Theory* 54: 179–234.

——. 2010b. 'Tonal and Structural Implications of Isorhythmic Design in Guillaume de Machaut's Tenors'. *Theory and Practice* 35: 57–94.

——. 2012. '*Les doubles hoqués et les motés*: Guillaume de Machaut's *Hoquetus David*'. *Plainsong and Medieval Music* 21: 137–73.

——. 2017. 'The Problem of the Vitry Motet Corpus: Sonority, Kinship, Attribution'. *Music Theory and Analysis* 4: 192–228.

Hiley, David. 1986. 'Ordinary of Mass Chants in English, North French and Sicilian Manuscripts'. *Journal of the Plainsong and Mediaeval Music Society* 9: 1–127.

Hoekstra, Gerald A. 1998. 'The French Motet as Trope: Multiple Levels of Meaning in *Quant florist la violete/El mois de mai/Et gaudebit*'. *Speculum* 73: 32–57.

Hofmann, Klaus. 1970. 'Zur Entstehungs- und Frühgeschichte des Terminus Motette'. *Acta Musicologica* 42: 138–50.

Holford-Strevens, Leofranc. 2005. 'Fauvel Goes to School'. In S. Clark and Leach 2005, 59–66.

——. 2011. 'Latin Poetry and Music'. In *The Cambridge Companion to Medieval Music*, ed. Mark Everist, 225–40. Cambridge.

Hoppin, Richard H. 1978. *Anthology of Medieval Music*. New York.

Howlett, David. 1991. Translations to accompany *Philippe de Vitry and the Ars Nova*. The Orlando Consort. Amon Ra CD-SAR 49.

———. 2005. '*Apollinis eclipsatur*: Foundation of the 'Collegium musicorum'. In S. Clark and Leach 2005, 152–9.

Hubble, E. P. 1936. *Realm of the Nebulae*. New Haven.

Hughes, David G. 2005. 'The Paschal Alleluia in Medieval France'. *Plainsong and Medieval Music* 14: 11–57.

Huot, Sylvia. 1987. *From Song to Book: The Poetics of Writing in Old French Lyric and Lyrical Narrative Poetry*. Ithaca and London.

———. 1989. 'Polyphonic Poetry: The Old French Motet and its Literary Context'. *French Forum* 14: 261–78.

———. 1994. 'Patience in Adversity: The Courtly Lover and Job in Machaut's Motets 2 and 3'. *Medium Aevum* 63: 222–38.

———. 1997. *Allegorical Play in the Old French Motet: The Sacred and the Profane in Thirteenth-Century Polyphony*. Stanford.

———. 2002. 'Guillaume de Machaut and the Consolation of Poetry'. *Modern Philology* 100: 169–95.

———. 2003. 'Reading across Genres: Froissart's *Joli Buisson de Jonece* and Machaut's Motets'. *French Studies*: 1–10.

Ibos-Augé, Anne. 2010. *Chanter et lire au recit médiéval: La fonction des insertions lyriques dans les oeuvres narratives et didactiques d'oïl aux XIIIe et XIVe siècles*. Bern.

———. 2014. '[…] Que ne dit "cief bien seans": Quoting Motets in the Eighth Fascicle of the Montpellier Codex'. Paper presented at the *Montpellier 8* conference, St Hugh's College, University of Oxford, March 20–1, 2014.

———. Forthcoming. 'Formules, lieux communs, stéréotypes? L'emploi de citations lyriques dans un traité spirituel: l'exemple du *Livre d'amoretes*'. In *Proceedings of La Formule au Moyen Age III*, ed. Olivier Simonin and Caroline de Barreau. Turnhout.

Jackson, Roland. 2003–8. 'Guillaume de Machaut and Dissonance in Fourteenth- Century French Music'. *Musica Disciplina* 53: 7–49.

Jaeger, C. Stephen. 2001. *Scholars and Courtiers: Intellectuals and Society in the Medieval West*. Aldershot and Burlington.

Jardine, Lisa. 1996. *Worldly Goods*. London.

Järnström, Edward and Arthur Långfors, eds. 1910–27. *Recueil de chansons pieuses du XIIIe siècle*. Vol. 1 ed. Edward Järnström. Vol. 2 ed. Edward Järnström and Arthur Långfors. Helsinki.

Johnes, Thomas, ed. and trans. 1808. *Sir John Froissart's Chronicles of England, France, Spain, and The Adjoining Countries, from the latter part of the reign of Edward II to the coronation of Henry IV*. 3rd edn. London.

Johnson, Mildred Jane. 1955. 'The Motets of the Codex Ivrea'. 2 vols. Ph.D. diss. Indiana University.

Jugie, Pierre. 1987. 'L'activité diplomatique du cardinal Gui de Boulogne en France au milieu du XIVe siècle'. *Bibliothèque de l'école des chartes* 145: 99–127.

Karl, Louis. 1924. 'L'Art d'amors de Guiart'. *Zeitschrift für romanische Philologie* 44: 66–80, 181–8.

Karp, Theodore. 1962. 'A Lost Medieval Chansonnier'. *The Musical Quarterly* 48: 50–67.

Kidwell, Susan Allison. 1993. 'The Integration of Music and Text in the Early Latin Motet'. Ph.D. diss. University of Texas at Austin.

———. 1996. 'Elaboration through Exhortation: Troping Motets for the Common of Martyrs'. *Plainsong and Medieval Music* 5: 153–73.

———. 1998. 'The Selection of Clausula Sources for Thirteenth-Century Motets: Some Practical Considerations and Aesthetic Implications'. *Current Musicology* 64: 73–103.

Körndle, Franz. 2010. 'Von der Klausel zur Motette und zurück? Überlegungen zum Repertoire der Handschrift *Saint-Victor*'. *Musiktheorie* 25: 117–28.

Krause, Kathy M. and Alison Stones, eds. 2006. *Gautier de Coinci: Miracles, Music, and Manuscripts.* Turnhout.

Kügle, Karl. 1996. 'Isorhythmie'. *Die Musik in Geschichte und Gegenwart*, ed. Ludwig Finscher. Vol. 4 of *Sachteil*, 1219–29. Kassel.

——. 1997. *The Manuscript Ivrea, Biblioteca capitolare 115: Studies in the Transmission and Composition of Ars Nova Polyphony.* Vol. 69 of Wissenschaftliche Abhandlungen. Ottawa.

Kühn, Hellmut. 1973. *Die Harmonik der Ars Nova: Zur Theorie der isorhythmischen Motette.* Vol. 5 of Berliner musikwissenschaftliche Arbeiten. Munich.

——. 1983. 'Guillaume de Machaut, Motette Nr. 22'. In *Chormusik und Analyse: Beiträge zur Formanalyse und Interpretation mehrstimmiger Vokalmusik*, ed. Heinrich Poos. 2 vols. Vol. 1, *Texte*, 29–41. Vol. 2, *Noten*, 11–16. Mainz and London.

Lakoff, George. 2004. *Don't Think of an Elephant: Know Your Values and Frame the Debate.* White River Junction.

Landwehr-Melnicki, Margaretha. 1968. *Das einstimmige Kyrie des lateinischen Mittelalters.* Forschungsbeiträge zur Musikwissenschaft. Regensburg.

Lavacek, Justin. 2011. 'Contrapuntal Confrontation and Expressive Signification in the Motets of Machaut'. Ph.D. diss. Indiana University.

——. 2015. 'Contrapuntal Ingenuity in the Motets of Machaut'. *Intégral* 28/29: 125–80.

Leach, Elizabeth Eva. 2011a. 'The Fourteenth Century'. In *The Cambridge Companion to Medieval Music*, ed. Mark Everist, 87–103. Cambridge.

——. 2011b. *Guillaume de Machaut: Secretary, Poet, Musician.* Ithaca and London.

——. 2015. 'A Courtly Compilation: The Douce Chansonnier'. In *Manuscripts and Medieval Song: Inscription, Performance, Context*, ed. Elizabeth Eva Leach and Helen Deeming, 221–46. Cambridge.

Leech-Wilkinson, Daniel. 1982–3. 'Related Motets from Fourteenth-Century France'. *Proceedings of the Royal Musical Association* 109: 1–22.

——. 1989. *Compositional Techniques in the Four-Part Isorhythmic Motets of Philippe de Vitry and His Contemporaries.* 2 vols. Outstanding Dissertations in Music from British Universities. New York and London.

——. 1993. '*Le Voir Dit* and *La Messe de Nostre Dame*: Aspects of Genre and Style in Late Works of Machaut'. *Plainsong and Medieval Music* 2: 43–73.

——. 1995. 'The Emergence of ars nova'. *The Journal of Musicology* 13: 285–317.

Lefferts, Peter M. 1983. 'The Motet in England in the Fourteenth Century'. Ph.D. diss. Columbia University.

——. 1986. *The Motet in England in the Fourteenth Century.* Vol. 94 of Studies in Musicology. Ann Arbor.

——. 1990. 'Cantilena and Antiphon: Music for Marian Services in Late Medieval England'. *Studies in Medieval Music: Festschrift for Ernest H. Sanders*, ed. Peter M. Lefferts and Brian Seirup. *Current Musicology* 45–7: 247–82.

——. 1992. 'Text and Context in the Fourteenth-Century English Motet'. In *L'Ars nova Italiana del Trecento* 6, ed. Giulio Cattin and Patrizia Dalla Vechia, 169–92. Certaldo.

——. 2001. 'An Anonymous Treatise of the Theory of Frater Robertus de Brunham'. In *Quellen und Studien zur Musiktheorie des Mittelalters*, ed. M. Bernhard, 217–51. Munich.

——. 2012. *Sources of Thirteenth-Century English Polyphony: Catalogue with Descriptions.* Lincoln, NE.

——, Margaret Bent, Roger Bowers, Mark Everist, and Andrew Wathey. 1982. 'New Sources of English Thirteenth- and Fourteenth-century Polyphony'. *Early Music History* 2: 273–362.

Lerch, Irmgaard. 1987. *Fragmente aus Cambrai: Ein Beitrag zur Rekonstruktion einer Handschrift mit spätmittelalterlicher Polyphonie*. Vol. 11 of Göttinger musikwissenschaftliche Arbeiten. 2 vols. Kassel and New York.

Lettenhove, Kervyn de, ed. 1882. *Poésies de Gilles Li Muisis*. Vol. 1. Louvain.

Levy, Kenneth. 1951. 'New Material on the Early Motet in England: A Report on Princeton Ms. Garrett 119'. *Journal of the American Musicological Society* 4: 220–39.

Lievois, Daniel and Mary E. Wolinski. 2002. 'Mout sont vallant cil de Gant: Een motet ter ere van de Gentse erfachtige lieden in het midden van de 13de eeuw'. *Handelingen Der Maatschappij Voor Geschiedenis En Oudheidkunde Te Gent* 56: 35–51.

Lintott, Chris J. *et al.* 2008. 'Galaxy Zoo: Morphologies Derived from Visual Inspection of Galaxies from the Sloan Digital Sky Survey'. *Monthly Notices of the Royal Astronomical Society* 389: 1179–89.

Lowes, John Livingston. 1914. 'The Loveres Maladye of Hereos'. *Modern Philology* 11: 491–546.

Ludwig, Friedrich. 1902. 'Die mehrstimmige Musik des 14. Jahrhunderts'. *Sammelbände der Internationalen Musikgesellschaft* 4: 16–69.

——. 1904. 'Studien über die Geschichte der mehrstimmigen Musik im Mittelalter, II. Die 50 Beispiele Coussemaker's aus der Handschrift von Montpellier'. *Sammelbände der Internationalen Musikgesellschaft* 5: 177–224.

——. 1905. Review of Johannes Wolf, *Geschichte der Mensuralnotation*. *Sammelbände der Internationalen Musikgesellschaft* 6: 597–641.

——. 1906. Review of Victor Lederer, *Über Heimat und Ursprung der mehrstimmigen Tonkunst. Zeitschrift der Internationalen Musikgesellschaft* 7: 404–14.

——. 1910–78. *Repertorium organorum recentioris et motetorum vetustissimi stili*. Vol. 1: *Catalogue raisonné der Quellen* (Part 1: *Handschriften in Quadrat-Notation*. Halle, 1910. 2nd edn Luther Dittmer. Hildesheim and New York, 1964. Part 2: *Handschriften in Mensural-Notation*, ed. Friedrich Gennrich. Frankfurt, 1961. Rev. edn Luther Dittmer. Assen, 1978). Vol. 2: *Musikalisches Anfangs-Verzeichnis des nach Tenores geordneten Repertorium*, ed. Friedrich Gennrich. Frankfurt, 1962. Reprint, ed. Luther Dittmer. Hildesheim and New York, 1972.

——, ed. 1926–54. *Guillaume de Machaut: Musikalische Werke*. Publikationen älterer Musik. 4 vols. Leipzig.

Lug, Robert. 2012. 'Politique et littérature à Metz autour de la guerre des amis (1231–1234): Le témoignage du Chansonnier de Saint-Germain-des-Prés'. In *Lettres, musique, et société en Lorraine médiévale: Autour du* Tournoi de Chauvency *(Ms. Oxford Bodleian Douce 308)*, ed. Mireille Chazan and Nancy Freeman Regalado, 451–86. Geneva.

Lütteken, Laurenz. 1997. 'Notation. VI.1–4. Mensuralnotation'. *Die Musik in Geschichte und Gegenwart*, ed. Ludwig Finscher. Vol. 7 of *Sachteil*, 323–35. Kassel.

Marchello-Nizia, Christiane. 1984. *Le Roman de la poire par Tibaut*. Paris.

Markstrom, Kurt. 1989. 'Machaut and the Wild Beast'. *Acta Musicologica* 61: 12–39.

Maw, David. 2004. '"Trespasser mesure": Meter in Machaut's Polyphonic Songs'. *The Journal of Musicology* 21: 46–126.

——. 2018. '"Je le temoin en mon chant": The Art of Diminution in the Petronian Triplum'. In Bradley and Desmond 2018, 161–83.

Mews, Constant J., John N. Crossley, Catherine Jeffreys, Leigh McKinnon, and Carol J. Williams, eds. 2011. *Johannes De Grocheio: Ars Musice*. Kalamazoo.

Meyer, Christian, ed., and Karen Desmond, trans. 2015. *The 'Ars musica' Attributed to Magister Lambertus/Aristoteles*. Farnham and Burlington.

Meyer, Wilhelm. 1898. 'Der Ursprung des Motett's: Vorläufige Bemerkungen'. Göttingen. Repr. in *Gesammelte Abhandlungen zur mittellateinischen Rhythmik*. 2 vols. Berlin, 1905: 2: 303–41.

Milsom, John. 2015. 'Making a Motet: Josquin's *Ave maria ... virgo serena*'. In the *Cambridge History of Fifteenth-Century Music*, ed. Anna Maria Busse Berger and Jesse Rodin, 183–99. Cambridge.

Minnis, Alastair J. 2001. *Magister amoris. The* Roman de la Rose *and Vernacular Hermeneutics*. Oxford.

——. 2009. *Translations of Authority in Medieval English Literature: Valuing the Vernacular*. Cambridge.

Mullally, Robert. 1998. 'Johannes de Grocheo's "Musica Vulgaris"'. *Music & Letters* 79: 1–26.

Nathan, Hans. 1942. 'The Function of Text in French 13th-Century Motets'. *Musical Quarterly* 28: 445–62.

Page, Christopher. 1989. *The Owl and the Nightingale: Musical Life and Ideas in France, 1100–1300*. London.

——. 1992. 'A Treatise on Musicians from ?c. 1400: The *Tractatulus de differentiis et gradibus cantorum* by Arnulf de St Ghislain'. *Journal of the Royal Musical Association* 117: 1–21.

——. 1993a. *Discarding Images: Reflections on Music and Culture in Medieval France*. Oxford.

——, ed. 1993b. 'Johannes de Grocheio on Secular Music: A Corrected Text and a New Translation'. *Plainsong and Medieval Music* 2: 17–41.

——. 1997. 'An English Motet of the 14th Century in Performance: Two Contemporary Images'. *Early Music* 25: 7–32.

——. 1998. 'Tradition and Innovation in fr. 146: The Background to the Ballades'. In Bent and Wathey, 353–88.

——. 2000. 'Around the Performance of a 13th-Century Motet'. *Early Music* 28: 343–57.

Paris, Gaston. 1883. 'Lancelot du Lac: Le Conte de la Charrette'. *Romania* 12: 459–534.

Parrish, Carl. 1959. *The Notation of Medieval Music*. New York. Reprint 1978. New York.

Payne, Thomas., ed. 1996. *Les Organa à Deux Voix du Manuscrit de Wolfenbüttel, Herzog August Bibliothek, Cod. Guelf. 1099 Helmst*. 2 vols. Vol. 6 of Le Magnus liber organi de Notre-Dame de Paris. Monaco.

——, ed. 2011. *Philip the Chancellor. Motets and Prosulas*. Vol. 41 of Recent Researches of Music in the Middle Ages and Early Renaissance. Middleton, WI.

Peraino, Judith. 1995. 'New Music, Notions of Genre, and the "Manuscrit du Roi" circa 1300'. Ph.D. diss. University of California, Berkeley.

——. 2001. 'Monophonic Motets: Sampling and Grafting in the Middle Ages'. *The Musical Quarterly* 85: 644–80.

——. 2011. *Giving Voice to Love: Song and Self-Expression from the Troubadours to Guillaume de Machaut*. New York.

Pesce, Dolores. 1986. 'The Significance of Text in Thirteenth-Century Latin Motets'. *Acta Musicologica* 58: 91–117.

——. 1990. 'A Case for Coherent Pitch Organization in the Thirteenth-Century Double Motet'. *Music Analysis* 9: 287–318.

——. 1997. 'Beyond Glossing: The Old Made New in *Mout me fu grief/Robin, m'aime/Portare*'. In *Hearing the Motet*, ed. Pesce 1997, 28–51.

——, ed. 1997. *Hearing the Motet: Essays on the Motet of the Middle Ages and Renaissance*. New York and Oxford.

——. 2013. '*Portare* and the *Mal mariée*'. Paper presented at the conference *Cantum pulcriorem invenire: Music in Western Europe, 1150–1350*, University of Southampton, September 9–11, 2013.

——. 2018. 'Montpellier, Fascicle 8 PORTARE Motets and Tonal Exploration'. In Bradley and Desmond 2018, 233–53.

Phan, Chantal. 1991. 'La tornada et l'envoi: Fonctions structurelles et poétiques'. *Cahiers de la civilisation médiévale* 34: 57–61.

Piaget, Arthur. 1897. 'Le *Chapel des fleurs de lis* par Philippe de Vitri'. *Romania* 27: 55–92.

Pieragostini, Renata. 2011. 'Rediscovering Lost Evidence: Little-Known Fragments with English Polyphony in Bologna'. *Music & Letters* 92: 343–76.

Planchart, Alejandro Enrique. 2003. 'The Flower's Children'. *Journal of Musicological Research* 22: 303–48.

Plumley, Yolanda. 2013. *The Art of Grafted Song: Citation and Allusion in the Age of Machaut*. Oxford and New York.

——and Anne Stone, eds. 2008. *Codex Chantilly. Bibliothèque du château de Chantilly Ms. 564. Facsimile and Introduction*. 2 vols. Turnhout.

Pruvost, Alexandre, ed. 1875. *Chronique et Cartulaire de L'Abbaye de Bergues Saint-Winnoc*. Vol. 1. Bruges.

Quinlan, Meghan. 2017. 'Contextualising the Contrafacta of Trouvère Song'. Ph.D. diss. University of Oxford.

Raitzig, Olaf and Angelika Raitzig. 2011. *Gotische Polyphonie, Motetten der Ars Nova: Codex Ivrea: Studien*. Berlin.

Randel, Don Michael, ed. 2003. *The Harvard Dictionary of Music*. 4th edn. Cambridge, MA.

Rankin, Susan. 2008. 'Thirteenth-Century Notations of Music and Arts of Performance'. In *Vom Preis des Fortschritts: Gewinn und Verlust in der Musikgeschichte*, Studien zur Wertungsforschung 49, ed. Andreas Haug and Andreas Dorschel, 110–42. Vienna, London, and New York.

Rastall, Richard. 1983. *The Notation of Western Music: An Introduction*. London.

Reaney, Gilbert. 1954. 'The Manuscript Chantilly, Musée Condé 1047'. *Musica Disciplina* 8: 59–113.

——, ed. 1966. *Manuscripts of Polyphonic Music. 11th-Early 14th Century. Répertoire International des Sources Musicales* B IV. Munich-Duisburg.

—— and André Gilles, eds. 1974. *Franco de Colonia. Ars cantus mensurabilis*. Corpus Scriptorum de Musica 18. [Dallas, Texas].

——, André Gilles, and Jean Maillard, eds. 1964. *Philippi de Vitriaco Ars nova*. Corpus Scriptorum de Musica 8. [Rome].

Regalado, Nancy Freeman. 1981. 'Des contraires choses: La fonction poétique de la citation et des exempla dans le "Roman de la rose" de Jean de Meun'. *Littérature* 41: 62–81.

——. 1998. 'The *Chronique métrique* and the Moral Design of BN fr. 146: Feasts of Good and Evil'. In Bent and Wathey 1998, 467–94.

——. 2006. 'Picturing the Story of Chivalry in Jacques Bretel's *Tournoi de Chauvency* (Oxford, Bodleian Library, MS Douce 308)'. In *Tributes to Jonathan J. G. Alexander: Making and Meaning in the Middle Ages and the Renaissance*, ed. Susan L'Engle and Gerald B. Guest, 341–52. London.

Reichert, Georg. 1956. 'Das Verhältnis zwischen musikalischer und textlicher Struktur in den Motetten Machauts'. *Archiv für Musikwissenschaft* 13: 197–216.

Robertson, Anne Walters. 1997. 'Which Vitry? The Witness of the Trinity Motet from the *Roman de Fauvel*'. In *Hearing the Motet*, ed. Pesce 1997, 52–81.

——. 1998. 'Local Chant Readings and the *Roman de Fauvel*'. In Bent and Wathey, 495–524.

——. 2002. *Guillaume de Machaut and Reims: Context and Meaning in his Musical Works*. Cambridge.

Roesner, Edward H. 1984. Review of *The Earliest Motets (To circa 1270): A Complete Comparative Edition* by Hans Tischler. *Early Music History* 4: 362–75.

——. 1990. 'The Emergence of *musica mensurabilis*'. In *Studies in Musical Sources and Style: Essays in Honor of Jan La Rue*, ed. Eugene K. Wolf and Edward H. Roesner, 41–74. Madison, WI.

——. 2007. '*Subtilitas* and *Delectatio*: Ne m'a pas oublié'. In *Cultural Performances in Medieval France: Essays in Honor of Nancy Freeman Regalado*, ed. Eglal Doss-Quinby, Roberta L. Krueger and E. Jane Burns, 25–43. Woodbridge.

——, François Avril, and Nancy Freeman Regalado, eds. 1990. *Le Roman de Fauvel in the Edition of Mesire Chaillou de Pesstain: A Reproduction in Facsimile of the Complete Manuscript Paris, Bibliothèque Nationale, Fonds Français 146*. New York.

Rokseth, Yvonne, ed. 1935–9. *Polyphonies du XIIIe siècle, le manuscrit H 196 de la Faculté de médecine de Montpellier*. 4 vols. Paris.

Rothenberg, David J. 2011. *The Flower of Paradise: Marian Devotion and Secular Song in Medieval and Renaissance Music*. Oxford.

———. 2016. 'The Gate that Carries Christ: Wordplay and Liturgical Imagery in a Motet from ca. 1300'. In *Music and Culture in the Middle Ages and Beyond: Liturgy, Sources, Symbolism. Cambridge*, ed. Benjamin Brand and David J. Rothenberg, 225–41. Cambridge.

Roy, Bruno, ed. 1974. *L'Art d'amours: Traduction et commentaire de l'Ars amatoria d'Ovide*. Leiden.

Saint-Cricq, Gaël. 2009. 'Formes types dans le motet du XIIIe siècle: étude d'un processus répétitif'. 2 vols. Ph.D. diss. University of Southampton.

———. 2013a. 'A New Link between the Motet and Trouvère Chanson: The *Pedes-cum-cauda* Motet'. *Early Music History* 32: 179–223.

———. 2013b. 'Transmitting a Compositional Process: Two Thirteenth-Century Motets'. *Musica Discplina* 58: 327–50.

———, with Eglal Doss-Quinby and Samuel N. Rosenberg, eds. 2017. *Motets from the Chansonnier de Noailles*. Madison.

Saltzstein, Jennifer. 2007. 'Wandering Voices: Refrain Citation in Thirteenth-Century French Music and Poetry'. Ph.D. diss. University of Pennsylvania.

———. 2010. 'Relocating the Thirteenth-Century Refrain: Intertextuality, Authority and Origins'. *Journal of the Royal Musical Association* 135: 245–79.

———. 2013a. 'Ovid and the Thirteenth-Century Motet: Quotation, Reinterpretation, and Vernacular Hermeneutics'. *Musica Disciplina* 58: 351–73.

———. 2013b. *The Refrain and the Rise of the Vernacular in Medieval French Music and Poetry*. Cambridge.

Saly, Antoinette. 1972. '*Li Commens d'Amours* de Richard de Fournival(?)'. *Travaux de linguistique et de littérature* 10: 21–55.

Sanders, Ernest H. 1962. 'Duple Rhythm and Alternate Third Mode in the 13th Century'. *Journal of the American Musicological Society* 15: 249–91.

———. 1963. 'Medieval English Polyphony and its Significance for the Continent'. Ph.D. diss. Columbia University.

———. 1965. 'Tonal Aspects of 13th-Century English Polyphony'. *Acta Musicologica* 37: 19–34.

———. 1973. 'The Medieval Motet'. In *Gattungen der Musik in Einzeldarstellungen: Gedenkschrift Leo Schrade*, ed. Leo Schrade, Wulf Arlt, and Higini Anglès, 497–573. Bern.

———. 1975. 'The Early Motets of Philippe de Vitry'. *Journal of the American Musicological Society* 28: 24–45.

———, ed. 1979. *English Music of the Thirteenth and Early Fourteenth Centuries*. Vol. 14 of Polyphonic Music of the Fourteenth Century. Monaco.

———. 1980a. 'Isorhythm'. *The New Grove Dictionary of Music and Musicians*, ed. Stanley Sadie, 9: 351–4. London and New York.

———. 1980b. 'Motet, §I. Medieval'. *The New Grove Dictionary of Music and Musicians*, ed. Stanley Sadie, 12: 617–28. London and New York.

Schmidt-Beste, Thomas. 2013. 'Singing the Hiccup – On Texting the Hocket'. *Early Music History* 32: 225–75.

Schrade, Leo. 1956a. 'Philippe de Vitry: Some New Discoveries'. *Musical Quarterly* 42: 330–54.

———, ed. 1956b. *The Roman de Fauvel; The Works of Philippe de Vitry; French Cycles of the Ordinarium Missae*. Vol. 1 of Polyphonic Music of the Fourteenth Century. Monaco.

———, ed. 1956c. *The Works of Guillaume de Machaut*. Vols. 3–4 of Polyphonic Music of the Fourteenth Century. Monaco.

Schramm, Wilbur Lang. 1933. 'The Cost of Books in Chaucer's Time'. *Modern Language Notes* 48: 139–45.

Schultz-Gora, Oskar. 1900. 'Ein ungedrucktes Salu d'amors nebst Antwort'. *Zeitschrift für romanische Philologie* 24: 358–69.

Setton, Kenneth M. 1976. *The Papacy and the Levant (1204–1571)*. Vol. 1. Philadelphia.

Sherr, Richard. 1988. '*Illibata Dei Virgo Nutrix* and Josquin's Roman Style'. *Journal of the American Musicological Society* 41: 434–64.

Smith, Norman E. 1980. 'From Clausula to Motet: Material for Further Studies in the Origin and Early History of the Motet'. *Musica Disciplina* 34: 29–31, 33–65.

——. 1989. 'The Earliest Motets: Music and Words'. *Journal of the Royal Musicological Association* 114: 141–63.

——. 1992. 'An Early Thirteenth-Century Motet: *Hodie Marie Concurrant/REGNAT*'. In *Models of Musical Analysis: Music Before 1600*, ed. Mark Everist, 20–41. Oxford.

Sombart, Werner. 1919. *Der moderne Kapitalismus: Historisch-systematische Darstellung des gesamteuropäischen Wirtschaftslebens von seinen Anfängen bis zur Gegenwart*. 2 vols. 3rd revised edn. Munich.

Spanke, Hans, ed. 1955. *G. Raynauds Bibliographie des altfranzösischen Liedes, neu bearbeitet und ergänzt von Hans Spanke*. Reprint with index 1980. Leiden.

Stäblein-Harder, Hanna, ed. 1962. *Fourteenth-Century Mass Music in France*. Vol. 29 of Corpus Mensurabilis Musicae. [Rome].

Staehelin, Martin. 1974. 'Beschreibungen und Beispiele musikalischer Formen in einem unbeachteten Traktat des frühen 15. Jahrhunderts'. *Archiv für Musikwissenschaft* 31: 237–42.

Stenzl, Jürg. 1970. *Die vierzig Clausulae der Handschrift Paris, Bibliothèque nationale, latin 15139 (Saint Victor-Clausulae)*. Publikationen der schweizerischen musikforschenden Gesellschaft, series 2, 22. Berne.

Stewart, Hugh, Edward Rand, and S. Jim Tester, trans. 1978. *Boethius, The Theological Tractates, De consolatione philosophiae*. London and Cambridge, MA.

Stones, Alison. 2013. *Gothic Manuscripts 1260–1320*. 4 vols. Turnhout.

——. 2018. 'The Style and Iconography of Montpellier folio 350'. In Bradley and Desmond 2018, 66–77.

Strubel, Armand, ed. and trans. 2012. *Le Roman de Fauvel*. Paris.

Strunk, Oliver. 1998. *Source Readings in Music History*. Rev. edn Leo Treitler. New York.

Sweeney, Cecile, and André Gilles, eds. 1971. *[Anonymous]. De musica mensurabili. [Anonymous]. De semibrevibus caudatis*. Vol. 13 of Corpus scriptorum de musica. [Dallas].

Switten, Margaret. 1995. *Music and Poetry in the Middle Ages: A Guide to Research on French and Occitan Song, 1100–1400*. New York and London.

Tanner, Heather. 2004. *Families, Friends and Allies: Boulogne and Politics in Northern France and England, c. 879–1160*. Leiden and Boston.

Terry, Patricia and Nancy Vine Durling, trans. 1993. *The Romance of the Rose or Guillaume de Dole*. Philadelphia.

Thomson, Matthew P. 2016. 'Interaction between Polyphonic Motets and Monophonic Songs in the Thirteenth Century'. Ph.D. diss. University of Oxford.

——. 2017. 'Monophonic Song in Motets: Performing Quoted Material and Performing Quotation'. In *Performing Medieval Text*, ed. Ardis Butterfield, Henry Hope, and Pauline Souleau, 136–51. Cambridge.

Tischler, Hans, ed. 1978. *The Montpellier Codex*. 4 vols. Vol. 4 trans. Susan Stakel and Joel C. Relihan. Vols. 2–8 of Recent Researches in the Music of the Middle Ages and Early Renaissance. Madison.

——, ed. 1982. *The Earliest Motets (to circa 1270): A Complete Comparative Edition*. 3 vols. New Haven and London.

Trachtenberg, Marvin. 2001. 'Architecture and Music Reunited: A New Reading of Dufay's *Nuper rosarum flores* and the Cathedral of Florence'. *Renaissance Quarterly* 54: 740–75.

Trowell, Brian. 1957. 'A Fourteenth-Century Ceremonial Motet and its Composer'. *Acta musicologica* 29: 65–75.

Tuchman, Barbara W. 1978. *A Distant Mirror: The Calamitous 14th Century*. New York.

Tyssens, Madeleine, ed. 1998. *Intavulare. Tables de chansonniers romans. Chansonniers français 1, a (B.A.V., Reg. Lat. 1490), b (B.A.V., Reg. Lat. 1522), A (Arras, Bibliothèque Municipale 657)*. Vatican.

Utz, Christian. 2016. 'Räumliche Vorstellungen als "Grundfunktionen des Hörens": Historische Dimensionen und formanalytische Potenziale musikbezogener Architektur- und Raummetaphern – eine Diskussion anhand von Werken Guillaume Dufays, Joseph Haydns und Edgard Varèses'. *Acta musicologica* 88: 193–221.

van den Boogaard, Nico H. J. 1969. *Rondeaux et refrains due XIIe siècle au début du XIVe: collationnement, introduction, et notes*. Paris.

van den Borren, Charles. 1924. *Le manuscrit musicale M. 222 C. 22 de la Bibliothèque de Strasbourg*. Antwerp.

van der Werf, Hendrik. 1989. *Integrated Directory of Organa, Clausulae, and Motets of the Thirteenth Century*. Rochester.

Vecchi, Giuseppe, ed. 1961. *Marchettus of Padua, Pomerium*. Vol. 6 of Corpus Scriptorum de Musica. Rome.

Vetter, Eddie. 1987. 'Philippe de Vitry and the Holy Trinity: An Early Manifesto of the Ars Nova'. In *Liber amicorum Chris Maas: Essays in Musicology in Honour of Chris Mass on his 65th Anniversary*, ed. Rob Wegman and Eddie Vetter, 4–14. Amsterdam.

Waite, William G. 1954. *The Rhythm of Twelfth-Century Polyphony: Its Theory and Practice*. Vol. 2 of Yale Studies in the History of Music. New Haven.

Walker, Thomas. 1982. 'Sui Tenor Francesi nei motett del '200'. *Schede medievali: Rassegna dell' officina di studi medievali* 3: 309–36.

Wallerstein, Immanuel. 2011. *Capitalist Agriculture and the Origins of the European World-Economy in the Sixteenth Century*. Berkeley.

Warner, Marina. 1976. *Alone of All Her Sex: The Myth and the Cult of the Virgin Mary*. New York.

Wathey, Andrew. 1993. 'The Motets of Philippe de Vitry and the Fourteenth-Century Renaissance'. *Early Music History* 12: 119–50.

——. 1998. 'Gervès du Bus, the *Roman de Fauvel*, and the Politics of the later Capetian Court'. In Bent and Wathey 1998, 599–614.

——. 2005. '*Auctoritas* and the Motets of Philippe de Vitry'. In S. Clark and Leach 2005, 67–78.

Wegman, Rob. 1991. 'Petrus de Domarto's "Missa Spiritus almus" and the Early History of the Four-Voice Mass in the Fifteenth Century'. *Early Music History* 10: 235–303.

——. 2016. 'Jacobus de Ispania and Liège'. *Journal of the Alamire Foundation* 8: 253–74.

Welker, Lorenz. 1998. 'Polyphonic Reworkings of Notre-Dame Conductûs in BN fr. 146: *Mundus a mundicia* and *Quare fremuerunt*'. In Bent and Wathey 1998, 615–36.

Weller, Philip. 1997. 'Frames and Images: Locating Music in Cultural Histories of the Middle Ages'. *Journal of the American Musicological Society* 50: 7–54.

Wibberley, Roger. 1975. 'English Polyphonic Music of the Late Thirteenth and Early Fourteenth Centuries'. Ph.D. diss. University of Oxford.

Wolf, Johannes. 1904. *Geschichte der Mensuralnotation von 1250–1460: nach den theoretischen und praktischen Quellen*. 3 vols. Leipzig. Reprint. Hildesheim, 1965.

——. 1908. 'Ein anonymer Musiktraktat aus der ersten Zeit der "Ars Nova"'. *Kirchenmusikalisches Jahrbuch* 21: 33–8.

——, ed. 1913–14. 'Ein Beitrag zur Diskantlehre des 14. Jahrhunderts'. *Sammelbände der Internationalen Musikgesellschaft* 15: 504–34.

Wolinski, Mary. 1992. 'The Compilation of the Montpellier Codex'. *Early Music History* 11: 263–301.

——. 1996. 'Tenors Lost and Found: The Reconstruction of Motets in Two Medieval Chansonniers'. In *Critica Musica: Essays in Honor of Paul Brainard*, ed. John Knowles, 461–81. Amsterdam.

Wolinski, Mary. 2008. 'Drinking Motets in Medieval Artois and Flanders'. *Yearbook of the Alamire Foundation* 6: 9–20.

Wright, Craig. 1994. 'Dufay's *Nuper rosarum flores*, King Solomon's Temple, and the Veneration of the Virgin'. *Journal of the American Musicological Society* 47: 395–441.

Yudkin, Jeremy, ed. 1990. *De Musica Mensurata: The Anonymous of St. Emmeram*. Bloomington and Indianapolis.

Zacour, Norman P. 1960. *Talleyrand: The Cardinal of Périgord (1301–1364)*. Vol. 10 of Transactions of the American Philosophical Society, New Series. Philadelphia.

Zayaruznaya, Anna. 2009. '"She Has a Wheel that Turns …": Crossed and Contradictory Voices in Machaut's Motets'. *Early Music History* 28: 185–240.

——. 2010. 'Form and Idea in the *Ars nova* Motet'. Ph.D. diss. Harvard University.

——. 2013. 'Hockets as Compositional and Scribal Practice in the *ars nova* Motet—A Letter from Lady Music'. *The Journal of Musicology* 30: 461–501.

——. 2014. 'Evidence of Reworkings in *Ars nova* Motets'. *Basler Jahrbuch für Historische Musikpraxis* 38: 155–75.

——. 2015a. *The Monstrous New Art: Divided Forms in the Late Medieval Motet*. Cambridge.

——. 2015b. 'Quotation, Perfection and the Eloquence of Form: Introducing *Beatius/Cum humanum*'. *Plainsong and Medieval Music* 24: 129–66.

——. 2018. *Upper-Voice Structures and Compositional Process in the* Ars nova *Motet*. London and New York.

——. Forthcoming 2018. 'New Voices for Vitry'. *Early Music* 46.

Zazulia, Emily. Forthcoming. *Where Sight Meets Sound: The Poetics of Late-Medieval Music Writing*.

Zimmermann, Ann-Katrin. 2008. *Studien zur mittelalterlichen Dreistimmigkeit*. Tutzing.

Zink, Michel. 1972. *La Pastourelle: Poésie et folklore au moyen age*. Paris.

SELECT GLOSSARY

These terms are defined *in the context of their use* in this *Companion*. Some terms may have broader or other meanings in other musical or historical contexts. For additional terms, see the index.

ARS NOVA   Literally, 'new art' or 'new technique'. *Ars nova* generally refers to a period in the early to mid-fourteenth century in France during which composers were experimenting with developments in rhythm and its notation.

CHANSONNIER   A songbook. While some chansonniers contain exclusively French songs, others also contain motets, as well as other genres. Some collections are notated, while others are not.

CLAUSULA   A polyphonic genre in which a newly composed and untexted voice (or voices) is added above a short segment of plainchant. Voices generally proceed in simple modal rhythmic patterns, more or less in a note-against-note or **DISCANT** style. Clausulae often functioned to substitute for melismatic passages of plainchant in **ORGANUM**, hence the frequently employed term 'subsitute clausula'. Some early motets consist of clausulae with poetry added to the upper voice or voices; conversely, some clausulae are motets stripped of their text(s).

COLOR   A term generally used to refer to the borrowed or newly composed melody of a tenor, most often irrespective of its rhythm. Many motets contain more than one color statement. Sometimes a second or subsequent color statement unfolds in a different rhythmic pattern than the first due to the tenor's rhythmic organization into taleae. The term is usually restricted to motets from the fourteenth century onward. See also **CURSUS**.

CONDUCTUS   A genre of vocal music for one or more voices that sets a single (usually strophic) Latin text, cultivated in the period *c*. 1160–1250. In polyphonic conducti, the setting is almost always note-against-note, which allows for clear textual audibility.

CONDUCTUS MOTET   A genre of motet with two, or occasionally three, upper voices singing the same Latin text, cultivated in the early decades of the thirteenth century.

CONTRAFACTUM   A term generally used to refer to the substitution of one text for another without making significant changes to the melody. For example, a French poem presented in the motetus voice might be replaced with a Latin text, thereby creating a contrafactum.

CONTRATENOR   Usually a newly composed, untexted voice that proceeds at approximately the same rate and in the same register as the tenor. The term is restricted to motets from the fourteenth century onward. See **MOTET VOICES**.

CURSUS   A term that is generally synonymous with **COLOR**; that is, a complete statement of the tenor's melody, irrespective of whether or not the second or any subsequent cursus is presented in the same rhythm. The term is usually restricted to thirteenth-century motets.

DIMINUTION   A process through which note values are replaced with shorter note values (i.e. longs become breves, breves become semibreves, and so forth; see **NOTE SHAPES**). A 'diminution section' often refers to the second section of a motet in which the tenor note values of the motet's first section are 'diminished'. At times the diminished note values are written out for the singer, but occasionally singers must make the mental adjustment on their own, as sometimes directed by a canon or new mensuration sign.

DISCANT   A type of polyphony in which a newly composed voice (or voices) is added above a melismatic portion of plainchant; both voices generally proceed in simple modal rhythms. Strictly speaking, the term refers to note-against-note polyphony, but it is often the case that the upper voice has two or more pitches per tenor note. Clausulae are composed in a 'discant style', hence the frequently employed term 'discant clausula'.

DUPLUM   A texted motet voice, usually above the tenor in register. Sometimes referred to as the motetus. See **MOTET VOICES**.

FASCICLE   A term that denotes a structural unit of the makeup of a manuscript, consisting of numerous folios. A manuscript often contains many fascicles. Sometimes fascicles are organized by genre or by number of voices, for instance, but this is not always the case.

FOLIO   A term that is used in numbering the pages in a manuscript. Folios are identified in two ways: by number, and by front (recto) or back (verso). For instance, a motet might begin on fol. 83r and conclude fol. 83v. When folios are bound together, this would require a page turn since fol. 83r occurs on the right-hand side of the manuscript, and fol. 83v on the left-hand side. Another motet might immediately follow on fol. 84r, which would be located on the same opening as fol. 83v, but on the right-hand side of the manuscript.

GRAND CHANT   A genre of **TROUVÈRE** song, often associated with the aristocracy and regarded as sophisticated and lofty in tone.

HOCKET   A compositional technique in which a melodic line is split between two or more voices, creating a 'hiccup' effect. Instead of two voices singing at the same time, one voice sings a note while the other rests briefly, then they exchange roles. Hocket sometimes serves a structural role; that is, it can recur at corresponding moments in successive taleae.

INTROITUS   A term that refers to the texted or untexted opening portion of a motet in which one or more voices sing on their own before the tenor – and, if present, contratenor – begin their articulation of the **TALEA**.

ISOMELISM   A compositional technique in which upper-voice melodic material recurs, sometimes following the repetition scheme of the tenor.

ISOPERIODICITY   In Continental motets, the term refers to the coordination of phrase lengths in all motet voices in such a way that the rests that conclude each period recur at the same point within each repeated tenor rhythmic segment. In English motets, the term refers to equal-length periods that are staggered between the motet voices; for instance, the tenor might state several nine-bar periods, the motetus might begin with a three-bar period that is followed by several nine-bar periods before concluding with a six-bar period, while the triplum might begin with a six-bar period that is followed by several nine-bar periods before concluding with a three-bar period.

ISORHYTHM   Literally, 'same rhythm' or 'equal rhythm'. A term coined in the early twentieth century that typically denotes a compositional technique in which the melody of the tenor is divided into rhythmically identical units of equal length. Early scholars of the motet used the term synonymously with isoperiodicity. Recent scholars have tended to apply the term to rhythmically identical segments in any voice.

LIGATURE   A group of two or more notes that are bound together, generally sung to a single syllable.

MELISMA   A term that denotes a group of notes sung to a single syllable of text.

MENSURAL NOTATION   A notational system developed in the later thirteenth century that afforded the possibility of notating a greater variety of rhythms and note values than had been possible with the **RHYTHMIC MODES**. Mensural notation differentiates specific **NOTE SHAPES** in which each figure is equivalent to either two or three of the next smallest note value: a maxima is equivalent to either two or (less frequently) three longs; a long is equivalent to either two or three breves; a breve is equivalent to either two or three semibreves; a semibreve is equivalent to either two or three minims.

MONOPHONY   A term used to refer to a single melodic line.

MOTET ENTÉ   Literally, 'grafted motet'. A genre of thirteenth-century motet in which two halves of a refrain begin and conclude a texted voice, respectively. Sometimes the term more broadly applies to any thirteenth-century motet with refrain citations.

MOTET VOICES   The names of the various motet voices in two-, three-, and four-voice motets are provided below. Typical registral placement is listed from highest to lowest, but voices frequently cross. The tenor and contratenor often exchange and/or share registers.

2v	3v	4v with Qu	4v with CT
motetus	triplum	quadruplum	triplum
tenor	motetus	triplum	motetus
	tenor	motetus	tenor
		tenor	contratenor

MOTET WITH MEDIUS CANTUS   A genre of motet, popular in England, in which the tenor occupies the middle range, that is, between the upper-voice triplum and the lower-voice motetus.

MOTETUS   A texted motet voice, usually above the tenor in register. Sometimes referred to as the duplum. See **MOTET VOICES**.

NOTE SHAPES   Maxima (◧); long (◪); breve (▪); semibreve (◆); minim (♦).

ORGANUM   A style of polyphony in which an untexted voice (or voices) is added above pre-existing plainchant. In organum of the late twelfth and early thirteenth centuries associated with the Notre Dame Cathedral in Paris, the added voice was florid; that is, there were numerous added notes for each tenor pitch. But when the declamation of the pre-existing chant was primarily melismatic, the polyphonic setting was often more or less note-against-note, resulting in **DISCANT**.

PAN-ISORHYTHM   A twentieth-century term that denotes passages in which the rhythms of all of the motet voices literally repeat from **TALEA** to talea.

PERIOD   A term generally used to refer to a segment or phrase of music in a single voice that concludes with a rest or rests.

PLICA   One or two hairline pen strokes added to certain **NOTE SHAPES** that indicates an additional pitch is to be sung, most often a step above or below the notated pitch.

POLYPHONY   A term used to refer to two or more melodic lines that unfold simultaneously.

PROSULA   A type of vocal music that results from the addition of syllabic text to a pre-existing melismatic melody.

QUADRUPLUM   A texted motet voice in a four-voice motet, often above the triplum in register. See **MOTET VOICES**.

REFRAIN   A short portion of text something like a proverb, often with associated music, that circulated between narrative poetry, songs, and motets.

RHYTHMIC MODES   Various rhythmic patterns of long and short notes. Although the rhythmic modes were employed in polyphony before the advent of the motet, it was not until the mid-thirteenth century that the modes became codified and were identified by number: 1. long-short (in modern notation, ♩♪); 2. short–long (♪♩); 3. long, short–long (♩. ♪♩); 4. short–long, long (♪♩ ♩.); 5. long, long (♩. ♩.); 6. short–short–short (♪♪♪). Rhythmic modes were notated using strict patterns of LIGATURES. For instance, a three-note ligature followed by several two-note ligatures indicates mode 1. Due in large part to the evolution of the motet, and as composers experimented with greater rhythmic variety, a new system was developed; see MENSURAL NOTATION.

RONDEAU-MOTET   A genre of motet in which the upper voice (or voices) is structured as a rondeau; that is, musical phrases recur in an alternating pattern, sometimes with text repetition. The tenor melody was thus also often laid out using a similar repetition scheme.

RUBRIC   Text, usually penned in red ink, that serves as a section heading in a manuscript.

TALEA   A repeating rhythmic segment, most often in the tenor. A motet typically contains several taleae. Sometimes the second half of a motet features taleae in DIMINUTION.

TENOR   A motet voice, often but not always lowest in register, that is frequently borrowed but sometimes composed anew. It can be liturgical or secular in origin. It is only rarely texted and usually moves along at a slower pace than the motetus, triplum and quadruplum. See MOTET VOICES.

TRIPLUM   A texted motet voice, often above the motetus in register. See MOTET VOICES.

TROUVÈRE   A term that generally refers to poet-composers in France who employed northern French dialects in their poetry and songs. Trouvères flourished from the late twelfth century until c. 1300. Hundreds of trouvère songs with music survive today, many in CHANSONNIERS; some trouvères also composed motets.

UNICUM   A term used to refer to a motet, song or text that appears in only a single extant source.

INDEX OF CITED MOTETS

For each cited motet in **Mo**, the **Mo** number is provided in parentheses after the motet title. The same applies to Guillaume de Machaut's motets; M numbers are provided in parentheses.

GENERAL INDEX

'Index of Cited Motets' for cited **Mo** motets and their **Mo** numbers

Mod 163, 163*n*53

MüA 108, 199, Table 9.1, 205*n*2

MüB 57, 57*n*40, Table 6.1, 136, 143, 218, 218*n*27

NL-Lu 342a 345, 345*n*25, 352

Noailles 7, 8, Table 1.1, 24, Table 1.2, 31*n*61, 40*n*68, 108, Table 6.1, 142*n*38, 178, 180–1, 181*n*22, Fig. 8.2, 191, 192, 194*n*9, Table 9.1, 218, 225*n*3, 226, Table 11.1, 228–31, 228*n*6, 228*n*7, 229*n*10, 229*n*12, 229*n*13, Ex. 11.1a, 231*n*18, 235–42, Ex. 11.3a, Ex. 11.3b, Ex. 11.4, 241*n*39, 244*n*6, 245*n*10

NYpm 978 123

O 24*n*45, 226*n*5, Table 11.1, 232

Ob 7 119, 122, 123, Fig. 5.3, 262*n*5, 285*n*44

Ob 20 120, 123

Ob 213 125, 125*n*50, 125*n*51, 125*n*52, Ex. 5.8

Ob 271* Table 5.2

Ob 594 122, 122*n*46

Onc 362 74, Ex. 4.6, Table 4.1, 119, 121, Ex. 5.6, 271

Oxf Add. 58

P Table 11.1, 236, 237

Pic 118*n*29

Pn 571 118*n*29

Pru 120

Ps Table 1.1

Q15 75*n*48, 125, 125*n*50, 350*n*50, 351

R Table 11.1, 228*n*7

Reg1490 Table 1.1, 23*n*35, 24, 24*n*45, 26*n*50, Table 9.1, 225*n*3, Table 11.1, 228, 228*n*7, 228*n*9, 229*n*11, 229*n*13, 237, 237*n*38, 241, 244*n*6

Robertsbridge 118*n*29

Roi 7, Table 1.1, 24, Table 1.2, 31*n*61, 40*n*68, 108, Table 6.1, 142*n*38, 176–81, 180*n*21, 181*n*22, Fig. 8.1, 191, 194*n*9, Table 9.1, 218, 225*n*3, 226, Table 11.1, 228–9, 228*n*7, 228*n*9, 229*n*11, 229*n*12, 229*n*13, 232, 234, 237, 241, 244*n*6, 245*n*10

S Table 11.1, 226

Sab 57

Str 341, 341*n*3, 343, 345, 345*n*25, 345*n*28, 351

StV Table 1.1, 23*n*35, 43, 43*n*4, 79*n*8, Ex. 4.2, 142, 142*n*35, 142*n*36, 218

To 225*n*2

Tort 57, 58*n*41

Trém 76*n*51, 159*n*28, 163, 296*n*24, 342, 345, 343*n*16, 345*n*25

Troyes 1949 Table 5.2

Tu 64*n*11, 112, Table 6.1, 179, 248*n*15, 254*n*29

TuB 75*n*48

U 24, 27, 199, 199*n*31, 226*n*5, Table 11.1, 237, 244*n*6

V 226*n*5, Table 11.1, 237

W1 4, 45–59 *passim*, Ex. 2.1, Ex. 2.2, 132

W2 1, 2, Table 1.1, 23*n*35, 25, Table 1.2, 55, 57, 64, 78*n*7, 104–8, 104*n*1, 104*n*2, 105*n*7, 105*n*9, Fig. 5.1, Ex. 5.1, 108*n*11, 108*n*12, 110, 119*n*31, 132, 133, Table 6.1, 142*n*38, 181, 194, 196, 199, Table 9.1, 205*n*2, 207, 209, 209*n*14, 212*n*20, 214, 225*n*1, 229*n*13, 236*n*31, 241*n*40, 244*n*6, 245*n*10, Ex. 12.1

WoC 73*n*41

X 24, Table 11.1, 228*n*7, 236, 237, 241

manuscripts (without motets)

F-Arras 444 Ex. 11.1b

F-Dm 526 248*n*16

F-LA 263 249*n*18

F-Pn f. fr. 372 254*n*29

F-Pn f. fr. 837 23*n*38

F-Pn f. fr. 1593 254*n*29

F-Pn f. fr. 2186 198*n*23

F-Pn f. fr. 23111 142

F-Pn f. fr. 24729 225*n*3

F-Pn lat. 1112 131, 249*n*18

F-Pn lat. 7378A 127*n*56

F-Pn lat. 10482 Ex. 14.1

F-Pn lat. 13091 142

F-Pn lat. 14452 249*n*18

F-Pn lat. 14741 127*n*56

F-Pn lat. 15181 281*n*39

GB-Cu 710 263, 263*n*14

GB-Mr [96] 66 248*n*16

GB-Ob 264 27*n*55

I-Rvat 307 127*n*56

Mary, Marian *see* Blessed Virgin Mary

materia 10, 61, 93*n*51, 287, 290, 298, 301
   meaning of 61*n*1, 287, 287*n*3
   See also Egidius de Murino

maximodus 92, *see also* modus

medius cantus *see* duet motet with medius cantus

Méliacin ou le Cheval de fust 18, 23, 39, 39*n*67, 141*n*33

mensural reinterpretation *see under* mensuration

mensuration 6, 123, 157
   in a Gloria in **Iv** 349–50
   in *Douce / Garison* 126–9, Ex. 5.9
   in *Firmissime / Adesto* 161
   in *Inter densas / Imbribus* 349
   in Machaut motets 98, 302*n*8, 328, 331, 333, 339
   in Machaut's *Rose lis* 302*n*8
   in *Portio / Ida* 347–9, 348*n*37
   in *Sub Arturo / Fons* 349, 350
   in *Tuba / In arboris* 161*n*41
   mensural combinations 125–6, Table 5.6
   mensural reinterpretation 11, 68, 348–51
   signs *see under* notation
   See also diminution

STUDIES IN MEDIEVAL AND RENAISSANCE MUSIC

Volumes already published

Machaut's Music: New Interpretations
edited by Elizabeth Eva Leach

The Church Music of Fifteenth-Century Spain
Kenneth Kreitner

The Royal Chapel in the time of the Habsburgs:
Music and Court Ceremony in Early Modern Europe
edited by Juan José Carreras and Bernardo García García

Citation and Authority in Medieval and Renaissance Musical Culture:
Learning from the Learned. Essays in Honour of Margaret Bent
edited by Suzannah Clark and Elizabeth Eva Leach

European Music, 1520–1640
edited by James Haar

Cristóbal de Morales:
Sources, Influences, Reception
edited by Owen Rees and Bernadette Nelson

Young Choristers, 650–1700
edited by Susan Boynton and Eric Rice

Hermann Pötzlinger's Music Book:
The St Emmeram Codex and its Contexts
Ian Rumbold with Peter Wright

Medieval Liturgical Chant and Patristic Exegesis:
Words and Music in the Second-Mode Tracts
Emma Hornby

Juan Esquivel: A Master of Sacred Music during the Spanish Golden Age
Clive Walkley

Essays on Renaissance Music in Honour of David Fallows:
Bon jour, bon mois et bonne estrenne
edited by Fabrice Fitch and Jacobijn Kiel

Music and Ceremony at the Court of Charles V:
The *Capilla Flamenca* and the Art of Political Promotion
Mary Tiffany Ferer

Music and Meaning in Old Hispanic Lenten Chants:
Psalmi, Threni and the Easter Vigil Canticles
Emma Hornby and Rebecca Maloy

Music in Elizabethan Court Politics
Katherine Butler

Verse and Voice in Byrd's Song Collections of 1588 and 1589
Jeremy L. Smith

The Montpellier Codex: The Final Fascicle. Contents, Contexts, Chronologies
edited by Catherine A. Bradley and Karen Desmond

CPSIA information can be obtained
at www.ICGtesting.com
Printed in the USA
BVHW08*1136240718
522338BV00017B/57/P